Dr. Larry Smith has written a compelling testament to human faith in his WWII historical novel *Darwin's War*. He writes about the airmen of the US Army Air Force's 416th Bombardment Group, his father Jack Smith among them. This book is a celebration of those brave aviators who daily faced life-and-death encounters. They stayed motivated and focused by believing in themselves, each other, and a higher power.

So true-to-life is Smith's narrative, the reader will feel transported back in time to that fiery shooting gallery that was the European Theater of Operations. Smith's words paint gripping pictures of battle-ready aviators, armed and airborne. Inside the cramped cockpit of their aluminum and Plexiglas A-20 Havoc bombers, the pilots manipulate a bank of controls. Behind him, in the turret, perches the turret gunner at the ready. Lying prone beneath the turret gunner inside the bottom of the plane is the belly gunner armed with a machine gun and camera. The Navigator Bombardier guides the formation to the target from his isolated Plexiglas compartment in the front of aircraft

Enriching the frontline bombs-away context, Smith interweaves provocative details about Adolph Hitler's death dance with eugenicists. Together, they justified—scientifically, philosophically, and patriotically— the führer's Final Solution. Hitler and the eugenicists would rid the fatherland of those unfit to breathe Deutschland's air. Ultimately, their plan expanded to include all of Europe.

The Nazis were on a mission. By war's end, they had systematically killed nine to eleven million people, including Jews, Gypsies, homosexuals, Catholics, Jehovah's Witnesses, and other social and political "undesirables."

Darwin's War shifts into cautionary tale mode with the author's insightful observations about eugenics. Smith cautions us not to underestimate those who preach about the "unfit"; left unchecked, eugenicists could gain fearsome support and momentum. Based on his meticulous research, Smith explains the origins of the eugenics movement, its influence on public policy, and what it has morphed into.

Darwin's War will resonate with military veterans, their loved ones, and people who simply enjoy a masterfully told story about actual Americans in wartime. The ninety accompanying photographs will enhance the reader's frontline experience.

Gail Chadwick,
BookSurge Editor

Darwin's War

Science, Politics, Warfare,
Faith and Sacrifice:
The 416th Bomb Group's
Sacrifices to Defeat Eugenics

L.N. Smith, M.D.

Bill,

Thank you for your leadership, service and Sacrifice

Larry N. Smith, MD

DRF Society meeting, Pensacola 2009

ISBN: 1-4196-8905-3
ISBN-13: 9781419689055
Library of Congress Control Number: 2008900726

Visit www.booksurge.com to order additional copies.

Table of Contents

Acknowledgments

Dedication

Introduction

Brief History of Group

Group Organization

Box and Flight Organization

Glossary

Bibliography and Footnotes

Larry Smith
10925 SW 27ᵗʰ Ave
Gainesville, Fl
        32608

352.332- 5626

Table of Contents

Acknowledgments

My first words of thanks must go to the members of the 416th Bomb Group who, like so many from their generation, were willing to stand and fight to prevent what would have been the enslavement of the world.

I also have to thank Mr. Ian Mactaggart form Braintree, England, who provided me with invaluable history of Wethersfield and the important historical facts about the 416th Bomb Group's time in England, while touring me through the old American air bases scattered across the English countryside.

Mr. Fabrice Dhollande from Rouen, France, personally toured me over the battlefields of Oissel and Rouen, France. His extensive personal knowledge and historical research provided insight into the tactics and missions of the allies during that period in the war.

I must thank Mr. James Royal for his invaluable advice and his patient editing of grammar and sentence structure.

To my family, I say thank you for tolerating me during this period and providing me the foundation on which I was able to complete the effort.

Thank You All

Dedication

This book is dedicated to the memory of my father Major Jack F. Smith, retired, United States Air Force, and all of those with whom he fought, especially to those who made the ultimate sacrifice, to help free the world of the tyranny that desired to destroy our struggling humanity.

I also want to dedicate this to my mother Rosalie G. Smith, RN, and all the women who served in support of our country, the troops, and their loved ones to help win this vital victory.

The larger dedication is to all the fine brave men and women who fought in, died in, and came home whole or maimed from the greatest conflict of their generation and of the world's to date.

Introduction

Conflict is not unique. It has been with us since the desire to procreate brought on the conflict of the selective genetic process. The real changes today have come in how we now define conflict and fight it. Just as the lethality by which we fight wars has evolved, our appreciation of its destructive force has consistently defined the nature of the conflict. Within this milieu of conflict, the forces that drive nations to war center on "policy" and the conflict that policy or the lack of policy brings.

Policy drives discussions and negotiations. It dictates the manner by which nations trade, governments decide or tragically fail to decide. Policy becomes the history that societies have survived or will endure in the future. Policy is the product of the yin and yang between the public and private policy-setting bodies that are in constant conflict with each other.

This policy conflict can be appreciated by examining the decades of conflicts and compromises that preceded World War II. The global policies of the late 1800s through the 1930s invariably led to the global conflict of the 1940s. Policies of science, economics, religion, immigration, and security pushed the global machinery of many nations into alliances and conflicts that were designed to ensure their Darwinian, Malthusian future. It was exactly because of the marriage of private and public policies that the men of United States Army Air Force's 416th Bomb Group (Light) were forced to endure the world's most destructive conflict ever witnessed by humankind.

We as free citizens of the earth will forever owe a debt for the sacrifices made by the men and women from all the nations who fought in all the theaters of war during World War II.

This book is about the experiences of the dedicated men of the US Army's Air Corps "Bantam" Bombers Ninth Air Force, IX Bomber Command, Ninety-Seventh Combat Wing, 416th Bombardment Group Light (BGL) during World War II.

This book not only acknowledges their sacrifices but also attempts to shed some light on the consequences of the misguided private and public policy actions that forced these men and women into the conflict we named World War II.

The desire to write this book has led me on an enlightening personal journey that begins in all children's minds when they imagine their parents' experiences in war and combat. I had opportunities to romanticize it more growing up as the son of a career Air Force officer by going to air shows with static and dynamic flying displays. These displays, coupled with combat reenactments, fueled my imagination of the entire experience. It is because of these feelings, along with a deeper appreciation of the accomplishments of the 416th, that I will try to capture the truly unromantic reality of their lives and experiences during their tenure together in World War II. In depicting their lives, I hope to interweave science's role in establishing private then public policy with the subsequent global consequences that brought these men to war.

The travel, research, personal experiences, and stories that led me to the writing of this book have become and always will be treasures for me. I hope I can convey the sincerity, intensity, and pain of all the heroic events these men experienced during this time of their lives.

Along the course of this journey, I realized I needed to understand the intellectual, scientific, economic, social, and nationalistic quests for resources that pushed the world into this cataclysmic war of mass destruction. This detailed examination helped reveal, when examined in conjunction with the evolving misguided scientific thoughts and beliefs of the times, what helped push the world into this abyss. It was within this milieu of universal misguided hatred that the men, soon to be warriors of the 416th, emerged. Their unselfish commitment helped to save us all from wrongly guided scientific racism.

This book is historic, combined with a small amount of historical fiction. The accounts are real as are the missions, but there has been some time compression to help create a concise, comprehensive story. The historical details of many of the stories have been told to me by the men who have lived with them as their personal and sometimes painful memories. I hope I can recount the details with the same intensity of the true experiences.

The 416th Bomb Group's time in the European Theater of Operations (ETO) started in January of 1944, lasting until the end of the war in Europe on May 8, 1945. During that time, the 416th Group consisted of the 668th, 669th, 670th, and 671st squadrons that collectively flew 285 separate missions. As the war progressed, the number of missions needed to be rotated out of combat was progressively increased, due to the need for experienced aircrews to "man" the planes.

The experiences of these dedicated men cannot be compared to the men and missions of any other group or squadron in the theater. Every aviator's Army Air Corps Group or squadron experiences were and always will be uniquely his.

This story is not intended to lift the 416th's importance regarding experiences, losses, or missions above that of any other group that served in the ETO or in the wider world conflict. I only intend to honor them, if possible, with this story while hoping it conveys the great sense of appreciation I have (and I hope others have) for their efforts and supreme sacrifices. They will not be forgotten. It is with the greatest humility that I try to honor the service these men gave while helping the reader understand the intensity of their time in this death-hungry world.

Brief History of the Group

The 416th BG (L) was the first USAAF A-20 group in the European Theater of Operations. The 416th flew 285 missions, dispatched 10,865 aircraft, and flew 10,009 sorties with 33,479 combat hours while in theater. The group dropped 11,119 tons of ordnance (bombs or rockets) with a large percentage of that dropped in the month of March 1945. There were forty aircraft lost and forty aircraft critically battle damaged. Eighty-five men were listed as missing in action (MIA); thirty were killed (KIA) and nineteen taken as prisoners of war (POW). The group received battle stars and citations for the air offensives in Europe, including Normandy, Northern France, Rhineland, Ardennes, and Central Europe, and a Distinguished Unit Citation for action from August 6 to 9, 1944, during the battle of the Falaise Gap shortly after D day. They were also decorated by the French with the Croix de Guerre with a silver star and the Corps Order of the French Air Force on July 4, 1945, for action between October 18, 1943, and May 8, 1945.

The 416th Bomb Group began its history when it was constituted on paper January 25, 1943. The group was intended to be an attack/bomber group with tactical targeting and bombing ability in formation, followed by fighterlike strafing attacks on the return flight from the target or in combination with the bombing of the target itself. This capability separated them from the standard designation of a bomber group earning them the designation A for "Attack."

The group completed proper organization and activation February 5, 1943, at Will Rogers Field, Oklahoma City, Oklahoma. There were fifty-one officers and two hundred forty-one enlisted men transferred into the group. The officers and enlisted men came from a large geographic region with many already having combat flight experience. The 416th was actually created by a separation from the Forty-Sixth Bombardment Group Light on February 15, 1943, at Will Rogers field and from then on was known as the 416th Bomb Group Light. This was where the administrative officers and staff learned how to manage the paperwork that militaries are known for.

The group was eventually assigned eight aircraft: six A-20 Havocs and two B-25 Mitchells, both twin-engine light bombers, with the A-20 Havoc being a better design for the attack roll. These planes were divided among the four squadrons with intense training that included code, link trainers, aircraft recognition, operation, and maintenance of the A-20s and B-25s, air navigation, radio, instrument procedures and many other important aspects of education. Physical conditioning was a critical and regular program carried out by officers and enlisted men. This conditioning combined sports as well as exercise programs.

It is important to note that without reservation every pilot, bombardier/navigator (BN), and gunner credits the success of the group to the dedicated abilities of the ground crews. These men worked every day at repairing flak damage, fixing engines, and ensuring that their plane was airworthy. Their outstanding efforts cannot be praised enough. By keeping the A-20 Havocs and later the A-26 Invaders in the air, the 416th could take the war to the enemy. Therefore, without the critical repairs, the success of every succeeding mission would have dwindled due to poor performance of the unrepaired aircraft along with the small number of remaining flyable aircraft.

Ground crews were educated in all aspects of the plane's design, maintenance, and repair. They would actually dismantle and then rebuild every part of the plane so that they would be able to do so when needed in theater. This skill could not be discounted in any way. Some of the pilots who brought back severely damaged aircraft appreciated the attention to detail the ground crews and crew chiefs had for "their planes." The ground crew only lent "their planes" to the pilots and aircrews for missions.

The group was assigned to fly the Douglas A-20 Havoc attack bomber. The Havoc, a twin-engine aircraft, was very fast and maneuverable. The two models used in theater were the glass-nosed bombardier version that carried the Norden bombsight and the solid-nosed attack version that housed six .50-caliber machine guns.

The Douglas A-20 Havoc had a service ceiling of up to 25,800 feet. It could fly as fast as many fighters with a top speed of 340 miles per hour. As a rule, the planes flew and bombed at fifteen hundred to twelve thousand feet at speeds of 200 to 240 mph. The plane was a stable bombing platform but, in a tight spot, the pilot could maneuver it like a fighter, an attribute many pilots came to appreciate. It flew well on one engine, which proved to be of great importance to many crews in combat.

Both planes carried two gunners and a pilot, with the glassed-nosed model carrying a fourth crewmember, the bombardier/navigator (BN) who rode in the nose of the plane. His job was a busy one of guiding the group to and from the target while also guiding the group through the flak fields. More importantly, he was responsible for releasing the first salvo of munitions from his plane. His dropping of bombs was the cue for the rest of the formation to drop their bombs on the target. The group flew in "boxes" of eighteen planes made up of three flights of six planes, bombing in flights of six.

Inside the plane the two gunners were separated from each other with one in the top rotating turret with twin .50-caliber machine guns; the other laid in the belly of the plane facing backward toward the tail of the plane. The belly gunner carried a handheld .30-caliber machine gun for aircraft defense and also had the responsibility of taking battle damage photos since he could see behind and below the plane on missions.

As a rule, the squadron's bombs were well placed, accomplishing their goal of destroying the target as the photos revealed. On occasion though the gunner may have missed the drop or shot the photos too early or late to allow the intelligence officers to gauge the success of the mission, a mistake that probably a few BNs appreciated on occasion, since they were responsible for the targeting and placement of the bombs. The intelligence officers were not as pleased though. They were then depending on follow-up reconnaissance photographs to assess bomb damage success.

Every mission was followed by a comprehensive debriefing of all returning aircrews. At debriefings the gunners, because of their view, could and did provide valuable information about ground flak gun emplacements, numbers of planes lost, and numbers of parachutes opened from which planes.

They were also detailed during the debriefings on how many enemy fighters were seen or shot down. They helped to fill in the gaps left from the pilot who was intent on keeping the fast-moving plane in tight formation and the BN who was busy keeping the formation headed in the right direction.

The group was moved to Lake Charles, Louisiana, for advanced training in bombing techniques in June of 1943, then on to Laurel, Mississippi, in November of 1943, for further refinement of the crew's skills and techniques. After Christmas the group headed by train to Camp Shanks, New York, for a January trip overseas on the converted French passenger liner *SS Colombe* out of New York City. Other crews were to follow in March on the *Queen Elizabeth.*

The group was stationed at Wethersfield Air Base, England, until September 15th, 1944, when they transferred to Melun-Villaroche Aerodrome, France, where they transitioned into the Douglas A-26 Invader (becoming the first bomb group to fly the A-26 Invader in combat). After the Battle of the Bulge, they moved to Laon-Athies Aerodrome, France, an old Luftwaffe base the Ninth Air Force had commandeered after being liberated by the US Army. Laon was to be their final active base in theater until war's end.

The majority of the missions of the 416th were flown in the A-20s out of England's Wethersfield Air Base between February 2, 1944, and September 14, 1944. To start, the group concentrated their efforts on buzz bomb sites. These missions were broken up with pre-invasion missions to marshaling yards, communication centers, bridges, German airfields, and supply depots, all designed to soften the way for the coming D day invasion. The group flew their two D day missions from Wethersfield Air Base with the now classic alternating black and white D day invasion stripes painted on the wings and fuselage of their Havocs. On that day, in the early morning, they bombed a crossroads named Argentan that was heavily trafficked by German reinforcements. In the late evening, the group flew on a German-held French marshaling yard named Serquex in the Pas de Calais region, the intent being to prevent Panzers and reinforcements from being moved to the critical and still voraciously contested beachheads. Both missions were successful but not without cost.

The fight over the English Channel on the first D day mission was punctuated by the group being witness to the vastness of the naval armada on the sea below them. Up to five thousand ships rode the waves of the channel, a spectacle that spread from horizon to horizon, as seen and appreciated from their altitude of only two thousand feet. The men fighting on the beaches appreciated this aerial display of power as the air armada flew over them. The projection of power must mean the possession of power.

Every flyer looking down onto the ships below knew that the brave souls inside were going into the jaws of the German death machine, many destined to never return to their homelands but instead to journey to their maker's greener pastures.

When the bomber group crossed the French coast witnessing the carnage on the beaches from two thousand feet, every air crewmember was reassured of his conviction, his sense of purpose and duty to take the war to the enemy. Even though the purpose and importance of the mission had been intensified by the sight of the beaches, it did not ease their consciences, as many civilians were killed on the group's first mission that day to Argentan due their concentration around the crossroads. The loss of innocent lives was always hard to deal with, even for the most seasoned flyer.

The second mission of the day was marred with many losses and aircraft damage. The objective was to prevent the Germans from moving any Panzer tanks, men, or materials to the front. Needless to say, heroics with selfless dedication was the order of the day, and was demonstrated in that airspace over the target.

While in England, many missions were dedicated to destroying the Germans' V-1 rocket launch sites positioned behind the French or Belgium coastal areas. This pilotless buzz bomb was designed to fly on a given path until its fuel was expended then fall to the earth and explode. They were quite powerful but thankfully not accurate.

Several stories about them have been shared with me. One my father told me one: It appears that after D day the English people were happy to rent rooms to US soldiers while they were on leave in London or elsewhere. The deal, though, was that the soldiers got the upper floors where the majority of the damage and deaths occurred from the V-1s when they hit. Another story was that aside from shooting the V-1s down with anti-aircraft fire or with chase planes, it became clear that fighters could simply parallel the V-1's course and gently tap or lift the wing of the buzz bomb in flight. The V-1 would then spin out of control into the English Channel or the ground. Apparently the gyroscopes in the V-1 could not correct for this change in flight attitude. This saved some ammunition but risked the plane and pilot willing to tip the V-1's wing with his own.

Several months after D day the group was transferred to Melun, France, Station A-55, on September 15, 1944. It was at this base the squadron began rotation into the new A-26 attack bomber. The 416th was the first group to receive and fly the A-26 into combat in the European Theater of Operations (ETO). They transitioned into the A-26 Invader during the months of October and November of 1944.

The Douglas A-26 Invader was a larger aircraft with more fire power and capable of carrying a greater bomb load a longer distance. It could carry a large internal bomb load as well as bombs on fixed hard points on the wings, for a total of four thousand pounds (nearly as much tonnage as the four-engine bombers).

The Invader was a twin-engine light attack bomber that cruised at 284 mph with a maximum speed of 355 mph. The plane was built in two models, the glassed-nosed C variant for the BN that could carry three men, and a solid-nosed B model that carried two men, with eight .50-caliber machine guns in the nose. There were also pod-mounted .50-caliber machine guns on the wings and, of course, the turret gunner's .50-calibers (that could be locked facing forward, increasing the firepower of the Invader). Overall, a heavily gunned aircraft that could destroy just about anything.

Anecdotally, an A-26 Invader is credited with shooting down an Me-262. This was one of Germany's twin-engine jet fighters, very fast and dangerous. The group's A-26-B models were initially led by the A-20 Havoc glassed-nosed model until the A-26-C model was delivered to the group.

During the 416th Bomb Group's combat time in France they flew support missions for Patton's Third Army with interdiction and frontline support missions during the breakout from St. Lo, France. The group flew one mission in support of General Montgomery's Operation Market Garden in the Netherlands and successfully pounded the Wehrmacht during the Battle of the Bulge in December of 1944 and January of 1945. This was followed with tactical missions that opened the Rhineland to the advancing allied forces.

The group was transferred to Laon, France, Station A-69, on February 11, 1945. It was from this base that the 416th would complete their tour of duty in the ETO, but not before setting several group records and flying several costly missions. It was from Laon in March of 1945 that one mission was flown over a very historic German town whose history contained insight into this now global struggle.

Organization Chart of the
416th Bomb Group (L)

United States Army Air Corps

✥

Ninth Air Force

✥

IXth Bomber Command

✥

Ninety-Seventh Combat Wing

✥

416th Bombardment Group (Light)

✥

668th – 669th – 670th – 671st Squadrons

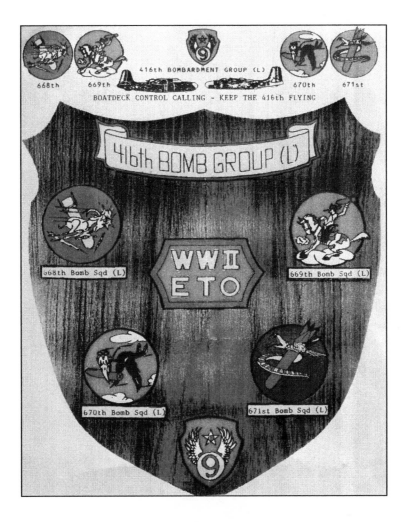

Group Standard

Standard of the 416th Bomb Group with the squadron insignias and Ninth Air Force insignia; Note Boat Deck Control recognition call sign. The 416th was the first USAAC group to fly A-20s and A-26s in combat. Reproduced with permission from Ralph Conte

Combat Flight Formation Organization

Box I (A)

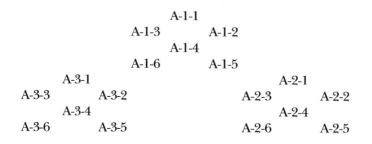

```
                    A-1-1
        A-1-3                A-1-2
                    A-1-4
        A-1-6                A-1-5
    A-3-1                            A-2-1
A-3-3        A-3-2              A-2-3        A-2-2
    A-3-4                            A-2-4
A-3-6        A-3-5              A-2-6        A-2-5
```

Box II (B)
Same Organization
3 Flights of 6
Designation B-x-x

Box III (C)
Same Organization
3 Flights of 6
Designation C-x-x

Prologue

This story recounts the reality of the daily lives of the aviators who flew with the 416th Bomb Group during World War II. It also details the consequences of the private and public policies that occurred during their early lives that subsequently resulted in the war they were to fight. This story begins at Wethersfield Air Base, England, in May of 1944, ending in mid-April of 1945 while the group is stationed at Laon /Athies aerodrome, France, station A-69. Their time in the ETO was punctuated with difficult missions, resulting in the loss of many lives.

Each phase of their service deserves attention and credit for its contribution to the entire effort of the war. The US Army Air Corps, which included the men of the 416th, had been flying and dying in the skies over Western Europe and Germany for many years before the first ground forces landed on the shores of Normandy. They would continue to fly and die as the Allies pushed over the Rhine to begin the liberation of the SS death camps along with the stalags of the Wehrmacht and Luftwaffe in the spring of 1945.

During the winter and spring of 1945, the group was making regular sorties into heavily defended German air space. Aircrews discovered the German war machine was far from destroyed or powerless. The German warriors, along with the citizens of Germany, were not going to surrender their country easily. The intensity of the resistance during these final months cost the 416th many lives before the war ended on May 8, 1945.

There is no single mission central to the story, but each mission is as factually correct as possible. Several heroic or tragic events from several missions have been recounted to bring credit to those men's sacrifices. These additions along with the time compression allows for some control of the vastness of the group's service from England to the final days in Germany. The events may be compressed in time but are historically correct accounts.

There are references to translations throughout the encounters with the German army or with the local French populace. The translations may not be grammatically correct for their native language. There is no intent to make this a foreign language textbook although every attempt for the proper use of grammar has been made.

Again, it is impossible to recount the heroics and sacrifices of every man in the 416th. I have tried to combine stories with events that portray the essence of their time in the ETO. I hope I captured their individual commitment that is multiplied with their group commitment in defeating that part of the Nazi war machine against which they flew sorties. Every mission was designed to help crush the Third Reich's hate-filled Fascism.

Many of these men trained together in the United States and then rotated into the group while it was stationed in Wethersfield, England. By the time the group moved to Laon many aircrews had completed their sixty-five-mission requirement for rotation out of combat.

Chapter One

For God alone my soul waits in silence.

– Psalm 62:1

Bat, as he was known by his fellow officers, was walking restlessly along the flight line. He had just completed his morning mission debriefing, recounting in as much detail as he could the 416th's forty-first mission with the group's intelligence officers. Having led the group on a difficult mission over the Aerschot marshaling yards this morning, he was glad it and the debriefing were behind him. He was equally happy to have made it back in one piece.

He had responded to the best of his ability to the questions they had asked as they tried to fill in the details about the mission. He had informed Operations, "There was a moderate amount of flak with no losses or injuries but most of the aircraft suffered flak battle damage." Time compression and tunnel vision caused by the intensity over the target always made it hard to recall all the details. It seemed that no matter how many missions the aircrews flew they never got used to the imminent fear of death once the flak started coming up. The fear pushed the crew's adrenalin levels into an ultra-focused survival mode forcing everyone to focus on the immediate risk or priority. Heart rates pushed to levels only young men with good arteries could tolerate as the increased cardiac output pushed the adrenalin to every neuron involved with survival. The mind focused through the eyes on only what was of immediate danger. Time seemed to stand still as every man tightened his reflexes like a cheetah ready to spring. Bat was still surprised he remembered anything more than keeping the pilot directional indicator (PDI) centered. Operations always seemed to want more answers than he or anyone else could recall. Nevertheless, with the proper guidance he found the Intel guys always got more out of the crews than he thought they could remember. Today seemed like any other mission until it had hit him—they all had made it back alive. As group leader, he knew he would have to relive the mission.

After debriefing all the crews, the operations and intelligence officers sat in their cigarette-smoke-filled Quonset hut, compiling the data into an after-action report. Once they completed it, the officers took the time to share the report.

"Bat, the mission was a good one. Bomb damage photos reveal that the group destroyed forty-five boxcars and two large buildings, one of which was a workshop. Heck, you guys decimated the turntable, along with the service tracks to and from it. To top it off, everyone returned alive and uninjured. A few planes will be grounded for a while due to flak damage but they could be replaced with some existing aircraft on the base now for the afternoon mission."

Drawing slowly on his Lucky, Captain Battersby had listened quietly to their comments. Exhaling from his smoke-filled lungs, Bat waited several seconds before responding to their report.

"Sounds good, guys. Doesn't sound like we'll need to go back there anytime soon."

He was happy about that, indeed.

In spite of the success, Bat was not quite ready to relax. Since he was not scheduled for the afternoon mission, he formulated a plan to take advantage of the perfect afternoon.

Bat climbed into his jeep, pushed the clutch in, and after pushing the starter button felt the small single-barrel carburetor-fed engine shake to a start. He quickly let off the starter button as a puff of grayish-whitish exhaust billowed out the exhaust pipe. Looking around the flight line, he could see the ground and sheet-metal crews were already hard at work repairing the planes that had taken hits over the target. Particular attention was being paid to the holes in the high-performance aluminum wings. Without smooth airflow over those wings, Bat knew drag would increase and cause lift to suffer. "I'm glad these guys know what they're doing."

Losing lift is not a good thing on any plane, particularly one flying in a combat zone. The fuselage was as important, but came second. He was glad to see that they were also checking for mechanical damage that may show up on the next mission at the wrong time. Battersby could not remember the last time he had flown a Havoc that did not have sheet-metal patches or carefully beveled Plexiglass patches designed to not compromise vision through the windshield or gun turrets. Once again, he was relieved that the guys who built or repaired these now damaged planes knew what they were doing.

"At least they did not have to clean a lot of blood out of any of them today."

He felt good about the mission, saying aloud, "Not a bad day at the office."

The engine pulled the jeep forward until it got up enough speed to allow him to grind into a second unsynchronized gear followed shortly by the little Willys Jeep's transmission being ground again into third.

On the Wethersfield Air Base, buildings and hangars were far apart. Bat was glad he rated a jeep as a captain. Indeed, the base was large and it had taken awhile to construct. The Air Corps needed the space for all the planes, taxiways, hangers, maintenance facilities, bomb storage, and barracks space. Built by the British but never occupied by them, it had been taken over by the Army Air Corps' 416th Bomb Group in January 1944. Like most things in life it had not come free to the US Army Air Corps. Uncle Sam was paying the English government a nice lease rate to use the base but that same government had just taken the land from the original landowners, over protest. These farmers had not wanted to give it up, stubbornly insisting that they were farmers. Even after the land was taken they farmed right up to the base fences. Anyway, the air force needed the space.

Turning to his left along the flight line, Bat headed toward the tower to put his plan into motion. Cruising along, he scanned the landscape. It was almost as if

Wethersfield sat on top of a plateau that sloped gently away on all sides. On the highest point sat the bomb dumps and ammunition bunkers. He was still impressed by how flat this area of the country was. He could see why this central to southeastern area of Britain was ideal for all the airfields that now covered it.

He thought about the small town of Finchingfield, just a few miles northwest of the base—a great place to bike to for lunch or just to get away from the base for awhile. He enjoyed visiting the cathedral or sitting outside the thatch-roofed cafes that bordered the small stream and pond in the village center. The English were friendly, making it that much nicer. Bat had found he enjoyed the city of London with its old-world architecture. To his surprise, he liked steak and kidney pie and particularly the English beer. He was looking forward to his R&R in one week on the south coast of England. Bat thought he would vacation here with his wife and family after the war.

He stopped contemplating the geography and architecture, and decided to take advantage of today. He had seen the new A-20 that had been ferried in yesterday over the northern route by way of Newfoundland, Greenland, Iceland, then here. It was a replacement aircraft for those that had been lost from battle damage or crashes over the last several missions. They would need it soon with all the damage the group sustained on today's mission. Knowing that rank has its privileges, Bat decided to take the new Havoc up today on its routine combat-clearance test flight.

All new aircraft were test-flown before they were introduced into combat with a full crew. The idea was to find any flaws in the plane before combat forced them out at the wrong time and the wrong airspace. Bat figured it might as well be him taking it up today, better than some desk-flying colonel trying to get some flight hours on the books to keep his flight status.

Gazing skyward as all good pilots do, Bat appreciated the cool air and blue skies while watching the slow, puffy, flat-bottomed cumulus clouds drift by, so typical for an early May high front. He was glad it had blown in and pushed the last cold front out, which had been hanging around for the last week. It was far from hot but nice to see the sun. Knowing the thermals caused by the sun's heat would make the climb out bumpy, he was pleased to see that the clouds topped out at about three or four thousand feet. Once above them, he knew it would be smooth sailing.

It was a day any pilot would love to be flying. The cool air was thicker, making for better lift and performance of any aircraft's wings, battle damaged or not. The air was crisp with a slight breeze that made a pilot happy to have his heavy flight jacket on to cut the chill.

A perfect day to fly, Bat thought. His drive to the tower was nearly over.

Wheeling into a turning stop, Battersby jumped out in front of the tower beside the large, black gravel circle with the two large white letters "WF" painted in the middle. With all the airbases around here, it helped to have anything that aided the pilots in identifying their base.

It's become more important now that Wing has added the 409ᵗʰ and 410ᵗʰ in this area, Bat thought.

Little Walden, or Hadstock, where the 409th was based, was just to the southwest. With all those A-20s sitting there, it could be easily mistaken for Wethersfield if a pilot weren't careful.

The chilled air encouraged Battersby to walk briskly between the military white path markers toward the two-story tower. He entered the tower's operation center. Instinctively he turned to the duty officer, who recognized the rank and immediately jumped to attention.

"Captain."

"At ease, Lieutenant," Bat said in his usual low, unhurried, almost-British manner while saluting.

"I want to schedule a test flight today in that replacement ship that touched down yesterday." He pointed in the direction of the ground crew's hangar area.

"Yes, sir. Let me check the log."

Opening the flight log on the desk in front of him, the lieutenant replied, "Sir, the plane hasn't been checked over by the crew chief yet. I can call and have them take a look at her for yuh, if you like. It may not be ready for a while, sir."

"Did they not fly it in yesterday from Ireland?" His right eyebrow rose.

"Yes, sir, they did." The young lieutenant was now anxious.

"Could it be flown back to Ireland today, if needed, Lieutenant?"

"Well, yes, sir, but I'm not sure it's been fueled since it got here, sir."

"Call the ground crew chief and have him put some petrol in her. I'll meet them at the hardstand in thirty minutes."

The lieutenant rang the ground crew chief's tent and spoke with Staff Sergeant Dullnig who answered.

"Ground crew," the cigar-chewing crew chief answered.

"This is the duty office in the tower. Will you see to it that plane niner-niner-eight is serviced for a test flight in thirty minutes? Captain Battersby wants to take her up for a routine combat clearance flight."

"Yes, sir, but it may take more than thirty minutes, sir."

"I suggest you should get on it then, Sergeant."

"Yes, sir, I'll get it done."

Staff Sergeant Dullnig spit and then bit hard on his cigar as he hung up the phone. Turning toward the fight line, he hustled over to a group of ground crew members who were working on one of the Havocs that had earned the worst of the battle damage from the morning's mission.

"You three go take care of getting that new A-20 ready for a test flight...niner-niner-eight," he barked out. "The captain wants to be airborne in thirty. Be sure she's fueled."

The three ground crew members looked at each other then over the sheet-metal repairs that this plane desperately needed. *How are we going to get all of this done, much less take time out for a perfectly good airplane?* the senior ground crew member silently lamented.

"Oh hell, an order is an order," he said. "Let's go, guys."

With the duties divided, they rendezvoused at the new Havoc, setting in motion the well-oiled process of prepping it for flight.

Leaving the tower, Bat ground the jeep's transmission on his way to the parachute hangar to request a chute for the flight. Stopping in front of the hangar, Bat spied a young airman packing a new chute on one of the packing tables. Several long tables were covered with silk chutes that had long cords running from the chutes down to the typical parachute harness that everyone wore on missions.

"Airman Coleman," Bat said, after looking at the airman's uniform.

Momentarily caught off guard, the young airman snapped to attention with a crisp salute. The captain cut a big toothy smile while saluting back.

"At ease." Bat knew he was a new airman.

"Coleman, do you have a chute available for me? I'm taking a test flight in the new arrival. Can never be too sure about when you might need one."

"I just happen to have two available, sir."

Airman First Class Charles W. Coleman was not so off guard as to not recognize an opportunity when he heard one.

"I only need one, Coleman."

"Yes, sir, but on test flights, ground crew can go along for the ride, sir. I thought… or was hoping…I could join you, sir…with your permission…that is, sir."

"What about your duties here, Coleman?" The chutes wafted in the light breeze.

"I can get help, sir. I've got a deal worked out with the other riggers to cover me anytime…if needed. How bout it, sir…can I come, sir?"

Bat looked the young airman in the eyes, where he recognized a similar eagerness he remembered from times past. True, there were no restrictions on ground personnel flying on test flights.

"OK, I'll see you in twenty on the line, Havoc niner-niner-eight. Don't forget to borrow a flight suit, it gets chilly up there."

"YES, SIR."

Coleman quickly turned around, then thought better of it. He turned back saluting Captain Battersby.

"Thank you, sir." Then he sprinted to the back of the hangar.

Coleman had always wanted to fly, after having seen the barnstormers come through his town when he was young. The memories of the Jennies and the old German triplanes of the flying circus still inspired him. He had hoped to have an assignment to a B-25 group, or even the heavies, since they both carried a flight engineer on each mission. That had not worked out, so now he was taking advantage of the next-best thing.

He talked eagerly with a couple of his buddies then was off again to sign out two chutes for the flight. "This seems to be a good place to start," he thought. "Who knows, maybe after the war I'll have my own plane."

As he drove to complete another part of his preflight responsibilities, the cool blue sky just kept calling to Captain Battersby. He stopped by the weather station to get a quick update, but mainly to get reassurance that it was going to stay a good day to fly. Bat listened halfheartedly to the report from the weather officer.

"Visibility fifteen miles plus, with light winds out of the northwest, clear skies as far as you could see."

Intel was the next stop. Bat jumped out of the jeep then walked casually up to the building. Walking through the door, he returned the salutes.

"At ease, gentlemen. Any Kraut fighters around lately?" he asked the Intel OD.[1]

"No, sir, sky's been clear for some time except for the occasional night fighter popping by to bomb somebody," replied the red-haired and freckle-faced lieutenant.

"Good, I'm going up for a while in the new bird. Don't want any surprises without a gunner on board."

"Yes, sir, I reck-un I do get the picture, sir."

Bat walked out the door into the sunshine. As he walked the well-worn path from the Intel building, a voice broke his concentration.

"Captain Battersby, what are you doing out here on the line? You aren't scheduled for the afternoon mission, are you, sir?" It was Lieutenant Ralph Conte.

Ralph, a bombardier/navigator (BN) in the 669th squadron, was a good man to lead the group or flight if you were on a mission. Everyone trusted him to get the group to the drop point, then put the eggs on target so that no one had to go back to do it again. Ralph had been with the group from the beginning but still had a ways to go until his sixty-fifth mission and his ticket home.

"That's correct, Ralph. I'm going to take up that new aircraft on a test flight."

"Anyone going with you?"

"An eager parachute rigger who can't wait to get into the air for some reason. Actually, it ought to be fun to see his reaction. Were we ever like that?"

"Heck, we're like that now. Have a good time. I'll see you at chow."

As Bat got back into the jeep, he thought he might try to write a letter home after the test flight. His foot pushed the starter button and the little engine sputtered to life. The recent pace of the missions combined with all the paperwork had kept him from his personal issues. Rank had its responsibilities too. He had neglected his letter writing. After shifting into third gear, he pulled his wallet out of his jacket pocket. He flipped it open to the picture of his new baby. The soft, pudgy face was pressed against the smiling face of his wife. He wondered how new babies smelled and sounded.

His wife had tried to describe it to him in a letter but somehow the appreciation for it was lost. Smiling broadly, he was amazed what had come from his R&R[2] thirteen months ago back in the states.

He could not wait to complete his next forty-seven missions so he could go home for a while. The promotions came all right. Maybe he would get called up to command, but he was not counting on it. Sixty-five missions was a lot, and he was not even at the halfway point.

---

1   OD, officer of the day
2   R&R, rest and relaxation, military slang for time off

He slipped his wallet back into his pocket, and observed the base during the drive across to the new Havoc. New aircraft were always taxied and parked close to the maintenance hangar. He could see the three crewmen topping off the tanks and walking the props to get the engines ready for start-up. As he watched the ground crew complete the preflight, Bat saw Coleman run up to the plane with two chutes and a lot of energy. The ground crew started showing him around but only as long as it did not interfere with their duties.

Battersby pulled up. The little four-cylinder engine sputtered to a stop.

"Over here, Coleman."

"Yes, sir, Captain," he yelled, slipping on his flight jacket as he ran up beside the captain, who was now walking toward the aircraft.

"Let's preflight and get going."

"Yes, sir."

Battersby led Coleman around the plane, instructing him about the preflight process. Bat and Coleman looked at the wings to check for leaks in the hydraulic fluid or fuel. They checked the brakes for leaks and the landing gear displacement, to be sure it was at least three inches. They checked the nosewheel snubbing pin and the wheel chocks. Bat explained to Coleman the purpose of the control surfaces on the wings and tail as they inspected them.

After they examined both engines closely for obvious oil or fuel leaks, Battersby led them to the cockpit. Bat climbed up first, with an eager Coleman not far behind. Bat stepped onto the left wing, turned the hatch latch, and lifted the long cockpit cover open, revealing the inside of the cockpit to Coleman. Stepping up into the now open fuselage behind the cockpit, Bat moved forward, put his foot down onto the seat, and then settled down into the cockpit. He adjusted the seat for his height. Sitting in the familiar pilot's station of the A-20, he could not help but notice that even the new planes had the smell of high-octane fuel mixed with oil, grease, and hydraulic fluid. He also noticed that the only thing this plane lacked was the smell of sweaty fear. He knew it would be there soon enough, and he turned back to Coleman, who was still standing on the wing.

"Lay down there, Coleman."

Bat pointed to the small crawl space behind and above the pilot's seat; it was used for storage or a place for pilots in training to observe.

Coleman did not care, and he was not going to be picky, anything for some flight time. He settled in on his belly looking forward.

"Not much room, but it works," Bat said.

"What's all that mean?" Coleman asked as he pointed at the cockpit's instrument panels.

Strapping himself in, Bat replied, "From the top down, this is the instrument panel with all the flight instruments, engine, oil, hydraulic, and fuel panel. It has all the readings about the engine's manifold pressure, oil pressure, rpms, engine temperature, fuel flow, and fuel gauges. Below that is the main electrical control panel. It has things like the cowl-flap control switches, oil-cooler door switches, and controls we use to get the engine running right. Here on the right side of the cockpit is all the communication equipment. Over here on the left are all the engine controls, flaps and landing gear controls."

Meticulously, Bat began the usual counterclockwise preflight cockpit check with his preflight checklist in his lap. All the pilots called it the "bible."

"Parking brake…on, fuel selector switch…on, cross-feed booster…off, generators…off…nose gun master switch off." Reaching down, he pumped the emergency hand-operated hydraulic pump, and watched the hydraulic pressure gauge to be sure it rose in response to the test. Bat turned to Coleman.

"What does that gauge behind me above the fire extinguisher read?"

"This large gauge above the fire extinguisher, the one that says 'emergency air brake pressure,' sir?"

"That's the one."

"Looks like," craning forward so he could read the gauge, "about 425 psi."

"Roger that, just need 400." Bat was happy it was 25 pounds above the minimum.

While Coleman checked the air pressure, Battersby had been moving on down the list.

"Control surface lever…unlocked." He instinctively took the control yoke in his hands, moving the control surfaces back and forth while making sure the rudder, elevators, and ailerons moved freely.

"Battery switches…on, oil cooler shutters." Battersby reached up, holding the oil cooler shutter switch in the open position for fifteen seconds. Then reversing it, he held it in the closed position until the shutters closed.

Battersby missed nothing, until the last preflight procedure was completed.

Coleman watched every move Bat made. He cataloged and put it all away in his mind, knowing he would need it someday. *When my turn comes to sit on the left side*, he thought, *I'll be that much farther ahead.*

Bat reached up, grabbed the hatch handle and pulled down the cockpit top. He then slid the left cockpit windowpane open, reached down and freed the engine primer pump. Immediately he set the propeller controls to increase rpm, supercharger on low blower.

Bat hollered out the window, "ALL CLEAR!"

He gave the ground crew the thumbs up. Bat waited until he got the thumbs up from the senior grounds crewmember, who then spun his right index finger and hand in a circular fashion for Bat to see. Bat flipped the starter-energizer switch to R and held it for fifteen seconds as he pumped the primer five times. This action created the familiar sound of the starter winding up before it engaged the engine's flywheel.

"CONTACT," Bat hollered out the window as he flipped the starter-engaging switch. It was the final switch needed for starting the starboard engine. He held the energizer switch closed; the big propeller resisted and then slowly began to turn. The engine and its big propeller began turning over slowly and then gained momentum.

The mass of the turning propeller, combined with the strength of the starter, forced the mass of the big radial engine to overcome its innate resistance to start.

After the fourth turn of the propeller, Bat flipped the engine-ignition switch. The spark plugs began firing in their synchronized order. The fuel in the proper cylinder head ignited as it completed its compression cycle, forcing the piston downward and bringing the next piston in the timing sequence into its compression then ignition stroke…**Whooom**…the engine erupted to life as it belched black then gray smoke out the exhaust manifolds. Fire blasted from the exhaust manifolds too, as the ground crews watched with fire extinguishers at the ready, just in case. The eighteen once cold, metallic cylinders of the radial roared to life, quickly heating to optimum temperature. The starboard engine was nearly ready to fly.

Bat flipped the mixture control to "Automatic Rich," then reached forward to the throttles in his center console, adjusting them so the engine idled at 700 rpms. Bat's eyes focused on the instrument panel as he watched to be sure his oil pressure rose above 25 psi. He needed the hydraulic pressure to reach at least 850 psi and his fuel-pressure gauge to read 15-17 psi. He watched the cylinder head temperature come up to two hundred degrees centigrade and the oil temperature level off at forty degrees. When the oil hit forty degrees, Bat reached forward to the electric panel and held the switch for the oil cooler doors in the "open" position for five seconds, partially opening the oil cooler shutters. He needed to keep the oil temperature at forty degrees in that engine. As the engine temperature climbed, the exhaust ports of the starboard radial began spurting only hot blue flames.

What a beautiful sight that is at night, Bat thought.

Satisfied with the right engine's performance, it was time to fire up the port engine. Looking at the ground crewmember, he thumbed up and hollered out the open window.

"All clear"

The ground crewmember gave the all-clear signal back.

Bat repeated the start-up procedure on the left engine. Oily black then gray smoke exploded from its exhaust ports as the engine roared to life. Within minutes, both engines hummed a deep healthy sound.

As the engines warmed up nicely, gauges all looked good, manifold pressure good, magnetos on and hot, hydraulic pressure holding in the green, cylinder head temperature in the green. "Generators…on." Bat flipped the switches to bring them on line, and the voltmeter responded appropriately. Bat prepared to taxi.

He looked out at the senior crewmember and held his thumbs-up sign. The crewman returned the sign, then looked toward the two ground crewmen who were standing behind the trailing edge of each wingtip. Having their attention, the senior staff sergeant turned his thumbs out and moved his forearms back and forth. The two men moved along the backside of the wing to the rear of the engine nacelles. They ducked under, and pulled the wheel chocks from under the wheel—a choreographed procedure done hundreds of times since their training days.

Battersby waited for the chief crewman to signal all clear and then called the tower for taxi instructions.

"Boat Deck Control, this is niner…niner…eight…A…alpha requesting permission to taxi, over."

"Roger, Boat Deck niner…niner…eight…A…alpha, you are clear for taxi to run up, over."

"Roger Boat Deck Control, this is Boat Deck niner…niner…eight…A…alpha, over and out," Bat responded in his meticulous and military manner.

Battersby checked to be sure the parking brake was off and looked out the window to the ground crew, now lined up saluting.[3] Bat returned the salutes, then pushed the throttles forward. He watched the manifold pressure increase as the extra fuel poured into the cylinder heads. The Havoc responded in the proper fashion.

Eager to get into the air, the two 1,600-hp Wasp radials roared with might as they pulled the A-20 forward. The nose gear turned only after moving forward a few feet, as Bat applied the appropriate left brake pressure and then increased the starboard engine's rpms just enough to help turn the big grounded bird. Once the plane was spun around 180 degrees, Bat released the left brake, balanced out the engine rpms, and began his taxi toward the runway.

The Havoc moved easily and eagerly down the taxiway as it headed toward the head of the runway. Bat set the manifold pressure at eight pounds, with the rpms at 1,000. The anxious newcomer rolled toward the head of the runway, ready to climb into the air.

"Who's that taxiing, Ralph?" asked Lieutenant Earl Hayter, as he walked out of the tower door. Ralph had just come from Operations after a briefing update on the afternoon mission.

"That's Bat and…Airman Coleman…going for a combat test flight of the new arrival."

"Great day for it…huh?"

"Sure as heck is."

"I was glad to get back this morning, not on the afternoon mission. I'm gonna sack out after mess. What about you?"

"I'm leading the second box this afternoon, got to get ready for the full briefing. Maybe I'll see you at chow tonight."

"Roger that."

Earl had known Ralph since the very early days in Wethersfield. Ralph had rotated into the 669th from the 670th some time ago. He flew with his pilot Dave Hulse mostly. Earl had never bunked with Ralph but they had flown many missions together. Missions bonded men together in a way only those who had lived through them could ever appreciate, and many things went unspoken afterward. Those who had journeyed together over occupied territory in the belly of an A-20 Havoc sometimes needed to

---

3   It was a standing order for the ground crews to salute as the planes began their taxi.

only motion or nod to make their point. More missions were yet to come; they both knew it.

Bat taxied into takeoff position at the head of the runway and then evenly applied the brakes. He wanted to get off the ground in a hurry, but was as meticulous as ever in his preparations.

The Wasp engines idled down, as Bat reduced the manifold pressure below eight and the rpms to 800. He held the brake pedals down, and reached beside the seat and picked up his checklist bible again. Reading aloud, he ran down the list.

"Upper cowl flaps closed…lower cowling flaps open." He lowered the handle into the half-open position and counted ten seconds to himself. He looked out the window to confirm their position.

"Flaps down." He pushed the flaps lever to the one-quarter down position listening as the hydraulic motor groaned as it pushed the pressurized fluid into the pistons that pushed the flaps down into takeoff position. Battersby confirmed they were down by the flaps position indicator on top of the engine control panel and then slipped the lever back into neutral.

"Cross-feed fuel boosters…off, propeller governor controls…increase rpms."

Bat laid the book down, pushed hard on the brakes, and then ran the starboard engine up and checked that engine's magnetos and rpm controls. The same procedure was repeated for the port engine. Everything was poised for action. Bat synchronized both engines, flipped the cross-feed fuel booster switch to on and called the tower for takeoff clearance. While getting same, he glanced over the instrument panel one more time, making sure everything was still in the green. He heard Coleman from the rear.

"Captain, why did you do that?"

"That cross-feed fuel pump supplies petrol to both engines during takeoff, just in case one of the fuel pumps fails. Don't mind trying to land on one engine, but it's tough taking off on just one."

"I get it." Coleman hoped he did not have to experience it.

Bat pushed the throttles forward. The Havoc revved up as the manifold pressures rose to forty-three inches of mercury. Bat let the brakes go, and the unloaded, undamaged, and smooth-skinned Havoc jumped to a rolling start. The sudden acceleration forced Bat against his seat and Coleman's feet back against the bulkhead. Unrestrained by Bat's pressure on the brakes, the Havoc began accelerating down the runway.

Coleman's eyes widened, amazed at how the A-20 accelerated down the runway. "Is it always like this?" Coleman blurted out, forgetting military protocol.

"It's only because we're so light on takeoff. No bomb load, extra fuel, or ammo to weigh us down."

Bat had forgotten himself how fast these little babes could roll out to takeoff speed without a bomb load.

"You guys do need longer to take off when you're bombed up."

When the plane hit 110 mph, Bat began pulling back on the yoke ever so gently. He wanted to lift the nosewheel off the ground. Using the cables attached to the yoke that ran through the pulley and drum system to the flight control surfaces, Bat's strength was multiplied a hundred fold as he pulled back on the yoke. This put tension on the elevator's cables that pulled them into their takeoff position. Bat began explaining to Coleman how you could feel the plane wanting to fly. Bat wanted to get airborne as much as the Havoc.

Desiring only to get into the air, the eager Havoc did its job without hesitation. The speedster began lifting the front wheel just inches off the runway. Exactly 464 square feet of wing surface pulled the Havoc effortlessly into the cool air.

Bat immediately shifted his thoughts to the process of converting the Havoc into the premier flying machine it was built to be. Waiting until they were fifty feet off the ground and moving at 135 mph, Bat retracted the landing gear. Using his left hand, he brought the gear lever into the up position, watching the hydraulic pressure drop as the wheels came up. As the gear locked into place, green lights signified that all three gear were up and locked. He saw the hydraulic pressure return to normal. Wanting better performance, Bat reached again to his lower left and pulled the wing flaps control lever back to the up position. The motor groaned as the hydraulic pressure fell and the flaps began retracting. Bat felt the plane's flight dynamics improve as he finished cleaning up all the drag.

"This little baby will climb like crazy if you give her a chance," Bat informed Coleman.

He loved the way the Havoc felt while climbing out on 75 percent power. Effortlessly it reached for more altitude as if it deserved it. The plane was still accelerating into the climb, as Bat called the tower for a heading.

"Boat Deck Control, this is Boat Deck niner…niner…eight…A…alpha on combat clearance flight, request heading for clear airspace, over."

The tower squawked back in a quick, static-infused sound "Boat deck niner…niner…eight…A…alpha, this is Boat Deck Control, turn left to two-seven-zero climbing to ten thousand, all yours after that, over."

"Roger that Boat Deck control, over and out."

By the time the conversation was over, Bat had completed his turn.

The well-balanced and highly powered light bomber could climb like a bat out of hell, and Battersby was not doing anything to stop it. He was enjoying the responsiveness of the plane. With the throttles steady, the airspeed increased as the Havoc climbed upward. The two propellers cut into the cool air with great efficiency, pulling the Havoc upward as Bat pulled the pitch and propeller rpm controls back to the climb position after he had completed the turn.

Climbing up through the first three thousand feet, the Havoc bounced around in all the thermals. Above the clouds Bat knew it would smooth out. Punching through four thousand feet, the Havoc got above the clouds. Bat felt the thermals die out through the flight controls and in the seat of his pants.

As they passed through seven thousand feet, the colder air that flowed around the wings generated good lift. Bat turned off the cross-feed fuel pump, set the supercharger at medium, and then reached forward to the electric panel. As he closed the cooling flaps on both engines, he instinctively said, "Cowl flaps closed."

"Why did you do that, Captain?"

"The cross-feed is for takeoff, don't need it now. Cowl flaps keep the engine cool on the ground, now that the plane is flying well above 165 miles per hour, the air flowing through the engine nacelles is enough to cool it."

"I get it."

"You have a good grip back there?" Bat turned his head slightly toward Coleman, to hear the answer better.

"Yes, sir, why do you ask?"

Coleman quickly found out, as Bat pulled the nose of the Havoc up into an aggressive angle of attack at a cruise speed of 280 miles per hour. He pulled back the manifold pressure that otherwise would have kept the Havoc climbing. At this angle and if he had not reduced the manifold pressure, Bat knew he could have caused a high-speed stall that would result in a spin.

At first, the A-20 charged upward into the sky. This was not going to last, as the airflow roughened over the wings while the airspeed bled off. The plane began to buffet, losing its ability to climb and if left unchecked, ultimately to fly. Watching the airspeed tail off, Bat knew it was about time to decrease his angle of attack. He eased the elevators down, then pushed the throttles forward. Bat waited for the Havoc to begin its drop back to controlled flight. The stall alarm went off, catching Coleman's attention. Instead of stopping, the plane's nose fell downward past the horizon and continued forward in a dive, using gravity to regain energy.

As it dove, Bat increased the manifold pressures slowly up until the Havoc hit 150 mph. Gently pulling back on the yoke, Bat activated the control surfaces so that the Havoc nosed up, entering into level flight. Pulling back the yoke still more, Bat edged the nose back into a climb of one thousand feet per minute while he pulled the manifold pressure back to fifteen pounds of mercury.

"Golly, that was great," Coleman exclaimed. "What was all that and what else will she do?"

Battersby again took the time to explain the physics of lift to the private. "The thing you need to remember, Private, is that in order to fly, the air has to flow over both sides of the wings. If it can't, then the lift is lost and the wings will no longer keep the plane in the air. That's why I pulled us out of that climb. We would have stalled out completely. After that it isn't much fun."

It beat being flipped over onto your back, Bat knew, *and then having to start your recovery upside down or, worse, in an upside-down spin.*

After regaining his airspeed, Bat turned to Coleman and said, "Hold on."

He pushed the Havoc's nose over. The shallow dive with the aid of gravity caused the airspeed to increase to 300 mph again. Turning the yoke hard right while pulling back slightly and then easing the throttles forward, Bat began rolling into a zero G aileron roll. Holding the controls steady, Bat brought the left wing over the right while twisting the fuselage like a corkscrew as the Havoc continued forward without needing to resist the pull of gravity.

With the Havoc's nose up slightly the natural horizon was suddenly turned upside down in front of Coleman's eyes. Coleman's heart began racing as his inner ear became confused. His brain was not in harmony with his eyes and ears. Coleman suddenly felt a little sick to his stomach as the big bird continued its roll. Coleman's eyes widened and his pupils dilated while he grabbed for the sides of his coffin-like compartment to fix himself inside it. Battersby grinned slightly as the Havoc continued its effortless roll to the right.

Bat kept the pressure on the controls, allowing the Havoc to continue rolling over onto its back. As the craft did as it was told, Coleman's youthful pulse quickened as his inner ear became even more confused. Coleman clung tighter to the walls of his compartment. He felt suspended in space.

The Havoc continued its roll to the right, and Bat kept the nose of the plane up. He let the plane complete its aileron roll back into its upright position, then returned the controls into a neutral attitude. He pulled the throttles back to fifteen pounds. Bat pulled the Havoc's nose up and resumed his climb at five hundred feet per minute into the deep blue English sky.

"Alright, Captain," screamed Coleman, forgetting protocol again in his enthusiasm "Let's do it again!"

"That's enough fun stuff, probably shouldn't have done that." Bat knew it was against regulations to have done it in the first place. He eased the throttles up to gain more altitude.

As the Havoc climbed, the temperature outside and inside the A-20 began to drop with each foot of altitude gained. Feeling the cold, Bat leveled the plane out at ten thousand feet knowing neither he nor Coleman was properly dressed for the unheated Havoc to go much higher.

"OK, that was fun. Now let's do some landing approaches." Turning back toward the base, Bat nosed the twin-engine speedster over, reduced the engine's manifold pressure and rpms, and the craft slowly lost altitude. Bat set his approach to the base.

"Boat Deck Control, this is Boat-deck niner…niner…eight…A…Alpha requesting approach for touchdown, over."

"Roger, Boat-deck niner…niner…eight…A…Alpha, this is Boat Deck Control, no inbound traffic in the pattern. You have direct approach in the pattern, over."

"Roger, Control, over and out."

Lieutenants Jack Smith, Hiram Clark, and Bill Tripp walked out of their Quonset hut toward the showers. They had left their fellow bunk mate Earl asleep in his cot. Missions were sweaty hard work. You had earned a good shower after one. The three young officers had only been in theater a month now and were still getting used to the realities of combat.

Looking up, Hiram heard the familiar synchronized drone of the twin radial engines of an A-20 Havoc off in the distance. "Hmm…that must be Bat on final."

"I heard from Earl he got the test flight," replied Bill.

"Great day for it," Jack said in a deep, slow Southern drawl, "ain't it?" He looked skyward. "Look at them clouds. It's a good day for fly-un."

"Gol-darn-it, Jack, could you be any more Southern?" Bill joked in his mocking New England best.

"Oh, hell, you damned Yankees won't ever get over it, will ya?" Jack's Southern drawl was so deep that during escape and evasion training (EET) in Ireland the instructors were unable to teach him any French without a Southern accent. They finally told him to act as if he were a mute if he were ever shot down and caught. He still had not lived that one down.

During their time in EET they were given clothes that resembled those of the French country folk. This was all designed to add to the realism of the hoax. After several days of not shaving, the pilots, navigators, and gunners were dressed in their French peasant clothes and then identification photos were made. These photos were used to make faux travel papers. They were issued other paraphernalia to help them succeed in their escape, such as a small amount of gold, French francs, German marks, a silk map of the region and, of course, chocolate. Each man always had the weapon of last resort—a .45-caliber sidearm.

EET also taught them how to contact the French underground and how to get them to assist you in your escape. No one wanted to go down in Kraut territory, but they all knew this training was effective and necessary. It had saved many a flyer from the POW camps.

The joking ended as the men continued their walk to the showers. Hiram glanced skyward in the direction of the lone Havoc's engine sounds.

With the base in sight Bat turned into the standard western approach. Completing his left-hand turn, Bat settled the Havoc into its final approach toward the end of the runway. He held a right rudder as the plane slid into a right crosswind. The synchronized drone of the approaching Havoc made everyone look skyward.

"Gear down." Bat spoke automatically as he performed each action. He pushed down the gear lever located on the left side of the seat.

Coleman craned forward to see where the lever was.

Bat and Coleman felt a subtle vibration throughout the ship as the wheel well doors opened. They heard the noise of the landing gear being hydraulically lowered. Bat reached to his trim tabs to stabilize the Havoc on final. He compensated some for the crosswind and the gear that now hung out in the slipstream. He watched the hydraulic pressure fall until he got all greens from the indicator lights on his instrument panel. He glanced at his hydraulic pressure gauge to be sure it had recovered to normal. The once smooth airflow around the airframe was now a roar.

"Flaps control set to landing."

Bat pushed the flaps' control lever into the proper setting. He continued the landing procedure, calling out maneuvers mainly for Coleman's sake. Bat knew the routine by heart.

"Throttles back to approach speed, manifold pressure thirty inches." The Havoc slowed to less than 150 mph on approach. Bat felt the Havoc develop that usual heavy feel with the gear and flaps down and a slower air speed.

"What do the flaps do?"

Bat responded to Coleman again in an instructor's fashion, as he scanned the instrument panel to be sure all was going according to protocol. He explained to Coleman that these maneuvers were designed to slow the plane by increasing the drag. Simultaneously the flaps generated more lift at the slower speeds. The flaps increased the surface area of the wing and changed the airflow characteristics so the wing had the low speed lift it needed to land.

Bat scanned the panel again then looked up to check his alignment with the runway.

"That's why they have to be partially out for takeoff when you're bombed up and full out for landing. This wing design won't give you the lift to fly at low speeds without them."

The need for flaps on this high-performance aircraft left little room for error on approach and landing. The plane had to land in a nose-up attitude just like it took off.

"Throttles back."

Coleman watched the airspeed quickly bleed off to less than 135 mph.

The hours of flight time in ferrying the aircraft combined with this test flight had finally produced what the test flight was designed to do, that is, bring out any potential faults or mechanical failures before the plane was flown into combat. A one-inch section of control cable that attached to the rudder-horn control yoke had accidentally been damaged during installation. More than six filaments in the braided cable had been cut. This severely weakened cable was under stress as Battersby held pressure against the right crosswind with down elevator and slight right aileron. Having slowed to less than 130 mph, the plane was about four hundred feet off the ground and slightly more than a mile from the runway when the failure occurred.

As the last thousandths of a millimeter of steel finally reached its breaking point the rudder cable snapped. It flailed wildly as the sudden release of constrained potential energy in the tight cable caused it to wrap around the elevator cables, locking the rudder into a right turn with the elevators positioned nose down.

With his control cables suddenly frozen, Bat recognized the seriousness of the problem. The Havoc began to drop nose first and the right wing dipped. Instinctively, Bat reached to be sure the flaps lever was at full.

Looking out the window and then at the instrument panel, Bat tried to right the plane's attitude with reverse aileron pressure. He could not pull up the nose. His instincts made him reach for the throttles to power up the right engine in hopes of correcting the right-wing drop while he fought to stay on approach.

Bat heard the starboard engine begin to power up as he adjusted the throttles. He felt the right wing rise while he watched the nose angle slowly to the left. For an instant Bat felt he was going to be able to set down without crashing.

Bat's pulse quickened as the first drops of sweat burned his right eye. His confidence rose.

The small success was short-lived. The starboard engine began to sputter. The fuel pump's heavy rubber diaphragm had been ripped from its fittings.

Battersby's adrenalin doubled as he heard the engine rumble to a stop. He glanced back to the instrument panel in time to see the fuel pressure in the engine drop to zero.

Bat started to think the problem through.

Engine failure starboard, the starboard wing dropping, losing lift, the port wing lifting up unrestrained as it lifts against the unbalanced loss of power on the right, and for some reason he could not raise the nose or use his rudder peddles. Battersby applied more left aileron, trying to raise the right wing to level the plane. He kicked on the rudder pedals to pull the nose to the left.

To increase the manifold pressure in the left engine, Bat throttled up quickly.

No good.

He heard the irritating stall warning erupt, and hit the emergency cross-feed fuel-booster switch to the right engine.

The Havoc shuddered as it started stalling at 112 mph. At this speed, even with full flaps and the 464 square feet of wing surface, the A-20 could not stay airborne for long. Gravity was winning.

Bat throttled up both engines by pushing the starboard throttle to the air-start position while he pushed the left-engine throttle handle to the bulkhead wall. Frantically he tried to get the right engine to restart while he strained against the last bit of control surface he had left. He tried to pull the nose up, but the ground kept getting closer. The two men could see only the deep green of the English countryside through the windshield.

With the nose having dropped well below the horizon, combined with the loss of altitude, Bat knew he did not have enough altitude to gain sufficient energy and airspeed to pull up.

"Captain!"

"I know."

In these final moments Battersby methodically tried to fire up the starboard engine, setting the propeller pitch and rpm control at their optimum for an air restart.

No longer flying, the Havoc fell at just over 100 mph and covered the short downward vector to the ground in seconds. The gremlin had shot from the first failure to the next in no time.

Bat felt the front landing gear hit first and then collapse. The nose crushed into the ground with a sickening, groaning metallic sound. Dirt began spewing from the front of the plane as it dug a deep furrow. The right wing struck the ground next. It was ripped from the fuselage, tearing fuel lines and the inboard fuel tank open as it tore from its bulkhead. Battersby thought of his wife and baby, and then wished he had written that letter. Continuing to skid, the plane rolled onto its back with the left wing pointing up, just after the fuel ignited.

With the fuel lines open, fuel began spewing onto the wing, aided by the pressure of the cross-feed fuel pump. The fuel showered the engine nacelle and instantly ignited when it hit the hot exhaust ports. Flames erupted and billowed all along the wing. Then the fumes in the open vapor-filled fuel tanks exploded, throwing metal shrapnel inside the open fuselage.

Looking out the side window, Coleman was unaware the wing had separated from the fuselage. Flames flashed in from the right side and rolled toward the cockpit—it was the last thing the airman saw.

Continuing its flaming, grinding swathe through the open field, the wounded bird completed its roll onto its back, crushing the cockpit, and then slowly came to rest less than three-quarters of a mile from the end of the runway. Except for the sound of the claxton and the emergency vehicles, everyone watched in quiet sickened disbelief as the oil-rich smoke blackened the sky over the crash site.

It took only seconds to end the earthly existence of two fine men.

Watching the tragedy unfolding before them Jack, Hiram, Bill, and Ralph realized Battersby was in serious trouble. It was over so quickly no one could believe it. The A-20 hit the ground at a thirty-degree angle nose first. Everyone knew the sound and what it meant. Instinctively everyone reacted, even before the emergency claxton sounded. They were ready to assist any way they could with what had just happened.

Ralph ran into the Operations building and called the fire-rescue crews to sound the alarm. The emergency claxton started wailing soon after the Havoc had come to a complete rest. Along with the others, Jack raced to the burning plane off the western end of the runway. The rest of the base along with the rescue personnel surged into action in a well-trained response to the emergency.

Ebony smoke billowed as orange flames roared upward from the burning hulk into the beautiful blue sky, reaffirming to all who had witnessed it the deadly reality of the risks so many men took every day. The sky was a place not reserved for humankind's presence by God, but one that they had ascended to with their own knowledge.

The heat from the burning wreckage overwhelmed many. It made it almost impossible for anyone to approach the wreckage, except the firefighters. The fire crew arrived and began their laborious ballet of dragging hoses and starting pumps to get water onto the fire. They streamed water on the left wing, which still had intact fuel tanks. This was their best hope—to keep the situation from becoming any worse.

Ready to chip in, the three pilots and the navigator arrived at the crash site, and jumped from the truck they had commandeered.

"Get out of the way," yelled the senior staff sergeant. "I don't need my crew trying to pull an overly heroic officer out of this mess!"

Jack, Bill, Hiram, and Ralph backed off, as the firefighters rushed around the burning aircraft.

On base it was not uncommon to see a bad crash landing or a plane burning after a difficult mission, but this was such a senseless waste. Thankfully, the two spiritless bodies that had been trapped in the burning plane did not care. The flames were painless to their mortal shells. In the crash two spirits were granted their freedom, violently and suddenly from the confines of their now lifeless bodies. They were soaring high on a flight of their own. Bat and Coleman had now completed the effortless flight reserved by God for man.

Their comrades stared at the burning mass and wondered how many more.

In spite of the morning losses, the afternoon mission to the Bois d'enfer No-ball site was started that day. Crewmen strolled into the briefing hut, took their customary seats, and focused on the mission at hand. The past—even the recent past—was the past.

Shortly after the briefing, forty aircraft cranked up to fly the afternoon's mission. The first two boxes scored good hits. The third box aborted when it could not find the target due to smoke. Returning home, everyone had to fly over the morning's crash site on landing approach. Ralph and Dave looked down on the burnt remains of the A-20, where work was still ongoing to remove the dead airmen's remains from the wreckage.

Once on the ground debriefings were completed and no losses were recorded. Operations noted the good bomb results. Bat would have called it "a good day at the office." For the surviving airmen it was another mission completed and one more closer to rotating out.

The aircrews headed for their barracks and then the showers. Chow and then a stiff drink followed if the men were not on flight status. The ground crews were already on the job repairing and readying the fleet of A-20s for the coming morning mission.

Chow was more a social time than culinary experience. Whether you felt like it or not, you had to feed yourself to keep up your strength. Following military tradition the officers dined in separate eating quarters from the enlisted men.

Jack and Earl had left the Quonset hut together heading toward their squadron's mess. Along the way, others from the 669th squadron had joined them. Settling into the line, they waited their turn while smoking and chatting. Earl spotted Hiram and Bill with some extra chairs at their table.

"Let's sit there, Jack."

Walking over to the table, Earl asked, "Mind if we join you guys?"

"Sure, have a seat. Glad to have ya," Hiram said.

"What happened to Bat up there today, Bill?" Hiram took a sip of coffee.

"Don't know. Looked like a stall, but I don't know why."

"Did the ground chief say anything?"

"No, fire pretty well took care of any evidence. What do you think?"

"When it's your time it's your time. Not much else to say." Hiram sipped his bitter coffee.

Bill and Hiram had become good friends over the course of their time together. It was a time that left little room for them or any of the others to bring new friends into their lives. Not that they wanted to—having seen the dark wings of death carry so many of their old friends away, they wanted only to deal with the friendships that they had now.

"Heard they said a few words in the afternoon briefing for them both," Jack added.

"I heard up at Operations they're gonna bury them over in the Cambridge Military Cemetery day after tomorrow," Earl said. "If I'm not flying, I'll make it."

The others shook their heads in acknowledgement.

The 416th had been in the fight only four months and a few days and death had already become a way of life for them.

It was a bad way to end an otherwise good day.

Chapter Two

The Early Days

*The volume of employment is determined by the point of intersection of the aggregate
supply function with the aggregate demand function...Consumption—to repeat
the obvious—is the sole end and object of all economic activity.*

– John Maynard Keynes, 1936

The 416th Tactical Bomb Group arrived in England in January 1944, months
before the deaths of Battersby and Coleman. They entered the fight for the first time in
March as they began their part in the preparation of the battlefield for the upcoming
invasion of the Continent. Their efforts were soon to be multiplied with the arrival of
their sister light bomber groups, the 409th and 410th in May 1944.

The 416th's first ten missions flown in March 1944 were directed against Luftwaffe airfields and the new German V-1 buzz bomb sites. To put it kindly, these missions
were at best educational, if not anticlimactic. Two of the missions were aborted when
the pilots failed to rendezvous with their fighter escort. On one mission cloud cover
prevented bombing. Another mission was marred by navigational errors, which resulted
in a visit to the outskirts of Paris. This miscalculation flew the group over the Luftwaffe's
anti-aircraft emplacements twice, resulting in nearly every aircraft receiving flak damage. Yet another mission had the bomb-release mechanism fail, causing the payload to
be released as soon as the bomb bay doors were opened. Bad weather kept the group
grounded for most of the month.

Only three of the ten missions resulted in what would be considered good hits,
but the group earned eight Purple Hearts, witnessed the startling realities of B-17s, and
B-26s falling from the skies over France and Belgium, and few parachutes were seen
opening as they fell. April was to prove to be much different.

Pulling back the covers, Jack rolled his lanky six foot two frame out of his cot
into the darkness of the Quonset hut.

"Damn, it's cold," he muttered as his socked feet hit the wood floors. For some
reason the blankets and long johns were never enough to cut the cold of the English
morning. Wethersfield was even farther north than London, putting it closer to the
same latitude as Newfoundland. Even with longer days and the stove, it got chilly at
night, no matter how much wood he burned in it. Knowing the way to the woodpile by
heart, he moved quickly through the dark hut and found a few more quarters of wood
to shove into the stove.

Smiling, Jack was reminded of winters back in Tennessee many years before this
war, when he'd get up to keep the fires going in his family's old home on the banks of

the Tennessee River. With the early spring plants starting to show, it would be nice there now, but still too early by the almanac's calendar to start planting.

Quonset hut living

Barracks at Wethersfield, England, from March 1944 until
September 1945. This base was much more comfortable than
all the forward-line bases (Melun and Laon) in which the
416th was stationed after D day. Each squadron was bivouacked
adjacent to its planes' hardstands. Each squadron had its own
mess hall adjacent to barracks at Wethersfield. The Quonset
huts could hold ten men and a potbellied stove. Today the
windows and stoves are collector's items for museums.
Reproduced with permission from Ralph Conte.

Walking back to the stove, Jack knew it wasn't quite how he remembered it to be back at home now. The thousand acres of good farmland along with his home had become the victim, or at best the not-so-willing participant, of the Tennessee Valley Authority's (TVA) dam system. The East Tennessee River Valley had been flooded from north of Knoxville all the way to the Ohio River. The old home was under it, in thirty feet of dark green water. No more floods but lots of electricity. Rural electrification, they called it.

Jack thought of all the good, rich farmland that had been lost, not to mention the loss of all the outstanding duck and goose hunting. All that remained of the family's heritage was a two-story house located on a river bluff next to Winton's Chapel Method-ist Church. This house was backed by seven hundred acres of rolling, wooded hills still owned by the family. The land for the church had been donated by his great-grandfather E.C. Montgomery and great-uncle John A. Winton. The chapel was named after John A. Winton's father, John C. Winton, who had been a central figure in helping to establish the Methodist faith in the East Tennessee Valley. Jack pictured the house and the church as he remembered them.

He could see the church and house looking out over the new body of water created by the TVA. On the far bank, across the body of water that lay in front of the old home place, a hill had an old red-stone quarry carved into its side. It protruded 150 feet upward from the water's surface and had another forty feet below that couldn't be seen. It was a shear, red rock face that had been patiently cut and dynamited out of the bluff before the lake had covered over a third of it.

It was the red-stone quarry in which all the Smith boys had worked while growing up in the river valley. In that quarry, they learned the art and danger of explosives along with the value of hard work. It was a life of hard work very similar to the lives of the men now fighting and dying in the service of their country, trying to win this war.

Jack thought back to the 1930s, before the flooding of the valley. He and his brothers had worked for the TVA, helping to build the dams. They had also worked for Roosevelt's Civilian Conservation Corps. He had enjoyed both jobs, but the most interesting part was excavating the Cherokee burial mounds that were up and down the river valley while working for the TVA. He was glad he had been assigned to work with the Indian reclamation crews instead of the regular cemetery crews. Somehow working in the Indian mounds seemed more important, and it was certainly more historical.

He knew, though, how hard it was for all the families up and down the valley to see their families exhumed from their resting places. His family had been lucky. Their plots were on the bluff next to Winton Chapel. A few Indian mounds too weren't going to be in the flood zone. They left them alone.

Jack knew his time with the CCC, like the commitments of so many others to the CCC during the 1930s, had become memorable and historic. He appreciated that the CCC, a nationwide work program, had helped shape the lives and politics of so many during its time. The general distrust of former Republican President Hoover and the chance to work a goods day's labor for a fair wage, had left many men and women his age Democrats for life.

Jack wondered how it had all come to this. From the farm, to the CCC, to the TVA, to this cold hut filled with good men willing to die for their country and their beliefs against an enemy who seemed to not believe in much of anything except death.

While finishing his work on the fire, he wondered where President Roosevelt and his programs would carry America in the years to come. As he focused on getting back to bed, he realized that he might never know, and left those issues for others to decide.

☙❦❧

Franklin Delano Roosevelt wondered too what he had gotten himself into and where things were going in this war that had already cost so much. It had been a long road to this moment in time. It was a road potholed with greed, distrust, worldwide market crashes, wars of imperialism, wars of retribution, interracial hatred, fear of immigration, and the rise of eugenics. It was a road that allowed for the irrational resurrection of ancient beliefs.

It had been a bumpy road for democracy also that led to Roosevelt being elected the thirty-second president of the United States in 1932. Roosevelt had campaigned against Herbert Hoover, who, with a slogan of a "chicken in every pot," promised a return to the abundance of the Roaring Twenties. However, Roosevelt's win marked the start of the worst of times for the Great Depression, despite the newly elected president's best efforts to get the country moving again. His election was quickly followed by the formation of "Roosevelt's Tree Army," officially called the Civilian Conservation Corps, or CCC, as it was also known. Such a broad plan to rework government and democracy, some would have thought, would be impossible from a man stricken with polio. With the increasing prominence of eugenics-driven movements that directed policy, those who suffered from any perceived degree of "unfitness" might be destined for removal from society. Yet Roosevelt proceeded with great ambition.

Designed to be one of the major themes in Roosevelt's New Deal programs, the CCC rose out of the administration's absolute need to get the American people back to work. The CCC fought a different kind of war in the 1930s—a war against the power of nature's ruthlessness. It was a war that in some ways was not much different than the international war the men who were working for the CCC would soon be fighting. The CCC intended to harness the resources of a large group of young, unemployed men in the mid-Depression era by putting them to work rebuilding the now decimated and unmanaged renewable resources across the country.

Roosevelt's programs fought against widespread economic problems. The Depression was fueled by the closure of over eighty-six thousand small businesses. Some five thousand banks were also shuttered, five of which were in the county next to then President Herbert Hoover's home. Defaults on home mortgages catapulted to 273,000 in 1932 alone, forcing families into the streets. As a result, the Gross Domestic Product had fallen to $41 billion from a high of $104 billion between 1929 and 1932. Major corporations were nearly idled, as exampled by US Steel operating at 19 percent of capacity. Unemployment skyrocketed, rising from less than 5 percent in 1929 to a high of nearly 25 percent in 1933. In the recession of 1938, the unemployment rate would peak again, at nearly 18 percent.

The significance of the stock market crash of 1929 and its contribution to unemployment was driven home by the fact that by 1933 stocks were worth 11 percent of their value in 1929. Investors who had overleveraged themselves lost $74 billion. It was a loss of value that could have been foreseen. During the 1920s, the American agricultural and industrial sectors were weakening. Farmers and industry overproduced, but both failed to increase wages to keep demand in balance with the "aggregate." Companies and individuals flush with cash speculated in the stock market, and even borrowed money to speculate, money that would sooner or later have to be repaid. Meanwhile, the industrial infrastructure was not upgraded, and consumers were progressively spending less and less, as their purchasing became more subsistence driven.

The American economic cycle was stifled even more by Germany's economic nightmare coupled with a slowing world economy. This decline was followed by the American crash in 1929, which had been preceded by a general economic slowdown. Hoover's hopes of "a chicken in every pot and two cars in every garage" did not and could not happen. On the other side of the Atlantic, the Germans wished they could buy chickens but couldn't get a big-enough truck to carry all the hyperinflated deutsche marks needed to buy one. The US market crash was preceded by a worldwide decline of stocks that began in 1928 on the Paris, London, and Berlin exchanges. The Berlin market and Germans in general suffered terribly. This suffering was feeding fuel to Hitler's fires of hate, hate that would help drive America into a war that would ultimately pull it out of the Depression but with a terrible cost. [4, 5]

In the early to mid-1930s American families, young high school graduates, and single men and women were all searching for relief from their newfound poverty and despair. Unfortunately they were searching penniless in an economy that was geared toward the consumer. Society had embraced the industrial revolution with such unrestrained vigor that it had grown almost unregulated. That growth came ultimately at the expense of the farmer, the fragile land, and the consumer.

During this period of despair, some industries and individuals did prosper, though. The contraceptive business was going great guns, netting $250 million a year. The movie houses collected their two bits hand over fist as people sought escape from the realities of their desperate lives. Fuller Brush salesmen were carrying the Fuller Brush Company to new revenue highs. J. Paul Getty was quietly acquiring controlling interests in petroleum companies across America. Howard Johnson's was born in Quincy, Massachusetts, due to the success of a playhouse across the street, as patrons of the arts would stop in for dinner before or after a play.

In spite of the paradox of an industrial, consumer-driven economy failing, an interesting number of successes did slowly appear that supported the economic theories of John Maynard Keynes. Keynes explained the concepts to President Roosevelt in an open letter published in the *New York Times* in December 1933. Keynes wrote, "The object of recovery is to increase the national output and put more men to work…Output is primarily produced for sale; and the volume of output depends on the amount of purchasing power, compared with the prime cost of production…Public authority must be called in aid to create additional current incomes through the expenditure of borrowed or printed money." In effect, Keynes advocated that the government should

---

4   *The Wall Street Waltz, 90 Visual Perspectives,* By Kenneth L. Fisher, Chapter 29, A Clear Warning, pages 70–71; 1987

5   American President, President Herbert Hoover; http://www.americanpresident.org/history/herberthoover/biography/printable.html

"prime the pump" of future consumption by spending now, especially with borrowed money. FDR seemed only too willing to get consumers spending again.

However, citizens struggled daily to just survive, let alone consume luxuries, with what money there was going to feed, shelter, clothe, and protect their families or themselves. This subsistence level—the baseline of Abraham Maslow's hierarchy of needs—was what Roosevelt wanted to help Americans transcend. Besides, he needed an enlarged and productive tax base to fill the empty coffers of the treasury. However, poor maintenance and caretaking of the land were to deter any such optimistic plan.

The American Industrial Revolution had spurred traditional conservation principles to the point that with the wanton harvesting of trees throughout the Midwestern and Western states, a recipe for disaster was looming. Modern farming equipment had allowed for expansion of farming lands at the expense of trees and natural barriers to weather. The replanting of cash crops and subsistence crops had drained the soil of nutrients, a situation that was complicated by a protracted drought in the early thirties. In the heartland of American, farmers were suddenly unable to grow crops.

Having been stripped of her ability to control the outcome of man's action, Mother Nature watched helplessly as the "Dust Bowl" exploded into the reality of the Great Depression. It was a painful example of the misuse of natural renewable resources. The Dust Bowl gave way to huge dust storms that buried homes and family farms, causing the decimation of untold acres of valuable farmland in the once fertile Midwest. This decimation dislodged hundreds of thousands of families from their traditional homes. The Dust Bowl would last upward of ten years, with the painful experience personified for all Americans by the lives of the Joad family in John Steinbeck's *The Grapes of Wrath*. It was a novel that arguably encouraged the prospects of socialism in America while further fueling the fears of Roosevelt's Republican distracters.

With the failed realities of the country's economic, industrial, and agricultural policies staring Roosevelt in the face, the administration designed the basic programs to help correct these problems. The CCC was one of the key programs to rejuvenate the country, restoring trees that had once sheltered the land from the now unchecked winds that blew across the Midwest and to help prevent erosion that was robbing the land of what little useful topsoil remained. The loss of trees in the barren soil coupled with unrestrained winds brought dust storms, and worsened the already-blighted existence of the families trying to survive in the Depression's path. This geological condition created one of Roosevelt's biggest economic problems—mass migration of families off the farmlands. The labor he needed to accomplish his goals was now in the inner cities, shanty towns, or working as migrant laborers all across America.

The newly elected president worked swiftly. Within a hundred days of his inauguration, FDR had signed the Emergency Conservation Corps (ECW) bill. The ECW bill married the strengths of the nation's young men to FDR's mission of reclaiming the decimated lands of the western states. The land recovery bill was only part of Roosevelt's reforms in his first hundred days. Other areas of reform included insurance for bank deposits (FDIC), refinancing for home mortgages (getting people back home), Wall Street reforms, four billion dollars in federal relief spending, legalization of beer, the Tennessee Valley Authority, and the Agricultural Adjustment Administration. After the days of laissez-faire capitalism in the Roaring Twenties, Roosevelt was carving out a new mission for government in the thirties, with reform bills the likes of which few had ever imagined.

While some policies helped increase output, others seemed to produce strange outcomes. For example, the Agricultural Adjustment Act (AAA) provided crop subsidies to farmers to not farm—and even destroy their crops and animals (which included the destruction of six million swine)—so that prices would rise. The political commotion rising from these policies was to continue for some time with protests of prominent officials not being heard. Speaking on behalf of disbelievers, Henry Wallace, then secretary of agriculture, exclaimed of such programs, "I hope we shall never have to resort to it again. To destroy a standing crop goes against the soundest instincts of human nature." Keynes was also critical of the policy of creating higher agricultural prices by limiting supply. In his open letter to the president, he wrote, "Thus rising prices caused by deliberately increasing prime costs or by restricting output have a vastly inferior value to rising prices which are the natural result of an increase in the nation's purchasing power." Walter Lippmann, a noted political commentator of the time, summed up the dissenting opinion when he wrote: "The excessive centralization and the dictatorial spirit are producing revulsion of feeling against bureaucratic control of American economic life."

Despite the criticism, Roosevelt created still other programs to "prime the pump" of consumption, such as the SSA, the SEC, and the NRA. With more of the so-called "alphabet soup" of his programs, Roosevelt did get money into the hands of consumers. By creating the Social Security Act (SSA) in 1935, he ensured a steady subsidy, but not a pension plan, to the elderly and infirm members of this consumer-driven economy that had few available consumers.

Contrarian political opinion surrounding the regulation of Wall Street hit a high note when the Securities and Exchange Commission (SEC) came into being. Uproar abounded when Joseph Kennedy was appointed by FDR to head the commission. Kennedy was referred to as a traitor to his class, and Republicans charged it was a plot to "Russianize everything worthwhile." In the long run, FDR's decision proved to be right, as Kennedy had a reputation as a shrewd speculative investor who knew the "good and bad" of the Street.

Meanwhile, the National Relief Act (NRA) was designed to help the industrial sector of the suffering economy, and was successful, to some degree. Under the act, labor gained collective bargaining rights, and women and children were freed from sweatshops and near-servitude. The act also allowed closer regulation of the workplace and industry. Ultimately, though, the NRA would falter, as overregulation with wage- and price-fixing proved to be unworkable The NRA along with the AAA suffered under legal challenges, with the Supreme Court ultimately declaring them invalid. Both finally slowly disappeared, dying the death of good intent but bad legislation. However, the Fair Labor Standards Act of 1938 did rise from the ashes.[6]

Another of Roosevelt's problems was finding some way to relieve the country of the debt of the Depression. The country had neither the money nor the tax base to remove the debt. The solution to the shortfall was made clear to FDR by John Maynard Keynes, who elaborated a mechanism by which the government could pull the American people from the Depression—deficit spending in the lean years, followed by surpluses to replenish the treasury in the boom years. The publication of Keynes's work *The General Theory of Employment, Interest and Money* in 1936 followed a meeting he had with President Roosevelt in 1934. After the conference, Keynes remarked: "Supposed the president was more literate, economically speaking."

Roosevelt seemed bewildered in his statements about the meeting with Keynes: "He left a whole rigmarole of figures" and "He must be a mathematician rather than a political economist." Yet despite Roosevelt's campaign promise to balance the national budget that "Hoover had created," he set about to spend money the government didn't have.

The real use and impact of deficit spending would come into its own in 1938, when a recession risked deepening the Depression and Roosevelt began the arguably successful financial funding and management of all government programs by running a large deficit. This deficit spending would continue during the war to record levels. When compared to the Gross Domestic Product (GDP) as a benchmark, the government deficit went as high as 120 percent of GDP during the war years of the 1940s.[7] After such an experiment, deficit spending would become part of the world economy. Keynesian deficit spending in the end would be loved and hated by many for years to come. In spite of Keynes's hypotheses on the value of deficit spending, many still credit the war economy of high production and rapid consumption coupled with good salaries for rescuing the American economy and its workers. [8, 9, 10]

Aside from the cost of the new programs, the enactment of these bills forced upon an unready nation the logistical nightmare of mobilizing, enrolling, feeding, housing, and providing for what would ultimately become a civilian "tree army" of three million men. Creating not only logistical problems, this process produced ideological concerns, as the military was called in to manage FDR's vision.

---

6   Fair Labor Standards Act of 1938: Maximum Struggle for a Minimum wage; Jonathan Grossman; US Department of Labor; http://www.dol.gov/oasam/programs/history/flsa1938.htm#content

7   *The Wall Street Waltz*, Kenneth L. Fisher, Chapter 74, In the Know, Or Heavily Snowed?; pages 168–169; 1987

8   Readers Companion to American History, New Deal, Houghton Mifflin; http://college.hmco.com/history/readerscomp/rcah/html/ah_064200_newdeal.htm

9   The Dust Bowl, http://www.usd.edu/anth/epa/dust.html

10   An Open Letter to President Roosevelt, John Maynard Keynes; http://newdeal.feri.org/misc/keynes2.htm

On April 7th—just thirty-four days after FDR's inauguration on March 4th, 1933—the CCC program had its first enrollee. Due to the colossal intent of the program and the fact that all the labor for the western projects lived in the east, it became clear to the administration and the ultimate civilian program director, Robert Fechner, that the military was going to have to play a major role in managing the complex and massive logistical problems. The undertaking had become so overwhelming to some that other ways to manage the problem arose. The chief forester, who was assigned the responsibility to mobilize the forces, fell from his office window to his untimely death. President Roosevelt wasted no time appointing Douglas MacArthur, the only four-star general in the nation, as the director of the CCC.

Over the objections of organized labor, which was in fear of military regimentation of labor, the military accepted the challenge and to their credit proved labor's fears unfounded. William Green of the American Federation of Labor (AFL), one of the largest unions, declared the military management smacked "of Fascism, of Hitlerism, of a form of Sovietism." Regardless, MacArthur saw this as an opportunity to make some form of recompense for the military's forced eviction of the Bonus Expeditionary Force (BEF) from Washington earlier in 1932. Thought by the Hoover administration to be generally squatters, the BEF was actually nearly 94 percent military veterans who wanted the acceleration of their $500 war bonus payments to help themselves and their families. President Hoover had ordered their removal and the military followed orders. Aside from MacArthur, a then eager Major George Patton led the eviction assault, both men destined for more noble efforts.

The involvement of the military in the CCC may have been as necessary as it was ultimately prophetic. Introducing young men from all over the country to the regimentation and discipline of the military helped lay the foundations for their future military service. This exposure would make their adjustment after December 7, 1941, to mess halls, barracks life, and command structure much easier. Coupling their past experience in the CCC with their new commitment to defeating the enemy at all costs, many of the American soldiers in the war had developed the tools for military success in the 1930s.

The military regimentation of the public works projects developed leadership talents that would prove beneficial in the war. The military's involvement required a command structure that naturally brought young military officers with leadership and administrative skills to the forefront. For example, Colonel George C. Marshall was recognized for his administrative skills, an ability that would serve the nation well in the 1940s, when Marshall served as military chief of staff, and later in the postwar period, when he worked as secretary of state and administered the Marshall Plan, which rebuilt the war-torn European countries. Also of note, as head of the program, General Douglas MacArthur honed the skills that were to shape the Pacific Basin for decades after the war.

The process of deploying FDR's programs revealed many cracks in the ability of the US to mobilize its population and resources. Utilizing the Army, Navy, Coast Guard, and Marine regular and reserve officers, the military command structure put the nation's military and its transportation system on a war-type footing. The country was forced to realize it was poorly prepared to deal with the reality of the mobilization and the moving of hundreds of thousands of men across the country. The military was also required to move the material to house, feed, and support the army of "civilians" doing the work of the nation. In essence, the military came of age at a time well before the development of this infrastructure would become of critical military importance to the nation. At the time of this great mobilization, America had the sixteenth-largest army in the world. *Fortune* magazine rightfully referred to it as the "worst equipped" military in the world, this in spite of its three-million-strong civilian CCC army.

In the face of the immense challenge, the enrollments started and the training began. All enrollees went through the traditional, military group physicals followed by inoculations, and then transfer to a military camp. From there they were assigned to camps or built them, living and working a military lifestyle. This lifestyle included military-type uniforms, drills, military discipline, and military chaplains with whom the men worshiped their God. Of course, the bleak barracks housing that was heated with potbellied stoves was included. The heavy equipment was military type. The base commanders and administrators were all from the services. In essence, the CCC was a paramilitary organization that worked hard and worked well.

As the program developed, the nation grew into a country of CCC believers. By 1934, the CCC had a legion of supporters: Republicans; the *Chicago Tribune's* owner and editor, Colonel Robert McCormick, a reformed Roosevelt hater; and even the Soviet Union. Without a doubt, the economy of the United States benefited from it. The workers in the camps were paid $30 a month and families received $25 allotment checks every month. Around $72 million in allotment checks were paid out over the early life of the program, stimulating the economies around the CCC camps. This massive infusion of dollars into local communities started the drive of all legislators to have camps placed in their states and communities. This infusion of cash saved countless businesses and started the road to the end of the CCC.

In some respects these local microeconomies supported the concept of consumer-driven market forces. The microeconomies created local demand and thereby increased output and downstream need for product materials. To paraphrase Keynes, aggregate buying power increased aggregate output, which required aggregate purchasing of a manufacturer's products and raw materials. Quite possibly this early phase of the recovery was the driving in of the pylons on which the rest of the recovery would be built.

By 1935, the CCC had started into its boom days, having built camps in every state in the union, as well as the territories of Hawaii, Alaska, Puerto Rico, and the Virgin Islands. The program would enroll up to 80,000 Native Americans, 250,000 veterans of the Spanish-American War and World War I, not to mention the millions of other Americans across the country of all ethnicities and races.

The CCC was involved in almost any area where their efforts would rejuvenate the landscape—fighting forest fires, draining soil, providing disaster relief, and doing other nonagricultural tasks. For example, the corps helped fight forest fires to the tune of 4,235,000 man-days; fires destroyed the basic work of the corps. The corps is credited with building 3,470 fire towers and ninety-seven thousand miles of fire roads. They also strung eighty-nine thousand miles of telephone line and planted over three billion trees to help stop the erosion of precious soil on more than twenty million acres of farms.

The CCC also worked with soil drainage. This task included the creation of 84.4 million acres of usable farmland from once unusable wetlands. This aspect of the program created new farmland roughly the size of Ohio, Indiana, and Iowa combined. This new farmland would be pressed into service soon enough to help feed America's coming war machine and military.

The CCC performed other key duties across the country. The Corps participated in disaster relief and aided farmers in times of natural disasters to protect livestock. They participated by responding collectively to the emergency, much the way a platoon, a company, or a division of soldiers would respond to an enemy assault. In addition, the CCC taught forty thousand men to read, and helped others gain their high school diplomas. It taught many skills that could be used after the minimum enlistment of six months, which could be extended to a maximum of two years.

The CCC was not the only large-scale government work program. Roosevelt's Tennessee Valley Authority was created to harness the Tennessee River to produce electricity. The program was as controversial as it was successful. The seeds of the TVA project were planted well before the Depression era. Its foundations came with the purchase of the property around Muscle Shoals, Alabama, in 1916 by the federal government. The government intended to build a dam to produce enough electricity to supply new factories that were to have been built in that area. These factories were to produce nitrates and phosphates for weapons during World War I.

However, the war ended and the property languished for decades. Ultimately, its time came with the Depression and Roosevelt's desire to open the Tennessee River to commerce, and the ongoing electrification of the region. TVA was also given the mandate to improve "the economic and social well-being of the people living in said river basin"—big, amorphous goals that were consistent with the times. Therefore, the TVA achieved other objectives: flood control, reforestation, assistance in agricultural and industrialization, and aid in national defense.

Opposition to the TVA was fierce, as private power companies sought to stop the project. Wendell Wilkie of the Commonwealth and Southern Company along with the Alabama Power Company and John D. Battle of the National Coal Association tried from 1932 to 1939 to have the Supreme Court declare the project invalid and unconstitutional, all to no avail. Opposition also came from the people of Tennessee, who had lived, farmed, raised families, and buried loved ones on the land that would be swallowed by the project.

With the government's powerful right of "eminent domain" the unwillingness of families to be displaced was overridden. Many were forced to vacate their family homesteads before the flooding. Their voices were heard the least or not at all, and many were left in as desperate a condition as before their displacement, if not worse. At this time in America's history, national necessities superseded personal needs and would for some time. The onset of a global, all-consuming war lay only a few years away.

Among the first dams to be built in the TVA system was Norris Dam, on the Clinch River, a long way from Muscle Shoals. The structure was named after George W. Norris, the strongest US Senate activist for the construction of the Muscle Shoals dam and the TVA project. Ultimately, Fort Sanders, Watts Bar, Chickamauga, and multiple other dams were built that would supply large quantities of electricity to the displaced and not immediately compensated population of the valley. The electricity would actually be used for purposes of national security, as secret government projects began to spring up around the country, such as in nearby Oak Ridge, Tennessee.

Oak Ridge—a sixty-thousand-acre secret city—was built in the East Tennessee Valley in 1942. Because of its location on the banks of the Clinton River, the city was built to support the nearby uranium-enrichment project named the Clinton River Works. Both massive programs were part of the larger Manhattan Project, which aimed to produce a nuclear bomb that might end the war. The Tennessee Valley was heartily pushed as the ideal location for these facilities by US Senator K.D. McKellar (D). He felt that because of the area's isolation in the rolling hills of east Tennessee, it would be an ideal location in the event of an unexpected explosion. With so few people nearby, it would reduce the risk of catastrophic loss of human life.

A more important reason to locate the uranium-enrichment facilities in the Tennessee River Valley was because of the large quantity of electricity that would be needed for the gaseous-diffusion process of enrichment. During its peak wartime production of uranium, the Clinton River Works consumed 7 percent of all the electricity produced in America.[11] With this energy, the Clinton River Works (later to be known as Oak Ridge National Laboratories) would produce the uranium that would be used, along with the plutonium from the state of Washington, to build the first nuclear weapons. These two critical neutron sources were used to provide the fissionable material for "Fat Man" and "Little Boy"—the names given to the first two nuclear bombs that would be used to end the war in the Pacific. Their prototype—known as "The Gadget"—was exploded in a remote desert area of the West.

The nuclear projects in the Tennessee River Valley would also consume huge amounts of money. Ultimately, of every dollar spent on the Manhattan Project, sixty cents went to the valley. Was this a fair Keynesian enrichment—priming the pump—of the valley's people over time? It cost the government and citizens more than money, as 14,700 tons of silver from the US treasury were consumed during the construction of the nuclear projects. Copper would have been the metal of choice, but it was strategically important, so silver was used as a conductor in the D-rings of the gaseous-diffusion

11   Secret City History: A World War II Secret City; http://smithdray.angletowns.net/or/sch.htm

facility at the Clinton River Works, code-named Y-12.[12] Therefore, money, silver, electricity and manpower produced the weapons that would end the Pacific war and launch the world into the protracted Cold War. [13,14]

In conjunction with the CCC, WPA, TVA, and the other New Deal policies, other dam projects such as the Hoover Dam and the Grand Coulee Dam would play important roles in the development of America's new prewar infrastructure. The Hoover Dam (or Boulder Dam), located in the Black Canyon of Nevada along the course of the Colorado River, had had its political and economic foundations laid in the 1890s. The California Development Company proposed and built water-diversion canals from the Colorado River into California's Imperial Valley. The project, however, was not designed to control the river's flooding, and the project and surrounding communities suffered a series of devastating floods that culminated in the flooding of Yuma, Arizona, in 1916.

The Hoover Dam had a long history. Although studies had been conducted as early as 1902 by the Bureau of Reclamation for a possible dam along the river, it was not until 1922 when the "Hoover Compromise" (named after Herbert Hoover, then secretary of commerce) resulted in the Colorado River Compact. Even with the Compact in place, it wasn't until 1928 that the project was authorized by Congress and then signed by President Calvin Coolidge. Its authorization had followed several failed attempts to pass the Swing-Johnson Bill that permitted the dam's construction. Protestors abounded: the state of Arizona, the private electricity lobby led by US Senator Reed Smoot of Utah, and *Los Angeles Times* publisher Harry Chandler, who had a vested interest in receiving water to his 830,000 acres of farmland downstream from the project. In spite of opposition, the project began, and at its peak employed more than five thousand workers, at a time in America's history when jobs were desperately needed.[15]

Following a surprisingly similar course to the construction of the Hoover Dam, the construction of the Grand Coulee Dam took many years to come to fruition. Like the Hoover Dam, interest in the Grand Coulee Dam began in the late 1890s. Irrigation was in critical need in the Columbia River Basin, particularly during the protracted and devastating droughts from 1929 through 1931 when dust storms of Midwest proportions raged through the river valley and the Northwest. The magnitude of the problem ultimately forced FDR into action, and he was virtually unopposed by legislators in funding public projects. By this point in the massive federal works era, congressional members were not willing to risk voting money away from their constituents. The severity of the

---

12   Secret City History: A World War II Secret City; http://smithdray.angletowns.net/or/sch.htm

13   TVA: Electricity for All, The Origins of the Tennessee Valley Authority, Opposition to TVA, The Dams and Their Builders, Agriculture and Conservation, The Displaced Peoples of Norris Basin; http://newdeal.feri.org/tva/tva01.htm

14   A Short History of TVA: From the New Deal to a New Century; http://www.tva.gov/abouttva/history.htm

15   The Boulder Canyon Project, Hoover Dam; William J. Simonds, http://www.nevada-history.org/boulder-project-by-simonds.html

Depression was one of the driving forces behind the success of much of the new legislation. So, the Grand Coulee Dam was funded, with construction beginning in 1933.

But, while government officials were willing to rubber-stamp FDR's projects, private interests fought mightily against the incursion of the government. The project faced the same resistance from the private power companies and other self-interest groups that the TVA and Boulder Dam projects had. In fact, opponents to the Grand Coulee Dam almost succeeded in stopping the project, after it was found out that FDR had funded it through the Public Work Commission as "Public Works Project No. 9." Roosevelt's attempts to avoid the need for congressional approval resulted in a 1935 US Supreme Court ruling declaring that the president didn't have the authority to construct dams on navigable waterways. Roosevelt responded by pushing through a "Rivers and Harbors" bill that allowed for the justification of this dam and the twenty others then under construction.

When the project was officially funded, an area of the Columbia River known as the "Grand Coulee" was selected as the site for the dam. It was an area of the river that had been carved through granite by glaciers during the last ice age. Employing upward of twelve thousand people throughout its construction, the dam project paid workers from 85 cents per hour, up to $1.20 an hour for skilled laborers. Despite the fact that the dam was under way, the project would still need help against its spoilers. Roosevelt's Department of the Interior and its associated Bonneville Power Administration called in Woody Guthrie in 1941 to help promote the dam. This public relations campaign would also contribute to the fame of Guthrie, a well-known avid Socialist, trade unionist, and regular contributor to the Communist publication *The Daily Worker* with his article "Woody Sez."

Guthrie, a political product of the Dust Bowl and Depression, had become a committed Socialist and anti-Fascist. Woody was promoting himself and the dam when he met a Harvard man, fellow musician and Socialist Pete Seeger. This association led Woody to tour the country with the Almanac Singers, an antiwar group, which is ironic given his previous stints in the Merchant Marines and the US Army. Woody did contribute to the project by writing twenty-six songs about the dam, two of which became well-known ditties, "Roll On, Columbia" and "Grand Coulee Dam." They reportedly earned him a grand total of $266.66.

In the year that Guthrie began touring the nation to promote it, the Grand Coulee Dam would be completed. It eventually produced electricity for the people of the Northwest, but more importantly for the defense industry. The dam supplied large quantities of electricity to the secret Manhattan Project's five-hundred-thousand-acre Hanford Engineer Works. Built by DuPont, the plutonium-production facility located in the wilds of the southwest section of Washington State went on—with the aid of large quantities of electricity—to produce the plutonium that was destined for delivery inside a nuclear bomb to Japan.[16, 17, 18, 19]

By 1939, the CCC and many other large government work projects were beginning to lose importance, as the prospects of war cast a shadow on both of America's coasts and its offshore territories. Fortunately, because of these government programs, the energy-production facilities were located in areas where power-hungry defense facilities would consume their energy and continue the work programs. The TVA, Hoover Dam, and Grand Coulee Dam projects as well as the CCC accomplished one other valuable thing—they helped to build the critical infrastructure that would allow America to become the war machine it was destined to be.

Congress and the Roosevelt administration began to think more globally about national defense as the Nazi ambitions of European domination paralleled the Japanese ambitions in the Pacific. The reality of the coming global conflicts is typified by Japan's response to a 1933 League of Nations request to withdraw its forces from Manchuria after Japan had completed its takeover in 1931 to exploit the area's natural resources. The Japanese had been in Manchuria since 1910 without a challenge, and the final assumption of power over Manchuria was as much a move to lessen Japan's dependence on America's natural resources as it was a drive toward military imperialism. The Japanese withdrew from the League of Nations in early 1933, signaling their global imperial intentions and weakening the authority of the already dysfunctional League.

Japanese imperialism had sown its seeds and grown its roots in the late 1880s with a victory over China that gave Japan control of Taiwan. Korea was next, when it came under Japanese control in 1910 after the Russo-Japanese war. The victory over the Russians had given Japan a small foothold in Manchuria as well—a foothold that was soon to be exploited for the wealth of natural resources the area held.

Japanese imperialism was fertilized in the economic soil of the late 1910s and early 1920s. World War I had brought great economic expansion to Japan, as it aggressively took over trading routes and partners in the Pacific and Indian Ocean basins that the Western powers had abandoned while fighting the war. During the 1920s Japan's false economy was challenged, as the Western countries reacquired their old trading partners in Asia. This shift caused economic pullbacks in Japan, helping to lay the foundations for the rise of military nationalism in Japan. Soon, the Japanese army's superior officers decided it was time to take control. Their efforts were aided by the 1923 earthquake that killed upward of 143,000 people, the strengthening of Chinese rule in Manchuria, the ongoing decline of the economy, and a weak corrupt central government.

Taking control of the government, the military spurred Japanese imperialism forward. In 1931, the Japanese military assumed governmental control in Manchuria,

16   History link Essay: Grand Coulee Dam – a Snapshot
History; File # 7264 http://www.historylink.org/essays/output.cfm?file-id=7264
17   Woody Guthrie Biography; http://www.woodyguhtrie.org/biography.htm
18   Woody Guthrie; http://en.wikipedia.org/wiki/Woody-Guthrie
19   Daily Worker; http://en.wikipedia.org/wiki/Daily_Worker

and assassinated the Japanese Prime Minister Tsuyoshi Inukai in May 1932.[20] The militarists soon forced the government to increase the budget for military armaments to 47 percent of total government spending while Japan's number one export, silk, had fallen by more than 40 percent after the end of America's Roaring Twenties.[21]

On the other side of the world, Adolf Hitler too displayed his imperial ambitions well before World War II officially began. Hitler had become chancellor and ultimately dictator of Germany after 1933. He soon grew his army, navy, and air force to colossal proportions, and put them to work by sending his army to reoccupy the Rhineland without firing a shot. For any objective observer, it would seem Hitler was spoiling for a fight, but the European powers, especially Britain, initially insisted on a policy of appeasement, thinking that the German führer would settle for much less.

While a few nations began rearmament, such as Sweden, which appropriated huge sums for bolstering its national defense in 1936 and 1938, many began to appease the German juggernaut. Typical of the policy of appeasement was that of English Prime Minister Neville Chamberlain, who spoke of "peace in our time," which meant backpedaling to Germany's aggressive posturing. It was a sad testament to a man's and mankind's inability to believe the worst, even when confronted by it. Chamberlain resisted the realities of Nazi Germany's ambitions, as evidenced in his writings to his sister after he read *The House That Hitler Built*. Written by Stephen Roberts, an Australian scholar, the book outlined the rise of National Socialism. In letters to his sister, Chamberlain wrote:

> If I accept the author's conclusions I should despair, but I don't and won't. Fortunately I have recently had a "scintillation" on the subject of German negotiations. It has been accepted promptly and even enthusiastically by all to whom I have broached it and we have sent for [Neville] Henderson [the British ambassador in Berlin] to come and talk it over with us.

Chamberlain's Pollyannaish vision of European politics and accommodative diplomacy would not hold against an aggressor like Hitler.

Winston Churchill had already outlined the failures of such diplomacy in a December 1937 speech before the House of Commons. He noted that on two occasions England had invited the German foreign minister to visit London, and that both invitations had been rejected. Churchill also focused on the relationship that England had with France by discussing its importance, saying that "the greatest significance to the

---

20   Japan; Contributor: Gary D. Allison, Ph.D., Ellen Bayard Weedon Prof. of East Asian Studies, Univ. of Virginia; www.pushsd.k12.ca.us/chana/staffpages/Mr._Eichman/worldhistory/wwii/japan

21   *Soldiers of the Sun: The Rise and Fall of the Imperial Japanese Army;* Meirion and Susie Harries; Random House;
copyright 1991; Part 3; chapter 13; page 139

relations we have with France," and how their democracies were "founded upon the power of the French Army and the power of the British Fleet."

Churchill's comments were designed to instill some realistic insight into Chamberlain's thoughts, but their main result was to cause the prime minister to fear that Hitler would read Churchill's comments. In reality, Hitler was neither interested nor concerned with the rhetoric of the English House of Commons. Hitler would pursue diplomacy with the English as long as it served his needs and no longer. This became even more obvious when, on October 1, 1938, Hitler occupied the Sudetenland in accord with the Munich Agreement, which had just been signed on September 30th by Neville Chamberlain, French Premier Édouard Daladier, Hitler, and his tagalong, Italian Premier Benito Mussolini. All the while Churchill warned, "The belief that security can be obtained by throwing a small state to the wolves is a fatal delusion."[22] It wasn't long before the wolves were coming for the rest of Europe.

While Europe tried placating the Germans, America had pursued a course of isolationism since the end of World War I, believing a head-in-the-sand approach was best. However, the age of self-imposed isolationism was about to be rapidly and uncontrollably brought to an end for America. Fortunately, as a result of well-funded government programs such as the CCC, the United States military was now well versed in the management and movement of massive quantities of men and material. This expanded ability of the military to "manage" was the very logistical necessity that would be required to win the coming war.

While it had done much to prepare the United States for war, the existence of the CCC was under threat. Not only had the prospect of war become the CCC's nemesis, but the economy was now working against it as well. From its low of 41.[22] in 1932, the Dow Jones Industrial Average had risen to 194.40 by 1937, and the increase was helping to spur the confidence of the country and the legislative bodies. It would go lower during the war, but the economy was stronger now and was growing with the pace of war preparations.[23]

Finally, it happened. Congress refused to make the program permanent over Roosevelt's objections, and December 7, 1941, sealed the CCC's fate. The corps had done its bit, and its time was over. America's well-conditioned and well-fed manpower and its recovering economy began focusing on winning a world war. [24,25,26,27]

---

22   *The Last Lion, Winston Spencer Churchill, Alone* 1932–1940; William Manchester, pages 1 to 350

23   *The Wall Street Waltz*, Kenneth L. Fisher, Chapter 22, The Silent Crash No One Noticed, pages 57–58; 1987

24   History of the Civilian Conservation Corps, www.cccalumni.org/history1.html

25   William Manchester, *The Glory and the Dream, A Narrative History of America –1932 –1972;* pages 1 to 93

26   James F. Justin, Civilian Conservation Corps museum, An online Museum of Histories, Items, Stories, links and Photographs regarding the CCC's. ; pages 1–8

27   www.emayzine.com, Japanese Economic History 1930's.

❦

The cold kept Jack moving, making him want to get his mind off it. He thought back to his decision to join the military in 1939. The fact that the farm was now at the bottom of a lake and that there weren't many jobs in Rockwood helped push him into it. His decision would lead him to train as an aircraft mechanic. Rising quickly through the enlisted ranks, he was given the opportunity to advance still further. Passing a college equivalency examination had allowed him the opportunity to be promoted to lieutenant. Having mustanged his way up through the ranks, he also had the ability to relate to men of every stripe.

He sat before the potbellied stove. Still working at getting the fire going to beat back the cold, Jack's thoughts wandered to home again. How were things back home now? A lot different, he figured. The family was different too. Bill was stationed in Burma, Frances at home, and Dick…

He thought about his older brother, Richard, a University of Tennessee magna cum laude engineering graduate, a lieutenant J.G. submarine officer aboard the *USS Corvina* in the Navy. He was gone now, along with eighty-one other sailors, and only a Purple Heart for Mom, Dad and the rest of us to remember him by. In Navy lingo, Dick was now "on eternal patrol."

Jack knew the *Corvina* had become a victim to some part of the war over there. As he understood it, Dick's sub had left on patrol from Pearl Harbor in November '43, it took on fuel at Johnson Island, and disappeared after that.[28] Jack found himself hoping that Dick had not suffered like his friend, whom Jack had witnessed struggling to get out of the cockpit of a burning plane. He sincerely and selfishly said a prayer asking that his mom and dad not have to mourn any more losses. Jack was glad he had sent his first wings home to mom as a keepsake, just in case he ended up in a burning cockpit.

Using one of the split logs to lift the handle on the door of the stove, Jack easily swung the door open, and stuffed a few more pieces of wood in. He closed the door with a small cut of wood they kept around for that purpose.

"Thanks," a voice whispered from the dark.

"No sweat." Jack crawled back between the blankets, waiting for the warmth to come and wondering how his brother Bill was doing in Burma.

Bill flew B-29s over "the Hump." He had written that he spent half his time ferrying gas in the bomb bay tanks to the forward bases over the Himalayas. He said that it seemed like he flew ten missions over the Hump to finally get enough gas there to fly one combat mission. Bill was flying a B-29 named, for some reason, *City of Pittsburg.* Jack hadn't asked where he got the name.

The Japs were tough fighters, so they said. Jack thought about Bill's near-fatal crash landing. It was in an article his mother had mailed from his hometown paper, *The*

---

28   Commander Submarine Force, US Pacific Fleet; USS Corvina; http://www.csp.navy.mil/ww2boats/corvina.htm

Rockwood Times. Jack was glad mom had sent it, but it made him realize just how quickly life moved. Yep, things were a lot different now.

His thoughts kept returning to the article. If the B-29 Super Fortresses had any trouble, there was no getting over the Himalayas. It wasn't hard for Jack to imagine how Bill's plane had been badly damaged and how, on the way back to the base, he had had to drop his bombs to try to gain altitude. In the article, Bill had said, "I was so low to the ground that when I dropped them the concussion from the explosion knocked my plane several hundred feet higher into the air. I was happy for that because it helped get me and the boys back to the base." Jack wanted to hear it from his brother's mouth.

He knew that the odds of at least one of his mother's sons coming home were better now than they had been before the Sullivans' losses. Like other families, his family could benefit from the terrible loss of all five of the Sullivan family's sons. After Pearl Harbor, the five Sullivan brothers had requested to serve together, and the Navy assigned them to the *USS Juneau.* All were lost in a single blow when the *Juneau* went down in '42. The military, particularly the Navy, now discouraged brothers from serving together. They even discouraged family members from serving together in the same branch or theater of war in an attempt to increase the odds of some of them returning home to continue the family heritage.

There was no safe place to be. Jack pulled the covers tighter. Maybe his sister Frances would be safe back in the states working in the defense factories. Francis was a "Rosie the riveter." Who would have ever thought it would all come to this?

Damn, April is going to be as cold as March, he thought. Rolling over onto his side, Jack tried to get back to sleep; he knew he'd be up early for the mission. He pulled the covers over his shoulders and closed his eyes. Sleep finally came.

Chapter Three
Preemptive Strikes

Yea, though I walk through the valley of the shadow of death, I will fear no evil.

– Psalm 23

Muster came quickly, with duty officers traveling from hut to hut and waking the morning flight crews. Everyone grumbled more for the cold than for the coming mission. After rubbing the sleep from their eyes, the crew's next priority was the morning's military and biological needs. Once these were completed, the flight crews began their tried and true dressing rituals. These rituals would give them the maximum amount of warmth from their clothing.

Well-bundled men slowly filled the base's well-marked walkways, as they headed to their mess hall. The four squadrons each had a mess hall, within which were separate messes for officers and enlisted men.

On their way to the mess, the pilots and crews walked past the notice board, stopping to read the morning's postings. It was mandatory to check the board every morning and evening. The board formed the lifeline to flying status and Wing's orders. The postings today had the usual flight status assignments for the pilots, navigators, and gunners on the afternoon mission. The flight status paralleled last night's posting for the morning mission.

The next order of the day was coffee and there was usually plenty of it; it made up for the so-called eggs. The powdered eggs were prepared so thick that they had to be cut into squares. Generally tasteless, the eggs whetted few appetites among the men. Better than the meal were coffee and a good smoke of a Lucky or Chesterfield.[29] But the SPAM was OK when it was available or stolen by the quartermaster from some other squadron. The only problem was that the cooks could never soak all the salt out of it, often leaving it almost too salty to eat.

"Time for briefing, guys, twenty minutes to briefing." The officer of the day rousted the occupants out of their respective mess halls.

Walking out of mess, the aircrews headed over to the big six wheeled deuce and a half truck that would take them all to the main briefing with Operations. The pilots met up with their navigators or gunners, as the crewmen settled into their usual seats in the back of the truck. Some stood, knowing that soon they were going to be sitting for a long time. After belching black exhaust from its stacks across the base, the deuce and a half bounced to a stop at Operations.

Climbing out of the back of the truck, the crews headed into the Operations building. They collected into small groups while waiting for the briefing to start. They

29   Luckies and Chesterfield — Two very desirable brands of American cigarettes popular among the aircrews at the time. Phillip Morris was also a popular brand.

sat or stood looking at the shade covering the map of this morning's mission, and everyone's mind drifted back to the price that was paid on yesterday's mission. The cloud of cigarette smoke began to thicken. Every puff on their Phillip Morris cigarettes signaled the nervous tension felt by the waiting crews.

Captain Griffin R. Beatty, the group's chief Operations officer, stood beside the covered mission board in front of the anxious, now war-hardened audience. He was flanked by his assistant, a young lieutenant. The door was closed, and Captain Beatty had the shade removed from the target map.

"Good morning, gentlemen. Let's get down to business. The Brits and American Intel are telling us that we've gotta to take out more of these rocket-bomb sites that we started flying against last month. So, we have another No-ball[30] site today."

In the past the 416th had been tasked with the destruction of many of the Luftwaffe's *Vergeltungswaffe*[31] launch sites. Their first three missions against the sites were flown in March 1944. Their missions to such sites were to peak in April 1944 with sixteen missions flown during the period of April 10th to the 30th. The group would go on to fly eleven more No-ball missions, six in May and five in June 1944.

Captain Beatty continued, "Men, the mission today will be to Bonnieres and Beauvoir, France, both buzz-bomb launching sites. Intel reports a lot of activity there, and believes theses sites to be near operational. We need to stop the construction of these sites. We have had good success destroying the Krauts' other launch sites, so let's make 'em pay with two good hits today."

It was a testament to Allied intelligence and luck that the purpose of the launching sites had been discovered before the weapon was actually used against London. As early as 1939 the British were watching the Baltic coastal areas around Peenemünde for rocket activity. It was not until May 1942, though, when a photo-reconnaissance flight, flown by flight Lieutenant D.W. Steventon produced photographic evidence of rocket activity. Photographic confirmation was finally obtained by Squadron Leader Gordon Hughes in 1943. Combining the photos with intelligence data of the Luftwaffe's rocketry program obtained from wiretaps, the British deduced that the Germans had progressed much further than anyone had suspected and would soon be able to launch long-range rocket attacks.

The British eventually identified Peenemünde as the research-production facility. This discovery resulted in "Operation Crossbow," in which thirty-six thousand tons of bombs were delivered to Peenemünde and other launch sites by Bomber Command's Number Five group over a period of months starting in May 1943. Over the next two years Allied aircraft of all types attacked research, production, and launch facilities with devastating results.[32]

---

30   No-ball missions were to German V-1 Rocket (buzz bomb) launch sites. The 416th was effective at destroying these sites but the Germans were equally effective at rebuilding them.
31   Vergeltungswaffe — German meaning "vengeance weapon." They were nicknamed "buzz bombs" or "doodlebugs" by the Londoners.
32   *Peenemünde.* 1943: Weapons of Mass Destruction; Global Security; http://www.globalsecurity.org/wmd/ops/peenemunde.htm

To avoid the aerial assaults, Germany moved the production of the V-bombs into an enormous reengineered gypsum mine near Nordhausen. With production protected from aerial bombardment, the Luftwaffe was able to produce and then deploy the weapon.

As Captain Beatty detailed the mission, Lieutenant Charles McGlohn's stomach tightened. He was thinking of the last two missions to these Kraut buzz bomb sites. Hell, he wasn't even sure what the damned things were used for, but they were trying to destroy them. Just yesterday the group had flown into France against the Bois de Ruit Rues No-ball site. The Krauts had extracted a heavy price from the group for that visit.

Everyone on that mission had been shaken by the amount and accuracy of the flak. The Krauts seemed to have focused their artillery against individual flights instead of just filling a zone of airspace with flak. Intel seemed to think the group had been targeted with radar-directed fire. McGlohn could still hear the distress calls from Lieutenant Arthur Raines. Raines's Havoc had taken fatal hits over the target, taking Staff Sergeants Glenn Bender and Jack Neilson down with it.

Meanwhile, Lieutenant William F. Cramsie with Staff Sergeants Gunners Charles Henshaw and Jack Steward were last heard requesting a heading back to base from somewhere over the channel. They and their Havoc were now resting at the bottom of those dark waters.

Two other crews had their planes shot up so badly that they were forced to crashland. Lieutenant Marion (Scotty) Street had his crew bail out, only to end up nursing his wounded bird across the channel to crash-land on the coast. Captain Lloyd Dunn had lost all his hydraulics, and crashed at the far end of the runway with his gunner Howard Worden injured on impact.

The 416th had suffered all around for yesterday's mission. McGlohn wondered what was in store for them today.

The briefing continued. Captain Beatty hadn't missed a beat.

"The lead navigators and pilots have already been briefed on flak positions located here, here, and here on the coast and around the V-1 sites here." He tapped the large map using a long wooden pointer.

"The best approach route to avoid the coastal gun concentrations up to that point is marked on your flight maps here and here. These guys are going to use everything they can aim to shoot us out of the air. G-2 says they have quad 20s all the way up to those damned 88s. So remember, use your evasive flight maneuvers so they can't zero in on you! Gunners and navigators call out those flak bursts."

Capt. Beatty paused, looking around the room to see if he had made his point strongly enough, and then resumed.

"Rendezvous point for fighter cover is here, east of the French coast at zero-seven-thirty, don't miss it. Turn onto the second-leg coastal approach heading, here, for these times designated on your flight map, here.

"One difference today, men. At this point here after crossing the French coast the two boxes will separate. Major Meng and Lieutenant Powell will lead A-Box on to

Bonnieres on this route to their IP.[33] Major Willets and Lieutenant Basnett will lead B-Box, turning south on this heading to bomb Beauvoir.

He tapped the point while looking out at the pilots and navigators.

"Navigators, remember your winds. After you cross the coastal approach point, turn on this heading and time. This will get you to the IP here." He tapped the map and looked out into the room. The faces looked increasingly stern.

"The drop today will be in flights, and all planes drop off their lead bombardier. Let's make it a good drop today so we don't have to go back." Captain Beatty looked around at murmurs of affirmation and head shakes of approval. No one wanted to go back to the same target.

The captain added: "I can't tell you about enemy fighters but I suspect that there may damned well be some around, so you gunners keep your eyes open. There is a large group of heavies from the Eighth going in deep right behind you, so…"

⚜

Indeed, there would be a large contingent of the Eighth Air Force leaving England that day. A combined force of 917 B-17 Flying Fortresses and B-24 Liberators were being escorted by 819 fighters into enemy air space. These fighters consisted of 124 Eighth Air Force P-38 Lightnings, 454 Eighth and Ninth Air Force P-47 Thunderbolts, along with 241 P-51 Mustangs, all dispatched from the island aircraft carrier that England had become.

Primarily assigned aircraft production sites, the bombers peppered locations all over Germany. Of the 643 B-17s sent on the morning mission, 17 bombed Cottbus, 127 hit Stettin, and 20 flew on Trechel. Meanwhile, 108 bombed Sorau and 16 hit Dobberphel. Other targets included Rostock, which saw 172 bombers overhead. Politz witnessed 52 bombers, and the industrial area of Arnimswalde was visited by 35 aircraft. The remaining 38 B-17 Flying Fortresses hit targets of opportunity.

The B-24 crews got their licks in too as 274 Liberators droned through the western-European airspace as they prepared to enter Luftwaffe airspace. The targets assigned and hit included Oschersleben (121 B-24s) and Berenburg (99 aircraft struck), while nine B-24s hit Halberstadt and nine flew on Eisleben. Targets of opportunity were hit by five Liberators.

On this April 11, 1944, both sides paid a dear price. For the Americans sixty-four heavy bombers went down, claiming nineteen lives, while thirty-one were wounded in action and six hundred were unaccounted for. Although arguably one of the most costly days in the war for the mighty Eighth Air Force, the Luftwaffe paid a high price as well. The tally at day's end credited the bombers with seventy-three fighter kills. The American fighter escorts claimed their share—fifty-one kills in the air and sixty-five on the ground. The trade-off came in the form of sixteen American fighter pilots missing along with their aircraft.

---

33   Initiation Point — IP, navigational point where the bomb-run to target begins

Other Eighth Air Force missions continued on that evening and night. They resulted in over two million leaflets being dropped by five B-17s on the French cities of Paris, Rouen, Le Mans, Rennes, Vichy, Lyon, Limoges, and Toulouse between 2300 and 0055 hours. Twelve B-24s from Harrington, England (home of the 801st and 492nd bomb groups), a special Operations unit, flew low-level carpetbagger missions that evening, supplying the French Resistance with needed men and material. No losses were recorded from either group.[34]

⚛

Captain Beatty continued: "A group of heavies and fighters like this are going to make for a large radar signal for those Kraut radar stations. I suspect that they may draw the bandits' attention away from you guys today, but I wouldn't count on the same for the flak. Bombardiers will take over at the IP. Bomb-run is upward of three minutes, so make it count. Bombardiers kill the rate[35] quickly, no time to make a mistake. Let's get this one the first time."[36]

Leaning over toward his pilot Dave Hulse, Ralph Conte whispered, "You get me there, I'll hit it."

"I'll get you there so don't miss." Hulse smiled.

Beatty's words gained their attention again.

"After the bombs drop, use your standard evasion maneuvers—diving left, recovering, then turning left at 230 mph on the heading indicated here with the time. This will get you to the next rendezvous point. You should pick up your fighter cover there for the return trip. Get home safe, gentlemen. Uncle Sam needs those planes back in one piece." He paused to look around at the faces. "Any questions?"

As usual, there were none.

"Let's synchronize. It will be zero-five-fifty in four…three…two…one, hack." Beatty pushed his watch's setting pin into position. The airmen followed.

"Dismissed, and good luck, gentlemen."

McGlohn and his crew left the briefing, jumped on the crew truck and counted heads. Getting the correct number of crewmen, McGlohn slapped his hand on the top of the truck cab, which alerted the driver they were ready. The truck moved down the

---

34   United States Army Air Force Chronology: Tuesday, April 11, 1944; http://paul.rutgers. edu/~mcgrew/wwii/usaf/html/Apr.44.html

35   Kill the Rate — Term used to describe the rate of closure and alignment as the Norden bombsight's crosshairs moved toward the target; one crosshair moved toward the other fixed crosshair. The phrase "rate of closure" signifies the aircraft's rate of closure towards the target's Maximum Point of Impact (MPI). When both crosshairs crossed on the MPI of the target, the bombs dropped automatically.

36   The 416th would make two more trips to Bonnieres and one to Beauvoir and would give up five lives and two POWs. The photo of Jedinak's plane afire amid ships displayed at the USAF Museum was shot on this mission.

flight line, dropping crews at their assigned planes. McGlohn and his crew jumped off in front of their plane's revetment.

Going through their takeoff routines mechanically, the crew cleared the Havoc for flight. McGlohn gave a thumbs-up from the cockpit.

The ground crew signaled back the all clear, and McGlohn cranked the engines. He let them warm up until he saw the green flare arch up into the sky from the tower. The mission was a go.

After the chocks were pulled from the Havoc's wheels, McGlohn released the brakes and eased the throttles forward. The engine roared. The Havoc slowly began moving forward as the spinning propellers overcame the downward force of gravity. Feeling the movement, McGlohn let the plane roll forward a few feet before turning the nosewheel toward the taxiway. He taxied the Havoc out when his slot in the flight's taxi order opened up.

Using his brakes, rudder, nosewheel and throttles, McGlohn controlled the A-20's roll down to the start of the runway, while keeping a safe distance from the plane in front of him. McGlohn waited his turn for takeoff by running through preparations. He ran up his engines, tested the magnetos, and set the turbochargers on low while he monitored the engine's performance.

With everything in the green, McGlohn settled back in his seat and waited his turn to burn some high-octane fuel on takeoff. The plane ahead of him rolled away and grew smaller. McGlohn pulled his Havoc to the head of the runway and lined up down the center. At nine seconds from seeing the plane ahead of him begin its roll, he pushed the throttles forward and let the Havoc's engines drink. As the twin Wasp radials voraciously gulped their fuel, the Havoc began a slow but steadily accelerating pace down the runway. Hurtling to takeoff speed, McGlohn gently pulled the yoke back and watched as the plane lifted itself from the ground. The runway slipped away below them.

Feeling the plane rise from the ground brought a smile to McGlohn's face. He loved it no matter how many times he had experienced it. At fifty feet, McGlohn brought the gear up, and then pulled the flaps control lever back to zero as he passed 150 mph. With the gear and flaps up and the supercharger running, the Havoc climbed to the designated altitude. McGlohn turned toward his flight leader, and slid his plane into the number two slot, on the right wing of Hulse and Conte's Havoc.

It had been a clean takeoff; all six planes filled in the second flight of A-Box in sixty seconds. Hulse continued the designated orbit with them, as the other planes rose to join their box. When A-Box was full, the planes gained altitude while continuing to orbit the airbase. A-Box waited on the eighteen aircraft of the second box to form up. Two spare Havocs joined the contingent, bringing the formation to thirty-eight aircraft.

After he completed another orbit around the base, Captain Hulse saw the last Havoc come into formation. He called on the interphone, "Hey, Conte, what's the heading?"

Conte heard the request and looked over his calculations quickly to be sure he had done them correctly.

"Major Meng should be turning right onto one-three-zero degrees for two fiver minutes, over."

Hulse followed Meng as the formation turned on course and pushed closer to their rendezvous point (RP) with the fighters. Reaching seaward toward the first RP, they climbed at 185 mph to twelve thousand feet, and leveled off to cruise at 240 mph aided by a tailwind.

McGlohn saw it was going to be an overcast day. "So much for the weather on this mission. I need to talk to those weather guys when I get back," he said to himself.

Reviewing his map, he saw they were headed into the Pas de Calais area. He knew there would be heavy flak there.

For practice Conte kept calculating the plot to the first RP. He noted the wind, heading, times, and landmarks when visible. He calculated for drift, and then recorded the calculations in his navigator logbook as they pushed toward the RP. He knew Lieutenant Powell, Meng's navigator, had them on course and he expected to hit the RP on schedule.

Scanning the sky to keep formation with the other planes, Hulse was the first to spot them. Their 25 P-47 Thunderbolt fighter escorts consisted of a mixture of aircraft from the 365th, 366th, and 367th squadrons of the Ninth's Tactical 358th Fighter Group.

Major Meng gave the escorts time to take their positions above the bombers before executing a port turn toward the French coast. The fighters quickly maneuvered into formation and settled into the same airspeed as the bombers. They were glad to be escorting bombers that flew at their speed. Seeing the fighters slide into position, Hulse called Conte, "What's the heading, over?"

"Follow Meng on this heading for three minutes, then turn onto one-two-fiver degrees for two-four minutes, over."

"Roger, turning in three minutes on this heading onto one-two-fiver degrees for two-four minutes, over."

"Roger."

In three minutes Hulse, his formation, and their fighter escorts followed Meng into a well-practiced, combined formation turn onto a southeastward heading out over the channel.

They were about to enter enemy airspace, and McGlohn knew they were now taking the fight to the enemy. His pulse quickened and his senses became more acute.

The flight across the channel was without incident. The two spare aircraft turned back for Wethersfield just before the French coast, as no planes had dropped out of formation.

Before crossing the French coast, McGlohn looked at his map, seeing where the flak might start up. He saw the lead ship starting to slip a little left, then a little more, then back to the right. The navigator was overcorrecting and then averaging out the maneuvers so the group stayed on course.

As the group pushed farther inland, the hazy blue sky began to fill with black puffs of Luftwaffe resistance, and the formation began their evasive maneuvers. Ralph radioed to Hulse to turn left onto a different heading for a set time then back to the right doubling that time. Ralph recorded his course changes in his logbook calculating the times and direction changes. Ralph knew he had to keep close track of the headings and times so that the flight would end the exaggerated left and right swinging back on course.

McGlohn imitated every evasive maneuver that Hulse and Conte made. He scanned the formation to be sure he kept his position in formation, as the planes slid back and forth through the sky.

"No close calls yet," McGlohn relayed to his gunners. "Call out any flak bursts or hits, over."

"Roger that."

As the planes slid or swung back and forth in their evasions, the German gunners constantly had to adjust their aim. It worked well on the way to the IP and on the way back to the RP. It kept them from being hit by the 88s and 105s, but the smaller-caliber guns could shift their aim quickly. So, there were always tracers shooting through the air. It wasn't perfect, but at least McGlohn felt he was doing something to make it harder for them to kill him from down there. He hated it more when the planes reached the IP. It wasn't far now.

Twenty minutes ago Conte had made the last scheduled course change, following Meng to the east to bring the group to the IP. Ten minutes ago the B-Box had left them. Now he knew the IP was only a few minutes away. He waited, and then comparing his heading with airspeed, time, and wind direction, he calculated that the group was ready to make the final turn onto the bomb-run.

"We're one minute out from the IP. Follow Captain Meng onto niner-eight degrees, and I'll take her after the turn," Conte informed Hulse.

"Roger that."

After waiting fifty seconds, Hulse saw Meng's Havoc begin the right-hand turn, and then heard from Conte at the same time.

"Turn now, Hulse."

Hulse turned his flight of six Havocs onto the bomb-run at the IP behind Meng.

"She's yours."

At the start of the bomb-run, Hulse turned part of the flying over to Conte, who started adjusting for the Havoc's position over the target using the Norden bombsight. As they completed the final turn, Conte raised the lever to open the bomb bay doors and listened as they opened and then saw the green indicator light pop on.

"Doors open."

"Roger that."

Paralleling Hulse, McGlohn completed his right-hand banking turn onto the bomb-run and opened his bomb bay doors. The other flights fell in behind Meng's first flight in echelon order. They formed a straight line of three flights of six Havocs tightly grouped one after the other with at least five hundred feet of altitude separating the flights. Their altitude centered around twelve thousand feet. The technique made it harder for the Luftwaffe gunners to zero in on a single altitude.

McGlohn, like all the others, knew this was the worst part of every mission, because no plane could evade the flak. There was only straight and level flight into and through the flak field.

It took teamwork to keep the plane flying level and straight in a flak field. Once Hulse leveled out onto the bomb-run, Ralph saw the green light and knew the bomb bay doors were open. All eyes were on him now as he unpinned his two gyros on the Norden, which passed direction and speed information up to Hulse's pilot direction indicator (PDI). Hulse kept the PDI needle steady, allowing Conte time to "kill the rate." The speed down the run had been set by Wing based on the type of bombs the group was dropping today. Conte adjusted for drift, wind speed, and direction, while Hulse kept the bird level and on course. The other planes followed Ralph's corrections. They did what he did, holding a tight formation regardless of the concentration or accuracy of the flak.

The flak came hard and fast. From some twelve thousand feet below, Deutsche *kanoniers* [37] were spitting flak from their 88-mm anti-aircraft cannons. The deadly 88-mm rounds were fused exactly for the altitude at which the 416th was flying, and the Krupp Steel manufactured cannons could hurl these artillery rounds capable of destroying the fuselage of an aircraft or the soft vulnerable bodies inside them swiftly and explosively. The powder exploded inside the shell casings sending the deadly artillery bullets whistling skyward out of the fire-belching barrels. The heavy 88s recoiled against the blast and then were quickly reloaded.

All the pilots in the formations could do was hold steady as the flak burst around them first in explosive orange and then in noxious black smoke. The sky clouded with the ebony death. The projectiles' fuses located in the tail of the shell had been set to detonate at the invading enemy air force's estimated altitude.

The moment between being scared and realizing you had been hit is always swift. McGlohn felt the aircraft shudder and then buck upward to the left.

"What the hell was that?" he barked across the interphone.

Zipping through the cockpit like angry hornets, the shrapnel stung the instrument panel as if it had been made of flesh. McGlohn recoiled and threw his arms in front of his face in a natural defensive maneuver. Smoke and sparks spewed out from the broken dials and switches. The shell had exploded just below cockpit level, slightly to the right and ahead of the nose of McGlohn's plane. The shrapnel had torn through the nose and belly of the Havoc. All six .50-calibers in the nose were destroyed, as they and the ammo canisters absorbed the bulk of the metal spraying into the Havoc. The fusillade of metal had ripped through the thin aluminum around the cockpit, only some of it stopped by the armor plate.

---

37   *Kanoniers* – gunner in artillery unit; artillery private

The hot metal projectiles found their softer target too. McGlohn's right arm and leg were ripped open, punctured in milliseconds by the vengeful German metal.

McGlohn was made aware of the success of the flak in less time than it took to make the injury. His nerves rapidly depolarized, carrying the pain up his right arm and leg where it stopped in the thalamus of his brain only long enough to be relayed to connecting nerves that transmitted the pain to the sensory region of his brain. McGlohn was immediately conscious of the magnitude of the injury.

"Damnit, those sum-bitches got me," McGlohn hollered into the interphone.

He took control of the yoke with his left hand, all he had left to keep the Havoc in formation. He instinctively ruddered and aileroned the Havoc back into formation to avoid a midair collision. With his arm and leg shot up so badly, he was going to have difficulty with rudder and engine controls. He moved his right arm, doing so with much pain.

Outside the flak kept streaming by.

His turret gunner J.W. Moran asked again what happened.

"We took a bad hit, damnit! So did I." Grimacing, he tried to keep the Havoc in tight formation against an unfavorable crosswind.

"Are you gonna be OK?" It was the belly gunner, Driskill.

"Hold on, guys, we're on the bomb-run! Moran, get in there and make sure those damned bomb bay doors are open and those eggs pickle off on the drop!" Breathing heavily with the pain now obvious in his voice, McGlohn focused his crew. "I don't know what's going to work from what's left of the controls up here."

Another German round detonated amid the formation of six Havocs, jolting McGlohn's plane again. From the rear and slightly above, it pelted all six Havocs in the flight with steel.

"Roger, I'm on it." Moran had just regained his balance after the last flak burst.

Moran scrambled out of the top ball turret and worked his way to the bomb bay. The four five-hundred-pound bombs seemed to hang precariously on their racks as if they could break loose any time. Another flak burst rocked the bombs in their racks, and he was eager for them to exit the plane. Moran plugged his headset into the bomb bay interphone jack and switched it to pilot.

"On station, Lieutenant. The doors are open."

"Roger that."

McGlohn found himself thinking that the last thing he wanted was a crash landing with a full bomb load nestled below the bomb bay fuel tanks. He liked the new A-20-Gs the group was flying, but he couldn't get used to having that much high-octane aviation fuel right behind the cockpit.

"Roger...steady now...come on, Ralph, kill the damned rate."

McGlohn's right leg was having trouble keeping pressure on the rudder pedal against the crosswind, and he struggled with his left arm to keep the plane in formation.

"Come on, Ralph, drop um, drop um."

Another well place flak bursts jarred Hulse's Havoc, tumbling the gyros of Ralph's bombsight and destroying all the calculations he had made since the start of the run.

"Damnit, Hulse, those Krauts nearly got us. Keep her level till I can line her up again."

Forced to recage the gyros and then unpin them again, Ralph started the targeting process all over. He worked quickly, closing the rate line with the direction, as Hulse kept the needle centered.

Ralph reached down and lifted the bomb-arming switch and engaged the pin. All green lights appeared on the bomb-armed panel. The arming servos had completed their duty.

As the crosshairs met over the MPI on the target, the electric bomb-release shackles popped open and the bombs fell away.

McGlohn saw the first bomb slip past Conte's bomb bay doors as they fell from their racks and began their descent to the target. He pushed the energized bomb-release switch on his control yoke, praying it worked too.

"Bombs away!" He hollered into the interphone mike.

Moran watched as the second row of bombs slipped out of their resting spot. He watched as the safety wires that prevented accidental arming of the bombs pulled clear as the bombs slid out of their racks into the cold air at twelve thousand feet.

The tips of the bombs nosed down, falling into the slipstream, which caused the impellers on the tips of the bombs to spin. The final arming mechanism had begun. Moran thought he could see the little ball bearings spit out the side of the arming mechanisms as the impellers spun around, but he wasn't sure. He really didn't care. He just wanted all of them the hell out of the plane. The bombs fell quickly out of sight, first below, and then behind the plane as they lost forward momentum and gained a downward curving velocity.

The impellers continued to spin in the high-velocity fall until the last ball bearing spun out of the arming mechanism. All four of the bomb bay's five-hundred-pound, high-explosive projectiles were now lethal.

Fully armed and deadly, the two bombs that had been hanging on wing racks joined their brothers on the fall to the target.

As the payload fell the bombs ignored the crosswind that had been calculated and then corrected for by Lieutenant Conte with aid of the bombardier's well-designed weapon, the Norden bombsight. The bombs fell along their calculated glide path that had taken the plane's airspeed, altitude, drift, and any wind directions into calculation. Whistling loudly now, the bombs quickly reached their terminal velocity and fell as if looking for retribution.

Retribution was swift. Because McGlohn could not keep his plane level and in tight formation, his bomb bay and wing bombs fell at a slightly different angle than those of the rest of his formation. The Luftwaffe *kanoniers* around the No-ball site could not hear the screams of their approaching five-hundred-pound angles of death. So intent on killing the enemy aircraft with their 88s, they never knew what was about to hit them. McGlohn's starboard wing bomb detonated on impact five feet from the very Krupp 88 that had fired the round that had wounded him and his plane.

Steel fragments and a body-shredding concussion from the detonation greeted the four kanoniers, their oberkanonier,[38] and their unterwachtmeister.[39] Luftwaffe battery eighteen instantaneously ceased to exist, suffering a more gruesome fate than the crew of McGlohn's plane. Their only redemption was that their deaths came so quickly that they were unaware of their soul's passing into Battersby and Coleman's world after the blast.

The blast also caused several 88 shells lying on the ground nearby to detonate, creating secondary explosions that added to the lethality of the first explosion. Caught out in the open running between batteries, the hauptwachtmeister[40] became a victim to the blast's shockwave, which blew him ten feet into the air. He landed with a broken leg and a penetrating shrapnel wound to the left chest.

The shockwave spread like a tidal wave, spreading to men in the nearby slit trenches. An *oberleutnant*,[41] *unteroffizier*,[42] and several *soldaten*[43] assigned to the defense of the *flugabwehrkanonen*[44] battery suffered only three ruptured eardrums among them as the shock wave passed over them.

Mercifully surviving this first deadly salvo, the young Wehrmacht soldaten were overcome by the fear of their helplessness coupled with the sudden alarming reality of their mortality, as high explosive detonations jarred the ground around them. Several of the young soldiers began praying out loud to their God, a God for whom they had quickly rediscovered deep convictions, after He had been stolen by Hitler.

Their prayers for salvation during this bombardment were timely, as the next salvo of explosions drowned out their prayers. The next wave of A-20s had dropped its eggs. The bombs had fallen in a tight pattern around the slit trenches, burying the group of young soldiers, killing only half of them first.

The No-ball site was suffering tremendous damage from the well-placed thirty-six thousand pounds of bombs dropped by the first two flights. The launch ramp was hit twice and blown into a useless pile of twisted steel and concrete. The control bunker shook off the well-targeted hits as the American projectiles ricocheted off its rounded concrete walls, as it was designed to do. The deflected bombs exploded nearby as they hit the ground.

The Allied attack on the Germans had been immense and destructive. They effectively destroyed the site, for now. England's people and cities would be very thankful for today's mission. It would mean less death dropping from the skies on their island nation in the future.

---

38   *Oberkanonier* — artillery private first class
39   *Unterwachtmeister* — artillery sergeant
40   *Hauptwachtmeister* — artillery battery sergeant major
41   *Oberleutnant* — infantry first lieutenant
42   *Unteroffizier* — infantry lance sergeant
43   *Soldat* — infantry private
44   German 88 mm anti-aircraft artillery battery

In a tight, left diving bank, the formation sped out of the bomb run flak zone with throttles pushed up, pouring the fuel to the cylinder heads. McGlohn struggled to follow his lead's maneuver. In spite of his efforts he missed the evasive maneuver, forcing his Havoc to fly through the black, powdery clouds of steel as the 88 shells exploded in front of them.

McGlohn reached over to push the throttles forward a little and tried to stay in formation. He was hesitant to push them too far, because he had no means to measure or know his airspeed.

After completing their evasive turn off the target, the flight had leveled out on their return leg. This allowed McGlohn time to join up with them and time to see the cloud cover that had been forming behind them.

Emerging from their shelters after the last flight's bombs had exploded, the Luftwaffe technicians, construction crews and Wehrmacht soldiers began the rebuilding process as the group of A-20s disappeared over the northwestern horizon. They were down but not out, and reconstruction began.

Up above the destruction, McGlohn struggled to stay in formation with Hulse's flight as the group headed for home. He still had to follow the evasive maneuvers of the lead plane to escape the flak bursts, and was not as good at it as he had been before he was wounded. Along with his crew, he heard the pieces of metal rip through the fuselage and wings from the undiminished flak barrage. Suspended in the flak barrage, all three crewmen were praying to their maker to help them get out of this as soon as possible.

"Oh hell, that's not a good thing."

"Lieutenant, are you gonna be OK?" Moran cautiously inquired with Driskill listening in over the interphone.

"Yeah…yeah, so far I'm OK, but I don't know for how long. Driskill, how long has that cloud cover I'm looking at been forming?"

"Just about since we left. It's pretty thick."

"Yeah, I can tell from here, that's not a good thing, guys."

"Are you bleeding a lot?" Moran was concerned.

"It's steady but doesn't seem too bad right now."

That response was more to reassure them than himself. His flight suit was bloody, and clotted blood pooled on the floor of the cockpit, and inside his flight boots. He still had the pain but at least he wasn't light-headed. He had been taught to look for bad signs that occur from bleeding too much. It didn't seem too bad yet.

The formation flew back toward the French coast along an imaginary line that was only visible on the map the navigator was using to get the boys home. Checking his times and direction, Conte recorded that they had crossed the coast and were now over the channel. The flight neared its descent point, where they would lose altitude and enter the cloud cover for their approach to the base.

Now outside the impending threat of flak, McGlohn began to worry about how he was going to descend through eight thousand feet of clouds without an artificial horizon, altimeter, airspeed indicator, rate-of-descent indicator, or his engine gauges.

Hell of a way to land a plane, he thought.

The formation continued its return flight over the English Channel. He was staying with the formation, knowing that he would have to follow the flight in doing what they did. McGlohn guessed they had crossed the French coast bomb line, and then radioed the lead.

"Boat deck two, this is two…fiver…one…H…hotel, over." Radio silence could now be broken.

"Roger that, two…fiver…one…H…hotel, this is Boat deck two, over," Hulse responded.

"Roger, I'm without instruments and I've been hit, bleeding some. I need to follow the flight down through the clouds on your lead, over."

"Roger that, how bad are you injured?"

"Don't know. I've been hit in my right arm and leg. I'm bleeding some, but feel OK."

"Roger that, just follow my lead, I'll radio you information during descent."

"Over and out."

Hulse began the process of radioing control and power settings to McGlohn so that he could descend into the clouds along with the rest of the flight. McGlohn watched as the first flight in A-Box disappeared into the clouds. His flight was right behind them.

Descending into the clouds, McGlohn felt his heart rate increase even more as the clouds suddenly enveloped the cockpit glass and then the entire plane. With visibility at zero feet, Driskill's and Moran's heart rates increased accordingly, belying the serenity of the clouds. Less than a minute into the descent, McGlohn began to realize he was risking his crew's lives and the lives of any plane in formation, because of his lack of instruments.

Remembering his position in the flight's formation, he pulled the yoke back and turned it slightly to the right. He applied a little right-rudder pressure despite the pain, while advancing the manifold pressure. The Havoc performed without hesitation; McGlohn quickly found the sunny clear skies again as the Havoc climbed out of the clouds.

With an immense sigh of relief he called to his gunners, "Moran, Driskill, listen up guys… I need to let you know our status."

"You OK?" Moran asked.

"I'm OK, but the plane's not. The instrument panel and flight-control instruments are all shot away. I don't have any way to safely fly through this soup. I think you guys would be better off bailing out. We're over the channel or maybe even the coast. You should get picked up soon."

Moran and Driskill thought about jumping.

"What do you think?"

Moran thought about Sergeant Cherry and Lieutenant Cruze, both of whom had drowned after landing in the channel. Air-Sea Rescue had been right there too.

"Remember Cherry and Cruze?" Moran suggested.

"Yeah, I remember."

"Me too. Think I'll stay put, how 'bout you?"

"I'm with you."

The thought of landing in the channel and then drowning in the cold, dark, choppy waters was not appealing. Just the thought of jumping, which neither had ever done before, was not very appealing either.

"What are you going to do, Lieutenant? Jump…or try to take her in?" Moran wanted to be ready.

"Well, everything seems to be working, except I don't have any instruments. My right arm and leg don't work too good, but I can use 'em. I think I can trim the plane and set the glide path. This should let her drop down real nice through the overcast. No way to know the attitude of the plane, but it might work, guys."

McGlohn had thought through all this before his crew asked. He remembered his instrument flight rules (IFR) officer's advice from Will Rogers Field—never trust your feelings in the clouds or at night. He figured he could land it, but he needed to warn his crew.

"By the way, guys, if I get her upside down or in a spin there may be no getting out of her then." McGlohn spoke in a hard, cold and understandable way.

"I'm with you, but can't speak for Driskill."

"Heck, I'm ready if you two are. Bring her in, Lieutenant!"

McGlohn went to work, reducing the manifold pressure and setting the rudder trim, the aileron trim, and the elevator trim in neutral so that the plane would cruise in straight-level flight.

He lifted his feet off the rudder controls while releasing his left hand's grip on the yoke. He had to see how the plane would fly. He was pleased to see his bird flew a level flight path. He could tell the crosswind would push him off course; he'd correct for that later.

Slowly he adjusted the three trim settings so that the Havoc began a slow descent.

"Here we go, guys."

McGlohn pushed forward on the yoke so that the plane nosed over into what he estimated to be a five-degree down angle. He pulled the throttles back, and began his power-off descent into the cloudy abyss below.

Moran saw the cloud cover coming from his turret bubble and said a hurried prayer. The clouds swallowed the plane again. Any perceived comforting feeling from the sunny blue sky was gone. A sweaty fear overcame them all.

Moran found himself reconsidering his decision not to jump. Accepting his fate, he put his life in McGlohn's hands, praying for God to guide him.

With its scared crew the Havoc descended through the clouds. McGlohn struggled to resist the impulse to adjust the controls for any perceived change in flight attitude. *Don't trust your feelings; they are not your friend right now.* The pain was a secondary issue now, as survival was the only state of mind that he could afford. The engines droned in their well-synchronized harmony, and the grayness passed by with no one daring to speak for fear of jinxing the descent.

Time seemed to be standing still for the crew of the Havoc as the craft descended through the disorienting clouds. McGlohn's hands shook as the adrenaline poured into his bloodstream, raising his heart rate, blood pressure, and sense of awareness. Moran's and Driskill's minds and bodies were in the same state; they realized there was nothing they could do to control their destiny now. Second thoughts about jumping crept into everyone's mind. Thoughts of their homes and families intermingled with their fear of death.

The Havoc's engines droned on in their steady synchronized monotony, creating an almost-soothing melody.

So far, so good, Moran thought.

Moran and Driskill had confidence in McGlohn, as most gunners have in all their pilots. They needed it now, for sure. The cloud cover became still thicker. Less sunlight penetrated to this depth, making their encircling captor a darker gray.

McGlohn kept resisting the urge to correct the Havoc's descent. He knew from training and experience that you could not trust your perception of orientation in the clouds, but it was still difficult to resist the impulse. With his eyes closed he steeled himself against the waves of vertigo.

He had developed several tricks to uncouple this impulse. He knew to ignore his mind's perception of the plane's attitude; he knew his brain's interpretation of the situation was wrong. He resisted looking out of the cockpit into the darkness around them. Instead he focused on the remains of his instrument panel while reviewing the settings of the rudder, aileron, and elevator trim tabs in his mind. As he studied the instrument panel he realized the now shredded panel had saved his life by absorbing all that Kraut steel.

The plane was close to being correctly trimmed with the proper power settings. He had to trust his training.

To occupy his mind, he began doing the math for their descent. He estimated it would or should take about eight minutes at a descent rate of one thousand feet per minute to clear the cloud base at two thousand feet from the ten thousand feet where it started. They were six minutes in now, so he started timing it on his watch and counting down the last two minutes. "Sixty, fifty-nine, fifty-eight… twenty-five, twenty-four…" Suddenly the dark shroud around them cleared. Beneath them the green patchwork of England's sparsely forested ground filled their retinas.

God, it was a welcome site that sent McGlohn's spirit, and then his heart soaring. He was the first to clear the clouds and alerted everyone. Sitting in the top turret with a 360-degree view, Moran saw it at almost the same time.

"Yee-haw! We made it, guys!" McGlohn erupted.

"Good job!" Two ecstatic airmen responded in unison.

Everyone thanked their God as McGlohn powered up the engines, pulled back aggressively on the controls to correct the steady but much-faster-than-expected dive.

McGlohn retrimmed the plane from the descent settings, and shook his head when he recognized that his airspeed and descent rate had been a lot faster than he had estimated. *Who cares now?* he thought.

Scanning the ground for landmarks, he calculated that he was northeast of the base, and he could correct for that. He put the Havoc into a gentle left-hand bank, radioed the base for approach instructions and more importantly, alerted the base to his condition, as well as his plane's.

"This is Boat Deck control, good to hear from you two…fiver…one…H…hotel. Stay on current heading. You are cleared for direct approach. Medical and emergency personnel will be waiting. We were worried when you didn't clear the clouds with your flight."

McGlohn then started his experienced and well-disciplined approach. Without any hesitation he put his gear down, flaps down, and reduced speed as he throttled back. With no instruments, he had to estimate every move.

He reached to his left, opened the window on his windshield, and then fired a red flare when he was close to the base.

"This is boat deck two…fiver…one…H…hotel asking for a look-over to be sure gear and flaps are down, over."

"Already done, ship looks good. You're on final now."

"Over and out."

McGlohn nosed the plane over onto the glide path toward the runway, while tolerating the searing pain that radiated up his leg as he controlled the drift of the Havoc with the rudder.

Flaring the plane just above the runway, he settled the A-20 down in a near-perfect three-point landing on the runway. McGlohn pulled the power back and rolled down the runway to the taxiway, turned left onto the taxiway, and then pulled the handle to open the cockpit.

He knew he wouldn't be crawling out, so he wanted to make it easy for the rescue people to pull him out. Shutting down the engines as the plane came to a halt, he sat there in his seat hurting, bleeding, sweaty, and tired, but happy; he just had to wait for some help to get out of the cockpit.

The emergency personnel didn't wait for the propellers to stop turning as they swarmed over the Havoc in their well-practiced ballet. Climbing up on the wings from behind, they moved to the cockpit and pulled the hatch open. They removed him from the tight quarters of the Havoc's cockpit, and he ached all over as they extracted him from his seat and then out of the hatch.

Moran and Driskill both clamored out of their gunners' positions as quickly as they could once the plane stopped rolling. All they wanted was to help their pilot.

With the emergency personnel already helping McGlohn, Moran and Driskill took a moment to appreciate terra firma. Looking each other in the eyes without speaking, they dropped to their hands and knees and kissed the ground while saying a thank you to their Almighty. Jumping up, they were quickly at McGlohn's side as he was slid off the wing, telling him what a great job he had done. No truer words were spoken that day.

A trail of bright blood was left across the fuselage and wing as he was pulled over the top of the ship onto the right wing. Carefully he was eased off the backside of the wing, and then placed onto a stretcher. Rescuers quickly carried him to the back of the waiting ambulance. Closing the doors, they raced off down the runway to the medical unit with the siren wailing.

Somewhere between the opening of the ambulance doors and their closing, the pain began to ease for McGlohn. Morpheus, who had been freed from *Papaver somniferum*[45] four thousand years before Christ's time by the Sumerians as opium, had begun to circulate through his brain. Once he penetrated the generally well-protected barriers of the spinal cord and brain, Morpheus began blocking the pain receptors from the substantia gelatinosa all the way up to McGlohn's hypothalamus and thalamus. Morpheus, the first alkaloid isolated from opium in 1803 by Sertürner, was better known as morphine, and was named after the Greek god of dreams, Morpheus. The "god" had been given to McGlohn by the medical corps on the wing of the plane just before they slid him off it onto their stretcher. With the morphine now blocking the receptors, the transmission of the pain to the higher cortical areas of his brain had ceased.

As the ambulance sped him back for aid, he began to feel warm. His nose itched and his mouth dried, while his pupils constricted and his skin flushed. McGlohn's conscious mind no longer cared that he was in pain because he was unaware of it.

Along with this interruption of nervous transmissions, morphine created other desirable benefits. Things just didn't seem as bad now, as McGlohn drifted off to fly through dreams beyond his control in an area of his mind that only Morpheus could open.[46]

∽✠⌒

The month of April would be filled with sixteen No-ball missions, five marshaling-yard missions—the second-most frequent target—followed by two coastal gun emplacements. On April 10, the 416th made history by being the first crew to fly a Window

---

45   *Papaver somniferum* – the poppy flower.
46   *The Pharmacological Basis of Therapeutics*, Ch. 22, Opioid Analgesics and Antagonists, pp 494 to 501; Alfred Goodman Gilman, M.D., Ph.D., Louis S. Goodman, M.A., M.D., D.Sc.(Hon.), Alfred Gilman, Ph.D., D.Sc.(Hon), et al.; Sixth edition.

mission in support of the Ninth Air Force's B-26 Marauder Group. It was an unusual mission clouded with secrecy.

There were other firsts in April as well. McGlohn would be awarded a Silver Star and a Purple Heart for his gallant efforts over the No-ball site that day.

March too had been costly. By month's end, nine men would be listed as missing in action (MIA) or killed in action (KIA). The reality of their lives in war had been driven home. They were sure more deaths were to come, but each man knew it wouldn't be he.

Chapter Four

Taking a Break

In this unamicable contest, the cause of truth cannot but suffer.
– Thomas Robert Malthus, 1798

Having been in theater three months now, the 416th would find April to be a busy month. April also brought some time off due to bad weather.

This morning all the crews were happy that there was no mission, and with some R&R available they figured they might as well take advantage of it. Only God and Operations knew what tomorrow would bring, and probably not in that order.

Jeeps were hard to come by for everyone except senior officers, which most of the men were not. A few officers went by the motor pool on the off chance of getting a ride into Braintree, where they could catch a train into London. Some had decided to take a bike ride or hitchhike around; England was good for those activities. Everything was close by. For hitchhikers it was not all bad. The people in the English countryside were happy to give an American a ride, but the real ticket was a bike. They were generally stolen back and forth among officers, enlisted men, squadrons, or groups. Most of the bikes had been bought when the group was in Northern Ireland receiving Escape and Evasion Training (EET). Once EET was completed, the group was transferred back to England. Most of the bikes made it to Wethersfield with the aircrews on the ride back in the C-47s. There was no honor when it came to transportation.

On this particular day a group of lieutenants had "requisitioned" five bikes from somewhere. They had put them to good use. Earl Hayter, Hiram Clark, Jack Smith, Bill Tripp, and Roland Enman headed out on a mission of their own this morning. They had hoped for some sights, heck, maybe even a good meal. Being nice to the local farmers had its rewards. Sometimes you could get a few eggs.

They were an interesting-looking group as they emerged from the base into the English countryside. They did not care. Getting off the base was the goal. Riding ten, fifteen or more miles at their age was nothing.

"Hey, anybody wanna ride into Finchingfield today?" Roland asked.

"It's close but we still have to be back by sixteen-thirty," Bill replied.

"Probably get some lunch there. What do you guys think?"

"Sounds good to me," Hiram chimed in.

"Besides, by the time we got to Braintree we'd miss the morning train," Roland added.

Earl interjected, "Let's just head out into the countryside toward Finchingfield and see what happens."

"Roger that." Jack took charge.

They turned northwest out of the base gate and headed into the early spring countryside toward Finchingfield.

Ralph Conte had met up with Lieutenant Wayne Downing during mess. They did not have passes today but also did not have any duty assignments for the rest of the day either, which was the next-best thing. The prospect of a free day gave the over-worked airmen time to catch up with some of their pastimes.

"You want to get in a few bridge games after mess?" Ralph asked.

"Yeah, sounds good," Wayne happily agreed.

"I'll try to round up two more players and meet you at thirteen-thirty in my tent. I need to write Norma before we play anyway."

Ralph and Norma had written each other since Ralph left at the start of the war, and they continued now through their war separation. It had been their plan to marry before the war, but circumstances of importance to the two of them had prevented that.

"All right, see you then."

Ralph headed straight for his hut thinking about what he wanted to say in the letter. Closing the door, he found he was alone in the hut. Ralph settled into his bunk, thought for several seconds, then started penning his thoughts. He could tell the words had an unfortunately sanguine feel, which he knew probably could not be avoided. The group had experienced some difficult losses and combined with the increasing pace of missions Ralph knew it was not going to get any easier. He appreciated now more than ever before that he may not make his mission quota.

Outside Ralph's small hut, activity covered the flight line as ground crews changed tires, rebuilt engines, and repaired sheet metal and Plexiglass. Trips were made to and from the boneyard as the ground crews scavenged whatever usable parts they could find.

Many pilots visited their planes to discuss with the ground crews the problems they had experienced on the last mission. Sergeant Ken Bailey, a ground crewman for *Daddy Land's Commando,* worked conscientiously to repair his Havoc. Ken had just spoken with Lieutenant Willard Land who flew *Daddy Land's Commando* the most into battle. He wanted to know exactly what kinds of problems Willard had experienced on the last flight. No one wanted a mishap on approach, takeoff or, even worse, engine failure over the target.

Work progressed on the A-20s on the off chance that the weather cleared, which would have made an afternoon mission possible. Armaments and ordnance were being loaded into the aircraft assigned to the afternoon mission if the duty arose.

Back in his hut, Ralph worked on his letter home, and thought of his job here as he wrote. Like Jack Smith and all the other multi-mission veterans, he had worked hard to earn his position in the group.

He knew he was different now, somehow. He was a long way from Paterson, New Jersey, where during the Depression his life was as hard as any "Dust Bowl" farmboy's life had been. Living in an ethnically diverse neighborhood of Italian-Americans, Polish-Americans, Russian-Americans, and African-Americans presented its own challenges. Everyone had a strong desire to achieve one way or the other. This desire, however, was hampered by the overwhelming lack of jobs.

Ralph and the others knew that college was never a reality for the vast majority of these Americans who lived there. Who could afford it? Other more important opportunities opened up for those too poor to attend. Everyone said that education was the goal, but in reality it was merely the avenue by which to reach sixteen, when you could drop out of school to find a job. This, like his other brothers and sisters, is what Ralph did.

When it was his turn to join the ranks of the employed, Ralph knew the drill. His two sisters before him were seamstresses earning six dollars a week each. His older brother made thirteen dollars a week working in a silk mill. All the money came home to the family. His youngest brother had entered the seminary at thirteen. At sixteen, Ralph left school and joined the CCC in 1934 and 1936 for two separate six-month stints. Between those times, he earned $10 a week driving a delivery truck for the silk industry—an industry that produced the very fabric that was to save the lives of many an airman in the years to come.

Of course, the lives of America's working men and women were to change after December 7, 1941. In January 1942 Ralph enlisted in the Army Air Corps hoping to be a pilot but, because of a hernia, he had difficulty passing his physical. During the enlistment process he also realized that he needed to improve his mathematical skills if he wanted to fly.

Undeterred and with the perseverance that was to bring him the respect of the group later, he continued to pursue an air career, and learned of two programs that were to change his life. Rutgers University was offering academic enrichment classes in algebra and trigonometry to help young men on their military entrance exams. He also discovered that some companies were financing the cost of repairing medical disabilities for young men wanting to get into the armed forces. For $50 the hernia was repaired, and after passing the math classes Ralph enlisted in June 1942. He was called up in January 1943, and then having earned his wings, was commissioned in July 1943.

Rutgers had paid off, as his test scores routed him into bombardier/navigator (BN) school even though he petitioned for pilot. He rotated through BN schools in Santa Ana, California, and then Roswell, New Mexico, being one of the sixteen to survive the weeding-out process in Carlsbad, New Mexico. He was then assigned to the 416th Bomb Group at Will Rogers Field. Now, after many difficult missions, he found himself sitting in this hut writing his beloved and dearly missed Norma.

Having read the letter over twice, Ralph slipped it into an envelope that he had addressed. He rolled out of his cot, and walked to the door hearing the old, familiar squeak of the hinges on his way to the Post. Walking along, he noted the dreary sky filled with patches of light gray clouds interspersed with patches of darker gray that formed a variegated gray wall that hid the blue sky. He was glad Wing had grounded the group today. It was not a good day to fly.

Since it was not raining, Ralph found that he was enjoying the long walk to the Post. His pleasure was interrupted when he ran into Captain William P. Thomas, the group's intelligence officer. Thomas also enjoyed the honor of being responsible for the censorship of all enlisted men's outgoing mail before it left the base.

It just was not Ralph's day. Conte saluted hoping that the captain would just walk by. Captain Thomas returned the salute, then spoke.

"Lieutenant Conte, do you mind stopping in at the Post to censor some of the enlisted men's outgoing mail?"

It was not a request but a nicely worded order. Stopped in his tracks as he brought his right hand down from his brow, Ralph turned to the captain.

"Yes, sir, I'll be happy to help out, sir," Conte replied without hesitation, then bit his tongue after saying it. This was not an honor or duty Conte enjoyed but he was a captain with the privileges that go with it.

"Good, I believe the Post is open now, Lieutenant."

"Yes, sir. Oh well, hadn't found a fourth for bridge anyway," he muttered as he turned.

"What's that, Lieutenant?"

"Nothing, sir. Just reviewing a few things out loud, sir." Ralph hoped the conversation would go no further.

"Very good, Lieutenant."

"Yes, sir."

Walking on, Ralph entered the Post and dropped his letter into the outgoing mail bag beside the postal counter. Looking behind the censor desk, Ralph saw his ol' buddy Wayne Downing censoring mail. Drafted too, for sure—no one volunteered for this duty.

"Wayne."

"Hey, Ralph."

Wayne had a slightly sinister smile.

"Usual censored words and phrases?"

"The very same," Wayne said and chuckled. "I see you ran into Captain Thomas as well." Wayne smiled incriminatingly.

"Oh, well, I hadn't found us a fourth for the game anyway."

Ralph picked up a chair, and placed it down beside Wayne. He sat down, reached over the desk, and took the first five or six letters off the top of the pile.

Opening the first one, he read the name on the envelope, then rolled his eyes. He had drawn "old lover boy's" letters. Ralph realized this stroke of bad luck was probably not out of random misfortune but more by careful design.

Wayne had been putting them back on top of the stack, not wanting this responsibility. Ralph noted the first four letters were all from the same enlisted man and were addressed to different women. Setting them out so he would not mix them up, he started reading and censoring. Ralph could not understand how "lover boy" had been writing four different girls in four different places in the states since arriving in the ETO. He still had not gotten caught. It was the censoring officer's responsibility to get the right letter in the correct envelope with the correct address. Surprisingly there had not been a mistake in all the many months this airman had been doing it. It was almost a game now to see which officer made the fatal mistake of mixing them up. God knows the flak "old lover boy" would catch if there were ever a mix-up.

Ralph completed the first four without error, then reached for a few more. Wayne followed.

"How'd you end up here in the 416th?" Ralph asked to pass the time.

"Well, that's a long one. I started in the Army Air Corps back in '41 before Pearl Harbor. I had been studying engineering at Denver University but had always wanted to fly, so I decided it was time to learn. It was funny really. I signed up for both the Army Air Corps and the Navy in the summer of '41. In November of '41 the Air Corps called me up first, then after Pearl I was headin' to war."

"What about before all that?"

"Probably like the rest of you guys. My dad lost his job in Duluth back in the Depression. I think that was in '32. We moved back home to Sioux City, Iowa. We lived with my grandparents there. I went to high school there too. Hey, it was pretty tough times for everyone then, how about you?"

"Well, I grew up in a pretty mixed neighborhood. Like you, we all ended up in the military after Pearl. Before that I drove some trucks and worked in the CCC. Didn't have any money, but it wasn't too bad."

"I know what you mean; heck, we were so poor we didn't know we were poor. We grew most of our food in the backyard and burned feed corncobs in the stove all night to stay warm. Sometimes we could find some coal by the railroad tracks that fell off the trains. That was nice, too; it would burn longer and hotter, but it was hard to come by."

"Kinda like here, huh?" Ralph added.

They went back to work on the letters for a while.

"You're Catholic, aren't you?" asked Wayne.

"Yeah, you?"

"Methodist, heck we useta go to church every Sunday." Wayne thought about how if he lived through this war he was going to carry on this tradition.

"So anyway, after graduation I enrolled at the University in Denver, and then moved on to the Army Air Corps. I did my basic flight training in Tulsa. I had a series of moves through Texas, and then oddly enough ended up in Savannah, where my squadron began training in dive-bomber techniques.'

"Dive bombers?"

"Believe it or not, the Air Corps had been impressed with the success of old Hermann Göring's Stuka dive bombers in Spain and Europe. They had decided to build a squadron of their own. We ended up with several Navy SBD Dauntless Dive Bombers. We painted over the SBD Navy designation, changing it to A-24, and removed the tail hook."

"How'd it go?"

"We dropped a lot of flour sacks in mock war games, but the unit was demobilized, and we were transferred to the 46th Bomb Group at Will Rogers Field in Oklahoma."

"Yeah, we all started there too," Ralph threw in.

"I learned to fly A-20s and B-25s that the observation-reconnaissance squadron lent us at the base. We were then transferred to Tullahoma, Tennessee, William North Field, I think it was. They taught us the basics of combat flying and bombing at a couple of bases, and then they transferred us overseas here to England to join the 2911th Bomb Squadron."

"So you were here before we were, huh?"

"We were the only American A-20 group in the ETO then. We replaced the 15th BG that had been moved to North Africa. I flew an A-20-B model on my first mission. We hit a German airfield. After that you guys showed up with General Backus at Wing and he took over the 409th, 410th, and the 416th. He was sent to Britain to assume command of the 2911th too. After my first mission with the 2911th I was moved into the 668th squadron here with you guys."

"What happened to the rest of the guys in the 2911th?"

"The 2911th was disbanded. Half the squadron was shipped out to become C-47 pilots and the other half to join the 416th. So, anyway, we've got one extra mission but they aren't gonna count it toward our sixty-five."

Ralph sympathized.

Peddling almost effortlessly, the lieutenants continued their quest. Covering a lot of ground, they enjoyed the early spring countryside in spite of the cloud cover. They still hoped to make it into Finchingfield to have lunch.

They rounded a curve in the dirt road and then dropped off down a short hill, when they noted a farmer plowing his field with mules. As the group coasted down the hill, there was talk of a plowing contest, but there were no serious takers.

"Ain't done that in a while," Jack said, almost melancholy. "We had two jarheads to pull our plow, then we got an old Massey 'bull' tractor." He was thrilled as a young man when his father got one of the first powered tractors in the valley after they had become available there.

"Let me tell you—tractors beat those old mules any damned day." He smiled as he thought back to the farm.

Tractors had made life so much easier and really allowed them to farm more land. Not that it mattered now. The whole farm was under TVA water. Jack and his brothers had learned a great deal from these new machines. On a farm, it was all about keeping the equipment running, so they had learned out of necessity about the mechanics of machinery and the engineering that made it all work. The technical skills they and all the farmboys in America learned back on the farm were still used today, in the air, on the ground, on the water, and even under the water.

The four brothers had learned enough that they built the first car they ever owned. They scavenged parts from wherever they could find them, even rebuilding some of the parts to make them work. This farmboy determination and willingness to make it work was a skill most men of the 416th had grown up acquiring. The Depression had taught them all not to waste and since many things were not available they had to keep what they had working. Rebuilding was a skill used by the 416th's ground crews today as they scavenged the boneyard for parts. The aircrews appreciated that it took a while to do but it was nice to have once done. This "can do" attitude had carried America and Americans through the Depression and now to the never-doubted victory in this war.

"Heck, it beats a stump ranch." Earl brought Jack back to the present.

Everyone laughed but they were not quite sure why.

Earl Hayter knew why. He had grown up plowing a stump ranch after his family had moved to Washington state back in 1926—three years before the market crash. At the age of sixty-five, his father, an ordained Baptist minister, moved the family from Kansas City to forty acres he had bought from a logging company in Washington. Earl and the family called it the stump ranch because it was literally forty acres of clear-cut forest now just covered in stumps and barren soil. Clear-cutting practices, Earl now knew, had helped contribute to the eventual deforestation and soil erosion that multiplied the misery of the worst years of the Depression.

Earl and the guys knew now that the entire world had been experiencing devastating change well before America's plunge into depression. They also knew for many of them the misery had been made worse by this war.

Even though America would suffer in the late 1920s and throughout the 1930s, the nation was yet to experience the kind of problems Germany had been wrestling with in the 1920s. Germany granted huge concessions to the postwar powers by signing the Treaty of Versailles. Because it severely disempowered and oppressed Germany, this treaty primed the pump for disaster.

The disaster began with Germany being forced to pay unbearable war reparations. That was on top of struggling to pay its own postwar debt. The Allies had taken possession of resource-rich land that had belonged to Germany before the war. Poland gained possession of Silesia, a mineral-abundant region in the eastern territory, as well as a corridor between Germany and Prussia. France "reclaimed" Alsace-Lorraine and its plentiful coal reserves, and the Saar was to be administered by the League of Nations for fifteen years. This confiscation of productive German land was responsible for some of the feelings of lost nationalism and shame—feelings that ultimately would be used to lead the resurgence of a fanatical nationalism.

Germans also had to live under the European attitude that Germany should never again be a threat to the rest of world. The victorious Allies believed the country and its people needed to be controlled at as many levels as possible. So, in addition to taking land and demanding financial reparations, the Allies prevented Germany from rearming. Such draconian punishments, Europe was warned in 1923, would be paid back handsomely, but the message fell on deaf ears. The Swedish book *Social-Demokraten* predicted: "Encircle Germany with zones…treat her as the dangerous lunatic of Europe, take every precaution against her, and one day Germany will break out of her cell with the demonic force of the lunatic."

In spite of Germany's 1924 "policy of fulfillment"—an effort to fulfill the accords of the Treaty of Versailles—a lunatic is what the nation ended up with. Unfortunately, this lunatic had armed himself with the now internationally supported propaganda of eugenic hatred, a pseudoscience of genetic racism.

Eugenics had become a form of self-serving genetic interpretation whose ideas of controlled human breeding had had its seeds planted in England by Sir Francis Galton (half cousin of Charles Darwin) in the late 1800s. Galton's early ideas were transported to and planted in America by Harvard biologist and geneticist Charles Davenport in conjunction with his contemporary Harry Laughlin. American and British genetic concepts embraced the belief that Northern European countries were the superior breeding stock, but this vision did not include everyone, mainly the privileged classes who were perceived as "fit."

The roots of the eugenics movement had grown deep in America's fertile land with the aid of financial fertilizer provided by the well-heeled and seemingly benevolent Americans and their cash-flush foundations. By the early 1900s eugenics had its own brand of cultural racism that came almost exclusively from America. Eugenics was the name given to the worst form of elitist klanism camouflaged by the facade of science. This "scientific agenda" paralleled the rising "social agenda" of the "second coming of the Ku Klux Klan." Indeed, the Klan's social policies and beliefs were "scientifically supported" by the eugenics organizations. Alcoholism, drug addiction, tuberculosis, seizures, blindness, eastern and southern Europeans, Africans, Jews, and Catholics were all to be blamed for the progressive decline of the superior gene pool of the social classes. The main goal of eugenics organizations had more to do with controlling the rate of procreation of the lower classes or the perceived genetically unfit than with enhancing their own fertility. [47, 48, 49, 50] America provided the money, and with this private money international support was garnered to support the eugenicists' "Better Breeding" agenda.

A series of letters between the British Eugenics Education Society (EES) and the Medical Research Council (MRC) outlined the growing influence of the former

47   *War Against the Weak: Eugenics and America's Campaign to Create a Master Race;* Edwin Black; Copyright 2003; Publisher, Four Walls Eight Windows
48   *From Darwin to Hitler: Evolutionary Ethics, Eugenics, and Racism;* Richard Weikart; Copyright 2004; Publisher, Palgrave Macmillan
49   *A Life of Sir Francis Galton: From African Exploration to the Birth of Eugenics;* Nicholas Wright Gillham; Copyright 2001; Publisher, Oxford University Press, Inc.
50   *Struggle for National Survival: Eugenics in Sino-Japanese Contexts, 1896–1945;* Yuehtsen Juliette Chung; Copyright 2002; Publisher, Routledge

while raising the dislike of the latter. In January 1926 Major Leonard Darwin (Charles Darwin's son), then president of the Eugenics Education Society, wrote to the Medical Research Council in an effort to get sanctioned medical support: "The chief existing danger to the race [English] appears to be due to the relatively high fertility of many inferior types." In response, the Medical Research Council privately referred to the EES as the "elderly or middle aged members of the leisured classes—who, I suppose, form the active spirits of the Eugenic Education Society." The MRC then went on to deny, yet again, the EES petition to undertake a study or form a committee to study the rates of procreation of "different classes." Throughout these series of correspondences over the years, the EES attempted to influence legislation and social policy, including state sterilization policies.[51]

England would not let its contribution to eugenics go unnoticed. In the "Statement by the British National Committee for Human Heredity" the British Committee had been appointed the controller of the "clearinghouse" for the International Committee for Human Heredity in 1934. The British Committee oversaw institutions and financial resources, specifically the "Kaiser-Wilhelm Institute for Eugenics and Anthropology in Berlin (founded partly by a Rockefeller fund and partly... by Roman Catholics) ... and the Kaiser-Wilhelm Institute for Psychiatry in Munich (...due to Rockefeller munificence...)." Later the statement lists other areas of responsibility, the Eugenics Records Office (ERO) and the Carnegie Institute of Genetics. The authors go on to recognize yet again England's role in the establishment of the theory of evolution and the coining of eugenics as a science.[52]

At the turn of the century, the study of eugenics spread not only in America but also in Germany. Alfred Ploetz of Germany, who wrote extensively in support of controlling the unfit, supported the eugenics movement. Coining the term *Rassenhygiene* (racial hygiene), he professed his position on racial and social health in his 1895 work *The Foundations of Racial Hygiene*. This was followed by the formation of the "Society for Racial Hygiene" in 1905 in Germany, which had been preceded one year before by Charles Davenport's Biological Experiment Station at Cold Spring Harbor. Built by Davenport with private American foundation money, the station was to study "the method of evolution." Davenport had self-proclaimed his mission to ensure the "fitness" of society by controlling the procreation of or eliminating those his organization had deemed "unfit" or of "inferior protoplasm." Not long after, the Eugenics Record Office and its superintendent Harry Laughlin cataloged the records of the locations and family trees of the unfit.

During this time international eugenics conferences were organized and attended, which gave a false validity to the movement. The organizational efforts for these conferences did reveal several distressing coming truths. Fritz Lenz, coauthor of a con-

---

51   British National Archives; Correspondence between EES and MRC 1925 to 1932; Ref: FO 1/1734 268033
52   Statement by the British National Committee for Human Heredity; British National Archives; Ref; FO 1/1733 268033

temporary eugenics text, spoke in Germany of America's lead in sterilization laws and practices. He also wrote Charles Davenport in 1923 in a sadly prophetic letter, responding to Davenport's request for a German contingent to attend the Second International Congress on Eugenics. Lenz responded:

> Europe goes with rapid steps toward a new frightful war, in which Germany will chiefly participate...I do not believe the time for international congresses has arrived so long as France occupies the Ruhr (with Afro-French soldiers that further enraged the believers of the Aryan purity)... I know that our race in it would suffer more heavily...but it cannot be avoided.

Such words were embraced by Hitler, even from his jail cell, where he welded the racial hate to his sword of power and then brandished. it. Soon he would use the vindictive power of retaliatory insults made upon Germany after World War I as one of the unifying magnets of his party.

While the flames of racial hate were being fanned across the world, they gave Germany through Hitler a new vision, through which to restore its national pride in the aftermath of the insulting reparations demanded by the Allies. These reparations were attacked by prominent authorities, such as economist John Maynard Keynes. At the conclusion of World War I, Keynes attended the Paris Peace Conference. There he witnessed America's Woodrow Wilson, Britain's David Lloyd George, and France's Georges Clemenceau build the framework for the next world war. On his return to England he wrote: "The Germans could not possibly pay what the victors were demanding." His insults of Wilson, "A blind, deaf Don Quixote," and Clemenceau, "A xenophobe with one illusion—France, and one disillusion—mankind" matched his equally derogatory words for George. Keynes rightly prophesied that the reparations would impoverish Germany, thereby threatening Europe. Deaf ears struggled to hear.

By the mid-1920s hyperinflation had made the German economy as painfully meaningless as America's and most of the world's economies were about to become. The German Central Bank running twenty-four hours a day could not keep up with the rate of inflation. The German populace living on fixed pensions could not buy food with their now worthless pension payments. Working people needed monthly raises just to pay the bills. Disbelief became meaningless, as disbelief was now a way of life.

Perhaps Germany during this time became an argument against the Keynesian hypothesis of deficit spending as a way to manage need. With the world expecting reparations to continue, but Germany becoming increasingly incapable of paying them, France mobilized troops into the Ruhr Valley, as a warning for Germany to continue its payments or else. The Germans were powerless to resist, and France's increasing military pressure lowered the threshold for the rise of eugenically driven German nationalism.

The Weimar Republic of President Hindenburg, which had attempted to bring democracy to the postwar nation, now had to deal with a creeping and growing anarchy on the heels of the assassination of its foreign minister Walter Rathenau. The fanatics were fracturing what little cohesion the Weimar Republic had.

Such utter economic ruin led many to question who was behind it all and when it would end. Surprisingly, some areas of the German economy prospered in spite of the hardships. Prostitution was rampant, as was the use of cocaine. The population traded money for commodities such as gold, diamonds, and real estate, opting for tangible real assets rather than constantly devalued paper marks. As the publisher Leopold Ullstein wrote, "People just did not understand what was happening…Somebody must be in the know, and that this small group of 'somebodies' must be a conspiracy."

In essence the German public was correct; the Allied European nations were the conspirators driving Germany to the edge. With currency valueless and prices astronomical, Germany experienced the opposite effect of the coming Great Depression. In Germany's case, money was everywhere but valueless, as prices climbed through the roof. In the coming American Depression, money was nowhere, but it was of tremendous value, with prices nearly nonexistent or overvalued.

In this hyperinflation period, the National Socialist Party took root, as unemployed veterans, disenfranchised peoples, and the weary young began looking for anybody who promised relief and could deliver it. By the start of 1921, there were three thousand members in the Nationsozialistische Deutsche Arbeiterpartei (NSDAP).[53] It would soon have its own anti-Semitic newspaper, a central secretariat and its own private army.

The Nazis made effective rhetorical work of the situation to entrench themselves in power. Every negative effect became a rallying cry for National Socialism. According to Stephen H. Roberts in his book *The House That Hitler Built,*

> It [National Socialism] survived because it had no fixed programme and could thus take advantage of every mood of national dejection and hatred. The 'dictate of Versailles' was always a powerful weapon, but there were many others, the loss of the Ruhr, inflation, unemployment, 'the tyranny of the Young Plan' (that had come after the failed Dawes Plan. Both were designed to force Germany to pay their reparations), and, of course, the old stand-by of anti-Semitism which was dragged out when there was nothing more topical.

Positioning Germany as the bullied underdog in this confusing and fluid period, the Nazis promised a return to glory, and won seats in the Reichstag, the national parliament, in the early thirties. The seats were won with broad-based political support from many sectors of society.

Having gained power in the Reichstag in 1933, Hitler empowered and challenged the nation to rebuild, re-arm, and prepare for war. He had all but eliminated every other political party and was now undisputed dictator of the country—a country

---

53   National Socialist Workers Party of Germany

he was determined to have reclaim its now occupied lands. The world was watching as he broke the Treaty of Versailles, and began mandatory military service in Germany. He pulled Germany out of the League of Nations, closing the doors for possible diplomatic dialogue. He defaulted on reparations as outlined in the Young Plan.

A key element of Hitler's plan to return Germany to its former glory was the military. Germany's military ground forces were secretly expanded as was its air force. In June 1933, British intelligence received secret information from the air attaché in Berlin, Group Captain J.H. Herring, that Hitler had ordered all civilian aircraft owners to register with the new Air Ministry. Herring commented, "A process of mobilization is in progress," and basically Hitler was "already engaged in building an air force." New pilots were being taught to fly gliders first, and then transitioned into powered planes. [54] The new German Air Force (Luftwaffe) was announced by Hermann Göring in March 1935. Not only was the National Socialist party developing its air force, German scientists had already launched the A-4 rocket prototype from the island of Borkum in 1934.

The A-4 project was to grow into the V-1 (buzz bomb) and V-2 rocket programs that later would rain death onto Britain's soil. By 1944 these German rocket programs would require a major combat effort to destroy them by the 416th Bomb Group in what were called No-ball missions. In the air-to-ground battles over these V-1 launch sites, death would come to some of the men from the 416th, while they succeeded in destroying these rocket sites, along with the enemy's ability to wage war.

Ironically, Germany obtained much of its knowledge of rocketry from an American. Rocket science pioneer Robert H. Goddard had conducted research and published the results with funding from the Smithsonian and the Guggenheim foundations. His work was intently followed by the Germans. Germany benefited from Goddard's work in gyroscopic control, gimbal steering of engines and moveable-rocket-fin or vane steering. Of particular importance to rocketry was Goddard's invention of the power-assisted fuel pump. The fuel pump, combined with all the other breakthroughs, helped to push German rocketry to the point of successful weaponry.

At the start of the war the American military had been given the opportunity to benefit from Goddard's work, but chose instead to have him focus on rocket-assisted airplane takeoff devices. This decision was surprising, given Germany's rapid adoption of Goddard's advances. At the end of the war a captured German rocket scientist was questioned about the V-2 program, and he responded, "Why don't you ask your own Dr. Goddard? He knows better than any of us."[55, 56]

The rise in power of the National Socialists came not only from the disenfranchised but also from a group of misled, misdirected, and propaganda-driven Protestants and Catholics who had fallen victim to a politically pressured, and thereby misguided church. From its early days, the Nazi party was forced to deal with the dichotomy of

54   *The Last Lion, Winston Spencer Churchill, Alone 1932–1940;* William Manchester, page 112
55   Goddard History, Robert H. Goddard: American Rocket Pioneer, http://www.gsfc. nasa.gov/gsfc/welcome/history/history.htm
56   Robert H. Goddard, father of modern rocketry, by Paul Jarvey; http://www.eworester. com/extra/goddard/

Article 24 of the party program that stated "the party is built on the base of a positive Christianity" while balancing that against the practices of the party. With the Nazi's policy of *Blut und Erde* (blood and soil), Hitler realized his party was at odds with the Lutheran and Catholic churches. It became obvious to Hitler and the party leaders that he was going to have to make Nazism into religion and Germany's religion into Nazism.

To this end, the party found its "philosophical leader" in the form of Alfred Rosenberg. Rosenberg was a German-born, Russian architectural student, a disgruntled Russian revolutionist, and a journalist for the Nazi party's paper *Der Völkischer Beobachter* (*The People's Observer*). Along with Hitler, he participated in the failed Munich Putsch, but he avoided imprisonment, unlike Hitler. Most ironically, Rosenberg was a Jewish anti-Semite, and developed the weltanschauung of "blood and soil." The rally cry soon became: "The Cross must fall if Germany is to live" as well as Hitler's line: "We wish for no other God than Germany."

A similar unifying eugenic belief had been espoused in 1904 when Sir Francis Galton spoke. "[Eugenics]…must be introduced into the national conscience, like a new religion. It has, indeed, strong claims to become an orthodox religious tenet of the future, for eugenics co-operates with the workings of nature by securing that humanity shall be represented by the fittest races."[57] George Bernard Shaw echoed this eugenic belief in the religion of inheritance and in 1904 said, "There is now no reasonable excuse for refusing to face the fact that nothing but a eugenic religion can save our civilisation from the fate that has overtaken all previous civilisations."[58]

Not just enthralling secular thinkers, eugenics was embraced by many religious teachers, who incorporated it into Judeo-Christian religious teachings. At the turn of the century Protestants, Catholics, and Reform rabbis saw eugenics as a way to strengthen their congregations' "germ-plasma," thereby ridding them of the weaknesses of alcoholism, congenital disorders, mental illness, and criminal behavior.

To his credit, Charles Davenport noticed the potentially destructive power of eugenics. He is credited with recognizing the ideology's potential for abuse. "Our greatest danger is from some impetuous temperament, who, planting a banner of Eugenics, rallies a volunteer army of Utopians, freelovers, and muddy thinkers to start a holy war for the new religion."[59] These prescient comments aptly displayed the danger lying in wait.

Hitler did exactly what they all had suggested, mixing the divine mysticism of Nordic power, purity, and God-given righteousness with this belief in Aryan "blood" superiority. Hitler looked for a leader who could combine these pseudoscientific beliefs into a religion to be taught from the pulpit. He found his religious collaborator

57   *Eugenics and Other Evils: An Argument Against the Scientifically Organized Society;* G. K. Chesterton; Copyright 2000; Editor, Michael W. Perry

58   *A Life of Sir Francis Galton: From African Exploration to the Birth of Eugenics;* Nicholas Wright Gillham; Oxford University Press; copyright 2001

59   *Preaching Eugenics: Religious Leaders and the American eugenics Movement;* Christine Rosen; Oxford University Press; copyright 2004

and propagandist in Pastor Ludwig Müller, a fifty-year-old *Wehrmacht* chaplain who was willing to work with the National Socialists and develop the "Nazi priestcraft." Hitler promoted Müller, who rose to become the bishop of Prussia in 1933

From their authoritative positions Hitler "orated" in political forums while Bishop Müller "preached" from Martin Luther's own pulpit, the role of the Lutheran Church acting as the National Socialists' hand servant. Müller spoke of Christian soldiers and crusades in a new age, evoking visions of better times to come with every citizen's responsibility to help achieve it through "Germany as our God." Whereas Hitler wove the fabric of politics into the religion, Müller wove the fabric of religion into politics, with the "conversion experiences" of the congregation signaling their conversion from God to Nazism. Soon no one could tell the difference.

The Nazi war of eugenics against the Protestants and the Catholics had started early. In July 1933 Cardinal Eugenio Pacelli (soon to become Pope Pius XII) agreed to a concordat with Franz Von Papen, then vice chancellor of Germany, that would allow the practice of Catholicism in exchange for the church removing itself from political processes. This separation of church and state followed the recent restriction of the church in Italy, which occurred with the establishment of the Vatican State in 1929.

Conversion proceeded swiftly. By 1934, Bishop Müller had "converted" through "submissive conversion" twenty-two of the twenty-eight regional churches. By September 1935 Hitler had converted, through the dictatorial powers of the Reich minister for Church Affairs, the evangelical churches and their congregations into a single "State German Church" with its "priestcraft." Paganism flourished as an Aryan German faith under the "German Faith Movement" that was led by their prophet Wilhelm Hauer. The masses followed.

The Evangelicals and Catholics protested, and manifestos against the Nazi religion were published and read. In 1934 a pamphlet titled "Studien zum Mythos des Zwanzigsten Jahrhunderts," credited to Dr. Wilhelm Neuss of the University of Bonn, attacked Alfred Rosenberg's thesis and conclusions about the scientifically organized a-religious state. However, the Church was afraid to publish the document, since they were being repressed and censored by the state. The Church's fear was well founded, as the Nazi party would eventually take over or close all the Catholic publishers and newspapers.

This suppression of the religious press was combined with suppression of religious education. From early 1937 to April 1939 the Nazi party would close all 5,006 Roman Catholic schools. Between 1941 and 1942, the closing of twelve monasteries and convents would follow the school closures, with pressure on the others until war's end. Finally, the united front of Catholic and Evangelical religious opposition led the Nazi party to an impasse. Neither religious body was ever free of the onslaught of the eugenic weltanschauung until the tides of war changed.[60]

---

60   Germany: Zone Handbook No. V: Rhine-Ruhr; Part 1: People and Administration; January 1944; Imperial War Museum, London, England

It was not just through the adulteration of religion that Hitler gained the broad base of membership in his party. He turned the Communists, the indecisive and the fearful conservative middle of Germany's politics, and the Jews into the pariahs of the "conspiracy" that caused all the German people's problems. Hitler's hatred of the inferior Gypsies, Polish, homosexuals, and Jews was used to inflate the egos of the "Aryans" by rationalizing it all with the misguided concept of eugenics.

Nazism became clear; it was justified with the fabrication of "Wagnerian mystical spiritualism" that was "a God-given" and forgotten gift to the Aryans; these elements were combined with an overstated, poorly understood concept of eugenics that was melded with the well-known concepts of hate-filled racism. Aryans, gods, genetics, mysticism, and the Nazis' Malthusian right to expand became the centerpieces of the party's mantra, and fascism grew.

With the scapegoats now clearly identified, the internal enemies of the Reich could be controlled and eliminated. With blind ambition fueling the "lunatic's escape," Hitler provided oration and promises, backed by violence to ensure success. He took great advantage of unfortunate, uncontrollable events such as the stock market crash of 1929 that required American banks to start calling in their loans from Germany. They were loans that Germany could not and would not repay. [61,62,63,64,65,66,67]

The eugenic, racist policies adopted by Hitler and his Nazi party were, by and large, plagiarized. International organizations with hateful rhetoric contributed to the practices occurring in Germany. During these difficult times America, unfortunately, was not so innocent. The foundation, rhetoric, and laws under which the Nazi party operated were easily traceable back to England and America. The ideas were the product of Charles Darwin, adulterated by Sir Francis Galton, Margaret Sanger, Charles Davenport, and Harry Laughlin. Davenport, the founder, and Laughlin, the superintendent of the Station for Experimental Evolution at Cold Spring Harbor, New York, exerted significant pressure on the public policy bodies in America from their scientific alter of eugenics. Laughlin wrote a model sterilization law that was used by twelve American states as their model for sterilization laws. By 1920 these laws were on the books in fifteen states—Indiana (1907), Washington (1909), California (1909, 1913, 1917), Connecticut (1909), Nevada (1911), Iowa (1911, 1913, 1915), New Jersey (1911), New

61   www.WorldHistory.com, Events preceding World War II in Europe.

62   www.WorldHistory.com, Causes of World War II

63   www.islandnet.com, Chronology of World War II, 1918 to 1939, Copyright © 1998–2004 Ken Polsson, pages 1 to 23.

64   www.pbs.org/wgbh, Commanding heights: The German Hyperinflation, 1923, By George J.W. Goodman, Copyright © 1981.

65   www.grolier.com/wwii/wwii, World War II Commemoration, Colonel Vincent J. Esposito, US Army; Head, Dept. of Military Art, United States Military Academy.

66   John Maynard Keynes, His radical idea that government should spend money they don't have may have saved capitalism, By Robert B. Reich; http://www.time.com/time/time100/scientist/profile/keyens.html

67   *The House that Hitler Built*, By Stephen H. Roberts, chapters; 3, 4, 8; Harper, 1938; reprint by Gordon Press, 1975

York (1912), North Dakota (1913), Michigan (1913), Kansas (1913, 1917), Wisconsin (1913), Nebraska (1915), Oregon (1917), South Dakota (1917).[68]

Fortunately, many legislative bodies feared passing such laws, afraid they would be used on themselves. Surprisingly and ironically, it is quite possible Charles Darwin himself would have been sterilized or eliminated from society due to his family's practice of interbreeding among close relatives. Darwin married his cousin, and produced arguably weak offspring.[69]

The sterilization laws in America were written only after support for the elimination of the "unfit" had been garnered from the medical community. Support for the control of the unfit came in the form of articles arguing for the mass sterilization of prisoners written by the future founder of the American College of Surgeons, Dr. Albert John Ochsner. This eugenic concept of mass sterilization was taken to heart by Dr. Harry Clay Sharp, who preformed involuntary castrations on the inmates of the Indiana Reformatory in Jeffersonville, to rid the world of future generations of criminals. His techniques were promoted in the *New York Medical Journal.*[70] The American model did not go unnoticed in Germany, which adopted a similar framework and modeling to justify its "racial hygiene" program. Racial hygiene would ultimately grow to become the "Final Solution."

America's complicity with "genetic racism" extended all the way to the Supreme Court, where in 1924 Justice Oliver Wendell Holmes Jr. delivered a horribly sad court opinion. Holmes opined: "It is better for all the world, if instead of waiting to execute degenerate offspring for crime or to let them starve for their imbecility, society can prevent those who are manifestly unfit from continuing their kind...Three generations of imbeciles are enough."[71, 72, 73, 74] The result of this arrogance was the forced sterilization of seventeen-year-old Carrie Buck from Charlottesville, Virginia, the defendant.

Justice Holmes had come by his eugenic sense of class superiority honestly. His father, Dr. Oliver Wendell Holmes Sr., was consulted to assist a mentally unstable newborn. When asked about extending life-saving efforts for the child, he is supposed to have said, "This consult should have been held some fifty years ago!" According to Hol-

68   *Eugenics and Other Evils: An Argument Against the Scientifically Organized Society;* G. K. Chesterton; Copyright 2000; Editor, Michael W. Perry ; pp151–152; (Social Hygiene, Vol. 6)

69   *Natural History:* Darwin & Evolution: Good Breeding: Darwin Doubted His Own Family's Fitness; James Moore; pp 45–46; November, 2005

70   *War Against the Weak: Eugenics and America's Campaign to Create a Master Race;* Edwin Black; Copyright 2003; Publisher, Four Walls Eight Windows

71   Eugenics: America's Darkest Days, Sterilization; http://iml.jou.ufl.edu/projects/Spring02/Holland/Sterlization.htm

72   Eugenics: A Faultline in History: Eugenics in America: Public Policy: Sterilization; Buck v. Bell Supreme Court case of 1927; http://129.41.238.103/eugenics/content/section_03/sterilization.htm

73   *Racial Science in Social Context,* John R. Baker on Eugenics, Race, and the Public Role of the Scientist by Michael G. Kenny; Isis, Vol. 95, number 3, Sept 2004, pp 394–419.

74   *The Unfit: A History of a Bad Idea;* Elof Axel Carlson; copyright 2001; Cold Spring Harbor Laboratory Press, Cold Spring Harbor, New York

mes, the right thing would have been the elimination of the perceived defective lineage many years earlier.

It is important to remember this was a period in American history where the Klan was resurging in great numbers, driven by a values agenda that was bolstered by the belief that so much of society's problems stemmed from eugenic weaknesses. So much so, that the eugenics societies, financed by the socially elite and well-heeled foundations in America, were advocating the elimination of alcoholics, the mentally infirm, diseased, insane, and inbred, all to preserve the "superior" Nordic gene pool that had built America. The societies succeeded in establishing the "genetic racist" practice of sterilization in many states.

America imported Sir Francis Galton's faux science of eugenics from the floundering unfunded eugenic societies in England. In America, eugenics became financially successful by pandering, and then by making it appealing to the egocentric philanthropic vein of the American nouveaux riches. With the proper funding achieved and sufficient fear of the unfit solidified in America, Davenport and Laughlin, as the ringleaders, exported it back to Europe in several international conferences that began the publication and dissemination of pseudoscientific hate.

America too was chastised for its movement into the fields of controlled breeding and sterilization when, on December 31, 1930, the Vatican issued a wide-ranging encyclical in which Pope Pius XI stated,

> That pernicious practice [eugenics] must be condemned which closely touches upon the natural right of man to enter matrimony but affects also in a real way the welfare of the offspring. For there are some who over-solicitous for the cause of eugenics…put eugenics before aims of a higher order, and by public authority wish to prevent from marrying all those whom, even though naturally fit for marriage, they consider, according to the norms and conjectures of their investigations, would, through hereditary transmission, bring forth defective offspring. And more, they wish to legislate to deprive these of that natural faculty by medical action [sterilization] despite their unwillingness[75, 76, 77]

The Church never gave up its quest in denouncing the eugenic movement and its supporters, such as Margaret Sanger. Sanger was an avid leader in the birth control movement, and a participant in the Neo-Malthusian[78] movement and later in eugenics organizations. She circled the globe speaking to any group who would listen. She

---

75   Casti Connubii, section 68
76   *War Against the Weak: Eugenics and America's Campaign to Create a Master Race;* Edwin Black; Copyright 2003; Publisher, Four Walls Eight Windows
77   *The Unfit: A History of a Bad Idea;* Elof Axel Carlson; copyright 2001; Cold Spring Harbor Laboratory Press, Cold Spring Harbor, New York
78   *The Works of Thomas Robert Malthus;* Vol. I; Copyright 1798; The Pickering Masters; William Pickering; copyright 1986

found fertile ground in England and other European countries but had suffered arrests and convictions in the United States for violating the Comstock Act, which prohibited, among other things, sending through the mail contraceptives or information on birth control. In spite of the legal resistance, she found many supporters for controlling the reproductive injustices of the economically underprivileged.

Sanger explained her method in typically eugenic terms. "We...sought first to stop the multiplication of the unfit," she wrote. "This appeared the most important and greatest step towards race betterment." In addition, Sanger herself supported aggressive anti-immigration legislation similar to the 1907 federal legislation. She stated: "Had these precautions been taken earlier our institutions would not now be crowded with moronic mothers, daughters, and grand-daughters—three generations at a time, all of whom have to be supported by tax-payers who shut their eyes to this condition, admittedly detrimental to the blood stream of the race."[79]

Sanger's efforts were met with acceptance in China but were challenged in Germany and Italy in the 1920s and '30s. As Göring was to have said, "The territory in which the Germans live is too small for our sixty-six million inhabitants and will be too small for the ninety million which we want to become." Germany embraced the concepts of resistive reproduction for the unfit while rewarding and encouraging a high birth rate of their eugenically defined "fit." The head of Italy, Benito Mussolini, stated that he wanted sixty million people for the second half of the century.

Just as there were resisters, there were also the opportunistic supporters of the eugenic and birth control concepts of the genetically engineered state. One would-be supporter had the opportunity to become a vocal advocate for eugenics during his time in prison, after his fledgling party's failed push for power in Munich. This ambitious World War I corporal began reading the publications about racial purification and control of the "genetically inferior." He was so impressed that he penned letters to two published eugenic scholars, Madison Grant, who authored *The Passing of the Great Race* (1916) and Leon Whitney, president of the American Eugenics Society. Hitler told both of his admiration for their published works and ideas. Grant's thesis argued that the destiny of the Nordic race was to lose its rightful place as leader of the world due to the influx and mixing of the Nordic races with less desirable cultural immigrants. This publication was reputed to be one of Hitler's favorites, referred to as his "bible." [80, 81]

Along with other contemporary eugenic writers and thinkers, the writings of Grant, an American-born and Columbia University-trained attorney, influenced Hitler's own book, *Mein Kampf (My Struggle)*. Grant was well positioned as chairman of the New York Zoological Society, trustee of the American Museum of Natural History, and councilor of the American Geographical Society. Hitler was a broad reader of eugenic litera-

---

79 *The Auto Biography of Margaret Sanger* (Margaret Sanger: An Autobiography); Margaret Sanger; Dover Publications; copyright 1938; pp 375–377

80 *War Against the Weak: Eugenics and America's Campaign to Create a Master Race;* Edwin Black; Copyright 2003; Publisher, Four Walls Eight Windows

81 *The Nazi Connection: Eugenics, American Racism and German National Socialism;* Stefan Kühl; Oxford University Press; Copyright 1994; Chapter 8; page 85

ture, though, ostensibly having studied in depth the publication *Foundation of Human Heredity and Race Hygiene* while in prison.

Madison Grant's own comments contributed to Hitler's propaganda, and laid the ideological groundwork for the Nazi Party. Grant argued, "Denmark, Norway and Sweden are purely Nordic…as they have been for thousands of years, the chief nursery and bloodline of the master race." Grant credited the Nordic bloodlines with flowing through "Dante, Raphael, Titian, Michael Angelo, Leonardo da Vinci," who "were all of Nordic type, just as in classic times many of the chief men and of the upper classes were Nordic." Grant further claimed that, "races must be kept apart by artificial devices …or they ultimately amalgamate and in the offspring the more generalized or lower type prevails."[82]

Fueled by this kind of legitimized socially scientific language, Hitler moved forward with solid foundations of "social genetic Darwinian selection." Hitler had found "someone to blame," and his hateful misunderstanding of genetics became obvious. He wrote,

> All the human culture, all the results of art, science, and technology that we see before us today are almost exclusively the creative product of the Aryan. This very fact admits of the not unfounded inference that he alone was the founder of all higher humanity, therefore representing the prototype of all that we understand by the word 'man'…If we were to divide mankind into three groups, the founders of culture, the bearers of culture, the destroyers of culture, only the Aryan could be considered as the representative of the first group.[83]

Hitler's confidence had been stoked by Friedrich Krupp, of industrial fame, who had sponsored a competition in 1900 that offered ten thousand marks to whomever could best answer the question, "What do we learn from the principles of biologic evolution in regard to domestic political developments and legislation of states?"

But even as Germany proceeded openly with its eugenic agenda, America was not without further blame. In 1934, ten years after the passing of the Virginia sterilization laws, Joseph DeJarnette (superintendent of Virginia's Western State Hospital) is quoted in the *Richmond Times* as saying, "The Germans are beating us at our own game." By 1934 Hitler and his henchmen had sterilized upward of fifty-six thousand unfit in the Reich. They were known as "Hitlerschnitte (Hitler's cut)."[84] The process was best outlined in a British secret report from 1943. In the section discussing the "health castes" the report states, "The individual 'health castes' depends not primarily on his occupation or even his national origin, but on his genetic qualifications as a breeder of good

82   *The Passing of the Great Race or The Racial Basis of European History;* Madison Grant; Copyright 1916; Charles Scribner's & Sons; Fourth revised edition, page 211-215, 222

83   *Mein Kampf;* Adolf Hitler; copyright 1925, Houghton Mifflin Company; *chapter XI, Vol. I*

84   *War Against the Weak: Eugenics and America's Campaign to Create a Master Race;* Edwin Black; Copyright 2003; Publisher, Four Walls Eight Windows

'Nordic Stock'....If the newborn is diseased or of bad ancestry, it is already downgraded. It is in fact held that it should not have been born at all." In July 1933, compulsory abortion was required of fetuses arising from parents of "inferior genetics."[85]

This eugenic idea of Nordic superiority had been strengthened in the 1936 Olympics, in spite of Jesse Owens's herculean effort in winning four gold medals. Germany finished as the leading medal winner with eighty-nine medals; the United States placed a distant second with fifty-six.[86]

The foundations for Nazi wholesale killing of the "unwanted" had been laid along with the outlines for Nazi wartime propaganda that would be beamed into England and America. The Nazi regime assumed the propaganda was falling on sympathetic ears. At this time in America's and the world's "evolution of thought and reason," scientific concepts and observations were being melded into the social and governmental culture as a form of a "society of science." Many in the global eugenic societies believed their science should become the driving principles of society, thereby selectively molding a healthier, genetically superior society and civilization.[87, 88, 89, 90]

In the 1920s America was wrestling with these evolving social-scientific concepts, which included the elimination of biblical creation. In a small Tennessee town a teacher and coach brought the depths of the struggle to light. The Scopes trial of evolution versus creationism would be fought in the summer of 1925 in the city of Dayton, located in Rhea County, Tennessee, just north of Chattanooga. Clarence Darrow would represent and defend John Scopes, a high school science teacher, against the charges of teaching evolution. Darrow faced William Jennings Bryan, a devout creationist who represented the State of Tennessee. Judge John Raulston presided over the trial's opening by reading the first twenty-seven verses of Genesis. In the heat and hubbub of a hot Tennessee courthouse the "monkey trial" proceeded.

While reporting the trial, Europeans wrote satire and the American press spoke of "yokels, bigots and rubes." Regardless, the verdict was returned guilty with a $100 fine, which was later reversed on a technicality. Bryan himself passed on five days later; some argued it was a reward for having done God's work. Thus, Tennessee's Butler law stood, and creationism was the manner of education for some time to come. This stood in stark contrast to the desires of many states to rid themselves of the undesirables, infirm, imbecilic, or physically challenged. These positions stood diametrically opposed

---

85   Germany: Zone Handbook No. V: Rhine-Ruhr; Part 1: People and Administration: The Health Castes; January 1944; Secret 1943; Imperial War Museum, London, England

86   MSN Encarta Premium-Multimedia-Summer Olympics Medal Standings, Berlin, 1936; http://encarta.msn.com/media_701701849/Summer_Olympics-Medal_Standings.html

87   *War Against the Weak: Eugenics and America's Campaign to Create a Master Race;* Edwin Black; Copyright 2003; Publisher, Four Walls Eight Windows

88   *From Darwin to Hitler: Evolutionary Ethics, Eugenics, and Racism;* Richard Weikart; Copyright 2004; Publisher, Palgrave Macmillan

89   *Struggle for National Survival: Eugenics in Sino-Japanese Contexts, 1896-1945;* Yuehtsen Juliette Chung; Copyright 2002; Publisher, Routledge

90   *The Unfit: A History of a Bad Idea;* Elof Axel Carlson; copyright 2001; Cold Spring Harbor Laboratory Press, Cold Spring Harbor, New York

to the constitutional and religious beliefs that had mobilized so many to win emancipation, only to have those freedoms cast into doubt by "egocentric eugenic reason" that was used to sterilize the undesirable and socially unequal masses.

As the fear of the undesirables increased, anti-immigration laws were passed across the country. Racism against those of Asian descent was becoming ingrained on the West Coast. Elsewhere, Jim Crow was growing, and by the late '20s and early '30s the situation was further complicated by the Fascist party of America going on the march.

During this era, fascist organizations sprang up, sometimes supported by German organizations. To quote Huey Long, when asked if fascism would come to America, he replied, "Sure, but here it will be called anti-fascism." In reality, Huey's antifascist name for fascism was to be called "eugenics." Two main fascist organizations were the Order of the Black Shirts and the American Fascist Association, both of which had been founded in Atlanta. This fascist movement was supported by the German-American Bund, which had grown from the ashes of the failed Friends of New Germany movement that had been created in New York by Nazi sympathizer Heinz Spanknobel in 1933. The Bund, like the Friends, failed to gather significant membership in spite of its eventual affiliation with the remnants of the KKK from the 1920s. This failure prompted a disaffiliation from the German homeland, even to the point of discouraging Germans to become members. After December 7, 1941, the organization was systemically dismantled, as the FBI arrested the leaders.

As in Germany and in spite of "reason," racism as religion was on the march and on the airwaves, literally, in the form of Father Charles E. Coughlin's National Union for Social Justice. At its peak, Father Coughlin's radio evangelism was an anti-Semitic racist group that boasted of citizens patrolling the streets looking for Jews and calling the New Deal "the Jew Deal," much as the German-American Bund had referred to FDR as a conspirator in the "Jewish-Bolshevik Conspiracy."

While he may have been inspired by the long affiliation of eugenics and religion, Father Coughlin pandered to his audience, such as those in Indiana and the Midwest, who were particularly strong believers in the power of eugenics. The National Union for Social Justice was swirling around supporting fascism and misunderstanding eugenic racism. Meanwhile, the hate-driven KKK and the policies of immigration racism were all bubbling in an "evil caldron" of hateful propaganda. [91, 92]

All these ingredients created a soup of despicable fascist racism that, if given the opportunity to congeal with the soon growing poverty of the Depression, could have changed the outcome of World War II on both sides of the world. Hitler, however, believed he had found supporters in this growing movement of American Eugenic

91   *Preaching Eugenics: Religious Leaders and the American Eugenics Movement;* Christine Rosen; Oxford University Press; copyright 2004
92   *The Glory and the Dream: A Narrative History of America, 1932–1972,* pp 57–58, pp 107–111. 1973

Klanism. [93], [94] As president, Roosevelt kept the caldron boiling until it boiled dry. Between 1932 and 1944 he harnessed the energy, controlling and redirecting it through the difficult times. He spent money changing the focus of America to itself, with a variety of self-improvement projects that helped Americans identify the real enemy, whose identity had been partially created by us.

With time the fashionable position of eugenics waned, resulting in the private foundations no longer funding the machinery of the eugenic organizations. As with the CCC, once a better focus and use for the money was found, the program passed into history. By the early 1940s the rats were fleeing the sinking ship of eugenics. The war America was being drawn into depended on it.

It was during these tumultuous times in America when so many young men like Wayne Downing, Ralph Conte, Bob Basnett, Jack Smith, Bill Tripp, Hiram Clark, Roland Enman, Don Sorrels, Al Damico, Robert Lee, and the other men of the 416th came of age.

Earl Hayter knew this time well, as his family had finally managed to build a house along with a barn from split cedar on the stump ranch. Working hard, they cleared enough stumps to plant a garden and a field of oat hay. His dad managed to come by a few milk cows, chickens, turkeys, and occasionally a few pigs. Earl, being the youngest of four brothers, always had plenty to do on the stump ranch, but it was never enough for the family to get by. They always depended on the county aid program for staples. Cornbread with beans—a meal Earl ate nearly every day with his family. Sunday was a day he looked forward to even if he had to attend Sunday school and then church. He looked forward to the Sunday meals the church congregation would provide twice a month. This meal broke the monotony of cornbread with beans. His mother, a proud religious woman, worked hard every day for her family. Taking pride in them and with them, she guided them along the straight and narrow.

The family had come a long way from Hayter's Gap, Washington County, Virginia, where in the 1700s the family had owned a large plantation until the founding patriarch passed. The plantation was eventually sold off. After the passing of several generations, with moves through several states, his father had ended up at the stump ranch just before the stock market crash. During the Depression Earl never had any idea he was really poor. It was not until he left the farm in 1936 after high school graduation and joined the CCC that he came to understand his poverty.

Working hard to earn a wage during his early years in the CCC helped him understand where he had come from and where he wanted to be. A good day's work for a fair wage and a square meal—it was not the best but he had known worse. While working for the CCC he met people just like himself. This experience allowed him to develop a different appreciation for America; seeing that many men lived like him let him understand his own circumstances. As it had for his brothers before him and so

93   American Bund: The Failure of American Nazism: The German-American Bund's Attempt to Create an American Fifth Column; Jim Bredemus; http://www.traces.org/americanbund.html
94   Hooded Progressivism: The Secret Reformist History of the Ku Klux Klan; Jesse Walker; http://www.reason.com/links/links120205.shtml

many other men and women, the CCC pulled his generation from the despair of the Depression, much as the Nazi Party arguably had pulled the German people from their despair.

With all the intelligence about Germany and Japan's aggressive intents pouring into government intelligence services from so many sources around the world, it should have seemed obvious to the Allied governments where things were heading. The people and the government of the United States were still trying to hide from the reality of it all in their isolationist policy.

America's hiding in an isolationist policy oddly enough did not seem to include the Pacific Ocean basin; America's "divinely inspired manifest destiny" was continuing westward with the annexation of Hawaii, Guam, the Philippines, and multiple small islands with names like Wake Island and Midway. Big and little islands were destined to soon be big players in the coming global conflict.

America's progressive expansion westward in the nineteenth and twentieth centuries, driven by and succeeding because of war, seemed to be divinely ordained. The term "manifest destiny" was credited to John L. O'Sullivan, and it seemed to capture the sense that America was blessed by God. In 1839, Sullivan described the zeitgeist that went with manifest destiny: "The far-reaching, the boundless future will be the era of American greatness....Its floor shall be a hemisphere—its roof the firmament...comprising hundreds of happy millions, calling, owing no one master, but governed by God's natural and moral law of equality." These were words that helped fuel many wars to come. They were words that were now being used to inspire and justify the doctrine of continued western expansion that ultimately would extend into the Pacific Rim.

Ironically, writings published before the War of Emancipation and at its end would galvanize many into disputing this moral obligation to emancipate the enslaved. In the same year as O'Sullivan's words, the words of Charles Darwin were published. *Voyage of the Beagle* recounted Darwin's experiences and observations from a world voyage; the document would win him respect in the naturalist and scientific societies of England and soon the world.[95] His concepts and scientific observations were the summation of years of reflection and observation of life on the planet, resulting in his work of comparative anatomy and geologic record. Later his seminal *On the Origin of Species* would challenge humankind's perception of or even the existence of a God.[96] Darwin's observations, when combined with the scientific observations of the Moravian-born monk Gregor Mendel, would lay the foundations that were to alter people's concept of themselves and more importantly their creator. Both men led solitary adult lives, the first by choice and speculated health reasons, and the other by design. Their writings would force the cataclysmic changes around the globe in the early 1900s.

Shortly after Darwin's startling claims, the civil war for America's "emancipation" was driven by the righteous belief "that all men are created equal." This belief supported the "moral righteousness" to prosecute a war driven by religious evangelicals under the concept of divine equality. Who at that time believed God would grace a country that

---

95   *Voyage of the Beagle;* Charles Darwin; Henry Colburn Publisher; 1839
96   *On the Origin of Species;* Charles Darwin; J. Murray: publisher; London; 1859

enslaved men? Not Evangelicals who earlier in America's history had helped fight and win American independence. This newfound American freedom was to be followed by the period of the "Great Awakening" or "American Revival." Even though the awakening led to an incremental increase in true believers, the foundation was laid for the armies who would soon fight a civil war for reasons of "moral humanity" and emancipation for God's people.

During the great emancipation conflict, the works of the Austrian monk Gregor Mendel would be published. His research consisted of the meticulous scientific cultivation of some twenty-eight thousand plants, which would lead to a presentation at the Natural History Society of Brunn in 1865 followed by its publication in 1866 in *Proceedings of the Natural History Society of Brunn.* Both the presentation and the paper met with little fanfare, but their significance would soon become apparent. [97, 98]

So, as some espoused divine equality and others began preaching eugenics, America continued to expand westward. Landing on the Pacific, the boundaries of manifest destiny were quickly becoming apparent, yet the doctrine poised the United States to move into oceanic territories, which put a nervous, economically insecure, and soon a eugenically driven and militaristic Japan on the western edge of the nation. [99,100,101,102,103]

After the overthrow of the Tokugawa Shogunate by the Meiji Restoration in 1868, Japan changed its economic and political course in the world. The Meiji policies were exemplified by their doctrine of *fukoku kyôhei* (rich country, strong military) adopted in 1868, followed by mandatory conscription in 1873 and the conquering of several Chinese island territories—Ryukyu, Bonin, and Kurile—in the late 1800s. Under the leadership of the Meiji, Japan was set on a course toward a Western style of imperialism and would use eugenics as ideological support for its policies.

---

97   Has Mendel's Work Been Rediscovered?, R.A. Fisher, MA., SC.D., F.R.S., (1890–1962), Galton Professor of Eugenics, University of Eugenics, University College, London, From Annals of Science,1, 1936, http://www.men.org/c/irapilgrim/men01.html

98   Gregory Mendel; Wikipedia, The Free Encyclopedia; http://en.wikipedia.org/wiki/ Gregor Experiments in Plant Hybridization (1865), Gregor Mendel; English translation, Http:// www.mendelweb.org/Mendel.html

99   An American Military History, Army Historical Series, Office of the Chief of Military History, United States Army, *The War of 1812;* Chapter 6; http://www.army.mil/cmh-pg/books/ amh/amh-06.htm

100   War of 1812, The history Channel; http://www.historychannel.com/perl/print_book. pl?ID=225473

101   The History Guy: The Mexican-American War; http://www.historyguy.com/mexican-american_war.html

102   An American Military History, Army Historical Series, Office of the Chief of Military History, United States Army, The Mexican War and After; Chapter 8; http://www.army.mil/cmh-pg/books/amh/AMH-08.htm

103   *Voyage of the Beagle,* Charles Darwin; Published by Henry Colburn 1939; Penguin Books 1989

Japan was convinced of its Malthusian-Shinto-Fascist future and set out to accomplish it.[104] Japan had seen the mechanism of its expansion, imperialism. Since the sixteenth century Japan had been witness to the good and the bad of imperialism. Having been visited by Dutch, English, and American mariners well before Admiral Perry's less then peaceful visit, the Japanese had been the victim of and witness to the "barbarians'" tactics and objectives through surrogate nations like China. Arguably, unfair treaties had been forced upon Japan in the 1850s, limiting Japan's opportunities for growth. However, the desire not to allow themselves to be contaminated by the "barbarians" forced at best an arm's-length relationship with the rising imperial powers. Japan had seen how the British negotiated "free trade agreements." Agree or face war—Burma having been the perfect example. Japan's desire to remain clean of outside contamination was balanced against the asymmetric power of the parties they were forced to deal with, thereby creating smoldering resentment toward the Western imperialists. During the 1860s assassinations of foreign sailors, officers, and diplomats became commonplace in the selected port cities where the "polluting barbarians" lived. Fueled by the teachings of the *kokugaku* (national learning) antiforeigner/antigovernment sentiment grew.[105, 106]

Japan's distrust, hatred, and fear of the Westerners combined with all the expectations of Japanese imperialism, expectations that included Japan's self-perception as the only true Asian leader. The nation needed only economic security to succeed in its plans. These plans resulted in a new form of "Japanese imperialism," imperialism not won without military conflict that would lead Japan to what it desired, *"itto koku"* (first-rate nation status). Once there, Japan would be freed from international dependence for natural resources.

This desire to be free of foreign entanglements grew stronger after Britain, France, and Russia forced Japan in 1895, via the Triple Intervention Accord, to give up the Liaotung Peninsula. Japan had won it by defeating China in the 1894–95 Sino-Japanese war, a war that China was forced to pay for with land and financial reparations imposed on them after the Japanese victory. Tensions were further escalated toward the West when Russia moved into Port Arthur on the peninsula in 1898.

It was during these final decades of the 1800s that capitalism was butting up against communism in the Manchurian regions. This worried the Western powers, particularly Britain. Seeing opportunities in strategic military and trade alliances, the Western powers assumed a watch-and-trade attitude toward Japan.

The Meiji overthrow of the ruling class had ensured the feudal status of the Japanese state. Simultaneously it instituted a program of military modernization with centralized socialization and militarization of its people through the resurrection of

---

104   *Japanese Militarism: Past and Present;* Dr. Harold Hakwon Sunoo; Nelson-Hall, Inc.; copyright 1975; Chapters 1–5

105   *Negotiating with Imperialism: Unequal Treaties and the Culture of Japanese Diplomacy;* Michael R. Austin; Harvard University Press; Copyright 2004

106   Mathew Perry & The Opening of Japan 1848–1860; http://www.navyandmarine.org/ondeck/1800perryjapan.htm

religious patriotism in Shintoism. Japanese villagers were to become "national villagers" who believed in the soldier's ethos, not at all dissimilar to the techniques used by the coming rise of Nazi militarism. The Japanese ruling powers channeled ideas and historical beliefs into the Japanese mainstream social consciousness, as absolute loyalty to the divine emperor was mandated.[107]

More importantly, Meiji Japan recognized the value of imperialism and its long-term objectives were spelled out by the statement, "We will learn all you can teach and then…we will fight you," which is exactly what the Meiji military took the time to do. Believing that the world was ultimately to be ruled by two or three nations, Japan set course to be one of them.[108]

Precisely because of the Anglo-Japanese Alliance (between Britain and Japan) that contained mutual security treaties and cooperative dialogue, war erupted between Japan and Russia, with Japan winning back the Liaotung Peninsula in 1905. This victory unfortunately encouraged the Japanese further in their belief of leadership as well as encouraging other Asian leaders to believe in Western vulnerability. Using the language of this document Japan would move farther into Manchuria and China. The roadway to world war was being built.

With the start of the new century Japan was positioning to enlarge its territories and independence. The Japanese military, either independently or with the plausible deniability of the government, began acting autonomously in the first half of the 1900s. China was seen as a paper tiger, divided and armed with ancient weapons. The Western nations wanted trade and were not prepared to fight on the Asian continent. Japan had doubled its military to thirteen divisions by 1904 and its navy nearly tripled in size. As part of its move to militarization, Japan wanted many children and a population that would allow it the ability to sustain a protracted war. By the mid-1920s the four main islands of Japan contained eighty million people. The belief in expansionism was supported by statements made by the Japanese ultranationalist Ikki Kita in the mid-1920s as he described his reconstruction of Japan. He stated, "Seven hundred million brethren in India and China cannot gain their independence without our protection and leadership….This will be achieved through the emergence of the strongest country, which will dominate all other nations of the world."[109]

Yet, while much of the rest of the globe was embroiled in World War I, Japan provided support to the Allies and avoided war with Russia through a nonaggression treaty. After the war, the Treaty of Versailles rewarded Japan with many German island territories, including the Marianas, Marshall, and Carolina islands. All were strategically positioned between Hawaii and the Philippines, and raised the concerns of then Presi-

---

107   *A Social Basis for Prewar Japanese Militarism: The Army and the Rural Community;* Richard J. Smethurst; University of California Press; copyright 1974

108   *Japanese Militarism: Past and Present;* Dr. Harold Hakwon Sunoo; Nelson-Hall, Inc.; copyright 1975; Chapters 1–5

109   *The Rising Sun: The Decline and Fall of the Japanese Empire: 1936–1945;* John Toland; Modern Library Publishing; copyright 1970, 1998 and 2003; Part 1; chapter 1; page 5

dent Woodrow Wilson. Such positioning seemed to threaten China, America's "Open Door Policy," and the trade routes to China, which were important to America.

In spite of the assistance Japan had provided the Allies during the war, anti-Japanese bigotry was growing in America and across the world. This racial prejudice was evident at the end of World War I when the League of Nations refused to include a clause "of racial equality" suggested by Japan into the League's covenant. Such a move would have gone a long way at that time to help ease tensions in the Asian nations, but it was a clause that may have cost Woodrow Wilson even more on the home front at that time.[110]

President Wilson, a member of the reborn and refocused Ku Klux Klan, was responding to the agenda of America's new national movement. The Klan had risen from its ashes as a values organization that, at its peak in the 1920s, had upward of five million members. It was an organization that spoke of and supported eugenics and hatred of immigrants, African-Americans, Jews, and Catholics, all the while professing and defending "white, Protestant values and beliefs of sobriety and community."

Eugenics-backed racism in the guise of the KKK flared all across America. The West Coast resented the Asian immigrants, while the Midwest, with the highest KKK membership numbers, went so far as to assassinate communists and socialists. Indiana, the northern state with the largest neo-KKK membership, even threatened the campus of Notre Dame in South Bend on May 17, 1925, only to be met and thwarted by a determined Catholic student body. The northern American cities became anti-black, as competition for jobs in the industrial areas of the country heated up. It was clear that the "New Klan" had a mission, a eugenic-fascist mission, but one that was supported even by the delegates to Washington with the passage of clearly racist laws controlling the hiring requirements of federal jobs in the District of Columbia. With Woodrow Wilson in office, "Jim Crow" had come to town and stayed on.

Indeed, it was Wilson who had endorsed the 1915 film *The Birth of a Nation* by D.W. Griffith, in spite of its poisonous racist propaganda. Cinema helped the eugenicists, and promoted their agenda, for instance, in the 1917 production of the *Black Stork*.[111, 112, 113] In the end it was easy to see that *The Birth of a Nation* and the *Black Stork* were hate-driven propaganda productions. These two publicly distributed films were followed by a failed 1930s attempt by Harry Laughlin of the Eugenics Record Office to

---

110   *Japanese Militarism: Past and Present;* Dr. Harold Hakwon Sunoo; Nelson-Hall, Inc.; copyright 1975; Chapters 1–3

111   *The Black Stork: Eugenics and The Death of "Defective" Babies in American Medicine and Motion Pictures Since 1915;* Martin S. Pernick; copyright 1996; Oxford University Press

112   *War Against the Weak: Eugenics and America's Campaign to Create a Master Race;* Edwin Black; Copyright 2003; Publisher, Four Walls Eight Windows

113   *The Unfit: A History of a Bad Idea;* Elof Axel Carlson; copyright 2001; Cold Spring Harbor Laboratory Press, Cold Spring Harbor, New York

distribute a German eugenic propaganda film in three thousand public schools, which was wisely prevented.[114, 115]

By and large, though, America was lucky. The Klan of the 1920s passed away under its own immorality and failed leadership, violating the very principles they espoused. If the Klan had enjoyed its peak of resurgence just ten years later, its success may have been much more devastating, driven as it would have been by the desperation of the Depression. Although this hatred waned in the '20s, its terrible legacy of racist damage took years to overcome. So while America's "New KKK" failed, Germany's National Socialist movement fell into its proper place in time to succeed. [116, 117, 118, 119]

Meanwhile, the perceived and justified fear of world racism fueled the progressive rise of social change in Japan. This change included a belief in "Japanese Social Darwinism," which stood in stark contrast to America's eugenic belief of Asian genetic inferiority. Japan wrestled with the concept of eugenic purity after having been introduced to the term first in 1881 by Fukazawa Yukichi. Familiar with Galton's work *Hereditary Genius*, he fought to protect the hereditary bloodlines of the samurai class from the Meiji social reforms that allowed intermarriage among the classes. These eugenic concepts were later expanded to include the problems of racial intermarriage of Japanese soldiers and workers living in the occupied territories of Taiwan, Manchuria, and later other areas of the Pacific region.

During the time of Japan's imperial self-awakening, Margaret Sanger, a self-proclaimed health care provider and member by marriage of the financial elite, visited the Sino-Japanese world in 1922. After first being denied a Japanese visa because of America's discriminatory immigration laws as well as the purpose of her visit, she managed to obtain a Chinese visa instead. Sanger, a person of strong conviction, presented herself as a woman who desired to educate other women on birth control, infant mortality, hygiene, and many other public health issues. The reality of her agenda eventually showed through her veneer of benevolence; her objectives were ultimately linked to and supported the negative eugenic concepts being developed and disseminated around the world from America, England, and the select European countries.[120] In her

114   *War Against the Weak: Eugenics and America's Campaign to Create a Master Race;* Edwin Black; Copyright 2003; Publisher, Four Walls Eight Windows

115   *The Nazi Connection: Eugenics, American Racism and German National Socialism;* Stefan Kühl; Oxford University Press; copyright 1994; Chapter 4; pp 48–50

116   Clash of Cultures in the 1910s and 1920s, *The Ku Klux Klan;* Immigration Restriction & The Ku Klux Klan; http://history.osu.edu/projects/clash/imm_KKK/KKK%20pages/KKK-page1.htm

117   Between the Wars: The Klan Rides Again; http://chnm.gmu.edu/courses/hist409/klan.html

118   *Dixiecrats Triumphant*, The secret history of Woodrow Wilson, By Charles Paul Freund, senior editor, Reason on Line; http://www.reason.com/0303/co.cf.dixiecrats.shtml

119   *Ku Klux Klan,* Wikipedia, the free encyclopedia; http://en.wikipedia.org/wiki/Ku_Klux_Klan

120   *The Auto Biography of Margaret Sanger;* Margaret Sanger; Dover Publications; copyright 1938; pp 317– 326

Japanese speeches Sanger referred to "cradle competition"—meaning the positive role of eugenics in forming a strong human race. She coupled this with the slogan printed on her publication, *The Birth Control Review,* which proclaimed "Birth Control: To Create a Race of Thoroughbreds." Yet these comments actually spoke to her true agenda of negative eugenics. [121,122,123,124]

In spite of the perceived benevolence of Sanger toward the high infant mortality rates, social hygiene issues, tuberculosis, and abuse of women (i.e., foot binding) in Japan, her real goals involved the negative control of birth and using eugenics to stop the rapidly procreating unfit. Such procreation, she perceived, was at the expense of the more slowly procreating superior class, which she had joined by marriage. Sadly, her views supported the Japanese attitude of racial and cultural superiority, thereby feeding the growing monster.

Although embraced by many, Sanger's ideas were questioned and rejected by the director of the Japanese Women Physician Association, Yoshioka Yayoi. Yoshioka feared a negative impact on the virtues of chastity, which would lead to a hedonistic attitude toward sex, with all the venereal and negative effects on reproduction. In spite of these views Japan did build on this eugenic concept. All these conflicting concepts of eugenics were selectively culled to support and encourage Japan's ambitions, as it looked to the richer nations around the world, while making plans to reach its goals in the 1920s.[125,126]

After World War I, the United States did little to change or respond in a more positive fashion to Japan. Treaties were forced on Japan to limit the number of battleships and cruisers that it could produce, pushing Japan in its desire for independence. By the end of the 1920s and the start of the Depression, Japan was poised to ensure its independence from Western countries and used Italy's march to fascism as an example to justify civilian militarism. Moreover, the American and world depressions brought tariffs and unfavorable trade relations to Japan from many of the Western nations.[127]

To exacerbate matters, America, in keeping with its "destiny," continued to strengthen its position in the Pacific, particularly Hawaii, which became a navy base. These were contrarian moves for so-called isolationists, which frightened and angered

121   *War Against the Weak: Eugenics and America's Campaign to Create a Master Race;* Edwin Black; Copyright 2003; Publisher, Four Walls Eight Windows

122   *Struggle for National Survival: Eugenics in Sino-Japanese Contexts, 1896–1945;* Yuehtsen Juliette Chung; Copyright 2002; Publisher, Routledge

123   *Eugenics and Other Evils: An Argument Against the Scientifically Organized State;* G.K. Chesterton; Edited by Michael W. Perry; copyright 2000

124   *Architects of the Culture of Death;* Donald De Marco and Benjamin D. Wiker; Ignatius Press; copyright 2004

125   *Killer Angel: A Short Biography of Planned Parenthood's Founder, Margaret Sanger;* George Grant; Cumberland House Publishing, Inc.; Copyright 1995, 2001

126   *Struggle for National Survival: Eugenics in Sino-Japanese Contexts, 1896–1945;* Yuehtsen Juliette Chung; Copyright 2002; Publisher, Routledge

127   *A Social Basis for Prewar Japanese Militarism: The Army and the Rural Community;* Richard J. Smethurst; University of California Press; copyright 1974; Ch II, pp 22–23

the Japanese, who already had control of Manchuria and were moving deeper into China as they pursued their own concept of manifest destiny.

While enlarging its naval station at Pearl Harbor, the United States began tightening the failing economic sanctions on Japan, although the sanctions did little to curb Japan's growing economy and appetite for resources. Imperialist policies of the United States and Japan were made worse by the now protectionist policies of both, which were strengthening the cold grip of the coming war. However, US sanctions designed to hurt the economy of Japan, in reality, did little to stifle it. The success of the Japanese economy was largely coming from the territorial expansion that allowed for the exploitation of the new region's resources and near-slave labor, combined with ever-increasing Japanese military spending. [128,129,130,131,132,133,134]

This excessive military spending would at its peak consume over 50 percent of government spending, and contribute disproportionately to the growing success of the economy. At the same time, the military began consuming disproportionately the resources that the conquests were designed to bring to Japan. By 1938, Japan's military investment in Manchuria and China was upward of 2.5 billion yen. Japan's territorial conquests became financial burdens, as guerrilla activities tied up thousands of troops, who were held back to guard important economic infrastructure sites. The vastness of China alone consumed resources that should have benefited the homeland but instead were used to allow the military to gain more ground, with the hope that prosperity would come with the next victory. The downward spiral for resources had begun for Japan; its strategic plan to acquire more would culminate on December 7, 1941, quickly followed by military advances into the Dutch West Indies and the Philippines. [135]

Before Pearl Harbor was attacked the deadly alliances were forming, as Italy began to go on the offensive. By the end of 1936 Italy had control of Ethiopia. Mussolini justified the invasion with the failures of the first Italo-Abyssinian War of 1895–96 and the perceived mistreatment of Italy at the Paris Peace Conference. He bemoaned

128   Louisiana Purchase, www.gatewayno.com/history/LaPurchase.html

129   The Louisiana Purchase, http://lsm.crt.state.la.us/cabildo/cab4.htm

130   The Avalon Project at Yale Law School; Thomas Jefferson- Message to the Senate of January 11, 1803 Regarding Louisiana; www.yale.edu/lawweb/avalon/presiden/messages/tj003.htm

131   Manifest Destiny: An Introduction; www.pbs.org/kera/usmexicanwar/dialogues/prelude/manifest/d2aeng.html

132   John L. O'Sullivan on "Manifest Destiny", 1839, Excerpted from "The Great Nation of Futurity," The United States Democratic Review, Vol. 6, Issue 23, pp. 426–430. www.mtholyoke.edu/acad/intrel/osulliva.htm

133   Manifest Destiny and Expansion in the Americas, http://humwww.ucsc.edu/gruesz/manifest.htm

134   Japan's March Toward Militarism, Bill Gordon; March 2000: http://wgordon.web.wesleyan.edu/papers/jhist2.htm

135   Japan's Economic Expansion into Manchuria and China in World War Two (parts one and two), James Graham, May 2004; http://www.historyorb.com/asia/japan_economic_expansion.shtml

the nation's fate at the end of World War I despite their sacrifices: "Around the hateful peace table Italy received but a few crumbs from the rich colonial booty gathered by others." He also used recent border clashes at Wal-Wal in 1934 to help justify the Ethiopia campaign. They were reasons and tactics not unlike those his fascist brothers in Germany were using to satisfy the questioning world about their expectations of reuniting their historical lands.

Mussolini scoffed at economic sanctions placed on Italy by the League of Nations. The sanctions came after the exiled emperor of Ethiopia, Haile Selassie, gave an impassioned speech, pleading for help and support from the now clearly powerless League. In spite of the League's attempts to help, the situation became another example of its failed attempts to enforce international sanctions. The sanctions were issued by a body with no authority or mechanism to enforce them, were ignored by those being cited, and actually reeked of the toothlessness of the sanctioning body. With Mussolini's "place in the sun" firmly under his control and the international community able to do little about it, the confidence of fascism in Italy and its Axis cohorts grew.[136, 137]

Hitler too was poised to take back what was once Germany's; after already having taken control of the Rhineland in March 1936, he wanted the Sudetenland. This too would come at the price of "appeasement and peace with honor."[138, 139, 140, 141, 142, 143]

During this time of difficult global issues, Earl Hayter and many of his fellow servicemen worked at whatever job the CCC gave them. After three years of voluntary and appreciated hard labor in the quasi-military CCC, Earl jumped at the opportunity to go to work in the Douglas Aircraft Factory in Santa Monica, California. Ironically, he was assigned to build the A-20 Havoc Attack Bomber—the very aircraft that he would be flying over Europe in just a few years. During his time with Douglas, he made enough money to take flying lessons at Van Nuys, the local airport. He did not know then that this flight training would open doors for him after the bombing of Pearl Harbor; he would apply to the Army Air Corps in February 1942.

Earl had closed a few doors too during his time in Los Angeles. He had become a little too enamored of the sights, sounds, and enticing opportunities of the area, falling

---

136   Armed Conflict Events Data, First Italo-Abyssinian War 1895–1896, http://www.onmar.com/aced/data/india/italyethiopia1895.htm

137   Mussolini Justifies War Against Ethiopia, Benito Mussolini, Scritti e Discorsi di Benito Mussolini, vol. IX (Milano, 1935), pp218–220; http://www.dickinson.edu/~rhyne/232/EthiopiaSpeech.html

138   www.WorldHistory.com, Events preceding World War II in Europe.

139   www.WorldHistory.com, Causes of World War II

140   www.islandnet.com, Chronology of World War II, 1918 to 1939, Copyright © 1998–2004 Ken Polsson, pages 1 to 23.

141   www.pbs.org/wgbh, Commanding heights: The German Hyperinflation, 1923, By George J. W. Goodman, Copyright © 1981.

142   www.grolier.com/wwii/wwii, World War II Commemoration, Colonel Vincent J. Esposito, US Army; Head, Dept. of Military Art, United States Military Academy.

143   *The Last Lion, Winston Spencer Churchill, Alone 1932–1940;* William Manchester, page 1 to 350

victim to the trappings of big-city life. To this farmboy, the pace and feel of the city would be overwhelming, leading him away from his God for the short period of time he was in California. It was also the time and place where he made the acquaintance of Helen, to whom he would write throughout the war, and even fly her namesake into battle. He would find his way back to his roots and spirituality after December 7, 1941. The big-city period of distraction would be forgotten as he was reunited with his God and true beliefs over the death-filled skies of Europe.

✧

"I'm not interested in plowing that field either. Let's keep going," Earl suggested.

The others figured Jack, the son of a sharecropper from Tennessee, would win anyway. Not a bad assumption, since they were right. For melancholy reasons of their own they stopped to watch the farmer for a short time, then rode on.

Riding in the middle of the pack, Roland kept checking the sun and the horizon intermittently to reassure them all. "Guys, we're doing OK with the time."

"Relax on the navigator stuff," said Bill Tripp. "We all have watches."

"Can't help it. I'm always watching the sun. Something I picked up while serving in the Merchant Marines."

"When were you in the Merchant Marines?" Hiram asked.

"Back in '39. I graduated from the Admiral Bullard Merchant Marine Academy and signed on with the Moore McCormick Lines as a cadet officer. I sailed the New York to South America routes aboard the *SS Uruguay* up through 1942."

By that time German submarines regularly patrolled the East Coast of the United States, the Caribbean Basin, and South America shipping routes. Mexico had felt the pressure from Germany after losing an oil tanker to one of Grossadmiral Karl Doenitz's U-boats. Mexico joined the war effort in May 1942, and Roosevelt indirectly rewarded the nation by establishing a farmworker program for Mexican nationals to come to America to compensate for America's labor force now fighting the war.

"I had heard about oil tankers getting hit by the Germans," Roland said. "I figured that instead of having a ship torpedoed out from under me, and not getting a chance to fight back, I'd rather apply for the air corps. I decided to fight the war a different way."

His navigational training in the Merchant Marines made him a natural for the bombardier/navigator position.

"I graduated from BN school, class 43-11, at Childress Field, Texas. Then got rotated in as an instructor, which was not what I wanted. That's when I learned that when you're in the military 'your butt belongs to Uncle Sam.'"

Everyone understood this truth and nodded their heads in agreement.

"So after a bunch of requests for transfer to a combat squadron, I finally got it and was transferred into the 416th in Florence, South Carolina."

No one spoke for a while as the group rode along with the green farm fields passing by on either side of them.

Earl changed the subject, "Let's see if we can find a farmhouse to get some fresh eggs. Heck fire, I'm so tired of powered eggs I can't stand it!"

"Golly, Earl, we've been real successful at that," Roland said, reminding them of their past failures with egg hunts. "Let's just save our time and play some cards back at the O-club."

They had all come a long way since Florence, South Carolina, where they had completed combat flight training. Earl had been in a different squadron there, and didn't get to know Jack, Hiram, and Bill until they shipped out together to Fort Hamilton, New York, in early 1944. The good news was they had a week's leave in the "Big Apple."

They rode on a ways, and then Earl piped up.

"Do you ever remember paying for a drink when we were in New York?"

"Can't think of a time, can you, Hiram?" Bill said. "I couldn't even get my wallet out fast enough to pay before the bartender told me it was taken care of."

"Wasn't that great?" Hiram said with a laugh. "All you could drink or eat in any bar you went into. What about all those dames—gee-whiz, could they shake a leg on that dance floor!"

"I can't wait to get back there," Bill added. "What a city."

Everyone grew silent on the thought of going home.

After a while Bill spoke.

"Heck, guys, the trip over on that liner wasn't so bad either. Those cooks fed us pretty good."

"It sure beats this mess hall grub we've had since getting here," Hiram agreed.

"I was seasick the whole way," Jack said. "Hell, I was never so happy to be back on dry land as when we landed in Scotland."

Everyone laughed, as they rode on toward Finchingfield. Cresting another hill the church tower came into view in the distance. Passing farmhouses along the way, the 20/20 vision of all the pilots allowed them to spy several chickens in the farmyards. They were scratching the earth for minerals and grit. Everyone had the same thought.

"Maybe we can get some eggs in Finchingfield," Earl said.

"Worth a try," Jack agreed.

Rolling into Finchingfield, everyone noticed the thatched grass roofs of the homes and businesses that surrounded the church on the hill in the center of town. With its tall distinctive bell tower, the church overlooked the small stream and the main part of the village sitting on both banks. Coasting downhill after passing the church, the officers reached the gray stone bridge that connected the divided village. They stopped on the other side and noticed a pub that sat on the corner overlooking the stream.

"Want to try that pub?" Roland asked. "Maybe they serve food."

"Let's go."

The officers propped their bikes against the wall or laid them on the ground. Everyone stooped as they walked through the low doorframe.

Two children sweeping the floor looked up at them as they came in. The boy, the older and taller of the two, approached them. He had made it a point to know the military uniforms of all the different countries fighting this war. Recognizing the US military's style of understatement, he knew they were pilots by the wings on their jackets. Snapping to attention with a sharp salute, he greeted them. The officers saluted back smiling.

"Go get Mum, Carolyn," the boy ordered.

The girl headed into the back of the pub, returning several minutes later with a young woman dressed in a country smock.

"May I help you?"

"We were hoping to get some lunch," said Bill.

"It's still a little early yet. What were you thinking of having?"

"Do you have any eggs?" Earl interjected.

The young matron hesitated. Since January 1940 the rationing office had severely limited her weekly rations to several ounces of protein, some canned goods, no sugar and very little tea. She was still able to buy some staples to keep the pub going. She had been growing vegetables in her victory garden, but it was a struggle to feed her family and still keep the pub open. She always seemed to have ale. If it were not for the ale and the American dollars spent here, she would have gone out of business some time ago. Most of the local men, her husband included, were off fighting the war.

She knew she could get some eggs and pretty much anything else she wanted from the local black market. She could purchase what she needed from the spive,[144] passing the cost on to the flyboys with a little markup.

"Would you like bacon with that?"

The officers lit up.

"Darn tootin', we do," Earl jumped in. "I'm so tired of SPAM I can't stand it."

"It will take a few minutes while I heat the stove." She needed time to get the food from the spive.

She hustled the children into the kitchen, where she gave them orders.

"Charlie, I need you to run down to Mr. Everest's home. Buy these things." She began scribbling on a piece of paper.

"Tell him they are for some Americans. I'll pay him after they pay me." She handed him the list. "Hurry now."

She turned to her daughter.

"Carolyn, please go set the table."

"Yes, Mum."

Heading over to the cabinets, Carolyn started collecting the plates and silverware. She began setting out once nice porcelain that was showing its age after five years of war. She smiled as she set it out, as if readying the table for a tea party. She handed every officer a spoon or a fork, as they waited for the hot food that would follow.

---

144   Spive—name of British black marketeer who could supply most anything someone wanted.

Empty, thick-bottomed pint glasses were set by the plates, and then Carolyn ran into the kitchen, returning with a yellow-glazed glass pitcher filled with cold well water. She carefully filled each glass with the help of the officers.

"Thank you, young lady," Jack said with a smile.

"You're very welcome, sir," she said, looking at Jack squarely with her green eyes. She headed back into the kitchen.

Finally, Charlie reappeared at the backdoor carrying a small, worn wicker basket with a small piece of cloth covering the contents. It was against the law to traffic and purchase things this way. However, there was really no need for secrecy, since everyone in the village knew who ran the black market, but it paid to be vigilant. The matron scooped out ten eggs and two rashers of bacon.

"What did he say the charge was?"

"Twice the regular for the Americans," her son replied.

"OK, let's get them prepared."

The mother scrambled the eggs while her son stoked the fire under the cooktop.

Producing a half loaf of bread along with some butter and cheese, she had her daughter set it all in front of the five hungry Americans. The smell of the cooking bacon filled the air.

Putting the eggs into a bowl, she set them next to the plate of crisp, fried bacon. Picking the two up, she walked out into the dining area. With their eyes glued to the bowl and plate, the airmen watched as the mother spooned an equal portion of eggs for each man.

"*Bon appétit.*"

Everyone just stared at first.

Earl broke the silence, "Heck, guys, they're gettin' cold."

That's all it took. They tucked into the food like a bear after hibernation.

They relished the flavor of real eggs, almost not wanting to swallow as the flavor slid over their tongues. The flavor took them back to places far from their present realities. The home-cooked bread opened memories that, for safety, had been walled off by all the young officers. The meal was eaten in a lot less time than it took to make, but not in an undisciplined manner, just with a great deal of enthusiasm. No morsel was left on any plate; even the breadcrumbs were consumed.

After their home-cooked meal of eggs, bacon, bread, butter, and cheese, the young officers thanked the matron profusely for her graciousness.

"What do we owe you, ma'am?" Hiram asked.

"That will be twenty pounds," the matron stated, hoping it would not be met with any objections.

Without hesitation Hiram turned to his fellow officers and collected the currency. He handed it to the matron, who accepted it with a smile that could be mistaken for a gotcha smirk. She pointed to the chairs by the fireplace and outside, and asked them to stay if they liked.

Being in no hurry, they accepted, and slowly got up from the table. Before long Jack was sleeping against a tree by the stream, while Hiram was dozing next to the hearth in the only overstuffed armchair in the living area. Earl and Bill were in the front yard passing a ball with the children.

Roland drifted outside, walking along the stream and looking at the colored homes with the thick, grass-thatched roofs. He had not seen any of these in London, and had been told that since the great London fire they had been forbidden. *Makes sense,* he thought, *probably burns like hell.*

Bill kicked the ball to the little girl and then walked to the doorway of the pub. He looked over at Roland by the stream, then at Jack sleeping with his back against the tree. Turning back to the main room of the pub, he took off his cap as he walked in. Looking around inside, he saw Hiram slumped in the chair by the hearth. From outside, Charlie and Carolyn came running through to the kitchen. Bill began to develop a slightly different perception of his hostess's generosity.

Bill could tell the pub was also where the family called home. Five years of war had taken their toll. Many things were old, in need of replacement, particularly the furniture. The curtains were worn but cared for. He noted the floors were swept clean and the pub was well dusted. The mother was working hard to keep it up. Running his hand through his hair, Bill realized that this war was all the two children here had known in their lives and would be all they knew for some time to come.

The weekly rations given to families in England did not consist of much. Bill smiled as he thought about all the victory gardens he saw in the yards of all the houses along the train ride into London. Even the homes in London had gardens. The gardens grew vegetables that citizens simply could not get any other way except through the black market. Not everyone wanted to support it. He knew it was taking from the boys at the front.

Food really does win wars, Bill thought. He remembered all the posters and flyers about food he had seen around London and the countryside. It was not a lot different back home.

Bill thought back before the war. He remembered his family growing up in a disciplined religious environment in New England. He had been a strong participant in his church in Massachusetts, as was his family. His father, a banker, and his mother together helped teach him of his community and social responsibilities. He had actually been encouraged to go into the ministry before the war. He was feeling the responsibility of those teachings now.

Going back outside, Bill gathered Earl and then Roland over. After Bill finished talking, they dug into their pockets and found some pound notes. Bill added two more to the pot, while walking over to the tree where Jack was resting. Bill kicked him gently.

"Time to get up, sleepyhead."

Jack stirred, and wiped his right then left eye with his left hand. He squinted up.

"Time to go?"

"Not yet. Let me ask you something."

Squatting down, Bill shared his conversation with Earl and Roland. "You in?"

Jack fished out a few more pounds.

Rubbing his belly, Hiram emerged from the doorway after waking from his nap. He stretched, and walked out into the day. Bill intercepted him, and related the cause.

"Thanks, Hiram." Hiram pulled several crumpled notes from his pocket.

"No sweat, Bill. It was worth it."

Bill walked into the kitchen where the mother was just tidying up the table. Bill caught her attention.

"We want to thank you again for your generosity."

"You're very welcome."

"We would like for you to have this." Bill extended his hand with the folded money in it.

She refused it vigorously, but Bill was steadfast.

"Please, we are grateful. This is important to us."

He took her hand and pressed the money into it, and then clasped her hand between his two. There were no other words, only a grateful, thankful locking of eyes that tightened Bill's throat. He shook his head, smiling slightly in an affirmative fashion.

Releasing her hand, he turned away. The cash would go a long way in helping the family. Besides, he knew his group of friends could all be killed tomorrow.

Walking out the front door, Bill said, "You guys want to hit the road? We have a bit of a journey ahead of us."

The officers went about picking up their bikes. They turned back to wave good-bye to the children, as they started across the bridge. Standing up and leaning forward over the bike handles, they weaved up and over the hill that now hid the location of their brief sanctuary of peace.

No one spoke much on the ride back. Rolling through the gate, they saluted the guard, with thirty minutes to spare before being declared AWOL.

The fiver current owners of the bikes managed to put them back from where they had "requisitioned" them, without getting caught. Not that there was any great penalty if you were caught, but it was more fun if you weren't.

Walking back to the tent they stopped to check the assignment board for any notices or changes of current mission assignments. Seeing their flight assignments for tomorrow, everyone began the process of steeling themselves for the next day's responsibilities. Their thoughts were interrupted by an announcement coming over the loudspeaker.

"All right, you officers, this is your chance to get even with us gunners. Baseball grudge match at 1730 hours on the ball field. Repeat, baseball grudge match at 1730 hours on the diamond."

Staff Sergeants Robert E. Lee and Ray Jones had laid down the challenge to the officers. Closing the microphone, they laughed aloud together as they left the Operations hut from where they had issued the challenge.

"That ought to get a few of them out there, you think?" Jones said.

"Let's go find out," Lee answered as they turned toward the makeshift field.

The challenge piqued the crew of airmen, who were ready for an impromptu game.

"Sounds like we've got a ball game, fellas," Earl said.

Jack and Hiram agreed.

"I want to hit the post first. I'll meet you guys there," Roland said.

"Haveta check the laundry," Bill added. "See you there."

The game presented some friendly competition and a reminder of home to the men. It also allowed the officers to forget tomorrow morning, when they were back on duty in the flak-filled skies.

"All right, we can't let them beat us again," Ralph said as he rallied his troops at the start of the ninth inning. "They're up by two games already."

They all remembered the walloping they had taken from the gunners' bats last time.

As the top of the ninth inning melted away, the officers of the 416th's four squadrons watched their side's last batter ground out to the shortstop on a poorly hit curve ball. The game was over. An 8-3 defeat was hard to swallow, even harder than the 5-2 loss last time.

Roland and Jack walked casually from the field and ran into Sergeants Jack Sittarich, Al Damico, and Constantine (Dean) Vafiadis along the first-base line.

"We'll get'cha next time, guys," Jack prodded.

"Ain't that what we heard last time?" Al joked.

"By golly, I believe it was, Al," Dean replied.

Kicking the dirt as they walked, Jack and Roland tolerated the ribbing as Dean, Al, and Sittarich recounted each painful inning.

"Dean," Jack interjected.

"Yes, sir."

"See you in the morning at briefing."

The ribbing ended.

Dean took a moment to respond. "Yes, sir, bright and early."

The officers headed one way as the sergeants went the other, each to their squadron's barracks.

As the officers headed back, Jack glanced over toward the flight line, noting a lot of activity in and around the planes. The ground crew chiefs Staff Sergeants Roland Dullnig and Ken Bailey were working their men hard repairing the planes. From the pace of the repairs and the number of trips to and from the boneyard, there was probably a mission scheduled in the morning. No one would know where until Wing sent the orders down sometime in the early morning hours.

Jack glanced westward and saw the clearing horizon as the sun set. The sun sat low in the horizon this time of the year and hour of the day. With double daylight savings time, though, it seemed to be up forever. England could still get noticeably cool this time of year.

Across the field, up the slope toward the armory, the ordnance crews loaded 150-pound general purpose (GP) and 500-pound high explosive (HE) bombs onto the bomb trains used to pull the bombs to each plane for loading. The sight of the work cut into Jack's appetite as he proceeded on to dinner.

"See you in the mess hall," Jack said to Roland.

Walking back to his tent, Jack noticed in an appreciative way the freshly cut wood alongside their month's supply of coal, which saved him time and labor.

He picked up several pieces of wood and coal as he walked into the barracks. Opening the vents and then the door on the potbellied stove, Jack checked to make sure there were still some hot coals in the bottom of the stove from this morning's fire. Carefully laying some kindling on the coals, followed by some larger pieces of wood topped with the coal, Jack gently blew on the embers a few times to heat them. He closed the stove's door. The kindling started to crackle, telling Jack it was time for chow.

Grabbing his heavy flight jacket off his bunk, he headed out the door. As he walked away he checked the stovepipe coming from the hut's roof to be sure smoke was rising from it. Meeting his friends at the mess hall, Jack shared cigarettes and conversation as they waited in line.

Having gotten through the chow line, Ralph sat down with Earl, Bill, and Hiram. Saying nothing, he listened to the conversation and tried to enjoy his meal. His ears perked up as he heard the story of getting real eggs in Finchingfield. He shook his head as he thought of the powdered eggs he would be eating tomorrow morning.

After censoring letters during the afternoon, he was in the mood to get a game of bridge going. Getting up from the table, Ralph spotted Wayne near the door.

"You still want to get in a game of bridge?"

"Sure, what time?"

"About thirty minutes in the Officers Club?"

"Sounds good."

"See if you can round up two more guys."

About twenty minutes later Ralph walked through the door of the O-Club and began looking for some players. Having stopped by his tent on the way to pick up the cards, he had almost brought his monthly ration of scotch to the club. Knowing he was on flying status in the morning, he had passed.

He saw Wayne at a table with another officer who played. Wayne greeted him, saying they had their foursome.

"Great, why don't we play right here?" Ralph said. "I've got the cards. Can someone get a score pad?"

Wayne opened a couple of cabinet drawers until he located some paper.

The officer at the table offered Ralph a shot of cognac.

"No, thanks. Just can't seem to get a taste for that cognac stuff. I prefer scotch or gin for my monthly ration."

The officer shrugged.

Ralph added, "The only thing I found cognac to be good for is starting fires in the stove. Couple a shots of that stuff on the wood, one lit match, and bingo, instant fire. Good as kerosene."

Ralph dealt the first hand, and the game was under way.

Earl walked into the club as Glenn Miller played his last note, the record scratched its way to the end of the recording, to be followed by Tommy Dorsey, a favorite of someone else's in the room. Earl caught Roland's eye from the corner table. He was sitting by the only window that was blacked out with paint, taped, and covered with a shade—not every German pilot had bad aim. He sat down with Roland at the table next to the stove. He knew why Roland had picked this table.

Declining a drink, Earl began a casual conversation with Roland, as Jack walked in smoking a Chesterfield. Jack looked around, then walked toward Hiram's table. He grabbed a chair and ignored the conversation while casually puffing his cigarette.

Those not on flight status were drinking whiskey, which always made Jack think of his younger brother, Bill. Before the war, Bill had been a consummate moonshiner back in their Tennessee hills. He actually made a good whiskey using copper components for his stills. He made quality stuff—blind customers were no good for business. *Blind airmen were no good either,* Jack mused. The extra money had helped out at home, but no one could ever tell Mom where it came from. Neither the Roane County revenuers nor his justice of the peace father had been happy about it. The revenuers helped by pressure from his dad eventually forced Bill out of moonshining. He was happy to get out by then, as the CCC and the TVA had brought some well-paying jobs into the valley that Bill enjoyed more.

It was going to be a short night, Jack knew zero-four-thirty came quickly.

Ralph and his partner Wayne had pretty well cleaned house in the bridge game. Ralph figured it was about time to turn in and not keep pushing his luck with the cards. They were all pushing their luck a little too much every day as it was. Thanking the guys, he and Wayne shook hands all around and headed toward the door.

Glenn Miller's "Moonlight Serenade" ended the night as the club emptied quickly and quietly. The firefly glow of the men's cigarettes spread out in a fanlike fashion across the base as the men strolled quietly to their huts.

Chapter Five

Waging War from Above

…I charge you further to submit to me as soon as possible a general plan
of the administrative material and final measures necessary for carrying out the desired
final solution (Endlösung) of the Jewish question…

– Hermann Göring, 1941

"Holy Toledo, Hulse!"

Ralph hollered into the interphone as a flak burst tossed him off the eyepiece of his Norden bombsight.

"Those sons of bitches are getting a little close!"

"Hell, Ralph, kill that damned rate and we'll get the hell out of here!" Hulse was equally worried about the accuracy of the orange-black puffs of death that were bursting among the formation.

Ralph repositioned himself on the eyepiece, dialing speed, altitude, drift, and wind into the early computer that the Norden was. Watching as the two crosshairs closed to the center, Ralph flipped the bomb-arming switch and waited for the two hairs to hit the auto-bomb-release point. Ralph knew they were close, and repeated over and over, "Hail, Mary, full of grace, the Lord is with thee."

Ralph was thrown uncontrollably from his bombsight against the wall of his compartment by the concussion of another exploding Luftwaffe anti-aircraft round.

"Damn it, those bastards got me!"

Yet another 88 round had detonated in front of and slightly below the nose of his plane. Nearly instantaneously the blast had been followed by shards of shrapnel penetrating through the Plexiglass nose of the bombardier compartment. Pieces of steel and glass had penetrated into Ralph's arms and legs, which had been pulled in to cover his face and chest.

"You OK down there, Conte?" Hulse's nervous voice sounded on the interphone.

Ralph recovered quickly to see that he was still in one piece, and then climbed back up to the Norden. Blood spotted his flight jackets and pants.

"Roger that, just ready to get the hell out of here!" Ralph repositioned himself over the sight, and again watched the crosshairs close on the center, just seconds from killing the rate.

"Bombs away!"

The shackles electronically sprang open, releasing the payload toward the Blanc Misseron marshaling yard. Ralph watched the last green light glow bright on his bomb-release panel, and then informed Hulse.

"Let's get the hell out of here."

Hulse had the same green lights in his instrument panel telling him all the bombs had fallen clean.

"Roger that, Lieutenant," came across the interphone, as gunner F.D. Allred affirmed his approval of exiting this airspace.

As he threw the switch to close the bomb bay doors, Ralph felt the Havoc bank as it dove to the left. The other five planes in the flight followed in formation, happy to get off this bomb-run.

Hulse kept the Havoc in an accelerating dive hoping to get out of the flak field quickly, and then turned onto the heading back to the RP for the flight home. He was not looking forward to the flight back over Ostend, Belgium, but that was the route home. They had taken heavy flak from Ostend before and Hulse, like the rest of the aircrews, were sure they would get it again.

As soon as the last flight in "B" box slid into formation they were happy to see the Brit's Spitfire fighter cover a couple of thousand feet above the A-Box in front of them. The aircrews knew the Brits would keep any Luftwaffe fighters at bay. Following the lead in A-Box the group turned toward home.

However, the Luftwaffe radar had not let the presence of the 416th go unnoticed. The *radartechniker*[145] couldn't believe his eyes—the flight's egress was the same route as their ingress. He quickly sent the information up the chain of command. The Ostend *flugabwehrkanonen*[146] batteries were alerted. Scrambling into action, the *kanoniers* began to elevate their tubes while the fusers adjusted the shells' fuses for the altitude of the approaching formation.

"*Feuerbefehl!*"

The barrels of the 88s erupted all along the battery line, sending their projectiles into the assigned airspace.

"Flak burst at twelve o'clock!" crewmen of the 416th relayed to their pilots as the skies filled with clouds of impending death.

"Turn onto 285 degrees magnetic now!" Lieutenant Palin interphoned to his pilot Major Campbell who was flying lead in A-Box with Palin. As lead navigator, Palin tried to turn the box out of harm's way. He aimed to get at least a ten-degree turn so the outside plane in the formation could avoid the flak field.

Palin started the calculations for time and distance before he gave a turn back to the left to bring them back on course. He started counting the seconds before he gave the order to turn left.

The *kanoniers* below were not concerned with the course changes; the batteries of radar directed 88s erupted, and the shells burst inside the A-Box, sending death in all directions. The shock waves blasted every plane in the formation and the aircraft were peppered with steel fragments from the shells. Unknown to Hulse and the crew, the return trip over Ostend had brought them a piece of Kraut steel that had torn through a hydraulic line supplying the nose landing gear.

---

145   *Radartechniker*, German: radar technician
146   *Flugabwehrkanonen*, German anti-aircraft canons, generally 88 or 105 mm canons

Captain Battersby and his BN Lieutenant Lytle were shaken by the accuracy of the flak bursts, as their A-20 absorbed the steel radiating from first fiery orange and then black balls of smoke. The impact also shook Conte, Hulse, Allred, and tunnel gunner Staff Sergeant D.J. Stephens. Even as they approached the relative safety of the channel, everyone wished they were going 430 mph instead of what seemed right now a turtle's speed—230 mph.

The group flew through the flak field out over the channel, miraculously without a loss.

"There's the coast."

Campbell noted the cliffs of southeast England through the slight haze in the distance. The flak field fell behind them as they moved out over the channel. The anxiety of the mission lessened as everyone in the group began to realize that they had survived another one.

Crossing the English coast, Hulse looked up in time to see the lead Spitfire pilot waggle his plane's wings and then turn his flight south toward their base. Hulse began his search for the large black ring surrounding the large white letters "WF," which was located just to the northeast of the tower. He really didn't need to see it, knowing Ralph would put him on the mark but it was always nice to realize he was home.

Not being first in the landing order, Hulse orbited with his flight and waited his turn to land. He had noted a slow but persistent drop in his hydraulic pressure. It wasn't enough to make him worry yet.

"Our turn, Hulse," Ralph communicated.

"Roger that, how you doing down there?" Hulse asked, as he turned on final.

"Bleeding seems to have stopped."

Ralph and the two gunners settled into their usual landing positions as they watched the ground come closer and closer.

Hulse lowered his landing gear lever, watching for the lights to turn green on his panel. The wing gear showed green first, as the nose gear lagged. The damaged hose was spewing hydraulic fluid into the wheel well. Hulse watched as his hydraulic pressure gauge indicated the expected fall in pressure. He also noted the pressure not returning as quickly as he would have liked.

Keeping the plane on its glide slope, Hulse flared the nose as they roared over the start of the runway. Pulling back the power, the Havoc settled its two main engine nacelle wheels onto the concrete. Easing the throttles back some more, Hulse began to drop the nose.

Ralph watched from his confining nose compartment. All he wanted now was to feel the ground under his feet again. This had been a particularly unpleasant mission, as he thought how close he had come to being hurt badly or killed.

"Hail, Mary, full of grace…Hail, Mary, full of grace…" Ralph repeated his mantra as he watched through the glass nose of the A-20 as the nosewheel prepared to contact the runway. He smiled as he thought of how many times he had watched this before, never growing tired of it. Particularly today, a touchdown would signify another return trip that counted toward the final trip home, back to the states. He was particularly happy that it would be a while before he had to see the ground approaching again.

"Hail, Mary, full of grace, the Lord is with thee…"

The nosewheel hit the ground as Ralph was in mid-prayer.

The nosewheel's undercarriage collapsed, and sent the nose of the plane down hard onto the tarmac. The hydraulic cylinders could not hold the weight of the plane as it hit the tarmac; the constant drain of the hydraulic fluid had become too much.

Ralph's eyes widened as he watched the nose of the plane slam into the tarmac. The deceleration immediately knocked him forward into the nose of the bombardier's compartment. Regaining his senses, he steadied himself, and then careened back in fear. Sparks and smoke started spewing off the nose of the plane as it ground itself down the runway.

"What the hell happened down there, Conte," Hulse called from the cockpit.

"Hell, if I know. Looks like the nosewheel went down. Did you have three greens for landing?" Conte screamed back. How ironic it was to have survived all those flak bursts with these wounds, only to die now here with this.

"I guess that don't matter now. As soon as we stop, everybody get the hell out of this fire trap!"

The crew didn't need the advice. They were not hanging around to see what happened after they stopped.

The plane continued down the runway trailing sparks and smoke until it veered to the left, finally leaving the runway as Hulse braked to a grinding halt about halfway down the runway off in the grass.

Crewmen burst out of the wrecked Havoc like jailbreakers desperate to escape the potential fire trap. They scattered down the field away from the craft.

Resting off the runway, the hulk did not delay the rest of the groups from landing. Planes continued to touch down in their disciplined fashion. A few crews noted the wreck at the side of the runway.

Hulse took the time to look at Ralph, who was covered in dried blood from all the small wounds that the shattered Plexiglass had caused.

"You OK, Ralph?"

"Yeah, I feel OK."

"You look like hell. Purple Heart for you, I guess."

Indeed it would be.

Hulse and his crew were driven to the debriefing, after which Ralph got a trip to the flight surgeon. After a little cleaning and careful extraction of many pieces of Plexiglass, the wounds were bandaged. Ralph was good to go again.

"Keep'em clean, and I'll see you in a week. I can't take you off flight status for this."

Mess was a welcome break as the squadrons gathered to review the day's results. Now among his squadron, Ralph wanted to settle down and start the long process of forgetting about the day's events.

"Hey, you look pretty beat up. Hulse try to kill ya up there today?" Earl was a joker.

"Not Hulse. Those damned Krauts were doing a good job of it all on their own," Ralph informed them as he tapped a Lucky from its pack and slipped it between his lips. The tobacco and paper crackled as the match lit the tip; Ralph felt the warm smoke enter his lungs. He remembered the blackness that followed the flash of the flak burst... wanting nothing more than to forget it.

Mess broke up with everyone heading to their place of choice for evening relaxation, happy to get away from the war just for a few hours. Everyone knew the early May morning would bring another mission, taking the men of the 416th over enemy-occupied France or Belgium.

Indeed, the next day of war came just like all the others, with only the small changes to distinguish it. The crews noted that their mission packages had been shifted from No-ball sites to marshaling yards and Luftwaffe airfields. Their morning and afternoon missions were to the Blanc Misseron marshaling yard. On the morning mission, the 409th had joined the 416th, with some close calls, as bombs from the 409th fell close to the 416th's formation. The afternoon mission was aborted due to cloud cover.

Despite the small setback for the 416th, the Allied war effort progressed unabated. All along the battle line, which extended from the French coast to Berlin, preparations of the battlefield were under way. Part of the preparation required the complete domination of the air by the Allies. Once this was accomplished, the prevention of transportation of German men and material was the goal of every air crew from every nation involved in the effort.

To this end, the American and British heavies were bombing day and night inside the German industrial heartland. Meanwhile, the light bombers of the Ninth Air Force fought to control the use and delivery of the output of the German war industry to the Wehrmacht, Luftwaffe, and Kriegsmarine. This would not come without cost to the 416th, as their efforts to helped ensure that the success of the coming invasion continued.

By late spring of 1944, each side of the global war effort had expended great energy in trying to accomplish military objectives to destroy the other. However, Hitler and his Nazi henchmen had other nonmilitary objectives to achieve, having wasted no time instituting their "Malthusian-Eugenic-Aryan" vision of the future.

Their plans had been put into action beginning in January 1933, immediately after gaining control of the government. By the end of March 1933, Dachau, Buchenwald, Sachsenhausen, and Ravensbrück concentration camps for the unfit were brought on line. The sterilization laws were passed, allowing for the elimination of the genetically unfit, followed by forced abortions on women with known genetic deficiencies; the fruits of private-policy initiatives, science, and financial influence were being put to work as public policy. Homosexuals, gypsies, and the diseased did not escape the cleansing effort.

In the midst of such efforts, the Olympics came to Germany in 1936, allowing the Nazis the opportunity to influence world opinion in a favorable way. Yet, it was the black American Jesse Owens who showed up the racist Nazis, who had been confident that they would dominate the games. Owens's four gold medals spoke volumes against Germany's racist project.

Further racially motivated maneuvers littered the path to World War II. Germany's October 1938 *Anschluss* (union) of Austria under racial pretensions was quickly followed by the eugenically driven brutal repression of the Austrian Jews with the opening of the Mauthausen concentration camp the following March. Right on the heels of the annexation of Austria was Kristallnacht ("Night of Broken Glass"), the German homeland's version of terroristic eugenic social cleansing. Thousands were sent to death camps while millions of deutsche marks in damage occurred and innocent lives taken. Taking place on November 9–10, 1938, it laid the groundwork for the ultimate expression of the coming total devaluation of life.

As the Nazi-backed Francisco Franco finally completed his takeover of Spain in March 1939, the German war machine was free to focus on other Malthusian-eugenic initiatives. The eugenic laws of sequestering the unfit were extended to become "euthanasia eugenic practices," removing the unfit permanently from society.

The move followed on the heels of Hermann Göring's appointment in December 1938 to resolve the "Jewish question." As rumors of the pogroms circulated, a Jewish exodus had been occurring, but not without international political complications. For example, of 930 Jewish refugees on board the ocean liner *St. Louis* in May 1939, just 30 were disembarked into Cuba and 287 into Britain. The United States and other nations refused entry to the refugees, and the rest were disembarked onto the European mainland, where 619 died at the hands of the Germans.

The racial cleansing continued wherever the Nazis went. The German invasion of Poland on September 1, 1939, brought Great Britain and France into the war, even though Poland was known to be indefensible from the beginning. The Nazis soon established the Warsaw Jewish ghettos. In January 1940 the Germans opened in Poland one of the most notorious concentration camps, Auschwitz. Soon after, the Nazis began forced immigration of Jews from every Nazi-occupied territory. Meanwhile, SS death squads were empowered to roam the Continent killing all "undesirables."

In July 1941 Hermann Göring issued an order to Gruppenführer Reinhard Heydrich that would be fateful to European Jews. He commanded to Heydrich, "I charge you further to submit to me as soon as possible a general plan of the administrative material and financial measures necessary for carrying out the desired final solution (*Endlösung*) of the Jewish question." The Gruppenführer responded with the Wannsee Conference in January 1942, which outlined the "Final Solution"—the complete and diabolic systematic extermination of Jews in concentration camps.

In the process of carrying out their eugenic solution, the Nazis used Zyklon-B, the first time the poison had been employed. Creating a bluish, almond-scented haze, Zyklon-B uncouples the oxidative phosphorylation of the cell's mitochondria, killing the inhaler quickly. With eugenic homicide going on at a massive scale all over Europe, the "eugenic culture of death" had reached its maturity. [147, 148, 149, 150]

While Germany was infamous for its Holocaust, the other theater of war offered similar atrocities. Under the auspices of Japan, vivisections and germ-warfare experiments proceeded unchecked. Having refused to sign the Geneva convention ban on biological warfare in 1925, Japan found the perfect environment to begin its foray into biological crimes. It would grow into Unit 731 after the invasion of Manchuria in 1932. There, Doctor Shiro Ishii started preliminary research in 1932 into "biologics" that by 1936 would grow into a six-square-mile "water-purification plant" with 150 buildings in which nine thousand human beings would be subjected to live experimentation and vivisection.

Japan also committed war crimes as it poured across Asia. Having been undeterred by world powers, Japan used poisonous gas 1,131 times in its campaigns in fourteen Chinese provinces, starting in 1937. Germ warfare was attempted five times between 1940 and January 1941. Only the unexpected death of Japanese soldiers halted the program temporarily. Undeterred, Ishii began field experiments in 1942 that resulted in deaths from bubonic plague, cholera, and anthrax. By June 1944, experiments were still proceeding as the Allies fought their way toward the island of Japan. Plans were under way to deliver biologics to the West Coast of America. The end couldn't come soon enough.[151]

The Allies' efforts in this struggle were being exerted across the globe, beginning with the Marines holding the line in the Pacific at Guadalcanal in 1942. The slow march up the Pacific Island chains, the struggle across Burma, the liberation of North Africa and Sicily, followed by the invasion of Italy and the liberation of Rome were to come. The liberation of the Philippines was followed by the Normandy invasion. No part of the globe was spared the scars and death of war.

The 416th was about to lose Captain Battersby and Airman Coleman on May 9th, and then the 416th would make a return trip to "Flak Alley" on May 12, 1944. The Beauvoir No-ball site had been visited before, and the trip back was to be equally costly.

---

147   The History Place: World War Two in Europe Timeline; http://www.historyplace.com/worldwar2/timeline/ww2time.htm

148   The History Place: Holocaust Timeline; http://www.historyplace.com/worldwar2/holocaust/timeline.html

149   The History Place: July 31, 1941: Heydrich ordered to prepare for Final Solution; http://www.historyplace.com/worldwar2/timeline/ww2time/order1.htm

150   Wannsee Protocol; The Jewish Virtual Library; http://www.jewishvirtullibrary.org/jsource/Holocaust/Wannsee_Protocol.html

151   World War II in the Pacific: Japanese Unit 731: Biologic Warfare Unit; http://www.ww2pacific.com/unit731.html

Chapter Six

Taking Casualties

Pray for us sinners, now and at the hour of our death. Amen.
— Catholic prayer

Standing in formation at Battersby's and Coleman's gravesides, members of the 668th squadron were about to pay honor to them. The Cambridge Military Cemetery was to receive two more of the best from the Ninth Air Force's 416th Bomb Group. It had already been witness to the burial of Lieutenant A.A. McDonald with his gunners, Staff Sergeants Leroy Barnard and Joseph J. Shields—three men from the 669th squadron of the 416th, who had died when the wing of their A-20 broke during a dive.

That day twenty-three other flag-draped coffins lined the grassy field as men from various groups were joining Battersby and Coleman. Unlike in life, the officers and enlisted men were not segregated in death, but buried side by side with the respect they all deserved.

Everyone noted the familiar presence of Lieutenant Chester Wysocki standing at the head of the graves of Battersby and Coleman. Wysocki stepped to the front of the assembled airmen. He stood silently with lips pursed tightly, looking at the faces of the airmen as they looked back at him. He began slowly, then with more resolve.

"Good afternoon, gentlemen. It's been a tough few days already this month. I want to say a few words about these two men and for those others who are no longer with us…They will always be…good men, unselfish men who bring the best from our country to fight this good fight in a foreign land, in the name of freedom…It is with great sadness…that I now stand before you…to honor the passing of a distinguished officer and airman, Captain William Battersby and Airman Charles Coleman. A reason cannot be given for this tragedy. An expert pilot and a good ship, but fate deemed it not to be a happy landing."

Wysocki paused to catch his breath.

"It will be hard to forget these two fine men, one who was more of a father than a superior officer. Who always had time to listen to your troubles, and give a hand when needed. Who bolstered morale when it was low. Who fought for the rights of 'his boys' when the going was rough…We won't forget. There is a place 'in the blue' where all eagles go to rest when their time is up. I hope he is now sitting in the front row with the best of them."

Wysocki looked down as he gathered himself to speak again. Around him the men had lowered their heads. No one escaped the intensity or the honesty of the comments. Each man knew that this day could be his day to join Bat and Coleman. Each man lived for today, with his goal to survive to the next. Some men did it better than others. Many a fine man woke one morning no longer able to hold his spoon steady enough to eat. Some cried sitting on their cots, not wanting to go or refusing to go. Others turned to alcohol as a way to hide or control the fear. There was no place to hide in or out of combat. You lived with it every day.

He regrouped and began.

"Private Coleman was a young man who was trained to not fail in his job. His purpose was to save lives when others had to jump from a doomed ship. He could not fail in his mission. A young airman whose time here with us was brief, but will not be forgotten. May he and Bat share the same pew in their new home."

Wysocki collected himself for the final send-off.

"Yes, Bat and Private Coleman, you will be with us when we break a bottle in Berlin, and when we drink a toast in Tokyo. When it is over, and we are home, America won't forget your breed of men, who made the supreme sacrifice for her freedom and democracy. We are proud of you, each and every one of us, to have served with you, and now, humbly in comradeship…we salute you. A-ten-shut!"

The entire group came to attention saluting the American flag as *Taps* was sounded out.

There was a period of silence, then the order.

"At ease…as you were."

As the officers and enlisted men returned from the cemetery and passed through Wethersfield's main gate, the morning mission over the Aerschot marshaling yard was landing. Some of the men headed to the tower to watch the approach and landing of the flights. Before the last A-20 settled onto the runway, the debriefings had already begun.

As it turned out, the mission was a partial success. The first box had hit the yard hard, but in doing so had obscured the target's aiming point with thick smoke. Lieutenant Jones in the second box was unable to drop and so aborted the run. All planes returned, and fourteen Havocs suffered severe battle damage. No casualties were recorded.

The following morning's run was aborted over the target since the lead navigator was plagued by a malfunctioning Norden bombsight. No flak, no fighters, no damage, no losses, and no hits were recorded at debrief. That afternoon, though, the mission was a go. Ralph Conte, Roland Enman, along with Albert Jedinak of the 671st squadron were walking casually toward the preflight briefing room. Pilots and other navigators were already there.

"Hulse, you ready for another?"

"Do we have a choice, Ralph?"

"Not that I've heard."

Lieutenant Robert Stockwell turned to his BN Albert Jedinak.

"You ready?"

"No sweat, Bob."

"Let's see where we're going this afternoon."

The box and flight leaders settled into their seats, and smoked nervously, which belied their outward demeanor of stoic confidence.

Captain Beatty entered the room.

"Good afternoon, gentlemen."

The shade came down that had been covering the map at the front of the briefing room. No one was surprised by the map's appearance. They had been seeing the same topography, longitude, latitude, ingress, and egress routes for many months now. The only change was in the course of ingress, rendezvous points, fighter cover groups, and target destinations.

The Operations officer quickly got everyone's attention. Almost instantly the cloud of sweetish blue smoke filling the room thickened as everyone pulled deeply on their cigarettes.

"We have an outstanding mission today, gentlemen, to destroy the Beauvoir No-ball sight. None seem to be operational yet and we plan to keep it that way."

Beatty turned to the map. This destination brought a sobering moment to all the aircrews as the Operations officer pointed to the Beauvoir No-ball sight.

"You should expect some cloud cover once you hit the coast. There's a stalled high front over the sites but that shouldn't give you any problems with bombing. Wind is out of the northwest at about eight knots and visibility is ten by ten. Return flight should be the same with good visibility all the way to approach." He turned from the map. "Any questions?"

No response. Beatty resumed.

"Standard staggered takeoff. Form up and head to the RP on this heading and time. Navigators, remember your wind direction and adjust as needed. You'll marry up with the fighters from the 9th's 358th squadron."

This last bit brought a round of mumbled approvals from the assembled crewmen, who were getting mentally ready to go in harm's way.

"They're the Thunderbolt boys you guys like so much. Lots of experience flying with the 8th's heavies before transferring to us."

Beatty again turned to the map as he spoke. "Here are your headings with times to the IP and target. Remember to keep that wind direction in mind for course corrections. You should have flight and box formation in front of you in the flight packet. Questions?" The officer looked around the room.

"We'll be dropping a mix of 150-pound GP and 500-pound HE. That means keep it tight and let's make this a good hit. Flak emplacements are thought to be pretty heavy on your run up to the target, as you all know, but be careful all the same. Flak positions are located here, here, and here." A tapping sound punctuated each "here."

The anti-aircraft sites were numerous, and since 1940 Germany had been developing arguably the best and largest air defense system in the world. Even with this force, the Allied onslaught continued night and day and from nearly every altitude. Now that the German air force was dwindling, though, more pressure was being placed on the artillery crews to bring down enemy aircraft. The Luftwaffe was feeling the pressure because V-1 sites were high priority to the high command, so they were high priority for the Luftwaffe.

After facing such extensive bombing, the Germans had become quite skilled with their anti-aircraft weapons. By this time in the war the *kanoniers, oberkanoniers,* and their *hauptwachtmeisters* manning the *flugabwehrkanonen* knew which aircraft to bring down first to disrupt the bombing effort. They had learned that it worked best to bring the lead ship down on the bomb-run so the group had to go around again and allow time for the secondary bombardier to get the flight or group back into position. The forced go-round gave the gunners more time to shoot the enemy invaders out of the sky.

Bringing the pointer to his side again, Beatty added: "Evade them as best you can, and be aggressive with your evasive maneuvers. We suspect there are some radar-directed batteries in the area."

The pilots, navigators, and gunners looked for the assigned entry point onto the Continent from the channel. Ralph saw that it was going to be hairy.

"Some good news," Beatty hastened to mention. "German fighters appear to be focused on the heavies, but just because you have a flight of P-47s for cover, don't let your gunners drop their guard. Stay alert up there. Any questions, gentlemen?"

Beatty heard none.

"OK, guys, make Wing proud on this one. Let's hack at 1530 hours in five… four…three…two…one, hack."

Every watch in the room clicked.

"Main briefing at 1545 hours, gentlemen."

The room began to empty. The last draws were pulled from cigarettes, and the airmen crushed out the glowing embers in the sand bucket, on the way to the bulletin board. The rest of the aircrews were there checking on flight-status listings for tomorrow. All but Lieutenant Gus Ebenstein were hoping to get a break.

Gus was anxiously perusing the listings.

"I see you made the morning mission roster," Roland joked. "Hell, you'll be home by summer at the rate you're going."

"That's the plan, that's the plan. I'm gunna kill as many of those Kraut bastards as I can, as quick as I can, and then get home."

Gus, a Jewish pilot in the 416th, was from New Jersey. He was well known for putting as much energy into his missions as he did his leave-time escapades.

"Listen, I got more missions than any of ya under my belt and I want the rest of them sixty-five there too as soon as possible. Let's go, we got five minutes to briefing."

"Yes, sir, General Ebenstein."

Once the men were inside the briefing room, Operations called the meeting to order. The men came to attention when the senior officer entered the room.

"At ease, gentlemen, take your seats."

Box and flight assignments were reviewed. The details of the mission were again reviewed, and were followed by a brief recon film of the bomb-run into the target, mainly for the benefit of the pilots and bombardiers. Ordnance loads were reviewed.

The crews smoked and listened intently to the briefing as each pilot or navigator recorded pertinent information for his group or flight. The backups to the group and flight leaders recorded the same info in case the lead ship was lost or the bombardier was killed by flak or fighter fire. Everyone took note of the hierarchy. The return route with RP was reviewed, and the senior officer provided the headings and times.

"OK, that's it for the afternoon mission. Any questions? Let's synchronize watches then…on my mark three…two…one—hack."

Again, the simultaneous cricket-like clicking quietly chirped across the room.

Hack Time

Done at the end of each briefing so that everyone would be on the same time to within several seconds; mission rendezvous with other aircraft, location of way points, and rendezvous positions depended on the navigators knowing the time traveled on a certain heading. Navigation along longitude requires time to be accurate.
(L to R): Lieutenant Roy Van Rope, R. Hackley, R. Conte, Captain. D. Hulse
Reproduced with permission from Ralph Conte

"All right then, good luck and make this a good hit!"

Shuffling out of the briefing, the flight crews could see the ground crews loading the bombs into the bays as well as the ammo into the Havocs' .50-caliber machine guns. Then the ordnance crews put the fuses into the bombs, a dangerous job if done wrong.

The other ground crewmen were walking the props, a ritual done for all aircraft with radial engines. The props belonged to the Havoc's two Pratt & Whitney R-2800 double Wasp, two-row, eighteen-cylinder engines. Its sixteen hundred horses slingshot planes across the sky, but the engine was harder to handle on the ground, much less to take apart and put back together for a failed bearing or thrown piston. If the props weren't turned, then oil settled into the bottom jugs[152] and so it couldn't lubricate the other pistons and moving parts during start-up. The loss of lubrication would cause unnecessary wear on the valves, camshaft bearings, and main bearings in the engine. If this happened consistently, the crew risked engine failure if a bearing overheated and failed. This could be particularly bad when the plane was at twelve thousand feet on its bomb-run. It generally took twelve to fifteen turns on the propeller per engine to pump the oil around and prevent any problems.

The ground crews were happy to walk the props to keep them from having to be removed or repaired. They had just buried a fellow ground crewman who was killed when the 2,350-pound engine he was working on tore loose from its engine mounts and crushed him to death.

As they drifted out toward the flight line the crews reviewed their taxi order and box assignments again. Before heading to their planes, though, all the air crews would go to the parachute building; no one wanted to fly without a safety net.

Parachutes were crucial on the A-20s, since the planes had no fire-extinguishing systems; fire meant bailing out. Once out of the plane, you were taken by the chute to the ground, where personal defense became the next issue at hand. The chutes and sidearms came at a price. Every crewman collected his personals, handing them to one of the first sergeants, who would register them in exchange for a sidearm, ammunition, parachute, and survival package. The mission aircrews knew that this was the first step in the long process of MIA/KIA documentation if they did not return.

Exiting the chute building, the crews diverged and walked casually to their squadron's deuce and a half, which would take them to their planes. On the way out Jedinak spoke casually with Stockwell about the upcoming flight. They placed their chutes and flak jackets onto the hood of the jeep as their gunners crawled into the back and stowed their gear in the middle. Stockwell cranked up the four little cylinders of the jeep, shoved it into first gear, and headed off to their aircraft.

Some of the flight crews preferred to walk to their planes if they were close by, while others rode in assigned trucks. A few rode bikes, which the ground crew would ride back off the flight line after takeoff.

Loading into the trucks, some men joked, some put their combat face on, while others smoked. All were repressing and controlling their fears as they settled into their usual spots. Exhaust belched from the diesel engine's exhaust pipe as the driver started forward. As he gained speed the crews rocked in unison. They knew they were all headed back to "Flak Alley."

Ralph Conte and his pilot Lieutenant Hulse jumped into their respective sides of the Willys Jeep waiting for their gunners to join them. Meanwhile, Lieutenant Roland Enman had drawn Lieutenant Marzolf and was flying second behind the lead in the

---

152   *Jug*—Cylinder head in which the piston resides. It provides a chamber for fuel and air to enter and exhaust to be pushed out of.

B-Box. Knowing the Krauts' preference for shooting down the lead plane, Operations had assigned each box a second flight crew with a bombardier/navigator just in case.

Having completed their preflight walk-around, the crews began climbing into their positions on the planes. The pilots started their cockpit preflights, while the gunners checked their weapons. The gunners went through their preflight rituals, ensuring that the servos and motors for the turrets worked, and moved the guns through their full fields of fire. Any abnormal function in the turret or guns would cause the plane to be scrubbed from the mission if it couldn't be fixed quickly. If the plane didn't fly, its crew didn't fly. If the plane was scrubbed, the mission did not count toward the magic number that sent the airmen home.

Post-Briefing Trip to Plane

Driving to the hardstand at start of mission after briefing.
(L to R): Lieutenant Ralph Conte, Staff Sergeant F. Allred,
Staff Sergeant D. Stevens and Captain Dave Hulse
Reproduced with permission from Ralph Conte

With checklists finished, the crews watched the sky above the tower, waiting for the day's colors to be shot so they could start their engines and then say their prayers. The tower personnel checked their watches for start-engine time. There had been no call from Operations to abort, so they raised the flare gun. The day's colors streaked skyward, breaking the relative silence of the flight line. Sight of the flare arching away from the tower prompted all the pilots to engage their engines' starters. High-pitched winding sounds came from the starboard engines of all the Havocs along the flight line just before the ignition of the powerful 18 cylinders of the Wasp radials.

Preflight Planning

Preplanning and maybe a little hamming before the mission,
navigator reviewing mission routes and waypoints with crew.
(L to R): Captain D. Hulse, Staff Sergeant D. Stevens,
Lieutenant R. Conte and Staff Sergeant F. Allred
Reproduced with permission from Ralph Conte

To meet the performance demands of American aircrews, the Wasp required highly precise engineering. All pistons of the eighteen cylinders were designed so that the explosions occurred in a perfectly timed circular sequence that allowed the camshaft to turn in a near-perfect circle. Arranged in a circle around a central cam, the pistons had an articulating rod running from the piston inside the cylinder heads to the cam. Once the starter began turning the flywheel that was connected to the camshaft, the pistons in turn moved in and out of the cylinder heads. On the compression stroke, the spark plugs would fire and detonate the high-octane gas vapor in the jug head, forcing the piston down and accelerating the turning of the camshaft. The faster the camshaft turned, the faster the propeller spun.

Suiting Up

Preflight suit-up of "flak jackets," which were felt to be of some
value in blocking shrapnel. Note heavy "flak helmet" or "steel
pot" on ground. Crews wore overhead gear when in combat.
(L to R): Lieutenant R. Conte, Staff Sergeant D. Stevens,
Captain. D. Hulse and Staff Sergeant F. Allred
Reproduced with permission from Ralph Conte

After the pilot first hit the starter, the propellers and pistons turned slowly at
first, but then faster and faster until all the cylinders began to fire off in their assigned
sequence. Then the engine exploded to life with a smoky fire emanating from the exhaust ports. The smoke, blown by the prop blast and breeze, carried the odor of burnt
oil and fuel across the base. As the engine heated up, the smoke from the ports would
turn into a blue-hot flame—letting the pilots know the ground crew had done a good
job with their maintenance.

The ground crewmen could see the exhaust flames as well, and were checking
each engine carefully to be sure it was running at its best. With fire extinguishers in
hand, they were also prepared to squelch the occasional fire that erupted from under
the engine cowling of a recently started radial. The extinguishers formed part of their
safety training. Each crew was educated every day about how to avoid a quick and gruesome death from the whirling propellers on the radials. The lessons were a mantra that
you repeated every time you approached a plane: Never approach the plane from the
front. Come in under the tail, and walk under the fuselage and behind the wheels.

Slowly the noise coming from the flight line increased to a deep guttural roar as
all the A-20s had both radials running at idling speed. The sound and the planes taxiing
all across the flight line inspired the ground crews and they saluted the aircrews inside

the Havocs as the taxi procession to the runway began. The aircrews saluted back with a different inspiration in their hearts.

Every ten seconds a plane would roll down the runway, so that a flight of six planes would be airborne every sixty seconds. The general rule was that a full box of eighteen planes should be airborne every three minutes, and the whole two or three boxes should be up in less than ten minutes. On a clear day that was pretty easy, but on cloudy days it was your best guess as to hitting the right position in the formation.

Ralph settled back into his plane's glass nose and watched as Hulse rolled the eager flying machine down the runway. Hulse lifted off, and began his orbit, waiting for the rest of his flight's Havocs to join the box. The aerial ballet had begun. To get in formation, Hulse, who was the flight leader, would fly out one minute, and then turn to his left 180 degrees and head back toward the runway. Every ten seconds he picked up one of his flight's planes, so by the time he reached the base he had all six planes in his flight. Hulse would then start an orbit around the base so that the next flight leader taking off would be able to climb to this altitude and slip his flight in behind him in the proper slot in the box formation.

The group followed this choreographed routine with the military precision that it had preformed hundreds of times before. This afternoon was no exception, and the first three flights of bombers had formed up their "high" box on schedule. They started their climb as the low B-Box formed up behind and below them. Hulse waited for the low box to form and join the high group. Once the two boxes were together in formation, Ralph advised Hulse of his first heading to reach the fighter rendezvous point. Soon, all thirty-six planes would be speeding to their target, producing in total upward of 115,000 horsepower, and carrying 108,000 pounds of bombs.

The pilots loved the high performance of the A-20 Havoc bomber. Next to the Brit's Mosquitos, the Havoc was one of the few bombers in the theater that could go to altitude with its supercharger on, with flight controls trimmed out, have its manifold pressure with water injection set, and stay right with the fighters in formation. The fighter boys loved this bomber too; they could keep the gas on instead of weaving back and forth flying slowly—and burning so much fuel—in order to stay with the heavies. At the same time, the sight of the "little friends" comforted the crews in any bomber formation on any mission. The fighter pilots had been instructed to stay within visual contact of the bombers for that reason.

Hulse found the fighters on station and watched as the fighter escort groups formed up with his bombers. Hulse called Conte for his second heading and time. Conte relayed it quickly.

Pilots Smith, Hayter, Clark, and Tripp had stayed with their navigator Roland Enman in the low box. They watched as Roland made a slight correction to the right that they all copied.

The two boxes of high-speed aluminum turned southeast in unison and headed out over the coast, leaving the smooth non-angular countryside of England for the white-capped English Channel. The coast of France was just visible on the horizon from this altitude. Little was said, as radio silence was strictly enforced on every mission.

After thirty minutes, Bill Tripp took the time to check on his gunners through the interphone.

"You guys OK back there?"

Hearing two "Rogers," Tripp focused his attention on holding formation in his flight.

The entry point on the coast was coming up. Everyone's adrenaline levels spiked as the Kraut flak rose to meet them, prompting Hulse to call Conte.

"Conte, what's the heading?"

Having already anticipated the evasive maneuvers, Conte replied. "Right to 150 degrees for ninety seconds then left to 75 degrees for two minutes. We'll correct back to the main heading of 130 degrees after that. I'll do my best to keep us out of this flak." Ralph remembered the Plexiglass coming at his face.

"Roger that."

Hulse had already begun the right-hand slow and banking turn to avoid the darkening sky in front of them. The group followed Hulse in the maneuver like a flock of migrating geese following the lead bird. No bird in this flock wanted a taste of that hot steel radiating from those bursts of German artillery.

Conte counted his time down and then called Hulse.

"OK, Dave, turn onto 75 degrees now."

"Roger."

The Havocs slid into the left bank. Hulse watched his compass dial swinging away from 150 degrees and slowly settling on 75 degrees northeast, as explosions of orange and then black puffs erupted to their right, peppering the outside members of the group with steel.

Pings and pangs ricocheted off the fuselages of a half dozen Havocs, causing all on board to hunker down a little more and tighten their flak jackets. The pilots pulled their heads down into their shoulders as much as they could and hoped the big radials on either side of them would stop most of the flak coming their way.

The group completed their left turn out of the new flak field. Running for one minute northeast gave the Luftwaffe *kanoniers* time to readjust their tubes and fuses.

The order came from the *hauptwachtmeister*.

"*Feuerbefehl!*"

All along the battery line the tubes erupted with fire, sending their payloads skyward.

In his navigator's compartment Roland Enman was counting since the last volley of explosions…eleven…twelve…thir…KAWAM….The sky around the low box exploded with the powdery black smoke of multiple 88 rounds. Ten of the eighteen low-box Havocs were knocked about in the small area of airspace they momentarily inhabited. Steel ripped through the wings and fuselages of the thin-skinned Havocs, forcing the gunners to flinch instinctively. Pilots Marzolf, Smith, Tripp, Clark, and Hayter struggled to resist the shockwaves as they surged through the flights.

"Holy cow!" came over the radio from Roland, as he grabbed hold of the sides of his compartment to steady himself.

"You see that?" Sittarich, in the third flight of the high box, called to his pilot.

"Multiple flak bursts…six o'clock low inside the low box."

Seeing the same thing, Stephens called Captain Hulse.

"Flak bursts, six o'clock low!"

"Roger that. Got it, Conte?" Hulse asked.

"Yeah…turn right now onto 135 degrees, hold for thirty seconds," Ralph calculated, as the cold sweat soaked his flight suit. He knew he had to stay focused and get the flight back on its heading of 130 degrees as he recorded the past evasive maneuvers into his navigator's logbook.

Hulse led the box into the turn.

Roland began his count again. His turn was already behind the mark as another salvo streaked skyward. The rounds detonated at their fused altitude. Fluffy black patches erupted all around and inside the B-Box. Other smaller anti-aircraft fire dotted the bursts of the 88s.

As the shockwave from the detonation lifted the tail of his plane, Vafiadis pulled his flak helmet down.

"Damn that was close, Lieutenant, you OK up there?"

"I'm OK," Jack replied.

"You two OK back there?"

Jack's tail gunner Ralph Hoffman replied quickly, "Roger that, those bastards almost got us, that burst was right behind us."

"Roger," Jack replied.

The shrapnel had already ripped its way through the tail structures. Jack had felt the erratic vibration through the control yoke as the burst peppered the tail. He automatically but cautiously tested his rudder controls—left…right…left…right—slipping the Havoc back and forth and then pushing the stick back and forth to be sure his elevators lifted and lowered the nose. Feeling confident, he refocused his attention first on his position in the flight, then in the box. He did not want to have a midair collision.

Hulse completed the turn with the two boxes following. Conte calculated his corrections to be sure they were on course to the IP, and then automatically recorded the series in his navigator's logbook. Every other pilot in the low box made the same adjustments.

The fighter pilots looked on the action from above.

"You seeing that down there, flight lead?" The wingman called to the lead P-47.

"You bet," the lead replied. "Don't want to be down there… poor bastards are gettin' hit hard. Let's go, guys, keep an eye out for bandits."

"Roger that, lead."

The bomber group slid out of the first flak zone as Ralph made fine adjustments to their course.

"IP in ten minutes, Hulse."

"Roger, Conte."

Flickering across the oscilloscope, the reflected frequencies from the two boxes of A-20 Havocs had not gone unnoticed by the radar *techniker*. The azimuth, speed, and directional targeting information was being fed to the slaved battery of four 88 mm *flugabwehrkanonen* from the gun-laying radar system.

The first flight of Havocs turned onto the bomb-run, and Ralph took control of the Havoc for the two-and-a-half-minute flight down the bomb-run.

Ralph opened the bomb bay doors as soon as Hulse leveled the A-20 on the run; the rest of the flight acted as if Ralph controlled them all as the first flights bomb by doors swung open. Ralph hit the bomb-arming circuit and saw the "bombs armed" lights in his circuit panel glow green. The pilots following Hulse and Conte did the same.

Hulse saw his arming lights come on too.

Just behind Hulse's flight, the second flight entered the bomb-run. The radar-directed 88s' projectiles immediately greeted Al Damico's A-20. A bright orange flash was immediately followed by the pings, pangs, and zips of steel hitting the wings and fuselage of his plane.

Al drew back from the all-too-familiar sounds, then looked out to examine the holes in the trailing edge and control surfaces of the right wing.

"We took a hit on the right wing. No fire, skipper."

"Roger, things look good here too," came back from Lieutenant Joe Meagher in the cockpit. "Keep calling those flak bursts."

Luftwaffe *kanoniers* manning the 88s sent repeated salvos of *tod*[153] upward into the helpless formation of Havocs. Each detonation added more smoke and steel to the airspace, prompting more calls of flak bursts from gunners and navigators that filled the pilot's earphones.

All the aircrews in the first three flights heard the steel impaling itself against their flying aluminum cocoons. Every aviator was experiencing the effects of adrenaline as it poured into the bloodstream from their overworked adrenal glands. Uncontrollably their pulses quickened, mouths dried, and blood vessels constricted, raising their blood pressure. These were all natural physiological mechanisms designed to help increase their situational awareness and their natural capacities for self-preservation.

Ralph finally killed the rate, centering the crosshairs over the target aiming point that was sliding underneath them. As the hairs centered, the gyros synchronized electrically and closed the bomb-release circuit. The bomb shackles opened and released the first rack of five-hundred-pounders. With the intervalometer set on zero, the next rack fell immediately.

"Bombs away!"

The words echoed through the radios of the other five Havocs in Ralph's flight as the pilots pushed their energized bomb-release buttons on the right side of the flight-control yoke.

The bombs finished arming themselves as they were falling to dead center on the aiming point. The V-1's concrete bunkers, slit trenches, and air-raid shelters were

---

153   *Tod*—(German) – death

filled with technicians, enlisted soldiers and officers. The *flugabwehrkanonens* positioned to the west of the site were to be spared the terror of eighteen thousand pounds of exploding steel projectiles as the first flight's bombs began to hit their mark.

The repaired launching ramp was first to be hit; that salvo destroyed the rails and part of the superstructure. The slit trenches were quickly proven to be useless protection to the soldiers, as the ground erupted around them, ripping limbs from torsos. Death came instantly to the *soldats* lying in the trenches close to the impact sites of the American ordnance.

Now it was time for the second box to lay its eggs. Jedinak's flight was following the first box along the bomb-run at 230 mph but five hundred feet lower in altitude. The bomb bay doors had already been forced open by the hydraulic pistons, and the lethal five-hundred-pound missiles were waiting their turn to do their duty. Every A-20 in the second box was taking the same withering fire as the first box had; meanwhile, the first box had powered into its steep, left-hand diving turn, and headed for safety.

"Steady, Stockwell…just about there…" Jedinak reassured his pilot, as Stockwell fought against the buffeting from the flak to keep the PDI centered.

In a moment, the Norden's automatic-release circuit closed, unharnessing the five-hundred-pound HE weapons from their resting spot. Jedinak had dropped the eggs, and now all he and the rest of the flight wanted to think about was getting the hell out of there. Yet, as the last five-hundred-pound high explosive left Stockwell and Jedinak's Havoc, an 88 round entered the bomb bay between the open doors, hitting the bomb bay gas tank. It exploded on impact. The tank, ripped open by the detonation, became an explosive fireball that tore through both wings' bulkheads and the armor plating that formed the front wall of the bomb bay compartment behind pilot Stockwell. The pilot's flight control surfaces were immediately destroyed, and the blast separated all the control cables between his yoke and tail controls.

With the first explosion Stockwell was knocked unconscious. The mixed metallic fragments had ripped through the armor plating designed to protect him, and then quickly destroyed his flak jacket as if it weren't there. Metallic shards did to his vital organs what they had done to his turret gunner. Stockwell, not yet dead, was initially spared the flames.

For turret gunner Staff Sergeant Hollis Foster only a thin layer of aluminum separated him and the bomb bay. It provided no protection when the steel and shredded aluminum ripped through it with only a little more resistance than when it tore into Foster's body. Shrapnel shredded his organs. He was dead before the fire consumed his soulless remains and before the second 88 round slammed into the tail of the now doomed Havoc.

After being flung against the nose of his Plexiglass compartment, Jedinak regained his senses. He started calling for Stockwell. He had felt both impacts, as had the tail tunnel gunner Sergeant Egan W. Rust. Both were shaken as never before. Disoriented by the first explosion, Egan was briefly blinded when the second round detonated in the tail and stunned him even more.

Death Came Quickly at 12,000 feet

Mission #46, afternoon of May 12, 1944
Direct flak hit amid-ship in open bomb bay of A-20 # 129 from
the 416th Bomb Group over the target area Beauvoir, France,
a No-ball (Buzz-bomb/ V-1) site; this was the group's second
mission to this site known as "Flak Alley."
Pilot Lieutenant Robert Stockwell (KIA), BN. Lieutenant
Albert Jedinak (POW), tail gunner Sergeant Egan W. Rust
(POW) and top gunner Staff Sergeant. Hollis Foster (KIA)
Jedinak and Rust were repatriated with Jedinak visiting
Stockwell's widow after the war. They were to marry later.
Photo on display in the USAF's Dayton Air Museum
Reproduced with permission from Ralph Conte

Moments before, Lieutenant Smith had seen the lead ship's bomb bay doors swing open, which prompted him to throw his switch. The green light on his instrument panel lit up, signifying that his bomb bay doors were open.

Hiram Clark and the other pilots did the same.

Roland watched as the crosshairs drew closer and closer to the target drop point. Sliding his hand over the arming switch, he lifted the safety cover on the bomb-arming switch located in the control box next to the Norden bombsight. He flipped the switch to arm the bombs and energize the release mechanism.

It was then that Stockwell's Havoc in the flight ahead of them took its almost-simultaneous hits. No one spoke; they only stared in disbelief as the flames erupted all around the fuselage. Everyone watched the plane slip to the right and out of formation.

Refocusing on the mission, Hiram moved his right hand to the bomb-release button located on his control stick. All the other pilots instinctively did the same, putting their thumbs on the drop button.

When Roland's Norden crosshairs met, his payload released. The rest of the flight followed suit. Impellers spun as the bombs fell from 12,500 feet, arming eighteen thousand pounds of mixed high-explosive ordnance.

"Bomb bay doors closed. Turn us for home, Pain," Roland called to his pilot. He looked up from his Norden in time to see Stockwell's inferno of an A-20 start into a flat spin.

"Dear God! Who's that going down?" Roland asked in horror.

"Stockwell. Looks like those guys bought it today. Ain't seen no chutes yet."

"Who could live through that?"

"Roger, what's the heading to the RP?" Pain asked as he prepared to pull the A-20 out of its evasive dive.

"Turn to two-fiver-seven for twenty, that's two-zero, minutes," Roland said. "That should put us there."

"Roger, turning to two-fiver-seven now."

The flight turned in unison onto a northwesterly course toward the RP, hoping they would find the rest of the group there to fly home with.

In the plummeting Havoc, Jedinak was unable to raise anyone on the interphone. He couldn't see the flames and had no way to know who was alive in the aircraft. Stockwell regained consciousness long enough to execute his last mental activity, reaching forward to sound the escape claxton. The instant the circuit closed his spirit passed and he was dead to this mortal world.

Hearing the alarm, Jedinak knew it was time to escape his isolated compartment in the nose of his doomed aircraft. The Havoc had started into a slow but accelerating flat spin. The pull of gravity on the burning bomber and the lack of flight controls were accelerating its fall to the green countryside below.

Jedinak could feel the acceleration, and knew he needed to get out now before becoming trapped. He released the emergency-escape handle and was startled not to see the hatch fly open. Then, he wrestled with his flak jacket, and finally shedding it, he grabbed his chute and snapped it into place on his harness. Lying on his back looking toward the cockpit, Jedinak kicked the escape hatch with his heel, trying to force the door open. He suddenly realized he couldn't lift himself from the floor of his compartment. He thought the centrifugal force of the spin had pinned him.

"Oh, dear God, not today," escaped his lips as a sense of serenity suddenly overcame him.

Looking behind himself, Jedinak saw a ring on his parachute harness that was hung between a strut and the wall of the fuselage. He nearly willed the ring free as he pulled it from between the structures. Feeling the acceleration of the spin increasing, Jedinak knew he needed to get out now before he really couldn't move. After squatting over the escape hatch, he kicked it repeatedly until it busted open. A rush of cold air followed.

Falling headfirst out the hatch, Jedinak slammed his head against the bottom of the plane as he hurtled toward earth. He heard the two propellers spinning on either side of him and prayed that he didn't become mincemeat as he tumbled away from the burning hulk. The centrifugal force was now so strong that anyone left alive in the plane would probably be doomed. He wondered if Egan or anyone else had made it out.

He looked down at the ground, to which he was accelerating faster than he would have liked. To slow himself, he reached for the ripcord and watched as the chute deployed and then slipped back between his legs. It didn't open correctly—the chute's lines were restricted by his right foot caught in the tension lines.

"Oh, damnit, can anything else go wrong?" he hollered as the partially opened chute spun him like a top.

He reached between his legs to grab the shock cords, and tugged them down until he could pull his right foot free of the lines. He let his feet fall below his head. The chute bloomed open above him. As his rate of descent slowed, he silently thanked his God. The rushing sound of his fall died away, and he was suddenly aware of the sounds of battle again. The shockwaves from the barrels of the guns below and the explosions above drowned out the drone of the rapidly departing American bombers.

After the first 88 round exploded in the bomb bay, Egan had not heard the emergency claxton or any communication and had assumed they were OK. Hesitating, he nervously looked around his compartment as the ship began to spin.

"Stockwell," he hollered into the interphone. "Are we OK, over?"

The aircraft accelerated its spin.

"Jedinak, do you read me, are we OK?"

Looking out the rear opening, he saw the flames lapping along the bottom of the plane. The heat warmed his face. Egan pushed his .30-caliber machine gun out the rear opening, and then turned to get his stowed parachute. After releasing his flak jacket, he snapped his chute to his harness. He looked down; he had put the D-ring on the left side.

"Ahh, damnit, Egan."

He unhooked his chute, turned it around, and then snapped it back to the harness. Looking out the opening, he saw a dark, man-shaped object fly through his field of view. It had to be Jedinak—only the navigators and tail gunners came out the bottom of the plane.

"Hell, it's now or never, Egan."

He pulled himself headfirst out the opening. Falling into the 250-mph slipstream, he was suddenly aware of the rushing sound of the air as it sped by his ears.

Tumbling in a tight ball, Egan counted, thousand four…thousand five…thousand six, up to ten, when he pulled his D-ring and prayed the chute would open. Feeling a jerk, he sensed his slowing descent toward the once rapidly approaching ground.

He saw another chute maybe a thousand feet below him, and then scanned the sky for others.

The burning Havoc, with Stockwell's and Foster's remains strapped in their stations, continued its accelerating spiral toward the ground. Jedinak watched his blazing Havoc spiral downward as it fell toward its final resting place. Tracers passed by and through the burning fuselage as the Luftwaffe's 20- and 37-mm anti-aircraft crews tried to destroy the remains. The Wehrmacht *soldats* and *offiziers* watching the two *fallschirm*[154] float to the ground were already organizing to *gefangen nehmen*.[155]

After the brisk descent, Jedinak saw that he was about to hit the ground in, of all places, a bomb crater. Hitting the angled wall of the crater, he fell toward the bottom and landed on his back. The odor of the wounded earth was mixed with the sulfurous fumes of explosives. The chute settled and draped the crater's edge. Using the tension lines to pull the silk into the hole, Jedinak began his escape and evasion protocol. As he took off his harness, he spied another chute coming down off to the south. Completing part of the ritual, he buried his chute, harness and group insignia with the fresh dirt around him.

He crawled up to the edge of the crater and witnessed the last explosions from the last flight's bombs. He knew he was out of the war, but he was eager to get back as his escape and evasion training began to come back to him. Seeing a thicket to the south—close to where the other chute had come down—Jedinak hunched over into a crouching trot and headed toward it, hoping to get cover. He made the edge of the thicket and ducked in on his hands and knees and crawled to a tree in the center. He caught his breath against a tree and watched anti-aircraft artillery erupt all around him. Between the salvos Jedinak heard rapidly approaching footsteps. He reached for his sidearm when he saw three well-armed German soldiers move in front of him at the edge of the thicket.

They pointed their weapons in Jedinak's direction, and he realized he was had. It wasn't hard to understand what they were shouting at him. He lowered his pistol and crawled out of the bushes. They hustled him in the direction of the other chute. Coming to the top of a small ridge, he looked down to see Egan sitting on the ground with two German soldiers pointing their weapons at him. Jedinak quickly found himself sitting beside Egan, and then the soldiers searched them. They took anything of any value except clothes and shoes.

That was the last Jedinak would see of Egan, since they were separated and independently interrogated. Their long journeys to separate POW camps had begun.

The bomber group was out of the flak fields, and the lead box had just completed its first circuit at the RP when the low box completed its transition into the group. The fighters circled above, scanning the surrounding airspace for any unwanted Luftwaffe fighters. The fighter pilots were sad at not seeing any, since most were still

154   *Fallschirm* — (German) – parachute
155   *Gefangen nehmen* — (German) — to take prisoners

looking to become aces. The bomber crews were delighted that there were no enemy fighters around.

Hulse turned the group toward the southeast coast of England, hoping the intel was correct that their egress route would be free of flak but maybe not fighters. Hulse led the group out over the coastline, away from the sharp-angled geometric divisions of the French countryside. He wanted to get back over the less-structured divisions of England.

Once over the channel tensions slowly lessened for each aircrew member. Bill Tripp felt the sweat under his heavy flak jacket and flight jacket as he reached for his radio dial. They had a ways to go before they were back at the base, so why not enjoy it? He turned the dial carefully until he tuned in the American Armed Forces Network. It was a tradition all the flights enjoyed on their return leg home, and was used as a homing beacon as well as for pleasure. Bill patched the music through to the other planes in the flight.

"Hey, guys, here it comes," he radioed to the other pilots.

Relaxing back, he watched as the other A-20s coursed through the sky. The pilots rocked their wings back and forth to the rhythm of the music while everyone still cautiously scanned the sky for bandits. Bill swore he had gotten to the point that he could tell the fast songs from the slow songs just by watching the other planes in formation. This "dance of the aircraft" was never discussed with command or any other squadron. The gunners never said a word either.

Bill swung the twin-engine bird back and forth in unison with the rest of the flight to "One O'clock Jump," which was followed by a Sinatra tune. Frank was followed by Benny Goodman. The fellas tried to enjoy the music. The vision of Stockwell's plane exploding into flames was still vivid, and kept them from truly enjoying the notes.

Heading Home

A-20 Havoc, the glass-nosed bombardier/navigator model
from the 669th squadron, airborne and leading the group or
flight home from the target.
Photographed from the number-two slot in the flight.
Reproduced with permission from Ralph Conte

At Wethersfield, the planes were returning. The last Havoc was settling down onto the runway and slowed to begin its taxi.

Earl completed his taxi to his revetment, and applied a hard right brake while he revved the port engine and swung the plane around in a near-perfect circle. Applying both brakes, Earl pulled off the power. The Havoc came to a stop, pointing out to the taxiway, ready for refueling and bombing-up for the next mission. In a practiced and meticulous counterclockwise manner he shut down the engines, turned off the fuel-booster pumps, shut off the magnetos, turned off the master switch, pulled on the parking brake, securing the plane as he had been taught. He watched the same militarily precise process of taxi, spin, shut down, and secure as his fellow 669th pilots put their birds to rest on their squadron's hardstands.

As he set his flak helmet down beside him, he knew this was not going to be a pleasurable debriefing. He rubbed his face and pulled back his hair with his right hand as he slid his flight cap and headset off. From what Earl knew, no one had taken any hits, and he hadn't seen any planes go down. Earl sat there for a few minutes looking around the cockpit smelling the sweat, oil, and fuel while thinking back to his first mission.

How difficult it had been to force himself to stay in formation that day when all the flak started coming up. He remembered listening to the sounds of steel shrapnel bouncing off or going through the skin of his plane. It was then that he realized some of that steel could go through him. On that first mission he had wondered what would happen if a piece of it did hit him.

That first day the hardest thing he learned to do was to fly through the middle of the black smoke of the flak bursts as he had been told to do and others around him were doing. It was always worse on the bomb-run because you couldn't maneuver, only fly straight and level. With sweat and prayer through the fire of battle, he had learned then what had now become his near-daily routine. He rarely gave it a second thought until today. He hoped he never saw flak like that again. Earl went through the necessary maneuvers to survive the mission but he never quit praying.

Earl reached up to open the hatch. He pulled himself up out of the cockpit and stood on his seat. As he scanned the area he could tell which planes had gotten to the barn before him. The ground crews were refueling them and crawling over them to examine every surface and piece of equipment for damage. They were looking for fluid leaks of any kind. It was a sight he had seen a lot. He stepped over the side of the cockpit, found the footholds and climbed down. The ground crew was securing his plane as he looked over at Hiram's plane and watched him climb out of his chariot.

"Hey, Hiram, good to see you."

Together they headed for the debriefing truck.

"One more under our belts, hey?"

"At least this one counts, Earl. We dropped those bombs on something."

They ran into Roland coming out from under his plane. He didn't look happy.

"Pretty tough up there today?" Earl asked.

"Hell of a way to make a living," Roland said.

All three chuckled because they knew in some respects it didn't matter. They were here to do a job and they were going to do it. Today was one more out of the way.

Every crewman knew that if you didn't drop your bombs on a target it didn't count as a completed mission. They also knew that's why having a good BN in your squadron was so important. He was someone to get you there and back, so that when you risked your life so flagrantly, it counted for something, even if on some missions you didn't know what you dropped the eggs on.

The *generaloberst stab offiziers*[156] of the Luftwaffe and Wehrmacht knew what Roland's, Ralph's, and Jedinak's flights had hit. They had received reports of how effective the 416th's strike on the Beauvoir V-1 rocket-bomb site had been. The repair crews and materials were already being ordered to the site as the 416th completed taxiing to their revetments.

The 416th's post-mission discussion sounded upbeat. The debriefing was detailed and productive from the point of view of Group Operations. The consensus among the leaders was that it was a good hit, but they would have to wait for photos from the

---

156   *Generaloberst stab offiziers* – (German) — general staff officers

stripped-down, unarmed, and high-speed P-38 recon aircraft for any bomb-damage assessment from this mission.

After the debriefing, the crewmen congregated around the Red Cross ladies, who had come out with hot coffee and donuts. Everyone appreciated having them there after the missions. It gave the guys a place to unwind, but today it was bittersweet.

Captain Mowry, the flight surgeon from the 670th, was at his usual spot after a mission.

"Any you guys need a shot today?" He was offering medicinal whiskey to anybody who wanted it.

"No, Doc, but thanks. I'm fine today," Wayne Downing replied, as he headed for coffee and a donut.

There were no takers today; everyone was more interested in the coffee, the donuts, and particularly the Red Cross ladies. The crews poured down coffee while smoking a few more cigarettes.

Wes Chitty, who hadn't been on the mission this afternoon, had come down to the tower to watch the returning planes. Seeing that all but one had come home, he headed over to the Red Cross hut for the dope. Wes poured a cup of coffee and sat down beside Wayne.

"How'd it go up there today?" Wes sipped his coffee. Then he leaned back in his chair and began a slow draw on his pipe.

"Stockwell, Jedinak, and the crew got it. Don't think anyone got out. Flak was as thick as I've ever seen it."

Wes blew the sweet pipe smoke out, and then sipped his coffee. Those comments coming from Wayne meant a lot.

Wayne lit a Lucky and took a deep draw. Like all the other airmen, he just tried to enjoy the rest of the day.

Chapter Seven

The Wizard War

Meanwhile the Wizard War was unfolding in its own strange way. The first five
stations of the coastal radar chain…had watched Mr. Chamberlain's aeroplane go and
come on its peace mission of September, 1938.

–Winston Churchill

"I can taste atomic fission; it tastes like lead." Later, in his journal he expressed amazement for
his part in the event, saying, "My God, what have we done?"

–Robert Lewis, copilot Enola Gay, 1945

While soldiers have always sought any edge in the life-and-death struggle of warfare, in the twentieth century increasing technological sophistication became a hallmark of each new conflict. For example, research into flight on the part of the Wright brothers and others led eventually to the deployment of aircraft in World War I, and then still later to commercial aviation. As the plane was to the Great War, thus radar development was to World War II. The second global conflict saw the extensive deployment of radar for defensive as well as offensive purposes. It became another key tool in warfare, and to be without it meant certain defeat. Generally speaking, the development of radar during the war occurred in three phases. The first phase was the development of detection and interceptor radar. The second phase was directional guidance and targeting radar, while the third was the countermeasure war.

In Germany, *Funkmessgerät* (radar) development was largely carried out by the *Gesellschaft für Elektroakustische und Mechanische Apparate*, or GEMA for short. Two other German companies also participated in radar research and development—Telefunken and Lorenz. The Luftwaffe worked closely in the development of radar defenses primarily with GEMA and Telefunken, but Lorenz also contributed. This cooperative development occurred only after the Luftwaffe became independent of the Wehrmacht and took control of air defenses. In 1936 GEMA provided the Luftwaffe with an early-detection radar called "Freya," or A-1, that operated at 125 MHz. The system was installed along the North Sea coastline in 1937 and ultimately would be used to create an extensive early-warning, layered defense ring around Germany.

Freya Radar

This early-model Luftwaffe radar was known as Freya (FuMG
401) LZ (*Lufttransport-zerlegbar,* or transportable by air) by
the Germans, or as Pole-Freya by the British. This model's
electronics provided the basis for all Luftwaffe radar systems.
*A Radar History of World War II: Technology and Military
Imperatives*; Louis Brown; Institute of Physics Publishing, 1999
Photo reproduced by permission of the National Archives,
photograph 111-SC 269043

Meanwhile, Telefunken independently produced targeting directional radar
that operated in the 570 MHz range, which was named Würzburg, or A-3, in 1941. The
Würzburg system was then added to the Freya system for targeting and guidance.

Telefunken also engineered fighter-borne radar called Lichtenstein that operated at the 50-cm wavelength. This system proved to be a great addition to the night
fighter interceptors.

All three systems—Würzburg, Lichtenstein, and Freya—were deployed together
to produce a layered radar system that identified approaching enemy aircraft with Freya,

and targeted them by knowing the altitude, azimuth, and distance using the Würzburg system. Then the information was passed to the fighter interceptor command, whose planes were directed to the bombers with the Würzburg radar system (usually two radar systems—one to track the enemy and the other to guide the interceptors) until they were close enough for the fighters to use their own Lichtenstein radar to close on the bombers.

The pilots' interceptors of choice for the radar were initially the Me-110s and Ju-88s. The advantage of the on-board radar was immediately clear: the German fighters could find the bombers on a clear or a cloudy night. But at first Luftwaffe pilots didn't like the system, since it limited the planes' performance. However, once successful intercepts were accomplished using the radar, the German pilots' attitudes changed, aided by the urging of Luftwaffe Captain Ludwig Becker. The Germans preferred the 50-cm wavelength, although they extended the wavelength on their fighter interceptors out to the 3.75-meter band, and by doing so improved the planes' effectiveness against countermeasures.

Lichtenstein Radar

The early model of airborne radar carried on a Luftwaffe
Me-110. The system known as Lichtenstein came in versions
that operated on different wavelengths, the 2-meter and 50-
centimeter models. The latter model was good for the final kill
but not for long-range tracking, which the 2-meter model was
better suited for.
It was used mainly in night-attack versions of the Luftwaffe's
air defense.
*A Radar History of World War II: Technology and Military
Imperatives;* Louis Brown; Institute of Physics Publishing, 1999
Photo reproduced by permission of the Imperial War Museum
CL 3299. Crown Copyright.

Britain's scientific community worked hard at understanding Germany's radar
capabilities. It actually took a commando raid on a coastal Freya-Würzburg site in Saint-
Jouin-Bruneval, France, to capture and bring home the essential components of the
Würzburg system. The system made it to British hands courtesy of 119 Scottish paratroopers and radar researcher R.V. Jones on February 27, 1942. Once the British under-

stood that the German systems operated at much shorter wavelengths than their own systems, they started their "war of countermeasures" to disable enemy radar. Such countermeasures included the British "Carpet" jamming system. Carpet techniques consisted of producing white noise, and were later used by the Americans. To work around these countermeasures, the Germans had to develop newer ground-based radar systems.

Besides high-tech countermeasure systems, a simple low-tech solution became commonplace in the skies over Europe after its first use in 1943. Initially successful but later less so, "Window"—known as "*Düppel*" by the Germans—was introduced by the British. Window consisted of aluminum strips cut to the wavelength dipoles of the transmitting radar. It was then dropped from airplanes. These strips reflected the radar waves back to the receivers, which basically overwhelmed the Germans' radar receivers and their operators' scopes, creating "reverse noise."

The Americans improved on the low-tech measure in several ways. They created strips of aluminum that were folded down the middle in order to create a right angle that increased the reflectivity. The strips were a twentieth of an inch wide and less than a hundredth of an inch thick. Each bundle of American *Düppel* weighed only three ounces. They were also cut shorter than the British strips. These modifications improved the efficacy of the countermeasure. Interestingly, by the end of the war three-quarters of all American aluminum-foil production went to make Window. So much foil was being diverted to war purposes that American cigarette producers and the Mars candy company switched from foil wrappers to paper.

Window would be introduced to the 416th and the Ninth Air Force on a special mission assigned to and flown by a small group of the 416th's airmen over the heavily defended, German-occupied port of Le Havre, France. The target was known for its heavy concentration of guns for port defense and anti-aircraft defense. On April 10, 1944, a small group of A-20s from Wethersfield were flown to a B-26 Marauder airfield in England. Led by pilot Captain Chester Jackson and navigator Lieutenant Ralph Conte, the group arrived at the Marauder base unsure of their mission. The mission briefing told them that they would lead a group of B-26 bombers, but they would fly two thousand feet below the Marauders' bombing altitude. Once at the target, the belly gunners in the A-20s were to drop strips of aluminum out the back of the Havocs. The pilots were then to maneuver about the airspace so as to give an unclear target for the Luftwaffe anti-aircraft gunners.

After takeoff the A-20s assumed their position in the formation. At the designated spot the aluminum strips spilled from the gunners' windows in the rear of the Havocs. Flying two thousand feet above the high-speed A-20s, the Marauders flew their bomb-run straight and level. The maneuverable Havocs were having a much different day as the German gun-laying radar fired on them. Fortunately, no Havocs were hit, but thousands of strips of aluminum fluttering to earth immediately behind them were destroyed. The Havoc crews watched as the B-26s loosed their loads and then turned for home without losing a single aircraft. The A-20s landed, to be met with only praise for the success of the mission as well as a newfound respect from the B-26 boys for the little hotrods the 416th flew.

Upon exiting his aircraft Captain Jackson was greeted by none other than General Dwight D. Eisenhower. "Ike" came to inspect the special planes that had made this mission such a success. Jackson was given the courtesy of escorting the general around the aircraft. In doing so, Jackson accidentally knocked the general's hat off while trying to look in the bomb bay. In spite of Eisenhower's disarming laughter, Jackson displayed his embarrassment for some time.

To say the least, the A-20 boys had their share of drinks bought for them that evening at the Officers Club. There they met the then well-known actor Robert Preston, who was losing badly at craps. The group flew to Wethersfield the next day. From then on, Window became SOP (standard operating procedure) for the Ninth Air Force.[157]

By the middle of Spring 1944, the Eighth Air Force was dropping upward of 355 tons of Window a month. This tonnage did not include that dropped by the Ninth Air Force and other groups across the theater or in other war zones. To help deal with *Düppel*, the Germans fielded the Würzlaus system, which was arguably the first Doppler radar. This system helped the German radar operators distinguish the difference between the falling aluminum strips and the moving bomber force. By detecting the shift in wavelength of the approaching bomber force the Germans could tell an approaching aircraft from the *Düppel*.

As Allied countermeasures developed greater effectiveness, the Germans were forced to develop the "Mammut" radar, which was an enlarged Freya that calculated distance and course, and the "Wasserman," for determining altitude. These systems increased the range of early-detection and targeting capabilities beyond the early Freya systems.

---

157   *Attack Bombers We Need You!: A History of the 416ᵗʰ Bomb Group*, Ralph Conte; copyright 2001, pp 48–49

Mammut Radar

This example of Mammut (FuMG 52) German meter-wave radar had long range and great accuracy with bidirectional capability. This model was used to detect incoming airborne formations at long range, thereby giving Luftwaffe interceptor aircraft, other short-range radar, and gun-laying radar an advance warning. The British referred to this style as Hoarding.

A Radar History of World War II: Technology and Military Imperatives; Louis Brown; Institute of Physics Publishing, 1999 Photo reproduced by permission of the National Archives, photograph 111-SC 269022

Chimney Radar

Chimney was the self-explanatory nickname the British gave
for this model of Luftwaffe radar. This Wassermann M II
(FuMG 402) could detect aircraft as far out as 210 kilometers
if they flew at or above 8,000 meters. For targeting it could
localize aircraft in a box of airspace 1,200 meters high by 300
meters long by 435 meters wide.
*A Radar History of World War II: Technology and Military
Imperatives;* Louis Brown; Institute of Physics Publishing, 1999
Photo reproduced by permission of the National Archives,
photograph 111-SC 269031

The "Würzburg-Riese" (Würzburg-Giant) system came quickly, and helped
Germany reestablish an effective air defense. To enhance their capabilities, several
Würzburg-Riese systems were linked to the improved Freya radar. The whole system
was in turn connected to searchlights and flak cannons. (Technically, this was a slightly
different system, named "Mannheim," but was commonly referred to as Würzburg.)
Despite the links between the radar, the German targeting system was limited by the
need for operators to reference targeting information, instead of having the *flugabwehr-*

kanonen completely controlled through the radar. Nevertheless, the system was a deadly combination that increased the 88s' efficiency threefold, and the loss of Allied bombers continued.

Würzburg Radar

This model of Luftwaffe Würzburg radar was used as the gun-laying radar for four to six anti-aircraft artillery pieces. It was effective and deadly as it vectored in the artillery rounds.
A Radar History of World War II: Technology and Military Imperatives; Louis Brown; Institute of Physics Publishing, 1999
Photo reproduced by permission of the *Bundesarchiv*
356/1845/8

Rail-mounted Würzburg Radar

The rail-mounted Würzburg D model was a smaller, mobile unit that could be transported to hot spots as needed by the military. The guns were on flatbed rail cars slaved to the radar.
A Radar History of World War II: Technology and Military Imperatives; Louis Brown; Institute of Physics Publishing,1999
Photo reproduced by permission of the *Bundesarchiv*
621/2943/24

While Germany improved its air defense through enhanced radar, its capabilities would have also been greatly aided by enhancements to anti-aircraft shells. A critical modification—the successful introduction of the proximity fuse—could have significantly impacted and arguably halted the Allied air campaign. Developed by the Allies, this miniature radar mounted in the nose of the artillery shell would detect the presence of an aircraft within a certain distance and would detonate at the position. Combined with radar guidance, this proximity fuse greatly increased the "kill percentage" of the shells fired.

Surprisingly, Germany's work on the proximity fuse and many other new scientific projects had been revealed to the British and their allies early in the conflict. The British government came into possession of a leaked report from Germany that became known as the *Oslo Report*.[158] The report also detailed the operation of Germany's navigational and targeting radars. These revelations helped Britain gain an edge in the German and British night bombings that had come to be known as the "Battle of the Beams." The *Oslo Report* was eventually passed to Reginald Victor Jones in November 1939. (Jones was soon to become a member of the Bruneval raid.) Winning the Battle of the Beams would prove to be decisive in these early days after the "Phoney War" of stalled aggressions from both sides had ended.

Germany too was in the espionage business, and fortunately missed its chance to understand Britain's radar capability. A 1939 zeppelin mission under the command of Colonel Wolfgang Martini, chief of Luftwaffe Signal Corps, was sent out to study the possible radar capabilities of the island nation. Monitoring only in the shorter wavelengths, the Luftwaffe completely missed Britain's longer-wavelength radar systems. As a result, the Luftwaffe did not target the stations throughout the critical air war known as the Battle of Britain, believing that Britain lacked significant radar capability.

Such a key mistake would seriously undermine the Germans' efforts to control Britain, and ultimately helped the Allies win the war. Radar was proving absolutely vital to victory as was superiority in other technological areas. Referring to this battle for technological ascendancy, especially for radar, as the "Wizard War," Winston Churchill wrote in The Grand Alliance,

---

158   *Oslo Report* — The validity of the report was questioned for some time but eventually was verified and the information put to use

A Botched Mission

The famous but failed German attempt to detect British radar
capabilities in August 1939 around the city of Aberdeen.
Colonel Wolfgang Martini (chief of Luftwaffe Signal Corps)
piloted this chartered zeppelin in an attempt to detect
the wavelength and location of British radar installations.
Measuring in the wrong frequencies, the mission was a failure
for Germany but a coup for Britain, since the failure to detect
any radio waves left Germany to believe that Britain had very
primitive capabilities.
*A Radar History of World War II: Technology and Military
Imperatives*; Louis Brown; Institute of Physics Publishing, 1999
Photo reproduced with permission of the Royal Air Force
Museum, Hendon, London, Photo P26. Crown Copyright

Meanwhile the Wizard War was unfolding in its own strange way. The first
five stations of the coastal radar chain…had watched Mr. Chamberlain's
aeroplane go and come on its peace mission of September, 1938. Eighteen stations from Dundee to Portsmouth began in the spring of 1939
a twenty-four hour watch, not to be interrupted in the next six years…
These stations were the watchdogs…they spared us alike grave losses in
war production and intolerable burdens on our civil defense workers.
They spared the anti-aircraft gun crews needless and tiring hours at action stations. They saved us from exhaustion of man and machine that
would have doomed our matchless but slender fighter force had it been
compelled to maintain standing patrols…they enabled the day fighters
to await their prey at the most favorable altitudes and aspects for attack.

The British prime minister understood well the significance of the battle for technology, and its potential effects on the outcome of the war. The gradual understanding of Germany's radar capabilities and the unsustainable Allied bomber losses from radar-guided planes and anti-aircraft artillery began the "countermeasure wizard war."[159, 160, 161]

On July 24, 1943, "Operation Gomorrah" was launched when 791 Bomber Command aircraft took off to decimate Hamburg. The sortie was the first wave of a series culminating in the July 29th raid. It was the first mission approved for the use of Window and it was devastatingly successful, leading to the subsequent coinage of the term "wizard war." Of 3,095 total bombers over target only 86 were lost, a loss rate of only 2.8 percent. While the Allied Bomber Command was delighted, the people of Hamburg were crushed by the success of the raids. A description from Robert Buderi's book on the wizard war best describes what the survivors and causalities experienced:

> Instead of fires, they [the pilots and crews of the July 29th raid saw only one—a gigantic inferno that sucked up air and suffocated thousands, while creating winds of fire that turned air raid shelters into crematoriums. The large stores of coal and coke in the cellars of nearly every house joined the conflagration. Sparks the size of coins rained down on those caught in the open. Human beings cooked in their own fat. Streets melted, trapping some residents temporarily alive in the asphalt.

Some forty-two thousand Hamburg residents—mostly children, women and the elderly—perished in the *feuersturm*.[162] This disturbing description would also accurately describe the quickly approaching fate of many German and Japanese cities.[163, 164]

The Luftwaffe was shocked by the success of the *Düppel* and other tactics, which merely ensured the rapid development of countermeasures. For every measure that Britain introduced there seemed to appear a countermeasure, which would be followed by a counter-countermeasure. In spite of Window and Carpet, US Army Strategic Air Forces in Europe lost 1,566 aircraft in the last seven months of the war to *flugabwehrkanonen*, not including those aircraft lost in tactical (the 416th and other groups) or British bomber groups. So, despite the countermeasures, losses persisted. But as Louis Brown in his book *A Radar History of World War II* asks, "What would the total have been without Carpet and Window?"

159   *The Grand Alliance, The Second World War*, Winston S. Churchill, pages 45–46;
160   *The Invention That Changed the World*, Robert Buderi; Touchstone Books, Simon and Schuster, copyright 1996
161   *A Radar History of World War II, Technical and Military Imperatives*, Louis Brown; Institute of Physics Publishing, copyright 1999
162   *Feuersturm*—(German)—firestorm
163   *The Invention That Changed the World*, Robert Buderi; Touchstone Books, Simon and Schuster, copyright 1996
164   *A Radar History of World War II, Technical and Military Imperatives*, Louis Brown; Institute of Physics Publishing, copyright 1999

Another key element in the wizard war was bomber guidance and targeting systems. The existence of German passive or active bomber guidance and targeting systems was hotly debated in the early days of the war by the British. Through prisoner interrogations and active monitoring, they eventually uncovered three distinct systems used by the Luftwaffe. Two of the systems were designed for the bombers to "ride" to the target. They transmitted signals to airborne bombers from the western city of Kleve, Germany, and the northernmost German province of Schleswig-Holstein, near Denmark. Wherever the signals converged the bombers dropped their payload. The more sophisticated third system—code-named "Y-Gerät," whose existence had been revealed in the *Oslo Report*—radiated a lobe switching signal for direction finding and an audio frequency for range. Using the system, ground controllers could lead pilots to the target.

Once these systems were understood, Robert Cockburn and his team at the Telecommunications Research Establishment produced its first jammers. This countermeasure seriously confused the radar systems, and skewed their target coordinates. In *The Grand Alliance* Churchill provided notes on the countermeasure:

> During 1941 we went on deflecting the German beams despite their various improvements. An example...on the night of May 8 the Germans planned two attacks, the first upon Rolls-Royce Works at Derby and the second on Nottingham. Through our interference with their beams [the attack was unsuccessful...The German communiqué claimed the destruction of the Rolls-Royce Works at Derby, which they never got near...The total casualties there were two chickens.

While Churchill poked fun at German efforts to attack Britain, the British pilots were having similar difficulties in hitting their targets.

The success of British bombing raids was seriously questioned after a review of the Battle of the Ruhr. British Intelligence learned that only about one-tenth of the bombs dropped over that target landed within two miles of the intended target. As a result, the British developed a land-based passive guidance system that utilized two separate transmissions. This system allowed the aircrews to monitor and plot their positions on oscilloscopes while in the air. It was extremely successful and, more importantly, accurate, and allowed more tonnage to hit the target area, thereby increasing the chances of a successful mission.

The Luftwaffe was not long in developing countermeasures though. They developed jamming systems that significantly hindered British radar. The systems functioned by feeding back radar-like pulses to the Allied bombers' receivers, thereby confusing the readings. Germany's most notable jamming facility was an old converted television station located in the Taunus Mountains, close to Frankfurt am Main. Because of the Germans' success with the jammers, the British were forced to develop the "GEE" and "Oboe" systems, so they could bomb in an environment where targets would be covered by bad weather for three out of five days. In spite of the modifications, the GEE, GEE-H, and Oboe systems were successfully jammed for most of the war.

The British countermeasures to German jamming were not always the most effective, but still proved useful. GEE suffered from inherent weaknesses. For example, it operated basically by line of sight. That meant it was dependable only for short distances, its accuracy was poor, and it was easy to jam. Oboe proved more beneficial. Initially a long-wavelength system, Oboe was converted later in the war to a microwave system that the Germans couldn't or didn't jam. For cover, it would broadcast in the longer wavelength, but the embedded microwave frequencies hid the real information and could be received by Allied bombers. Near the end of the war the majority of Allied bombing missions, including those of the 416th, were flown under radar guidance and targeting.[165, 166]

It is interesting to note that in spite of the rapid and effective development of radar and radar countermeasures in the ongoing wizard war, the German infrastructure for managing air raids was quite low-tech—the general population. In April 1933, well before German aggression had become apparent, the Nazi Party founded the *Reichsluftschutzbund* (National Air Raid Protection League), an odd organization to have in a country that was professing peace and nonaggression. Initially a volunteer organization, the league had become obligatory for all German citizens by 1935. In essence, the league's role was to provide air-raid shelters and first-line fire protection to the people in their assigned area or subarea. The league would also post roof spotters to look for planes and fires. Its obligations were taken over by the Luftwaffe in 1940. By 1943 the group had twenty-two million members.

The *Reichsluftschutzbund* worked in conjunction with the *Sicherheits und Hilfsdienst* (Security and Assistance Service), which was formed in 1935. *Sicherheits und Hilfsdienst* was a mobile force that dealt with the heavy rescue work that was necessary after every Allied bombing mission on a German town. By 1942 the burden became so overwhelming that the organization was reformed as the *Luftschutzpolizei* (Air Defense Police) and was controlled by the *Deutsche Ordnungspolizei* (German Order Police). The remains of the *Sicherheits und Hilfdienst* were transferred to the Luftwaffe, where they became motorized air-protection battalions used to fight fires, rescue civilians, and clean debris. Each city had its own *Luftschutzwarndienst* (Air Raid Warning Service) that would collate data received from other locations in order to sound the warning at the appropriate location. It also was responsible for sounding the all-clear signal.

By the start of Hitler's aggression on the citizens of Europe the German people were layered in protection, often provided by some of the most high-tech devices in existence. Stating with the ring of radar that detected aircraft hundreds of miles away, the protection extended to a layered system of defenses and reaction systems, both mechanical and human, that were designed to allow the citizenry and military to survive. The efficacy and success of this system was arguably superior to any other system during

165   *The Invention That Changed the World*, Robert Buderi; Touchstone Books, Simon and Schuster, copyright 1996
166   *A Radar History of World War II, Technical and Military Imperatives*, Louis Brown; Institute of Physics Publishing, copyright 1999

the war after 1941. The Germans would need it, as the 416th and the rest of the Allies brought the war and their high technology to the enemy.

⚜

Walking back to his tent after the debriefing, Hiram noted it was getting chilly again. He stopped in at Operations to check with Weather to see what was up. The weather officer told him that a cold front was sliding in from the northwest and it might get chilly, but that it shouldn't stay around long. It wasn't supposed to affect operations.

Hiram was the last to get back to the barracks. The others were sacked out on their cots. Hiram informed them about the weather.

"Weather tells me it's going to be cold tonight, probably for a couple more days."

The guys roused themselves, and Hiram continued.

"We need to get more wood. Jack, we got any coal left from our last ration?"

"We got a new bag the other day."

"We could use some wood though, fellas," Hiram added.

Earl jumped in, "Hey, I cut my share this week. Somebody else needs to scrounge some." He rubbed his sore hand.

"I'll go get some," Bill piped up and turned to Hiram. "You wanna help?"

"Sure."

The two headed out to see what they could find.

Earl got up to see if his laundry was back. He asked the guys, but no one wanted to join him. Once out the door, he met Roland, who was on the way back from the Post. Roland's hand was brimming with letters.

"Any for me?"

Letters from home made everyone happy. It was nice to hear about family and friends back home and even better if it was your girl. Mail was a moment to be savored, a private time that almost allowed the men to escape from the reality of their current lives.

"Got a couple here for you." Roland shuffled through them and pulled out two.

Earl looked at the letters and was delighted to see one from Helen—a girl he had met in Los Angeles while he was in cadets. Earl had given her a ring the last time he saw her, before being shipped to the East Coast. He wanted to get back to the hut to read it.

"Are the other guys in the hut?"

"Yeah, they're sacked out," Earl said. "They'll be happy to see you."

Roland walked into the Quonset hut and passed out the mail to the eager recipients. He laid the letters on the cots of those who weren't there.

At the laundry area, Earl was pleased to find his clothes were ready. Picking up Bill's, Hiram's, and Roland's clothes as well, he paid the English lady. Earl slid his letters into his front shirt pocket, and then put the parcels under both arms. He began the walk back, all the while praying the laundry ladies hadn't starched everyone's briefs again. He and the squadron had learned the hard way that nothing was worse than starched briefs at twelve thousand feet. Nearing his Quonset, Earl's thoughts drifted to Helen, and he looked forward to reading her letter.

Meanwhile, Bill and Hiram had succeeded in getting a fair amount of wood, enough to get them by for a few days along with the coal, they figured. They would have to protect it or it would get requisitioned by the other officers in their bivouac area.

"All's fair in love and warmth," Bill said with a sigh.

They stacked the wood in their woodpile just inside the door. Bill was delighted to see the letters on his cot and shot straight for them. He lay back on his cot to enjoy the read. First, he opened his letter from Joanne, sliding it out gingerly and trying to minimize the damage to the envelope. He started reading equally slowly, savoring each word from home.

And so began a period of relaxation and winding down in the hut. Roland turned on the pieced-together radio, which he and Jack kept working by scrounging parts from the boneyard. Roland's prewar training in the Merchant Marines combined with Jack's technical and mechanical skills were always appreciated around the tent. After the glowing vacuum tubes had warmed up enough, he carefully tuned the radio to get the best reception. It wasn't perfect, but it worked.

The guys looked forward to Lord Haw-Haw's daily propaganda broadcast out of Berlin. It was even fun listening to the female broadcasters, who were always trying to convince the soldiers that their girlfriends were back in the states playing around with the F-4s, those who had failed to qualify for military service. Lord Haw-Haw signed on and began his broadcast while the men focused on their letters.

Ralph poked his head in to see if anyone wanted a card game. Every nose was buried in a letter. He waved good-bye and walked out of the hut without saying a word. He could see there were no bridge players in there today.

As Lord Haw-Haw prattled on, Jack opened his letter from Rosalie. The censored areas jumped out at him.

April 1944

Dear Jack,

Things are going well here. I have been working in a hospital in (blank area) and occasionally they send me down to a medical facility by the (blank area) River at a place called the (blank area). There is lots of security everywhere. The place covers a large valley. Someone told me something like sixty thousand acres. Trucks and construction equipment are everywhere. There are buildings with restricted areas where only special people can go. Some of the facilities have funny names. I don't know what the names mean but I did finally piece together that no one was allowed to know what the other areas were doing or what the other people from the different sites were building. I have treated some bad injuries from some of the construction sites but thankfully no deaths, mostly injured hands and bad cuts to the head.

Your mom and dad are doing fine. I see them around town every now and then. Frances is doing fine. She is still working in that Glen L. Martin aircraft factory up north. Last time we talked she seemed interested in teaching after the war. They don't have any new information on your brothers right now. They are really hoping for a letter from you all soon. They did say Bill had been flying a lot of missions lately. I guess you know what that means more than the rest of us. I've included a few cuttings from the Rockwood Times I've been saving for you. Hope they get to you OK. There's a story about your dad and brother Pat.

Jack stopped reading. He was remembering what his mom had written in her last letter after Pat had left home to start basic. "Your father cried with great sorrow."

Jack had never seen or known his father to cry, only to be a hard-working sharecropper. He had sat for thirty-two years on the county court, and had been a justice of the peace and a member of the Sixty-Third General Assembly as a state representative from his district in Nashville, Tennessee, from 1923–25. He was a strong man. Jack picked out the article with his father and youngest brother's picture on it. He scanned the headline and then dove into the article.

E.D. Smith Gives Last Son, 17-Year-Old
Pat Smith, For Service in the U.S. Navy

Two Rockwood Families of Same Name Given
Four Sons Each For Country – One a Gold Star Boy

The Smiths of Rockwood are patriotic, there being two families of that name in town with four sons in the service, one of which proudly but sadly has changed the blue of the service star in the window, to a gold star, in memory of the son who has given all to his country—Wednesday – Flag Day—Mr. Smith accompanied his youngest son only seventeen years of age, to Knoxville to sign for him to enter the Navy.

The other Smith boys, sons of Mrs. Susie Smith, are Harold, Fletcher, Clay, and Marvin, and are scattered in various branches of the service.

*Mr. Smith was heard to say, "All my boys, one who will never come back, volunteered."…
"They are all buying war bonds and sending them home regularly."*

Jack stopped and set the cutting down. He wasn't sure that there might not be more left on the field of honor for his parents to mourn. Three blue stars and one gold star hung in the front window of his mother's home now. He knew his family wasn't the only family in this fight. He looked around the hut at the four other men here with him now. Men from all over America and the world were fighting this fight alongside his brothers. They all had to win this war. Reaching for the smaller press clippings, he perused them quickly. Jack found little interest in the brief recounts of the missions. He returned his attention to the letter.

I am staying in Rockwood right now with Vern and ride to work every day with a friend. We are lucky; since we both work together we get some extra gas ration coupons. Vern sends her love and looks forward to the day you come home.

Mary and Martha are doing fine now but Mary was sick a little while back. Vern gave her the last can of pineapple that she had been saving to bake a cake, anything for your sick child. Mary enjoyed it. Oh, the girls won second prize in the scrap metal drive but had to give up their tricycles to win. We hope it helps.

It's been so long since we have had any bananas or other fruit. Living together the way we do lets us get more out of our ration books, still not much sugar, coffee, or meat around though. Thank God, Mom and Dad still have the farm. Dad brought us a ham from a hog he slaughtered last fall along with some vegetables Mom had put up then. It was the first meat we'd had in months.

I am looking forward to you coming home. I truly enjoyed the dinner in Knoxville when you were home last. Do you have any idea how much longer it will be?

Jack knew he had a ways to go yet to sixty-five, and he didn't want to jinx himself by talking or writing about it.

The newspapers around here make it sound like it's going to be awhile. We all hope and pray that it's sooner than later. This war has gone on long enough. Vern's sewing needles are all dull and the girls need new shoes but the money really isn't there. If Vern's sewing needles give out, I don't know what we'll do. I guess we will need to try and find some way to sharpen them. The girls are already using string to hold their underwear up, all the elastic is gone.

I'm sorry about the quality of the paper but it's all we can get right now.

Well, I need to get to bed now. I get up so early that if I don't go to bed early I won't get enough rest. Can't wait for your homecoming, be careful. I'll write again soon.

Love,
Rosalie

Jack laid the letter down on his chest and stared into the curved roof of the hut and thought about Rosie's words for a while. He picked up the newspaper clippings and read through them all again. He wondered what it would be like back home. He could tell from the letters and the little news they did get here that America and his little piece of it were changing. He wondered what he would have to go home to.

❧

Neither Jack nor Rosalie had any idea how important the Clinton River Project was going to be to America, until August 6, 1945. The coming reality of August 6 would be brought about by people like Rosalie, who worked diligently to serve their country on a variety of projects—from Enrico Fermi's first self-sustaining chain reaction of neutrons, in his nuclear reactor under the squash court at the University of Chicago on December 1–2, 1942, to the creation and construction of complex and secret facilities in Hanford, Washington; Oak Ridge, Tennessee; and Los Alamos, New Mexico. It was the hard work and determination of all the good men and women in the CCC and TVA that had made a success of Oak Ridge National Laboratories, known before and during the war as the Clinton River Project. Commissioned as part of the Manhattan Project, the code name of the entire top-secret nuclear program, the plant was crafting the deadly product of its design by this point in the war. Dedicated Americans had built the electrical power system and the developing industrial infrastructure in eastern Tennessee that allowed the project to succeed. Just as the CCC and other Depression-era relief programs had reshaped American lives and politics, men like General Leslie R. Groves and Dr. Robert Oppenheimer and their colleagues were getting ready to reshape the lives and politics of the entire world.

The August 6th mission would succeed from the combined results of these widely separated projects and a long series of political and economic events. These events culminated in the forced fission of a plutonium-cored weapon inside what was referred to as the "gadget" at the "Trinity Site"—the first of the three nuclear weapons America would ultimately possess at that time. The Trinity Site was also known as site "S," and was located in the desert, fifty miles from Alamogordo, New Mexico, next to a place known by two Spanish names, *Obscuro* and *Jornada Del Muerto*, by the locals. They mean, respectively, Dark and Expedition of Death.

The Manhattan Project, its operation and design, objectives, and final goals were known to only a select few in the highest levels of the military and government. Or so it was thought, despite references to the program by other members of the Allied forces. The British referred to "it" as "tube alloys," and Stalin had apparently been fully apprised of the weapon's capabilities by a complex network of spies (Fuchs, Gold, Rosenberg, and Greenglass). Some, such as World War I ace Eddie Rickenbacker, would argue that the White House itself supplied Stalin with his knowledge of the project's design and objectives.[167]

Whatever the case, a complicated project was spread across America and was heading toward completion in the hills of eastern Tennessee and the deserts around Alamogordo. The scope of the project would become clear to the world on August 6, 1945, when a B-29 Superfortress named the *Enola Gay* (after the mother of pilot Paul W. Tibbets Jr.) took off at 0245 from the 509th Composite Group stationed on Tinian Island. The Japanese people and their government were made devastatingly aware of the Manhattan Project's true potential when Colonel Tibbets flew the B-29 over its target, where Major Tom Ferebee, the bombardier, dropped the approximately

---

167   *Rickenbacker*; Edward V. Rickenbacker; New York; Fawcett Crest; Copyright 1967

nine-thousand-pound uranium-235 bomb called "Little Boy" on Hiroshima. It was the first of two nuclear weapon devices in US possession and the second such device to be exploded on the Earth's surface. Detonating nineteen hundred feet above the city, the bomb killed upward of eighty thousand residents.

Ferebee wasn't aware of the type or potential magnitude of the weapon he had dropped until it detonated in a blinding flash. He had been handpicked by Tibbets because of his skill with the Norden bombsight. According to Ferebee, Tibbets had said that Ferebee was "the best bombardier who ever looked through the eyepiece of a Norden bombsight." Although the mission navigator Theodore J. Van Kirk doubted the Norden bombsight's capabilities, Ferebee had confidence in it. Speaking of the bombardier, Van Kirk said, "He was like a magician with that bombsight." He then qualified his remark by adding, "The Norden bombsight was supposed to put a bomb in a pickle barrel from thirty thousand feet. All I said was they must have had a very, very large pickle barrel."[168]

At the time of the detonation, copilot Robert Lewis pounded Tibbets on the shoulder shouting, "Look at that! Look at that! Look at that!" He was pointing to the swelling mushroom cloud characteristic of nuclear explosions.

After a bit he remarked, "I can taste atomic fission; it tastes like lead." Later, in his journal he expressed amazement for his part in the event, saying, "My God, what have we done?"

In Hiroshima, the single nuclear explosion consumed a radius of one and a half miles from the center point of detonation; people, animals, plants, and buildings were all consumed by the release of a massive amount of energy of unprecedented power.

Even after Hiroshima and the resumption of conventional bombing, Japan rejected a second warning and an appeal for its unconditional surrender from President Truman. Therefore, Truman approved another nuclear drop. On August 9, 1945, Major Charles Sweeney flew his B-29 *Bockscar* over Nagasaki after aborting the run on the primary target, the Kokura arsenal. He dropped "Fat Man"—the last nuclear weapon in America's arsenal at that time. The 10,200-pound plutonium bomb detonated sixteen hundred feet off the ground, annihilating an estimated forty thousand immediately and thousands later from radiation sickness and nuclear fallout.

This second nuclear blast over Nagasaki was the event that finally obtained the unconditional surrender of the Japanese military and government that the Allies had requested. Unfortunately, the Japanese military resisted just long enough to allow the Russians to involve themselves in the Pacific campaign by invading Korea. Their proxy occupation of half the Korean peninsula helped Stalin pursue the pre-1905 policies of instability, which were now renewed by reclaiming territories that they had lost to Japan earlier in the century.[169]

---

168   My tribute to Tom Ferebee, bombardier on the Enola Gay; http://home.att.net/
~sallyann4/ton-ferebee.html
169   Soviet Aims in Korea and the Origins of the Korean War: 1945–1950 New Evidence
from Russian Archives; Woodrow Wilson International Center for Scholars; http://www.
wilsoncenter.org/topics/pubs/ACFB76.pdf

Beyond the sheer material consequences of the bombs, the blasts left lingering moral questions. Truman's decision to use nuclear weapons would be second-guessed, rightly or wrongly, for generations to come.[170, 171] With the bomb now a reality, death could come in one blinding, vaporizing flash instead of as raging firestorms. Yet such firestorms, on more than one mission, had killed more civilians at one time than the detonation of a single nuclear weapon ever would.

∞

Like the others in their cots, Roland and Hiram were absorbed in reading their cherished connections to home, as the invading cold front started to filch the heat from their hut. Roland quietly read Marguerite's letter, drifting back to their meeting while he was in training in Texas. Their romance and commitment grew during his time as an instructor there. He missed her. The relationship had not come without some pain. He realized the complexity that the relationship had caused at home, a relationship that had led him to him divorce his wife. His family had never been happy with his first whirlwind war marriage anyway, and now it was even more complicated. He shivered as much from the letter as he did from the cold. His family had quit writing as much as they had, but he persisted in writing to them.

Hiram interrupted Roland's thoughts with a chuckle. "Where does this guy come up with all this crazy stuff?"

Lord Haw-Haw was going on and on about how the Americans were being stooges for the Bolsheviks. He propagandized about how they were going to be destroyed by the Communists if they persisted in helping them. They all listened as he encouraged the Americans to wake up and to defect to help the Germans stop the Russians.

The guys got good laughs from it all, so the brass didn't jam it. Besides, the troops enjoyed the music, which helped beat back the thoughts of flak on the next mission or the one they had just completed.

"Damn, I thought this winter was over," Hiram complained. "I guess not, it's getting chilly."

Jack agreed.

Rolling out of his cot to get the fire going, Jack walked by the door and picked up an armload of wood. He opened the door of the Franklin-like potbellied stove only to discover that the ashes needed to be cleaned out.

"Someone needs to give me a hand here. I'll scoop if someone will carry out."

Roland eased off his cot and looked around for something to carry the ashes in. "Well, what do you recommend?"

"Get that empty coal sack over there in the corner."

"Good idea."

---

170   The Atomic Century, The 1940's, http://www.dpi.anl.gov/dpi2/timeslines/1940s.htm
171   *The Glory and the Dream, A Narrative History of America 1932–1972*, William Manchester, Chapter 11 pp 308–311, Chapter 12 pp 371–388.

Working quickly as a team, they finished the job. Then Roland carried the sack out as Jack built up the kindling on the little bit of paper they had scraped together. Lighting the match almost inside the stove, Jack carefully touched off the paper's edges all around and then slid the smallest kindling over the flames. Almost willing the wood to ignite, he saw the small pieces smoke and then begin to burn. Jack placed small pieces of wood on top of the burning kindling and paper, then placed larger pieces of wood on top of it all. The larger pieces began to smoke, so Jack placed three pieces of coal on top of them, and then eased the door closed. *Another successful mission,* Jack thought, as he lay back down on his cot.

"Good job," Hiram commended.

"No sweat."

Earl came into the tent pitching the packs of laundry to the rightful owner and telling them what they owed him as they caught it.

"Thanks, Earl," was repeated around the room.

"How's Lord Haw-Haw today?" Earl asked. "Germany still winning the war?"

"Just the usual stuff," Hiram chuckled.

"I wonder if the Russians hear the same thing where they are, only in Russian," Earl added. "Have they played any good music yet?"

His propaganda report complete, Lord Haw-Haw began signing off.

"Here at the Reich center Hamburg, station Bremen and station DXB, this is the end of our news in English. In thanking you for your attention I would remind you that our next transmission of news in English takes place at a quarter past nine Greenwich Mean Time and will be given from the Reich station Hamburg, station Bremen, station DXB on your 31-meter band. Good night."

"That's it for the laughs tonight, guys," Hiram mocked. "Old Lord Haw-Haw is off the air."

"It's almost chow time anyway," Bill said. "That will be good for a few laughs too."

Hiram reached over to tune in the American radio station for some music. He made some delicate adjustments to the tuner dial, finally getting it set so the reception was as clear as it was ever going to be, and then fell back onto his cot.

The growing warmth from the stove along with the music began to relax everyone as they got back to reading their lifelines to home.

In his barracks along with his fellow officers, Ralph settled into his cot using his flight jacket as a pillow. They too had made a run to the Post and now enjoyed their letters from home. Ralph had received two letters.

Ralph was reading Norma's first letter again, and thinking of the last time they were together. It had been a long time since he had seen or held her. Reading the letter made him want now more than ever before for his sixty-fifth to arrive. Before reading any of the letters he received from her, he put them in order of their post date, from oldest to the most recent. This way he could take pleasure in reading the letters in their proper order. Reaching over, he picked up Norma's next letter, and opened it carefully so as not to tear the envelope. He'd be able to put it back in, saving it to be read later if he wanted.

About this time everyone in the barracks noted the rapid change in the weather.

"Hey, Ralph, work your magic on that stove, how 'bout it?"

"I need to teach you guys how to do this," Ralph joked. "What are you going to do when I'm back in the states? Freeze to death?"

"Ah, Ralph, you're the best with that thing, we ain't letting you go home. They're goin-ta raise the mission minimum to eighty so you have to stay."

Ralph thought about Norma and knew it could happen, as it had happened before.

"You guys sure as heck better hope not. They've done it before," Ralph said.

The men in the tent became solemnly quiet as they realized just how right Ralph was. It hadn't been such a funny joke after all.

Ralph got up out of his cot to begin his cognac magic on the wood in the belly of the stove. With two shots of cognac, a lit match…**whoosh**…the fire blazed to life. Everyone let out a fake cheer of appreciation punctuated by one Bronx cheer. The hurrahs were followed by a slow but steady warming of those flanking the stove. The guys farthest from the stove had a while to wait. The fire took time to heat the stove's metal enough to warm them all.

After the fire was going well, Ralph opened his footlocker. He reached into the right corner and pulled out a small bottle of reconstituted powdered milk he had gotten at morning mess today. He pulled a small chipped saucer out from under the stove and then poured the milk onto the saucer. After he put the bottle away, Ralph went back to reading his letters from home.

The stovepipe in Ralph's barracks joined those across the camp in pouring out smoke that smelled of burning wood and coal. For the few quarters that didn't yet have a fire, small bands of men of all ranks could be seen scrounging for wood. At the far edges of the base some trees were being brought down by those bivouacked close to them. Once the fires were burning, the next priority arose.

Slowly men were collecting in groups and moving toward the mess hall in their squadron's bivouac area. As the lines formed outside the mess halls, the men worked at staying warm. Cigarettes started burning, feet stamped, and hands rubbed against one another; everyone was eager to get inside. The airmen talked about the cold front; no one talked about the day's events or had any thoughts about tomorrow's possibilities. Once inside, the officers and enlisted men ate the meal in an equally bland way. Coffee with cigarettes topped it all off, before everyone began their determined evacuation of the mess hall for the warmth of their potbellied stoves.

Returning to his hut after mess, Ralph was greeted by the comforting warmth of his creation. He kicked open the stove door with his right foot and threw in two logs, which sent sparks flying up the stovepipe. After closing the stove's door with his foot, he walked over to the naked bulb hanging down in the center of the hut. It hung over a small table with one chair and three stools. Ralph turned the switch.

"Thank God for generators," he said aloud.

The bulb radiated harsh light, which caused Ralph to quickly turn his head away from it. The light was appreciated, though, because it let the guys enjoy their off-hours after meals.

He threw his heavy flight jacket on the bed, and then reached into the zippered pouch on the side of his B-4 to retrieve a deck of cards. Ralph stepped over Poontang, asleep beside his cot; she had drunk all the milk from the bowl. The cat was curled up asleep on the floor about a foot away from the stove.

Ralph reached down and stroked the cat along its back, waking Poontang briefly. Still laying on her side, the cat arched her back with all four legs stretched out; her foot pads and claws were extended out fully. She opened her jaws wide with a big yawn, sticking her rough red tongue out at the same time. She relaxed, looked up at Ralph, purred briefly, and then curled back into a ball, wrapping her tail around her body, and fell back to sleep.

"How's Poontang?" Hulse asked as he walked into the toasty-warm hut.

"Taking real good care of her, this cat keeps the mice away."

"I don't know about that, but I do know I'm ready to play some cards," Hulse replied. "So start dealing."

In the mess hall, Ralph had been able to talk up another game of bridge. He went about getting the game ready as the other two officers walked into the hut. No one was much interested in going to the Officers Club tonight because they were all on flight status in the morning. As a rule, that meant no drinking. Most of those on flight status had settled into their own "home away from home." A few headed over to relax with a scotch and water at the Officers Club, but not many.

Ralph shuffled the deck and dealt the first hand. Bids were made by his partner and the game began. Ralph felt good about the hand, which proved to be an accurate premonition. When the game wrapped up, it was Ralph and his partner who had won.

Bridge could be a great game, Ralph thought, *time passed quickly.*

But now the cards were put away and the table cleared. The two visiting officers headed for their hut as Ralph and Hulse stretched out on their cots. As much as they didn't want them, thoughts about where they might be going in the morning crept into their minds.

As the day got older, the evening grew colder, and the blankets were pulled tighter. Ground fog began forming in the low areas around the base and countryside as the chilled air caused the suspended water vapor to condense. Fires were stoked by cold men all around the base as sleep came slowly. Eventually sleep came to all and let them drift into its mindless embrace.

The next morning's mission was to be followed by many more missions into France and Belgium for the 416th. The push to gain complete air dominance was under way. By the end of May the group had flown thirteen missions against Luftwaffe Aerodromes, nine against marshaling yards, six against No-ball sites, one coastal gun emplacement, and one radar site. The cost to America was twenty-two men killed or listed as missing in action.[172]

Across every theater of operation, action was nonstop. The Allies were fighting and dying on all fronts as the Soviet troops recaptured Sevastopol. The Allies assaulted the Gustav Line south of Rome, which was followed by the Wehrmacht's retreat from Anzio to the Adolf Hitler line, later renamed the Dora line. (Hitler did not want his name associated with it for fear of negative propaganda value). Meanwhile, German troops surrendered to the Russians in the Crimea.[173] In the South Pacific, the Allies were consolidating their holdings on Aitape, Hollandia, and New Guinea, while invading Biak Island, New Guinea, on May 27. [174]

By the start of May and certainly by the end, the Nazi regime was feeling the pressure of all-out war against it. In what appeared to be a demonstration of the Nazis' desperate need for materials, Himmler offered to trade Jewish prisoners for war materials or cash. He ordered Rudolf Höss to Auschwitz to oversee the eugenic extermination of the Hungarian Jews, who were being shipped there from Hungary. By May 24, 1944, an estimated one hundred thousand Jews had been killed, and half of the estimated Hungarian Jews had arrived at Auschwitz. The Third Reich was feeling the pressure to complete their criminally deranged, eugenic, genocidal exterminations before the world exposed them.[175]

The invasion of Normandy by the Allies and the ultimate liberation of the continent that held the death camps were to come, with the 416th doing its share in the effort.

---

172   *Attack Bombers We Need You: A History of the 416th Bomb Group*; Ralph Conte, copyright 2001

173   The History Place: World War Two in Europe Timeline; http://www.historyplace.com/wordwar2/timeline/ww2time.htm

174   The History Place: Timeline of Pacific War; http://www.historyplace.com/united-states/pacificwar/timeline.htm

175   The History Place: Holocaust Timeline; http://www.historyplace.com/worldwar2/holocaust/timeline.html

Chapter Eight

The Crossing

Anyone who has to fight, even with the most modern weapons, against an enemy in complete command of the air, fights like a savage against modern European troops.

– Field Marshal Erwin Rommel

"Clouds and rain, fellas. Ain't gonna be much flyin' today," Hiram observed as they left morning mess.

Clouds, rain, and fog shrouded the British Isles this first day of June. The bad weather was partially caused by the warm water of the Gulf Stream that brought moisture-laden air that mixed with the cooler air over the Isles. The resultant clouds and rain grounded nearly the entire British and American air forces that day. No one in the 416th complained much, though, having been lucky enough to have slept in since there was no muster for a morning mission.

After mess, the airmen hung around their huts enjoying the morning. Gus Ebenstein seemed to be the only one particularly upset about not flying today. He wanted to get his mission quota over with, and didn't let anyone forget it.

"OK, Gus, we get it," Earl finally succumbed.

Hiram added, "Don't you have a leave today anyway?"

"Hell yeah, heading to Braintree to catch the early train into London. The Officers Club there in Soho opens around ten-hundred hours. Guess I'll see you two sometime tomorrow." Gus walked away.

"Maybe you will, depends on the weather," Earl said, as he looked around at the sky. "Got the duty tomorrow. If this holds up I'll be on standby. I'm heading down to the flight line to check on Helen. What about you?"

"Not a bad idea. My bird has been shot up pretty bad lately by those Krauts."

After snagging a couple of bicycles, the two officers headed off to the flight line. They encountered most of the flight crews examining their aircraft, stopping occasionally to chat. Eventually the two cyclists diverged as they headed to their planes' hardstands. Flight crews were talking with their ground crews all along the line as they got their hands dirty packing bearings or turning a wrench—teamwork that built esprit de corps. The mission success involved everyone, and the ground crew knew it.

As the repairs continued on the weather-grounded aircraft, the United States Army Air Force was busy elsewhere. In the Pacific, consolidated B-24s were flying missions against the Japanese-held Kurile Islands, while B-25 Mitchells flew anti-shipping missions, all from Alaska. Cover was flown by P-38s. Burma, India, and China would see their share of missions as the 10th and 14th air forces flew B-25s against bridges, ammo dumps, gun emplacements, barracks, and troop concentrations.

The Pacific atolls were busy as well, with A-20s, B-24s, B-25s, P-38s, P-39s, and P-40s from the 5th, 7th, and 13th air forces attacking assigned targets and targets of opportunity. The Japanese, like the Nazis, were feeling pressure from every side along their overextended and under-defended frontiers.

Other Allied positions got their licks in on the Nazis too. The Soviet Army was threatening the Wehrmacht's eastern front, after having repulsed "Operation Barbarossa"—the Nazis' attempt to invade the Soviet Union by holding the line between Leningrad, Moscow, and Stalingrad. This victory came at a great human cost to the Russian people and to the Wehrmacht's Sixth Army at Stalingrad.

On the southern front America's 12th Tactical Air Force in Italy flew sorties against front-line troop concentrations, bivouac areas, motor transports, railways, road and rail junctions, bridges, and trains. Fighter sweeps looked for targets of aerial or ground opportunity.

It was only in England with its noncompliant weather that the Allies had to take a breath. Only one hundred of the 9th Air Force's B-26s mounted missions from the island. The missions were directed against enemy airfields and coastal gun emplacements from Belgium to the Cherbourg Peninsula.

The next several days saw the ongoing buildup of troops, material, trucks, and tanks on the mainland and coastal areas of England. It was becoming harder to keep secret. Harbors were filled with naval vessels of all types. Troops were bivouacked in English homes and in large camps. Large areas of the English countryside were off-limits to civilians and even most military personnel. Everyone knew the day was coming but when and where was the secret. Soon, "Operation Overlord" would be unleashed.

Available to very few eyes, the plans for Operation Overlord were concealed in documents stamped "BIGOT" (the reverse of the identification for mail "TO GIB," To Gibraltar). The responsibility of planning the invasion had fallen to British Lieutenant General Frederick Morgan after the 1943 Casablanca Conference. Overlord was a monumental strategy that began consuming the output of the US economy almost immediately. With painstaking attention to detail, Morgan drafted an immense plan, which required the creation of new weapons of war and the integration of logistics and time schedules. Such complexity was reduced to a short statement made by General Dwight D. Eisenhower, supreme commander of the European Theater of Operations. Eisenhower said the goal of Overlord was "[to] land amphibious and airborne forces on the Normandy coast between Le Havre and the Cotentin Peninsula and, with the successful establishment of a beachhead with adequate ports, to drive along the lines of the Loire and the Seine rivers into the heart of France, destroying the German strength and freeing France." This statement went to the heart of the issue but could be accomplished only if, as learned in the skies over Britain between July 30 and September 15, 1940, air supremacy belonged to the Allies.

The Germans' goal of total air supremacy, *Unternehmen Adler* (Operation Eagle), had begun in the skies over the British Isles in 1940 as Hitler planned for Operation Sea Lion, the Nazi invasion of Britain. During those critical months contrails crisscrossed the skies over southeast England as Luftwaffe Air Marshal Hermann Göring sent medium bombers and their fighter escorts over England day after day. Spitfires and Hurricanes greeted every wave, having been given advance warning by the English radar system.

Göring attempted to accomplish in a few months against the English what would take the Allies years to do against the Luftwaffe—obtain air supremacy before the invasion. The opportunity to attrite the air power of both the Germans and the Japanese finally presented itself on December 7, 1941, when the now global conflict brought the overwhelming war machinery of the United States into the fray.

Lieutenant General Frederick Morgan went to work a year later, knowingly or not, applying Sun Tzu's principles in *The Art of War* to the Allies' "Europe first" objective. Examples of the Allies' purposeful or accidental use of the ancient Chinese text can be found throughout the war. Surprisingly, the ancient treatise outlined the complexity of modern warfare. Sun Tzu's seven critical "initial estimations" were seemingly applied by the Overlord command planners. Sun Tzu asked the would-be warrior the following questions:

1. "Which ruler has the 'tao' [the way to survival or extinction?"

The advantage here went to the Allies after December 7, when US sentiment fell strongly to entering the war. The eugenic, Nazi principle of "to the victor the spoils" would fall in the Allies' favor. After extensive attacks across Europe and the obligation to defend much wide-ranging territory, Hitler had lost his capacity to wage unlimited warfare. This capacity was to become the overwhelming forte of the Allies.

2. "Which general has greater ability?"

Arguably Hitler had made the correct choice in placing Field Marshal Erwin Rommel in command of the Western front. Yet, when Hitler enforced his own faulty military judgments, which were supported by his own sycophantic command structure, it overrode Rommel's true strategic and tactical strengths. Again, the advantage fell to the Allies.

3. "Who has gained Heaven and Earth?"

This question was never to be in doubt, since the Allies' aircraft, naval, tank, arms, and munitions industries around the world began producing the weapons to conquer both realms.

4. "Whose laws and orders are more thoroughly implemented?"

The Nazi war machine was disciplined and determined. There were no allies to bicker with, and no other nation's generals with postwar demands to negotiate with. In Hitler's mind this war had truly become a question of Aryan survival, undertaken through total war. This completely controlling and distracting belief allowed the Allies to gain the advantage.

5. "Whose forces are stronger?"

Individually no single nation would fare well against the Nazis or the Japanese or, for that matter, Italy. Paraphrasing what Churchill had already said, England's navy and France's army were the keys. But their objectives had to be married for the nations to succeed early on in the conflict, and they weren't. Eisenhower would see to it that the collective might of the European allies would become a deadly well-coordinated military machine.

6. "Whose officers and troops are better trained?"

This advantage also fell to the Allies, since they had secured the vital natural, technological and sexual reproductive resources. The world's oil reserves, farmlands, and mineral resources were theirs. These resources provided them the time to train, enlarge, and deploy their militaries, enhancing their ability to take the destructive powers of war to the ever-shrinking frontiers of the Axis powers.

7. "Whose rewards and punishments are clearest?"

For the Allies victory was perceived as the preservation of a way of life. The true depths of the atrocities inside Germany were known to just a few but threatened the opportunities for the people of the free world to live their way of life.

The Allied command continued evaluating the logistics as Sun Tzu had elucidated. Waging war is an expensive undertaking, as demonstrated by Japan's escalating military budget in trying to maintain the war effort in Manchuria and by America's public debt, which at the high point exceeded its gross national production by 20 percent. That is, America owed more than it could make in a year. Defense expenditures of the US government represented 20 percent of the GNP, and up to 90 percent of total federal spending. The Russians also knew that waging war was expensive, and so they left only charred earth behind as they retreated in the face of Operation Barbarossa. This move forced the Wehrmacht to overextend its supply lines, and resulted in the pivotal Battle of Stalingrad.

By denying the enemy its economy and thereby its ability to resupply its troops, the Allies gained the advantage. In words from the treatise on war, "It takes a thousand pounds of rice to get one pound of rice to the man fighting at the front lines." The Japanese and the Nazis could have mitigated this problem as Sun Tzu recommended, by "[treating] your prisoners well." Sun Tzu suggested that conquerors treat the occupied populations with respect, so that they would help you. Yet, all three Axis powers failed at this task, making the Allies a welcome liberator.

The ability to plan offensives was becoming the talent of the Allies. From Guadalcanal up through the Pacific and in Africa, Sicily, and Italy, the Allies had learned the logistics of a successful amphibious campaign. The Allies' general staff followed *The Art of War*'s recommendations for the Normandy invasion. Sun Tzu advised: "The realization of warfare is to attack the enemy's plans, next is to attack their alliances, next to attack their armies, and the lowest is to attack their fortified cities." To attack the enemy's plans, the Allies denied the Nazis access to an expanding network of resources. To attack their alliances, the Allies forced the weaker Italy to capitulate, which demanded that the Wehrmacht take over the defense of its third front in the south. At the same time, Japan could not assist Germany in attacking the Soviet Union on a second front, since the Japanese were forced into the Pacific to ensure the supply of oil and war materials after the total American embargo in 1941. Allied troops attacked the Axis's armies by ringing the Axis powers and forcing them to fight individually on multiple fronts, and thereby shrinking their frontiers. The Allies avoided attacking fortified cities until absolutely necessary, for instance, deceiving the enemy by continually attacking the Pas de Calais area while avoiding the fortresses there and on the Cotentin Peninsula.

The biggest advantage achieved by the Allies was that Hitler put his armies into difficulty often by not comprehending the battlefield. Sun Tzu advised against the leader who does "not [understand] his army's tactical balance of power [ch'üan] but undertakes responsibility for command. Then the officers will be doubtful." Instead of relying on his generals, Hitler took command of his armies at inopportune times and asked them to perform impossible tasks. Sun Tzu's prediction of doubtful officers was borne out by Colonel Klaus von Stauffenburg's failed assassination attempt against Hitler.

Sun Tzu's concept of military disposition became the next issue for the planners. The various forces had taken many of the actions recommended by the Chinese master. Sun Tzu advised: "One who cannot be victorious assumes a defensive posture; one who can be victorious attacks…Those who excel at defense bury themselves away below the lowest depths of earth. Those who excel at offense move from above the greatest heights of Heaven. Thus they are able to preserve themselves and attain complete victory." While Germany was busy building a defensive posture from Denmark to the Franco-Spanish border, the Allies were preparing to move to the greatest heights, and to annihilate the enemy with minimal losses.

In planning the offensive across the Continent, the Allies proved they understood the concept of mechanized warfare, having integrated the combined-arms approach to blitzkrieg. Marrying the attack aircraft to the mobility and firepower of the tank would prove a deadly combination over the plains of France. This concept of combined arms warfare was developed by the British after World War I but aggressively and successfully used by the Germans at the start of the Second World War. The real fruits of this strategy would be born out on the day of the Normandy Invasion, with naval, air, and infantry power overwhelming the fixed positions of the Wehrmacht. Or as Sun Tzu said, "This is the strategic disposition of force [hsing]."

To have strategic military power, Sun Tzu advises the warrior that "one who employs strategic power [shih] commands men in battle…Thus the strategic power of one who excels at employing men in warfare is comparable to rolling round boulders down a thousand-fathom mountain. Such is the strategic configuration of power." Here the Chinese strategist suggests that the commander must have complete control over very determined fighting forces that are willing to ceaselessly throw themselves at the enemy. The Allied attack had been ceaseless since 1940, and had been accelerating every year after that. The bottom of the hill was Berlin and Tokyo. The logs and boulders were the planes, bombs, and men who hurled themselves day after day into battle after battle all around the world. The weight of the onslaught was burying the Axis powers.

In a section titled "Vacuity and Substance," Sun Tzu elaborates on how a military should operate. He writes, "Now the army's disposition of force [hsing] is like water. Water's configuration [hsing] avoids heights and races downward. The army's disposition of force [hsing] avoids the substantial and strikes the vacuous." The effective commander, argues Sun Tzu, attacks where the chances of victory are already high, and avoids the battles where the army is at a disadvantage. The Allies used a similar strategy as they moved into Europe. First, they assaulted Rommel's rear guard in Africa, landing behind him and forcing him to fight on two fronts. Then, they filled the vacuum by attacking Germany's southern flanks through Italy. Next, they slid into Europe through the narrow corridor between Caen and the Cherbourg Peninsula. Both locations were of critical strategic value to the Allies, having been assigned top priority in the early phase of the assault. In each instance, the Allies operated like water, moving into regions where they had a clear strategic advantage.

While they took the advantage where they could, the Allies could not follow all of Sun Tzu's rules for military combat, due to the varied nature of terrain and warfare. The campaign in Italy fell victim to the mountains. There the Wehrmacht dominated the heights, thereby preventing the complete destruction of their forces. The Allies tried to execute the other rules by avoiding traps, allowing retreating forces to escape and stopping to allow the Wehrmacht to regroup after the liberation of France and "Operation Market Garden." After the pause, the powers assaulted one another in the Battle of the Bulge, which marked the start of the invasion of Germany and the destruction of the Wehrmacht.

Throughout the war the Allies followed in varying degrees the tactics presented in a section of *The Art of War* called "Nine Changes." To be a successful commander, Sun Tzu recommends,

- "avoiding entrapping terrain"–which America did by island hopping in the Pacific and not invading in the Pas de Calais coast of France where the Germans had anticipated and planned for the invasion.
- "uniting with their allies on focal terrain"–which the Allies did in Burma, Africa, and Europe by bringing the displaced militaries into the fight and using them to assault the common enemy. Uniting with the Chinese, the Poles, the Free French, and others against the Axis powers empowered the Allies.
- "not remaining on isolated terrain"
- "making strategic plans for encircled terrain" – avoiding and exploiting
- "fighting on fatal terrain" – battles in Corregidor, Bataan, Guadalcanal, and Bastogne were fought from immobile defensive positions. Guadalcanal and Bastogne proved victorious but were constantly in doubt. Fighting for the strategic.
- "avoiding the wrong roads"
- "avoiding strong armies and fortified cities" – which Operation Overlord was designed to do
- "not contesting all terrain" – more commonly a tactic of the Pacific war as islands were bypassed, leaving the Japanese troops to fend for themselves without resupply possible.

Finally, "Nine Changes" warns of the total breakdown of authority:

- "There are commands from the ruler that are not accepted" – which was evidenced in the final unwillingness of Germans to follow Hitler at his downfall

Sun Tzu's suggestions in a section called "Maneuvering the Army" were conducted on a global scale, with armies maneuvering over, around, and through the fighting on what the strategist named the "Nine Terrains." To ensure victory, the clever commander will configure the terrain to the army's advantage, Sun Tzu argues. The Allies accomplished this task on a variety of scales, from platoon skirmishes to larger efforts, such as island bombardments prior to invasion, and massive efforts never before possible, such as the overall preparation of a continent for the D day invasion. Part of this preparation included incendiary attacks—which Sun Tzu recommended. These attacks became the forte of the Allies, who destroyed the enemy using the strategic, tactical, and support advantages that came with air superiority. Such air superiority led to firestorms in German and Japanese cities, napalm dropped on troop concentrations, and flamethrowers used at the most personal of levels to incinerate the enemy at close range, the last of which was commonplace in the Pacific Theater of Operations.

Espionage was to become a critical element in favor of the Allies. Sun Tzu focused on spies because they could offer an advantage to a general. He enumerated five types of spies—"local spies (people within the occupied towns), internal spies (government employees), double agents, expendable spies (spreaders of disinformation), and living spies (agents who return with their reports).[176, 177, 178] Information supplied by the fifth column from the French, Dutch, Swedish, and Polish underground, to name a few, empowered the Allies' intelligence arm. Intelligence from a number of sources—people within the occupied towns, government employees, and spreaders of disinformation— was used to great effect. The use of spies also benefited the enemy, as the 416th would learn.

The first phase of the Allied air war over Europe was to destroy the Luftwaffe. The American Eighth Air Force began its daylight missions into occupied Europe, as the Brits challenged the Luftwaffe at night. Every mission that Bomber Command and the Eighth Air Force flew was designed not only to destroy the enemy's capacity to wage war but more importantly to lure the fighters of Göring's Luftwaffe into a war of attrition that overwhelmingly favored the Allies. Drop tanks, which stored extra fuel, carried the heavily armed and durable P-47s to the outskirts of Germany as they escorted the B-17s on their missions in the fall of 1943.

In December of that year the "little plane that could"—the P-51—entered service over the skies of Europe. The redesigned and Rolls-Royce Merlin-powered P-51 Mustang had switched roles from a mediocre ground-attack fighter-bomber to that of arguably the best air-supremacy fighter of the war. Equipped with drop tanks, wing tanks, and an internal tank behind the pilot, the Mustang was capable of carrying sufficient fuel to reach Berlin from England and still return.

By January 1944 the Luftwaffe was losing the battle. In March, the Luftwaffe lost 56 percent of their available fighters. By June they had lost 2,262 fighter pilots—25

---

176   *The Art of War; Sun-tzu;* Translation by Ralph D. Sawyer; copyright 1994, pp 163–229
177   *The Wall Street Waltz: 90 Visual Perspectives;* Illustrated Lessons From Financial Cycles and Trends; Kenneth L. Fisher; copyright 1987; pp 168 & 186
178   *Great Battles of World War II;* John MacDonald; copyright 1986; pp 132–143

percent of them in May alone. The sky was filled with the aircraft of the nations allied against the eugenically driven Nazi Malthusians. Flying with near impunity, the American Ninth Air Force began its tactical campaign, or second phase of the air campaign, at "D day" minus sixty days. This phase consisted of isolating the battlefield by interdicting road, rail, rail yards, and bridges. Beginning twenty-one days before the ground invasion, the Ninth Air Force assaulted Luftwaffe airfields within a 130-mile radius of the invasion landing zones. Once the invasion began, the tactical air war would shift to battlefield interdiction and front-line support.

The strategic air war would carry the Eighth Air Force on a series of operations during the last days before the execution of "Operation Neptune"—the actual invasion operation of "Operation Overlord." June 2-5, 1944, found the heavies flying the deception missions of "Operation Cover" into the Pas de Calais area. Bombers and fighter-bombers of the Eighth would also interdict airfields, bridges, and coastal gun batteries. The Eighth flew carpetbagger missions into France, supplying the predominantly Communist French underground with agents, supplies, and materials to support the coming assault. [179,180,181,182]

❧

The 416th's role in the first two phases of the air war—bombing key sites on the Continent—had been accomplished in April and May 1944. Now, five days before the D day invasion began, no one at Wethersfield Air Base knew when or where it would happen, but the air was filled with the anticipation.

June 2nd greeted the 416th's crews on flight status in the usual way; it was a good day for flying, so it was a good day for fighting. Wing Operations had assigned the 416th another No-ball site. Operations wanted to prevent these weapons from creating problems during the invasion, for either the assault forces or rear logistics.

The second day of June proved to be a good one, with a solid hit on the Gorenflos V-1 target. On the third, the group targeted the Chartres Airdrome, deep inside France, one of the group's deepest penetrations over enemy territory. This attack was followed by an assault against the St. Pierre du Mont coastal gun emplacement on the fourth.

June was certainly shaping up to be a busy time, thought Lieutenant Bob Basnett, as he came to a standstill on the runway. Now, he was just happy to see the nose of the

179   Army Air Forces in World War II: Combat Chronology of the US Army Air Forces: June 1944; http://www.usaaf.net/chron/44/jun44.htm

180   D-Day 1944: Air Power Over the Normandy Beaches and Beyond: The US Army Air Forces in World War II; Richard P. Hallion, Air Force Historian; http://www.ibiblio.org/hyperwar/AAF/AAF-H-DDay/

181   Frequently Asked Questions for D-Day and the Battle of Normandy; http://www.ddaymuseum.co.uk/faq.htm

182   Eighth Air Force Historical Society: Timeline; http://www.8[th]afhs.org/combat1944a.htm

plane spin around 180 degrees in the revetment, and hear the engines shutting down, first the left and then the right. Bob made sure he had secured his Norden, and sat back to rest a few minutes while waiting for his ears to quit ringing. It seemed like it took longer after each mission for his hearing to return to normal. Well, it was time to go.

After removing his flak jacket, Bob opened the bottom hatch and dropped the heavy jacket out the opening. Thwop! He heard it hit the ground heavy. The chute followed, landing on top of the jacket with a similar sound. Basnett dropped out through the hatch feetfirst, careful not to catch his shoulder holster on the edges of the hatch. Hitting the ground with his legs straddling the jacket and chute, Basnett picked them up. Lieutenant Marzolf was climbing down from the cockpit as Bob stepped out from under the nose of the plane.

Both men looked into the sky beyond the end of the runway. They heard an A-20 on final approach with just one engine running hard.

"Who's that?

"Don't know. You got any idea, Sergeant Wellin?" Their gunner had just walked up beside them.

"I think it's Captain Conant. I believe it was them I saw get hit right before we came off target."

"Could be bad," Marzolf said. "They still have a five hundred hanging by its back shackle on that left wing."

The Havoc approached the end of the runway.

Conant was holding the rudder against the over-revved right engine while he pushed the aileron against the engine. He was trying to keep the left wing up, as he slipped toward the tarmac. He hoped the gear would come down when it was time. The hydraulic pressure had been dropping slowly as he nursed his flak-damaged bird over the dark water of the channel.

His navigator, McBrien, sat in his compartment with his eyes closed reciting the Lord's Prayer and wondering if he should have jumped. All communication with the group had been lost just after McBrien felt the German flak that wounded him. He had been unaware of the fire that had destroyed the radio and VHF equipment.

McBrien had relayed his injury to Conant. After that there was nothing to do but pray. McBrien didn't want to end up like that new guy, Nikas, and his two gunners, Newkirk and Scott. On yesterday's mission over Chartres Airdrome...MIA. They had taken hits just over the French coast on the way in. Nobody had seen any chutes.

Now, the Havoc was dropping farther, almost on the runway.

Conant hoped he had brake fluid so that he could stop once he was on the ground. He quickly checked the air pressure in his emergency brake air bottle. The dial read more than 450 psi. Lowering the landing gear lever, Conant heard the hydraulics strain to open the wheel well doors and move the gear. The hydraulic pressure dropped to zero as the hydraulic pumps strained to keep the fluid flowing and the pressure up.

Conant watched the dials anxiously, forced to wait as the ground sneaked up to meet him. Finally the gear lock-down and gave Conant the three green lights he was praying to see. Reassured, he hit the runway hard, which exacted a grimace and a cringe when he thought about the bomb hanging off the left wing.

Conant pulled the throttles back, slowing the plane, and then gradually applied his brakes. He wanted to avoid accidentally jarring the armed five-hundred-pound weapon out of its shackles as he eased the Havoc to a slow rolling stop. Feeling the Havoc slow to a controllable speed, the pilot made sure he had control of the steering and then nurtured his wounded bird to the side of the runway. As soon as possible, he sounded the escape alarm, and then, letting out a necessarily quick sigh, Conant began shutting down the engine. Before the propeller had come to a stop, his crew had moved away from the Havoc. Soon the emergency crews arrived with the ordnance-disposal men.

After an examination, McBrien's wounds were not found to be that serious, so he made the debriefing, which was followed by a trip to the flight surgeon and then to the Red Cross tent for coffee.

Mess was a beehive of scuttlebutt; everyone's leave had been canceled and those on leave had been called back to base.

"They've got us locked up pretty tight tonight, have you noticed?" Ralph asked his mess table.

"They've doubled the guards at the gates too," Earl said. "I couldn't get my laundry today."

"Somethun's up," Bill said. "Probably another one of those mobilization drills. Boy, was that a screwup back in April or what?" He got chuckles from all the others around the table.

"Well, I had a three-day R&R to Torquay canceled," Hiram lamented.

"Yeah, it's pretty nice there," said Ralph. "I was down that way with Sittarich and Damico last month. Hotels are nice. Heck, they got palm trees growing down there. Never thought I'd see that in England."

"Well, heck fire, I may never know now," Hiram complained.

Roland changed the pace of the discussion.

"I'm headin' to the O-club, guys. Anybody interested?"

"Won't be doin' us no good. They got it off-limits too," Jack said.

"Heck, I'm gunna go hit the sack then. See you guys later." Roland left.

"Not far behind ya, Roland," Jack said, as pulled the last draw on his cigarette, and then crushed it out in the ashtray.

The mess hall emptied more slowly than usual, since there was no place else to go. When they were sick of just sitting there, Ralph, Hulse, and Hiram decided to call it a night. Walking back to their Quonset huts, Hiram noted the clouds blowing in.

"Think we'll be flying tomorrow, fellas?"

"We'll know at 0430," Ralph said.

"Yeah, Weather ain't sure what's going on," Hulse said. "They think it's about fifty-fifty we'll be flying tomorrow." He looked up, then said, "At least that's what they told me before mess."

Hulse's comments quieted the talk during the final few paces to their cots.

The gaggle of officers split up, heading in different directions to their own barracks.

"See you guys later," said Ralph.

Everyone around the base slowly retreated to their homes and settled in for the night.

On Monday morning wake-up, clouds, intermittent rain, and grounding weather greeted the crews. But the weather didn't stop the ground crews who were patching up every serviceable aircraft. They had been tasked with ensuring that every plane that could fly would be ready to do just that.

After morning mess the flight crews "requisitioned" some bikes and headed down to the flight line. Along the way the officers noted a lot more activity than usual. Various crews were scavenging thoroughly around the boneyard.

"Gee whiz, they sure got those guys workin' hard today," said Jack, as he peddled his bike along the flight line.

"Busy as bees," Earl agreed.

"Hey, Dullnig!" Earl hollered out to the staff sergeant. "What's with these black and white stripes you're paintin' on the wings and fuselage?"

Normandy Invasion Preparations

Mission Maid A-20 nose art. Note the invasion stripes and
British soldier in left background.
Lieutenants on bikes at Wethersfield, which were bought
in Ireland during Escape and Evasion training; bikes were
coveted like gold.
(L to R): Lieutenants William (Bill) Tripp, Hiram Clark, Jack
Smith, Leo Poundstone and Earl Hayter
Reproduced with permission from Ralph Conte and Larry
Smith

Normandy Invasion Preparations

A-20 painted in D day invasion strips with maintenance
ground crews repairing landing gear. Here young combat
veterans visit ground crews on or after D day.
(L to R): Lieutenants Hiram Clark, William (Bill) Tripp, Earl
Hayter and unknown
Reproduced with permission from Ralph Conte and Larry
Smith

"Don't know, Lieutenant. Just been given orders by Operations to paint 'em all this way," Dullnig hollered back. "You guys are gunna stick out like a sore thumb up there."

"I wonder if it's just ours or are they painting everyone's?" Bill wondered out loud, as they looked around the squadron's revetments.

Bill spotted Sergeant Ken Bailey and called over to him. He was working on *Daddy Land's Commando.*

"You guys going to paint *Commando* with those stripes?"

"Yessir, got the orders this mornin'," Ken replied, as he continued his duties.

Ken had been with the 416th since the Lake Charles, Louisiana, days. He had come over on the same liner from New York and was assigned to *Daddy Land's Commando.* He was well respected for doing a good job in a difficult place.

"Dullnig," Earl shouted down the flight line. "You guys painting the whole group's planes?"

"Hell yeah, and they want it all done today. They're gunna have us here all day and half the night gettun' this done."

Engine Work

Pre- or post-D day engine work by the ground crew.
Note D day stripes on the wings.
Reproduced with permission from Ralph Conte

Never-Ending Maintenance

Photo was on or after D day, as evidenced by the invasion
stripes on the wing. Note the bomb on the wing's hard-point.
The bomb is not fused, since you can see the open tip without
the impeller arming fuse. On September 24, 1944, Technical
Sergeant Richard L. Haptonstall, a crew chief, was killed when
an engine he was overhauling tore loose from its supports,
crushing him to death.
Reproduced with permission from Ralph Conte

The day moved on without a break in the weather—a bland, gloomy, overcast day that belied the state of mind of the supreme commander of the ETO. General Eisenhower was receiving weather reports on a regular basis from Group Captain J.M. Stagg, the senior meteorological advisor to the supreme commander and his invasion staff.

Using weather data from June 3rd and 4th, Eisenhower had decided to postpone the planned invasion on the 5th of June. Group Captain Stagg continued to study the limited available data from weather balloons, aircraft weather sorties, surface-ship data, and land readings. Projections of the weather over the channel on June 6, 1944, were based on data from June 4th, and then reaffirmed in the early morning hours of June 5th. After seeing the predictions, the meteorological officer and representatives of the Royal Navy and the United States Army Air Force cast their votes on whether the weather was acceptable for an invasion. The result: two to one in favor of a clearing over the channel on June 6th. Along with clearer weather, all the multiple minimum requirements that each service branch needed to accomplish its mission would be present. Stagg presented this result to Eisenhower, who was well aware that the animal was ready to be loosed. Keeping it contained too long could result in compromises. The Nazis had their five types of spies operating round the clock too.

Eisenhower gave the order, and the radio broadcast that signaled the start of the invasion was sent. French men and women listening to the radio heard the BBC broadcast the critical lines from Paul Verlaine's poem *Chanson d' Automne, "Les sanglots longs des violins de l'automne."* Although the code was understood by German intelligence, Rommel had gone home for the sixth, doubting the ability of the Allies to successfully launch an invasion in the bad weather. [183, 184, 185]

All across the island aircraft carrier that England had become, preparations accelerated. Airborne crews, glider crews, deception units and Army Air Corps tactical air-support crews prepared for the onslaught.

At Wethersfield, Dullnig was completing his tour of the flight line, checking that all maintenance issues were completed as well as all that dang painting. It had worn into late Monday afternoon, and they had long since received their 0500 orders to paint and repair the planes for a maximum effort. That painting had to get done.

Throughout the day the men of the 416th had listened to aircraft of all type fly by the base. They were unaware of the destinations of the planes but the Germans along the French coast felt the reason, as tens of thousands of pounds of high-explosive ordnance fell on their concrete coastal gun emplacements, while they sat deep inside. Little did they know what would be greeting them at first light.

---

183   Analysing and Forecasting the Weather of Early June 1944; ECMWF; http://www.ec-mwf.int/research/era/dday
184   *Great Battles of World War II;* John MacDonald; copyright 1986; pp 132–143
185   Doctor on D-Day; Claude Matuchansky; *Annals of Internal Medicine,* 2001;134: 1075–1076

The day rolled on, with some clearing of the skies as mess wrapped up. The activity in the sky slowed some, at least in the sky around Wethersfield. After mess most everyone headed back to their barracks, but a few officers went over to Operations.

Walking in the front door Dave Hulse, Ralph Conte, Jack Smith, and Roland Enman confronted the officer of the day after a quick salute.

"What's up, Major Price?" Conte broke in. "Why you guys got us locked up so tight?"

Looking at the officers, Price hesitated more from ignorance than insight.

"Don't know, Ralph," Price began. "Orders came down from Wing to do it. The only other thing they said was to prepare for a maximum effort with orders to follow. We haven't heard anything since. I'm in the dark just like you fellas."

"Major, what's up with painting the planes with those crazy stripes?" Jack demanded. "We're gunna stick out like a sore thumb up there painted like that."

"Orders—that's all I know, guys."

"Well, sumthin's up," Jack replied. "Sumthin' big, I bet."

"You got that right, Jack," Roland added.

"Thanks, major." Hulse saluted, prompting the others to salute and follow him out the door.

The group headed back toward their barracks.

The day grew long in the tooth as every conceivable reason for the extra base security, the stripes on the planes, and the cancellation of all the leaves were discussed by every rank across the base. As the sun set on double daylight savings time, everyone became aware of the increasing air traffic. Slowly at first and then with a growing intensity, the darkening sky began to fill with the sound of aircraft.

"What do you think, guys?" Ralph asked.

They all listened as more and more planes lumbered eastward. Through the darkening skies the young officers noted C-47s and the occasional small group of B-17s or B-24s, before darkness took visual identification away.

Every man suspected the reason that they were here was about to begin. Getting back to their squadron's bivouac, they found nearly everyone else had been outside watching the ever-enlarging aerial armada heading southeast.

Chapter Nine
Protecting the Beaches

If I didn't have air superiority, I wouldn't be here.
– Gen. Dwight D. Eisenhower, 1944

I still feel bad about all the innocent French people I killed.
– Ralph Conte, 2004

Heading to the morning briefing Hulse and Conte met Major Price with his navigator, Lieutenant Hand. Before they were able to say hello, the operations officer ordered everyone inside and stood there until the last officer entered the room. Turning to two armed guards, he ordered the door closed and locked. The guards stepped outside as the door closed behind them.

The operations officer walked to the front of the room. He signaled and the assistant operations officer dropped the curtain that was covering the map of France. Over the next thirty minutes the officers were apprised of their role in "Operation Neptune," which they learned was the assault landing portion of Operation Overlord.

The day had come, and everyone felt the importance of the mission. Their pride in being a part of it bolstered their spirits. Ralph and Hulse scanned the room, noting it was an unusually large group this morning as more than half the men had been assigned for this maximum-effort mission. After studying the map, everyone saw the road junction of Argentan, France, marked as their target for the morning.

After breakfast, the morning progressed with the usual combined group briefing. Familiar faces populated the room—Wayne Downing, Earl Hayter, Bill Tripp, Charles McGlohn and the ever-ready Gus Ebenstein. Gunners Dean Vafiadis, Ralph Hoffman, Al Damico, and Robert E. Lee listened to the briefing and were understanding more and more that every minute good men would be dying on the beaches of Normandy.

They all had flown missions over France and Belgium destroying targets. Now they realized they were flying in support of their men who would be dying. They were all ready. At last came the mission the A-20 Havoc was designed to deliver—frontline interdiction and support of ground troops.

The briefing ended, and everyone followed their usual routine out to their planes.

Dean lay in the grass behind his Havoc and watched the clouds build up, and then turned to Hoffman.

"You think they're going to send us up in this soup?"

"Heck, I guess that's why we're sittin' here. They haven't decided yet."

In spite of the early-morning briefing, the fifty-six Havocs assigned to the early mission sat in their revetments waiting for the go sign.

Similarly, sitting in the Operations hut, the OD waited for the word to come down over the teletype from Wing. Reclining with his feet on the only desk, the OD drew on his cigarette, flicking the ashs in the trashcan just as the phone rang.

"Operations," he answered. "No, sir…No, sir…Yessir, I'll let you know, sir…first thing, sir…yessir."

He hung up the phone. Going back to his cigarette, the young officer put his feet back on the desk just as the teletype awakened. The order had come. He picked up the phone again.

"Tower, this is Operations…It's a go. Give'em the green…yeah…yeah…I'll be there in a minute. Hanging up the phone, he quickly picked it up again, rang up the colonel and informed him it was a go."

Hanging the phone up a second time, he headed out the door.

On the way over, he saw the tower officer fire the green flare into the sky. It brought the flight line to life, and everyone headed for his assigned aircraft.

Ready to Roll

A-20 Havoc taxiing from hardstand in Wethersfield, England,
on or after D day.
The wing hard-points are carrying five-hundred-pound bombs
on glass-nosed "C" model.
Reproduced with permission of Ralph Conte

Major Willets led the train of A-20s along the taxiway, and at 1300 hours he sat at the head of the runway. Running up his engines, he tested his magnetos and fuel pumps. Willets pushed his throttles forward, accelerated the A-20 to takeoff speed, and then rotated skyward. He was followed by fifty-five aircraft at ten-second intervals. Willets orbited the base until the formation of A-20s was completed. He then turned the A-Box south-southeast toward Maidenhead at an altitude of two thousand feet on their first leg of the mission.

"Hell, we're gunna be flying low all the way on this one, it looks like to me," Basnett relayed to his pilot, Lieutenant Marzolf.

"Shoot-fire, that's OK with me. I don't want to fly up or come back down through that soup today anyway."

Bob agreed. That environment was when pilots got vertigo or had midair collisions. Either one was deadly.

Making the group's second turn toward the battlefront, Willets headed out over the channel. He watched the waves roll onto the English beaches. Flying at only two thousand feet, he realized he had little room for maneuvering if the group encountered any flak.

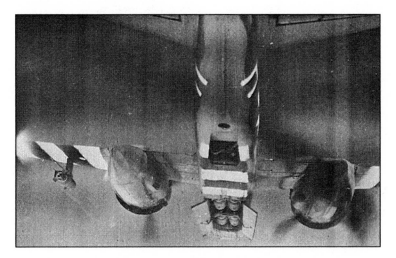

Into the Belly of the Beast

A-20 in flight on mission around D day. Note D day markings. Excellent view of open tail gunner's space in the belly, behind open bomb-bay compartment. At 12,000 feet it could get very cold on winter and even summer days. The bomb bay is loaded with four 500-pound bombs and wing hard-points carried two extra 500-pounders. This photo also makes you realize why bailing out for the navigator and pilot, with the propellers so close, was not an inviting prospect. It was the pilot's job to stop both engines and "feather" both propellers before bailing out. Photo reproduced with permission of Squadron/Signal Publications

After ten minutes on this heading, the aircrews began to notice a few ships on the horizon. A few minutes later, the sea was dotted, and then soon covered with ships of all types. Their flight plan took them directly over the American invasion beaches, which were backed by a powerful naval armada that extended from north of the British beaches to south of Omaha and Utah Beaches. In was an inspiring site.

"God Lord, Hoffman, do you see all this?" Dean marveled at the vastness and diversity of the armada passing below them.

"Heck yeah, there must be a thousand of them." Hoffman saw ships continue to come into view on the horizon. "I'm gunna get a few pictures of this."

"Roger that," Dean responded.

Hoffman grabbed his camera and began snapping photos of the ship-dotted sea below them.

"Have them make me a few copies."

"I'll try, Dean," said Hoffman between snaps.

The inspiring sight did not go unnoticed by others as the speedy A-20s passed over the armada.

"Hulse, I see why they painted our wings now," Conte thankfully observed.

"Me too."

"We might have been dodging our own side's flak if those guys down there didn't know we were on their side. Damn with all that firepower and at this altitude we wouldn't stand a chance."

The display of power dazzled the crew members as the fifty-six A-20s passed over the battleships, cruisers, destroyers, and landing ships of all kinds. Strict radio silence among aircraft was maintained, though, as the formation continued toward the French coast.

American beachheads with multiple scattered plumes of black smoke rising from them started coming into view. The two beachheads that the Allies wanted—Omaha Beach and Utah Beach—were still in dispute, particularly Omaha, but the tide was turning. Closing in on the no-man's-land of Omaha and Utah, the group was greeted by the sight of burning vehicles, destroyed landing craft, and the silhouettes of what appeared to be bodies. Their attention was quickly redirected to their own situation, as poorly aimed and sporadic tracer fire arched skyward.

The men of the 416th had no way to appreciate the true reality of the struggle that had been engaged at 2200 hours on June 5th when the armada had set sail from England. Since that time, British and American paratroopers had been dying at places that would have seemed inconsequential at any other time in history.

British paratroopers began fighting and dying at 0020 hours on June 6, endeavoring to capture the Pegasus Bridge over the Orne River. At 0100 hours American paratroopers of the Eighty-Second Airborne jumped and landed in France but were dispersed all across the countryside. Disorganized at first, in the region of Saint Mere Eglise, small groups joined together to complete their objectives. They accomplished their goal of taking Saint Mere Eglise by 0430 hours while American infantrymen occupied the Marcouf Islets off Utah Beach.

From their landing craft stationed off the beaches, troops watched as the land before them erupted in explosions of fire, smoke, dirt, and human body parts. The shelling of the American beachheads from the naval armada began at 0530 hours, and was followed at 0600 hours by bombs from the United States Army Air Force and British Bomber Command. The landing craft hit the beaches at approximately 0630 hours. The dying started immediately.

Long before the 416th's flight over the battlefield, Wehrmacht *soldat* Franz Gockel had crawled from his protected, but not indestructible, hole in the earth. Struggling to regain his senses and urgency as the bombardment slowed, he began to evaluate the situation around him.

With first light breaking over the grassy hills behind him, he saw his comrades around him—some alive, others dead and dismembered. Craters covered the hillside where his *maschinengewehr*-armed[186] pillbox had been positioned. Looking out over a narrow draw at the northern end of Omaha Beach, Franz had no idea it was an objective that had to be taken by the Americans that day. Although a narrow draw, it provided access for men and tanks from the beach into the hedgerows of France behind it.

Through the smoke that still covered the beaches from his pillbox, Franz peered down at the surf's edge and was surprised to see the first wave of landing craft hitting the beach. Reacting instinctively, Franz called to his *maschinengewehr* team for assistance and ammo. The well-trained soldiers began the process of repelling the coming assault. Franz's *maschinengewehr* began spewing its deadly missiles with guttural burps of fire, a sound unfamiliar to the young American soldiers who were exiting their Higgins boats onto the shores of France. It was a sound that the young Americans would quickly come to recognize with great fear. Franz's *maschinengewehr* and the hundred others pointed at the beach did their duty, as America's youth began to die in waves. The beach began to change from its natural, dark sandy color to a dirty red.

"Noch mehr Munitionen…Noch mehr Munitionen!"[187] Franz hollered to his squad members, as he raked the beach before him. He heard the occasional "zing" or "thump" of return fire as it zipped past or hit his pillbox.

As the assault continued, Franz's bullets ripped the life from the young Americans below, and pinned them down on the beach to wait for death. The varied fire of rifles, grenades, machine guns, mortars, and bracketed artillery fire descended on the invaders from positions along and behind the hills, ensuring the invaders could not move. With the Germans commanding the heights over the beach, the Americans returned fire with little effect.

Four hours before the 416th's flight over the beaches, the general in charge of the US First Army that was invading, Omar Bradley, was on the verge of abandoning Omaha Beach but committed his reinforcements instead. The soldiers kept pouring onto the beach. Having already changed several barrels of his weapon, Franz continued his fire unafraid. His initial fear had given way to vengeful enthusiasm mixed with

---

186 *Maschinengewehr* – (German)—machine gun
187 *Noch mehr Munitionen* – (German)—More ammunition…more ammunition

prayer as he raked the beach and hillside before him. The second wave of landing craft deposited yet more men for him to kill. Franz had seen his own men around him die, only to be replaced by others who, like him, had been conditioned for years to resist an enemy known to be bent on their destruction.

Franz robotically continued his slaughter of the Americans on Omaha Beach, while the US Army Second Ranger Battalion assaulted and ultimately captured Pointe du Hoc, only to find the artillery that could have threatened both the American and British beaches was not there. Pushing inland the Rangers found some Wehrmacht artillery pieces hidden in the woods back behind the bunker. Taking the initiative the Rangers destroyed these cannons but the overall cost was yet to come. The successful assault on Pointe du Hoc was to be followed by two days of German counterattacks that took the lives of all but ninety American men defending it. Death scoured the battlefields that day, swinging his sickle with impunity on both sides of the belief line.

At Omaha Beach, Franz continued firing into the ever-increasing swarm of olive-drab objects below him, seeing some stumble and others fall under his fire. He had noted the slow but progressive movement of the enemy ever closer to his position. He welcomed them into his "Gate to Hell."[188]

Franz kept the fire pouring down on the Americans as he slowly began to realize that his position was about to be overrun...

⚜

Looking down on the beaches from two thousand feet at approximately 1400 hours, the men of the 416th had no idea that Franz Gockel had been taken prisoner. The slopes leading to his position were draped with the bodies of more than two hundred American soldiers. Franz had done his job well, but the testament went to the American soldiers who finally overran his position. Instead of seeking vengeance for his lethal efficiency, they took him prisoner.

As they passed the beachhead, Lieutenant Royal, Willets's navigator, passed a course change to his pilot. Responding without question, Willets made the turn, and the group followed. Flying at 230 mph at only two thousand feet allowed the aircrews to appreciate their Havoc's performance. The ocean zipped by below. With no fighter coverage today, the crews wanted to get in and out fast. Watching the ground pass and the sensation of speed build, the aircrews steeled themselves for the coming IP.

The formation passed by Sainte Mere Eglise and St. Lô as they approached the IP for their run on Argentan. Argentan had become a busy road junction for the Wehrmacht, which was now using the area to move men, material, and ammunition toward the beaches.

"Ten minutes to IP, Marzolf," said Basnett to his pilot, and then gave an altitude correction. "Drop to one...seven...zero...zero feet, that's seventeen hundred feet, roger?"

"Roger that. You guys see any flak or bandits out there?"

---

188   Franz Gockel was taken prisoner on Omaha Beach and later wrote a book about his experience, *The Gate to Hell*

Marzolf had indirectly ordered his crew to keep their eyes open, which would help all the exposed bombers.

Conte called, "Hulse, get ready. I'm gunna have to bomb manually, can't use the Norden from this altitude. I'll line you up."

Then Conte called back to his tail gunner.

"Stephens, do you read, over?"

"Roger sir, 10–10."

"Get that camera ready, this will be quick."

"Roger." Stephens readied the camera and himself for the bomb drop.

Willets was the first to see the people of Argentan running for cover as the planes roared in toward the outskirts of their target. Some Wehrmacht trucks sat in the woods next to the road; others were traveling through the town.

On the lead flight of Havocs, the bomb bay doors started swinging open.

Royal saw the aiming point approaching quickly and the heavy traffic on the roads.

"Bombs away!" The mixture of general-purpose and high-explosive ordnance burst from the first flight.

Argentan

June 6, 1944 was a good day for Lieutenant Bob Basnett on
the 416th BG's first D-day mission.
Reproduced with permission of Andy Fluxe

The second flight led by Basnett began seeing and feeling the shocks of the first flight's bombs below. Trucks, infantry, and French civilians began burning and dying. as the ordnance detonated on first contact. The bombs indiscriminately killed or destroyed anything in their shrapnel-filled blast radius.

Having lined his pilot and flight on course down the bomb-run, Basnett was unsure of his release point. He had already armed the bombs but was having difficulty judging his speed and bomb-release trajectory from this low altitude. Mistaking a road junction on the west side of town as the maximum point of impact (MPI) Basnett reached for the bomb-release switch.

"Bombs away!" Basnett toggled the release switch, sending his and five other Havocs's payloads toward the target.

The bombs whistled out the bomb bay and off the wing hard points. The impellers spun and armed the predominantly five-hundred-pound high-explosive bombs as they plummeted. Falling short of the city, they impacted a forested area a hundred yards west of Argentan that paralleled the road coming out of the town.

As the flight zipped away from the powerful explosions, Basnett's tail gunner was busy snapping pictures of the impact site.

"Good Lord, Lieutenant!" Wellin yelled. "I think you hit something big back there." He snapped his last few frames.

The flight banked hard right, taking the target zone out of view and ending Wellin's photo responsibilities. For the first time since approaching the bomb-run, the flight held the same altitude as the throttles were opened, accelerating the high-performance Havocs. Everyone felt the g-forces of the turn and heard the engines revving, happy to be heading home.

Moments before, Dean Vafiadis watched as the bombs from Basnett's flight exploded, creating a great deal of secondary explosions, which surprised him.

"Hoffman, look below ya."

"Holy cow, what the heck is all that?"

Hoffman heard "bombs away" in his headset, catching him off guard as he scrambled to get the camera up and ready.

The third flight's bombs fell just short and to the right of the first flight's salvo. Homes, families, soldiers, and German trucks exploded. Death came to many.

Conte watched his lead flight's bombs hit just beyond the MPI, and had released his bombs a second before theirs. Sailing free, they performed their duty flawlessly, all but one. This lone five-hundred-pounder struck the roof of a home to the right and ahead of the MPI. It crashed through the ceiling, and then through the floor of the room where a mother and her three children were huddled in fear. Slamming into the earth just below the wooden floor, it stopped.

Crying screams came from the children as explosions continued to shake their little cottage, while the mother stared in disbelief at the tail fins of the merciful dud that had hit their home. The rest of the town's homes and families would not fair as well.

Gus Ebenstein released his flight's bomb-load of death hollering, "Take that, you Kraut bastards!" Gus's bombs did their job in cleaning up any missed opportunities from the earlier salvos. He banked off the run and headed back for the RP.

After regrouping southeast of the St. Lô area, the group turned northwest toward home. It was then that Ebenstein's turret gunner, Newell, noted that the Havoc flying third in their flight was heading westerly, away from the group.

"Where's that new guy going?" Newell asked his pilot.

"Your guess is as good as mine," crackled back.

"Hell, if that kid stays on that heading he'll hit Cherbourg," Newell said. "They'll shoot his ass up over there."

"Holy shit! Hold on, guys!"

Wagging his wings to maintain radio silence yet signal his intentions, Ebenstein banked hard left and dropped out of the lead. He turned toward the misdirected Havoc. Accelerating in a shallow dive and then leveling off, Gus closed at 310 mph. He pulled up into a shallow climb, and bled off energy to slow to 250 mph. He slid into position on the right side of the misdirected plane. Finally getting the young pilot's attention, Gus gestured with his right thumb the direction he wanted the kid to turn. The rookie nodded.

As he banked right, Gus looked over his shoulder to be sure the kid was following. Seeing that he was, Gus set course for the RP trailing the rest of his flight. Just before the beaches Gus took the lead again, as his number three settled into the correct spot in the formation.

As they approached the beach, the group was again greeted by sporadic and inaccurate small-arms fire. From their point of view, the scene below them had not changed much since their first crossing.

For the men on the ground, though, things had changed a lot. Omaha had been secured, and the US Army's First Infantry Division, the Big Red One, and the US Twenty-Ninth Infantry Division pushed inland. Order was coming from chaos on the beach and behind it, as makeshift units began forming. These units soon began taking important military objectives. As tenuous as it was, the foothold was ashore.

The Wehrmacht was not waiting for the Allies to consolidate their holdings. Rommel's Panzer divisions were being mobilized and thrown into the fight. The 416th was about to encounter the lethality of a Panzer division.[189, 190, 191]

Debriefing went well for the first group back from the run. Much to Basnett's surprise, G-2 was all over his gunner's photos. Calling him back, G-2 informed Basnett that his bombs had fallen on an ammunition convoy, destroying it nearly completely. Listening intently, Bob kept asking himself, "Who am I to correct G-2 by telling them it

189   The World at War: Operation Overlord; Richard Doody; http://worldatwar.net/article/overlord/

190   *Great Battles of World War II;* John MacDonald; copyright 1986; pp 132–143

191   Second World War History: D-Day: The Normandy Invasion (June 6–25, 1944); http://www.secomdworldwarhistory.com/battle_of_normandy.asp

was just pure luck?" Such is the fate of war. Bob had prevented ammunition of all types that would have been thrown against his fellow countrymen and allies if it had reached the front.

Much later and just before the second mission of the day, Jack found himself hoping the afternoon mission, which had actually become a 2000 hours, early-evening mission, would be as successful as the morning sortie as he crushed out his cigarette. He was surprised to hear from Dean Vafiadis and Ralph Hoffman how little resistance they had met. There were no casualties or battle damage, and even better, no Me-109s or Focke-Wulf 190s were seen. Riding to the Havoc's revetment together, Hoffman told Jack about photographing the bomb blasts from seventeen hundred feet. Tonight they would be dropping from about three thousand feet.

Earlier in the day, Rommel's Twenty-First Panzer Division had launched their counterattack at approximately 1400 hours. They were ordered to fight their way to the beach at Luc sur Mer between Sword and Juno beaches and "throw the fishes back into the sea." By now, in the early evening, Panzers were threatening the beachheads of the Canadian and British forces while the 416th was taking off for its second sortie.

Major Meng led the A-Box and was followed in order by another A-20 and another, starting the process of forming the bomber group. A few minutes later, Jack accelerated his heavily loaded Havoc down the runway. Rotating, he climbed to altitude to join the third flight of B-Box. He checked his routes and way points as he followed the flight leader into position.

Staying below the clouds, the formation of thirty-nine Havocs made their second turn and headed out over the channel toward the Pas de Calais area north of Rouen. The Serquez marshaling yard was their target. This interdiction strike was chosen for the same reasons as the morning mission—to prevent the movement of any of the Wehrmacht's men, material, or Panzers south to the beaches. The Twelfth and Twenty-First Panzers were slowing the Canadian advance on Caen already, but were suffering terrible losses at the hands of fighter-bombers. If more Panzers were thrown into the fight, it would create significant problems for the invading forces.

Meng had been informed of the importance of this mission. He understood too that this was a well-defended region of France. For years the Allies had been deceiving the Germans into believing that Pas de Calais was the planned invasion area. Now they continued the deception by flying into this fortress area at only three thousand feet without fighter cover. Meng knew from the briefing that flak would greet them soon. The bomb drop would be without the aid of the Norden too; here all the low-level bombing training back in the states would pay off.

Approaching the French coast, Meng was surprised with the amount of flak that was suddenly streaking up to greet his formation. At this altitude it wouldn't take long for the German gunners to adjust their aim. It also didn't take long for those damned shells to reach his formation. With the shells exploding all around the formation, he followed his navigator's recommendations for evasion even though the gunners below quickly adjusted for the moves. Meng began to understand why the Allies hadn't landed here.

As they crossed the coast and turned for the IP, the flak weakened. At four minutes from the IP, Meng thought maybe the worst was behind them. Such thoughts were not to be the case; the Pas de Calais region was well defended with major radar installations that were part of the Reich's home-defense chain. Besides, at three thousand feet the group was in range of every type of anti-aircraft cannon in the Luftwaffe inventory, including the rifles and machine guns of any soldier who cared to take a potshot. The cannons were well positioned on the ground below. Hitler, and therefore his command staff, had believed this to be the area where the Allies would land to begin the invasion. Würzburg gun-laying radar had had the 416th on their scopes for some time. They were now ready to help themselves to the pickings.

Slammed against his straps while being blinded by the initial blast, Meng was so shocked by the explosion that he was totally unaware of the volume of steel that was passing through his cockpit and around his frail body. Spared any physical injury, Meng immediately became aware that the burst had disabled his left engine. Out his left window Meng saw flames and thick smoke pouring from the remains of his engine and nacelle.

"Major, we're on fire!" yelled Staff Sergeant Francis Glynn. "The left engine is on fire!"

"Roger that, I'm on it."

Meng shut off fuel pumps and electricity to the burning engine while trying to keep in formation. After feathering the prop Meng evaluated his options.

The rest of the lead formation had not suffered as badly, but had sustained damage as the accurately targeted anti-aircraft shells had exploded within the formation.

Meng finally realized he had to drop out of formation. Diving in a slipping fashion away from the burning wing, he tried to extinguish the fire. He was rewarded; starved of fuel, the fire went out. He leveled off at eighteen hundred feet.

"Listen up, guys," spoke Meng through the interphone, "I've got the fire under control. I'm heading back to base, but don't know if we can make it. We've still got to get past the coastal flak. You can jump or stay. I'm going to try and bring her home."

Without hesitation the crew agreed to stay, and Meng proceeded with preparations.

"OK, now listen up. We need to lighten the load, so you guys dump whatever you can once we're over the channel."

Meng opened the bomb bay and released his payload. The bombs plummeted into a grain field, destroying a large area of future food stock that so many nations were now fighting for. Now relieved of three thousand pounds of bombs, the lightened plane responded deftly, as Meng felt the controls become more nimble.

In the number-two slot of the third flight of A-Box, Lieutenant C.C. Mish with Staff Sergeant C.J. Clark and tail gunner Sergeant R.P. Chustz watched as Meng banked out of formation with the engine fire.

"Holy cow! The major just got hit," Mish hollered over the interphone. "He's falling out of formation!" Just as he finished the statement Mish and his crew felt their Havoc shudder as they were slammed against their straps. Mish felt the Havoc begin an unplanned and uncontrolled banking turn to the right.

"Lieutenant, we're on fire. The right engine is on fire," came the call over the interphone.

A-20 Havoc on fire

**A-20 Havoc dropping out of formation because of flak hit to
starboard engine causing fire.
Reproduced with permission of Andy Fluxe**

The well-placed burst of Luftwaffe anti-aircraft fire from a mobile quad 20-mm had destroyed Mish's engine and ignited the fuel tank behind it. Burning aviation fuel had already ignited the tire in the wheel well and the smoke was turning a sooty black as it billowed from the nacelle. The following rounds had ripped the wing's trailing edge, disabling any control over the wing. Mish realized he was unable to control his plane and could not slip away from the fire. He tried to rudder away from the flames by holding the reverse aileron, and tried to remember his feathering procedure. He was not going to be able to put out the fire or control the plane, and he was losing altitude quickly as he heard more and more small-caliber anti-aircraft rounds passing through his plane. Mish reached forward and hit the emergency claxton and repeated three times over the interphone to abandon ship.

There was no hesitation, as flak jackets were removed and chutes hooked to the parachute harnesses. First, Chustz fell from the plane and was followed by Clark and then Mish, who crawled out over the fuselage and carefully avoided the flames as he rolled off the fuselage behind the right wing. All three men pulled the D-ring as soon as they exited the plane. All three knew they had little altitude for the chutes to open.

Three chutes blossomed over the Serquex marshaling yard, prompting orders to the Wehrmacht *soldaten* to capture them as prisoners. Chustz, Clark, and Mish hit the ground in the order of their jump, after watching their Havoc auger into the French countryside and create a massive fireball and concussion. Before they could free themselves from their chutes, they were prisoners.

As Meng and then Mish dropped away, the formation continued forward with Captain Gerald McNulty of the 668th squadron moving up from second to take the lead. Lieutenant Francis Burseil of the 670th squadron, McNulty's bombardier/navigator rose to the responsibility.

"IP in thirty seconds, Captain."

"Roger," said McNulty as he completed his maneuver to take the lead.

Flak continued to erupt all around the aircraft as the next flight began their right-hand turn onto the bomb-run just as the 20- and 37-mm anti-aircraft batteries along both sides of the bomb-run opened fire. They were delighted to see these big birds at such low altitudes. It improved their chances of getting a kill.

Major Campbell, who led the second box, prepared to follow McNulty onto the bomb-run when all hell broke loose. He had seen Meng's plane take the hit, then burst into flames. Sweating bullets like all the A-Box crews ahead of him, he watched in amazement as the sky before them became blacker than anyone could remember. They were equally impressed with the extraordinarily thick tracer fire coming up from below them.

Following Campbell in the second box, Lieutenant Jack Smith saw all the flashes and then the tracers zooming up at them.

"Dean, Hoffman, do you guys see this? Damn! The tracers are so thick you can walk on' em."

Every tenth round was a tracer, so they knew there were ten times as many rounds that they didn't see. At just three thousand feet every crew member knew they were just too tempting for the Krauts. The second box continued forward and prepared themselves for their turn on the gauntlet called the bomb-run.

"My God, two minutes of this!" Campbell heard someone speak over the radio. He silently concurred, and hoped Palin was ready.

Unlike other bombardiers, Palin liked opening the bomb bay doors before hitting the IP. Reaching to throw the switch that opened the doors, Palin was suddenly slammed against the wall of the Havoc's Plexiglass nose. Like the other crew members, he was shaken and disoriented by the blast. The 88-mm shell had exploded in front of the starboard engine. The explosion had viciously separated the three propeller blades from the hub and crankshaft of the engine. As the shockwave and steel passed the propeller, six of the Wasp's front-row engine cylinders had explosively separated from the engine. Shrapnel had torn through fuel, oil, and hydraulic lines and tanks. Now the engine was failing. Fire engulfed the wing.

"Damnit, Palin, what happened?" Murdoch Campbell swore out loud, as he surveyed the instrument panel for information.

The equally shocked Palin struggled to regain his composure.

"Hell if I know! I can't see a thing!"

Campbell worked to make sense of the instruments while keeping the plane in the air. Pouring power to the port engine, Campbell went through the feathering procedure for the starboard prop. He didn't know that there wasn't a starboard prop left to feather.

"Thompson, what the hell can you see from there?" Campbell barked.

Fuel was pouring from the starboard engine's open fuel lines and from the so-called self-sealing fuel tanks that could no longer self-seal. Aviation fuel mixed with hot metal—a recipe for danger. When it hit the hot exhaust manifolds attached to the engine remnants, the high-octane fuel ignited, setting the wing ablaze.

"Major, we got problems!" Thompson screamed. "The whole starboard wing is on fire and…and…hell, half the engine is gone! What are we going to do?"

Campbell looked out the right side of his cockpit and saw the roaring fire. The instrument panel's fuel gauges continued to fall as his fuel fed the fire. Every second that it burned it was eating its way through the critical aluminum wing supports. Campbell felt the A-20 sliding out of formation with no way to stop it. He was unaware that the shrapnel had cut the control cables to the right wing's ailerons.

Watching in disbelief, the rest of the B-Box slid past Campbell as his Havoc fell below and to the right. The formation sped past. Having seen the hit, Captain Dunn immediately moved up into the lead.

Campbell's tail gunner Harold Hatch called out: "Major, that ground is getting mighty close!"

Left unchecked, the fire would eventually ignite the fumes in the fuel tanks and the whole ship would go up with it. The left engine was still doing its job supplying the needed airspeed for the plane to stay airworthy, but the laws of physics wouldn't let a plane fly on one wing, or worse, if it was blown to pieces. Campbell made his decision.

"Listen up! Abandon ship, repeat abandon ship!" Campbell ordered. "Bail out now, repeat, bail out now!" He flipped the abandon-ship claxton while pulling his escape-hatch handle, which turned on the red emergency light. Campbell released his seat straps and waited to be sure his crew got out before him.

While checking his chute, Palin opened the escape hatch in the floor of the navigator compartment. The hatch flew open, and the gunpowder-scented air rushed into the nose of the plane. He was more worried about hitting his head on the way out of the plane or worse falling into the propellers or the fire.

"Geronimo!"

Palin fell out the opening, but had forgotten to unplug his headset. It snapped free from its jack as gravity and the plane's velocity separated them.

Campbell heard Palin's final word as he left the ship. *That's one,* he thought.

Thompson was not far behind, exiting through the escape panel on the side of the plane behind his top turret. Meanwhile, Hatch stripped off his flak jacket and slid out the rear opening immediately after he had snapped on his chute.

Staying with the plane a few more seconds to give everyone time to bail out, Campbell was shocked as several 20-mm rounds ripped through the right floor of the cockpit passing through Plexiglass roof of his cockpit. Campbell clambered out as fast as he could. He had been unable to trim the stricken ship out in level flight, and was afraid that would keep him from a safe escape. Having seen the anti-aircraft rounds pass through his cockpit he knew nothing would keep him from escaping the doomed ship. After climbing out the escape hatch, he slid across the fuselage to avoid the right wing's fire and then fell off to the left. Starting his count while praying the chute worked, he pulled the D-ring. In less than two seconds he was jerked upward and realized the chute had worked perfectly.

Seeing three chutes maybe five hundred feet below made him feel good. His crew was out.

"Thank you, thank you," he quietly said out loud, thanking his Almighty and knowing his most important job had been done.

Flying on for another five seconds, the now-crewless plane became an aerial fireball as the vapors in the right wing's fuel tank exploded, separating the right wing from the fuselage. The explosion ignited the bomb bay fuel tank, adding to the spectacle. Spinning downward to its high-velocity death, the burning hulk accelerated toward the waiting soil of France. It slammed into the outer edge of the marshaling yard, detonating the payload and consuming a 37-mm gun mount and its crew with the ensuing blast of three thousand pounds of high explosives.

The four silk chutes drifted calmly down through the ongoing barrage. One by one their thankful cargo hit the ground. The first two were quickly rounded up by the now waiting Wehrmacht *soldaten*. Hatch and Thompson's war was done.

Landing several thousand yards away from Palin, Campbell was immediately aware of a large group of soldiers approaching him from the east. He feared his life was now in jeopardy. Working quickly and efficiently to remove his parachute harness, he instinctively reached for his .45-caliber sidearm as the Wehrmacht infantrymen raced toward him. Pulling his weapon, he comically chambered a round as he prepared to defend himself.

"I'll be damned if I'm going to die here without taking some of you with me!" He hoped to appear menacing enough to slow the advancing soldiers. He found himself second-guessing his bravado.

Suddenly he heard German voices from behind. He turned sharply to see two *soldaten* with their *unterfeldwebel*. The *unterfeldwebel* took control of the situation as he repeated a statement over and over. Campbell got the meaning and laid down his sidearm. He surrendered it to become a *Kriegsgefangene*[192] for the duration of the war.

Moments before, Dunn had taken leadership of the second box as they turned onto the bomb-run. Arrington was now the lead bombardier.

"Arrington, have you got it?"

"Yessir, Captain Dunn, I've got her!"

Watching for the target, Dunn saw the marshaling yard come into view directly ahead of his flight. Harry Arrington calculated the drop in his head since he couldn't use his Norden bombsight. Trying not to be bounced around too much as the flak ex-

---

192   *Kriegsgefangene*—(German)—prisoner of war

ploded around them, Arrington prepared. Having flipped the switch to open the bomb bay doors at the IP, he waited for the primary impact point to slip into his field of view as he calculated the drop point.

Every pilot in the first flight of B-Box was delighted to see the bomb bay doors swing out from the belly of Arrington's plane. That meant they were two minutes from the drop. Almost in unison their doors swung out into the 200-plus mph slipstream. They had quit thinking of Campbell now, and were praying that what they had just seen didn't happen to them. Well into the run now, all the crews wanted these bombs out of their planes and falling toward the target. Every pilot's thumb was on the bomb-release button mounted on his yoke, ready to get rid of the eggs. Having witnessed hits first to Meng and then to Mish and Campbell, the pilots were focused on making their evasive left-hand bank and dive toward home as soon as their eggs were on their way.

Arrington felt the plane shudder yet again. He watched the ground pass by below him, and was anxious to get on with it. He saw the aiming point slide into view. As they closed in on the aiming point, he waited until he was sure the target was right.

"Bombs away!"

The crew was happy to hear it. The five-hundred-pound eggs fell in twos out of their nests. The planes shook as each pair escaped their shackles, causing a small bounce upward in the plane as the hard-point-mounted bombs fell away. The pilots could barely wait for the all-clear sign to close their doors before starting their evasive maneuvers.

The *kanoniers* had a different plan for the boys in the air though. The radar system had bracketed the group's drop point, which made that point in space at three thousand feet not a good place to be. *Hauptwachtmeister* Raake directed his *kanoniers* with great efficiency and accuracy today. His *kanoniers* were setting fuses and then firing at a deadly rate and with great accuracy. He gave his men the *Feuerbefehl* just before the bombs would drop from the bomb bays. He knew how long the planes would be passing overhead, having timed from the opening of the doors to the last bomb leaving the planes. For these two minutes Raake had the Amerikaner bombers at his mercy. The eight *runde*[193] from the *hauptwachtmeister's* eight *kanones* rifled their way out of the 88s' barrels. Traveling at maximum velocity, the shells took three seconds to reach the proper altitude and then exploded as their tail fuses detonated at the preset altitude. Fulfilling their *Wehrmacht verpflichtung*,[194] all eight of the 88 *runde* exploded on the mark. This salvo of 88s found their targets.

Feeling a violent shudder of their previously stable flying platform and hearing the corresponding explosion, Jack, Dean, and Hoffman were jolted inside their compartments. Lurching up in response to the concussion from the 88s' detonation, the right wing fell back down as if it were pulled. Shrapnel had sprayed through the right wing and engine nacelle, cutting fuel lines and hydraulic lines. The starboard engine cylinders absorbed the greatest amount of the shrapnel and energy of the shell's detona-

193   *Runde –* (German)—rounds or artillery shells
194   *Wehrmacht verpflichtung—*(German)—German army obligation

tion that blew off five of the second-row jugs. Still trying to run in spite of missing nearly a third of its jugs, the now injured engine pumped out oil, fuel, and smoke rapidly.

Jack could tell from the oil pressure readings on his instrument panel that it wouldn't run much longer. He reacted to the loss of power, the potential for fire, and the changes in the instrument readings. Jack throttled up the left engine while looking out the right windshield as he began the feathering process in the right engine. He had to get control of the engine to cut drag and prevent the windmilling of the propeller. Running down the oft-repeated emergency checklist, Jack feathered his right engine, then proceeded: fuel pumps off, magnetos off, throttle off, prop pitch full open. He was relieved to see the engine shut down and the propeller spin to a stop. While watching to be sure that no fire started, he called out.

"Dean, Hoffman, you two OK back there?"

"I'm OK," Hoffman responded

"How bad is it?" Dean added.

"I'm OK, but the right wing and engine look like hell!"

"Damn right it does, but look at that flak!" Jack redirected everyone's attention to the real enemy while he balanced his rudder and ailerons against the pull of the powered-up left engine. They stayed in formation but he knew it was going to be tough to hold it.

"Dear God, Jack, that sky is looking bad!" Dean had the same increasing anxiety in his voice.

Having seen the other three ships get shot out of the sky, Dean prayed as he'd never prayed before. Hoffman was doing the same as they both reached out for spiritual comfort.

The sky was filling with orange-red explosions that turned into benign-looking black puffs as the 88 *runde* exploded. The pilots and bombardiers watched as the puffs of death were slowly vectored in on the flights by the Würzburg- and Würzlaus-directed gun-laying radar. Their two-minute bomb-run had now become a brush with eternity.

"Can you guys see anything to shoot at?"

"Hell, yes! At this altitude I can see all kinds of targets!" Hoffman affirmed.

"Then open up on those bastards!" Jack ordered. It was in direct violation of Wing's standing orders.

Hoffman and Dean knew too that firing at anything but enemy aircraft was not approved, but they didn't care. They wanted to get even. Spinning the turret around, Dean found a target, carefully sighted, and then unleashed his .50-calibers on a 37-mm gun emplacement. It took a few moments for the rounds to reach their target but when they did the *kanoniers* felt their wrath.

"Got one, Ralph!" Dean yelled as the first seventy or eighty rounds poured onto the 37-mm gun position shredding the Luftwaffe loader and gunner. This silenced the gun, and Dean moved to a new target. "How 'bout you?"

Ralph ripped rounds from his .30-caliber sending his copper-jacketed retribution toward the flashes of anti-aircraft artillery below the ship. The sudden impact of the ammunition on a quad 20-mm mobile gun mount surprised and scattered the German crew after one of them crumpled to the ground when a round penetrated his helmet then skull.

"Hell, I don't know, but I'm givin' 'em hell!" Hoffman said as he laughed back.

Jack managed to keep his speed on the one engine and continued along the bomb-run with the rest of his flight. He slid his thumb over his bomb drop switch and sensed, while praying, that they were close to the drop site. He was ready to get the hell out of there. He wasn't sure he was going to be able to stay in formation with what was left of his engines. Dropping the bombs would lighten his plane. The release mechanism merely awaited Jack's command to drop the armed five-hundred-pounders.

Dean and Ralph were actually having a good day of it. Since opening fire, they felt sure they had taken out several AA gun emplacements. It also got their minds off the serious situation. The rest of the formation was that much the happier for it too.

"Hell, Jack, I'm killing some of those bastards!" Dean shouted over the intercom while he turned the turret looking for another gun emplacement.

"Kill one of them sum-bitches for me," Jack said in anger, while trying to keep the plane in a tight formation with all the explosions around them.

Captain Dunn's plane released its payload, and Jack followed his lead, pushing his energized bomb-release button and sending his payback earthward.

All green signaled on the bomb bay release indicator, but not on the wing bombs.

"Oh hell!"

Jack realized they were going to have to fly home with them—armed bombs. He had armed them after turning onto the bomb-run. He threw the switch to close the bomb bay doors. Knowing he couldn't turn into the dead engine, Jack put the nose down and banked to the left, just as a well-placed 88 *rund* exploded below and to the right of the cockpit. All three men thought the same thing: *Dear God, not again!*

Jack realized that if he had turned right the Kraut 88 would have hit them dead amid ships.

The already-wounded Havoc was pounded with multiple pieces of *Deutsche stahl*, which had entered through the bottom of the plane. The shrapnel had taken out several of the hydraulic systems, and fluid now sprung from the wounds. One piece of unrestrained steel had ricocheted around the cockpit until it hit Jack in the left elbow, along the ulnar nerve. After a brief shocking pain ran up and down his left limb, the whole arm went to sleep.

"Damnit, I've been hit!"

"How bad?" Hoffman sounded scared.

"Don't know, just can't use my left hand and arm. No blood anywhere!"

"Are you going to be OK?" Dean asked carefully.

"I think I can keep the plane flying, but we're losing hydraulics."

"Stay in touch."

After recovering somewhat, they continued the evasion. Jack was forced to turn farther away from the rest of the formation. Turning into the dead engine meant a stall and crash. He then entered a shallow short dive, and after completing the evasion maneuver, leveled off after hitting 300 mph in the dive. Jack listened to the chatter of the Havoc's machine guns as Dean and Ralph continued to hammer the gun crews on the terrain below them. Jack assessed their situation.

"A bad arm, one engine out, with hydraulic pressure falling—can it get any worse?" Jack found his mouth so dry from fear that he was unable to chew his gum. He wondered if this could be the one, as his mind briefly wandered back to his Methodist church in the Tennessee River Valley. He was shocked back to reality when a 37-mm round tore through the right wing.

Ralph's and Dean's thoughts were following the same line as Jack's, while the rest of the 416th finished their mission.

Flying the number three slot in the last flight of the third box, Lieutenant Wipperman had seen all the planes that took hits and fell out of formation. He and his crew had also seen most of the ordnance fall on the target. He was equally surprised to have seen the Panzers in the marshaling yard fire their cannons up at the formation. He just had to drop his load and then they were off. As he approached the target, he observed the destruction that had happened just before.

Having seen the A-20s come in at this low altitude, the tank commanders had elevated their barrels and added their firepower to the fight. They had been oblivious to the bombs that had slid out of the approaching Havocs' bomb racks and begun their fall to the marshaling yard below, which was crowded with troop transports, Panzers, and self-propelled weapons. The impellers in the bombs had armed the fuses and spun as if they were pinwheels falling toward their target. With the sound of battle and engine noise of the Wehrmacht's weapons, no one had heard the whistle of approaching death.

The first bomb had landed squarely in the middle of a troop concentration. The shrapnel and concussion instantaneously separated the souls of twelve red-cheeked *soldaten* from their now useless bodies. Seventeen-year-olds who were seconds before pretending to be tough men were now oblivious to their mortal bodies being shredded by the salvo. They were young *soldaten* who never had a chance to prove their valor or worth in combat, unlike the veteran Panzer crews twenty yards behind them. Seconds later, the Panzers took the direct hits of high-explosive projectiles. Veterans of the Wehrmacht's eastern-front engagements were now being incinerated inside the remnants of their tanks.

The bomb pattern had widened around the railyard, as the payloads found the ground. Clouds of dirt, rock, fire, and shrapnel sprang from the center of each detonation, shredding men and machines equally as the mortals cried out for protection from the death falling all about them. Bombs from the Havocs above had done their duty that day—killing men, and destroying multiple rail tracks and mechanized weapons. It was a small military achievement that would be unknown to the allies dying on the beaches, but not to the Wehrmacht and the Luftwaffe. German families would be notified of their losses.

The marshaling yard was sustaining damage, but not as totally as it could have. Due to the intensity of the flak, which caused the loss of two lead aircrews, the air raid had become disorganized and less effective than it should otherwise have been. Regardless, the yard was being damaged enough to prevent moving any Panzers toward the beaches. A locomotive had taken a direct hit, and spewed steel and scalding steam in a fifty-yard radius, killing and burning Wehrmacht *soldaten* and French rail men. Flatbed rail cars were destroyed by the attack, along with the Panzer tanks they were hauling. On the ground, several motorized guns and several Panzers were destroyed along with their crews. There was loss of human life on both sides, but tipped well toward the Americans' advantage, as the concrete air-raid shelters located in most rail yards filled to overflowing.

Bombs had continued pelting the ground. Several salvos overshot the target and headed toward the city. The bombs had but one mission and the inescapable force of gravity as their ally—they sought the ground dispassionately. The misdirected salvo blasted its first target, killing two hundred children in a fraction of a second. Thousands of pounds of high explosives shattered their orphanage and ended their lives. The people of the city would live with their loss, as would the crews of B-Box, who would always remember. The bombs, however, would never suffer with their consciences. That day, the hands of Providence opened wide to comfort all the innocent souls, particularly the children, as they entered their new home.

Like every other crewman who had flown down this bomb-run, Wipperman was ready to get off it. His thumb was on the energized bomb-release button. He had seen so many planes go down today that he feared today might be his day. Then, he felt an 88 round go straight through the outer third of the right wing and explode just above it, showering the upper surface of the wing, the right engine, and the fuselage. The right engine belched black smoke and then caught fire. The fuel lines, fuel tanks, cylinder heads, the wing, the fuselage, and Staff Sergeant Henry Ahrens's top turret absorbed the brunt of the shrapnel.

Looking directly at the burst, Henry didn't even have time for his brain to comprehend what was happening, as shrapnel ripped through the side of the plane. Having effortlessly passed through the aluminum shell and the Plexiglass of the turret, the steel had entered Henry with the same degree of ease. More than half the heavy steel that entered the turret passed directly through his body. In spite of his prayers, Ahrens's spirit was separated from his body, never having to experience the pain of the wounds.

Another round caught the plane hard, hitting below the left wing's engine nacelle. Fire and black smoke erupted. The left engine had lost seven of the bottom cylinders from the two radials, and the wheel had fallen out of its well due to the concussion and the complete loss of hydraulics. Oil, fuel, and two of the bottom pistons came flying out of the nonfunctioning engine.

Wipperman reacted immediately. He knew that the ship was no longer airworthy and in a few minutes it was going to be a death trap.

"Bail out...Repeat, bail out!" He called to Ahrens and Sergeant Louis Mazza.

"Henry, Henry, what the hell happened?" Mazza called.

"We're bailing out, Maz," Wipperman hollered into the mouthpiece. Smoke was now filling the inside of the ship as it crept toward the explosive fuel tanks.

"Roger, bailing out. I'm right behind you!"

Wipperman pulled his hatch handle, while Maz pushed his .30-caliber out the rear escape route. After shedding his flak jacket and securing his chute, Maz crawled out right behind it, oblivious to the blood dripping into his gunner's compartment from Ahrens's lifeless body above him.

Wipperman was still unstrapping himself from the seat and then finally pulled himself out of the cockpit into the 280-mph slipstream as the plane accelerated in its fall. Wipperman bounced off the fuselage and then fell over the back of the right wing, just escaping the fire. He pushed off the side of the plane trying to separate himself from the plane to avoid the tail; he pulled the rip cord. The chute opened, and he felt the jerk. He looked up to see the chute blossoming open, and then scanned below him to find the top of Maz's chute floating down. Tracers headed up toward both of them.

"Those damned Krauts are still trying to kill us!" Wipperman yelled, shooting back a raised middle finger.

Over to his right the spiraling Havoc crashed into the earth and created a fireball that was followed by explosions from the detonation of the six five-hundred-pound bombs. Wipperman looked around for the third chute and realized what had happened. When he looked below, it was the last view that he had of Maz.

Landing a quarter mile apart, they both struggled to get out of their harnesses. Then they heard the Germans running toward them. They could hear the *unterfeldwebel* yelling, "*Gefangen halten,*"[195] and his *soldaten* responding, "*Jawohl, Herr Unterfeldwebel.*"[196] By the time both men had removed their harnesses, they found themselves looking down the barrels of bolt-action 8-mm Mausers. Following orders, the *soldaten* began searching Wipperman and Mazza, taking their sidearms and escape packages. They made the two men walk in different directions, beginning the process of separating them into the officers' and enlisted men's POW camps.

In the air, the 416th zoomed toward home, with some injured birds praying that they would make it back. The formation was crossing the coastal gun emplacements and was again taking fire. Fortunately, the Havocs absorbed the steel this time and none fell from the sky. Unfortunately, two gunners were wounded slightly by shrapnel, adding more Purple Hearts to the day's tally of medals.

Having cleared the coast at just fifteen hundred feet, Meng had avoided the coastal artillery batteries with a little careful flying. He again offered—but didn't order—his crew the option to bail out over the channel. He felt sure that with all the rescue crews on the channel waters today, they would be sure to be rescued. Again, the crew chose to fly on with the skipper, come what may. Finally, Meng caught a glimpse of the English coast, and felt some relief. They were going to make it, he thought. Fly-

195   Gefangen halten – (German) – Take them prisoner
196   Jawohl, Herr Unterfeldwebel – (German) – Yes, sir, sergeant (infantry)

ing over the coastline, he set course for Wethersfield, thankful that this mission was just about over. Now seeing his base, Meng set his flaps, dropped his landing gear, crabbed the A-20 onto the runway, and rolled it down the taxiway onto his hardstand.

Twenty minutes later, the first planes began to return. The Havocs with wounded landed first, and ambulances rushed in to meet them at the usual spot. Then, the rest of the Havocs began peeling off in order from the flights. The remainder of the formation finished landing in twenty minutes, while two Havocs that had taken hits over the coast had landed away from the base on a coastal emergency strip. The tower became a crowded place today as the beat-up Havocs with their wounded aircrews inside came home. The men in the tower noted the missing aircraft, and quickly figured who had been inside, and they mourned.

After the post-mission briefing, the men drifted back to their huts. They were shaken by the ferocity of the combat and relieved to be back. They broke up into their groups and tried to regain some sense of normalcy.

As they walked into their quarters, Earl asked Hiram, "Hey, is it true that Jack got hit today?" Others were already calming themselves on their bunks.

Looking Earl in the eyes, he hesitated and then tiredly responded. "Jack, Vafiadis, and Hoffman went down right after the bomb drop. They haven't landed yet. Operations has listed them MIA."

Bill Tripp and Roland Enman looked at Hiram and said nothing. They had seen their friends go down, but never anyone with whom they had trained and lived. Jack's absence was noted and felt.

Americans in the Skies

Flight of A-20s from the 416th, 668th, and 671st squadrons.
This mission is believed to be passing near Le Havre, France,
and is well over 2,000 feet, so it occurred after D day. Note
the wing racks have no bombs, so the planes are probably
homeward bound.
Photo reproduced with permission of Squadron/Signal
Publications

"Sweating It Out"

This photo was taken in June 1944 in Wethersfield, England,
at the tower, where nonflying officers and crews of the 416th
would congregate to "sweat out" the mission; counting the
returning planes from the mission was a ritual taken very
seriously by all. Note the ambulance positioned for possible
causalities.
A plane with casualties would fire a red flare to alert ground
and rescue crews, and would land first.
Reproduced with permission from Ralph Conte

   While the bulk of the 416th had landed, one plane was still out there trying to get
home. Jack was struggling along at one thousand feet on one engine. As they crossed
the channel, he had seen the flak bursts that had silhouetted the rest of the formation
off to the northwest. He had decided to steer clear of the action. He had correctly reasoned that he could sneak by the enemy while they shot at the formation instead of him.
He had plugged along behind the main group, lagging progressively farther behind.
   Jack could see the cliffs rising from the channel's edge and thought, *We need altitude.* He worked to increase the manifold pressure in the left engine. The supercharger
had quit working when the second blast hit under the left wing. The only good news was
that the feeling in his left arm had started coming back, but now it hurt like hell.
   "Dean, Hoffman."
   "Yeah?"

"We've got a heckuva problem here. Damned bomb-release mechanisms didn't drop the wing bombs," Jack moaned. "Someone needs to shoot the guy who designed them."

"You're right about that," said Dean, "but at least they're still hanging in the racks instead of nose down by the back one." The A-20s had a terrible problem: sometimes just the front bomb-release mechanism let go, leaving the bomb nose down and armed, hanging in the bomb bay or on the wing.

After all the missions he had flown with Jack, Dean could tell when the news was good, bad, or life threatening by the tone of Jack's deep Southern drawl. This tone was not a good one. "What's the situation, Lieutenant?"

"You guys may want to think about jumping. We ain't got much hydraulics and I don't know about brakes. Heck, we still got two bombs hangin' on the wings. It might be a bit safer for you to bail out. Wouldn't blame you none if you did." Since the flak hits over the target, the Havoc had been losing hydraulic pressure, and all the while Jack had been hoping that he had enough left to get his bird on the ground. He knew he could land with the wheels up, but with two five-hundred-pounders on the wings, it didn't make for a pretty picture.

"What are you doing?" Dean asked.

There was a long pause as Jack took a deep breath through his nose, and exhaled deeply while rubbing his forehead with his sore hand. He replied, "I need to get her wheels down first. If they drop, I figure I'll try to bring her in. Hope she stops before the barbed wire. If the wheels won't drop from their wells…well, hell, I guess we're all jumping then."

Dean and Hoffman needed no explanation for what Jack meant by the "barbed wire." They had seen what was left of a plane and crew three weeks ago when they hit the wire with a five-hundred-pounder hanging on the wing.

"I'm with you, Jack. Bring her in," said Dean as he settled into his gunner's compartment and waited for whatever was coming.

"I'm with you too, Lieutenant," Hoffman said.

"Listen—dump out everything not nailed down. We need about five hundred feet to get over these cliffs and find a place to land."

"We're on it," said Hoffman. He started dumping his ammo cans, flak helmet, and flak jacket, which followed his gun into the channel waters. Dean pushed his ammo cans out his escape hatch followed by the .50-caliber shell casings covering the bottom of the turret. Dean smiled as he thought about all the damage he had caused. Jack emptied his nose guns of their ammo by ripping off round after round. He watched them splash into the waves a thousand yards ahead.

The altimeter responded, and the Havoc cleared one thousand feet, giving Jack a view of the countryside. About three miles inland he spotted an emergency strip.

"That's the one."

Going straight in, Jack began his landing ritual. Reaching to his right, he pushed the landing gear lever to the down position and listened for the hydraulic cylinders straining as they pushed open the wheel well doors and lowered the wheels. Jack heard the pumps whining as they ever so slowly found enough fluid to get the wheels down. In a herky-jerky fashion they finally came down, giving Jack three greens on his indicator lights. One problem down.

Tentatively he brought the lever controlling the flaps down to 25 percent to see if they would respond. The hydraulic motor whined and slowly lowered the flaps to the desired position. *So far, so good,* Jack thought as he put the Havoc into the final glide slope. "Hold on, guys, we're only gunna get one shot at this."

"Roger."

"Heck fire, we got the wheels down anyway. Sure hope the brakes work and those dang bombs don't fall off."

Closing his eyes Dean sat back in the turret. He then heard the quiet prayer coming from Hoffman below him. Dean also began a short conversation with his God. He had been lucky, surviving all these missions, but he was now counting on Jack to bring him home.

Steeling himself, Dean encouraged Jack: "Put her on the ground, Lieutenant!"

"No sweat," Jack replied, belying his true condition. The droplets of salty perspiration dripped from under his flight helmet, first running down his forehead and then into his eyes or off his nose. He wiped his eyes free with his jacket sleeve as they closed in on the end of the runway.

Jack settled the Havoc into the approach. Lining up on the centerline and looking down the runway to the far end, he prayed that he could set it down and then slow to a stop. He would rather ground loop[197] than hit the barbed wire; at least that way the bombs might not explode.

The runway was coming up quickly, as Jack eased down to the ground, keeping his airspeed a little higher than he might need. Glancing quickly at the windsock, he saw there was a good headwind, so he backed off the throttles but still kept good lift. To land, he wanted as low a relative ground speed as possible when he touched down but enough lift to keep from stalling.

He had just passed the start of the runway. He pushed the plane down without reducing power by easing in a little forward pressure on the yoke. As he descended, he held the rudder steady. Flaring the nose, he eased the throttles back and brought the main gear to the tarmac. The touch jolted them all, and now Jack had to fight to keep the plane on the runway. He pulled back on the throttles slowly as he felt the wheels hit and hold the ground. Then he eased back on the manifold pressure until the nose dropped. He tried to steady the plane.

"Hold on, guys!"

The airspeed bled off quickly now, to about 95 mph. As he pulled off the power, Jack readied himself to steer the Havoc with the nosewheel. He pressed the rudder pedals forward to apply the brakes. Instinctively, he cut the throttle and looked to his right, yelling, "No brakes! Hold on, I'm gunna hit the emergency air bottle."

---

197   Ground loop – when a plane spins in circles on the ground without flipping over

Reaching to the emergency backup system, Jack pulled the handle to release two hundred pounds per square inch of pressurized air onto the brakes, to lock the wheels. The pressurized air rapidly escaped to the brake slave cylinders in the three tricycle landing gear brake systems. The brakes began to squeal, heating rapidly, as the rubber tires skidded along the ground and smoked. Having never done this before, Jack realized he had no steering. The wheels were completely locked.

"Shit! The brakes are locked. I guess it *can* get a hell of lot worse!" Nearing the end of the runway, the trenches and barbed wire loomed. "Damnit, we ain't gunna make it! Hold on, we're going off the runway!"

Dean closed his eyes, and took his cross in his right hand and lifted his words to a higher power.

Jack knew there was no stopping this twenty-thousand-pound giant on a dime, so he systematically cut the fuel pumps, hydraulic pumps, and magnetos to prevent a fire. He finished by feathering the prop. As the air pressure on the brakes declined, the plane began a repetitive two-step—skidding then rolling toward the runway's edge.

Completing his first conversation with God, Dean tightened his hold on the turret, and quickly renewed his conversation. Hoffman was already planning his escape the second the plane stopped, as he watched the plane slow through his gun opening.

All three braced for the impact. Jack cringed with eyes open, ducking his head as low as his seat harness would let him. The first impact, they knew, would be followed by the detonation of the five-hundred-pounders. Praying hard, Jack felt his deep Methodist roots overcoming him again, wrapping him in generations of security. Jack could only watch the inevitable chain of events unfold.

Alternating between rolling and skidding, the Havoc careened onto the grass at the end of the runway just when the last drop in air pressure released the brakes completely. The nosewheel hit the raised edge of a trench. The Havoc lurched to an abrupt stop.

"Get the hell out of here!"

Dean really didn't need to be told; he was already heading out his escape hatch. Jack wrestled with his escape hatch and then threw it open as he called for everyone to get out. He then released his seat harness. Once free, all six feet and two inches came out of the hatch, moving fast for such a tall guy in such a small space. Jack rolled off the backside of the right wing, meeting Dean as he came out of his hatch behind the upper turret. Hoffman had also burst free, and the three sprinted from the Havoc. They could hear the alarm sirens of the rescue vehicles approaching. A jeep pulled up.

"You Yanks OK?" a very English voice greeted them.

"I'm OK, what about you two?" Jack asked.

"Heck, I'm still in one piece, so I guess I'm OK." Hoffman laughed.

"Me too," said Dean, joining the laughter.

The immediate release of immense strain had left them giddy.

Laughing too, Jack replied, "Well, at least the bird is still in one piece too."

As they ran away from the scene, Jack looked back at the A-20 and said, "Damn, we were lucky today." He wondered why those two bombs hadn't fallen off the racks and why the bombs weeks before had, killing the crew and destroying the plane.

"Sure as hell were. No sweat though. Just wasn't our time, Jack," Hoffman said, relieved to be able to say it.

"I wasn't wantin' to give up the ghost today either," Dean agreed.

The emergency crew truck pulled up beside them, and a voice yelled, "You three—let's go!"

Along the way to one of the three small buildings on the airstrip, Jack, Dean, and Hoffman eyed two other A-20s from their group parked along the runway. Both had taken 37-mm rounds through their inboard wing tanks, forcing them to land before running out of fuel. The jeep rolled to a jerky stop and let the three of them off in front of the personnel building.

The three walked up toward the building, seeing Lieutenant DeMun with his gunners Rosenstein and Carney chatting with Lieutenant Hand and his crew, Staff Sergeants Alden and Ballinger. Sitting down outside the only door, Jack lit a Lucky with a shaky hand, and then leaned over and held the lighter with both hands to steady it as he lit Dean's and Hoffman's Phillip Morris cigarettes.

Hand looked at Jack. "That was a damned good landing, Smith. Didn't think you fellas were gunna make it."

"Thanks," was all Jack could say as he took a deep draw on his cigarette. He looked out over the base and then up into the sky. The daylight was almost gone. He saw the sunset in an entirely different way now; the sun seemed brighter, the air smelled fresher, and the cigarette tasted much better. More feeling was coming back into his left arm, and he was happy that the injury did not seem to be permanent. He was hoping that by the time they got back to base all the feeling would return.

"Smoke?" extending his pack toward the other crew.

Nothing else was said as they looked out into the new world before them. After finishing their smokes, the crews reported in to Wethersfield.

As the sun descended on June 6, Operation Neptune's first day of war was drawing to a close. Ground crews at Wethersfield were busy examining and repairing the damage done to their aircraft by the flight crews. It was not hard for them to imagine the intensity of the battle these Havocs had flown through several hours ago, particularly those ground crews cleaning the blood from their A-20s. Back in May, Colonel Mace had given the ground crews a simulated briefing so they would know what went on inside the briefing hut twice a day, but they all knew there was no way to simulate what these men flew through day after day.

Simulation was not what the armies who landed on the beaches of Normandy experienced either. Darkness was allowing the consolidation of the day's accomplishments while thousands of dead were being accounted for.

Chapter Ten
Consolidations on the Continent

If they kill their horses and eat the meat, the army lacks grain.
– Sun Tzu

After the Allies gained a foothold in Europe, resupply became the order of the day. The oldest problem known to warfare was the potential Achilles' heel of the largest amphibious landing in history. To supply the forces at the front, the Allies constructed two prefabricated harbors—code-named Mulberry—off the landing beaches. Mulberry "A," for the Americans, was anchored on Omaha beach at Saint-Laurent, while Mulberry "B," for the British and Canadians, was constructed off Arromanches. By June 9—just three days after D day—the harbors were fully functional, and began deploying the some four million tons of supplies that would pass through them in the first one hundred days of the invasion.

In spite of Mulberry's success, every invasion planner knew from the beginning that to get that proverbial pound of rice to each soldier at the front, dependable natural harbors were needed. So, capturing natural ports that could withstand storms, bombardments, and a high volume of ship traffic was the priority. Because it met these criteria, Cherbourg was of critical importance to the Allies. As one of their first major objectives, the Allies had plans to liberate the German-occupied French harbor fortress sitting at the tip of the Cotentin peninsula. By June 18, the Americans had cut across the base of the peninsula, setting the stage to follow. Then, the Americans began their assault of Cherbourg from behind, following the battle plan outlined by the Japanese conquest of Singapore four years earlier. By capturing the city on June 30th the Americans kept supply lines flowing, since Mulberry A had fallen to the enemy of all campaigns—weather, in the form of a storm of record proportions—the day after the siege of Cherbourg began.

After supply had been relatively stabilized, the processes of consolidating and expanding territory could begin, with air power playing a significant role. Havocs from the Ninth Air Force's 409th, 410th, and 416th bomb groups had been supporting the front-line efforts since June 6th by interdicting the bridges, rail yards, and road junctions that the Wehrmacht had to use to mount a counterattack. Missions to obscure places such as a bridge at Lessay, the Balleroy road junction, the Vitre railroad bridge, and a place soon to become famous, the Falaise railroad junction, had been flown by the 416th, and more missions were to come. After D day, No-ball targets hit the 416th's radar screen again, as the Nazis fired up the first buzz bomb rocket attacks against England.

As a retaliatory measure against the Allies for their invasion of the continent, Hitler had fired the first of his *vergeltungswaffe,* or vengeance weapons, into London.

London needed these launch sites destroyed, since its citizenry began dying in great numbers under the onslaught of doodlebugs.[198]

Defending London from these flying bombs was not easy. Having been conditioned to fight manned bomber aircraft, the English had positioned their anti-aircraft artillery around London. As a result, the fighters got first crack at the incoming V-bombs over the channel and coastal areas. If the V-bomb made it through the fighters, then artillery gunners had their chance. However, even if it was hit, the V-bomb still had the opportunity to complete its mission, since it would fall to the ground in London. Counterintuitively, a better defense of the city would require moving the artillery away.

After many appeals from General Pile, the officer responsible for the artillery defense of London, he was finally granted permission to move the batteries to the coast. This herculean effort was accomplished in three days and required the movement of twenty-three thousand personnel, the laying of thousands of miles of telephone cable and the integration of 180 90-mm American anti-aircraft guns donated by General Eisenhower. Along with the guns came the Bell Labs SCR-584 gun-laying radar and M-9 tracker. When married to the guns, these devices provided the targeting, speed, and accuracy needed to change the balance in the air battle over London toward the defenders. Then the Allies coupled the high-tech defense with the newly developed "proximity fuse" in the artillery shell. The doodlebugs now had to fly through a fighter screen followed by a radar-directed artillery barrage and then another layer of fighters. This three-level defense reduced the rate of successful V-1 assaults to around five percent.[199, 200] The buzz bomb faced a new gauntlet.

Since Belgium and France had become the launching ground for the vast majority of the V-weapons, it had been and currently was the target of the bombers from the 416th Bomb Group. Missions by tactical aircraft against French No-ball sites in June and July diverted resources away from the front line and behind-the-lines support against enemy logistical tactical strikes, but they were missions for which the A-20 was designed. By the end of July the bombing had destroyed most of the sites that were in range of London, while the rapidly advancing Allied forces prevented the construction of more launch sites.

In spite of the intensive effort to destroy the launch sites between June 12 and July 21, 1944, the Germans still managed to launch 4,059 V-1s at Tower Bridge, the relative center of London, which was used as a target reference. By March 1945 a total of 9,251 V-1s had been hurled at England, with only 2,419 "vengeance weapons" actually hitting a target in England. Over two thousand had been shot down or knocked off course by brave RAF fighter pilots, who would position their wing under the V-1's wing and flip it out of control. With its gyros disrupted, the original "cruise mis-

---

198   British nickname for V-1's or buzz bombs
199   United States Air Force Museum-WW-II Combat Europe-V-1 Buzz Bomb; http://www .wpafb.af.mil/museum/history/wii/ce28.htm
200   Fighter Factory: Aviation Institute of Maintenance: German V-1 Buzz Bomb; http:// www.fighterfactory.net/airworthy-aircraft/buzzbomb-v1.php

sile" would spin out of control to the ground. The anti-aircraft crews claimed 1,971 kills, while barrage-balloon crews snagged 278 of the low-flying missiles.

When London was relatively secure, Antwerp became the next city that required protection from the V-bombs after D day. Antwerp was a critical supply port that disbursed upward of ninety thousand tons of supplies a day. This task fell to a quickly assembled, twenty-two-thousand-strong American-British-Polish anti-aircraft artillery brigade that had been organized under "Antwerp X," the secret plan to protect the Belgian city from Nazi disruption. The American SCR-584 gun-laying radar and particularly the proximity fuse, which initially had been denied use on the Continent for security reasons, aided the air defense.

The anti-aircraft and searchlight brigades, battalions, and groups battled non-stop for 154 days to prevent the V-1s from hitting the vital supply port of Antwerp. Not until April 1945 did the last V-1 bomb fall against the city, bringing the total missiles launched there to five thousand. They had carried a total of five million pounds of high explosives. The vast majority—some thirty-six hundred—never reached their target. This size of this aerial assault was the reason command decided to shift tactical missions toward the V-1 launch sites. It was on a mission into southern Belgium that Staff Sergeant Elpidio "Al" Damico would find himself utilizing all the skills developed during his escape and evasion training in Ireland.[201, 202, 203]

⚜︎

The A-3 flight was less than thirty seconds behind the A-2 flight that had just turned onto the bomb-run as planned over the northwestern France town of Ligescourt. They were experiencing the same merciless pounding that the other flights had endured. Like every crew member on the run, Damico wanted nothing more than to drop these bombs and then get the hell out of there. He wondered why the Window missions didn't seem to be so effective today. Kissing his cross that hung around his neck while saying a prayer, Al watched the flak bursts move closer and closer.

"Flak bursts at two o'clock low and ten o'clock high," Al called out to his pilot. German steel continued shredding all the planes in Al's flight; the airframes were sustaining tremendous structural damage. By God's grace none of the planes had suffered any mechanical failures or loss of young men's souls yet. Al doubted that this luck would hold out much longer.

Watching in terrifying amazement, Damico and the rest of the crews in A-3 were stunned by the volume of anti-aircraft fire today. All the pilots held steady on the bomb-run, though, as they had been trained, even as the barrages detonated around them. Wings, tail structures and fuselages were pierced through and through by the screaming

201   V-1 Flying Bombs; http://spartacus.schoolnet.co.uk/2WWv1.htm

202   Antwerp X: The AAA War Against the Buzz Bombs: Skylighters, the Web site of the 225th AAA Searchlight Battalion; http://www.skylighters.org/buzzbombs/index2.html

203   *A Radar History World War II: Technology and Military Imperatives*; Louis Brown; Institute of Physics publishing; pp 395-396 copyright 1999

metal bumble bees. Damico listened as the steel passed effortlessly through his plane and prayed that all it hit was his plane. Al's prayers were heard that day just as his plane was hit.

Feeling the concussion of the blast, Al was banged around inside his gunner turret. The flak had ripped through the plane's shell and then careened through his compartment. Just as Al leaned back, a large piece of German steel sliced through one side of his compartment, passing directly in front of him, and then went out the other side of the plane. Other pieces tore through the compartment, and Al wrapped his flak jacket even tighter. It was a protective maneuver he had done for every mission he had flown, and it had done its job today by deflecting a few small pieces of steel that would otherwise have found Al's flesh.

Al sat silently looking at the two holes on either side of his compartment. The path of the steel had gone right through where his head should have been. If they were shot up any more, he knew the plane might be his death trap. Kissing his gold cross again, he closed his eyes and said a silent prayer. *Hell of a mission,* Al thought to himself as he looked out at the right wing and noticed a small amount of hydraulic fluid leaking over the trailing edge of the wing. "Oh, that's not good."

The flight was moving down the bomb-run with Al's flight-lead bombardier killing the rate as quickly as he could. Al was temporarily relieved when he heard "bombs away" in his headphones. Listening to the shackles release, he looked into the bomb bay to be sure all the bombs had dropped clear. Watching as they fell, Al swore he could see the bombs bouncing off the concrete bunkers that housed parts of the V-1 facility. "Golly, what do they make those things out of, Lieutenant?"

"Hell if I know. Why you want to know, Damico?"

"The damn bombs are just bouncing off."

"Well, nothing we can do about that. Are we clear?"

"Yes sir, all clear."

As the bomb bay doors closed, Al turned toward the tail and crawled back into his gun turret. Lieutenant Harris banked hard left into a steep dive to get out of the flak, and Al felt the change in G's."

Swinging the turret around, Al could see ground flashes from the variety of anti-aircraft fire the Germans were throwing at them. Watching some flashes in front of the downward-banking left wing, Al was suddenly stunned when the 88 round exploded in front of and below the left engine nacelle. "Holy cow, did you guys see that?" Al hollered into the interphone.

The detonation lifted the left wing up almost out of its banked position, from which it fell back quickly, jarring the whole plane. The left engine was smoking almost immediately. Al could see fluid and smoke coming from around the engine cowling, as small flames lapped out of the newly created openings.

"That's not good."

"What's that, Al?" the pilot asked.

"Fire and smoke coming out of the left engine along with some kind of fluid."

"That explains the loss of oil pressure and hydraulics in that one. Do you see anything else?"

"Lots of holes and lots of smoke in that left wing!"

The Havoc began to lose altitude rapidly as it banked into the dead engine. The fire grew. Al could see the ground approaching a lot quicker than he liked.

"Lieutenant, that fire is getting worse, I'm gone!"

Al ducked out of the turret and reached for the escape hatch. He stopped to tell the tail gunner to get out too. Looking into the tail gunner's compartment, Al saw it was empty.

Now he really moved. Al shed his flak jacket and flak helmet. After correctly hooking his chute, Al fell out the escape hatch into the slipstream. He didn't count long before he pulled the rip cord; the ground was too close. The chute jerked him upright, allowing him to see that he had done the right thing by pulling the cord quickly. He couldn't be more than five hundred feet off the ground. *Coupla more seconds, and, heck, there wouldn't be an Al Damico,* he thought as he floated down.

Looking around for the plane, Al hoped to see some more chutes, but he was turned the wrong direction, and he was almost on the ground. He put his feet together and rolled to the ground as he made contact. Reaching for the chute's quick-release, Al struggled and then finally jettisoned his chute and harness.

Now in a kneel he looked around for cover. Having landed in a large clearing, he needed to hide. How many people had seen him jump? Looking to his left he spied some thick undergrowth maybe fifty yards away. Moving quickly in a hunched-over position, he thought, *This is not good.*

Ducking into the undergrowth, he moved deep into it and stayed low to the ground. He was impressed by the sound and concussions of the group's punishing bombardment of the No-ball site. Settling back into the thicket, he hoped the undergrowth would provide enough cover while he thought about how the hell he was going to get back to US territory. What had he been told about how to find the Libre Francais Résistance?

"First things first," he mumbled as he took inventory of his escape packet. "Let's see."

Al found his evasion photos along with some French, Belgium, and German money. "Check." A .45-caliber sidearm. "Yep, loaded and two extra magazines." He then located his most important item. From inside his flight jacket he pulled out his stick of pepperoni. He never flew without one, and smiled, looking out through the underbrush. *What now?* Al thought as the explosions from the group's bombardment stopped and the drone of the departing aircraft faded.

It was then that he heard the footsteps in the woods behind him. He listened to the crackle of leaves get closer. "Oh hell," he muttered, trying to burrow deeper into the undergrowth, until he smelled the humus of mother earth and hoped he was hidden enough to remain unseen by the enemy.

Holding his .45 at the ready, he remembered he hadn't chambered a round. He needed to, if the gun was to be of any help. Slowly he drew the slide back as quietly as a forty-five would let you, then let it slip forward to chamber the first round. That's when he heard, "*Américain, ne vous déplacez pas. Nous sommes ici pour vous aider. Faites comme nous disons.*"[204]

Al looked up and had no idea what the heck they were saying, except he knew it was French, not German.

"*Venez ici maintenant!*"[205]

Looking them in the eyes, Al figured out their intent by the pantomime of the two Frenchmen. Crawling out of the thicket, he walked to the spot the Résistance fighter was pointing to. They immediately took his sidearm and extra clips. Sitting him down, they began removing his boots and anything else that looked American. At first, Al resisted but when he saw their seriousness, he let them proceed.

Reaching for his escape packet, the shorter of the two Frenchmen opened it and put everything in his pockets, except for the escape and evasion photos. Watching the two work, Al realized they had done this before. They produced some clothes from a backpack that resembled the clothes he had on in the photos. Al took off his flight jacket and pants, getting rid of anything that would identify him as an American, including his GI issue underwear. After he put on the old clothes, he realized that except for a lack of a beard he really looked French. They headed out quickly from the No-ball site toward the southwest. The shoes they gave him were too small and hurt his feet, but they were better than no shoes at all.

"*Venez avec nous, Nous nous cacherons dans la forêt pendant le jour et voyagerons seullement pendant la nuit, Vous comprenez?*"[206]

"Ah, sure thing, fellas, whatever you say," Al replied, having no idea what they were talking about. "At least you left me my pepperoni."

Walking between them, Al started the first steps of a difficult fifteen-day journey through the German-occupied northern French countryside. He hid in the woods by day, and nibbled on his sausage and the occasional piece of stale bread or rare drink of water. Al wondered when it would end. Night was the worst. Al could hear the German patrols moving along roads or trails but could not see them. He was constantly afraid they would walk right into him. With the help of his guides he evaded the German patrols until they encountered an Allied unit. Al was never more thankful, and shook the hands of his saviors many times, while gulping several drafts of water from a soldier's canteen.

Damico's absence was felt by his fellow gunners of the 668th. Conflict, however, did not mourn Al's absence long, as missions continued coming down from Command to Wing, ending up in the Operations building of the 416th at Wethersfield. However, the logistics of resupply were again creating problems for the advancing Allied forces.

---

204   *Américain ne vous déplacez pas. Nous sommes ici pour vous aider. Faites comme nous disons* – (French) – American, don't move we are here to help you, do as we say.

205   *Venez ici maintenant* – (French) – Come over here now

206   Venez avec nous. Nous nous cacherons dans la forêt pendant le jour et voyageronsseullement la nuit. Vous comprenez – (French) – Come with us. We will hide in the forest during the day and travel only at night. Do you understand?

Cherbourg was continuing to resist surrender and Allied occupation. Resources were being used daily in the struggle to take the port that could be used elsewhere. To clear this impasse, a massive air strike against the harbor fortress was planned.

As American ground forces continued up the Cotentin Peninsula toward Cherbourg, the city was listed as a target by the IXth Bomber Command HQ on June 22. The orders were sent down to the 97th Combat Wing's HQ. Cherbourg was to be a complex mission requiring multiple heavy and light bomber groups to hit the target in sequence without hitting each other.

During the briefing the pilots and navigators leading the 416th on the mission began to realize that pinpoint arrival and departure times were critical to its success. Any significant miscalculation could potentially cause loss of life.

As they shuffled out of the briefing, Ralph asked his pilot: "Hulse, did you get us posted to be deputy on this one?"

"Heck fire, Conte, at least we're not leading this one. That is, of course, unless Captain Jackson and Lieutenant Maltby get shot down."

"Let's hope not." Ralph imagined having to take the lead on this one.

"Yeah, 'let's hope not' is right," Jackson chimed in, surprising Hulse and Conte. He was walking out behind them. They strode to the trucks that would move them to the planes, and joined others doing the same.

Staff Sergeant Robert E. Lee walked up to his pilot, Lieutenant Daniel Shea. "Hey, Lieutenant, you ready to go get 'em?"

"Sounds like a tough one."

"Ain't been any easy ones yet, sir," Lee said, as they recognized their tunnel gunner Staff Sergeant Francis Falk crawling into the back of the truck that would take them to their plane's revetment.

"Falk, save us a seat," Lee hollered.

"Done."

The men were in the air in what seemed like moments. Jackson accelerated down the runway followed by Hulse and Conte. In three minutes the first box was airborne. In six minutes both boxes were airborne. Jackson followed his navigator's recommendations and turned south toward Maidenhead. He had to hit the next waypoint on schedule so he could hit the IP on time. Otherwise, the bombs from the other groups before or behind them, dropping from one thousand feet above them, might hit the 416th.

Timetables were kept, and Lieutenant Maltby called up, "IP in five minutes."

Jackson checked his watch—twenty seconds ahead of schedule.

"One minute to target, Captain. Window should be out ahead dropping now, sir."

"Roger that, Maltby."

Artillery erupted from the fortress below, sending their happy hellos skyward into the high and low boxes of the 416th. The Luftwaffe and the Kriegsmarine had been fortifying the fortress since 1940 and were making good use of it today.

"Hold on, guys, here it comes. Flak bursts at ten, twelve, and one o'clock. Looks like they've got our altitude," Lee relayed to Shea.

"How bad is it?" Falk asked. He was unable to see the sky ahead.

"Not too bad, but they got our altitude. Its gunna be rough," Lee shot back. "Burst at twelve low."

One by one the flights turned onto the IP, opening their bomb bays and praying for the navigators to get it over with. Shea held his bomb-release button down, and watched the bombs fall from the other planes in the formation from his number-four position. Then, getting all green lights on his indicator panel, he closed his bomb bay doors. All gunners assigned to photos were shooting pictures instead of bullets as the flights passed the MIP.

Lee was just about to call another set of flak bursts when he was thrown to the deck of his turret. The A-20 was forced upward after a 150-mm artillery shell exploded just beneath it. Shea, Lee, and Falk had never felt a blast so large. Immediately the plane started dropping out of formation. "Oh, shit, not again," Lee said.

Theirs wasn't the only plane hit that instant, as the number-five slot in his flight took a 150-mm shell in the right engine and wing. It, however, managed to hold course.

Shea watched in awe as all the needles in his panel gauges flipped in the wrong direction. His left engine was out, since the shrapnel had destroyed his fuel pumps and fuel lines, and punched several holes into his left engine's crankcase. The blow had knocked several piston rods out and pushed one piston out the top of a jug. Hydraulic lines in both wings were shot, creating an oily mess along the trailing edge of both wings. Shea tried to feather the prop and fought to keep the plane in the air. He quickly learned that the left engine wouldn't feather as the propeller spun out of control in the slipstream.

Havocs over Cherbourg

Eight A-20 Havocs all appear to be solid-nose "B" models with D-Day invasion stripes, flying over Cherbourg, France. This complex mission was flown after D-Day to destroy heavy gun emplacements and help the army capture the vital port city. This complex mission was flown with many other aircraft types and groups involved.

The 416th had two planes shot up that crash-landed on their return to base. One piloted by Lieutenant. D. F. Shea with his gunners Staff Sergeants Robert E. Lee and F. G. Falk crash landed in France on an emergency strip completed just three hours before they landed. The other flew back to land at Wethersfield. The 416th suffered no losses but much battle damage all around.

Wethersfield also became the emergency landing strip for a Consolidated B-24 Liberator, a B-26 Marauder and a British Halifax Bomber that day.

Reproduced with permission of Wayne Downing

"Mayday! Mayday! This is fiver-seven-one…T…Tango," Shea radioed. "Repeat, Mayday! Mayday! Fiver-seven-one…T…Tango. I'm hit and going down. Will try for Normandy, over and out." Shea nosed his Havoc into a dive to gain energy, while keeping his left engine on the outside for the turn to the northeast.

"Roger fiver-seven-one, good luck," came back from the radio.

The Havoc was falling fast. Having started with good altitude, Shea figured they could make it to friendly territory. With good aerodynamics in the wings you could cover a lot of ground by keeping airspeed in a downward glide. He hoped they had enough altitude to get back behind American lines near the Normandy beaches.

Shea watched his pressure gauges slowly head to zero as his hydraulic fluid drained out over the back of his plane's wings. His left engine had been out since the first flak burst, but now he saw the manifold temperature rising in his right engine. He watched as the right engine's fuel pressure gauge surged, and at the same time the engine revved and rumbled, revved and rumbled. Even worse, his fuel level was dropping.

"Listen up, guys. I don't know if we're going to be airborne much longer. We're close to American lines, so you can jump."

The two crewmen listened, and then Lee responded, "I'm staying with you, Lieutenant."

"Me too," Falk cautiously agreed.

Continuing to lose altitude, Shea scanned the landscape ahead of him looking for a strip, any strip. Passing the southern end of Utah Beach, Shea saw a straight flat strip, which he immediately decided was his landing zone or crash site, whichever it became.

"Listen up, fellas. I'm going in, last chance to jump." Shea said, and added that the Havoc had now slid below twelve hundred feet.

"You brung us this far, Lieutenant, so put her down," Falk said.

Shea lowered his flaps and then turned his attention to lowering his wheels. He figured it was a waste of time but would try anyway. After dropping the lever to the down position, Shea heard the hydraulic pumps whine as they tried to pump the last of the hydraulic fluid through the shredded hydraulic lines. Shea finally got three green lights on his indicator panel, which let him know his wheels had locked down. He had no way of knowing the last pound of hydraulic pressure had secured them in position.

Shea lined up on the runway aiming at the thirty feet of marston mat that the engineers had laid. As he did, he saw a P-38 at the far right end with a C-47 across from it on the left. Both had bellied in. *So,* he thought, *we're not the first to use this strip. Well, at least they left me room to land.* Never had a more serendipitous timing of events prevented a disaster. Just three hours before, the engineers had finished the emergency-landing strip inland behind the American beaches, and they were still in the process of laying the metal marston mats when the wounded aircraft started landing.

"You guys lay down back there. Prepare for a rough landing."

Not having to be told twice, Lee and Falk braced themselves in their compartments as they had been taught in basic. Lee thought back to his first close encounter with death. Odd that it came to him now. Facing death nearly every day now seemed almost commonplace. Even as the three of them fell toward their destiny, he couldn't help but think of the crash landing he had survived in Lake Charles, Louisiana, while still in training. He now found himself in almost the same painfully remembered situation as then.

⚜

Coming back from a night training mission, Lee could see very little as he looked out through the Plexiglass of his turret into the fog. The night landing was complicated by the smoke from an oil rig fire about two miles upwind of the runway. This made the ground fog that had settled in, with its eight-hundred-foot ceiling, that much thicker. Lee's pilot, Lieutenant Bob Duthu, was the instrument instructor pilot for the group. He made Lee feel secure that they would make it in OK. Lieutenant Robert Jones, the BN in the nose, wasn't worried either. As the plane settled in for approach, the crew knew that one plane had already crashed on approach. The glow of the blaze was visible in the northwest through the fog, like the oil rig fire. As Duthu descended through the murk, Lee suddenly saw the ground and recognized the flight line, not the runway.

"Pull up, Duthu, you're landing on the flight line!"

The engines roared as Duthu applied power, pulled back on the yoke and turned toward the right to bank upward out of the descent. He circled back around, but began experiencing vertigo in the heavy fog laced with thick black smoke from the oil rig. To make it worse, the oily residue from the rig fire was covering the windshield. As the plane banked back toward what Duthu thought was the field, he had become so disoriented that he could no longer fly the plane. After losing the pilot's orientation completely, the plane lost altitude and nosed into a dry rice field at over 200 mph, crushing the glass nose of the plane. As the nose curled in around him, Jones died almost instantaneously. By the grace of the good Lord, Jones never had time to become aware of his impending passing.

On impact, the tail of the plane broke off just behind the bomb bay, flipping the rudder and elevators over onto their backs. Lee was left hanging out the open end. The momentum of the plane pushed the two separate parts of the fuselage forward while at the same time dragging Lee along the ground with the tail structures, his head bouncing along the ground as it skidded through the rice field. Duthu, trapped in the cockpit, was severely injured by the time the fuselage had finally dug itself to a stop.

Coming to his senses, Lee slowly unhooked his seatbelt and crawled out of the twisted and deformed mass of aluminum that was once the plane's tail superstructure. Stumbling around, Lee saw the other part of the fuselage and slowly made his way to it. He hollered out, but he got no reply. Seeing the nose of the plane crushed and nearly buried, Lee crawled up onto the wing and then the fuselage. Looking into the cockpit Lee found Duthu pinned in by the instrument panel that had collapsed around him. Lee hollered through the cockpit's Plexiglass canopy, after trying to pull open the escape hatch, which was jammed shut. "Duthu, you OK?"

"Go for help, Lee. I'm stuck here. You need to get help."

Lee tried several times to open the hatch, but couldn't. He rolled off the fuselage and stumbled to a road, where a car finally stopped to help. He accepted medical attention only after he made the people around him aware of the need for the rescue team to help the crew in the crashed plane.

༄

As the plane descended toward the new emergency landing strip, Lee found himself thinking more of home and peace time. He was another Tennessee boy, with a solid Southern tone to his voice. The son of an attorney, he had grown up in Pulaski. His life had always been comfortable, but his family was never rich. During the hard years of the thirties his father was paid with livestock or foodstock, but there still seemed to be some cash around. After high school Lee enlisted in the Army Air Corps. Having flown and soloed his first plane before joining made him think the air corps might give him a chance to fly. He was not to be that lucky. The flight surgeon found some weakness in his eyes that made him ineligible to be a pilot but not so bad that he couldn't be a gunner. It had been a long road to this spot, descending to the ground in a wounded bird and having put his life in God's hands. It made him try harder to look into the future, and not dwell on the present. He thought about his plans after he completed his required missions and then rotated home. The first thing on his list was spending time with his new wife. He missed her dearly, not having had much time with her before rotating out with the group to the ETO. After spending time with her, he wanted some time with the family. He missed the fried chicken, taters, beans, corn bread, and fried okra with Sunday dinners. Oh, howdy! After some time at home doing nothing, he figured he would start working toward a degree at the University of Tennessee, maybe in the law, like his father.

Lee pulled his shoulders up higher and braced for a hard landing as he heard the overheated engine begin to misfire and rumble as the pistons sucked in the gas.

Shea wrestled the flight controls against the crosswind coming from his left while balancing the rudder against the pull of the right engine. He passed over the runway high but down the center. His right engine rumbled but didn't stop as the cylinders sucked in the fuel. Shea chopped the power and dropped the bird toward the runway.

The Havoc hit long, slamming onto the packed earth runway just beyond the metal marston mats, bouncing up and then slamming down again. The landing jarred the occupants so hard that their prayers and promises with God increased as their fear of death intensified. Rolling down the center of the runway, Shea pressed his brakes only to find he had none. Having hit long, the Havoc was not going to stop on the earthen strip. He quickly pulled the emergency air brake, only to hear the high-pitched hissing of pressurized air as it escaped from all the punctured tubing. The air never made it to the brake cylinders. Shea relayed the news to his crewmen.

"Hold on! We're going off the end!"

Passing the end of the runway, the Havoc hit the first mound of dirt, slamming hard against it and ripping off the front landing gear. Milliseconds later the rear wheels hit the mound and were ripped from the wheel wells, tearing open the fuel tanks as they separated themselves from the nacelles. The Havoc sailed another ten feet over the ditch behind the mound, where the last of the Havoc's energy was expended. The crew was jarred violently as gravity jerked the twenty-thousand-pound aluminum cylinder to the ground. There was no noise, only the smell of aviation fuel mixed with hydraulic fluid and oil.

Regaining his senses, Lee yelled to Falk, "Let's go!"

Lee swung the escape ax, knocking the Plexiglass escape panel out behind the turret, then crawled out onto the fuselage just in front of the vertical stabilizer. Falk was out the escape hatch right behind him, and both men headed toward the nose of the plane to help Shea. They saw him wrestling with the cockpit's escape hatch, which had been buckled closed by the impact of the crash. With Falk's help, Lee used the ax and chopped the cockpit open. Together they pulled Shea free of the cockpit and headed down the right wing, and then jumped to the ground. Lee was the first off the wing, landing five feet from a young infantryman whom he immediately recognized as his friend and fellow offensive guard from his Pulaski, Tennessee, high school football team.

"Booger Burton, what the hell are you doing here?"

"Holy cow, Lee! Hell fire, I reckon the same damned thing you are—trying to stay alive!"

"Your damned right about that, Booger!" They gave each other a big bear hug.

"Come on, she may blow," Shea hollered, turning and running toward the crashed P-38 as a hiding place. Booger and the crew followed.

As he ran away, Lee thought to himself, "How many more of these am I gunna have to go through?"

The devastation of the Cherbourg harbor fortress continued for some time as wave after terrifying wave of aircraft passed over, dropping death from above. Aircraft from other groups suffered damage too, as the defenders weren't going to give up without a good fight.

The men of the 416th had settled onto their runway at Wethersfield, happy to be home with only one known loss and the three MIAs that went with it. The other wounded Havoc had limped back to base behind the formation. The 416th wouldn't be the only planes coming to roost at Wethersfield today. Over the next several hours the crews of a B-24, B-17, and B-26 nursed their wounded birds down onto Wethersfield's welcoming airstrip. The visiting aircrews shared their experiences from the Cherbourg mission, and the 416th happily reciprocated.

Normandy ended up being to the liking of Shea and his two gunners. They didn't hurry back to England, taking time to visit the remnants of a German military headquarters and to savor a few bottles of good French wine. The war did eventually find Lee, Falk, and Shea, and loaded them on to a C-47 Dakota that flew them home to Wethersfield.

Chapter Eleven

Sealing Their Fate At All Costs

There has never been a closer fraternity than the one that existed among the
pilots of a squadron fighting together high in the sky.
– Eddie Rickenbacker

All in the valley of Death
Rode the six hundred
– Alfred, Lord Tennyson, 1854

As soon as the Allies got their foothold on the Continent through victories such as Cherbourg, they began their plans to push the Germans out of France. Strategically important, the war of logistics was being progressively lost by Germany. After the capture of Cherbourg, interdiction became the mission of the 416th and similar air groups. Road and rail junctions were destroyed as well as the occasional troop concentration. Also on the mission list were the fuel dumps that held the lifeblood of any modern army, but particularly the Wehrmacht. Without resupply, without that pound of rice, an army cannot resist or attack. Germany's last source of natural oil reserves—Romania—was being threatened as the Russians advanced on the southeastern front. Slowly but surely the Germans were being pushed onto their heels.

As the weather finally cooperated in favor of the Allies, July was to be a busy month for all the Army Air Corps as they supported the ground forces on the difficult push eastward. The ground war would change course as the Wehrmacht's resistance stiffened. Hedgerow after hedgerow confronted the ground forces as they fought their way inland from the beaches. Rear supply logistics were being aggressively resolved, allowing the power of the invasion to be turned eastward.

The German positions began to fall one by one. On July 3rd, after pressing ever farther westward, the Russians liberated Minsk, in Belarus. Less than a week later, Canadian and British troops captured Caen, France, and yet another week later US troops liberated St. Lô, France, where "Operation Cobra" would begin on July 24th. Operation Cobra would see the Allies sweep deep into France using armored divisions. Finally in open country, the US troops headed toward Brest, Argentan, and Paris, while the Canadians and British fought toward Falaise, where some four hundred thousand German troops would be encircled.[207, 208] Also, Hitler was forced to plan a purge of his own

---

207   *Great Battles of World War II;* John MacDonald; copyright 1986; pp 120-131

208   The History Place: World War Two in Europe: Timeline; http://www.historyplace.com/worldwar2/timeline/ww2time.htm

command staff after the failed assassination attempt on him on July 20th. The seemingly impenetrable defenses were falling.

Due to the success of Operation Cobra, Paris could eventually be liberated. Although more a moral victory than a military objective, Paris was a symbol for the Allies, if for nothing else than Charles de Gaulle's march into the city. De Gaulle had helped to consolidate and organize the underground Résistance of France. Headquartered in London, he orchestrated through Jean Moulin the consolidation of the eight minor Résistance groups into one major group named the *Conseil National de la Résistance* (CNR). The vast majority of the French Résistance in Paris and the countryside was a mixture of Communist and socialist forces. Regardless of its membership, the CNR proved to be important in coordinating carpetbagger missions, which resupplied Résistance fighters through airdrops of weapons and other resources.[209]

The successes of the Allies that summer would later be overshadowed by the discovery of the accelerated eugenic atrocities of the believers in the "New Genetic World Order." In early June forty thousand children were kidnapped from Poland and taken into Germany as slave labor or for other unknown reasons. Over the summer of 1944 the Auschwitz-Birkenau Death Camp documented a record number of eugenic murders, exceeding nine thousand in that camp alone. The godless slaughter was proceeding in other camps at the same accelerated rate, as the Nazi leadership understood their days were numbered and that the same fate awaited them.[210, 211]

Yet, that summer Jewish extermination was also interrupted for the first time, as the Allies increasingly pressured the Germans. Swedish diplomat Raoul Wallenberg went to Budapest to secure the safety of thirty-three thousand Jews by giving them diplomatic protection. Meanwhile, the Russians liberated the Majdanek concentration camp, outside Lublin, Poland, where some 1.5 million human beings had been murdered for reasons only a eugenic bigot could understand. Medical experimentation was being interrupted, as pressure to evacuate or accelerate the death of Jewish prisoners began to interrupt the experiments of SS officer and physician Josef Mengele, whose goal was to try to double the birth rate for the *Lebensborn* project by understanding the genetic reason for the birth of twins. Vivisection of twins was his preferred technique. The Allies' approach forced an end to the Nazis' human experimentation on high altitude, low temperature, sterilization, freezing, incendiary bombs, and infectious disease.[212, 213, 214]

209   *Conseil National de la Résistance* (CNR); http://www.spartacus.schoolnet.co.uk/FRenr .htm

210   The History Place: Holocaust Timeline; http://www.historyplace.com/worldwar2/ holocaust/timeline.html

211   The Jewish Virtual Library; http://www.jewishvirtuallibrary.org/jsource/holo.html

212   *Majdanek;* The Jewish Virtual Library; http://jewishvirtuallibrary.org/jsource/ Holocaust/maidanek.html

213   The History Place: Holocaust Timeline; http://historyplace.com/worldwar2/ holocaust/timeline.html

214   The History Place: World War Two in Europe: Timeline; http://www.historyplace.com/ worldwar2/timeline/ww2time.htm

All the while that summer, interdiction missions continued for the Ninth Air Force Bomb Groups. Interruption of the Wehrmacht's ability to resupply, reinforce or retreat sent the 416th over the Continent on some of their longest missions on record. The 416th came to know well their many targets—Wehrmacht headquarters, fuel depots, railroad and road bridges, marshaling yards, and concentrated strong points. In support of Operation Cobra over the German-occupied French countryside, the men would fly many missions over villages and towns where their bombs would kill friend and enemy alike.

Even with the success of the 416th on the battlefield, one major change had affected their overall sense of security at Wethersfield. The V-1 sites they had struggled so hard to destroy now hurled death toward their English sanctuary. Regardless, they flew as often as the weather allowed or when called upon by command. The success of these July missions, which the 416th had flown in conjunction with every other bomber group in the ETO, helped to open the way to the Siegfried Line, on Germany's western border, for the soldiers fighting and dying on the earth below them. As on the ground, death came to the men in the air, taking four from the 416th this month and wounding two.

The stage was now set for the pincher movement that the Allies had been driving forward to accomplish. A series of battles was about to unfold that were to be anchored at Argentan and Falaise, France—towns the 416th had visited before. The scope and objectives of these battles created a corridor that narrowed every day as the Wehrmacht retreated toward Germany. The Allies wanted very much to seal the exit routes from this trap, and the 416th was granted the privilege to help accomplish this objective.

Allied airpower continued to prepare and soften the enemy front, which by August had become more a fighting retreat by the Wehrmacht than a picture of classic counterattacks. Constantly harassed from the air, the Wehrmacht could never consolidate a position to mount a counteroffensive from.

Airpower's role in the success of the Normandy campaign was best described during a conversation between General Dwight D. Eisenhower and his son, Lieutenant John S.D. Eisenhower, a recent graduate of the US Military Academy. While riding through the liberated countryside of Normandy in late June with his father, the younger commented about the lack of road discipline, with convoys bumper to bumper and moving very slowly. "You wouldn't get away with this if you didn't have air supremacy."

The senior replied, "If I didn't have air supremacy, I wouldn't be here."[215]

Throughout the invasion, the Allies effectively exploited their overwhelming numerical and technical superiority of fighters; fighter-bombers; light, medium, and heavy bombers; and the airlift capacity of the Air Corps. As they prepared to move deeper into the Continent, airpower was about to play some of its most critical roles.

---

215   The US Army Air Forces in World War II: D-Day 1944: Air Power Over the Normandy Beaches and Beyond; Richard Hallion; Air Force historian; http://www.ibiblio.org/hyperwar/AAF/AAF-H-DDay/

As Operation Cobra fanned out across the central and southwestern French countryside, a thorn in the Allies' side continued to resurrect itself. In performing its Lazarus act, the Wehrmacht was able to resupply their frontline troops over a major rail bridge that crossed the Seine River at Oissel, France. The Air Corps had been tasked to destroy this bridge on multiple occasions, starting the month before "Operation Neptune." To complete the mission, the Ninth Air Force sent twenty-four B-26 Marauders from the 397th Bomb Group on May 8, 1944. This assault was followed by thirty-six Marauders from the 386th BG on May 9, and thirty-two Marauders from the 387th BG on the 10th. These groups were successful in damaging the bridge, but German efficiency and French forced labor rebuilt the bridges.

Follow-up missions on June 29 and July 4 by the 344th BG were sent to destroy the repaired rail bridge. The group committed twenty-three and twenty-eight aircraft, respectively. The bridge suffered damage, but repairs quickly followed and train traffic resumed. Soon after, the invasion of Europe required resources to be expended elsewhere, until August, when the focus of the Normandy effort turned toward Germany.

Resurrection

Southern span (Tourville side) of Oissel-Tourville Railroad Bridge on May 25, 1944. Repair activities took place after Ninth Air Force's B-26 Marauder attacks in early May 1944. This bridge was critical to the Wehrmacht for resupply early in the battle for Normandy, and then later for retreat in August '44. A and C are sections of temporary tracks. B is a temporary bridge. D is anti-aircraft artillery, while E is barge activity.
Reproduced with permission of Fabrice Dhollande and the National Archives A18228

Oissel-Tourville Rail Bridge on June 12, 1944

A close-up photo of bomb damage to the southern Tourville
span from May '44 missions. It was repaired because the
critical riverbed support pylons were never damaged or
destroyed.
The diversion bridge on the east side of the damaged span is
clearly intact.
Reproduced with permission of Fabrice Dhollande and the
National Archives A18270-54840 AC

Oissel-Tourville Rail Bridge in June 1944

Note the bomb patterns around the bridgeheads and island
span. Anti-aircraft artillery of many types were located on both
ends of the island and along the ingress and egress routes;
trains were again crossing the bridge.
Reproduced with permission of Fabrice Dhollande

Glowing red hot on the dark side of the open doorway, the Camel cigarette
between the young lieutenant's lips accompanied a cup of black coffee in his left hand.
Wishing he were asleep instead of being up on duty tonight, the officer leaned against

the hinged side of the closed doorway of the Wethersfield Air Base's Operations building at 0100 hours. Sipping his coffee, he thought, *It's an odd term "Officer of the Day," with me here in the middle of the night.* Pulling on his cigarette to make the embers glow hotter, he looked up into the western sky, contemplating the clouds with the occasional break that allowed the stars to twinkle through. His thoughts were interrupted by the sound of the teletype machine coming to life.

The slightly startling sound of the teletype responding to the incoming message quickened his heart as his adrenaline level rose in a Pavlovian response to the sound. He knew the consequences that were about to come as a result of the machine responding to its commands. Crushing his Camel under his right boot, he blew the smoke out of his lungs from the last puff and walked toward the machine, being sure to close the door behind him as he maintained light discipline. He was greeted by the rapid fire of the typewriter keys striking the ink ribbon then the paper. He began to read the morning's mission description from the orders as they came down from the 97th Combat Wing Headquarters in Mark's Hall, Earls Colne Airfield in Essex. The machine chattered as the paper began rolling out into the collection tray, giving the naïve lieutenant and the experienced German spies who had tapped into the communication lines their first glimpse of the sortie. The teletype chattered on as the OD began reading:

OIRAK OIYAA V OILAI

FROM 97TH COMBAT BOMB WING
TO 409TH BOMB GROUP
416TH BOMB GROUP
ATTN: SIGNAL OFFICE
ADVANCED INFORMATION COPY OF PARA. 5. OF FIELD ORDER TO FOLLOW

Following Target Information:

A double track bridge in two sections over the Seine River to an island in the river. East bridge had three spans of steel girders and was 620' long.

Beginning on 10 May 44, these bridges have been attacked, repaired in part and re-attacked with varying degrees of damage. About June 1st, a single track diversion bridge was completed immediately to the east of the south bridge (30' away from the original bridge), was knocked out and rebuilt several times. On August 3rd, in 48 hours, this diversion bridge was again rebuilt and connects with the regular tracks at the north end of the island. A light foot-bridge spans the river between the diversion bridge and the original bridge, probably used by repair crews. The new diversion bridge is of light steel or heavy timber construction. This is the only complete railroad bridge across the Seine River north of One, and possibly three German Divisions are moving by this route to the battle area.

410th dispatched yesterday but did not attack due to 10/10 cloud cover.

X. GENERAL INFORMATION
    (10) VABT
    (11) BOX LEADERS WILL REPORT TO COMMAND CONTROL ON
CHANNEL"C" WHEN CLEARING TARGET AREA.
    COCBTWIG 97

OPERATIONAL PRIORITY BT
SECRET SENT IN THE CLEAR AUTH: LIEUTENANT COL. MC AFZX
97ᵀᴴ COMBAT BOMB WING
APO – 140
6 AUGUST 1944

FIELD ORDER NO. 164-471
MAPS: NORMAL
1. B. (1) REF. CURRENT BOMB LINE.
(2) NINTH T.A.C. WILL FURNISH FIGHTER ESCORT FOR THIS WING.
2. THIS WING WILL ATTACK TARGETS IN FRANCE.

    ZERO HOUR: 06/1930B

"Oh heck," escaped the lieutenant's lips while he read the orders as they rolled off the teletype. He knew this was going to be a tough one. He continued reading.

3. B. 416ᵀᴴ GROUP:
(1) 4901E/22 AND 23
(2) 2 BOXES OF 18 BOMBING BY FLIGHTS OF 6
(3) WITH P-38'S AT 4919N 0000 AT 12,000 FEET AT ZERO HOUR PLUS 10 MIN.
(4) BASE TO MAIDENHEAD TO SELSEY BILL TO 4919N 0000 TO 4980N 0013E TO I.P.
TO TARGET.
(5) TARGET RIGHT

Watching the printed pages come out, he kept reading, reviewing in his mind the processes he was about to set in motion. He waited for the bomb-fusing information to come across before he alerted the ground and ordnance crews to start preparing the planes and fusing the bombs.

(10) 6 X 500 LB. G.P. FUSED 1/10 SEC. NOSE 1/100 SEC. TAIL ON REF. 033065; FUSED
WITH INSTANTANIOUS NOSE 1/100 SEC. TAIL ON REF. 031077.

Sergeant Dullnig blinked his eyes slowly, instinctively reaching for the ringing phone. He knew why it was ringing. "Ground crew," he answered.

Dullnig wrote down everything the lieutenant on the other end had to say. He listened as he heard the planes' loading lists and estimated flight times.

"Roger, Lieutenant, I'll get on it now, sir," Dullnig replied, and then hung up the phone. He dressed, and headed out of the tent after waking the others to start the preflight muster of the ground crews. Seeing Sergeant Bailey, Dullnig acknowledged him, "Morning, Ken."

"Morning, Sergeant," Ken yawningly replied. "Ready to get 'em ready?"

"Let's get it done."

"You bet."

Ordnance crews were next on the alert list for the young OD.

Activities gained intensity all along the separated squadron's flight lines. The bomb trains began running back and forth to the bomb dump as the ordnance crews' started bombing up the Havocs. Bomb fuses were set as ordered and safeties were placed on the fuses. Fuel tanks were topped off, and machine gun magazines were filled with ammo.

At 0400, Operations officers moved from barrack to barrack waking up the pilots and navigators who would be leading the group over the target. Some airmen grumbled, others cried, while others crawled out of the sack saying very little, but regardless, they all started the process of preparing to go to war.

After leaving the briefing for lead pilots and navigators, the aircrews headed for breakfast, more interested in coffee than food.

"Hey, Ralph," Jack said, as he and Earl walked up to the chow line. "What's the word this morning?"

"Looks like a tough one, fellas," Ralph informed them matter-of-factly. "Another rail bridge over the Seine. Pretty well protected, looks like."

"Any other groups with us?" Earl asked.

Reaching for his silver and tray, Ralph eventually answered, "Yeah…409th is supposed to hit it with us."

"Sounds good," Earl said as they looked for three seats together.

Breakfast was a quiet event that ended as unceremoniously as it had begun.

Jack, Earl, and Ralph left together, separating at the truck where Ralph joined Hulse and their gunners at the jeep. Jack and Earl met up with their gunners behind the deuce and a half.

"Morning, Lieutenant," Dean said to Jack, as the former crawled into the back of the truck after extending his hand back to fellow gunner Ralph Hoffman to help him in.

"Morning, Dean. Hey, Hoffman, glad to see you could make it," Jack ribbed, as he watched Hoffman complete his climb over the tailgate into the bed of the truck. Hoffman extended his hand for Jack.

"Ain't we lucky? Any idea where we're going today, Lieutenant?"

"Golly, Hoffman, your guess is as good as mine. Operations will let us know where, here in about five minutes, I reckon."

Hoffman grunted, "Yeah, that's for sure, sir." He hauled Jack up over the tail-gate.

"I've heard some scuttlebutt that it's a tough one. We'll see," Earl informed Jack and his crew as well as those who overheard.

Jack knew better, but played along. They couldn't talk about it, even though they'd talked with Conte who'd just come from the briefing. No other words were shared as the truck rolled on toward the Operations building.

The truck rolled to a slow stop in front of Operations. A few who were smoking finished their cigarettes, crushing them out in the bed. Everyone stood up and waited his turn to jump off the back of the truck and then lit up.

The Operations briefing began a little differently from usual.

"Good morning, gentlemen," the Operations officer began. "Wish I had great news for you this morning, but I don't. We've got a tough one ahead of us. We've been requested for this mission by Brigadier General Anderson, the CO of Ninth Bomber Command himself. He asked for the 416th to attack this target and destroy it. Not only is it tough, but it's critical we succeed."

He paused to be sure the faces in the crowd understood the gravity.

"The target today is the Oissel railroad bridge over the Seine River." he continued, as the curtain came down from the map at the front of the briefing area. "As you can imagine, the flak is going to be thick because the Krauts are protecting this thing tooth and nail. All they've got left west of there are ferries and barges to cross the river. To the East is Paris with the only other major bridge system and that's off-limits. The Krauts are using it to supply about two hundred thousand ground forces between Falaise and Argentan. Since the St. Lô breakout, the Krauts have been trying to get a sustained counterattack going. That's where we come in today, fellas. We need to close this resupply and escape route today. A lot of groups have tried but the Krauts keep fixing the damned thing. Let's not let the general down."

The briefing proceeded as usual after that. Fighter cover was reviewed along with ordnance and box responsibilities. High box was to hit the center of the south railroad bridge, while the low box aimed for the center of the northern span. Flak positions and emergency-landing strips were pointed out. The crews were made aware of their approach to the target and their return home.

The Operations officer explained: "Form up as usual over the base, turn to Maidenhead to Selsey Bill to four-niner-one-niner north to four-niner-zero-eight north, zero-zero-one-three east to the I.P. and then on to the target. Bomb at twelve thousand feet or below cloud base down to but not below ten thousand feet. Got that?" He looked around to make his point, and then continued. "Cross the French coast at twelve thousand feet at this entry point. Winds will be generally west by northwest. There are no alternate targets today, gentlemen, so let the Krauts have everything we bring with us. Any questions?"

He paused to look over the now-steeled and anxious faces, but no one responded. He said, "All right then, synchronize at 0530 in…six…five…four…three…two…one and hack. Let's go, men."

The ride to the flight line was quiet as each man thought about his responsibilities. Stopping at each assigned plane, the truck for the 669th squadron was slowly emptying. Jack, Dean, and Hoffman jumped out somewhere near the middle; they were in the first flight of the second box, which provided them some time before taxiing. Jack was flying number-two slot next to Major Napier and his BN Lieutenant Madenfort. Having talked with Earl before leaving Operations, Jack found out that Earl was flying in the third flight of his box along with Captain Meredith Huff and Bombardier Lieutenant Kupits as lead. Hulse and Conte were leading the second flight in the first box.

"All right, guys, let's get this thing in the air," Jack remarked as they moved to their respective hatches. After completing the preflight, Jack looked at his watch. Two minutes to zero hour. He turned his attention toward the tower, waiting to see the day's colors go up. On the mark the colors arched skyward, prompting Jack to signal his ground chief that they were good to go.

Smoke billowed out from the Havocs' exhaust manifolds all along the flight line, as the big radial's jugs begin consuming the organic remains of the Triassic period that they had been waiting for. Eighty combat-ready radials roaring at various speeds drowned out all other noise on the base. The odor of burnt oil mixed with aviation fuel drifted across the base as the planes waited on their hardstands. The taxi order began, and the Wethersfield base personnel had gathered at various locations to watch the orchestrated takeoff. Father Penticoff took his usual position by the runway.

Jack sat in the cockpit of his A-20 with his hands on the throttles and feet pushing the brakes. When he saw Napier roll past his hardstand on the taxiway, Jack kicked up the throttles and released the brakes, rolling out behind Napier while keeping the prescribed distance from his tail. Napier taxied to the head of the runway, and Jack was behind him.

"You guys ready back there?" Jack asked.

"I'm good," Dean replied.

"Same here, Lieutenant," followed Hoffman.

"We're next," Jack informed them, as he counted ten seconds while watching Napier's Havoc accelerate down the runway.

Jack pushed the throttles forward and released the brakes. The Havoc's roll down the runway was accompanied by the high-pitched roar of its twin radials, which harmonized with the sound of the propellers cutting the air. Hitting takeoff speed, Jack rotated the nose of the Havoc skyward. He started his fifty-second countdown as he raised the gear and then the flaps. On hitting fifty of his count, Jack put the A-20 into a coordinated left-hand banking turn, and saw Napier heading toward him on his return leg. Turning in behind Napier, Jack formed up in the number-two slot and spotted the number-three plane fill in after its forty-second run.

So it went, plane after plane, until all eighteen aircraft filled the low box, which was flying five hundred feet below and behind the first box. Forty planes were now in formation, including one spare and three Havocs out in front of the first box on the Window run. Ten minutes from takeoff the fighter cover rendezvoused with the group as Lieutenant Osborne led the group toward Maidenhead then out over the channel toward the target. On reaching the west coast of France the spare A-20 turned back to the base. No other plane had fallen out of formation for it to replace. Forma informed Osborne of the new heading, and Osborne turned onto same. The thirty-nine Havocs continued unmolested by bandits or flak, only to find the ground and the bomb-run to the target covered by clouds.

"Osborne, I've got nothing here but ten-by-ten cloud cover. I don't even see any breaks. What do you think?"

"If we can't see it, we can't bomb it, Forma. Let's take it to the barn and try again this afternoon."

"Roger that."

After transmitting the mission's recognition codes first, Osborne addressed the group. "This is Boat deck one-seven-eight-A-alpha to group. Target cover ten-by-ten. Let's take 'em back to the barn." He completed the circuit across the bomb-run, fortunately not receiving any flak or encountering any Luftwaffe fighters. The Window crew ahead of them was already busy pushing bundles of aluminum foil out through their bomb bays, hoping that they were jamming radar if any was there.

The 409th Bomb Group had been sent this morning but had also returned home with full bomb loads. Both groups had been prevented from completing their mission by the clouds. The 416th knew that more Germans were entering the fight every minute that bridge was up.

❦

While fights were occurring all along the front, in Germany just two days before the Oissel Bridge mission, Hitler had exterminated upward of five thousand officers and conspirators believed to be associated with his assassination attempt. The Wehrmacht, now sufficiently motivated, was preparing the 2nd, 116th, 1st SS and 2nd SS Panzer units for a counter-attack called "Operation Lüttich" to be launched against the US Third Army on the day after the Oissel mission. Operation Lüttich aimed to stymie Operation Cobra. A determined Wehrmacht Panzer force put up stiff resistance to Canadian forces on a southern push, after the Canadians had just liberated Caen. The Allied advance was about to begin and would destroy or drive the Wehrmacht from all of western France.[216]

It had been a surprisingly orderly and successful retreat for the Wehrmacht since the American breakout at St. Lô combined with the British and Canadian assault from the north. With clever military planners and logisticians, the Wehrmacht made the retreat much less difficult and costly than it could have been. Long before the well-defended strategic retreat, the Wehrmacht and the Kriegsmarine had been storing materials and supplies along the Seine River in barges. Some carefully camouflaged and others not at all, the barges sat in the shallow channel sides of the many islands in

216   World War 2 Timeline 1939-1945: Western Europe 1944; http://www.worldwar-2.net/timelines/war-in-europe/western-europe/western-europe-inde

a large bend in the Seine River between Oissel, Tourville, Rouen and Elbeuf. Even if they were hit as targets of opportunity by patrolling Allied fighters or attack bombers, the barges never completely sank since the water was so shallow. They would settle to the bottom, and then at low tide the damage was repaired, saving the material that was generally on the deck of the barge. The large, 180-degree turn of the otherwise broadly serpentine course of the Seine River was about to become one of the most heavily defended and contested areas at this time of the war. This geographic area—now a magnet for the opposing militaries—had been a center for warfare long before, predating even the fiery sacrifice of Joan of Arc.

Situated just to the northwest of Paris, the city of Rouen was to become a focal point of action. The metropolis sits in a river valley surrounded by high ridges that are geologically the same as the Dover cliffs. The Wehrmacht and the Luftwaffe controlled these ridges and from this high ground the two branches of the German military controlled both the ground and air approaches of this strategic area.

Snug between the ridges and the Seine River, Rouen had long ago established itself as a major port city between the sea and Paris. All manner of ships from around the world had loaded and unloaded cargo or been built or repaired there. What followed this commerce was a strong economy that brought traffic, which necessitated the construction of bridges. The addition of shipping via railroads required rail bridges. Rouen's marshaling yards directed many of the trains hauling goods to or from Paris. As a result of this, the cities close to Rouen that shared the same turn of the river had prospered from their neighbor's success. Unfortunately, this prosperity was the exact reason their towns had been important during the Wehrmacht's advance into France and now had become the very center of their retreat. Geology, geography, and economy had created the perfect location to meet the needs of a mobile army on this bend of the Seine River around Rouen, France. Armies have to be fed, supplied, reinforced and repaired—logistics, the Wehrmacht and the Allies knew this. As a result, powerful armies were converging on this area with one goal—the total destruction of the other. With the Wehrmacht controlling the rail and road bridges, Oissel and Rouen became the focus of the Allies' tactical air assaults.

The Oissel-Tourville rail bridge had suffered and survived many attempts to be destroyed. During the Wehrmacht's advance into France in 1940 the bridge system over the Seine was destroyed, and required extensive repair to those bridges that could be repaired or forced the construction of new bridges. The Oissel-Tourville bridge had been rebuilt by the Wehrmacht with the help of the local French workforce. Between 1942 and 1944 several more bridges had been constructed across the Seine between Elbeuf and Rouen.

Yet, as early as May 1944 the Air Corps had begun its tactical assaults on the bridges around Rouen and Oissel, continuing the preparation of the battlefield for the coming D day invasion. These missions in May '44 were directed against the Oissel-Tourville bridge. Flown by the USAAF's, Ninth Air Force, B-26 Marauder Bomb Groups, these missions successfully damaged the southern span of the bridge. This was the first of many missions to this soon-to-be-well-protected bridge, which played a critical role in the retreat of the Wehrmacht out of France. After the May attacks, the bridge was repaired with the aid of the local workforce.

The bombing and rebuilding of bridges showcased how the cloak-and-dagger business of spying played its role in the war. The Oissel bridge had been destroyed in 1941 by the French Résistance, which was trying to slow the Wehrmacht's advance into France. Undeterred by the damage to the bridge, the Wehrmacht quickly saw to its repair using their engineers and the local labor force. As the repairs progressed, reports were filed with the proper local civil authorities. Upon completion, this local civil authority received the final report detailing the repairs. The report was properly filed, while a copy was clandestinely passed to the Résistance through a civil servant spy, a crime of espionage against the German occupiers that was punishable by death. Gestapo agents or, more commonly, spies were constantly on the hunt for them as the cat-and-mouse game continued over the many years of the occupation. Undeterred, the Résistance would find ways to inform London of the status of the repairs. Not long after London received the information, another air mission would be scheduled against the bridge.

German Intelligence was not without its tricks either. Many times the repair of downed bridges was delayed for several days. This delay was not from lack of manpower or resources, but to give the Résistance time to file its reports while Allied air reconnaissance took pictures to confirm the bomb damage. After the recon planes had flown over, repairs began with uninterrupted earnest. Deception was an important part in keeping this escape route functional.

Not long after the May missions, the Oissel-Tourville bridge was reopened to train, Panzer, and foot traffic. This rail bridge held several significant advantages for the Wehrmacht that would confound and frustrate the Allies over the next four months. The designer of the bridge had created a nearly bomb-proof structure. Built across an island between Oissel and Tourville, the bridge spanned the two courses of the river and the island. The northern span at Oissel crossed the navigation channel and continued on across the island to the southern span that crossed the shallow southern branch of the Seine. The designer had sectionalized the bridge so that no two parts depended upon the other. Each span was connected to the other at each pylon but supported its own weight between the pylons. The rail bed consisted of sectional units built of steel I beams, and then cross-linked with the same parallel steel I beams that were strengthened by steel angle beams. Steel sides were then added and X-linked for support. The tops of the two sides were jointed by a roof of the same steel I beams and X-linking. To make it even stronger, a steel plate floor was laid and riveted down, like the rest of the structure. In essence, the Oissel-Tourville railroad bridge was a battleship on land. If one span was dropped, it could be raised, repaired with steel plates, placed back on the pylons, and riveted to the adjoining section. Then tracks were laid and it was operational. It was the perfect bridge for a war, ugly but very serviceable.

Another unplanned but greatly appreciated gift the bridge provided to the Wehrmacht was its width. Because of the bridge's width, German Panzers of all types could cross it as soldiers walked alongside. Many Panzer IVs and Tigers were first driven north across the bridge to resist the invasion and then escaped south across this bridge to fight again. The Wehrmacht strategically preserved men by having trucks, tanks, and armored personnel carriers cross bridges with only the driver. In the event of an attack, only one man was lost. The logic was that by separating crews from their equipment only one—not all—could be lost in an attack, leaving one or both to fight again.

The Wehrmacht had not relied solely on this bridge to escape. As was their strategic plan at most bridges, they had built a wooden bridge on the east side of the Oissel bridge to be used for trucks, troops, armored vehicles, and tanks. This wooden bridge would serve them well after the 416th's attack on the sixth of August 1944.[217]

While the retreat of the Wehrmacht did not include any radar, it did offer plenty of resistance to would-be air attackers. Even though the coastal defense radar system had worked well before the invasion, radar now did not lend itself to the retreat. Regardless, the Luftwaffe had solidly defended the bridges over the Seine River around Rouen. The 88s had been positioned outside the target areas as the outer ring of defense on the ridges and fields surrounding the four cities. Inside this ring, the 20- and 37-mm anti-aircraft artillery had been placed on the bluffs of the aircraft approaches and at the bridges themselves. Initially the Luftwaffe had positioned many of the 20-mm guns at the bridges, but the carnage to the gun crews was so devastating with each Allied bombing run that they were forced to move farther away from the bridges. But the Oissel bridge offered a great defensive field of fire for the German gunners because of its island. The Luftwaffe knew that the Allies always came over the bluffs and then turned onto the bomb-run, following the river's course west to east at Oissel. Therefore, they positioned their artillery accordingly. From Elbeuf all along the peninsula to Rouen, the Luftwaffe waited with a range of 20-mm to 88-mm anti-aircraft cannons for the Allied attacks.

The Oissel-Trouville Bridge had other guardian angels. Out of the last five days clouds had obscured the target on four. This morning's mission was no exception. The Wehrmacht soldiers, Kriegsmarine seamen, and Luftwaffe *kanoniers* were happy to hear the drone of the enemy planes fade into the distance without the whistle and explosions of falling bombs. The Wehrmacht had made great use of this weather by pushing as much as possible across all the available river forges.

❦

Crossing the bomb line heading west, Osborne complied with orders and reported the status of the mission to Operations on channel C. Operations was not happy. As they entered the east coast of England, the aircrews, particularly the pilots, were relieved to see breaks in the clouds, which would make landing easier. With Osborne leading, the group landed in the same order as takeoff. Once on the ground, the pilots taxied their Havocs back to their hardstands for refueling and orders. Hulse and Conte crawled out of their plane along with others up and down the flight line. The ground crews busied themselves with refueling and a possible afternoon mission.

---

217   Personal Historical Record of Oissel Rail Bridge; Fabrice Dhollande

Conte walked up to Forma. "I couldn't see anything either. You made the right call. Maybe we'll get 'em this afternoon."

"Sorry, I just didn't want to waste a mission. Let's go over to Operations to see if we're going to get a break in this weather."

"Good idea."

Ralph and Forma headed toward Operations, and were joined by Major Napier and Lieutenant Madenfort.

Taking advantage of the downtime, the aircrews relaxed in, on, or around their revetments while the ground crews went to work. They refilled the fuel tanks that supplied the sixteen hundred horses attached to each wing with their high-octane lifeblood.

Seventeen hundred hours rolled around, and with it, the order to suit up from Operations. Preflight was given at 1730 hours. The green flare again arched from the tower, starting the taxi and takeoff procession. The first A-20, piloted by Lieutenant Osborne, lifted off at 1806 hours. For the second time today Osborne saw the P-38 fighters from the Ninth's TAC fall into formation with them right on schedule. Osborne relayed to Forma, "Fighter cover on station."

Flying south over Maidenhead, Osborne waited for the coast and then turned off Selsey Bill at 5006N – 0126E as the group turned southeastward out over the English Channel airspace. There the gunners were cleared to fire a few rounds to check their guns. Fire burst out of the barrels of the .50- and .30-caliber guns. The recently liberated French coast became visible through the clouds and haze. "Coastline coming up, Forma," Osborne relayed to his navigator.

The group saw a much different sight on the beaches of Normandy than what they had seen two months earlier on their morning D day mission. Looking down on the Normandy beaches from twelve thousand feet today, instead of the two thousand feet as on D day, the aircrews could see the tracks worn into the sand from all the wheeled and tracked equipment being unloaded. Piles of supplies were stacked on and behind the high-water mark on the beaches. The sunken or partially sunken parts of the prefabricated Mulberry docks were also visible. Much of the docks had been lost to the storms that had followed the landings. Even better, there was no one shooting at them…yet. Seeing that no one had dropped out of formation, the two spare aircraft on the mission turned back northwest toward Wethersfield. No mission for them today as the group proceeded toward the IP.

Flying over the bomb line that was now well past the beachhead, everyone knew the ante had just gone up. The bomb line is an imaginary line that separates hostile territory and airspace from friendly. Every crewman could feel his focus on the mission intensify, as much from fear as duty.

"Conte, what's that over there by Lisieux?" Hulse asked.

"Whatever it is, it must be two or three miles long. Looks like a Kraut convoy going west to me. What do you think?"

"Looks like a Kraut convoy to me too. Record that for debriefing. They may send a few P-47s their way."

Ralph hoped that other pilots or gunners noted the same convoy so that at debriefing the validity of the observation could be confirmed. He still had not lived down sighting a battleship off the French coast on one mission. It had turned out to be a small island. Operations had gotten really excited about the sighting but were not happy with having wasted a mission to go look at an island. Ralph's thoughts were suddenly interrupted by the first concentrated flak bursts coming up from Elbeuf.

"Roger that, turn onto a heading of eight…five degrees east at 4940N – 0157E in eight minutes, sir," Forma transmitted to Osborne.

"Turning onto eight…five degrees east at 4940N – 0157E in eight minutes," Osborne repeated.

The two boxes flew on until Osborne turned onto the new heading. The other thirty-five aircraft followed their lead's turn, settling in behind him in tight formation as they closed on the initiation point.

Forma called up to Osborne, "Near our waypoint 4928N – 0142E. Turn onto the new heading in one minute."

"Roger that, turning onto the IP."

Having been alerted this morning by the aborted missions, the *Luftwaffe kanoniers* knew if the weather cleared there would be bombers over soon. They didn't know if it would be fighter-bombers or larger, but they knew they would be right on schedule as the weather front moved out above them. With hazy skies and broken clouds at eight thousand feet there would nowhere for the A-20s to hide this afternoon.

The *kanoniers* had grown tired of bomber missions over their bridge; they were ready for some payback. Spotters on the ground had identified the type, course, and speed of the 416th's two boxes long before they had gotten to the target, and had relayed the information to the anti-aircraft crews. The German gunners now had a close approximation of the group's altitude and course. They knew the Americans would come straight down the river to avoid accidentally dropping bombs into the city of Oissel. They had trained their guns on the airspace over the target on both the inbound and outbound course of the bomb-run. They had a few spots on the route home for the 416th to navigate through as well. Their artillery pieces were loaded with angry retribution today.

"Flak at twelve o'clock low, Osborne," Forma shouted.

"Roger." Osborne pushed a little left rudder with some right aileron to allow the ship to slide right while holding altitude, and the formation followed.

"We're close, Captain. Forma should be turning soon," Conte informed Hulse.

"Roger that, Ralph."

"IP coming up, Osborne," Forma noted by his charts, his heading, time, and landmarks, "in ten seconds."

"Call the mark," replied Osborne.

"This isn't going to be easy. There's so much haze and those damned clouds could get in the way. I've got visibility of three to five miles at best."

"Do the best you can. When we hit the IP, she's all yours. Let's kill the rate and get this run over with."

"Roger that. Turn now," Forma said, as he positioned himself over the Norden sight's eyepiece while preparing to open the Havoc's bomb bay doors.

Osborne turned right onto the bomb-run at the IP at twelve thousand feet. The rest of the first flight of A-Box followed, and opened their bomb bays when they saw Forma open his. The first flight formed up tightly as the flak concentrated around them. Heart rates soared, as anxiety mixed with fear and anger in this life-taking corridor.

Conte and Hulse turned the second flight of A-Box onto the bomb-run at 12,700 feet and just fifteen seconds behind the lead flight. Conte noted the coordinates as they hit the IP, and threw the switch to open the doors. Within seconds all the bomb bay doors in the six-plane flight were open. Twenty seconds behind them the third flight of A-Box lined up down the bomb-run with doors opening at 11,800 feet. Captain Jackson served as lead pilot and Lieutenant Maltby as the flight's bombardier. The three navigators of each flight were now bombardiers, unpinning their Norden gyros, dialing in the calculations to hit their primary target at 49°20'06.02" N - 1°06'09.65" E, while flying their west-to-east bomb-run to the target. The six bombardiers in both boxes were doing the business that had brought them to this deadly pocket of air over this densely defended enemy target.

The sky around them erupted again and again with the detonation of 88 rounds from the occupied French city of Elbeuf. Immediately the crews and planes were banged around the sky and in their compartments. No evasive maneuvers now. Elbeuf's salvos were soon joined by rounds from the 88s on the ridges and valley surrounding the bridge. Artillery crews on the island joined in, as the tracers from their 20- and 37-mm guns created a barrier through which the 416th had to fly.

Hulse and Conte's flight took the brunt of the first salvo. Fused to detonate at 12,500 feet, the rounds spared the flight crews below that altitude from the flak but not the shockwave. The second salvo was fused to detonate between 11,000 and 12,500 feet by their gunners. When the rounds detonated, all the ships in the first box shuddered from the concussions, while shrapnel penetrated the thin aluminum shells of the Havocs.

Shrapnel sprayed through Lieutenant J.R. Monroe's A-20 as the German anti-aircraft round exploded above and behind the inside trailing edge of his Havoc's wing just at the level of the top gunner's turret. Feeling the concussion knock down the tail of his plane, Monroe regained control and then called to his gunners. His calls went unanswered.

"Come in, Felkel and Gandy, do you read?"

Slowly regaining his senses, Felkel answered, "Loud and clear, Lieutenant!"

"You OK?"

"Yeah…yeah…I'm OK, sir!"

"What about Gandy?"

"Gandy…Gandy…Do you read, over?" Felkel called. Sliding around in his compartment, he looked up into his buddy's position, only to see Gandy's slumped but breathing body.

The shrapnel had shattered the upper turret's Plexiglass shell, which had been followed instantaneously by the maceration of Sergeant Robert S. Gandy's vital organs. His blood flowed downward and pooled on the turret floor, before it flowed down toward Sergeant James Felkel's tunnel position.

"Lieutenant?"

"Yeah?"

"Gandy's hit bad, sir."

Silence followed, and then, "Roger that, can you help him?"

"I'm on it," he said, as he crawled up into Gandy's space.

Nothing more was said as the Havoc closed on the target.

The battle continued.

"Damn those sumbitches," Conte hollered as he was knocked off his Norden bombsight by another detonation before killing the rate. Buffeted about by each salvo of exploding 88s, Osborne, Hulse, and Jackson fought to keep the needle on the center mark of their PDI.[218] Each deadly salvo filled the sky with red-orange balls of fire, which melted into gray-black clouds of smoke that belied the hot German metal radiating out from the red-orange center.

Regaining his balance and composure, Conte repositioned himself back on the Norden sight in time to see the MPI[219] sliding into the upper edge of the bombsight's field of view. Just a few more seconds and he would have to unload his bombs. Forma's flight had already killed the rate with Osborne having held the PDI steady, dropping their five-hundred-pounders on the southern span of the bridge at 1956 hours.

"Let's get the hell out of here," Forma yelled when he saw all green on his bomb-release panel.

Osborne needed no encouragement as he kicked right rudder and turned hard right on the ailerons while pushing the yoke and throttles forward. Lowering the elevators and rolling the ailerons put the eager A-20 into a steep, high-speed dive. All the pilots followed, keeping a tight, well-disciplined formation.

Seconds later Conte saw his Norden's crosshairs align over the MPI just as another salvo of 88-mm shells were sent skyward by the well-trained *kanoniers*. The anti-aircraft men were firing eight rounds per minute through their Krupp 88-mm tubes. Rocking all the ships in Conte's flight from the concussion, the artillery penetrated the skin of the ships in the second flight. Conte was happy to see the green lights on his panel start glowing, and he pressed himself against the side of the ship for stability, so that he could send a prayer to his God. Metal ripped through or ricocheted off the fuselages and wings of the second fight, while the eggs fell from their nests toward the southern span of the railroad bridge below.

---

218   PDI – Pilot Directional Indicator, which was used to control left and right drift of the plane on the bomb-run. Drift was relayed to the pilot's instrument panel's PDI by the Norden bombsight.

219   MPI – Main Point of Impact on the target for the salvoed bombs

Nearby, Lieutenant McManus felt the explosive concussion directly below his plane, which was quickly followed by searing pain in his legs and back.

"Dear God, I've been hit, LaPorte," McManus screamed into the intercom. "You guys OK back there, over?" Waiting briefly for a reply McManus repeated, "Are you guys OK back there, come back?"

McManus had no way of knowing his requests were falling on the nonhearing ears of his two gunners, Sergeant John A. LaPorte and Gerald A. Hart, both bodies now lifeless in their blood-coated aluminum cocoons.

The shrapnel had also cut into the fuel and hydraulic lines of the right wing, igniting the fuel flowing out of the open lines. McManus continued to watch the lights turn green and then looked up from his number-six slot at Hulse and Conte's plane. He saw Conte's bomb bay doors begin to close. McManus followed Conte's lead, and then grimaced and kicked right rudder while pushing the yoke forward and to the right. Painfully he reached for the throttles and pushed them forward while listening to the radials drink the high-octane fuel he was pouring into them. The plane nosed over with the other planes but continued to fall out of the formation as the right engine stopped but continued to burn.

McManus noted the cockpit filling with smoke as he slipped into unconsciousness from blood loss. Blood poured into his retroperitoneal space from his right renal artery, which had been lacerated by the German steel when it penetrated his back. He lived long enough to turn off the bomb-run but not long enough to look back to see the results of the drop. McManus, LaPorte, and Hart began their downward spiral inside the belly of the fatally wounded A-20. Eventually the right wing burned off, putting the Havoc into its final high-speed spin. The Havoc burrowed into the ground and exploded, as the fumes filling the fuel tanks ignited on impact. The ranks of heaven's warriors had just grown by three more souls.

Oissel-Tourville Rail Bridge

Mission # 116, August 6, 1944
This day the 416th flew two missions on this railroad bridge.
The morning mission was aborted due to cloud cover, but
the afternoon mission was flown with significant losses. Arrow
shows direction of attack. Note bomb craters scattered across
both shores and island from earlier missions. This mission
helped to seal the fate of many retreating Germans in an area
known as the Falaise Gap, after the Army breakout from the
hedgerow country at St. Lô. For destroying the southern span
of the bridge the group received a Distinguished Unit Citation.
Four planes were lost, with significant loss of life, and every
plane sustained flak damage.
KIA Lieutenant Colonel W. W. Farmer; Lieutenants Douglas T.
Sommers, Thomas W. McManus, A.J. Welsh; Sergeants John L.
Johnson, Stanley R. Zakliskewicz, John H. LaPorte, Gerald A.
Hart, J. E. Hay, J.A. Buskirk, R.E. Wright, S. G. Novak.
Reproduced with permission Ralph Conte

Back in the third flight and just behind McManus's flight, Lieutenant McGlohn
had watched as McManus's aircraft took the flak burst immediately below the open
bomb bay. Bombing from one thousand feet below McManus's flight, McGlohn had
a bird's-eye view of the hit. He shuddered from fear as he flashed back to his own
brush with death some months before. Shaking it off, he refocused his attention on
the mission, and watched his lead as the first bombs fell from the belly of that aircraft. McGlohn instinctively pushed his bomb-release button, and then directed his

attention to the bomb-release panel lights as another salvo of 88s detonated in front of the flight. The artillery buffeted the planes as the shockwave and shrapnel passed over and through the fuselages of the Havocs. As the last bomb fell from the racks, the right-hand evasion turn began. Bomb bay doors closed, and then it was right rudder, right aileron, throttles forward, and nose down.

McGlohn was glad he had made it through the run without being hit as he watched the Wing's commanding officer, Colonel Backus, slide his Havoc into McManus's number-six slot. Backus had flown "tail-end Charlie" in the number-seven slot. McGlohn and the rest of the flight crews appreciated the colonel's commitment to the mission. He didn't have to fly this one but he had. They all knew the courage it took to do this, and it earned him the respect of the airmen.

The second box was on its way over the target, and had witnessed all that had gone on as the A-Box flew through.

"Dear God, did you see that? It's going to get hairy," Jack commented over the intercom to his two gunners, Hoffman and Vafiadis. "Call out those bursts and let's get this one over with."

Jack was flying number two in the lead flight of the second box, and had opened his doors at the IP. He continued to follow Major Napier down the run. The flak continued shaking the planes as box two's lead flight killed the rate down the run.

"Major, you've got to keep the PDI steady or we're gunna miss this damned bridge by a mile," Lieutenant Madenfort relayed up to Napier. Another salvo of flak detonated around the flight, showering Napier's and three other aircraft in the flight with a rain of steel.

"What the hell do you think I'm trying to do?" Napier barked back. "The read-out isn't right. Abort this run. Repeat, abort this run. We'll go around again."

Following a short pause, Madenfort said, "Roger that." He closed the bomb bay doors while caging the gyros on the Norden bombsight. The whole time he was thinking to himself, *Dear God, get me back home on this one and I promise...* Then he said to Napier, "She's all yours, Major."

Seeing the doors close on the number-one ship, the other five ships in the first flight of the B-Box shut their Havocs' bomb bays and waited to see what was next. Lieutenant Smith followed Major Napier as he continued the right-hand turn at twelve-thousand feet without dropping altitude. Everyone soon realized they were going around again.

Jack informed his crew.

Hoffman and Vafiadis said nothing as they checked their flak jackets and then pulled their heads tighter to their shoulders.

Flights two and three watched as Napier turned off the target without dropping. They quickly lost interest, though, as they approached the MPI over the target. Earl Hayter watched the second flight release its eggs from twelve thousand feet—about seven hundred feet higher and only eighteen seconds ahead of his flight. He watched as his flight's bombardier, Lieutenant Kupits, flying with pilot Captain Meredith Huff, neared the target. Earl had energized his bomb-release switch as they flew down the bomb-run. Flak bursts greeted them all at the bomb-release site as the Norden automatically released Kupits' bombs.

"Now!" Earl released the first row of five-hundred-pounders from the belly of his plane. The first row of green lights came on, and were followed by two more as he felt the bombs salvo rapidly. There was a zero intervalometer setting so they fell quickly. Earl's bombs witnessed the first box's accomplishment of destroying the southern span of the Oissel bridge. They also witnessed the second flight's bombs hitting the northern span, and destroying it as a usable escape or resupply route for the Wehrmacht, but they had not dropped it. Seeing all green, Earl flipped the door-close switch, and followed Captain Huff into the right-hand dive.

Two months to the day since D day, the 416th was contributing to the success of the retaking of France by the Allied ground forces. The disabling of the bridge was yet to be appreciated, since the group was still far from safety, flying over this heavily defended enemy airspace.

Osborne's lead flight was now climbing after pulling up from the dive. Gravity was now the enemy as it pulled on the Havoc, stealing back all the energy the plane had gained in the dive. After completing the 180-degree turn Osborne was ready to level the flight out when the sky about them blackened with high-intensity red-orange bursts of flak that quickly turned black. Osborne's A-20 took the first hits from the well-directed anti-aircraft fire from the city of Elbeuf. His plane's right engine and wing were perforated with hundreds of pieces of steel, which destroyed fuel pumps, hydraulic pumps, magnetos, hydraulic lines, and cylinder heads.

"Good God!" came across his headset. "They just about took off the right wing," yelled his turret gunner, Staff Sergeant Kelly.

Osborne didn't need to look out the window to confirm it; his instrument panel told him all he needed to know. No fuel pressure, no hydraulic pressure, propeller rpm control gone and engine rpm surging up and down. "Any fire, Kelly?"

"Negative on the fire, but a helluva lot of smoke is comin' from under that engine cowling!"

In response, Osborne shut off the fuel, oil, and hydraulics to the engine, and began to feather it, stopping the windmilling of the propeller. Smoke continued to billow from the engine nacelle as he applied left rudder while powering up the left engine to keep the plane leading the formation.

Only a tenth of a second after Osborne's near-direct hit, Lieutenant Welsh's Havoc, flying number six in Osborne's flight, took one in the left wing. The nose-fused 88 had detonated on impact and separated a portion of the wing from the aircraft, ripped holes in the fuel tank and ignited it, and destroyed the rear row of the radial's jugs. It stopped the engine cold, having bent the crankshaft, which now screeched terribly.

Seeing the severity of the wound, Sergeant Wright frantically informed Welsh, "We're on fire! Hell, half the damned wing is gone! What are we gunna do?"

Looking out the windshield Welsh saw the damage, which quickly became secondary when he saw fire consuming the wing.

"Hellfire, you'd think they'd be puttin' fire extinguishers in these things by now." Welsh instinctually flipped the emergency-escape switch, setting off the claxton, while at the same time communicating with his crew. "Bail out, abandon ship, abandon ship!" With the cockpit and fuselage filling with smoke, Welsh released his emergency-escape handle, causing the canopy to fly open. Wrestling with his seat's straps he prayed to get out before the wing came off or the remaining fuel exploded. The smell of cold sweat and fear filled the cabin as every second stretched into an hour.

Welsh's gunners Kelly and Novak were both nearly out of the plane by the time Welsh freed himself from his seat. Novak was the first out of the plane and he spun around in the thin air of ten thousand feet. Kelly exited less than a second later. Welsh pulled himself up and out with the aid of the escape strap to his right rear. Navigating along the back of the cockpit and fuselage, Welsh aimed his exit to avoid the tail structures and death or terrible injury if he hit them on the way out. Starting a slow roll to the right, the Havoc began to feel the gentle, yet all-controlling pull of gravity as its horizontal airspeed was gradually transitioning into a vertical trajectory. Now facing the tail structures of the plane Welsh slid down to his left and then he rolled off the back of the burning wing and prayed as he fell. He was blessed as the tail structures continued their upward transition, allowing him to fall past them unmolested.

"Thank God, they all three got out," relayed Lieutenant Douglas Sommers to his crew. Flying number three in the third flight of A-Box, Sommers had just witnessed Welsh's hit and fire. Sommers was hoping to escape any hits inside the flak zone where Osborne and Welsh had just been hit. His crew, Sergeants S.R. Zakliskewicz and John L. Johnson, were thinking and praying for the same. Their prayers were greeted by a well-aimed anti-aircraft round detonating ten feet below and eight feet in front of the left engine. The shrapnel reached upward as the left wing of the Havoc passed over the detonation site. The steel ripped through the wing and engine hardware, cutting fuel and hydraulic lines. The engine lost five bottom pistons, and precious engine oil began to pour out.

Sommers glanced out the left windshield thinking, "Hell, this isn't supposed to happen to me." He cut the fuel flow, hydraulic flow, and magnetos in the damaged engine. As he feathered out the prop, he kicked up power in his right engine. In spite of his efforts, he saw the fuel and hydraulic levels continue to drop from both sides of his control panel. He reviewed his map to identify two possible emergency-landing sites.

"This is two-zero-zero-F-foxtrot. I'm dropping out of formation, heading to emergency-landing site Alpha-13, repeat, Alpha-13, over and out." Sommers turned out of the formation toward his emergency landing.

As A-Box's lead flight was exiting the killing space over the target, the third flight of B-Box had just pickled off their eggs. As it started its post-bombing evasions, the third flight of B-Box was taking the same pounding as all the others.

Napier's lead flight of B-Box was close to their second turn on to the IP and had fallen in behind the third flight of B-Box. "Damnit, Madenfort. This PDI still isn't reading right," Napier shouted to his bombardier.

"We have to turn on to the run in five seconds."

"Roger that…" Napier's communication was interrupted by the blinding flash and concussion of an 88 detonating in front of the lead Havoc. The fragments radiated out, penetrating the glass nose of the navigator's compartment. They tore into Madenfort's right forearm and lacerated his right temple, even cutting down into the temporalis muscle after lacerating the temporalis artery and the frontal zygomatic branch of the facial nerve. Shrapnel continued its upward trajectory and then exited the upper rear of his helmet, lodging in the bulkhead in front of the pilot. The piece of steel had ricocheted off the Norden bombsight just as he was leaning over it. Madenfort fell backward into the rear of his compartment and ripped off his flak helmet in order to apply pressure to the wound. He counted fingers and limbs to be sure everything was still there, and to check to be sure his brain was still working. In spite of the flak helmet, Madenfort had sustained a wound that disoriented him and prevented him from bombing. The blood streamed across his face.

Major Napier rolled the lead flight of B-Box back onto the bomb-run at the IP. Heading down the run for the second time the crews looked out into the peppered blue-black sky. Looking around, they could see that they were the only flight left on the run. They were a juicy target for all the anti-aircraft crews.

"Abort, Major, abort. I've been hit…I can't bomb."

"You gunna make it?"

"Hell, I don't know, but I'm bleedin' real bad."

"Hell, this PDI ain't workin' anyway. We couldn't hit the broad side of a barn with it, damnit. You hold on; we're gettin' the hell out of here."

The rest of the flight never saw Napier's bomb bay open, and guessed incorrectly that they were going around a third time. The flak continued as the flight passed over the target, but this time they were all relieved when the major pushed the nose of his Havoc over into the escape maneuver they had been waiting for. Gaining speed to over 325 miles per hour in their dive, the flight started its three-G rotation back up into a climb and hoped to level out at ten thousand feet without any losses. Unfortunately, lady luck wasn't to hold them in her hands any longer.

Group Operations Officer Lieutenant Colonel W.W. Farmer flew number three on Major Napier's left wing, and was following Napier's lead up. When Farmer passed through 9,900 feet, moving at only 220 mph now, the German gunners found their range. The 25 Krupp 88-mm tubes erupted with fire, from around the town of Elbeuf. This salvo was quickly followed by another; the anti-aircraft gun crews could reload and fire again in less than ten seconds. Napier's flight was starting to level out at ten thousand feet as the first vectored salvo of high-velocity projectiles collided with them. The rounds detonated all around the flight in a tight, well-targeted pattern. Farmer and his crew felt the concussion, then the pain. The steel burst through the cockpit, ripping Farmer's instrument panel into pieces while doing the same to him. The right wing burst into flames as the fuel tank spewed its contents into the wing and the bomb bay. Sergeants Hay and Buskirk were knocked against the walls of their gunners' compartments. Hays could see the fire in the starboard wing and the faltering engine.

"Oh damnit, Buskirk, we're hit bad!"

"Roger that!"

"Colonel Farmer, do you copy, over? Colonel, do you read, over?" Hays prayed that the colonel was OK.

Colonel Farmer heard but could not respond, as his level of consciousness fluctuated, but he was still aware enough to see his cockpit was filling with smoke. Determined to complete his last obligation of freeing his men from this doomed ship, he leaned forward and flipped the emergency claxton relay closed. He felt the heat of the first of the flames that lapped into his once secure cockpit. Straining against his seat straps, he reached toward the escape hatch handle. Farmer could feel his spirit separating itself from his dust-derived body. He struggled against the flames, the straps, and death's cold grasp.

Hearing the claxton, Hays and Buskirk needed no more encouragement as they made their way to their escape hatches. Shedding their flak jackets they opened them, then made sure their chutes were snapped on correctly before escaping from their aluminum pyre. As they fell through open hatches, both men watched as their colonel's plane fell with no signs of his exit. Both men pulled the D-rings on their chutes together. Both noted they were only separated by a thousand feet. The Krauts saw the two chutes blossom open too and began firing their 20- and 37-mm anti-aircraft batteries at them until just before they hit the ground, where they now found themselves separated by about five hundred feet. Quickly regrouping, they headed west toward what they hoped would be safety.

Jack and Dean witnessed Farmer's hit as they leveled out in the number-two spot. Jack watched as Colonel Farmer's plane flew level for a while. Looking into the cockpit of the injured warrior and aircraft, Jack saw his fellow pilot reach forward wrestling with the escape hatch as the fire spread along the wing and into the cockpit. He and Dean watched as the plane rolled to its right, exposing the inside of the cockpit that was quickly filling with flames as the colonel struggled against the will of death that had filled his cockpit.

"Bail out, Colonel, abandon ship, get the hell out before it blows, Colonel Farmer," Jack and the other pilots frantically relayed to the dying pilot inside the mortally wounded ship. Jack watched as two bodies fell from the rear of the ship while the Havoc continued its fall out of formation. All the crews watched as the right wing on the colonel's Havoc burned on the way down then slammed into the ground, becoming a fiery ball.

"Oh damn it, guys, the colonel bought it today," Jack relayed to his gunners, Dean and Hoffman.

"Yeah, I saw it. Looks like Hays and Buskirk made it out all right. I wouldn't want to be down there with them right now. Too damn many angry Krauts down there for me," Hoffman replied.

Many of the Germans were wishing they weren't there right now either. Repeated salvos of well-placed five-hundred-pounders were doing their share of destruction and soul-harvesting. The first flight had dropped the southern bridge span and killed several men of the repair crew and many of the Seventh Army soldiers being moved across the bridge. The second flight destroyed more of its assigned span while taking out a Panzer and its crew, who were waiting to cross the bridge. With the excessive carnage caused from earlier missions, the Luftwaffe had moved many of the guns from the immediate vicinity of the bridge. Now defended from each end, the island was an ideal location for targeting enemy aircraft.

The successful attack had eliminated effective German evacuation and reinforcement potential over the Oissel-Tourville Bridge for some time to come. Now, for General Bradley's and General Patton's American ground forces, it was a matter of sealing the fate of the trapped Wehrmacht. To encircle the Germans, the Americans drove toward Argentan, while the Canadians pushed toward Falaise. By August 19, the narrow remaining corridor of escape for the Wehrmacht's Seventh Army and Fifth Panzer Army would be reduced to a gap only two miles wide, which ended in a crossing of the River Dives. Over the remaining days of August the Wehrmacht pushed what it could through this narrow corridor, and many men were lost, thus earning it the nickname *Das Korridor des Todes.*[220] By August 22, thirty thousand Germans had managed to cross to relative safety, but ultimately ten thousand were killed in the corridor. Some fifty thousand were taken prisoner after the corridor was closed. The mission had been a success, but the final cost was still being exacted from the American aircrews.[221]

⚔

In the intense artillery fire the flights and boxes had become separated, so flights paired up the best they could in order to head back to the RP to begin their trip home over the channel. Others were in much worse shape.

Sommers was still wrestling with his controls, trying to keep his critically wounded A-20 in the air. His crew had completed many prayers, and by now had made many promises that they would have to keep if they survived this one. Continuing to lose altitude, Sommers fell from formation into the territory of the smaller-caliber anti-aircraft crews. He considered trying to avoid the tracers, but his gauges told him to fly as straight and level as possible to get to the closest emergency-landing site. The occasional round of the Luftwaffe's 20-mm guns passed through the wings and fuselage, hitting with a bang and rocking the ship.

Sommers flew on while watching his gauges fall, as all the fluids drained out through the open wounds in the wings. He had lost interest in the location of the rest of the group with wanting to get on the ground with a happy landing. At five thousand

---

220   *Das Korridor des Todes* – (German) – The Corridor of Death

221   *Great Battles of World War II;* John Mac Donald, pp 140-143; Macmillan Publishing Company, 1986

feet Sommers informed his crew, "Listen up, guys. We might not make it. We're losin' fuel, hydraulic fluid, and oil fast. You may want to jump."

"Hell, I ain't jumping down there in among those Krauts. They've been gettin' their asses whipped for days now. Those sumbitches are just as likely to kill us as take us prisoner," Zakliskewicz replied without hesitation.

"I'm with him," Johnson followed, as the ship was rocked again by a 20-mm round passing through the rear fuselage. Johnson saw the hole it left, closed his eyes, and quietly said, "Dear God, get me through this."

"All right, hold on then, guys. I'll push her as long as she'll let me," Sommers replied, and then silently prayed for some divine lift to ensure that the Havoc made it to the base.

Sommers and his crew sat silently inside the lone A-20. The crew felt their isolation, and prayed that no German fighters discovered them before they reached safety. Wide-eyed and nervous, Johnson and Zakliskewicz scanned the sky for the little black dots that would rapidly grow into the silhouettes of Me-109s or Fw-190s—two deadly shapes that a wounded A-20 were no match for.

As they escaped the airspace around the bridge, the flak stopped, making the crew feel safer but not safe. The occasional tracer round came their way as they passed over small, isolated Wehrmacht ground units covering the retreat for the main body of soldiers. But the bomber—now flying at two thousand feet—did not present itself long as a target.

Still struggling to keep the plane in the air, Sommers recognized the terrain below him.

"Thank God, there's the bomb line," Sommers said. "The emergency strip is close. Maybe we can get a drink at the O-club. Those guys in the 406th aren't shy about turning one up, I hear." Sommers knew the 373rd and the 406th fighter groups were stationed at Tour en Bessin, better known as A-13. After D day it had become a front-line fighter base and emergency-landing strip that was not much farther west.

As he flew on, he began to feel better about his decision to stay with the ship. The instrument panel told him that he was low on everything vital, as the fluids that keep the plane aloft and alive had drained away through the shrapnel holes. He turned a little north onto a new heading that he had calculated would take him to the base. Sommers saw the runway some five miles away.

At the airstrip ground crews of the 406th were readying a P-47 fighter-bomber with gas, rockets, and .50-caliber rounds when they heard the sound of a radial engine approaching from the east. Thinking it might be an enemy bomber, everyone responded as the air-raid siren began to wail. Running for anti-aircraft guns or trenches, the men prepared to defend the base. When the silhouette of the American A-20 bomber was recognized, the siren stopped, followed by the all-clear being sounded. Ground crews immediately recognized that the plane was going to land on their strip, and for only one reason—it was damaged. Running for the emergency equipment, the flight and ground crews watched the silhouette grow larger.

Sommers heard the roughness in his starboard engine as the last of its fuel drained away from the shrapnel-riddled fuel tanks. It ran for several thousand more revolutions before stopping completely. The pilot reached for the cross-flow booster switch in hopes of getting fuel from the port tanks to the starboard engine. He pulled the throttles for the starboard engine back to the air-start position, hoping it would fire up when he hit the ignition. Praying that he could keep his 250 feet of altitude, he yelled out to the engine: "Come on, girl, fire up. Dear God, let her fire up."

His mind raced through all the emergency procedures he had been taught but had never really had to use. He simultaneously turned on to the final approach while trying to restart the right engine. After setting the magnetos, he flipped the ignition switch and then threw the lever that would lower his landing gear. He waited to hear and feel the gear as they fell out into the slipstream. Nothing happened. Sommers looked at his hydraulic fluid readings; they were at zero. He despaired for a moment, and then he heard the belching of the starboard engine as it caught. Drinking in the fresh fuel, eighteen cylinders roared to life. But it was not to last. The starboard engine roared once more, and then misfired repeatedly as the last of the fuel was consumed. Now he could see the end of the runway, but it provided little reassurance as the right engine sputtered to a stop. Gliding forward at a hundred feet in altitude, a mile out from the runway, they couldn't jump but weren't going to make the approach. "Hold on, guys. We're goin' in short on our belly!"

Both gunners braced themselves for the shock of a rough landing while continuing to make promises they would live by if granted the grace of a safe landing.

Pulling back on the yoke, Sommers raised the nose of the gravity-gripped Havoc, only to push it back down when the low airspeed threatened to stall the plane. The runway was out; he just wanted to clear the trees. An oak's top branches reached up to hit the leading outer edge of the Havoc's left wing and jerked it down. Sommers fought to correct the roll to the left, only to be thwarted as the right wing and propeller struck another oak.

Sommers felt his heart rate and adrenaline level soar as he wrestled to right the earth-bound aircraft. Johnson and Zakliskewicz had wedged themselves tighter into their emergency-landing positions. Prayers and promises from all three verbally or silently were sent, asking for salvation and forgiveness.

The pilots and ground crews watching from the base knew what was about to happen. They had lived it before, when wounded Thunderbolts and Lightnings on final approach had augered into the French countryside. They watched as the A-20 rolled hard right, bringing the left wing high and the tail higher still. The outcome was inevitable.

The Havoc's nose fell forward into the trees, bringing the cockpit into contact with the oak branches. Looking out at the ground, Sommers watched his windshield shatter when it was struck by the thick upper branches. His hands and arms instinctively went up in a defensive posture. Slamming into the upper trunk of a tree, the right engine and nacelle were torn from the wing, hastening the Havoc's deadly cartwheeling through the trees. Leaves flew and branches snapped, but the tree trunks first resisted the force of the aluminum object and then snapped against the force.

As the nose of the Havoc slammed into the ground, the forward momentum of the plane pushed the cockpit against the trunk of a tree. Sommers was crushed. Johnson and Zakliskewicz were aware of their worldly gift only slightly longer, until the Havoc rolled over onto its back and then slammed into the ground, taking the men together. The remnants of the fuel, hydraulic fluid, and oil ignited. The now burning wreck finally came to rest upside down with the right wing severed off at the nacelle. The tail—broken but not completely ripped off—lay with the rest of plane on the French soil. It was twisted upward against the trunk of an oak. Black, oily smoke rose from the fires that were consuming the remains of the plane and the three bodies of America's finest inside. The ground crews rushed to the site to see if they could help.

By the time Sommers and his crew passed to a more peaceful place, all six flights of the mission had cleared the death-filled airspace over the target. Osborne was leading his flight of five planes as well as his second flight from A-Box. Just as A-Box had lost flight three, so had the second box lost its flight two. No one wanted to believe that the two missing flights had been shot from the sky.

In actuality, the two missing flights were riding home on a different route. This route took them over a battery of anti-aircraft artillery in the town of Pont Audemer, which fortunately was on stand-down. However, the sight and sound of the approaching A-20s changed that condition. The cannon crews responded to the blaring alarm that signified approaching enemy aircraft, but the flak crews had little time to cut their fuses to the range and set the direction of their cannons before the Havocs had left. They did manage to fire several meager, inaccurate salvos in the direction of the Havocs.

Meanwhile, the four flights led by Osborne were being targeted by a heavier concentration of artillery with better gun crews at Pont l'Evéque. On the first salvo Osborne's left wing was hit with shrapnel, tearing its way through the aluminum under-surface and shredding fuel lines, hydraulic lines, and fuel tanks before exiting through the upper surface of the wing. Osborne felt the left wing rise and then level out as he corrected for what he knew was a bad hit. The engine was spared, but the landing gear tire was punctured.

"Damnit, we took another hit," Osborne relayed to his gunners, "and the damned bomb line is only a few minutes away!" Flak exploded all around the A-20s, peppering them again with German steel.

Conte watched as Osborne's lead ship stumbled and then pulled back into the lead spot in the formation. Conte could see the fluids draining out through the holes in the top and bottom of his wing.

"Hulse, it looks like Osborne has taken a bad hit. Do you need to check on him?"

"Roger. Boat deck one, Boat deck one, this is four-fiver-two-H-hotel. Do you copy, over?" Hulse waited.

"Roger, four-fiver-two-Hotel. This is Boat deck one, over."

"You OK up there? That looked like a bad hit, over."

"Roger. Losing fuel and hydraulic fluid fast. Think I can make it home, over." He said it, but Osborne wasn't really sure. The fluids were draining quickly.

"Roger. Keep us informed, over and out," Lieutenant Hulse said, and then spoke to Conte. "Did you get that? How's it lookin' to you up there?"

"Hard to tell, but he's losin' fuel fast. He might make the coast, probably not the base."

Osborne was coming to the same conclusion as he watched the fuel gauges drop.

Some five hundred feet below, Captain Napier flying lead and then Lieutenant Jack Smith with his gunners Vafiadis and Hoffman had grimaced as they witnessed the near-direct hit on Osborne's wing. No sooner had they seen it than all the ships in their box were rocked by the orange-red flashes of 88- and 150-mm shells detonating at or below their altitude. The artillery crews firing the guns were wanting some payback for the poundings they had been taking since the Americans broke out of Normandy at St. Lô in July. Jack felt his ship rocked by a hit to its left wing. Feeling as if the ship had almost stumbled in midair, everyone aboard knew what had happened.

"Holy mother of God, Jack," Vafiadis hollered. "We've been hit!"

"How bad is it, Dean? Any fire?"

"No fire that I can see. How about you?"

"Don't see any. Don't see any smoke either. Gauges all readin' in the green. Pressures and temperatures all in normal range."

The ship was jolted again by a flak burst below and behind the right wing.

"Holy shit," came from the cockpit. "Did those sumbitches get us again? You OK, Dean?"

"Lieutenant, you with us? You OK?"

"This is Smith. Yeah, I'm OK—how 'bout you?"

"I'm OK. Do you see any fire?"

"Negative on the fire, but the tail is really shot up," Ralph interjected.

Dean jumped in, "Fluid is coming off the trailing edge of the right wing really badly."

"Roger, we've got a fuel leak but the pressure is holdin'. Hold on," Jack said. "Check that. Fuel and hydraulics are dropping, but the pressures are still good. We should make it."

"Roger, Jack," Dean replied. He and Hoffman could calm down for a moment. They both had flown a lot of missions with Jack, and had gotten lots of holes punched in the ship, but Jack always got them home. This was not the worst they had seen while hoping Jack's and their luck held out.

Jack was thinking the same thing as he watched the gauges fall ever so slowly—faster than he wanted, though, knowing that they might not make it across the channel.

The four flights led by Osborne flew west across the bomb line. Once over it, Osborne turned to channel C and radioed out, "Boat deck control, this is Boat deck one, over."

"Roger, Boat deck one. This is Boat deck control, we copy."

"Mission complete. Boat deck returning to base, heavy losses, over."

"Roger. Mission completed, over and out."

With each mile Osborne knew he wasn't going to make it across the channel. In the distance he could see the Normandy coastline through the haze and clouds.

"Four-Fiver-two-H-hotel, this is Boat deck one, over."

"Read you loud and clear. You OK, over?" It was Hulse.

"Listen, four-fiver-two, I aint gunna make the base. For that matter I don't think I'm gunna make the coast. Those sumbitches shot me up pretty good. I'm gointa try to put her down at B-18 on the beach. Roger that, over?"

"Roger, Boat deck one. Good luck, over and out," Hulse replied, glad he was not being knocked about the sky by artillery rounds anymore. He would have to move into the lead when Osborne dropped out.

Osborne knew the mission was going from bad to worse. Being shot up and losing fuel was being made worse now as the sun disappeared below the horizon. Landing in the dark was hard enough, but in a bleeding plane, it was nearly impossible. He knew there wouldn't be any lights on the runway this close to the front. No one wanted to invite night attacks.

Earl Hayter, flying the number-five slot in the third flight of B-Box, was happy that they were just below the altitude of the artillery detonations. They still felt the concussions, but were spared the hits from the shrapnel that tended to go upward and out. Earl still heard some steel ricocheting off his ship, as the occasional round detonated at or below his altitude. All the pilots in the third flight had seen Osborne and Smith take their hits and were thankful that it wasn't them. Earl was worried that Jack's luck was running out and that his hut might be a little less crowded tonight.

The flak bursts slowed and then stopped as the four flights cleared the bomb line and slowly escaped the range of the Krupp cannons. Everyone from pilots to gunners breathed a sigh of relief as they entered friendly airspace.

"Boat deck two, Boat deck two, this is eight-fiver-one-S-sierra, over," came over Napier's radio.

"Roger, eight-fiver-one. This is Boat deck two, good to hear from you, over," Napier responded, having wondered where they had gone. The missing flights were found.

"Roger, we are on your six and will be in formation soon, over."

"Roger."

The separated flights closed in on their comrades, as Osborne began his descent toward the Cristot emergency field. With the runway in sight, Osborne began his landing procedure. "Listen up, guys," he said. "I'm gunna try to land her at alternate site B-13. We're runnin' low on fuel and hydraulics, and I aint promising we're gunna make it. It might not be a bad time to bail out. I'll leave it up to you. We're passing through three thousand feet now."

The intercom was silent as everyone considered their options.

"I'm with you, Lieutenant," Forma replied, which was followed by Kelly's and Lagerman's commitment to stay with Osborne and the ship.

"All right then, here we go," Osborne said, as he nosed over and pulled back on the throttles hoping to save some petrol for landing. Fuel was really the least of his problems as he dropped through twenty-five hundred feet and set up on final.

The British ground crews and pilots knew what was at stake in a night landing, as they watched the A-20 approach. Since occupying the base shortly after D day, they had seen a few American planes land here after their daylight raids. They were less optimistic about this night landing. Regardless, they watched as the plane's wheels and flaps came down. They saw that the pilot had a good approach, but it wasn't until he got closer that they made out the flat tire.

Osborne could not have made a better call to land here. Easing down, he felt the wheels hit and then grab. The flat tire resisted rolling, causing the nosewheel to slam down. Osborne cut power and tried to correct the plane's sudden yaw toward the left flat tire. He knew that there was no stopping it now, as the A-20 began an uncontrolled series of ground loops. Moments later, the flat tire's undercarriage finally gave way, and broke off at its attachment to the wing's wheel supports inside the nacelle. Slamming to the ground, the left wing was bent upward but did not separate from the plane. Finally stopping after skidding off the runway, Osborne gave the order to abandon ship and set off the emergency claxton. No one hesitated, wanting out before a fire started.

British ground crews arrived with rescue and fire-fighting equipment as Osborne and his crew raced from the destroyed Havoc.

"Hey, Yank, looks like you made a mess of this one," ribbed a major in the Canadian Air Corps. He had pulled up alongside Osborne and Forma, who stood some distance from their permanently grounded A-20.

"Yessir," Osborne replied, as he and Forma saluted the superior officer. "Lot of paperwork now, sir."

"Don't worry about that now, Yank. Let's get you and your crew a jigger of scotch to celebrate a good landing."

Osborne leaned against the major's jeep and pulled his flight helmet and head-set off. "Yessir, I think we're all ready for a shot."

"Amen," Forma mumbled while staring at the ground, happy to be alive.

"Climb aboard, gentlemen. I'll ferry you all to the pub," the major ordered.

Well before Osborne had landed, Lieutenant Hulse had assumed the lead of A-Box. The box continued west across the French coast and out over the channel as they chased the waning daylight. He wanted to push the group along a little faster in order to save some daylight for landing, but not knowing the condition of the other ships, he stayed with the standard operating procedure and flew at 220 mph.

Jack watched his instrument panel, unhappy with the rate the fuel levels were dropping in the right tank—much faster than they normally would on the way back. It was flowing out through all the flak holes. He knew that the engine would fail soon, and he would have to land on one engine in the dark. But new problems were beginning to trouble him—surging oil pressure in the left engine and climbing temperatures in the cylinder head. He could deal with one engine out, but not two. He pulled out his tactical map and looked for emergency-landing strips along the English coast. There was an RAF fighter base at Tangmere, just under the flight route back. That was his new destination.

"Hoffman, Vafiadis, I'm gunna put us down at a British airfield just over the coast south of London called Tangmere. I aint sure we're gunna make it to Wethersfield. Hell, I aint sure we're gunna get to England, but we're still flying and I aint wantin' to get wet. The left engine is gunna quit soon, and the right one musta took a hit in the oil system from that first burst. Anyway, it's actin' up some, but I don't know why. I don't want to order you, but you guys can jump if you want. I wouldn't blame you none."

"If you're staying, I'm staying," Hoffman came back.

"We've come this far together, might as well finish it," Dean answered, although he was thinking about jumping this time if things changed.

"I'll do the best I can," Jack informed them, knowing he could do no less. They flew on for fifteen minutes more, and then Jack heard the right engine falter and then stop. The fuel had stopped flowing to the jugs. Jack went through his feathering procedures while continuing to worry about the left engine. The oil temperature was running hot now all the time. His speed started to sink as the cylinder-head temperatures rose. He didn't want to push the engine any more than he had to, so he let the ship slip out of formation.

"Listen up, guys, I'm gunna try to restart the right engine. If the petrol levels start dropping too fast, I'm gunna shut her down. We need the fuel to get us home even if the left engine is overheatin."

Jack threw his cross-feed booster switch. After resetting the throttles, magnetos, and fuel pumps, Jack hit the ignition switch. Everyone listened as the engine spun back to life. The eighteen pistons completed revolution after revolution. The Havoc's airspeed increased slowly and then stabilized at 200 mph, as Jack watched the cylinder-head temperatures rise in the left engine and the oil pressure fall. Jack watched uneasily as the oil temperature increased correspondingly in the left engine. Reaching up, he held the oil-cooler-flap switch in the open position for twenty seconds, and then saw the oil temperature drop to fifty degrees. He knew the left engine wasn't long from failure, but every little bit helped.

He worried now about finishing the flight over the channel on only the right engine, which was pouring as much fuel out into the air as it was burning. Jack knew he didn't want to bail out into the channel at night. He prayed silently, lifting an unselfish request for some help in getting his crew back safely. He didn't know his prayer was along the same lines as the requests of Dean and Ralph, who were asking for intervention on Jack's behalf so they would get home.

The group passed by the darkening Dover cliffs as they turned north over Selsey Bill onto their final heading toward Wethersfield. Hulse and Conte were anxious to get everyone on the ground before it got too dark. Hulse called Conte, "Hey, Ralph, how much longer to base?"

"I'd say about twenty minutes or so," he said after checking his maps and times.

"Got it. Maybe it won't be too dark."

"Roger that," Ralph anxiously agreed with his pilot.

By this time many pilots were looking for places to land their damaged planes before it was too dark. Lieutenant Parker, who had been flying number two to Osborne, was already having difficulty seeing Hulse flying in Osborne's place. Parker, looking over his flight map, decided he was going down at Northolt. The same site had also been chosen by Lieutenant C.J. Anderson, Captain R.B. Prentise, and Lieutenant J.R. Monroe. On approach Monroe fired a red flare into the sky.

"Felkel, I'm taking her in now at Northolt. Flare's out. How's Gandy?"

"Not good. Not much I can do for him. Hope the doc can help him. He's hurt bad."

"Roger that. We'll be down in a few seconds," Monroe said.

From first to last, all four planes landed within two minutes at Northolt

Monroe taxied to the emergency vehicles waiting on them. As soon as he had stopped, the medical rescue crews swarmed his Havoc, and took Gandy to the medical facility. Little could be done, and Gandy's spirit passed on.

Hulse flew on, leading the remainder of the flights that would make it home.

Jack could just make out what should have been the white cliffs of Dover. They were now a dusky gray as the sun edged lower and sent up its last, dust-filtered orange rays toward the returning group. The ground and shadows blended into one at this time of dusk, making depth perception that much harder. Flying at five hundred feet, Jack didn't want to lose any more altitude or they wouldn't make it over the cliffs. He had been trying to stretch the remaining fuel by running the engines at their lowest possible rpm, leaning out the mixture in order to stay in the air.

"We need to lighten our load again like last time, or we aint gunna make it."

Looking out of his top turret, Dean had been watching the cliffs get closer and closer as the plane got lower and lower. He was in full agreement.

"I'm gunna get rid of these bombs," Jack said. "You guys throw out anything we don't need, roger?"

"We got it," said Dean and Ralph. They started dumping ammo, guns, and ammo boxes out the tail gunner's opening.

Jack opened the bomb bay doors while energizing his firing switch. He waited a few seconds to be sure he had enough energy to release the bombs from their cradles. The crew felt the plane jerk with the release of each bomb, but Jack didn't try to keep the Havoc at altitude. He wanted every foot he could get, as he listened to the left engine sputter and then surge. The temperature in the jugs continued to rise, while the oil pressure fell. The A-20 climbed another 250 feet as the load was lightened. After reading the altimeter, Jack felt better about clearing the coast. "Another 250 feet, fellas, looks good."

Dean crawled down inside the belly of the plane and watched the bomb bay doors close, and then glanced at Hoffman. Dean gave him the thumbs-up. Hoffman flashed a toothy smile, and thanked God as they listened to the left engine's unsteady performance.

Jack watched as the cylinder-head temperatures in the left engine exceeded safe levels, while the oil pressure dropped close to zero. The engine would probably soon seize and catch fire. Jack couldn't synchronize it any more to the right engine, as it surged and rumbled from the overheating. The fuel was still flowing out much faster than he wanted, and reaching to his throttles he pulled back the left engine's handle. The left engine's sound was reduced to a rough, irregular idle and then disappeared. Jack turned off the fuel pumps and then the magnetos, and feathered the prop.

"Dean, Ralph, had to shut down the left engine. It was gunna cause a fire. All we've got now is the right engine. It's running OK as long as the petrol holds out. You can still jump if I can get her up to a thousand feet."

"How's the fuel?" asked Ralph.

"Right now, its gunna be close, can't say fur shur, though," Jack replied.

Ralph and Dean had crash-landed with Jack once before on their D day mission when the plane got shot up pretty badly. They had come back over the channel on one engine then. They had been happy to see these white cliffs along England's coast that day, but were ecstatic after Jack had landed on one engine with a lot of helpful prayers. They had walked away from that one without a scratch. They figured they would trust him again to get them back alive today.

"I'm with you," Ralph said, and was quickly followed by Dean's affirmative.

"OK then." Jack set his final heading toward Tangmere off Selsey Bill. He watched the fuel levels fall as he wondered if they would make it to the landing strip. As he turned the bleeding Havoc onto its final approach to Tangmere, the last photons of light painted the outline of the runway. Jack opened his left window and fired a red flare to alert the ground personnel of his status. Then he turned to the instrument panel. Airspeed OK, flaps down, control your drift against the one engine. He pushed the landing gear lever down and listened as the wheel well doors opened and the gear dropped into the slipstream. Easing down and keeping the nose up just a little, Jack waited for the main gear to touch down. Both main wheels hit the runway together, first skidding, then rolling as they started carrying the weight of the plane. Jack knew it was too late now as the front wheel hit the ground. He reached to the throttles and pulled the power off the right engine. Jack pushed the brakes gently, hoping they would work without putting the plane into a ground loop. The plane started to slow, and came to a stop well before the end of the runway. Easing the plane off onto a taxiway, Jack pulled the plane onto the grass.

"Let's get out of this thing," Jack ordered as he flipped the alarm and freed himself from the cockpit's seat straps. Dean and Ralph were out before Jack had opened his hatch.

Providence had shone itself on Jack and his crew twice now. How many more times such grace was to be bestowed on them was known only to Him. The only thing Jack Smith, Dean Vafiadis, and Ralph Hoffman knew was that they were going to fly into more life-threatening situations. They hoped Providence would continue to shine on them. Today, such Providence had not been universally spread. There was no rhyme or reason for it; it was just the way things go up there. Some had bought the farm today, while some came home to the barn. One thing was for sure—Coleman and Battersby's heavenly pew had gotten more crowded.

Crashed Havoc

This crashed A-20 Havoc from the 669th squadron (2A) was believed to have gone down in the vicinity of the Oissel-Tourville Rail Bridge. The photo was taken on or after August 6, 1944.
Note: German Guard generally notified whether remains of airmen were still in the plane. Crashed planes were stripped for armaments and parts.
Reproduced with permission of Fabrice Dhollande

Thanks to the efforts of the 416th, the Oissel-Tourville Rail Bridge would see no more train traffic for the duration of the Normandy campaign. The southern span was destroyed by the 416th's efforts; however, the northern span was damaged but reparable. Repair material stored in a tunnel close by allowed for work to begin as soon as necessary. Even though trains never crossed the bridge again, German engineering still made it possible for men and machines to be moved across the river. The Germans rerouted traffic along the eastern diversion bridge, then across the center and northern spans. Panzers, trucks, and armored vehicles continued to make it across the Seine.

After the sixth of August, interdiction missions interspersed with front-line troop support became the business of the 416th. They were difficult missions that required precision bombing. Six days after the Oissel mission, the men of the 416th found themselves taxiing to the runway for a close air-support interdiction mission back to an area they knew well. In coordinated attacks with other groups, they bombed a Wehrmacht troop concentration near Argentan. The push was on for American troops to link with the Canadians at Falaise while destroying the enemy's ability to wage war in the process. The mission was devastating to the Wehrmacht. It wouldn't be the last destructive air assault against the retreating Wehrmacht.

"Operation Dragoon" was launched on August 15 with the landing of the Allies on the French Riviera. Shortly afterward, in northern France, the Allies shut the Falaise Corridor on August 20. The still-retreating Wehrmacht would see the Ninth Air Force and its 416th back over the Seine on August 27, on a mission to destroy the remains of their retreating divisions. These divisions were being ferried over the Seine near Rouen with the aid of Kriegsmarine barges. Multiple groups from the Ninth Air Force came to the attack, dropping fragmentation bombs on the docks, barges, and ferry areas of Rouen. The Wehrmacht suffered great losses of men and material. On the same day the Canadians halted their advance as the bombs fell. With the Wehrmacht only a mile away on the white-faced ridges surrounding the valley, the Canadians waited and then occupied the city on August 29th.

Rouen, August 1944

Rouen, France, after air attacks from the Ninth Air Force in
August 1944.
Many fighter-bomber attacks by the Ninth Air Force's TAC
Groups contributed to the carnage.
Reproduced with permission of Fabrice Dhollande

With decisive routs such as at Falaise, the Wehrmacht had suffered significant casualties in a very short period. As the Wehrmacht honored their fallen, burial details took men from the fight. Logistics and tradition were again forcing the German military leadership to realize that delaying actions had become the only military means to postpone the inevitable end. The Nazi supreme commander felt differently, and plans were being laid for the coming counterattack.

The passing of summer into fall would bring changes for the Nazis. The pressure to complete the murder of all the Jews, homosexuals, gypsies, spies, conspirators, and every other undesirable was becoming more difficult and required changes in their Final Solution. Gestapo personnel began arresting Jews in Amsterdam in early August, arresting and transporting Anne Frank, among others, to her death from typhus. On August 6, the same day as the 416th's Oissel Rail Bridge mission, the Nazis began the Lodz ghetto evacuation in Poland, ultimately transferring sixty thousand Jews to Auschwitz for liquidation. The killing continued even as France was slowly liberated after the closing of the "Corridor of Death." [222, 223,224,225,226]

The 416th had given twenty-two missing or killed in the effort, while earning a Distinguished Unit Citation for their Oissel Rail Bridge Mission on August 6, 1944. But the end of August and early September held significant changes for the 416th. Their "Life of Riley" at Wethersfield was about to end as the war front moved farther east, pushing their targets out beyond the fuel capacity of their planes. It was time to move on to the Continent.

Bird of Prey

Fw-190 shot down near Rouen, France, in October 1944;
Left to right: Officers Robert Kehres, Shapiro and Shaffer
Reproduced with permission of Robert Kehres

---

222   *Attack Bombers We Need You: A History of the 416th Bomb Group;* Ralph Conte; copyright 2001; chapter 7
223   Western Europe; World War 2 Timelines 1939-1945; http://www.worldwar-2.net/timelines/war-in-europe/western-europe/western-europe-inde.
224   History of the Oissel Rail Bridge and Battle for Rouen, France; Fabrice Dhollande; Personal Records and Historical Research
225   The Normandy Campaign: June-August 1944: Great Battles of World War II; John MacDonald; copyright 1986; pp 132-144
226   Anne Frank 1929-1945; Jewish Virtual Library; http://www.jewishvirtuallibrary.org/jsource/biography/frank.html

German Burials

Wehrmacht burial ground in Rouen, France, in October 1944.
The Canadians occupied Rouen in August '44. It appears two
soldiers were actually buried in each grave.
Reproduced with permission of Robert Kehres

Chapter Twelve
The Business of Brest

There are fortified cities that are not assaulted.
– Sun Tzu

In nearly every part of France, September was a modern combat general's dream of fighting and dying. It began with the British and Canadian drive north along the coast toward Calais. Americans were spreading out into central and northwestern France like the head of a cobra, but supplies were still needed all along the front because Cherbourg harbor was still not totally functional. Since the Allies still needed functioning port facilities, the city of Brest, another fortress harbor city, became a military objective. The pressure of resupply pushed Eisenhower to order the destruction of the German garrison at Brest, as the fortress resisted assault, refusing to surrender. The Ninth Air Force, along with many groups from the Eighth, were assigned the mission of bringing Brest to its knees. The 416th warmed its engines as the navigators repeatedly calculated the time and distance to target. This was going to be long and difficult, but they would do it.

❧

Burning bright green and leaving a smoky trail in its wake as it arched upward from the tower, the flare fell onto the runway, setting in motion the first of six straight missions to Brest. Havocs waited to propel themselves down the runway at ten-second intervals. It wasn't a particularly great day for a 0730 takeoff, but the pilots weren't making the calls. Operations had received orders, and the group was going to carry them out. But by day's end the 416th had not distinguished itself, and for that matter wouldn't earn any accolades until its fourth mission over Brest. To say the least, the group's bombardiers had struggled with cloud cover over the target, complicated by a few Havocs running out of fuel on their first three attempts to bomb the harbor. However, September 5 brought a mission that allowed the 416th to earn some marks as they put bombs on the target. On the following day their expertise showed, as recon scored five out of six flights as excellent. Unfortunately the afternoon mission of the sixth brought cloud cover, requiring bombing from just two thousand feet, which produced just marginal results.

Weather held the group earthbound until the tenth, when other conflicts called the 416th away from Brest. The Allies were closing in on Nancy, in northeast France. Together with the 410th BG (L) and a group of Ninth Air Force B-26s, the 416th attacked a well-protected ammunition dump, with good results. Nancy was liberated five days later, but not before the 416th made one last trip over Brest on September 14. Again, it was a day fraught with problems as weather brought cloud cover to the target and prevented bombing. After aborting the bomb-run, the group flew back home to Wethersfield as low as three hundred feet, due to cloud cover. However, since low-altitude flying burns more fuel than normal, six Havocs were forced to make emergency landings in Cherbourg. This mission helped Command finally decide to move its light bombers closer to the front, where they could better do their job of frontline support and interdiction.

Business of Brest

Brest coastal gun emplacements taking a pounding from well
placed salvos from the 416th BG in 1944
Reproduced with permission of Andy Fluxe

Along with the other 416th bombers making impromptu stops, Lieutenant Wayne Downing also put down, but in Normandy. Downing had developed a "mysterious" oil-pressure problem in his A-20, *The Pink Lady*. While in Normandy, Downing took the liberty of spending several days before returning to base, for reasons most men at the base understood.

After Wayne's first tour of sixty-six missions, he was given some leave before reassignment. He immediately headed over to the environs of Cherbourg, to propose marriage to an American nurse he had met at a dance while on leave in London. Norma, an Army nurse, had been working in a Bristol, England, hospital in the early years of the war. Her unit was moved to the Cherbourg region three weeks after D day. Norma was happy to accept, and they spent three weeks together on their honeymoon in France, after being married twice in one day—first by the mayor of Cherbourg and then by a US military chaplain. The laws of both countries had to be satisfied so the marriage would be legal. After the honeymoon, Norma would stay in the Cherbourg region for a while, but would follow the advancing troops all the way to the Ardennes Forest. Her life and her company's lives and safety would be threatened during the Battle of the Bulge, as German troops advanced toward the coast from around Bastogne. Her husband, who had been reassigned to the 670th squadron of the 416th, fought even harder to stop them.

But today, on this day in September 1944, it was his desire to see her that prompted the development of oil pressure problems that required the "emergency landing" in the Normandy area. Wayne spent a few more days in the company of his wife, but the war called him back, as it did all soldiers.

Changes were coming as the Ninth Bomber Command realized the war was outrunning the ability of their flyers to get to it. Orders were cut, since a suitable frontline base had been found for the 416th, in the newly liberated city of Melun, just thirty-five miles southeast of Paris.

Melun offered useful infrastructure for the advancing Allies, after its liberation by an American armored unit on August 23, 1944. But before the city and the massive Melun-Villaroche Luftwaffe airbase surrendered, the Luftwaffe had used its remaining ordnance and planes to bomb the surrounding villages and base in the hopes of delaying useful Allied occupation of it. Again, the Luftwaffe violated a simple principle of Sun Tzu, by not providing well for the prisoners or those people in the area you occupy. The base itself had been bombed, but, worse, had been laced with booby traps and mines. The occupation of the base would not be easy, but began on September 15.

In preparation for a large-scale advance, practice mobilizations had taken place at Wethersfield prior to the D day landings, but this order to move to Melun was the real thing. The first of several waves of ground crews and all other support personnel left on the 15th. From Wethersfield, they went by train to Southampton. After picking them up from that port city, the ferry boat *Lady of Man* rendezvoused with an LST at sea, where the group was transported to shore on Utah Beach. The ground crews witnessed the aftermath of battle there and when they were trucked through the surrounding countryside, including the town of Carenton. Eventually a transport squadron of C-47s would finish the move, and bring them to Melun.

Meanwhile, air crews were to fly their planes to the new base, but not until they completed their last mission from Wethersfield. September 16 took them to Bergen op Zoom, Belgium, in support of Operation Market Garden—a mission that took the lives of one 669th air crew, Lieutenant Andre J. Vleghels and his gunners, Staff Sergeants Roger W. Rice and Clay E. Young. On the same sortie, another Havoc from the 669th was lost, but the crew survived.

After that mission, the flyboys completed the move to Melun-Villaroche Aerodrome. On the 23rd of September the air crews flew their war-weary A-20s over the English Channel for the last time, heading to Melun, where they found only one of three runways in working order upon arrival. But the flight over Paris inspired the crews, motivating them to look forward to their first leave. Leave wouldn't come right away, but it would come, and they were ready. Lieutenant Gus Ebenstein and Staff Sergeant Robert E. Lee were determined to make the most of the Parisian nightlife, doing just that the first chance they were given.

Paris was ready for the Americans. The City of Light had seen many invading armies come through its gates over the last thousand years, only to go out them later. Just as they had absorbed the Germans in 1940, just as they had cheered the arrival of the Vichy Government shortly thereafter, so they cheered the Résistance government in August 1944 and the arrival of Charles de Gaulle. Thus they cheered the Americans. Those who have been the conqueror or the conquered know how to play this game. It wouldn't be long, though, before even America would be considered an occupying military force within the French state. The French would soon be happy to see them leave.

But in Melun the Americans were just settling in, with very little to settle in to. Melun became a pup-tent city for some time—a long way from comfortable Wethersfield. Most of the buildings had been destroyed by the Luftwaffe before they left. Those buildings still standing were taken over by Command, Logistics, Maintenance, and Technical Operations. That left the ground for sleeping airmen, who bivouacked in their squadron area. Makeshift mess tents were set up, and in time the men adapted. It wasn't a particularly good time to be on the ground sleeping in a tent, as the weather was growing colder day by day.

Mess was a lot different too. Suddenly powdered eggs weren't as bad as they had seemed, when K rations became the mainstay of the 416th's diet. Efforts were being made to get the mess halls up and running, but as with everything, logistics was the problem. So K rations remained the order of the day.

With time, things improved. Larger tents began to arrive, along with the ever-loved potbellied stoves. Stovepipe chimneys were shoved through the openings in the tents' roofs. With these small conveniences, life started to look a little better. Lieutenant Leo Poundstone became the hero of the 669th by improvising a heated shower system from a bathtub and a borrowed pipe, which ran the water to the showerheads. A wood fire provided the heat to warm the water.

The Early Days at Melun

Melun in mid-September 1944: quite a transition from heated
Quonset huts at Wethersfield to sleeping bags and pup tents
at Melun. The base required a great deal of repair to bring it
to full operational readiness, but the group accomplished the
mission.
Reproduced with permission of Robert Kehres

Traveling on Their Stomachs

Krations for breakfast, lunch, and dinner. The priority to
construct a mess hall at Melun fell to each squadron.
Reproduced with permission of Robert Kehres

For many of the country boys this was not too bad a setting, having grown up
hunting or fishing for several days at a time. Jack Smith remembered when he and his
brothers would go hunting for days along the banks of the Tennessee River, sleeping at
night with only a blanket. Comparatively, this was high cotton, even if not like Wethersfield. Jack knew it could get a lot worse.

The group worked hard at improving the base for the military as well as for
themselves. Eventually things started to seem like home, as mess halls, medical facilities, recreational facilities, and operations were all up and running. More importantly,
an Officers Club was finally opened. The base would continue to be cleared of mines
and booby traps for some time, but the worst was over. A large arsenal of German propaganda leaflets and bombs had been left behind by the Luftwaffe. The paper came in
handy to start fires or manage some bodily functions.

In Transition

From September 1944 through February 1945, the 416th was
in transition here at Allied Air Base A-55 in Melun-Villaroche,
France. Here are members of the 669th squadron: (L to R)
Lieutenants Roland Enman, Julien Allen, Jack Smith and Earl
Hayter.
Reproduced with permission of Earl Hayter

Great Kindling Too

An unknown airman holds German propaganda leaflets,
which would be dispersed by a leaflet bomb, in the left
background.
Reproduced from personal collection,

Life even settled down to the point that leave time hit the radar screen, allowing men time to explore that Parisian nightlife that young men have often dreamed of. Warm showers and tolerable living quarters with their homemade wooden floors set great expectations for the airmen.

All Dressed Up and Ready to Go

The 669th crew is ready for its leave to Paris. The quarters
were a change from the Quonset huts back in Wethersfield.
The small building in the right background is the latrine. The
small tent to the left is a makeshift mess hall. The men slept
in the tent to the right. (L to R): Unknown airman, unknown
pilot, Captain Dave Hulse, Lieutenant Ralph Conte and
Lieutenant Jack Smith
Reproduced with Permission of Ralph Conte

When the men finally made it there, Paris brought good food that accompanied good times. Paris was also all Lee and Ebenstein had hoped for. Lady Godiva on a white horse ended Lee's evening on top of his magnum of French champagne. But pleasure eventually had to give way to the business of waging war, and it took the 416th back to the air. The war had moved along at a rapid pace in spite of their absence.

In September, the Allies would move across the Continent taking key cities. Forces crossed the Somme and liberated Dieppe, Verdun, Artois, Rouen and Abbeville, while Brussels was freed by the British Second Army. An important port—Antwerp—was finally taken without damage by the British Eleventh Armored. Then they set up anti-aircraft defenses to protect the port from V-1s. The port city of Calais was surrounded on September 6 in a bid to stop the long-range Krupp guns that had been shelling the southeastern English coast for nearly four years. But, it would take until the 30th to finally capture the port and silence the guns. Britain was now to be threatened by only the V-1 and V-2 terror weapons.

As operations proceeded, France began to reorganize itself. On September 9, Charles de Gaulle formed a new government, with the Communist Résistance well represented. Debts were to be repaid to the estimated one-hundred-thousand-strong well-armed, predominately Communist Résistance. De Gaulle was in no position to resist them or their demands. The next day "Operation Market Garden" was approved by Eisenhower, giving British General Montgomery the opportunity to continue the momentum that was driving the Allies ever closer to Berlin. The strategy aimed to capture key Dutch bridges, which would accelerate the advance into Germany, but it fell one bridge short, at Arnhem in the Netherlands. The British suffered terrible losses of paratroopers, and after eight days of struggle, bleeding, and death, the British retreated.[227, 228]

Nevertheless, the Allied onslaught continued. Two days later the French port of Le Havre surrendered, which provided another location to keep supplying the breakneck Allied advance. Resupply, especially of fuel, would cause a headache for the armies not involved in Operation Market Garden. On the southwestern Atlantic coast of France, Brest finally fell to the Allies on the 18th.

September 29 brought the last two missions of the month to the 416th. Both missions had very different, German-sounding names as the crews flew into German airspace for the first time. The group was now conducting its first missions into airspace that had been reserved for the B-24 Liberator and B-17 Flying Fortress heavy bombers of the Army Air Corps mighty Eighth Air Force and British Bomber Command's Lancasters and Halifaxes with their long-range fighter escorts. The first two missions into German airspace over Bitburg and Jülich would prove to be costly for the 416th.

Germany was in the bombsights of the 416th and the airmen found the airspace well protected. The morning mission to Bitburg cost the 670th squadron Lieutenant Arthur Nordstrom and Staff Sergeant Robert Miller. Fellow crewman Staff Sergeant Joseph Gossett escaped the doomed A-20 that had been split in two by a direct hit and spent the remainder of the war in a POW camp. Also lost were Lieutenant Tonnis Boukamp of the 669th and his two gunners, Staff Sergeants Russell J. Colosimo and Jeong S. Wing, all of whom escaped the burning plane, only to join Gossett as a prisoner. So, the Bitburg marshaling yard and German soil had claimed their first 416th airmen just as they had been taking the lives of the Eighth Air Force and Bomber Command crews for years.

More casualties were to follow that afternoon when Staff Sergeant William J. Daniel was mortally wounded over the Jülich marshaling yard, bleeding to death alone in his gun compartment from a lacerated artery. On this mission five ships were lost, taking Lieutenants F.W. DeMand, A.C. Burns, R.W. York and R.C. Morehouse—all listed MIA—and their gunners, R.J. Troyer, C.W. Middleton, L.A. Ashton, H.J. Wilds, L.A. Zygiel, and A.J. Burgess. Only Ashton and Middleton were taken POW. Germany demonstrated that it was still in full command of its airspace. On that day over Jülich, no planes escaped damage. The ground crews saw the intensity of the battle in the damage done to the Havoc's airframes, which had seen too many hours and too many missions during which they sustained too much damage to keep going. The 416th's war-weary birds of prey were due a rest and would soon be getting one.

On September 29 that opportunity for rest arose, as the replacement aircraft began to arrive. Douglas A-26 Invader gunships were beginning to fill revetments that

227   World War 2 Timelines:1939–1945: Western Europe 1944; http://www.worldwar-2.net/ timelines/war-in-europe/western-europe
228   The History Place: World War Two in Europe Timeline; http://www.historyplace.com/ worldwar2/timeline/ww2time.htm

had once housed the venerable A-20 Havocs. Training began immediately. Over the next thirty days, individual squadrons would stand down to receive transition training to the new Douglas A-26 Invaders. Some crews received only one introductory checkout flight in the new Invader, and then were ordered to fly their A-20s to England where they would exchange them for the A-26. Their second checkout flight was flying the Invader back to Melun. The 416th would earn the distinction of being the first bomber group to fly the A-26 Invader, as well as the first to fly it into combat. Slowly the face of the massive Melun airbase changed from that of an A-20 group to that of an A-26 Invader airbase. But the beloved A-20 still had a role to play. The glass-nosed A-26s had yet to be manufactured, so the reliable glass-nosed A-20s were pressed into service as group and flight leaders. New planes brought new pilots and personnel to the 416th, replacing those men who had been promoted, rotated out, or lost to the enemy.

The A-26 Overtakes the A-20

At Melun the 416th became the first USAAF group to receive
and fly the new Douglas A-26 Invader, seen here as two of the
669[th's] A-26s are in a climbing turn with the war-tested and
deeply loved A-20 Havoc leading. In spite of its larger size,
the A-26 could outperform the A-20 in speed, altitude, range,
firepower, and bomb load. The A-26 would go on to serve with
the USAF until after the Vietnam War.
Reproduced with permission of Ralph Conte

Circling in on the final leg of its approach pattern to Melun, the C-47 dropped its gear and flaps as the young officers in the cargo compartment contemplated their assignments. Lieutenant Carl Weinert looked out the window at his new home and began counting the rows of tents on the ground, but didn't get very far before he realized the immensity of the airbase. Leveling out into its glide path, the Dakota took the base from Carl's field of view, and he slipped into reminiscences.

Carl had completed his group training in South Carolina about three weeks ago, and had been shipped over on a converted liner out of New York. Like all the other passengers, he had worried about U-boats on the trip over, but fortunately the convoy didn't encounter any. He went through his EET training in Ireland, and afterward was shipped to Melun as a replacement pilot in the 669th squadron of the 416th. Carl was joining Lieutenant Don Sorrels, pilot and assistant Operations officer, who had just rotated into the 669th. Even though it didn't look like home, it was nice to have a place to finally call home.

Finally, the pilot settled the twin-engine transport onto the runway. Having made a perfect landing, the pilot taxied the plane toward the tower. Ground crew members ran under each engine nacelle and shoved chocks around the wheels. A few moments later the flight crewman swung the cargo door open. The sunlight and fresh air rushed into the stuffy cargo bay, making Carl and the other four replacement pilots blink but appreciate the fresher air of the French countryside.

After letting his eyes adjust to the brightness, Carl walked to the rear of the aircraft to grab his B-4 flight bag off the mail sacks. Stepping to the door, he waited and watched the ground crew attach the ladder to the plane. After the ladder was anchored, Carl handed his B-4 down to one of the ground crew. Then he put on his hat and slid his footlocker toward the door. The ground crew set it on the ground behind the wing, while Carl climbed down to the tarmac. Quickly retuning the salute to the ground crewmen, Carl asked, "How do we get to the HQ, Sergeant?"

"Welcome, sir. We've been expecting you. The truck there will take all five of you to HQ. It's the third building on your left, sir, over that direction," replied the airman. "We'll get the lockers there in a minute, sir."

"Thanks," Carl replied while grabbing his B-4 and then heading to the truck.

The other replacement pilots climbed out of the belly of the C-47.

Sitting in the open bed of the truck with the other pilots, Carl looked around the base to appreciate its size and the number of aircraft on the hardstands. It was a mixture of A-20s and A-26s, both of which he had trained in. He couldn't believe the size of this place because of how close it was to the front.

"Big place, huh?" Carl said to his fellow lieutenants.

"Sure as heck is. I wonder which plane is mine and where my squadron is," replied one fresh-faced lieutenant.

Carl looked around and shook his head in agreement.

Flight line at Melun A-55

In spite of their haphazard and disordered appearance,
these rescue and transport vehicles were highly organized.
The vehicles of the 416th were forced to adjust to their
inheritance—land pockmarked by bomb craters and
destroyed structures.
Reproduced with permission of Ralph Conte, Earl Hayter and
Wes Chitty

The other lieutenants looked around, to see that Carl was right, while noting the unrepaired runways full of bomb craters. The officers didn't know that most of them were caused by Luftwaffe attacks on their own base as the Germans evacuated it. They just knew that it didn't look good. It was then that they began to develop an appreciation for where they were. They rode the rest of the way without speaking, just noting the bomb craters as they drove past them.

The truck moved along the flight line toward a wood frame building with HEAD-QUARTERS painted in black block letters on the door. The passengers were pushed forward as the truck rocked to a stop.

"Heck, that was rough as a cob. Does he have a driver's license?" asked one pilot, not realizing that it was something he would have to get used to.

Climbing out over the truck's closed tailgate, the officers hit the ground one after the other and turned toward headquarters, while putting on their hats. Walking the well-worn path to the door, Carl and the others removed their hats and placed them under their arms. Carl opened the door into the HQ. A lone three-stripe sergeant sat behind the only desk in the room. He quickly stood up, sharply saluting the growing group of officers. The covey of officers returned the courtesy and dropped their B-4s in a series of thuds. As if conditioned, the young officers all unzipped the side of their B-4s, to produce their orders.

"At ease," Carl ordered, while zipping up the side of his B-4. He handed his orders to the sergeant.

After reading over the paperwork, the sergeant remarked, "Yessir, we've been expecting you. We sent these requests for replacements up to Wing some time ago. Let me get you to your squadrons, sirs." Collecting all the orders from the officers, the sergeant worked his way through the typical pile of government forms. Finally completing the paperwork, he handed the officers their squadron and tent assignments.

"The truck will drop you off at your squadron's bivouacs, sirs. Your cots and footlockers will catch up with you, sirs."

Carl read his orders, and then watched as the sergeant turned his attention to efficiently collecting and filing the orders into a folder with other papers. He then placed the folder with Carl's file in a cabinet behind the desk.

"Have a seat, Lieutenants. It will be a few minutes."

"Thank you, Sergeant," Carl responded, while looking around the office. He finally spotted a collapsible chair in a corner by the desk. With his B-4 he walked over to it and sat down. The sergeant went about his filing without talking, except when needed. Not feeling compelled to start a conversation, Carl looked at the blacked-out window. *Light discipline*, he thought.

The door to the HQ swung open and the airman from the flight line walked in. "Footlockers will be in the jeep behind you, gentlemen. Anything else, sir?"

"No, thank you, that will be all," replied one of the lieutenants.

Becoming bored after several minutes, Carl walked outside. A jeep pulled up in front of the HQ. On the back of it footlockers were stacked on top of each other and tied down with rope. Another truck was heading toward the HQ. Ducking back inside, Carl picked up his B-4, thanked the sergeant and informed the others that their ride was here. It was a long drive to Carl's new home, as the truck stopped first at the 671st squadron, dropping off the replacement pilots, and then drove to the 670th. After nearly forty-five minutes, Carl was the third pilot out of the truck, and followed the driver along the path to his tent.

Walking into the tent, Carl found some pretty bleak quarters. He wondered where he would fit in, as the sergeant dropped his footlocker on the wood floor.

The sergeant said, "The quartermaster will deliver your sleeping cot soon, sir. Anything else, sir?"

With a quick salute Carl responded, "No, that's all." Then he quickly added, "Thank you, Sergeant." The sergeant closed the tent door behind him. Carl was suddenly alone in his new home and feeling like a stranger.

Home Sweet Home

Melun A-55 had been an occupied Nazi airbase. The Germans
had bombed, burned and booby-trapped everything as they
left. During the occupation of the base, Americans took great
care to avoid loss of life from the booby traps. When it rained,
the base became potholed and muddy.
Reproduced with permission of Ralph Conte, Earl Hayter, and
Wes Chitty

The C-47's radial engine fired up in a cloud of oily, dark smoke ejecting from its exhaust ports, which was blown back by the prop blast. The plane shot down the runway, and suddenly the pilot had begun his climb. Soon the plane banked to the left, toward its next destination with a load of outgoing mail.

"Hey, Roland, maybe we'll get some more of that fudge like your family sent us last time," Hiram joked as they all watched the C-47 heading west.

"Well, if I did, I ain't telling you guys. That's for dang sure," Roland shot back, knowing he'd share every piece without even having to be asked.

As the group approached their tent, Roland was the first to notice the new arrival. Carl was taking his cot from the quartermaster. Waiting until they were close enough to start a conversation, Roland offered a hello in a reserved, almost distant tone.

"Hi," replied the newcomer in a friendly way. "You guys the owners of this tent?

"Yep," said Bill.

"I was assigned here by the sergeant at HQ. It looks like it might be a little tight in there though." Carl looked into the tent, noting the board floors with the naked bulb hanging next to the stove that was surrounded by cots with a footlocker slid under each one.

Carl had to get used to his new home, which had been improvised with anything available. All the wood to build the floors and racks in the tent had been scrounged from the ruins of buildings that the Luftwaffe had partially destroyed. There was the stove in the center with the smokestack running out the top of the tent. Hanging from homemade hangers at each cot were the B-4s, holding each officer's clothes and the personal belongings not found in the footlocker. The wash basin was filled with water and rested on the stove top. *All the comforts of home,* thought Carl.

No one spoke to Carl right away; no one needed to or really wanted to. There was little room left in anyone to start new friendships. It's not that they didn't want to get to know the new guys or let the new guys get to know them; it's just that there was only so much left in each of the veterans for the friends they knew now and for the friends they had already lost. It's a burden that all men who face death together learned to limit as much as possible. Standing outside the tent together, Carl asked, "What do you guys want to do?"

"Don't know. Let's take a look," Hiram replied.

"Roland, want to pitch some shoes before mess?" Jack asked, as a way to avoid becoming the new guy's guide.

"Sure, let's go," said Roland, recognizing his chance.

The two headed off to the horseshoe pits.

Earl volunteered to get some wood to get them through the night, and turning quickly he scampered off to find some wood for the shrinking wood pile.

Bill looked at Hiram, who shrugged his shoulders and turned to Carl. Hiram said, "Come on, let's see what we can do."

The three entered the tent thinking about the logistics of getting another cot comfortably into the tent. Bill, Hiram, and Carl eventually decided how to make enough room. It was tight, but it worked, and left room for everyone to still have some space of their own. Bill and Hiram both hoped it was a temporary situation, a thought that was soon to be sadly prophetic.

"What's your name?" Bill opened the dialogue that he knew would lead them down the road to a potentially painful friendship.

"Carl. Carl Weinert. Just came in from England with four other replacements on that C-47 that just took off. What about you? What's yours?"

"I'm Bill Tripp. He's Hiram Clark," Bill said, extending his hand to shake.

"Nice to meet you." Carl grabbed the extended hand and then offered his to Hiram.

"Where was your training?" asked Hiram.

"Started off like everyone else. Transitioned into Bamboo Bombers in Yuma, and then moved to South Carolina for advanced tactical training. New York was nice, but can't say the boat ride over was fun. Kept thinking about all those darn U-Boats that were out there. Golly, though, I enjoyed the food. It was great, had waiters in white gloves serving us on china plates. Hot dog, rank has its privileges. Almost hated to see us dock, except for those submarines. How long have you guys been here?"

Hiram looked over at Bill, who let him lead off. "Pretty much since the beginning, hoping to rotate out soon."

"That's good. What's the routine around here?"

"Not much, you'll catch on quick. If this weather holds, we'll be on a mission tomorrow. They probably won't select you for a few days," Hiram said.

"Why not? I'm ready."

"They think the new guys need a few combat test flights first, but not always. You'll go soon enough, so don't be in such a hurry," Bill reassured Carl in a somber, matter-of-fact tone, while thinking of the last two missions of September.

Carl realized that this wasn't training anymore. He wasn't sure how to feel or what to say, so he said nothing, and just shook his head in the affirmative.

Dean let the horseshoe go as his right arm completed its arch forward, no longer thinking of anything except the successful ringer he knew he had just thrown. Sailing closed end over open end, the shoe reached its apogee and then fell toward the stake. His teammates watched it fall open end out, right before clanging against the post in a perfect ringer.

"All right, Vafiadis," said Sittarich, as he slapped Dean on the back.

"Holy cow, Jack! They beat us again," said Enman dejectedly. "Let's not play these guys again. I'm going to the tent."

"I'm right behind you, Roland. Good shot, Dean," Jack grudgingly acknowledged.

"Thanks, Lieutenant, but how 'bout one more?"

"No…no, I think we've had enough. We'll see you guys at mess." Jack returned to Dean, anxious to get to the tent to relax before mess. But before leaving, he asked, "How's Hoffman?"

Since rotating into the Invaders, Jack and Dean had lost their Havoc tail gunner, Ralph Hoffman, to another pilot's plane. The A-26 required only one gunner because of the remote targeting system, through which one gunner controlled both twin .50-caliber turrets with a periscope system. Very similar to the B-29 system, they'd been told. They both missed talking with "Swede," as he had become known, and had enjoyed his friendship.

"Doing OK, likes his new pilot."

"Good. Tell him hello for me."

"You got it," Dean replied as they headed their separate ways.

Having chopped all the wood he was going to, Earl tossed the ax to the ground. Cradling the wood in his arms, he headed back to the tent. On the way he realized he had worked up quite a good sweat. That meant that he would have to have his uniform cleaned. A couple of French ladies ran a local laundry service in Melun, which was four miles away. They had a little drop-off and pick-up service that was quite handy.

"Hey, want some help?" Jack's voice came from behind.

"Heck yeah, you guys carry this." Earl graciously accepted the offer. Splitting up the load, Earl asked, "How'd the horseshoes go, fellas?"

"Don't ask," Roland quickly answered.

"That bad?" Earl pushed them for the whole story.

"Aw heck, Jack Sittarich and Vafiadis cleaned our plow," Jack began.

Through his smile Earl tried to provide some consolation, "After all, they are gunners. Got a better eye than you two."

Their idle chat was interrupted by the sound of a multi-engine aircraft's un-synchronized engines approaching with one sputtering. Men across the base looked skyward.

"Sounds like a heavy," Earl noted before the silhouette of the troubled plane appeared over the low horizon, just above tree level.

"Yeah, it don't sound too good either," Jack concurred.

The dark silhouette grew larger and slid to the left as it lined up on its approach to the runway. A red flare arched from the copilot's side of the cockpit.

"This isn't gunna be pretty," Roland muttered, as the flare drifted down, glowing red in the twilight. "Looks like a Brit."

Smoke trailed out of the feathered number-three starboard engine as the landing gear fell out of the wheel wells. More and more men around the base turned their attention skyward toward the approaching Lancaster. The number-one port engine was smoking, running rough and irregular as the pilot throttled back and dropped the big bird onto the mile-long runway. Touching down on the main landing gear, the plane began to slow. While it was rolling forward on these two wheels, the engine power was reduced more, and the bird settled back onto its rear wheel. The Lancaster pilot shut down the smoking engine, cut the gas, feathered the prop, and the plane slowed on its roll down the tarmac. Number two and four were powered down, and the big blades spun slowly to a stop as both engines shut down. The pilot completed the plane's roll to a stop at a spot off the runway, where he had been directed by the tower. As soon as the Lancaster stopped, emergency crews were at the plane. Hatches popped open, and the rescuers crawled inside to attend to the crew's needs.

Around the base, those men with duties went back to work. Those without watched as bodies were removed from the now obviously bullet-ridden fuselage. Four bodies were eventually laid under the right wing. The pilot and his right-seater climbed out of the plane. Walking over to the bodies, the pilot could be seen identifying the young men's remains for registration. The copilot knelt beside the first body, head down with his forehead in the palm of his right hand, as if praying. Everyone watching knew why. A jeep pulled up, collected the two pilots and then pulled away toward Operations.

All the airmen on the base turned away.

Earl, Jack, and Roland walked on and said nothing. After entering their tent, they dropped the wood on the pile by the stove, estimating that it would be enough to get them through the night.

"Dang, this October weather is unpredictable. Heck, it might snow tonight," Earl joked, as he felt the air cooling around him. Digging out his casual dress from his B-4, Earl changed clothes while he was introduced to Carl.

"Earl, meet Carl. What did you say your last name was?"

Avro Lancaster

British Bomber Command's Ovro Lancaster heavy bomber
that made an emergency landing at Melun, after being shot
up on mission. Visiting air crews were entertained at the
Officers Club and stories were swapped between air crews.
Reproduced with permission of Earl Hayter and Wes Chitty

"Weinert," Carl replied to Bill.

"Yeah, Carl Weinert…Earl," finished Bill.

"Hey, nice to meet you, Carl. I'm Earl Hayter."

"Nice to meet you, Earl." They shook hands.

"Where you from?" Earl finished dressing and then collected his dirty uniforms
for the French ladies.

"I'm out of the Midwest. What about you?"

"Northwest," Earl responded, as he walked out of the tent. "See you later, guys,"
He was going to the laundry area and then maybe the Post.

Jack and Roland went through the same introductory protocol with Carl as they
settled down in their cots. The men relaxed in the downtime, and just listened to the
sounds of war overhead. A-26s coming and A-20s going continued in the skies. *The
669ᵗʰ's turn to transition over to the A-26 was coming*, thought Jack. They were ready. After a
while, he looked at his watch—mess time was approaching. He finally got up and built
a fire in the stove. Its crackling heat was appreciated by the rest of the men in the tent,
and it would be good when they got back from eating and the club.

Throughout dinner Carl stayed with Bill and Hiram, and now he was with them
on the walk to the Officers Club. Dinner had not been the social time that Carl remembered mess to be when he was in the states. Back there the officers had a separate mess
from the enlisted men. Here, everyone ate in the same mess, but the officers had a separate area to eat in. He realized again that this wasn't "training." At dinner he had been

introduced to Don Sorrels, another new guy, and met Dave Hulse and Ralph Conte. He had learned their roles in the squadron and what to expect.

On the way to the O-Club, the three men ran into two officers that Bill and Hiram knew well—Lieutenants Wes Chitty and Wayne Downing.

"Hey, guys, how you doin'?" asked Hiram.

"All right," Wes replied as they joined up and continued to the club.

Bill broke the silence of the walk: "Did you guys find out anything about that Lancaster that landed today?"

"Some Canadians flying out of England," said Wayne. "They got shot up really bad coming back from the target. Seems some Kraut fighters got them in their sights, killed four of their guys before they shook 'em. They were all pretty glad to get back."

That ended any conversation for a while. They walked on smoking, before the inevitable happened.

"Who's the new guy?" asked Wayne, having put off asking about the new face with Hiram and Bill.

"I'm Carl Weinert. Got in today, came in on a C-47 with the mail." Carl extended his hand.

"Yeah, I saw that one come in. Nice to meet you. I'm Wayne Downing and this here is Wes Chitty."

Carl shook both men's hands.

"We're in the 670ᵗʰ," added Wayne. "How 'bout you?"

"The 669ᵗʰ, with these guys."

"Good bunch of guys."

Bill and Hiram took that as a sincere compliment, coming from Wayne. Wayne was a well-respected officer around the 416ᵗʰ because of his early days with the A-20s and his commitment to the effort. He was doing his second tour.

"How are the fellas in the 670ᵗʰ treating you these days since you started your second tour?" asked Hiram.

"Not bad, miss seeing some of the guys from the 668ᵗʰ, but all in all it's OK. Still wish they had given me a P-38 to fly, as I requested. But flying *The Pink Lady* with you guys is all right; she's gotten me this far. How about you, Carl? Are these guys showing you the ropes?"

"Yeah, only got here today. Did I hear right, that this is your second tour?"

"Yeah, nothing great, but hell, somebody's gotta win this war for you fellas," Wayne joked with a big smile.

"Sure, Wayne, single-handed, I'm sure," Bill shot back.

The five young officers opened the door of the O-club.

Bill walked up to the Gramophone and selected the Glenn Miller tune "In the Mood." He missed dancing with his girl, Joanne, and remembered the several one-day passes he had had with her between duty stations, before shipping out overseas. She loved to dance, and he had loved dancing with her ever since they started dating in high school. The record started spinning, with the saxophones blowing out the melody, followed by the trumpets. When the clarinets cut in, Bill's feet ached to swing him across the floor. The trumpet solo started and he could almost smell her perfume. *How many more missions?* Bill thought to himself.

Hiram and Carl had sat down at a table, joining the others already there. Hiram introduced Carl to a few of the other pilots and administrative officers. They both accepted a drink from one of the other men, and then leaned back to relax. The talk was of all the activity on the flight line and everyone offered guesses as to tomorrow's target. Scuttlebutt abounded, as it always did. Slowly the talk centered on the new Invaders.

Jack walked in, slowly making his way toward Hiram's table.

He was immediately introduced to Carl again.

"Yeah, we've met," said Jack as he sat down. He joined in the conversation. The men were giving Jack and Carl flak. They were the two tallest pilots in the squadron—at 6 feet 2. The men were ribbing them about sticking out of the cockpit on flights.

Through it all, Carl was trying to fit in and getting a feel for the whole thing. He looked around the room, noting the meager decorations with a few tables and chairs. Carl could tell that this building had been used by the former German owners. The former occupants hadn't done a good job completely destroying it. He didn't know the officers were lucky to have gotten it. Any building of value had been confiscated by Operations and Command.

He was surprised to see German pictures and a few German propaganda posters tacked to the walls. One poster read "Cannon fodder for Bolshevism," which ridiculed Americans for being the puppets of the Russians. Another print was of American soldiers turning to skeletons. The men were dying row after row as they marched into cannon fire. Across the top of the poster was printed "THE 'D' MARCH." He wondered why the guys would leave them up. When he looked down for his glass, he noticed the coasters. The guys used actual German propaganda leaflets, those with five questions that were designed to make soldiers question their mission here in Europe. After a while, he understood the humor, and why they left them up. He reasoned that the effect and success of propaganda just depended on whether you were winning or losing the war. He noticed *A Stars and Stripes* news release from July of '44 that was stuck on the wall, and left the table to read it. It read:

Spearheading the great onslaught on the Continent was a dawn attack by Havocs and Marauders against German armor amassed ahead of the British east flank in Normandy.

"What was this from?" Carl turned to an officer sitting close by.

"We flew on a German strongpoint a few days before that came out. What was the name of that place?"

"Something like Giberville, I think," someone replied.

"Yeah, that was it. Heck, I don't think we even dropped our eggs on that place. Those gunners shot us up pretty bad, took the lead BN out, if I remember rightly."

"Heck yeah, and we weren't the only ones bombing that place. I heard there was something like eight thousand tons dropped there with 24s, 17s, and even the P-47s got in on that one," reminded another lieutenant sitting at the table. "We got our licks in too."

Moving to the next press article hanging close by, Carl read,

Approximately 150 Ninth Air Force Marauders and Havocs yesterday continued the assault on Brest harbor, dropping more than 200 tons of bombs on the fortress guarding the Atlantic port in an attempt to force the surrender of the fanatic Nazi garrison that has held out for more than…

Glancing to the next one Carl read on,

Storming over the line in Normandy, more than 300 Marauders and Havocs virtually isolated Caen by cutting the main rail lines running into the battle area and smashing two bridges within the city itself.

"What happened here?" Carl cautiously asked.

"Just what it says," someone answered.

"Yeah, but they shot the hell out of us. I don't think anyone made it back that day without some flak damage," Hiram kicked in, quieting the conversation.

Carl realized that he shouldn't push it anymore. He went back to poking around, and saw a detailed typewritten notice on the wall. Getting closer, he saw that it was a Distinguished Unit Citation.

FROM: 97TH COMBAT BOMB WING
TO: CO 416TH BOMB GROUP (L)
PRIORITY CONFIDENTIAL

FOLLOWING MESSAGE RECEIVED FROM COMMANDING GENERAL IX BOMBER COMMAND, QUOTE, MY REQUEST THAT YOU ASSIGN THE 416TH BOMB GROUP OF YOUR COMMAND TO ATTACK THE OISSEL BRIDGE WAS PROMPTED BY MY GREAT CONFIDENCE IN THE GROUP'S ABILITY AND COURAGE. THE BOMBING OF THE BRIDGE ON 6 AUGUST FULLY JUSTIFIED MY CONFIDENCE. IN SPITE OF INTENSE OPPOSITION AT THE TARGET, THE ACCURACY OF THE BOMBING WOULD REFLECT CREDIT ON A GROUP BOMBING ON A PRACTICE RANGE. AS A RESULT A TROUBLESOME AND IMPORTANT TARGET, WHICH HAD ALREADY COST IX BOMBER COMMAND FOUR PLANES LOST AND MANY DAMAGED, WAS ALMOST CETAINLY DESTROYED.

Carl realized yet again that he wasn't in training any more. This was a new world, one that required more, potentially much more.

PLEASE INFORM THE GROUP OF MY ADMIRATION FOR THE COURAGE AND BOMBING ACCURACY DISPLAYED. OISSEL WAS AN IMPORTANT AND DIFFICULT

ASSIGNMENT SUPERBLY ACCOMPLISHED. ANDERSON QUOTE.

TO THIS COMMENDATION, I WISH TO ADD THAT I AM INDEED PROUD TO BE THE COMMANDING OFFICER OF THE WING IN WHICH THE 416TH BOMB GROUP (L) IS SUCH AN EFFICIENT AND OUTSTANDING MEMBER.

DEEPLY REGRET THE LOSSES IN YESTERDAY AFTERNOON'S MISSION, BUT AT THE SAME TIME, I WISH TO COMMEND YOU HIGHLY FOR THE SUPERB BOMBING ATTACKS CARRIED OUT AGAINST YESTERDAY'S TARGET, THE OISSEL BRIDGES, AND UPON THE COMPEIGNE MARIGNY MARSHALING YARDS ON 5 JULY 1944. YOUR DESTRUCTION OF THESE TARGETS WAS OF GREAT MILITARY VALUE AND IMPORTANCE.
SIGNED
BACKUS

A Certified True copy
/S/ Harold L. Sommers
HAROLD L. SOMMERS
Captain, Air Corps
Operations Officer
669th Bombardment Group (L)
416th Bombardment Group (L)

Carl rubbed the back of his neck and felt a cold sweat.

Looking around again, he saw the other new guy, Sorrels, sitting at a table in the far corner. He decided that that might be a better place to be. As he walked across the room, a new number started on the Gramophone, "Kalamazoo" by Glenn Miller. Miller, like so many other men over here, had been lost in a plane accident somewhere over the English Channel earlier in the war. "No more music like this," Carl said aloud.

"What's that?" asked Hiram from a nearby table. Hiram stopped Carl before he reached Sorrels.

"Oh, nothing, I was thinking about Glenn Miller going down in the channel. Did you guys hear anymore about that?"

"Naw. Damn shame, though, But when your number's up, it's up, Carl. Not a damned thing you can do about it. Golly, he could sure blow that trombone, huh? Gee-wiz, I'm going to miss that." Everyone shook their heads in silent agreement.

Carl spotted a bridge game and a low-stakes poker game. All the games shared the light of three bulbs strung down the center of the room. Not a lot of words were being shared. He sipped his drink and waited for someone to talk.

After a while, the club started to fill up, and the quiet mood gave way to the louder din of multiple conversations. He was cornered before he made it to Sorrels.

"Carl, where you from?" Wes Chitty asked from another table.

Eager to share some conversation, Carl responded, "Illinois, up around Chicago. What about you?"

"I'm from South Carolina."

"Yeah, did some training in Columbia before coming over. I was there during D day. Didn't you guys come through there too?"

"A lot of us spent some time there."

"Did you fly on D day?"

Wes leaned back in his chair, and drawing deeply on the pipe resting in the right side of his mouth, reflected on the question. Blowing the smoke out from the left side of his lips, he responded, "Yeah, we were there." He didn't want to revive the memories and blew more smoke. He reconsidered. "We lost ten men on that afternoon mission over Serquex. Those damned German Panzers can use their main guns as anti-aircraft cannons too. They shot us all up pretty good."

Wayne joined in. "Hell, we bombed from three thousand. It's no wonder they shot us up. Even the 20-mm guns were chewing us up. I don't look forward to something like that again." Wayne took a drink "We were lucky any of us got home that day."

Jack added, "Major Meng got hit bad over the target, had his port engine on fire. No one thought he was going to make it, but he did. Somehow he got that dang fire out, limping her back to base." The men nodded in confirmation.

Jack added, "He was danged lucky to live through that one."

"So, Carl, what'd you do in Illinois before the Air Corps?" Wes wanted to change the subject.

"Not a whole lot. Started at DuPont as an office clerk in '39 after high school. Didn't last too long with DuPont. I decided to give college a try, so I went to the University of Illinois in '40 to study engineering. For a while I tried to make it in baseball there, and even played semipro with a team in Chicago. I had seen too many good friends try and fail, ending up baseball bums, so I focused on school, and gave up baseball. Got drafted in '43 and now I'm here."

"The baseball stuff sounds pretty good. What positions can you play?" asked Bill. He had walked over to the table, after overhearing the baseball part.

"Oh, a kinda utility player. I played a little first base, shortstop, or third base. It didn't last long, though. I figured out I had to find something a little more dependable."

"I played some ball in high school," said Bill. "It was fun. We need to get you on our team. Those dang-gum gunners and ground crews are killing us every time we play 'em. How's your hittin'?"

"Not bad—250 to 275."

"Good. We'll use you this spring when we start up again."

"All right, sounds like fun." Carl felt a little more comfortable with the group now that he could fit in.

Don Sorrels had made his way over to the bridge game that Ralph Conte and the others were playing. Saying hello, he began a conversation that eventually led to him being dealt in for the next game.

Friendships began to form, and old ones were renewed, as Jack walked over to the bridge game, "Hey, Don, how you-a doing?"

Sorrels looked up, recognizing his old friend from Yuma flight training school, where he and Jack had flown Bamboo bombers together before transitioning into combat aircraft. Happy to see a familiar face, Don stood up and shook Jack's hand. "Good to see you, Jack. How long you been with these guys?"

"Since March. It's good to see you, how was California?"

Don had been transferred there after their time at the Yuma, Arizona, twin-engine flight school.

The conversations continued and the evening slowly ended.

Human nature's desire for companionship happened whether wanted or not.

Chapter Thirteen

Invaders at the Gates

Life belongs to the living, and he who lives
must be prepared for changes.
– Johann Wolfgang von Goethe

Awaking to the sunrise of early autumn, the men of the 669th mustered out to breakfast first, and then the flight line, to begin their transition training to the A-26. Preflight introduction briefings were held, after which the crews were taken down to the flight line. Awaiting them were four shiny but slightly used Invaders, which were much bigger than the A-20s sitting in the revetments. Wasting no time, the instructor began the preflight checklist as the crews listened intently. Relieved that the checklist was very similar to the A-20s, the pilots noted the differences for future reference.

The gunners were taken aside to be introduced to their new turret and aiming system, while the ground crews were being bombarded with detail after detail of the Invader's new upgrades and mechanics. Ground school began to weary the veterans long before the time came to fly the new weapons.

As the pilot walk-around continued, the officer in charge of the process began to detail the new 2,000-hp radials.

"OK now, fellas, you're gunna find these babies are hot," began Lieutenant Claude "Brownie" Brown. "So hot that they had to have specially designed cylinder heads to keep 'em cool. Remember these pistons generate tremendous heat in those combustion chambers. So much heat that the cylinder-head cooling fins had to be cut extremely thin in order to allow the heat to dissipate so that the engine could run at its maximum performance."

This need for uniformity in the cooling fins created special engineering challenges that were solved by the introduction of a block-milling technique, in which all the cylinder-head cooling fins would be milled from a solid block of metal at the same time. Once this method was perfected, the Wasp radial became the engine of choice for the light- and medium-bomber fleets.[229] Innovation had advanced the A-26 to the level of fighter performance in a light-bomber airframe.

"Any questions?" Brownie scanned a group of faces that seemed strangely hardened and focused to him, making him wonder if this was his future. "OK, then, this wing is a lot different than you're used to, as well. It works on a principle called laminar flow. This baby is high performance, as you're gunna see here in a little while, when you fly her."

---

229   Pratt and Whitney R-2800 Double Wasp- USA; http://www.aviation-history.com/engines/pr-2800.htm

"Now listen up—this is important," Brownie commanded. "It may just help keep you alive."

Every pilot's ears sprung to attention.

Aware of his audience, Brownie gestured to the wings, and explained, "These wings and flaps are different than you guys are used to using on the A-20. These flaps are designed to help these babies have lift at low speeds. Got it? With the A-20's standard flaps, the A-26s would have problems generating lift at low speeds You see, the designer of the A-26 Invader's high-performance wing—Ed Heinemann, I think was the guy's name—figured out that by installing this new double-slatted flap system along the tailing edge of the wings he could get the wings to generate enough low-speed lift to keep this type of plane in the air."

Brownie passed his hand along the flaps that were full out for demonstration purposes, before he continued proudly.

"No other twin-engine bomber in the inventory has this type of flap system. It was a critical upgrade for the Invader's high-performance wing. That's why they have to be full out for takeoff when you're bombed up and out for landing. These high-performance babies don't fly well without them. Any questions?"

Each new innovation and change of flight characteristic was discussed with the pilots in order to help them to understand how this plane was going to fly and how it compared with the plane that they were already so skilled at manipulating.

In his demonstration, Brownie eventually reached the cockpit, and he released the spring-loaded ladder on the right side in front of the wing. He showed everyone how to climb up the ladder using the spring-loaded slots on the side of the plane as hand and footholds.

After all the introductions to the new features, now was the time that the pilots got their hands on the machines. The first 669th pilot to fly the Invader—Hiram Clark—climbed up to the pilot's seat, while Brownie sat down in the loader's seat to the right and slightly behind the pilot. Originally designed as a space for the 75-mm cannon that could be fitted in the plane, it was now an instructor's seat, since the cannon was never added to the airframe. Preflight checklists were repeated, with Brownie teaching the engine-start sequence. Following the proper order, Hiram started up the big bird. Taxiing to the head of the runway, Hiram followed as the instructor took him through the preflight run-up.

"Now for the takeoff roll. Now listen up, this is important. You see, the Invader lifts off in a flat, high-speed takeoff, not in a tail-down attack, like the A-20. This new, high-speed, high-lift wing pulls the wheels, fuselage, and us off the runway in one steady upward ascent. So don't go jerking back on the yoke like you're useta doin' or we're gunna end up dragging the tail, and that don't look good on your record."

"Roger that."

When he pushed the throttles forward, Hiram felt and heard the power of the big radials—not ten feet from his head—as they accelerated down the runway. Hitting 150 mph, he was tempted to rotate the Invader up, but Brownie kept telling him to hold it. Hiram then felt the Invader lifting into the air and accelerating.

After cleaning up the airframe, Hiram and Claude pulled the Invader into a climb and leveled off at seven thousand feet. Along the way Brownie taught Hiram about the radial's supercharger and water-injection system, which gave the machine its speed and power. Hiram was impressed with the performance, but was about to be more impressed with the stall.

Brownie spoke: "All right now, pull the nose up and pull back on the power. That's it. A little more…a little more."

Watching the horizon fall away as the nose rose, Hiram felt the plane slowing as it tried to climb upward against gravity while losing the energy to do so. The stall alarm sounded, catching Hiram's attention, but instead of rolling left or right the plane's nose fell forward. The Invader's attitude passed the horizon and continued forward, but now it was in a shallow dive and gaining energy.

"Now, raise the manifold pressure to eighteen pounds and let her gain some speed in the dive," instructed Brownie.

Hiram slowly began increasing the manifold pressure, and pushed the throttles forward until the Invader hit 150 mph in its dive. Gently pulling back on the yoke, Hiram activated the control surfaces so that the Invader nosed up and entered into level flight. Pulling back the yoke a little more, Hiram moved the Invader's nose back into a climb of one thousand feet per minute while keeping the manifold pressure at eighteen pounds.

"Good job, Lieutenant. Follow directions well, and this newly designed high-speed wing on this aircraft is ideal in stalls. As the lift degrades along the wing, what lift is left is slowly transferred out toward the wing tips as the airspeed falls and drag increases. This transferring of the lift to the wing tips results in a flat, nose-down stall configuration, just like we had."

It's a stall characteristic that any pilot would love.

Hiram turned the Invader for home, and on the way was introduced to the outstanding single-engine performance characteristics of the Invader. Hiram was impressed that this plane could take off, climb, and land easily on one engine.

This routine was repeated time and again as the 669th pilots and crews acquainted themselves with their new weapon of war—one they were going to put to good use soon.

The next day the 669th flew to England early, only to fly back with their new Invaders. To personalize the planes in which they spent the most dangerous hours of their lives, the pilots selected nose art and names for the new aircraft, which kept the ground crews busy adding the adornments.

Ken Bailey found himself with a new pilot, Carl Weinert, as well as a new plane. He painted the Invader's new name—*Tom Swift's Flying Machine*—on its nose. Ken was happy seeing the new bird here finally. Its smooth-skinned fuselage lacked the endearing dents, pocks, and aluminum patches that characterized the war-scarred Havocs. At least the Invader wouldn't need any repairs soon.

Brownie was glad when the group took ownership of the new planes and the training schedule was completed. He walked along the flight line looking at all the Invaders filing the revetments where A-20s once stood. He had just received orders that he would be staying on with the 416th for a while. They had assigned him to the 671st squadron, which was OK with him. He wouldn't have to move his quarters.

A-26 Invaders on the Flight Line

Flight line at A-55, in Melun, France. This is an example of just
one squadron's area. The entire base occupied many square
miles and included small villages. From hardstands the planes
would taxi based on the flight and box formation that they
would occupy after takeoff.
Reproduced with permission of Earl Hayter

His quarters had been garnered by privilege of rank. He and the other instructors had exercised their rights after arriving at Melun by requisitioning a building. They then turned it into their barracks and their transition Operations building. Eventually the 671st ended up adopting it for their squadron's operations too.

Now, walking along and smelling the familiar odors of fuel mixed with oil and exhaust, Brownie scanned the flight line again. He was pleased with the job they had accomplished but realized he was tired and ready for a nap, right now. He found himself not the least bit interested in flying for a while. Reaching the 671st Operations building, Brownie sauntered through the door and addressed the two corporals there as he passed through the office and into his quarters behind them. Without removing his clothes or shoes, Brownie hit the rack and wasted little time falling asleep. Sleeping from the late evening until morning, Brownie was oblivious to his roommates coming and going. At daybreak he was rousted awake by their jovial antics.

Brownie crawled out of bed and began to shave in the chill of the building.

"Turn up that heater, somebody," echoed a voice.

Someone did just that, and stoked the homemade oil-burning heater that they had jerry-rigged right after moving in to this unheated building. Several minutes after, Brownie could smell and feel the heat. Black smoke poured out the chimney, which was actually a stove pipe sticking out below the eaves.

After the shave, Brownie changed his clothes and then asked, "You guys ready?"

"Yeah, let's go."

Mess was again a culinary experience of salty SPAM with powdered eggs. Brownie didn't care, though; he found it filling. As he was chewing another mouthful, he heard the shouts of "fire" followed by cries for help. Bodies jostled against each other as everyone tried to exit the mess at once. Upon exiting the mess tent Brownie saw his quarters on fire.

"Holy cow!" He ran toward the burning building. The blaze wasn't huge, and he thought that it might be controllable. He barged through the front door and ran to the back just in time to see one of his roommates toss a bucket of water onto the oil heater, which had overflowed. Burning oil was confined to the area around the heater until the water hit it. Immediately, the oil spread across the water and brought the fire with it. The men scrambled away from the fire, and on the way out helped the corporals grab files and paperwork.

Brownie looked at the fire in amazement and disbelief. The fire crews were running toward him.

"Hell, boy! What's wrong with you? Don't you know you ain't supposed to put water on an oil fire?" barked one of the firemen.

"Heck, it wasn't me." Brownie quickly defended himself.

The fire was eventually controlled, but the building was no longer usable. As the firemen wrapped up their job, they were startled to find several unexploded German booby traps in the burned building. Brownie realized just how lucky they all were. He decided that sleeping in a tent might not be so bad after all.

Making One Hundred

Infamous and famous *MISS LAID* with one of its air crews:
(L to R) Sergeant Evans, Lieutenant Lenard and Sergeant
Driskin.
Reproduced with permission of Robert Kehres

In exchange for their new A-26s, the 416th had to pilot their A-20s to England and surrender them. But as it turned out, not all the A-20s were flown home. One Havoc from the 670th was singled out for having reached a significant waypoint in its brief career. Only one plane could lay claim to the distinction of having flown a hundred missions on the same engines with the crews never having to abort a single mission due to mechanical failure of any type. The honors fell to the A-20 named *MISS LAID* and to the pilot and crew who flew it the most—Lieutenant Hugh Monroe and Staff Sergeants William Kidd and Steve Risko. This accomplishment earned the ground crew chief, Technical Sergeant Royal S. Everts, an air medal.

As a tribute to the airworthy craft, the *MISS LAID* was painted and renamed *La France Libre*. It was then flown to Paris by the crew most associated with it, as well as Everts, and was dedicated to the government of France in a large ceremony. The Ninth Air Force's chief of staff, Brigadier General Strahm, presented the plane to General Martial Valin, the French Air Force commanding general, and the French air minister, Charles Tillon. The name was christened by French actress Monique Rolland. While the ceremony provided a good diversion and accolades for the sometimes overlooked value of the ground crews, it was a sideshow to the real business of the 416th. This was not to be the end of *MISS LAID*, however. The name, along with the plane, had earned the respect of the group, so it was continued. The A-26 Invader that replaced it was painted and named in its honor.

The Free France

The original A-20 named **MISS LAID** had survived a hundred
combat missions and was renamed **La France Libre** and then
given to the French government. The center figure is believed
to be Lieutenant Jack Smith. The airmen on his flanks are
unidentified. This was most likely a staged photo op, since Smith
did not fly the plane to the dedication. Note the one hundred
mission bombs painted on the nose with the American and
French flags.
Photo reproduced with permission of Squadron/Signal Publications

MISS LAID's Face Lift

The A-20 Havoc renamed **La France Libre** takes off for its
dedication ceremony. The crew most identified with the plane
flew it to the dedication in Paris. The fate of the plane is
unknown.
Photo reproduced with permission of Squadron/Signal
Publications

MISS LAID Part Deux

This A-26 is actually the second **MISS LAID**. The one hundred-
plus missions painted on this plane included the A-20's
missions. It would not be possible for any A-26 of the 416th to
have one hundred missions by war's end.
Reproduced with permission of Wes Chitty, Wayne Downing
and the 416th BG reunion group

Hayter's Nose Art

Lieutenant Earl Hayter named his A-26 Invader *Classy Lassy Helen*, after a young lady named Helen, whom he had met and dated while living in Los Angles before the war. The relationship didn't last, but the plane did, carrying Earl on many missions until April 1945, when he completed his sixty-fifth mission.
Reproduced with permission from Earl Hayter

Other descendants of the A-20 were named in honor of their forebears, and pilots had ground crews paint the noses of their new A-26 Invaders. Lieutenant Earl Hayter was not one to break tradition, and had his chief paint the name of his girl-friend on his new craft. The new craft was called the *Classy Lassy Helen*. So Invaders were receiving their christening from nearly every crew as they began flying the A-26 into hostile airspace. Transition didn't mean complete stand-down. No, the war needed every able body it could get to defeat this ruthless enemy. No one had waited on the 416th as they transitioned into the Invaders; in fact, the Allies continued to sweep across Western Europe and up the Pacific Island chains toward the homelands of the enemy.

As the year moved into autumn, the war was progressing swiftly on all fronts. Early October brought the end of the Polish resistance, as the Polish home army surrendered to the Germans. Farther east, Russian military men were not sitting still, as they occupied Estonia. After nineteen days, Soviet troops ended their assault on Riga by October 29 and captured the Latvian capital. In midmonth Athens was liberated, while on the same day Erwin Rommel committed forced suicide for his role in the failed assassination attempt on Hitler. Just a week later on October 21, the Allies accepted a massive German surrender at Aachen, taking prisoner some ten thousand Wehrmacht troops.[230]

In the Pacific, Japan was feeling the pressure increase when Okinawa came under aerial attack by the United States military on October 11. A week later saw Japan's major base on Truk being bombed by fourteen B-29s, which was followed in two days by the landing of the US Sixth Army at Leyte Gulf in the Philippines. The invasion led to one of the most decisive naval victories for the United States Navy, the Battle of Leyte Gulf. This naval battle witnessed the first Japanese kamikaze attacks against the Americans—the ultimate expression of genetic fear and social brainwashing.[231]

The eugenics war was squeezed even more in Europe, as an uprising of the *Sonderkommando* in the Auschwitz crematorium resulted in the destruction of the number-four furnace. The *Sonderkommando*—a hated but coveted position held by Jews in the death camp hierarchy—normally disposed of corpses. By destroying the furnace, they managed an act of defiance against their oppressors and achieved some redemption. However, the Nazis pushed on aggressively with their agenda. The Hungarian government capitulated to the Nazis, who seized control of the government on October 15. Until then, international pressure had stopped the Hungarian government from transferring people to the death camps. Once in power, the Nazis quickly transferred undesirables of all types to the furnaces. To expedite the transfers, Adolph Eichmann arrived in Hungary on the 17th. As the Soviets advanced, Auschwitz closed its gas chambers on October 30, and plans were made for transferring the detainees.[232, 233]

World pressure and the overwhelming force of worldwide militaries were closing in on the two aggressor nations that had put the concepts of eugenics into its structured, government reality. Across the globe, people were dying in order to end this

230   The History Place: World War Two in Europe Timeline; http://www.historyplace.com/worldwar2/timeline/ww2/ww2time.htm

231   The History Place: Timeline of Pacific War; http://www.historyplace.com/unitedstates/pacificwar/timeline.htm

232   The History Place: Holocaust Timeline; http://www.historyplace.com/worldwar2/holocaust/timeline.html

233   Sonderkommando; The Jewish Virtual Library; http://www.jewishvirtuallibrary.org

distorted public policy, and the 416th hadn't sat still throughout their transition period to the Invader.

A cloudy autumn saw the 416th undertaking missions in western Germany. Missions were flown October 2 to the Aachen area without success, as weather obscured the target. On the sortie four other Ninth Air Force Groups failed to bomb the target. October 3 and 5 brought the same disappointment. On the sixth, the Havocs found their mark on the Düren marshaling yard, after weather had shut them out the day before. On October 7, Brigadier General Backus from the ninety-seventh Combat Wing flew with the group against the Trier supply dump. It was a good run, but cost the group three men, all listed as POW. October also cost Lieutenant Samuel P. Leishman, Sergeant Eugene Shempren, and Sergeant Joseph Siracusa, who all lost their lives on a training mission. Sorties continued until October 18, when the entire group finally stood down to complete the transition to the Invaders. The transition training continued, but not without losses. Falling from the sky in a spin, Second Lieutenants Miles and Kelly along with Sergeants Morrissy and Pepe died as their Invader never recovered from the spin. One man did escape the plane but died when his chute didn't open; the others passed on inside the belly of the doomed Invader.

The year was ebbing to a close, and November brought five missions with no losses, as the pilots of the 416th had to learn formation flying in their new chariots. The bigger plane had less visibility out of the right side of the cockpit, which brought a degree of timidity to the pilots. No one wanted a midair collision. With time, formations tightened as crews developed confidence in the flight characteristics of the new planes. Bombing results improved right along with their confidence.

For one member of the 416th November would bring a milestone. Lieutenant Gus Ebenstein reached his magic sixty-fifth mission on November 19. He was fortunate that it was a "milk run" and landed safely but exhausted, needing to be helped from the cockpit.

Gus was a committed Jewish pilot, a New York City kid with lots of Greek and Italian friends, all of whom would find their places in the war. He had left high school in 1938, ultimately joining the United States Army Air Force after hanging around New York for a while. By war's end he would be one of 550,000 Jewish service men and women.[234] In the service he trained to be an aircraft mechanic. But fate found Gus, who was befriended by a colonel on the rise to general. This officer encouraged him to learn to fly. After passing a college equivalency exam, Gus joined the ranks of mustang officers like Lieutenant Jack Smith. Gus trained with the founding members of the 416th, and had soon found himself at Wethersfield in January 1944.

Gus rivaled Wayne Downing on the race to be the first to the magic number. He had been eager to get his ticket home, and wanted as many assignments as possible. Yet, until his last five missions Gus had not worried about dying. Suddenly his rush to get it over with had collided with the reality of getting killed. On his sixty-first, sixty-second, and sixty-third missions his Havoc's wings and rudder were riddled with flak holes. As he

---

234   Statistics on American Jews in World War II; http://www.jewishvirtuallibrary.org

was making his sixty-fourth run, Gus felt the anxiety mounting, which made the trip that much more difficult. Perhaps it was a foreshadowing, but on that mission Gus escaped from a piece of Nazi shrapnel that missed his head by only six inches. It was during these difficult times that Gus found his God, but between times, he thought little of Him. He had already joined the ranks of 2,046 other Jewish airmen who had earned the Distinguished Flying Cross.[235] Gus had earned his by rescuing a new pilot who had become lost on the way home to Wethersfield on an earlier mission.

It was on his sixty-fifth mission that he earned his place in the group's folklore, just by following orders. After becoming frustrated on the third go-around to bomb an overcast target, Gus wagged his wings and then dove out of the formation. Back in October, orders had come down that if they were unable to bomb the target, the planes were cleared to bomb "other German territory"—targets of opportunity. So, that's exactly what Gus did. Having left formation, he dropped altitude and opened his bomb bay doors at one thousand feet. Upon seeing a German town, he let loose and "bombed the heck out of those lousy Kraut bastards." Gus knew that if he had gone down, things would have been tough for him, but he had accomplished two goals: he had gained credit for his sixty-fifth and killed some of the enemy. He was helped from the cockpit of his plane, survived his debriefing, drank Dewar's scotch with his crew chief, and then stole a jeep and headed off to Paris.

Not long after his final mission, Gus would rotate home. His fun-loving approach on leave would be missed.

November would see the war of eugenics diving to great depths. Some fifty thousand Jews and other so called undesirables were forced to march from Budapest to the Mauthausen death camp in Austria. As the Allies neared, the Nazis undertook measures to cover up their atrocities. At Auschwitz, guards and other military personnel waited on orders from Heinrich Himmler to destroy the crematoriums there.[236] As autumn froze into winter, the 416th would have to prepare for interdiction and frontline support missions against the Wehrmacht's coming counterattack in Belgium's Ardennes Forest.

---

235   Statistics on American Jews in World War II; http://www.jewishvirtuallibrary.org
236   The History Place: Holocaust Timeline; http://www.historyplace.com/worldwar2/
holocaust/timeline.html

Chapter Fourteen

Chasing Plankton

Oil is like a wild animal. Whoever captures it has it.

– J. Paul Getty

Germany's leadership finally found time to catch its breath, after giving up substantial territory to the Allies. Yet, as 1944 wound down, Allied forces found themselves as victims of their own rapid advance. During fighting in the Ardennes, the Allied push stalled, roughly dividing the forest in two. The Allies claimed the western portion, which ran nearly to Arnhem, Holland—where the British had been recently forced to lick their wounds after a retreat. Logistics had been stretched with the swift move eastward, and winter was coming on. Cold weather was now layering itself over the silence of the battlefield, bringing yet another front with which the soldiers would have to contend, since they had no winter clothes and equipment. Thoughts of Christmas, peace, and a trip home couldn't help but slip into the minds of the Allied soldiers sitting in their trenches or flying at twelve thousand feet. Wehrmacht leadership felt differently, though.

Invigorated by the Allied loss of momentum, the Wehrmacht gained the time needed to reinforce its western defenses. Behind this stabilized front, an army of devastating power and mobility was amassing. Foot soldiers, Panzers, and paratroopers were orchestrated into strike forces using Sun Tzu's concept of battlefield deception. Hiding men and material in forests, farmhouses, haystacks and any other natural or man-made sanctuary, the Wehrmacht was producing a powerful deception. Oblivious to the build-up in front of them, the Allies prepared poorly for the coming winter.

This plan for salvation of the Fatherland had arisen in staff plans in mid-September, as the Nazis' supreme commander ranted on about the failures along the western and eastern fronts. Hitler's leadership knew that with the progressive fall of Romania to the Soviets, the last natural source for crude oil was being lost to them. All that remained were their reserves on hand and their scientists' ability to create the synthetic alternatives that they had been using since before the war. This lack of resources was about to unhinge the Wehrmacht's ability to wage modern war.[237] In 1938, Germany could provide one-tenth of its oil needs from indigenous sources, while importing the remainder from places such as Poland, Romania, and Hungary. Recapturing these places early in the war became critical to the Nazi war machine.[238]

---

237 *The Ardennes: Battle of the Bulge: The European Theater of Operations:* United States Army in World War II; Hugh M. Cole; Chapters 1; http://www.army.mil/cmh-pg/books/wwii/7-8/7-8_Cont.htm

238 Germany Zone Handbook No. V: Rhine-Ruhr: Part I: People and Administration: January 1944: Secret 1943: Chapter III

This fact had not been lost on the Allies, as Britain's Bomber Command began in December of 1944 by sending ninety-three Lancasters from No. Three Group against the Hansa benzol plant at Dortmund. The campaign proceeded against targets throughout Germany. All chemical plants dealing with carbon-based chemistry were potential places for alternative-energy production. This first assault was to be followed by missions against the synthetic-oil plants at Leuna and Pölitz, the Meiderich benzol and oil plant near Duisburg (three times), Osterfeld's benzol plant, the oil refinery at Scholven-Buer, and the IG Farben chemical plants in Oppau. The Krupp steel plant in Essen was not neglected, as 349 Lancasters, 163 Halifaxes and 28 Mosquitos blasted the facility on the evening of December 12th and morning of the 13th.

Destruction of oil and oil-refinery capacity had been on the Allies' mission list earlier in the war. Several attempts to destroy seven oil refineries in a nineteen-square-mile area in Ploesti, Romania, showed little benefit for the immense sacrifices. The region was assaulted in June 1942 and August 1943 by American B-24s from the Eighth and Ninth Air Force out of Egypt. The bombers took devastating losses, particularly on the August 1943 raid, which gave the flyers five Medals of Honor, and yet oil production was interrupted for only two to three weeks, and had resumed its pre-strike production within that period. These oil facilities were of tremendous importance to the Reich, so men and material for the defense and maintenance of the facility were top priority. [239, 240, 241]

Equipped now with A-26 Invaders and ever closer to the action at their new home in Melun, the men of the 416th were ready to prove themselves again. Their first mission would give them that chance.

⚜

All the pilots, navigators, and gunners were mustered to the briefing hut by 0500 and settled down into their customary seats. Listening with the same degree of mounting anxiety as with any preflight briefing, the men relaxed slightly when they heard this was to be a milk run. Dean Vafiadis and Jack Smith listened intently. They knew in reality that there was no such thing as a milk run, but it was good to hear anyway. Jack scanned the room, noting all the new faces mixed with the old vets. The recently promoted Joseph "Joe" Meagher was sitting with his gunner and navigator.

The briefing was over unceremoniously with the customary "Hack," as the Operations officer clicked in the stem of his watch. The briefing room was filled with motion as men began their ritual migration to the chute hangar and then the trip to the flight line.

239   RAF History: Bomber Command: Campaign Diary, December 1944; http://www.raf
.mod.uk/bombercommand/dec44.html
240   Tidal Wave, The August 1943 Raid on Ploesti; Air Force Historical Studies Office;
http://www.airforcehistory.hq.af.mil/popTopics/ploesti.htm
241   Ploesti Oil Raid Operation Tidal Wave; http://www.ww2guide.com/oil.shtml

After crawling into the bed of the truck, Bill Tripp turned to Jack: "How many more for you?"

"Eleven more. How 'bout you?"

"The same."

"No sweat."

"Yeah…no sweat, Jack."

Jack turned to Dean: "How 'bout you, how many more?"

"I've got six. They can't come soon enough," answered Dean, as the truck rolled out.

The men reached their new planes and started their preflight checklists. Dean confirmed that the turrets turned and that his targeting periscope was operational. He alerted Jack: "Lieutenant, I'm good to go."

"Roger," said Jack, as he continued running through the preflight getting ready to fire up the engines. Seeing the day's colors to start engines, he completed the preflight sequence and then looked out at the ground crewman giving him the thumbs-up. The ground crewman lifted his right arm and spun his right index finger and hand in a small circle. Flipping the ignition switch for the starboard engine, Jack watched it come to life. The roar from all eighteen cylinders inside the cylinder heads was almost deafening. Jack set his air-fuel mixtures and then fired up the port engine.

A few planes taxied out. Lieutenant Colonel Willets flying lead in A-Box turned his Invader onto the runway. Willets revved his engines and then cut them back to idle. All the planes waited in takeoff or taxi position and everyone kept their eyes on the tower waiting for the green or red flare. It was an easy system, green for "go" and red for "no go."

Moments later, green streaked up and then arched over the runway. Before it had reached its apogee, Willets had pushed his throttles forward. Ten seconds later, twenty-two-year-old Captain Joe Meagher in his A-20K model Havoc followed. Joe was flying the Havoc because there still weren't enough glass-nosed Invaders to fill the lead and deputy slots in formation. Regardless, he felt right at home as the A-20 lifted off into the thick, cold air of December.

Uncensored Photo

A-26 Invader taking off from Melun in January 1945. Back of
photo reads, "Passed by theater censors 1-24-45 Jack F. Smith
1st Lieutenant For release."
Personal Collection

"Burg, you got the directions to this Saarlautern place were hittin' today, over?"
"Yessir."
"Good, this is number sixty-five for me. I don't want to mess it up."
"I'll take good care of you sir, over."
"No sweat."

As the last plane joined the third flight of B-Box, Willets turned both boxes toward the RP, where they were to join up with three B-26 Marauders equipped with the GEE radar-directed bombing system. Cloud cover was thick, preventing visual bombing, which necessitated the British navigational bombing aid. All thirty-six planes in the group were to drop when the Marauders dropped. German troop concentrations had been detected in this area, so along with other Ninth Air Force Groups, the 416th was trying out a saturation bombing technique. It wasn't a mission that required as great an accuracy as they were used to delivering. Just because the Army wasn't moving forward didn't mean the Air Force wasn't going to hit targets.

Clearing the cloud top at four thousand feet, the group climbed to their assigned altitude and after ten minutes saw the B-26s at the RP. Moving into position ahead of the two boxes, the three Marauders turned the formation of thirty-nine planes toward the IP.

"Doubt those Krauts can hit us through this stuff," said Bill to his gunner.

Scanning around with his periscope, his gunner agreed hopefully.

Dean Vafiadis was enjoying his new toy. Sitting in his chair in the middle of his gunner's compartment, which was attached to the periscope shaft, he swung around in circles, supposedly scanning the sky for bogies, but really just for the fun of it.

"Ten minutes from the IP, Colonel," said Lieutenant Royal to Willets.

"Roger" just escaped Willets' lips when bright red-orange bursts erupted around and through the formation.

Radar didn't care about the cloud cover, and the Marauder-led formation began receiving the first of many salvos of 88- and 150-mm anti-aircraft fire directed by the gun-laying radar batteries below. Every ship in the A-Box shuddered from the first salvo. Earl Hayter looked over at Bill's plane wondering if this was going to be the one for him.

Explosions filled the sky again as the men in the formation realized the B-26s were flying the beams, not trying to avoid the flak. Meagher realized it was going to be a long ride to the target.

Flying in the A-1-2 slot, Joe was focusing on the B-26s and watching for the bomb bay doors to open on the lead plane. Now on his sixty-fifth mission, he already had his orders rotating him back to the states in his right front pocket. His packed B-4 was waiting for him on his cot at the base. He had been told that a DC-3 supply plane would arrive this afternoon, and that he could catch it to England and then pick a ship home or maybe ferry a plane back. He was just waiting for the doors to open so he could drop these damned eggs and then turn his plane homeward for the last time. That was all Joe could think about at this moment. But kismet was not on his side today.

Flak Bursts in the Formation

Flight of A-26s in box and flight formation. Note the full flight complement of six planes in the upper left corner, while only three align in the upper center and four in the mid-right flight. The black clouds are flak bursts. The photo suggests that this mission took some losses. Photo was taken from the low box.
Personal Collection

Exploding below and to the right of his cockpit, the 150-mm round radiated shrapnel in all directions, the detonation made Joe's A-20 sound like a pinball gallery, as the shower of shrapnel peppered and penetrated the shell. Joe felt his plane bounce and then fall back in a bone-jarring jolt. A gunpowder smell from the detonation filled the cockpit.

Almost instantaneously aware of his injury, Joe tried to regain control of the plane; he grimaced as the higher cortical areas of his brain made him aware of the excruciating pain in his right ankle. The steel had shattered the distal part of the fibula where it met the talus bone of the ankle, and then penetrated into the ankle proper. Still with lots of energy left, the undeterred shrapnel had penetrated the ligaments, muscle, and skin of Joe's medial ankle, and then exited through his boot. It had effectively destroyed the articulation of his right ankle—the one that controlled the right rudder.

"Son of a bitch," exclaimed Joe, when his consciousness of the pain caught up. Fighting to overcome the distraction, he scanned the instrument panel, and saw the manifold pressure in the starboard engine dropping quickly. His airspeed now fell below two hundred miles per hour. Reacting quickly, he pushed the throttles up in the left engine while feathering the starboard engine and banking down to the left, away from the dead engine to get out of formation. Pushing the yoke forward and to the left Joe applied pressure to the left rudder pedal and immediately suffered pulsating pain in his right ankle as the right pedal rose and compressed his foot. With every move, the bones in his fractured ankle grated together. He saw blood coming from the holes in his flight boot, running down toward the heel and pooling on the flight deck under the rudder controls. It was coagulating into a liver-red glob.

After scanning the panel, Joe discovered that the interphone was destroyed as was the radio. More shrapnel than he knew had made it through the bottom of the ship and violated his small sanctuary. He needed no more information to come to grips with the reality of this dilemma.

During the blast Staff Sergeant Joe E. McCreary and navigator Lieutenant J.J. Burg had experienced the same disorienting concussion, but were both spared any injury from the shrapnel. They felt the plane bank off to the left and worried that it was out of control, but quickly realized that the turn was too well coordinated.

Shaking his head back and forth while rubbing his face with adrenaline-driven quivering hands, McCreary realized how much worse it could have been. He tried to raise anyone on the interphone, all the while asking the Almighty for guidance. Should he jump and take his chances with the Germans or stay with the plane to take his chances with Meagher? He couldn't believe Joe's luck. His last mission! He was scheduled to go home. Contemplating his current predicament made McCreary realize it might be his own last mission in more ways than one, and his prayers shifted from guidance to salvation.

Burg too was worried this might be his last mission. His prayers came with more solemn intent, as he began to list his personal regrets while planning his escape from the plane. He felt the plane continue its turn down to the left and watched the compass rotate 180 degrees. As the plane leveled out and dropped into the clouds for cover, Burg realized the captain was trying to get them back home. Feeling his prayers were answered, he began to get his sense of control and confidence back.

Burg checked on his pilot asking, "Captain, you OK?"

Burg waited for a reply then he repeated the question. He correctly reasoned the interphone was out. He settled into his lonely space and again contemplated his options, just as McCreary was doing in his gunner's compartment.

Meagher was contemplating his options as well. He couldn't leave the plane without telling his crew to bail out. Was McCreary alive? He could fly the plane out of here as long the damaged left engine kept running and his ankle held out, but the pain was growing worse every minute. Joe decided to stay with the plane, to get it and his crew back to free territory. He could belly in or wheel in, depending on the landing site. He worried about his navigator becoming trapped in the nose, if he had to belly in.

"First things first," he said out loud. "We need to get into some clouds!" Heading toward the thick bank in front of him, Meagher trimmed up the plane as best he could and slowly dropped down through them using only the instruments. He let out a sigh of relief as the wounded Havoc lumbered into a cloud bank, which felt like a comforting, protective blanket instead of the menacing deadly shroud it could sometimes be. Using the cloud cover to avoid any Luftwaffe fighters and any 20- or 37-mms spraying tracers at them, he kept the plane on course. Once deep inside the clouds, he opened his bomb bay door and salvoed his bomb load. He didn't care where they landed—anywhere would be a target of opportunity—and more importantly, he had completed number sixty-five.

Smith, Hayter, Tripp, and Vafiadis had watched Joe's Havoc take the hit. But now priorities had changed, and everyone refocused on the lead Marauders. Several minutes later their bomb bay doors swung open. The formation continued to be showered with flak, with steel ripping and tearing its way through the polished aluminum of the A-26s. Jack and Dean found themselves hoping it was someone else's turn to get hit this trip. Dean's boyish interest in his new targeting system had been forgotten when death had begun to reach up to them. Since D day they had had their fill of close calls.

With his attention on the belly of the lead B-26, Willets watched for the bombs to drop. His finger rested on the energized bomb-release button.

Ahead of him, the bombardier-navigator in the B-26 sat with his eyes glued to the GEE oscilloscope bombsite. Watching the two lines approaching the bomb-release point, the navigator knew that when the two lines crossed at the right point, the formation was in the position that corresponded to the geographic position of the target below. Watching the two lines converge, he was anticipating the automatic bomb release when a 150-mm flak explosion knocked him off his perch. Responding to the blast wave the B-26 reared upward, then settled back into position. After insulting the Germans, the BN regained his composure and watched the lines converge. "Bombs away!"

The thirty-eight planes released tons of death in the direction of the enemy below. The Wehrmacht *soldaten* heard only the roar of the *Flugabwehrkanonen* around them. Oblivious to the massed quantity of death falling their way, the concentrated masses had no idea of the number of Ninth Air Force groups targeting the area this morning. Death was going to fall for some time today.

As soon as their salvos were gone, the Americans turned toward home, accelerating in a dive, hoping to get out of the flak field as quickly as possible.

Flying some distance before dropping out of the bottom of the clouds just eight hundred feet off the deck, Meagher leveled off and continued west, with the left engine smoking but not quitting. Knowing the distance back to the bomb line, his airspeed, and heading, Meagher estimated that they were probably out of German airspace by now. He was a little unhappy about not seeing any good spots to land. Joe nursed his wounded bird along until he spied the comforting bright yellow of several good ol' American-made Caterpillar tractors leveling off a field. *The Krauts don't use yellow,* he thought as he turned onto an approach toward the field. Buzzing the field at fifty feet, he hoped the crews would pull their tractors off so he could land. Joe pulled up sharply to the left, keeping his dead engine on the outside of the turn so he wouldn't lose lift and stall. After heading back into the clouds, he circled and dropped out of them. He could see the field was now clear. As he turned on final, he knew he needed to get the gear down. Pushing the lever down, Joe heard nothing except the pump activating. The hydraulic lines and pumps were empty, no way to lower the gear. Joe rapidly began getting his gear down manually. After pushing the gear lever down to neutral, he pulled the T handle to release the hydraulic control on the wheels. Joe began bouncing the nose of the plane violently, in order to force the landing gear to drop out of the bays, as he had been taught to do in training, never actually having done it. Then...**THUMP!**... he heard and felt the heavy thud of the wheels falling out, and figured that it was working, but with the ground coming up fast there was no time to worry about it. Joe throttled back and dropped his flaps, somehow leveling out on a textbook emergency approach.

The touchdown was better than they could have hoped for. The wheels hit the supporting soil—compacted by heavy dozers—which allowed the Havoc to roll and skid along. Meagher, Burg, and McCreary hadn't completed their talks with God as the plane's moving wheels made them know that this mission wasn't over yet. Meagher, enduring the pain in his ankle, bringing the wounded Havoc to a stop.

Burg and McCreary were happy to be able to get out of the plane, and moved quickly to the cockpit to check on their captain. After opening the emergency hatch, they turned their energies to helping Meagher get out.

"Great job, Captain. Damned fine flying," said Burg, but became concerned about his pilot when he saw all the blood in the cockpit.

"Heck-fire, you're right about that. You did a damn fine job bringing her in," said McCreary, as they released Joe from the seat's harnesses and carefully lifted him from the cockpit.

That's when they became aware of just how badly Joe's ankle was injured, as he informed them, in no uncertain terms, to be careful. After seeing his pain, they took great care in moving him out of the cockpit then getting him over onto the wing, Burg slid off the trailing edge to the ground, and turned to help McCreary slide their pilot off the wing. Partly carrying Meagher, they got safely away from the plane and fell to the freshly compacted earth. Its musty smell was somehow comforting to all of them. Rummaging through the medical kit McCreary had taken from the cockpit, Burg gave Meagher an amp of morphine into the right thigh. He grimaced and then realized that his prayers for his crew had been answered. He gladly accepted the slow relief, and slid off into drug-induced tranquility with a small thankful smile.

Mission Accomplished

A-26 Invader from the 669th squadron (2A markings) in flight
returning from target.
Personal collection

Having escaped the flak fields, Willets followed the B-26s until they hit the second RP. All three Marauders banked to the right as they headed for home. Willets continued the formation on its current heading for ten minutes longer, and then got a new heading from Royal. Applying slight left rudder with left aileron and back pressure on the yoke, Willets completed a coordinated left-banking turn. In unison the formation followed Willets onto the final leg home.

"Colonel, we're at the bomb line, sir. Time to report to Command our mission status, over," Lieutenant Royal informed his lead.

"Roger," Willets replied, and then radioed.

Willets completed his report and then began the formation's descent into the cloud cover. Every flight followed Willets into the fluffy surface of the cloud cover, disappearing six at a time.

Earl felt the clouds steal his vision when his Invader descended into the suspended water vapor. He could no longer see the big planes beside him. Immediately he directed his attention to his instrument panel, which became his new eyes. He scanned his instruments, and then quickly glanced out the windshield hoping that he wouldn't see the fuselage of an airplane filling the view. Every pilot in the group felt the same anxiety, as they slid down through the darkening gray around them. They all felt their cold sweat and fought to control it, hoping the flight behind them didn't overtake them or that they didn't drift into the plane beside them. At eight hundred feet Willets popped out of the overcast and saw the winter brown of the French countryside. The other four Invaders in his flight appeared through the bottoms of the clouds, and were more dispersed than when they entered.

Peeling off from his flight, Willets lowered his flaps, dropped his gear and touched down first. All the others followed the orchestrated sequence of orbiting the base and peeling off to land in the order they took off. With no wounded to land first, the thirty-four Invaders and one Havoc landed within ten minutes. Debriefing was quick, except for the pilots reassuring Intel that the mission was no milk run.

The ground crews were aware of how difficult the mission had been. They were already shaking their heads about the damage done to their new planes. The repairs began in earnest, as the aircrews went off to relax.

Carefully sipping his Red Cross coffee, Earl moved the hot liquid rapidly around his mouth, allowing it to cool. The heat forced Earl to think about something other than Joe Meagher's Havoc falling from formation. Operations had already listed the crew as MIA.

"Hey, Earl, any word on Joe?"

Earl looked at Jack, and shook his head.

Jack sipped his coffee and said nothing. He'd check with Sorrels later. As the assistant Operations officer, Sorrels should know something sooner or later.

❧

A cold December continued on, as the lines of both opposing armies stabilized. As the hard of winter approached, one side appeared arguably deceptive or naively complacent, while the other side deceptively prepared for aggression.

As the Allied advance stalled, the German leadership tried to regroup and mount a counteroffensive. Five plans based on Hitler's basic strategy had been discussed and then submitted to Hitler and his military chiefs. Arguments by General Jodl to narrow the scope of the attack while maintaining its strength were ultimately rejected by the Führer, and then by his command staff of lackeys. The unanimity was not surprising, given the wholesale liquidation of the officer corps that had taken place in response to the failed assassination attempt on Hitler. It served as a reminder to all the general staff officers who were still in command.

Finally, Hitler approved a large, sweeping, double-pronged attack known as "The Grand Slam." The plan had serious weaknesses, which Field Marshal Von Rundstedt understood. Initially, Von Rundstedt tried to distance himself from the plan, but later referred to the general idea as "a stroke of genius." Perhaps understanding the large probability of failure for the logistically unsupportable scale of the operation, Von Rundstedt saw the end coming sooner than later. The military promised eighteen infantry and twelve armored divisions, which were then strengthened to include five motorized Luftwaffe anti-aircraft regiments, twelve Volks artillery corps, ten rocket brigades, and assorted infantry units. Hitler himself promised fifteen hundred aircraft of assorted vintage, including upward of one hundred jet fighters. Throughout the preparation of the campaign, the real logistical problem for the Wehrmacht would be—as it had always been—fuel. If the Germans diverted fuel for the counterstrike, other fronts would suffer. Nevertheless, *Generalfeldmarschall* Keitel promised 4,250,000 gallons of fuel for the counteroffensive along with a special fifty trainloads of ammunition.

The two generals responsible for the operation were well aware of its strategic shortcomings. Both General Von Rundstedt and General Westphal knew the plan was too ambitious to reach Antwerp—the force was too undersized to achieve the massive scope of the plan. In the execution of the strategy, both saw the potential for a World War I-type salient, in which the Allies would surround and destroy the Wehrmacht in the process. Von Rundstedt offered an alternative plan that, if followed, would have better secured the opportunity for success. Hitler ridiculed the plan as small minded, lacking the audacity for grand success, and thus the "Grand Slam" moved forward.

As the war shifted constantly against the Germans, surviving the climate inside the higher offices of the Third Reich had become an art form. Humbling oneself to the Führer had become more an act of self-preservation than an open expression of commitment. Responsibility of command down to the smallest units had been assumed by the Führer or else acquiesced to by sycophants. With the leader in charge of every detail and the generals distrusted, failure was assured. Sun Tzu had been ignored again.

Finally, Hitler's strategy went into effect, leading to what would be called the Battle of the Ardennes, or more colorfully, the Battle of the Bulge. On December 16 the First SS Panzer Corps along with the Sixth Panzer Army silently ordered for battle in front of the US Army's Third division of the 394th infantry. The Panzer corps was bolstered with the 227th Volks Grenadier Division, the 12th Volks Grenadier Division, and the Third Parachute Division. In an atypical fashion, the Panzers were to support and then exploit an infantry breakthrough. The 227th Volks Grenadiers faced the American 393rd Infantry while the Wehrmacht's Third Parachute Division on the left flank of Wehrmacht assault would be thrown against the US Fourteenth Calvary Group, which was backed by the inexperienced US Ninety-Ninth Division. The absence of enemy activity and cold weather had conspired to lull the Allies into a sense of watchful complacency.

At 0530 hours on December 16, 1944, the Wehrmacht began their third invasion of Western Europe in the first half of the twentieth century. Massed Wehrmacht artillery let loose the opening salvos of the Ardennes offensive upon the 394th, who believed it to be outgoing fire. Wehrmacht Artillery from 75-mm up to 210-mm heavies poured death into the US divisions along the line. Command and frontline troops quickly realized that the outgoing had become incoming. Having reinforced their bunkers, the

US corps suffered few casualties during the one-hour bombardment. The Wehrmacht was slow to exploit the artillery barrage, and the offensive began with tentative probes into the American lines. Contact with American forces was made along the line early, and later in the day Sergeant Eddie Dolenc of B Company, defending the town of Losheimergraben, met the advance of the Forty-Eighth Grenadier Regiment from a shell hole created by the morning's bombardment. After the Forty-Eighth Grenadier Regiment completed their cautious advance through the woods, wire, and minefields, their assault began. Firing from the protection of his shell hole, Dolenc was last seen piling the gray-coated grenadiers in front of his position as the *soldates* advanced into their own "gate to hell," reminiscent of Franz Gockel's *maschinengewehr* position on Omaha Beach from which he cut down the advancing Americans. Dolenc's fortune was not to be as benevolent as Gockel's was to him. The assault was repelled with the aid of mortar teams dropping their rounds nearly on top of B Company. This tentative approach was not to last, though, as the Wehrmacht probed and advanced slowly until the morning of the next day, when a hole was opened between the Ninety-Ninth and Fourteenth Calvary. By December 18 the floodgates were beginning to give way and the onslaught was about to begin, as the Wehrmacht exploited their breakout over the Eifel highlands. Bastogne would soon be surrounded, and any ideas that soldiers had of getting home by Christmas were pushed from rational thought.[242]

Having tactically delayed committing their Panzers, the Germans pushed the responsibility of creating a breakthrough onto the infantry. Determined American resistance delayed the breakout and allowed time for the Allied defenses to stiffen. For the first time since Operation Neptune, the American military was on the defensive and on occasion fighting a delaying retreating action. While the Americans suffered a few significant reverses early in the German counteroffensive, they would not be on their heels long, as German forces were consistently having problems with supplies.

Logistical problems became inexorable. By December 21 the Wehrmacht's need for ammunition was documented; the consumption of twelve hundred tons per day exceeded the planned pre-D day rate. It would soon become obvious as the counteroffensive waged on that resupply failures were taking their toll on the Wehrmacht's ability to advance. Panzer Lehr Division reported that it was out of fuel and was short of ammunition by December 28th. Indeed, much if not all the failure of the operation was attributed to the inability of the Wehrmacht to transport supplies, not from the lack of them. Because the infrastructure was so destroyed by Allied air missions, the Germans were reduced to using horses to move supplies. In fact, during the Ardennes counteroffensive, German infantry divisions contained more horses than their World War I counterparts. What little logistical support there was found itself falling victim to interdiction by Allied aircraft after December 23. Eventually the Wehrmacht's counteroffensive stalled, not from a true lack of fuel, but from the inability to move the fuel to the front.

---

242   *The Ardennes: Battle of the Bulge:* United States Army in World War Two: *The European Theater of Operations;* Hugh M. Cole; Office of the Chief of Military History, Department of the Army; 1965; http://www.army.mil/cmh-pg/books/wwii/7-8/7-8_2.htm;

This failure to transport supplies can be appreciated by the 10th Waffen SS Panzer Division, which sat outside Bonn with eight consumption units. ("One unit" was defined by the Wehrmacht as the amount of fuel needed to move the vehicles of a combat unit sixty-three miles.) The division was unable to be mobilized to the fuel-starved front, and so the front went without. All the infrastructure needed to fight a modern war—rail lines, rail bridges, road junctions and bridges—had fallen victim to the Allied tactical air campaign. Sun Tzu's principles had been proven true—the historically well-disciplined, logistically minded German war machine succumbed to the inability to get the pound of rice to the front.[243]

Before the Battle of the Bulge, between December 2nd and 15th, the 416th undertook missions over road junctions in the German towns of Kall, Erkelenz, Dilsburg, Schleiden, Germund, and Heimbach. After the start of the German counteroffensive on the 16th, the poor northern-European weather prevented effective Allied aerial attacks. But, when the weather cleared—on the 23rd—the 416th's mission package changed to tactical interdiction. From the 23rd to 29th of December the group went after the arteries of the Wehrmacht. Starve the Ardennes offensive was their goal.

To accomplish this goal, they hit the Saarburg bridge, Waxweiler marshaling yard, the Zulpich railroad, the Münstereifel communication center, the Hillersheim railroad junction, the Eller bridge, and the Keuchinger bridge. While the 416th bombed these targets, other Ninth Air Force groups either joined them or attacked targets of their own. Fighter-bombers attacked the front lines, destroying vehicles needed for resupply and reinforcement. Panzers were destroyed or damaged. With no way to repair them, the leading edge of the Ardennes counteroffensive began to grow hungry and then falter from starvation for supplies.

By December many new faces had been introduced to the 416th. Older veterans who had hit their sixty-fifth missions were being transferred into command positions, rotated into instructor slots, or just sent home. December was when many of the new gunners, pilots, and navigators were to get their first taste of combat at twelve thousand feet. Christmas Eve and Christmas Day gave many their introduction to death.

⚜

"Hey, Sergeant Cheney, what do you think of these new birds?" Lieutenant Reese asked his gunner over the interphone.

"Pretty nice, but I miss havin' someone to talk to back here," came a chuckling reply. "What's the name of this place we're hitting today again?"

"Z-u-l-p-i-c-h...Zul-pich is how they said it...Supposed to have some Krauts there. Some kinda road and rail junction. Anyway, we were told to stop them from using it."

"Roger that," said Cheney.

Reese concentrated again on keeping a tight formation.

---

243   *The Ardennes: Battle of the Bulge: United States Army in World War II:* The European Theater of Operations; Hugh M. Cole; http://www.army.mil/cmh-pg/books/wwii/7-8/7-8_2.htm ; Chapters 2 & 25

"I never thought I'd be spendin' Christmas Eve flying over Germany trying to get my butt shot off," said Cheney.

"Me neither, Sergeant. Me neither."

Watching his lead, Reese turned onto the bomb-run and opened his bomb bay doors in unison with the rest of the flight. The first salvos of Luftwaffe anti-aircraft rounds were streaking skyward.

"Here we go," Reese said.

"Roger."

The well-aimed anti-aircraft shells hit the formation hard. One round claimed an A-26 in the first flight. Smoke billowed from the right engine, as Lieutenant Reese Robertson sat stunned by the blast, wondering just what the heck had happened. He had never thought he'd ever get hit by flak, something else had happened. Quickly he realized that he was wrong, and he found himself battling to keep his bleeding bird in formation.

Reese immediately called his gunner, "Cheney, do you read me, over...do you read me?" M.W. Cheney had ceased to read anybody or anything just milliseconds after the 150-mm round had exploded below and behind the ring wing of the Invader. Steel and aluminum had shredded his flak jacket, with similar effect to his body.

The right engine hadn't fared much better. Reese was forced to concentrate on the bomb-run, while he feathered his right engine, trying to remember the proper sequence while concentrating on all his other duties. "Throttle closed...propeller governor, propeller gov...there it is...switch to decrease mph. Let's see...car..bor..ate..or control to idle cut off...oh heck-fire." Reese was falling from formation and pushed the throttle forward to increase his good engine's manifold pressure to 18 mm Hg. He went back to feathering: "Rudder trim...rudder trim." Before he had time to check his airspeed, the bombs were falling from the lead plane, and he lurched toward the bomb-release button on his control yoke and felt his Invader shudder as each thousand-pound bomb fell from its rack.

He glanced at his instrument panel to see the rpms racing in the right engine. "Oh hell, what did I forget?" he muttered, as he reviewed the feathering sequence in his head. "Oh yeah." Reese pushed the propeller-feathering control down and watched the windmilling in the right engine slow and then stop. "What's next?...cowl flaps closed... oil-cooler switch...door switch...closed." He looked out the right window to see if all was going well, and saw the flames lapping out of the back of the engine cowls that had not been closed. "Oh, hellfire," escaped Reese's lips as he tried to slip the plane to the left away from the fire.

"Fuel container selector valve to...off, fuel booster switch to...off." Frantically he wrestled with all the complexities of the failed engine, which were now complicated by the blaze. He had long since lost his position in the formation. They were executing their escape maneuver, leaving Reese alone in the flak field. Reese was rocked by a second blast, which left him again temporarily disoriented. After recovering, Reese saw the fire growing in the right engine, which was made worse by the fact that his left engine was losing fuel pressure after the second blast. Reese knew the Invader was about to buy the farm and he didn't want to be in it when it did. He called over the interphone: "Bail out, Cheney. Repeat, bail out!"

Reese flipped the emergency claxton and unstrapped himself from his seat while simultaneously reaching to the top of the cockpit to turn the handle of his emergency hatch. It jerked open as the 280-mph slipstream caught it. Reese called to Cheney one more time. Then pulling himself upward, he slid out the opening, and was quickly sucked out of the cockpit over the right side of the aircraft. Reese fell for several seconds before pulling his chute open. Anti-aircraft rounds whizzed past him until he hit the ground with a dull thud. The impact knocked his breath out. Like all the others, he was quickly captured by the Wehrmacht.

Idling down, the engine noise across the base slowly decreased, as the returning A-26s and the few remaining A-20s were put to bed by their pilots. Ground crews started their evaluation routine before beginning their repairs, all except Reese's crew. They stood or lay in the grass by the hardstand for a while, believing Reese and Cheney would show up soon. Eventually the crew realized that they weren't coming back, and drifted over to the debriefing hut to see if they could find out what had happened. It wasn't pleasant when they did. After learning, they shared a smoke as they walked back toward the flight line. They needed something to do, and there were plenty of shot-up planes to fix after this mission. One of the crewmen was drafted by airman Ken Bailey, who was working on his plane Tom Swift and needed help. The other crews quickly put the remainder to work.

This evening, mess was a quick affair, since everyone wanted to get ready for Father Penticoff's Mass. This was the first Christmas in theater for the 416th and many men in the complement had found a new outlook on religion since the group had started flying missions.

"Ralph, what time to do we need to head over to the hangar?" Hulse asked his good Catholic friend.

"You going?"

"Yeah, I thought I might. Heck, it's Christmas Eve. Besides, I heard a lot of the guys from the 669th are going."

"It's a pretty good walk, so I figure maybe 2300, so we can get a good seat too."

"Sounds good."

Later, as they made their way to the parachute hangar that had been set up to accommodate Mass, Ralph and Hulse were greeted by all the 669th pilots. Ralph found himself chatting with Roland Enman, Jack Smith, Earl Hayter, Bill Tripp, and Hiram Clark as they walked to the hangar.

"Jack, what's a good Southern Methodist boy like you doing here?" Ralph joked.

"Same thing you are, brother—gettin' right with the Lord... gettin' right with the Lord."

"Amen to that, Brother Jack," said Earl, as they moved to their chairs.

The men shared Christmas stories until Father Penticoff stepped to the make-shift pulpit, and quieted the overflow crowd that had jammed themselves into the hangar.

Looking out on the sea of faces, Father Penticoff was glad that he had prepared a sermon that would speak to all denominations. He didn't care what religion the men in front of him practiced. He was in the business of helping and saving souls, so that's what he was going to do. "Let's hope we don't get an air raid tonight," he opened, getting some chuckles but no laughs. He then began his first overseas Christmas Mass. Every crew on flight status lingered a little longer in their prayers. The men sung and broke bread together as Christmas Eve became Christmas Day.

Rousted from his sleep, Don Sorrels rubbed his eyes. "Christmas, huh?" He crawled out of his sleeping bag, which was covered with two woolen blankets. As the new guy in the tent, he was the farthest away from the stove. The summer and early fall warmth had faded and it was really getting chilly this late in December. It didn't help his mood that all the other men were still in bed.

Don began his morning ritual and then left to eat. As he walked in the predawn, he thought it was odd that he was the only pilot on flight status from his tent, but then remembered that he didn't write the orders.

"Hey, Don, looks like it's me and you today," said a voice from the darkness behind him. Recognizing the voice, he turned to see his good friend Bob Svenson coming out of the darkness from the direction of his tent.

"Yeah, the rest of my guys are still in the rack," Don replied.

"Well, let's go get a cup of joe. To heck with them."

"I'm for that."

They opened the door to the mess hall.

"Where ya wanna sit?" Svenson asked, after they picked up their breakfast.

"I don't care. See any seats?"

"There's a couple back there by Captain Prentiss and Lieutenant Burseil."

"Great, they're leadin' our flight this morning. Maybe we can get some info from them before the briefing," Sorrels added.

Sitting down with their flight leaders, Don and Bob shared greetings.

"Hey, Captain, where we going today?" Don inquired.

"Heading into Germany…east of Bastogne…trying to destroy a command center," said Prentiss. "Krauts set up there after the start of the offensive, have been sending orders to some Panzer corps near the front, they say. Same areas as yesterday's run. Flak looks to be pretty heavy." He sipped his coffee nonchalantly.

With a mouthful of eggs Svenson added: "This is our third trip in two days to that area. Command must have some good intel about what's going on there." He swallowed and scooped another spoonful and piled on a piece of **SPAM.**

Don smiled, and said: "Don't give 'em too much credit, Bob. They've been wrong before."

After finishing breakfast, the crews moved to the trucks over the snowy ground. Kicking a small drift of snow with his heavy, fleece-lined flight boots, Svenson said,

"Hope we don't have any more of those damned air raids. I sure as hell hate jumping into those foxholes when they're full of snow."

Burseil shook his head in agreement. "Amen. At least they haven't hit anything yet."

All four men thought back to the nightly air raids of last week. The raids began after the Germans started their offensive in Belgium. Fortunately, all that had resulted were some bombs hitting close to the 671st squadron's bivouac area. No causalities were taken and no damage to the base or planes. The only damage had been to the men laying in their slit trenches, out in the cold.

Now, walking into the briefing hut, everyone was happy to feel the heat. No one was really in a hurry to get to twelve thousand feet in an unheated Invader.

"Good morning," greeted them, as the Operations officer stood to start the briefing. "This morning we're going to Münstereifel. Krauts have a command and communications center there. Colonel Willets will be leading."

Some forty minutes went by quickly as the mission details were revealed. With the ending of the briefing, the conversation was light with no mention made of the mission. In the early-morning darkness the glowing embers from the nervous cigarettes spoke volumes about how the men felt as they moved slowly toward the truck after receiving their chutes and sidearms.

After completing the ride to their Invaders, the men crawled into their planes, continuing the ritual that all those years of repetitive training had conditioned them to do. It was an inspiring morning ceremony that the rising sun had grown accustomed to seeing —the cylinders of the 2,000-hp radials on the new A-26s started heating up. The ceremony was—in the sun's measure of time—something very new to witness. In humankind's existence, the ceremony seemed old, but exhilarating all the same. Over the last forty years, though, the sun had not grown accustomed to seeing unnatural looking objects leave the ground and fly. Now over the last five years it had witnessed the aerial armadas of warring nations flying from nearly every continent. For day after day, on continent after continent, over these past many years, the morning sacrament of this war—by its warriors to its massive destructive aerial capacity—became airborne. This Christmas Day the sun greeted the formation with its light glinting off the tips of the synchronized harmony of spinning propellers. It watched not only the 416th but bombers and fighters from nearly every group in the theater rising from the ground on the way to their assigned targets.

God watched with quiet reserve, and examined his policy of free will. These spinning propellers owed their existence to the organic residue left from the deaths of trillions of trillions of Mesozoic phytoplankton. Their decaying corpses still contained the energy of the sunlight they had fixed using the carbon atom and their chlorophyll molecular machinery before their death. Other plant and animal species that had been buried with them at the bottom of earth's anoxic equatorial Jurassic seas began cooking there for the next two hundred million years. These organic remains that had been left to decay under the earth's heat and pressure, finally became a mass of complex hydrocarbons containing the volatile high-octane gasoline that was now exploding on compression cycles in the cylinder heads of all these man-made Wasp Radials. The once-living matter had decayed into other compounds like the lubricating oil that was now protecting the moving parts of the Invader's high-RPM engines from the destructive forces of friction. This organic residue, was almost all controlled by the Allies by this time in the war, but soon would empower the Muslim world in ways they had never imagined capable of before. During the 1930s Saudi Arabia's Ghawar oil field was about to become the focal point of all the world's energy consumers. Hitler had been striving to capture the Russian then the Saudi fields since the beginning of the war. Now, near the end of it, his army was killing and dying to capture any petroleum reserves that could be taken from the Allies on its drive to the channel.

The 416th turned onto the first leg of a mission that would take them over Bastogne and Malmedy.

"Flak bursts—two o'clock low," came across the pilots' headsets throughout the formation. The first shots were low, but no one was waiting around to see if the next bursts were at altitude and direction. Turning twenty degrees left for one minute and then back right for a minute and a half, the formation stayed out of the main flak fields. After correcting to the left for thirty seconds, the group was back on course. Flak continued to rise, and pushed the group left and right in twenty-degree or greater turns and forcing them to run that course for at least a half-minute.

"Damnit, Burg, they're on us today. How much longer to the IP?" called Lieutenant Miracle to his navigator. A close burst had just rocked their Invader.

"Looks like ten minutes, sir. Leads coming back on course now."

"Can't be soon enough. These Krauts are protecting sumthin' down there," added Staff Sergeant Galloway from the cold confines of his gunner's compartment.

Moving successfully through the first flak field did little to relieve the fear and anxiety of the men flying toward the target. At their altitude they were within range of every anti-aircraft gun that the Luftwaffe and the Wehrmacht had in the area. Today they seemed to be using them all too. Tracers flew in front of, behind, and around the formation even if there weren't any bursts of the high-explosive stuff around them.

"Looks like the colonel is turning onto the bomb-run," crackled across the headset of Lieutenant Kehoe.

"Roger that, Gillespie," Kehoe replied to his gunner, "Holy cow, look at that flak!" All the air crews watched the sky darken as the big stuff rose to greet them.

Miracle was leading the second flight down the run and watched as the first flight dropped its bombs. "Burg, you ready to drop?"

"Roger. MPI in sight and closing the rate fast. Just keep the PDI on line. Damn, those Krauts have us in their sights today. Keep her steady, sir, steady and—"

Miracle felt the plane shudder and heard the aluminum skin of the Invader shred all around him. The 37-mm rounds were ripping through the nose of the Invader, and killed Burg just as indiscriminately. Miracle almost simultaneously felt the concussion from the right side of his aircraft. Shrapnel spewed out in all directions from the direct hit at the base of the wing, where it attached to the bulkhead of the fuselage. Shrapnel sprayed into the cockpit, gunner's compartment, and the main fuel tank immediately behind the right engine. Fire erupted from the right wing's nacelle as the last bit of life drained from Staff Sergeant Arthur Galloway.

Miracle had felt the hot steel rip through his right arm, side, and leg. One small piece had found its way into his right neck. Slashing its way through the skin and then the enveloping fascia of the vascular compartment, the steel sliver had severed the jugular vein before exiting out the right lateral larynx. Miracle began to gasp as the blood flowed from his neck, but—worse—into his airway from the larynx injury. Spitting up blood, Miracle was unable to speak as the frothy blood bubbled out of his mouth. Unable to move his right arm or leg, Miracle watched the ball in his artificial horizon begin to angle. The Invader slid to the right.

Using his left hand, Miracle flipped the emergency alarm, unaware that he was the only living body still in the plane. Drifting in and out of consciousness, Miracle felt the A-26 begin its ever-accelerating spin, praying for a miracle as he bargained during his lucent periods.

Pilots in Miracle's flight passed over the drop point even as they watched their lead's Invader begin its fall into a slow death spiral. Closing their bomb bay doors, they fell into formation behind the number-two ship and banked hard left.

In the flight behind Miracle, Lieutenant Kehoe watched in horror; his breath came quicker, and he prayed that he would be able to escape the same fate. Summoning his composure, Kehoe pushed his bomb-release button, feeling the pair of thousand-pounders fall from his wing shackles. As the last two small green bulbs signaled, his Invader was rocked by the blast of an 88-mm round, which had detonated inside the left wing. Concussion, steel and fire followed. Oil gushed from the left engine and burned away instantaneously in a black billowy display. In the gunner's compartment, Gillespie was just recovering from the shock and looking out his port window to see the flames and smoke. Thanking God that he was spared injury, he ripped off his flak jacket, snapped on his chute, kicked open the emergency hatch on the starboard side, and dove out head first. Kehoe had already left the Invader, greeting Miracle, Burg, and Galloway on their new journey.

When he landed, Gillespie was searched by his new jailors and then began his long walk to the stalag.

Meanwhile, the last flight continued its accelerated exit off the bomb-run and was pulling up from the dive, and running toward the RP. Seeing the fighters there, they formed up and turned for home.

"We gunna be OK, Lieutenant?"

"By golly, I sure hope so. I plan to get this bird home," said Lieutenant Willie Green to his gunner. "I didn't make it to sixty-five to get shot down today."

Green was battling with a right engine that was losing oil and a left engine with decreased fuel pressure, but both were still running well enough to keep him in formation. On his final mission he just wanted to get to the base in one piece. He knew he was scheduled to rotate back to the states and that was just fine with him.

After an uneventful trip back, Green shut down the superchargers, fuel pumps, generators, magnetos, and hydraulics, and he unstrapped himself from his pilot's seat and let out a deep sigh of relief. His ground crew greeted him on terra firma as he stepped off the last rung of the ladder. He'd made it.

Green and the other airmen attended a painful debriefing. The group learned that they had hit the target, but many flights had to bomb alternate targets due to smoke. Even worse, five men were missing.

Captain Prentiss left the debriefing and walked toward the mess hall with his navigator, Burseil. "Briefing at 1330 hours for the afternoon mission," he said as he blew the smoke from his first cigarette after the mission.

"Yeah, I'll see you there," Burseil replied, as the two spilt company, neither really hungry for afternoon mess.

Death had become a way of life around the world by now, a condition not re-served just for the 416th. A new war—a civil war—was being waged in Greece, as the Communists and the non-Communists fought for power—the result of a failed power-sharing attempt. France would avoid its civil war by agreeing to the demands of the mainly Communist Résistance.

As Germany's counteroffensive moved into its second week, the Allies were tak-ing numerous casualties across the Ardennes, but so were the Germans. In Bastogne, the American 101st held on, while Patton's Third Army was on the verge of relieving them. The British Thirtieth Corps and America's US First Armored and US Second Armored stopped the advance of the Wehrmacht's Fifth and Second Panzer Divisions southwest of Liege on December 25th. The very next day the Third Army broke through to Bas-togne. The fighting was intense, since the Germans felt that this was their last best ef-fort. Great sacrifices were now a daily occurrence on all sides of the war.

Even as the Allies approached, the death camps continued—even hastened—their eugenic agenda, which was built on the foundations of the euthanasia policies of the central government. The end of the "final solution" was thankfully approaching as the Wehrmacht and the Luftwaffe expended themselves in last-ditch attempts on both of Germany's fronts.[244], [245], [246] As early as 1939 the Nazi regime had begun killing the retarded, deformed, epileptic, syphilitic, or senile as well as anyone with a known genetic disorder. Great efforts by the Bishop Clemens von Galen in August of 1941 to stop the murder resulted in some cosmetic changes by the Nazis but did little to help or stop the slaughter, ultimately costing the heads of three priests. This monster of eugenic euthanasia had under Nazi tutelage grown into the nightmare of the Final Solution, a

244   The History Place: Holocaust Timeline: Nazi Euthanasia; http://www.historyplace. com/worldwar2/holocaust/h-eitanasia.htm
245   The History Place: World War Two in Europe Timeline; http://www.historyplace.com/ worldwar2/timeline/ww2/ww2time.htm
246   *The Ardennes: Battle of the Bulge: The European Theater of Operations:* United States Army in World War II; Hugh M. Cole; Chapters 22-24; http://www.army.mil/cmh-pg/books/wwii/7-8/ 7-8_22.htm

solution that thankfully was approaching its finale as the Wehrmacht and the Luftwaffe expended themselves on both of Germany's fronts.[247], [248], [249]

Afternoon Mission

The ground crews load an A-26 Invader with thousand-pound bombs. This A-26 was assigned to the 670th squadron (F6) in Melun, France.
Personal Collection

Christmas afternoon brought as few gifts as the morning had for the 416th; sacrifices were expected as the afternoon briefing drew to a close.

"Listen up, men. This is an important target. Our guys are takin' a poundin' up there in Belgium around Bastogne. The Third Army is breakin' through to them there." He pointed to a spot on the map and then another. "Let's take this rail junction out of the game for 'em. Any questions? OK, then let's go get 'em."

Sorrels stood up with Svenson and they walked to the door.

"Svenson, see you at the Christmas party tonight."

"Yeah, no sweat, see you there."

They joined the other men going out to the flight line.

247 The History Place: Holocaust Timeline: Nazi Euthanasia; http://www.historyplace.com/worldwar2/holocaust/h-eitanasia.htm
248 The History Place: World War Two in Europe Timeline; http://www.historyplace.com/worldwar2/timeline/ww2/ww2time.htm
249 The Ardennes: Battle of the Bulge: The European Theater of Operations: United States Army in World War II; Hugh M. Cole; Chapters 22–24; http://www.army.mil/cmh-pg/books/wwii/7-8/7-8_22.htm

After he had made his way to his plane, Prentiss walked around the Invader, noticing the upgrades in armor that the Douglas Company had added. After this morning's mission he appreciated more than ever before the new Dural plate that surrounded his cockpit and then ran the length of the Invader's fuselage below the wing to just past the gunner's compartment. As he prepared to fly, he ran over the finer points. Nose-wheel snubbing pin…engaged…pitot head covers…removed, oil and fuel reserve levels checked. Then he climbed aboard and settled into his pilot seat, thankful for the armor plate in front of and behind him. He knew it wouldn't stop a direct hit, but after seeing so many planes with more than seventy flak holes just today, he knew the plate would stop a lot.

Down the flight line Major Price was starting his preflight. "Lieutenant Hand, everything in order down there?"

"Yessir, good to go."

Price began his duties inside the cockpit like every other pilot, navigator, and gunner began theirs. Price looked at gauges, checked fluid levels and turned switches…hydraulic fluid levels…normal, hydraulic purolator…Price turned the handle four times and then checked to be sure the carburetor filter control was set on "direct."

Sorrels checked his oil-cooler doors, holding the switch in the open position for fifteen seconds, and then flipped both back to the closed position and held it for fifteen seconds.

Svenson checked his radio while others worked their way to the fuel-selector switches. For many, it was the same routine as every morning or afternoon.

The flare arched upward and every pilot checked that his cross-feed was on, throttles…one-quarter open, propeller governor controls…"increase mph," supercharger blower on…"low." Starter energizer switches were moved to R along the flight line—starting the familiar sound of radial engines about to explode to life. Eventually all the engines erupted, causing needles and dials in every cockpit to spring to life.

After liftoff the group took its first heading to the target. Everyone who had taken off was present except Major Price, who had aborted and landed at an emergency strip when his right engine cylinder-head temperature rose to dangerous levels. Sitting at the end of the runway, he watched the formation head northeast as Prentiss moved into the lead slot, taking Price's position.

Don Sorrels, in the second flight of the high group, could see the weather report had not been as accurate as he would have liked. Heavy scattered clouds sat smugly at several different altitudes, and worse yet, the cloud base was nearly solid in some areas, which might potentially hide the primary and secondary targets. Looking out ahead, he could see the cloud cover rise up to the group's altitude as they moved closer to the target. They would all have to fly in formation through the clouds. Not a good thing.

The group was lucky though. As they flew over the target area, the clouds began to clear. Don watched Captain Prentiss, in the lead, turn onto the bomb-run at the IP. That's when Don, Bob, and the rest of the flight realized how seriously the Luftwaffe was going to protect their lifeline twelve thousand feet below the 416th.

"Lieutenant Burseil, she's yours," said Prentiss in a ritual manner that both officers had grown accustomed to.

"Roger, sir," was all Prentiss heard, as the first salvo of anti-aircraft fire hit the flight. Prentiss was jolted unconscious by the 88-mm round that detonated immediately below the cockpit. The blast was enough by itself, but combined with the shrapnel, neither Burseil nor Prentiss survived, and their bodies were partially dismembered by the explosion. Also on board, Staff Sergeant Daniel Brown was flying his fiftieth mission and did survive the first blast, but not the second—a direct hit—just several seconds later. Filling with smoke from the fires, the A-26 nosed over and arched into a steep dive.

Lieutenant Bob Svenson, flying as Prentiss's deputy, reached to throw the switch to open his bomb bay doors. He was ready to begin his banking turn onto the run. Eleven seconds before, a Luftwaffe *kanonier* had fired another round through his *Flugabwehrkanone*. The 88-mm round rifled upward in a perfect trajectory to hit Svenson's plane. It entered immediately behind the cockpit, just inside the front of the bomb bay as the doors were opening. Detonating inside the cavity of the plane, the round ignited one of the fragmentation bombs that Svenson was preparing to drop. Gunners John Simmons and Alvin Wylie never had time to come to terms with their maker. Having attended Father Penticoff's Mass last night, they had spoken with him and now were meeting him in spirit.

Sorrels saw the explosion rip nearly in half the only A-20 on the mission. Don knew who was flying it, and he immediately radioed, "Svenson, bail out! Can you read, over? Bail out! Damn it, Svenson do you read, over? Bail out!"

Don called over and over, as he followed Brownie and Kerns into their banking turn onto the run. Watching to his right, Don saw the A-20 beginning to spin uncontrollably downward, leaving a trail of black smoke from the fires that were raging in both wings. He continued calling, as he remembered all the times he and Svenson had spent together in cadet training, and all the transition flying until they ended up together here in the 416th. Don's calls went unanswered.

The blast in the bomb bay had instantly separated the mortal from the immortal in the cockpit and the gunner's stations. The fires were doing the rest. As the plane fell, Don prayed, even as he witnessed both wings separate from the Havoc at five thousand feet. The fuselage had become a spinning aerial torpedo. There would be no getting out now. A few moments later it had driven itself deep into the ground. The exploding earth fell nearly straight back down, filling the hole that had now become the graves of Svenson, Simmons, and Wylie.

Looking for chutes that had never opened, Don spoke to his God on the men's behalf, "God, please bless 'em." And then he had to turn back to the fight.

Ahead, watching Brownie's Invader bounce in the flak field, Sorrels was now ready to get the hell out of here. "Come on, drop 'em, Brownie," escaped his lips, as he readied his release button. Another salvo exploded around the flight as Don saw Brownie's eggs leave the nest. His followed quickly.

Chaos was swarming on the ground, as thousand-pound, high-explosive bombs mixed with fragmentation bombs exploded along the bomb path. Railroad tracks were ripped from their cross ties, and the flailing steel had cut several men in half as it sailed through the congested rail junction. Explosions destroyed trucks, tanks, and railcars and the ability of the Wehrmacht to move its rice to the front.

After hitting 300 mph in a left high-speed dive on his escape, Brownie leveled out, hoping to get out of the flak field. The gunners below were mainly interested in the planes that hadn't bombed yet, and kept their guns firmly pointed to the bomb-run and cut their fuses accordingly. The sky continued to fill with death as the last of the flights dropped its salvo and then dove for safety.

After Prentiss was lost, Major Dick Wheeler assumed the lead of Prentiss's flight. He knew there was no use staying on the run without a bombardier, so he closed his bomb bay doors. Then, for some reason Pilot Campbell made a diving right turn off the bomb-run, and the other three Invaders in the flight followed. Pulling up, Wheeler looked at his map for a heading to the RP. Then Wheeler realized that the three remaining planes in his flight were scattered across the sky, putting them all at risk for being attacked by enemy aircraft. Responding to the situation, he radioed the remaining planes and began the process of regrouping.

Unfortunately, the disarray had not gone unnoticed. A flight of Luftwaffe ME-109s had witnessed the slaughter and the resulting disorganization of the remaining bombers. Seeing a terrific opportunity to capitalize on the situation, the Luftwaffe squadron zeroed in on its disorganized prey from several thousand feet above. Wheeler was desperately trying to get his Invaders back in formation.

The Germans came in quickly.

"*Nimm die drei am links, Gruppe zwei. Gruppe eins, komm mit mir und die zwei am rechts angreifen. Gut jagen!*"[250] said the Luftwaffe *fluchtkommandeur,*[251] as the 109s targeted their apparently unprotected victims below.

In spite of the terrible losses and disasters of the day's mission, the twists of war were about to bring fortune to Wheeler's vulnerable Invaders. Hiding in the sun just one thousand feet above the 109s, a flight of P-38s were still waiting for an opportunity like this. They had been providing high cover as the bombers went in on the run. The lead pilot in the Lightning fighter group recognized the ME-109s for what they were. He called to his other pilots, "Bandits, eleven o'clock low! They're going after the bombers! On my lead, angle's four, take the bandits on the right. Tally ho!"

The Lightnings winged over to port, keeping the G-forces low. Never losing sight of their prey while pulling back on the stick, they completed their nose-down aileron roll and slid in above the 109s into an excellent angle of attack. The heavily weaponed nose of the Lightning fell into the best angle to kill the bandits below. Nosed over and hidden by the light of the sun behind them, the now diving fighters began their silent and high-speed stalking of their Luftwaffe prey.

---

250   *Nimm die drei am links, Gruppe zwei. Gruppe eins, komm mit mir und die zwei am rechts angreifen. Gut jagen* — (German) – Take the three on the left, group two. Group one, come with me and attack the two on the right. Good hunting!

251   *Luftwaffe fluchtkommandeur* – (German) – air force flight commander

"Ducks in a barrel, guys. Let's get 'em," said the lead pilot. It was exactly what the Luftwaffe flight leader was thinking about the disorganized Invaders coming into his sights some two thousand feet below.

As he looked at his scattered flight, Wheeler didn't like what he saw. He glanced around and spotted the 109s diving out of the sky. "Bandits, three o'clock high," he called to the rest of the flight. He hoped his gunner would start putting some lead in their direction soon, and ordered: "Fire at will!"

"Roger, I'm on 'em," said his gunner.

Dick could see the spinning spiral-painted noses of the 109s as they closed the distance between them. He was startled when the guns of the 109s flashed with tracers, which zipped passed the nose of his plane. He felt the vibration of the rapid-fire chatter from the fifties in the top turret. *At least we're givin' 'em somethin' back,* he thought. Dick hoped the tracers he saw heading up would hit their mark before those coming down hit theirs. He then noticed tracers streaking past the nose of the 109, tracers coming from another direction. Wheeler thought, "What the hell?"

With a sudden change in attitude and then direction, a 109 turned away from his attack on Wheeler's ship and pushed over into a steeper dive. The 109 passed within fifty yards of the Invader's nose, and tracers chased and peppered the 109's fuselage. One or two seconds after the Messerschmitt dove past, a Lightning came flashing by in hot pursuit, barrels blazing fire with tracers that chased down the 109. Getting a smile on his face, Dick said a prayer of thanks, but was suddenly amazed to see tracers chasing his savior, tracers from another 109 in hot pursuit of the first Lightning.

He radioed to his savior: "They're hot on you, watch out." He didn't know whom he was radioing or if he was even on this channel.

"Roger" was all the came back.

The third set of tracers was quickly followed by a 109 flashing by the nose of Wheeler's plane in gun-blazing hot pursuit of the P-38.

"My God, did you see that?" Wheeler called to his gunner.

He heard: "You ain't seen nothin' yet."

With tracers again flashing in front of Wheeler's windshield, another P-38 with nose guns spewing fiery death zipped by, chasing the second 109 that had just passed. Dick watched as all four fighters maneuvered to escape while pursuing to kill. They evaded or pursued each other like a twisting, burning snake falling from the sky. Wheeler suddenly realized that he had more important things to do than watch a dogfight.

He radioed to his broken flight: "Everybody tighten up! Get ready for more bandits! Anybody see any more?" He wanted to get the rest of these men home alive.

Nevertheless, Wheeler watched as the first two planes of the downward-spiraling dogfight disappeared into the clouds. Just as the last two were heading that way, Wheeler saw what appeared to be a flak burst close to the left wing of the last P-38. The blast destroyed its port engine, and it began pouring smoke. The speeding twin-tailed fighter flipped over onto its back, disappearing into the clouds. Wheeler watched as it slid seemingly out of control into the clouds. He uttered another silent prayer for the pilot, who he thought was destined for a tragic end. Then he appreciated that the two P-38s had saved his crew's bacon and changed his prayer to reflect how thankful he was.

"Did anybody see the squadron marker on those 38s?" Wheeler asked when he finished his prayer.

"No, sir," came back from multiple pilots and gunners.

Too bad, thought Wheeler. *I'd like to thank them.*

The other 109s had passed through the flight without scoring a hit. They too were more interested in escaping the tracers that were riddling their plane's fuselages. The Lightnings had succeeded in chasing the Luftwaffe away, and it turned out that they had even scored a few kills, after the gun-camera footage was reviewed.

Dick called again to his flight, ordering everyone to form up tight on him if they hadn't already. With the men behind him, Dick set a course for the RP, praying that there would be no more flak or fighters along the way.

Christmas was an unholy day for the 416th, as death rose to kill them, while they dropped death to kill those below them. Death was being spewed in every mode of lethality that the Allies and the Axis powers had designed. There were many unique ways to die that day, and the 416th had experienced just a few. As the group settled its Invaders down onto the runway, the survivors thanked their God for another mission behind them.

"Drink?" asked Conte.

"Don't mind if I do," replied Jack Smith, with a smile on his face.

After pouring straight scotch, Ralph handed Jack the short glass.

"Here's to the end of this war," Ralph toasted.

"Amen, and to number sixty-five," Jack said.

"Whichever comes first…whichever comes first," said Ralph with a laugh, and Jack joined in, as they clinked glasses.

Christmas night had come with clouds and cold weather. In spite of high spirits, the cold was driving men from the Christmas party back to their tents, where at least they could get a good fire going in the stove. Despite the bleakness of their existence at Melun, the crews knew it was a lot better than those Army guys had it on the front, or worse, Bastogne.

December ended with two missions into Germany to bomb bridges. In return, the Luftwaffe offered two night air raids on the Melun Airbase, driving everyone in the 416th out into the cold. After the first air raid it became obvious that the Germans still had spies in the area. A burning flare had been positioned at the end of a runway, which gave the German bombers a clear reference point. This raid was followed by two weeks of extra guards, and everyone was restricted to base. It wasn't the best way to start a new year.

Photographs:

A-20 Flight Crews Wethersfield Airbase and London, England

෴

A-20 Nose Art

Florence, South Carolina, 1944

These smiling, fresh faces would serve together throughout
the war: (L to R) gunner Staff Sergeant Dick Holloway, pilot
Lieutenant Earl Hayter, and gunner Staff Sergeant Frank
Melchoir.
Reproduced with permission of Earl Hayter and Ralph Conte

Men in Training – February 13, 1944

Members of the 416th trained in Florence, South Carolina,
before being shipped to New York and then Europe. Back
row: (L to R) Lieutenants Carlton J. Hubbard, Jack F. Smith,
unknown, unknown. Front row: (L to R) Lieutenant William
(Bill) Tripp, unknown, unknown
Reproduced with permission of Joanne Tripp

Proud Airmen

A-20 *El Conquistador* on June 22, 1944. Back row: (L to R)
Lieutenant Gerald McNulty, pilot; unidentified crewman; Staff
Sergeant Raymond Addleman, gunner. Front row: (L to R)
Lieutenant Frank Burseil, bombardier-navigator; unidentified
crewman; Staff Sergeant Howard White, gunner.
Reproduced with permission of Ralph Conte

May 10, 1944

(L to R): D. Stephens, gunner; pilot unidentified; and F.
Allred, gunner.
Reproduced with permission of Ralph Conte

Belle of the Ball

The infamous Pink Lady with Homer Hudson. crew chief,
at Station Melun-Villaroche (A-55), France. The A-20 Havoc
had serial number AF43-10170 and belonged to the 668th
Squadron. The plane was regularly flown by Lieutenant
Wayne Downing, pilot; Staff Sergeant Ken Hornbeck, turret
gunner; Sergeant Ed Dickson, bottom gunner/cameraman;
and Homer Hudson, crew chief.
Reproduced with permission of Wayne Downing

Unique Nose Art

Homer Hudson, crew chief, created the notorious nose art
of the Pink Lady. To count the number of missions, Hudson
shellacked the labels of whiskey bottles brought back by crews
on leave onto the painted likenesses of bottles. With sixty-five
bottles shellacked, the crew had earned their ticket home.
Reproduced with permission of Wayne Downing

Thumbs-Down

Staff Sergeant Ken Hornbeck on the wing of A-20 Havoc with
the emperor's thumbs-down for the turret gunner. Note the
large flak hole in the top of number five. Reproduced with
permission of Wayne Downing

Claudene II

This A-20 was likely shared by many different crews; note
the lack of detail in the nose art. This glass-nosed "C" model
would carry the Norden bombsight used by the bombardier.
Note crewman sitting in the Havoc's nose.
Reproduced with permission of Ralph Conte

Little Angels?

**There seems to be some doubt expressed in the nose art of
this solid-nosed "B" model of the A-20 Havoc called** *Little
Angels?*
Reproduced with permission of Wayne Downing

A-20 Havoc *IRISH*

Reproduced with permission of Andy Fluxe

A-20 Havoc *OUT HELLN*

Reproduced with permission of Andy Fluxe

A-20 Havoc *PRETTY JANET*

Reproduced with permission of Andy Fluxe

A-20 Havoc *DENVER DARLING*

Reproduced with permission of Andy Fluxe

A-20 Havoc unnamed nose art

Reproduced with permission of Andy Fluxe

A-20 Havoc *MOAN IN' GUS*

Reproduced with permission of Andy Fluxe

Passing the Time

Between missions was the time to play and relax: Lieutenant
Earl Hayter on guitar accompanied by Staff Sergeant Ralph
Hoffman, at Wethersfield, England.
Reproduced with permission of Earl Hayter

Escape and Evasion Fake ID

An escape and evasion photo like this one became part of the
airmen's faux papers to be used if they were captured. The
photo of Lieutenant Earl Hayter was taken while in Ireland,
where the 416th was learning EE procedures.Reproduced with
permission of Earl Hayter

Ready for R&R at Wethersfield

Lieutenant Jack Smith is dressed for leave, in Wethersfield,
England.
Personal collection

On Leave

**Lieutenant Jack Smith negotiates in Soho, the Italian district
of London. Also in the district was the USAAF Officers Club.
Personal collection**

On Leave in Soho

Lieutenant Jack Smith photographed his fellow warriors, in
the Soho district of London.
Personal Collection

A Camp Pet

Pets played an important part in airbase life. The group took
care of this puppy in Wethersfield, then a pet cat named
"Poontang," and later in France, a German shepherd named
"Distemper."
Distemper was left behind by the Germans when they
evacuated Melun.
Personal collection

A Survivor

As a pilot in the 669th Squadron, Lieutenant Harry Hewes parachuted out of his damaged A-20 during a mission to the Amiens marshaling yard on May 27, 1944. The Luftwaffe anti-aircraft severely wounded his legs as he descended. He saved his own life by using his belt as a tourniquet. Hewes was taken to a German hospital in Paris, from which he was liberated when Paris was freed by the Allies. He was repatriated but listed as "Severely Wounded in Action" (SWA).
Reproduced with permission of Wes Chitty

Ready for Combat

June 3, 1944 – The men pictured here (L to R) – Staff
Sergeant F. Allred, pilot D. Hulse, Lieutenant R. Conte, and
Staff Sergeant D. Stevens – prepped for Mission #65 to the
Chartres Aerodrome in France. This long mission was one of
the deepest penetrations into German-held airspace.
Reproduced with permission of Ralph Conte

Young Airman

Lieutenant William (Bill) Tripp with his wings.
Reproduced with permission of Joanne Tripp

Photographs:
Moving onto the Continent

❧

Melun-Villaroche Aerodrome, France September 1944 to February 1945 with transition to the Douglas A-26 Invader

❧

Laon-Athies Aerodrome, France February to War's End

Melun-Villaroche, France, September 1944

Living arrangements changed significantly when the 416th
moved onto the Continent in September 1944. Sitting (L to
R): Lieutenants Roland Enman, Leo Poundstone, Jack Smith,
and Earl Hayter. Standing man is unknown.
Personal collection

A Wounded Heavy

An American B-24 Liberator on hardstand at Melun, after
making an emergency landing because of battle damage and
loss of life on a daylight bombing mission.
Reproduced with permission of Wes Chitty

Remains

Signs of Luftwaffe losses were present at the USAAF-occupied
base at Melun. These are the remains of an FW-190.
Reproduced with permission of Wes Chitty

Melun in Ruins

Melun was bombed by the retreating Luftwaffe, reaffirming
the general disregard that the German military held for
others. Although denying the enemy the use of facilities was
an accepted military tactic, killing civilians had become part
of the German dictum by this point in the war.
Reproduced with permission of Wes Chitty

The Original *MISS LAID*

The original *MISS LAID* was renamed *La France Libre*
and presented to the French government.
This Havoc had flown one hundred consecutive missions
without aborting, earning honors for the ground and air
crews.
Reproduced with permission of Bob Kehres

For Pete's Sake

This A-26 Invader aircraft was flown by Lieutenant. Wes
Chitty with his gunner, Staff Sergeant Vincent B. Rocco, on
the March 18, 1945, mission over Worms, Germany, its last
mission. It was shot up so badly that it was washed out of
service, but fortunately its crew wasn't. The name was said to
have come from the wife of pilot Wayne Musgrove (pictured).
Reproduced with permission of Wes Chitty

On Top of His World

Staff Sergeant Vincent B. Rocco above his gunner's station on
an A-26 remotely operated gun turret. Rocco flew with Lt. Wes
Chitty.
Reproduced with permission of Wes Chitty

A-26 Invader *BULA*

Reproduced with permission of Andy Fluxe

A-26 Invader *"LASSIE COME HOME*

Reproduced with permission of Andy Fluxe

A-26 Invader *MAGGIE'S DRAWERS*

Reproduced with permission of Andy Fluxe

A-26 Invader *DORIS LEE*

Reproduced with permission of Andy Fluxe

A-26 Invader *RUTHIE*

Reproduced with permission of Andy Fluxe

A-26 Invader *MISS MILDRED*

Reproduced with permission of Andy Fluxe

Angels of Mercy

After *For Pete's Sake* washed out, this A-26 became the new
bird for Chitty and Rocco. The "angels" are (L to R): Sergeant
Rocco, gunner; Sergeant Tyson, asst. crew chief; Staff Sergeant
Silvia, crew chief; and Lieutenant Wes Chitty with his pipe,
pilot. Chitty and Rocco flew this plane from March 18 until
they rotated into a "C" model to lead missions.
Reproduced with permission of Wes Chitty

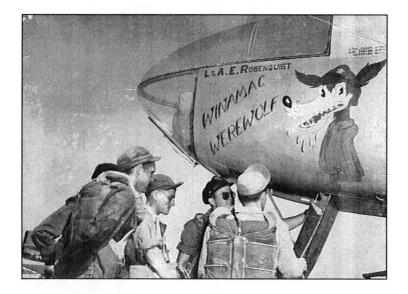

Winamac Werewolf

This glass-nosed "C" model A-26 Invader was flown by
Lieutenant Wes Chitty, when he led flights and groups. Chitty
and Rocco flew this plane until war's end.
Reproduced with permission of Wes Chitty

A Fresh Face

A young Lieutenant Carl Weinert in the cockpit of an A-26
Invader. Carl joined the squadron in late 1944 and served
until the end of the war.
Reproduced with permission of Carl Weinert

Chapter Fifteen
A Cold Day in Hell

Get those damned planes in the air
– 97ᵗʰ Bomb Wing Command

After providing a peaceful escape for all the air crews, Hypnos was dutifully driven from the lead crews at 0330 hours by the OD's adjutant. Shaken out of his grasp and back into the realities of their responsibilities, the crews began their routines.

Rubbing the sleep out of his eyes, Ralph instinctively checked the stove, by flipping up the handle and then pulling open the door. The fire was still burning. A little wood was all that was needed. Finding a few pieces lying beside the stove, he shoved them in, and closed the door. Rubbing his eyes again, he heard the fresh wood crackling, knowing the heat was to follow. Ralph kicked Hulse's foot. "Come on, sleepy. Let's go."

"I'm awake, just waitin' for you to get that fire going," said Hulse, throwing the blankets back as he rolled out of the cot. "Oh, heck, it's cold today. What happened?"

"Don't know, but better dress extra warm today," said Ralph, as he began his meticulous dressing ritual, paying more attention to detail this morning. It was vital at twelve thousand feet in an unpressurized, unheated aluminum shell to be able to stay warm. Ralph knew it was going to be cold at altitude today, but he didn't know it was going to be well below zero. Heck, he didn't know the thermometer went down that low. Nevertheless, the clothes went on thick—long johns followed by a pair of silk socks, then a layer of paper wrapped around each foot, followed by a pair of heavy socks, another layer of paper, then silk socks again. He pulled on fur-lined pants and then fur-lined flight boots that would barely fit over the socks. Ralph knew the routine now, so he could squeeze them on. Ralph followed his ritual every time he flew, and it hadn't failed him yet. Each flight crewman had his own dressing ritual to stay warm. Today the ritual was going to be critical.

Following Hulse out of the tent, Ralph was soberingly greeted by cold air, a light dust of snow-like frost covering everything, and a thick ground fog that seemed to cling to everything and then freeze. Ralph's breath was visible as he exhaled. He watched as the condensed vapor seemed to add to the thickness of the fog instead of dissipating.

"I can't imagine we're going up in this stuff today."

"Hard to say, let's see what the Weather guys have for us and what they think the target is going to look like."

"I bet he says it's cold and foggy." Ralph chuckled, and got a similar response from Hulse. "Can you see the truck?"

"No, I'm sure it's there though."

"Yeah, right," Ralph agreed.

Ralph and Hulse could hear, but not see, the fuel trucks and bomb trains rumbling around the flight line. They knew the routine, and were grateful that the crew chiefs and ground crew took such great care of the planes. Hulse wondered out loud, "How do the ground crews see what they're doing out there in this stuff? They seem to be working all the time."

"I suspect they get a break when we're on the mission. Not much for them to do if there are no planes here to fix."

"You know, I'm going to ask them when I get back."

"That's an idea."

Walking on in the fog, Hulse and Ralph found the jeep with Lieutenant Colonel Willets and his navigator, Lieutenant Royal, waiting to take them to the morning briefing. Ralph and Hulse crawled into the back, crouching over against the cold. Royal drove slowly into the fog, with everyone straining to see ahead.

When they finally saw the lights of the Operations building through the fog as the jeep came to a stop, the airmen happily jumped out and headed for coffee and the warmth of the building.

As they got closer to the briefing room, Ralph and the guys were gradually joined by the rest of the morning lead crews. Roland Enman said that the other crews looked like ghosts as they came out of the fog toward them. Mumbled conversations ended as the men join up by the Operations building. After a short, cold congregation outside the door of the briefing hut, they moved inside. The door was closed tightly behind the last officer to enter, and they all quietly settled into their seats, looking intently up at the mission board covered with a black sheet. Cigarettes burned brightly with each deep draw.

After dropping the sheet covering the mission board, the Operations commander opened the briefing. The new pilots and navigators listened intently as the veterans took it all in stride. To the experienced flyers the briefing seemed to finish almost as soon as it had begun.

Later, after the briefing, the bomber crews walked to mess. They silently noted the less-than-ideal flying conditions. The weather was still lousy, with the fog thickening as dawn neared. As usual, it always seemed coldest then. A quick SPAM-and-powdered-egg breakfast was washed down with lots of coffee and followed by cigarettes. The men knew what they had to do next—the cold, slow truck ride to the combined briefing.

The truck rolled up to the Operations building through the fog, allowing the ghostly fog-shrouded bodies to climb out the back of the truck. Moving through the fog, the crews made their way to the building and squeezed hurriedly through the door to get out of the cold. A few new faces sat in the chairs, but on whole it was about the same mix of veteran and rookie flight crews as yesterday's New Year Day's mission to Mont Le Ban troop command post. The officers and sergeants settled into their usual places, drinking more coffee and smoking more Luckies.

Looking around the room, Bill asked, "What's with all the captains and majors on this mission?"

"You didn't hear? HQ started crediting ranking officers with an extra quarter of a mission for every group or flight they lead, so more brass have been flying to get their quota sooner," Hiram informed his friend in sarcastic way.

"Well, good for them," Bill grumbled back. His musings were cut short, however, as Operations swung down the curtain from the mission map. Quickly everyone quieted.

The mission plan was reviewed and the men received the routine details—RPs, fighter escort, the route to IP, bomb loads, MPI, intervalometer settings, flak positions along the run, and the complex coordination of the attack. Navigators and pilots automatically plotted the routes in their heads while calculating fuel consumption and takeoff weights, as the briefing continued. Attention was then directed to the bomb-run, which brought a few audible few groans when the Operations officer mentioned the four-minute run down the valley. The room's air became noticeably thickened by tobacco smoke resembling the fog outside. The weather report was more detailed this time, for the pilots' sake. It would be a cloudy takeoff, but it should be all clear after getting to altitude. Everyone got counseled on the need for tight formations so that no one would become separated in cloud formations. Significant details to avoid flak emplacements were then reviewed.

Then the Operations officer walked to the projector in the center aisle. The lights went out, and a beam flashed onto the wall. It was a recon film taken by F-5s out of the Thirty-Third Recon Squadron and showed the terrain along the bomb-run. Throughout the film, the men were shown significant landmarks en route to the target, while the bombardiers were shown the main aiming point. Operations went over and over the importance of a tight formation so everyone would appreciate the need to put the bombs on the Simmern Bridge. All the pilots and bombardiers knew that a one-degree error in the fight formation at twelve thousand feet resulted in a big miss on the ground. A miss resulted in a wasted mission, and someone had to go back to do the job right. No one wanted that, knowing that it might be him going back. The cigarette smoke filled the room like the chilled fog outside as everyone thought about those four minutes on the bomb-run. Clouds or no clouds, they knew that was a long time to fly straight and level waiting on the bombardier to line up on target and then pickle off the eggs. No fun at all.

The room was silent for a few seconds, and then the Operations officer asked, "Any questions? Then let's synchronize at 0530...in twenty seconds...and...three...two...one...hack."

Looking up from his watch and out into the faces of the young men sitting in the briefing, the Operations officer closed, "Dismissed, gentlemen, and good luck." His final comment started chairs squeaking and knocking together followed by the sound of shuffling feet and mumbled conversation.

Once outside, the men began the preflight rituals again. Waiting for them somewhere outside the briefing room was good old "Distemper"—a German shepherd that had been left by the Germans. It was tradition to rub his head as the crews left the briefing. No one took any chances, sometimes waiting in line to get the canine's lucky blessing by rubbing his head or giving him a pat. Distemper had just stopped by for all the affection. He had been adopted as one of the base's pets. For whatever reason, he shook constantly, which earned him his name. Everyone figured he must have had distemper at one time and so he was abandoned by the previous owners of the base, maybe left as a spy. Either way, he was appreciated now. It was hard to come by this much affection, as a rule, as shaky as he was, and he was glad he had found a home here with the 416th. After his blessings were given to all who wanted them, he wobbled off to the mess hall to check on scraps. He knew there was always a good meal there about this time of the morning, lots of eggs and meat. He couldn't have asked for a better setup.

The rituals continued. After checking out their chutes and sidearms, the men pulled on their bulky, fleece-lined flight jackets while walking toward their squadron's idling deuce-and-a-half. With all this ground fog, they knew it would be hard to drive or ride a bike across base today, much less fly. While walking to their trucks, everyone looked for their lucky charms. Even if they had lain on hands with lucky old Distemper this morning, many crewmen still went looking in better places for more substantial blessings and reassurances. Given the weather alone, not to mention the Germans who would soon try to kill them all, it was a good day to seek some higher blessing before the mission.

They knew Father Penticoff was always close by the door of the briefing hut. He was just visible through the fog, out behind the trucks, setting up his makeshift pulpit from which to give blessings and absolutions before the mission. Many a Catholic and non-Catholic alike were stopping by to get their anointments this morning. Ralph, having been a good Catholic boy before the war, walked up to Father Penticoff's pulpit. For some reason, this morning he particularly wanted to see the priest; he wasn't taking any chances. Closing his eyes as Father Penticoff blessed him, Ralph gratefully accepted. While getting up, he looked the priest in the eyes and said, "Thank you, Father."

"God bless you."

The next airman slid in and kneeled before the pulpit. Ralph turned and moved on like all the others, toward their destiny.

Father Penticoff noted that this morning he was a lot busier than usual. Many new faces he didn't immediately recognize had stopped by. Losses and rotations were bringing new airmen to the group faster than he could learn their names. He knew that no one wanted to fly in today's soup, which caused the men to seek assurances. He had had unexpectedly large turnouts before. The midnight Christmas Mass was standing room only, as Catholic and non-Catholic, officers and enlisted men all filled the hangar and overflowed out onto the flight line. From the pulpit he sought the salvation of souls only, a trait every airman respected and sought from him. Father Penticoff ministered to the inner spiritual needs of the men who nearly every day were offering up their lives to win this war.

By January 2nd, the Germans' Ardennes counterattack had been halted, allowing the worm to turn. In spite of losses of more than forty thousand American soldiers in the Ardennes, the Allies were preparing to assault the remains of the Wehrmacht's Army Group B, which had suffered an estimated sixty-five thousand-plus losses in the Ardennes. The Allies' official counterattack would begin on the third, but the Ninth

Air Force and the 416th would start a series of interdictions days before to hamper the Wehrmacht's retreat and reinforcement potential. The success of the Allied counterattack would lay the footing for the big push into the Rhineland.

Today would take the 416th to the Simmern Bridge to begin the interdictions. Battles were still raging across a long front, and everyone knew the group would be committed again and again to the battle arena. Recent orders had come down from Command that put the A-26s to work doing what they were designed to do. Low-altitude bombing followed by strafing runs were about to become part of the 416th's repertoire. These strafing missions in high-intensity war zones were going to prove very costly to planes and crews.[252, 253]

All the crews could hear the last of the bomb trains running from the bomb dump, as the ordnance crews finished loading the ships and putting in the fuses. Even though they couldn't see them, the airmen could hear the last chains of .50-caliber ammo being loaded into the nose-gun's magazines. The closer the men got to the revetments, the quieter it became, as the ground crews were completing their assignments on each aircraft.

On their way to their planes, Earl and Jack walked together through the fog that Weather had referred to as a "heavy mist."

"Damnedest mist I've ever seen, how about you?"

"Reminds me a little of England, only colder."

"Yeah, you're not kidding," said Jack as he walked under his ship's left wing, heading toward the tail. "See you later, Earl. Good luck."

"No sweat. See you back at the barn."

"Roger."

Earl faded into the "mist."

Jack was standing behind the tail of the plane.

On reaching their assigned planes, crewmembers would walk to the back of the plane, near the edge of the tarmac, to complete their personal preflight duties. It was always at this point in the preparation when both the butterflies in their bellies and the adrenaline in their blood increased their need. Besides, no one wanted to do it at twelve thousand feet where it was freezing cold, and was made worse by having to nearly undress to relieve your bladder. The story had already been passed around about the B-17 boys who flew with condoms, which they used to evacuate themselves after the relief tubes froze up. They would get a kick out of dropping condoms filled with frozen urine on the Germans. The problem, though, was avoiding frostbite on the important parts while making the bomblets.[254]

Having completed the first part of the preflight, Jack zipped up, Turning to walk under and around his plane, Jack chatted with the ground crewmen while waiting on

---

252   The Ardennes, Battle of the Bulge; http://www.army.mil/cmh; Ch 25
253   Attack Bombers We Need You, A History of the 416th Bomb Group; Ralph Conte; Ch 11; Copyright 2001
254   A Matter of Some Urgency, Lois Eveland memoirs of Col. Ivan Wayne Eveland, Retired officer, 2002

Vafiadis as he did the rest of the preflight inspection. Jack watched as the other crews completed the prop-walking. As cold as it was today, prop-walking was like pumping molasses around in those engines. Crew Chief Staff Sergeant Dullnig had told the crews to walk the props five extra times each today because of the cold.

Sticking his head out of the side of the plane through the gunner's compartment hatch, Dean asked, "Hey, Lieutenant, you about ready to go, or are you gointa stand around out there all morning? We aren't gettin' any closer to gettin' this mission over with you standing around, are we?"

"Didn't know you were here. Heck, let me finish this walk-around and we'll warm 'em up. Everything OK with your guns?"

"Everything seems OK here, but it's going to be damned cold up there today. Hope nothin' freezes up."

"Hell fire, you're right about that. It's gunna be colder than a well-digger's ass in January up there."

"Aaa-men to that," said Dean, mocking Jack's Southern drawl. Dean pulled his head back inside the belly of the plane and sat down in his small chair attached to a rotating periscope that gave him a view above and below the plane. Anxiety forced him to run through his preflight routine again. As he finished up, he heard Jack climbing into the cockpit.

"Got your headset on?" Jack asked over the intercom.

"Roger, read you five by five," Dean answered.

After several minutes Dean heard but barely saw the starboard engine crank off, which was followed by the port. He recited a favorite prayer while rubbing the cross hanging from his neck. He was thinking to himself the entire time, *Get back safe on this one, Dean, and you're heading home.* He was glad he'd taken a blessing from the father this morning.

Farther down the fog shrouded flightline, Earl completed his checklist and began his ignition sequence, winding up the starboard followed by the port engine. Both engines turned over slowly at first, and then finally caught with a belch of ebony exhaust as all the cylinders sprung to life. Earl idled down both engines to give time for the oil and other fluids to warm up on this especially cold morning. Looking left then right seeing only fog, he thought, *They can't be serious about this.* He could barely make out the tip of the Invader's wings. "Not a good sign," he said.

"What was that, Lieutenant," asked his gunner.

"Oh, nothing." Earl felt the engines smoothing out as the temperatures began to rise. The air-fuel mixtures would be burning better in the cylinder heads that were now up to their proper operating temperatures. Scanning the instrument panel, Earl could see all the gauges were reading in the green now. This was a good start, and things were looking better. "OK, Helen, bring me home again," he said to himself, as he thought about his girl in Los Angeles, after whom he had named his plane.

Still farther down the flight line, Bill and Hiram were standing at the edge of the tarmac, completing the first part of their preflight duties. Bill jokingly asked Hiram, "Great day for a mission, huh?"

"Yeah, can't see your hand in front of your face. They want us to fly in this stuff? They'll scrub this one, for sure; they have to. Golly, even if we get off, how are we going to land in this stuff?"

After having a good laugh about the weather report, Bill left Hiram and walked toward his plane and started his preflight. Hiram walked down the flight line and turned back to holler, "See you back at the barn."

Giving him the thumbs-up, Bill hollered back, "No sweat!"

Up in his plane, Bill couldn't see the tower this morning, and hoped he'd be able to see the flare in this pea soup. More so, he hoped it would be a red flare, which would cancel today's mission. This was one morning he'd be happy to put it back in the barn.

Hiram continued down the line; he had drawn the A-Box—a slot in the first flight; he would be one of the first off the strip. He could hear A-26s all along the line spinning up and then firing off the eighteen cylinders of their Wasp radials. It was almost eerie in the thickness of the fog to hear these unseen weapons of war growling awake on this cold morning. Hiram thought about how close he was to finishing his required sixty-five.

Climbing up into the cockpit after the walk-around, Hiram sat down at his throne to survey his chariot of death's instrument panel. Checking the intercom first and then moving counterclockwise around the cockpit, he finished his preflight. Everything was a go and he moved into his engine-ignition sequence after getting the all-clear from the ground crew. He threw the ignition switch and listened intently as his starboard engine wound up, engaged, and then sputtered for twenty seconds to an uneventful stop.

"Damned cold weather," Hiram muttered under his frosty breath, and he began his cold-weather start-up procedure again, holding the spring-loaded primer switch open for fifteen seconds while the starter cooled. Hiram repeated the start sequence, and after a prolonged effort, the Wasp finally started with a deep, smoke-filled roar that quickly blended into the fog. The engine ran rough as Hiram primed and throttled the eighteen cylinders until he was satisfied that all the readings were going in the right direction.

"Damned cold weather, worse than the damned Krauts," muttered Hiram again, as he turned his attention to the port engine. Several seconds later the port engine spun up, lumbering to a slow start with a cloud of smoke. Both engines continued running roughly at first and then smoothed out as they cleared their throats by sucking in the life-giving gasoline and air. To show their life, they spit out hot blue flame through the exhaust manifolds. Hiram and his fire-breathing chariot were now ready for war.

Guided by the ground crew, since visibility was limited, Lieutenant Hiram Clark prepared to taxi to the runway. Rolling up to the taxiway, Clark held on the brakes while he pushed up the throttle handles separately. The two Pratt & Whitneys roared with power as fuel poured into the now-hot cylinder heads. He put his supercharger setting on low, and pushed hard on the brakes that were straining to hold the plane back. Hiram checked the rpm, after switching off the primary magnetos in order to check the backups. Both magnetos seemed to work well. Satisfied with their performance, he calmed the engines while easing off the brakes. He looked through the hazy, ice-covered windshield toward the tower. "Damn, I wish these things had some deicers on them," said Hiram to no one in particular.

"You're right about that, sir." It was his gunner Sabadosh trying to look out through the frost-covered windscreens of the gunner's compartment.

The tower personnel were looking out into thickness of the fog and worrying about it too, but not nearly as much as the flight crews were. With over twelve hundred per cubic centimeter of air, the water droplets were just 0.01 mms in diameter, but the tower personnel knew they could be enough to cancel this mission. It was just enough suspended water to create a slightly wet surface on the tents, jeeps, clothing, and wings of the planes. Coupled with the below-freezing temperature it became ice. This water created a none-too-easy situation for the Operations OD to opt for the green flare. Staring out into the gray abyss, the major hesitated; he wanted confirmation from a higher source before committing men and machines into combat today. It was hard enough to send men to die on a perfect day, and he wasn't in a hurry to send them on a miserable day. Walking to the base phone, the Operations officer called HQ. "Can I speak with the colonel, please?… Hello, sir…yes, sir. This is the officer of the day in the tower. Colonel, are we a go in this soup?"

"Major," began the man on the other end, "I don't like this any more than you. Have you called Command to see what Weather and Operations have to say?"

"No, sir. We haven't talked with them. We can ring them up if you like, sir."

"Yeah…yeah…OK, do it. Let me know what they give you on weather over the target and what to expect on the way to it. Got that?"

"Yessir."

The major hung up and shook his head in a worried way. He turned to the sergeant in the tower with him, "Sergeant, get me Command."

"Yessir."

The sergeant picked up the receiver and spoke. "Command, this is Melun tower. The major wants to confirm mission status here, hold on."

Taking the phone from the sergeant's hand, the major inquired, "This is the Operations officer at boat deck requesting reconfirmation from Command to launch the group. We are socked in solid here. We also need weather over the target and any updated changes."

"Hold on," the voice responded.

The major nervously tapped the table with his fingertips. Apprehensively looking across the room, he saw the table with the flare pistol loaded with the green flare, while the red flare sat next to it. A veteran pilot himself, he knew what every pilot on the line was thinking right now. Lifting his gaze from the flare gun, he looked out through the frost-covered windows into the void of the fog and mumbled, "This is a no-go day."

"What was that, Major?" asked the sergeant.

"Nothing." He swallowed hard while shaking his head slowly from side to side. He couldn't imagine they were going to let this happen.

"Melun, this is Command. It's a go for takeoff. Get them over the target. We have clear weather there. If there's fog with you, it clears at nine thousand feet. Fighters are already en route to the rendezvous point. Get those damned planes in the air, Major!"

"Yessir," answered the major quickly, realizing he was talking to someone up at Command much higher than his rank and grade. Hanging up the phone, the major turned to the base phone to call HQ and inform the old man.

"This is the tower, sir. Yes, sir, Command says it's a go. Cloud ceiling at nine thousand feet, target should be covered, but we've got pathfinders just in case...Yessir, fighters are en route...Yes, sir, I'll do it now." The major hung up and reached for the flare pistol lying on the table. Following a moment of sweaty apprehension, he walked out into the cold morning fog. He slowly raised his right arm, and pointed the barrel at a 45-degree angle upward then pulled the trigger.

The green flare exploded from the pistol's barrel, propelled out by the twelve-gauge shell's power. The flare set in motion a chain of events with consequences the major could have barely imagined. The flare's fog-muted green was nearly imperceptible through the opaque mist. With the sun not visible this morning, the flight crews couldn't even see the horizon.

"There it is, guys, let's go." Seeing the flare, Lieutenant Colonel Willets and his crew at the head of the runway acknowledged it. The thirty-six cylinders began revving up. With the brakes released, the A-26 started its roll down the runway. As the plane accelerated, Willets was having difficulty seeing the sides of the runway, much less ahead. He wondered if Operations really knew how bad it was out here. He pressed on.

He had lined the plane up in what he thought was the center of the runway, hoping as he throttled up that the plane would pull forward until it reached takeoff speed so that he could rotate it on up without going off the side of the airstrip. With no crosswinds, he wasn't worried about rudder corrections on takeoff, just about getting into the air. The plane hit takeoff speed, and he felt the craft lift off the runway. Blinded by the weather, the pilot resorted immediately to flying on instruments—watching the ball, checking the artificial horizon, and following his climb indictor and altitude. At fifty feet, he started cleaning up the aerodynamics of the plane—landing gear up, flaps up, nose up, watch the artificial horizon, watch the wing attitude indicator. No fast movements, steady, steady. Are we still climbing? How's the manifold pressure? Are we still climbing on the altimeter? The rate of climb indicator OK? What are my power settings? Wings level, no stall buzzer? As he climbed through the disorienting fog, he anticipated the morning sky opening up before him. "God bless us," he said as the propellers dragged the A-26 upward into the dark heavy fog.

After the flare and Willets' roll, the procession had begun, with Invader after Invader following. Lieutenant Evans, in the A-2-1 slot, moved his Invader into takeoff position behind the first flight's A-1-6 plane. Precisely ten seconds after the Invader in front of him had disappeared into the fog, Evans throttled forward to take off. "Flaps down, fuel settings rich, manifold pressure climbing—everything in the green so far," thought Evans as he scanned his instrument panel. Rolling forward into the fog with the throttles pushed up, the plane power-lifted off while Evans read his instruments for orientation. It seemed a little more difficult than normal to get off the ground, but he was climbing. He stayed with the instruments, and cleaned up the airframe so the plane would fly better. He soared through the fog and out into the early-morning light at nine thousand feet. "Thank you," came from his lips, as he waited on the others to form A-Box. This orchestrated ten-second takeoff sequence was repeated routinely down the flight line as it always had been and always would be, even after today's mission.

Rolling into position behind Evans, Lieutenant Hiram P. Clark and gunner Staff Sergeant J.W. Sabadosh watched Evans disappear ahead of them. The last thing to evaporate from sight was the blue-red fire from the exhaust ports. Hiram powered up his engines as Evans disappeared, noting a brief hesitation in the port engine, which quickly cleared. He then powered down. At eight seconds, Hiram ran the engines up again to takeoff power, and released the brakes. The eager Invader lurched forward rolling into the white abyss, while Hiram made subtle adjustments, as it became the lone Invader on the runway.

As it had to all the thin-skinned aluminum Invaders that morning, the fog had condensed onto Hiram's wings and fuselage. The antennae and all the noncritical flight surfaces were coated with this thin but measurable layer of water. Sitting in the cold fog had created the best possible conditions for icing, which was the worst possible condition for pilots and crews.

As Hiram's Invader rolled down the tarmac, the next plane slid in behind him. Lieutenant Ralph Conte sat in its glassed nose. Conte and Hulse watched Hiram's exhaust ports disappear into the fog. Ralph immediately looked to his left, as was his tradition on every takeoff, looking for Father Penticoff. Rubbing the moisture off the glass inside the nose of the plane, Ralph could just make him out through the ice-covered glass. He was standing in his usual place on the runway, offering a blessing to any crewman who would take it. Ralph gratefully accepted another blessing, as would a lot of other crews.

He settled into his lucky spot in the exposed nose of the Invader for his takeoff ritual, "Hail Mary, full of grace, hail Mary, full of grace…pray for us sinners, now and at the hour of our death…Hail Mary, full of grace…." Ralph repeated the words as the big twin radials revved up, causing the ship to vibrate in that old familiar way. Hulse released the ship's brakes, and Ralph felt the ship lurching forward and he was prompted to say more "Hail Mary's." He would repeat them until they were well into the air. He knew he needed forgiveness for all manner of names he had called the Germans during his other missions and for the names he would be calling them today when they started shooting at him. Today would be no exception. The Invader roared down the runway.

Hiram was having difficulty getting to takeoff speed, as the port engine hesitated slightly and then recovered, which was followed by the spinning propeller gripping the cold, foggy air again. The rpms were surging up and down as Hiram lifted the nose slightly. The plane was heavy and sluggish. The airspeed increased finally, lifting the plane slightly into the air. Hiram saw the hundred-yard marker flash by the cockpit, and realized that he had taken too much runway to get to takeoff speed. He was at a point of no return now, and reacted quickly by pushing the throttles forward as he saw the end of the runway slide beneath the plane. He was at less than one hundred feet. Raising the landing gear and the flaps, he still felt that the plane was not responding as it should. From its 120 feet, the plane began to lose altitude. It was an emergency, and he knew it. Hiram lunged for the throttles, pushing them up to full manifold pressure. The starboard engine spun up even more; the rpms surged, while the port engine hesitated again and then failed completely. They were not gaining altitude on the one engine, as they were supposed to.

The A-26 was a pilot's dream to fly on one engine in good weather, but not in this freezing, foggy morning. The rpms dropped to critical in the left engine. The eighteen cylinders were starving; the fuel had been stopped between the carburetor and the injector valves of the pistons due to icing. The carburetor was iced so badly that the venturi and the throttle plates were both blocked.

This bad situation was worsened by the malignant progression of rime ice forming on the lifting surfaces of the wings. The icing on the wings was enough of a problem by itself, but the plane's high takeoff speed was also forming a small upper and lower rim of glaze ice on the leading edges of the A-26's high-performance wing. Rime ice, glaze ice, and carburetor icing had combined to create a deadly situation. This combination of problems was turning an outstanding airplane into an unflyable, fully-loaded thirty-six-thousand-pound piece of aluminum, and it was barely in the air.

Then, Hiram felt it happening, the plane stalling as the ice disrupted the airflow over the wings. The ice caused the plane to lose the most critical element for flying—lift. The nose started dropping as the Invader experienced the first part of a tail stall caused by the excess ice on the horizontal stabilizers. Hiram worked feverishly to recover, but the ice was way ahead of him. By coating the wings and disrupting the air flow, the ice had changed the stall characteristics of the wings. With the ice, the outer edges of the wings were thicker than the inner, which caused the Invader to stall differently and at a much higher speed than usual.

"Oh, hell! Failed engine, no lift, max power starboard, wings stalling." Hiram's mind raced for a workable solution as the ground drew horrifyingly close. "We're gunna belly in!"

The ball in the artificial horizon showed all black now as the nose of the plane had passed the horizon long ago going in the wrong direction. Hiram was sweating profusely now with the worst of all kinds of sweat, that cold adrenaline-driven, life-or-death sweat that few people have known. Working to keep the plane in the air, Hiram pulled on full flaps, praying it would be enough to get some lift from his Invader's wings. Even if they had reached the proper speed, the elements were against them, and therefore, so were the unbreakable laws of physics and flight.

Hiram and Sabadosh had not cleared the fog for a chance to witness the beauty of the dawn above them. All they could see now was the ground, as the plane accelerated toward it. Hiram was straining at the stick, pulling it back and praying they would gain enough lift and airspeed before they augered into the ground. The ice had frozen the Invader's elevators. The Invader was going the only place it could—down. Hiram knew that now.

"I'm sorry, Sabadosh."

"Oh, God," was all Hiram heard back.

The plane slammed nose first into the ground at over 125 mph. Burrowing into the ground, the aluminum nose collapsed as it dug into the earth. The men had no time for further thought or regrets, a great blessing.

As the plane's forward momentum pushed it farther into the warmth of the earth, the four one-thousand-pound bombs nestled in the bomb bay had been knocked free of their imprisoning cradles by the first impact. They went about their unemotional duty. On the first impact the two lower bombs had been dislodged from their cradles, which armed them. The next event was inevitable. The first bomb to hit the bomb bay doors exploded. Then the rest of the bombs went off in echo. Four thousand pounds of high explosives detonating nearly at once was a sight that was as horrifying as it was spectacular. The four crater-generating projectiles detonated sequentially, but to an observer it would have seemed like one huge simultaneous detonation.

The four-thousand-pound blast-wave instantaneously vaporized the thin pliable shell of the aircraft. The durable but not indestructible engines and their nacelles had been ripped from the wings and orbited away from the center of the crater, as the ever-expanding ball of fire became a wall of cremating death. The shockwave produced by the blast was propagating outward, destroying anything in its path.

The officers and the ground crew around the tower were overwhelmed by the blast wave. Men were knocked to the ground, while the tower's windows blew inward as shiny slivers of shrapnel. The Operations building suffered a similar impact and fate. At first, the officers and enlisted men thought they were being bombed, but when they realized what was happening, they responded. The emergency claxton began sounding, and the base sprang to life in response.

The slowly enlarging aerial armada was continuing its progressive reach for the sky, as Ralph's A-2-3 plane was rising through the air immediately behind Hiram Clark's plane. Busy praying, Ralph had not seen Hiram fall from the sky, but all three in the plane had felt the shockwave and appreciated a muted orange brightness from below. They didn't have much time to think about it, as they suddenly cleared the fog into an early dawn light. Ralph said his last "Hail Mary" for a while. Looking for the lead flight as it banked back around to pick them up, Ralph immediately noticed Hiram's plane was not in formation where it should have been. While they joined up with the group leader, Ralph noted that they were in the proper slot in the flight, but as they moved in, Ralph wondered where Hiram's plane was.

"Boat deck one, over."

"Roger, this is boat beck one."

"Have you seen Clark, over?"

"Negative."

"Roger, will keep a look out, over and out."

"Roger, over and out."

Ralph hoped it was a mechanical failure, while praying that the bright flash and the concussion weren't what he feared it might be. "Hail Mary, full of grace," Ralph repeated once more while looking down toward mother earth.

Ten seconds behind Conte's plane, Lieutenant R.J. Lackner and gunner Sergeant A.F. Musserre flying A-2-4 sped down the runway. Lackner noted that they had left the runway longer than usual, with very poor aircraft performance. Struggling to keep the plane in the air, Lackner raised his gear while dropping his flaps, hoping this maneuver would help generate lift. Both engines were failing due to that gremlin of carburetor icing; his manifold pressures dropped, causing his airspeed to fall off even more.

Unable to do anything about it, he felt the plane stalling at not more than one hundred feet. The plane shuddered as it fell from the sky. Lackner was lucky; his plane fell in a flat, slightly nose-up stall, and violently slammed and skidded down in a belly landing that distorted the plane's frame around the bomb bay. As the plane continued to careen, the distortion of the airframe twisted the bomb racks, which freed three of the four deadly cargo from their restraining shackles. This left only the armed bomb in the rack hanging precariously by its back support and dangling its armed detonator fuse above the other unarmed bombs. Three thousand pounds of cold heartless death were lying in wait on the bomb bay doors below, wanting only to do their job. The Invader continued skidding and bouncing across the ground, throwing dirt in all directions. Groaning as it slid into a sideways position, the propellers dug up French soil as if they were crazed steam shovels, throwing it in every direction. The engines finally stopped, as the appallingly bent propellers dug into the soil for one last try at flight. The Invader at last came to an abrupt stop; the tip of the left wing arched into the ground, causing the last bit of the plane's momentum to lift the big piece of flightless aluminum briefly into the air until gravity slammed it back to God's earth. This last jarring movement rocked the deadly, ticking time bombs in the bay in a less than gentle way.

Lackner radioed to Musserre, "Get the hell out of here!"

Both men scrambled out of their seats and tumbled through their emergency exits. They met up by the left wing and wordlessly looked each other in the eyes before dashing from the time bomb they had just crashed landed. Finally, Lackner hollered to his gunner, and he led them toward a ditch he saw fifty yards to their right.

At last the precarious support holding the dangling thousand-pound bomb finally gave way. It fell as the two men dove into the small but deep ditch fifty yards from the plane. Like the blast before it, this explosion rocked the area. The concussion was overwhelming to the senses of the two cowering and now disoriented airmen. God's presence and all his mercy were called upon at that moment by two men who believed now more than ever before. Their faith escalated a thousandfold for all the reasons one can only imagine, as the numbing and disorienting concussion ruptured their eardrums, bloodied their noses, and finally passed over them. They were overwhelmed with a sense of doom as they lay in the ditch.

With their bleeding noses and ears, both slowly recovered from the concussive disorientation caused by the blast. They were thankful to be whole as Lackner suddenly felt the dirt falling from the sky landing on them.

"Take cover," he hollered.

Both men suddenly found themselves praying that a piece of the plane didn't land on them. Finally the rain of earth stopped. Shaking his head, trying to get oriented, Lackner turned toward Musserre, "You OK?"

"Yeah, I think I'm in one piece. How 'bout you?"

"Well, if I look as bad as you do, I'm not sure."

"You look like hell, sir."

"I guess we both made it then."

"Thank God," Musserre replied.

"Amen to that!" Lackner responded with all sincerity, never to doubt again.

Both would never forget the intensity of this near-death experience or the harsh reality of the magnitude of devastation they carried to the enemy.

As the second shockwave passed over them, the personnel still gathering around the tower were again reminded of their responsibilities, while the fire and rescue crews raced for their equipment. In a span of thirty seconds, two aircraft were lost. Two men found their deliverance, while two others found themselves believing more than ever before in theirs. The rescue crews were racing in the direction of the explosions, praying it wasn't as bad as they imagined it to be.

Lieutenant J.H. Roberts with Staff Sergeant Raymond P. Windisch flying the A-3-4 slot were in formation behind the second A-Box flight. Roberts had seen the Invader take off in front of him and had pushed his throttles forward at nine seconds after. Following takeoff protocol, Robert's plane was reaching takeoff speed, but just wouldn't lift off, even after a long roll down the runway. It was then that he saw the end-of-runway warning marker from the corner of his eye. Reaching to the throttles, Roberts pushed the power settings up while pulling the wheel back, as if trying to lift the plane off the runway himself with just his sheer will. The nose lifted slowly from the tarmac, and the plane seemed to follow. Roberts thought, "Thank God, we're gunna make it…Come on…Come on!" He pulled the gear-up lever while, almost but not quite, breathing a sigh of relief. It would have been premature; the ice-laden Invader shuddered, then faltered.

"Hold on, Windisch! We're going in!"

Roberts recognized that there was no keeping the plane in the air now, and began bracing for an unwanted, unplanned impact. Windisch grabbed what he could to brace himself against, as the stricken Invader fell to the ground.

The plane plummeted like an aluminum pancake, hitting the ground just beyond the runway. The landing gear, which were not completely retracted yet, hit in a perfect three-point landing, but with such force that the tricycle gear collapsed into their compartments. Then the belly slammed into the ground. The pilot and gunner suffered a bone-jarring deceleration shock from the impact, but braced themselves even more for the second impact after feeling the plane bounce back into the air. It struck again with a back-breaking vengeance. With all their might, two thousand horses spun each of the two Hamilton-Standard propellers that were now chewing their way through the soil as if plowing a field. The left propeller cut into the ground effortlessly until encountering a large glacier boulder just under the surface, which ripped the prop from the crankshaft and sent it upward over the tail of the plane. After cartwheeling across the ground, the prop finally embedded one blade into a small mound fifty yards from the sliding plane. The crew was blessed that the propeller didn't impale itself into the side of the aircraft, potentially ripping open the bomb-bay gas tank or worse.

From the resulting hole in the left engine's crankcase spewed oil, which leapt onto the hot fins of the jugs and instantly burned off. The cloud of smoke spun off the left wing as the plane stuttered out of control toward its fate. The resistance caused by the left propeller hitting the boulder had swung the right wing hard to the left, and had thrown the occupants outward and away from the plane's center, as the centrifugal force had increased before the propeller tore loose. With dirt flying everywhere and prayers streaming outward, the plane finally spun to a halt. Smoke billowed from the port engine as the last of the oil cooked off the jugs.

"Damn it, Windisch, I'm trapped! This damned hatch is jammed! Help me!"

"I'm on it!"

Windisch wasted no time, and clambered out of the gunner's area toward the cockpit. He saw Roberts pulling the escape-hatch handle. Together they started pushing and pulling at the jammed hatch. Finally manhandling it open, Windisch reached into the cockpit to help Roberts out. Together they slid off the fuselage and hit the ground racing for cover. Running for their lives, they saw a small depression not much farther ahead, but as they dove toward it, they were blown off their feet and thrown twenty feet over the ditch. Roberts saw the remnants of half an engine sail past before they painfully hit the ground. Both men lay there stunned, disoriented, and semi-comatose for some time, unsure if they were dead or alive, as dirt and debris fell about them.

It had all happened quickly. Some four thousand pounds of high explosives and thousands of gallons of fuel had created a third huge fireball and a third crater on the outer edge of the runway. The blast had vaporized their plane. Watching in shock, the two crewmen were slowly realizing for the first time the type of death they had been carrying to the Wehrmacht for years. Rescue personnel reached the site shortly after the blast, and began their search for survivors using the light of the burning fuel in the blast craters to see.

Despite three horrific crashes, the Invaders kept to their takeoff on schedule. A-3 had been rolling down the runway as Roberts' plane was seconds from crashing. The pilot behind Roberts successfully lifted his plane off the runway into the dark, disorienting water droplets. That was when the crew saw the orange fireball and felt the concussion of the explosion. The concussion was so much more powerful than any flak burst they had ever encountered; it blasted the right wing upward almost sixty degrees, forcing the pilot to correct the marked change in attitude. The concussion threw the two men against the insides of the aircraft. Both were stunned by the magnitude of the blast and looked toward it in disbelief. The men realized what had happened to Roberts and Windisch, and prayed that it didn't happen to them. "How we doing, sir?" warily came across the pilot's headset.

By now all the flight crews were aware of the causes of the blasts. They were all thankful that it wasn't them, and prayed that it wouldn't be them.

The planes that had made it into the air were readjusting, since pilots were taking much longer than usual to reach altitude. Evans was just about to pull through the cloud cover and join the circling Invaders.

"OK, OK…We're doing ok…good airspeed, climbing at one thousand feet per minute, manifold pressures good, oil and hydraulic pressure in the green with engines running hot. The artificial is OK and the climb indicator is good, wings level. I think we're going to make it."

Just about ten minutes after takeoff, Evans' plane drove out of the cloud cover at nine thousand feet. The men aboard found some relief in the ever-increasing daylight. Evans radioed the tower to have them notify the rest of the group about the flight-position changes.

Lieutenant Jack F. Smith and gunner Staff Sergeant Dean Vafiadis had successfully lifted off the runway and were gazing down at the fires at the end of the runway as they passed over. Both Jack and Dean were thankful it wasn't them, but also hoped that their friends were all OK. Jack's plane was performing well. Finally popping through the clouds, Jack was able to see the other six aircraft in their proper positions, except in the wrong flights. Jack quickly responded to the change and joined up with the proper flight in the A-3-5 slot as the flight moved out to the group staging area.

Lieutenant Earl Hayter pulled his *Classy Lassy Helen* out onto the taxiway. He was having difficulty seeing out into the blanketing whiteness of the fog, which was compounded by a constant banging noise on his fuselage. His windshields were iced over, making it even more difficult to see the runway. Sliding his left windshield open, he stuck his head out to see the side of the taxiway better, as he headed toward the runway that he hoped was coming up soon. With the windshield open, he discovered the banging sound was the ice being slung off the propeller blades against the side of his ship. But all he had been hearing from the tower was to "get those damned planes in the air." Operations wasn't happy with the takeoff ritual today; they had a rendezvous time with the fighters, which, if missed, could compromise the mission schedule or have it canceled completely.

Earl felt the pressure but didn't let it interfere with his ritual, which was very important, not only to him but to his crew. The ritual was always the same and had sustained them through many dangerous missions. Earl thought back to his time in California before the war, when he had lost contact with his beliefs while living in the Los Angeles area. That digression hadn't lasted long, as he had quickly found his right path again, after dueling in these aerial chariots of death. He wasn't going to change his beliefs now or ever again.

While taxiing down the flight line, Earl scanned his instruments as he sang out loud his favorite hymn, "If Jesus Goes With Me."[255] When he turned onto the runway, he slid the left window open completely so he could see the runway markers. The fuselage was no longer being hammered by the ice slung off the propellers, which gave Earl some confidence. He looked at his compass, took a heading down the runway, put his hands on the throttles, and closed his eyes while reciting out loud, "Thy will be done." He had recited the line from the Lord's Prayer at the start of every mission. The crew appreciated it too. Earl knew his destiny was beyond his control the second he pushed the throttles forward, which he did without hesitation.

The Invader charged into the lonesome fog, quickly disappearing from everyone's sight as it eagerly became airborne, while Earl sang on,

> It may be in the valley, where countless dangers hide;
> It may be in the sunshine that I, in peace, abide;
> But this one thing I know—if it be dark or fair,
> If Jesus is with me, I'll go anywhere!

Pausing after the last line to scan his instrument panel, check his heading, and monitor engine performance, he recited, "Thy will be done." He had followed his instrument takeoff routine flawlessly, and the plane responded perfectly to his commands, and climbed into the isolating fog. Earl sang on,

> If Jesus goes with me, I'll go anywhere!
> 'Tis Heaven to me, where'er I may be, if He is there!

Earl completed a few more verses, and finally penetrated the ceiling of the fog and burst into the morning sunlight. He sighed relief. Approaching his assigned position in the flight, he smiled when he noticed the sun was melting the ice on the windshield. He was happy now, knowing that he was not going to have to fly the whole mission with his head out the window. The freezing air was rushing into the cockpit, so he slid the window closed and immediately felt warmer.

Damn, how I wish these things had a heater, Earl thought.

Earl took up the number-four slot in his flight, while two others filled in numbers five and six.

The crashes and iced-up planes were just the start of the other ground delays. Even though the first flights had seen the green flare, plenty of crews had not seen it, due to the thickness of the fog. Many were wondering if the mission was a go or a scrub. Many planes were still in their revetments with their engines idling.

Pilot Lieutenant Robert Rooney knew they were behind schedule as he felt the plane's vibration. The well-tuned radial engines were roaring on either side of the

---

255   "If Jesus Goes With Me"; Gospel song written by C. Austin Miles, 1908; http://www. cyberhymnal.org/htm/i/f/ifjesusg.htm

cockpit. They were so close that if you reached too far outside the cockpit, the blade would take your hand off. Rooney started his acceleration down the runway, but realized sooner than the others that he was getting reduced performance from his starboard engine. He wasn't reaching takeoff speed quick enough to get off the ground. He had seen the ice on the wings when he saddled up, and now while trying to look out these ice-covered windows, he reasoned that his carburetor was iced.

Quickly responding to his assessment before he ran out of usable runway, Rooney throttled back and applied the brakes hard. He strained as he stomped the pedals down, hoping the plane would stop before the end of the runway. The plane was slowing but he saw the marker for the end of the runway, and pushed the pedals harder. The brakes were already gripping as tight as they could, short of failure. Simultaneously, he was wrestling the plane to the right side of the runway when the wheels finally locked. The plane skidded fifteen feet to a stop—just twenty feet short of the end. Blowing out a big sigh of relief, Rooney gasped, "Oh, God, thank you." He taxied forward to the outside corner of the runway, while his hands and legs slowly quit shaking. He hoped that parking here would prevent any collisions from the following aircraft.

"Let's get the heelll outta here!" ordered Rooney through the intercom. The two crew men scrambled out. Once on the tarmac, they ran far off to the right, away from the plane in case someone hit it on takeoff. Both knew what a mess that would make.

Don Sorrels watched as Lieutenant G.O. Van Meter began his run and then watched the Invader disappear into the fog.

Van Meter managed to inch the Invader off the ground slightly, only to suffer the same aerodynamic failures as the many aircraft in the first flight. He struggled to keep the plane in the air, but to no avail. The plane passed over Rooney's parked Invader, and then hit the ground hard in a twenty-degree nose-down right bank. The ground crews had already started scattering as soon as they saw the big lame bird flying over at such a low altitude. Rooney hollered to his gunner to follow him, as he sprinted toward the fallen Invader.

The tip of the right wing hit the ground first, sending the plane into a series of cartwheels. Like an unbalanced top, the plane slowed. In the middle of the fourth cartwheel, the Invader finished its acrobatics, with the right wing separating from the fuselage and ripping open fuel lines and tanks. Seconds later the plane exploded.

The rescue crews were knocked senseless as the shockwave passed over them from such a close detonation. Rooney was thrown backward, while his parked Invader took shrapnel from the aluminum radiating out in all directions. For Van Meter and Staff Sergeant Kiker, the explosion sent their quintessence on that final mission, where they met their fallen comrades at heaven's gate.

Rooney realized his good intentions were of little use.

Powering up his four thousand horses, Don Sorrels was next in the takeoff order. He released his brakes and started his roll toward the heavens. As the plane accelerated, Don glanced over the Invader's instrument panel—speed good, manifold pressures good, oil pressure good, hydraulic pressure good, air speed—zero! Don's eyes opened wide as his mind was catching up to the reality of no airspeed. His heart rate immediately responded to the magnitude of the emergency, and it pounded in his chest. Don quickly realized that every other flight parameter he could monitor was in the green; only the airspeed read zero, but all he had to do was look out the window to prove that the reading was wrong. He pushed the throttles to the firewall and watched for the runway markers to plan his liftoff point. The manifold pressures rose normally, causing the propellers to chew faster and faster into the thick air. Pulling the yoke back at the three-quarter point, Don hoped to become airborne and realized that if he didn't lift off soon, he would have no room left to abort. It would be ugly at the end of the runway if he didn't clear.

The heavy Invader finally responded to Don's commands, lifting off the runway into the cold foggy air. Watching the runway disappear beneath him, Don caught a quick glimpse of an Invader sitting on the end of the runway, maybe seventy-five feet below him now. It was almost as if a ghost Invader were parked there. Don knew better. *Hell, that was a close one,* he thought. *Someone didn't make it.*

Don had heard the explosions before his roll down the runway, and knew that things were a lot worse than he was aware of, but that was all secondary now. Right now his attention had to be focused on getting this bird airborne. After raising the gear and the flaps, he climbed at full throttle—twelve hundred feet per minute. The Invader slashed through the fog into the morning radiance, which almost blinded him.

While worrying that he was going to have to fly the whole mission without an air-speed indicator, he looked for his flight and slot. Don saw his lead plane on the inbound leg. Turning into the flight, he took up the B-2-4 slot, immediately behind the lead. The lead's starboard wing man was in place, but there were still spots left to fill. Watching his airspeed indicator flicker and then slowly come to life, he was relieved as the warming sun thawed the invaluable inlet tube that allowed the indicator to function. "Thank you, God, for small favors," Don prayed.

The last Invaders left the confines of the ground and popped through the top of the clouds – one after the other, on perfect schedule. But overall the mission was still behind. The P-38 Lightnings and P-47 Thunderbolts had been waiting for some time at the RP.

"Angel wings, angel wings, this is boat deck one, come in, over," radioed Colonel Willets to the black specks flying in a tight orbit at the rendezvous site.

"Roger, boat deck one, this is angel wings one. Read you five by five. Good to hear from you. We thought you guys had been scrubbed, over," said the lead fighter.

"Roger, angel wings one, we are on final, flying zero-niner-zero. Do you see us, over?"

"Roger, have you in sight now, will take assigned positions, over and out."

"Roger, angel wings one. Happy hunting, thanks a lot, over and out." Willets continued on his current heading toward the fighters. He would receive a new heading from his navigator once they reached the RP.

The fighters scooted around the sky like flights of widgeons, finally settling into their position two thousand feet above the flight, moving occasionally to the left or right. The fighter boys liked flying cover for the A-26s because the bombers' speed matched their own. Now with these 26s, all they had to worry about was to avoid becoming complacent, getting caught flatfooted by a Luftwaffe squadron of Messerschmitt Bf-109s or Focke-Wulf FW-190s. That could make for a very bad day for them, but an even worse day for the bomber boys down below.

Closing on the target, the group flew through a weak and inaccurate flak field. No hits were recorded by the Luftwaffe, but a few ships took some damage. Happy they met such little resistance, each flight released its payload with good aim. The twenty-four thousand pounds of bombs from each flight hit the bridge's approaches, the riverbed and the surrounding countryside, but the bridge suffered only scars from the shrapnel of the close explosions. Turning toward home, the crews were unaware that this would be the first of five missions to this stubborn and nearly indestructible Simmern bridge.

Indeed, a third of the 416th's missions for January would be spent flying sorties in this airspace. The battle to open the doorway into Germany was beginning, as the Allied ground forces prepared for their January counteroffensive that would push the Wehrmacht back inside the Western Wall of Deutschland by February. The Soviets were closing just as hard from the east.

In the face of deep Soviet incursions into their occupied territory, the Nazis nevertheless advanced their eugenic agenda. Already, on the eastern front the Soviets were driving toward Budapest, which would be liberated on January 6, saving upward of sixty thousand Jews and others who were "unfit." With many goals of the Final Solution still to be accomplished, the SS began death marches for detainees of concentration and death camps, from outlying areas toward protected camps. Meanwhile, the Soviets were preparing for a winter offensive that would begin on the twelfth of January. The Soviet assault would bring the liberation of Warsaw on the seventeenth and the liberation of Auschwitz the next day, but not before the evacuation of sixty-six thousand detainees by their murderers. It is estimated that by this time two million people had been liquidated at Auschwitz. And the killings continued inside Germany, as the combined efforts of the world's armies pushed to achieve unconditional surrender from the Nazis.

The Soviet offensive would also result in yet another rift among the Allies. On January 6 Churchill was reported to have encouraged Stalin to begin the offensive, in order to relieve pressure on the western front. Ironically, on the eighth, Hitler agreed to transfer the Sixth Panzer Army to the eastern front, which was followed four days later by the start of the Soviet offensive. After the war, this assistance was used as a concession during a rift that developed over the Soviets' refusal to honor war debts. Stalin rationalized the position by arguing that the start of the Soviets' January offensive negated the debt, because the Soviets saved the Americans and the British on the western front. This statement is of questionable accuracy, since the Wehrmacht was already on the retreat in the west after the third of January.

January brought challenges in the Pacific too. Iwo Jima and Okinawa were on the planning table for the Americans. Capturing these two island fortresses was critical for providing airfields and logistical support bases for the final assault on the mainland of Japan. In these two invasions would be revealed the ferocious intensity of the Japanese defense of their home territory. Losses to both sides would be so large that it would lead to calculations of unacceptable causalities if the Americans invaded the Japanese mainland. But technology was about to obviate the need for such an invasion, as work progressed in nuclear labs at the Tennessee Clinton River Engineering Works, Los Alamos labs and Hanford Engineering Works in the Grand Coulee area of the Columbia River.

Other less-scientific projects were progressing inside the United States, as the FBI investigated 19,299 separate allegations of sabotage. By war's end—aside from the eight German saboteurs who landed in New York and Florida in 1942—no internal acts of direct sabotage were ever discovered by the FBI. This statistic seemingly ran in conflict with Stalin's and Churchill's knowledge of the Manhattan Project's "Gadget." Indeed, so advanced was Soviet knowledge that, before the decade was out, Russia would detonate its first nuclear bomb.

Just as the new was developing, the old was passing on or metamorphosing. As early as 1940, American eugenic programs started dying out from lack of funding, or they were quietly reinventing themselves into less-obvious organizations. The sum of their past works was resisting with all its might the world armies, navies and air forces. The men who made up these armed services trudged forward carrying their form of death to the enemy. [256, 257, 258, 259, 260, 261]

Jack walked into the tent, holding the door open for Earl. As soon as he entered, he noticed that Hiram's cot was gone, along with his B-4 and foot locker. There were a few items left on the small table next to the stove, as well as his month's liquor ration, some unopened packs of Chesterfields, and a pack of matches. Bill was sitting in his own cot looking at the empty space and rubbing his eyes clear as Jack and Earl walked into their cold home. Nothing needed to be said; both men immediately felt the loss.

"You OK, Bill?" Earl asked.

"No sweat." Bill hid his true feelings, as they all had learned to do.

"What about Hiram?" Jack inquired, not really wanting to hear the truth.

Shaking his bowed head back and forth, Bill said, "Hiram bought it on takeoff, bombs blew up when they went in…wasn't anything left of either of 'em."

Jack sat down on his cot and rubbed his face back and forth with the palms of both hands, quietly saying a prayer for having survived sixty-three missions and two crash landings, thankful that by the grace of God he was still here. He thought of his lost

256   Chronology of Jewish Persecution, 1945; http://www.jewishvirtuallibrary.org

257   Army Air Forces in World War II; http://www.usaaf.net/chron/45/jan45.htm

258   Timeline of Pacific War; http://historyplace.com/unitedstates/pacificwar/timeline.htm

259   Federal Bureau of Investigation; FBI History; http://www.2.fbi.gov/libref/historic/history/historicdates.htm

260   White House Statement on the Sentence of Nazi Saboteurs; August 8, 1942; http://www.jewishvirtuallibrary.org

261   Rhineland; http://www.army.mil/cmh-pg/brochures/rhineland/rhineland.htm

friends, silently saying a blessing for them. Jack looked up out of his hands while lying back on his cot. His heavy, fur-lined flight boots hung over the bed's end.

Bill looked around the tent and realized that after nearly one year Hiram was the first really close friend they had ever lost. Jack had a couple of close calls, but this one was for real. Bill's life was different from that moment forward. He would not seek a life in the church, having once been courted to attend seminary school. His beliefs in the goodness of mankind and of a God in heaven changed. He swore to live differently—with great energy and no regrets from that point on. Lieutenant Bill Tripp hated the senseless loss of his good friend and brother-in-arms Lieutenant Hiram Clark. Bill questioned why any god would allow a fine man to die so pointlessly. Hiram's death was mourned, and one man's life was profoundly changed forever.

Earl didn't say a word. His thoughts just repeated over and over, *Thy will be done.*

Carl and Roland walked in, already well aware of the loss. Carl realized yet again the reality of the world he had entered. He knew the others felt the loss of their friend more than he did. Having only been with them three months, he didn't have the history that the others had developed from the beginning of their time in theater. He did know that Bill and Hiram had become very close friends over the last several years. Roland and Carl said nothing as they laid back on their cots.

Fatigue was beginning to overtake the ones who had just returned from the mission. The restless fatigue kept sleep from coming but made you want it even more. Hiram's fate couldn't escape their minds.

Pushing through January, the 416th helped open the way for the Rhineland invasion. Flying into German airspace that was still heavily defended by the Luftwaffe, the 416th learned the Third Reich was far from finished. The Allied armies on the ground found the Wehrmacht was not just going to give up either.

January brought more sad news to Jack Smith. The form letter arrived that informed him of his father's death on January 16, 1945. He was not eligible for leave nor were his brothers Bill and Pat.

Jack sat on the on the edge of his bunk several days later reading the letter from his mother as tears came to his eyes. She blamed the war for taking her husband and oldest son. Jack read where his father never recovered after sending his fourth son to war. Jack was glad he had given her his first set of wings in case he joined his brother. He had learned a lot about death and wished he could have been there with her at the funeral.

Chapter Sixteen

Finding a New Home

If you kill enough of them, they stop fighting.
– Curtis E. Lemay, WW II

All around, the borders of Germany were crumbling. By February 1945, Germany would be fighting to hold the Allies' western advance along a line extending from Arnhem in the north (the site of Montgomery's ill-fated Operation Market Garden) to Basel in the south, on the Swiss border. By February 7th this line of German defense would be an outline of Germany's West Wall, or the Siegfried Line. The line wouldn't hold long.

On March 1st, American General Omar Bradley would launch "Operation Lumberjack," which would open the Rhineland campaign. As part of the plan, America's Third and Seventh Armies would push to the Rhine, and would reach it by March 17th, inside a salient extending from Mainz south to Mannheim. At the center of this salient was the small town of Worms, whose defenders would extract significant losses from the 416th on the 18th of March, 1945. Lumberjack would also give the western Allies their first push across the Rhine River over the Ludendorff railroad bridge at Remagen, Germany. Eisenhower was slow to exploit the capture, however, pushing only ten miles deep and twenty-five miles wide with five divisions, fearing a lack of logistical support.

During this period of advancement between January and March, the Eighth Air Force heavy bombers were shifting from strategic to tactical bombing operations, since the front lines and the strategic lines were merging. Marshaling yards, communication centers and rail bridges began showing up on the Mighty Eighth's mission boards. Tactical fighter-bombers prowled the countryside. Pilots of the 416th used their new A-26 Invaders in combined bombing-strafing runs. Targets were moving farther east as the ground campaign succeeded in pushing the Wehrmacht closer to Berlin.

As they began to infiltrate Germany, western Allies began targeting those locations that offered the opportunity to exploit the scientific advancement and discoveries of the Nazis. In a bid to structure the postwar environment to its advantage, the Americans planned "Operation Overcast," in which military intelligence swept across Allied-occupied Germany scouring for scientists, technology and equipment that could be taken back to the United States. The basic technology for cruise missiles, wire-guided missiles and torpedoes, jet aircraft, rocketry, and stealth technology were all for the taking inside the West Wall. Medical experiments of unspeakable horror had been and were still occurring across the eugenic wasteland of the Fatherland, producing unethical but sadly valuable research data. All were acquired by experimenting in a godless way on living subjects resulting in the deaths of thousands of men, women and children.

Results from altitude, temperature, toxicology, infectious disease, sterilization and radiation experiments—all of unspeakable terror—had been recorded in camps across
Germany and its occupied territories. This data would be confiscated and exploited by
whoever could retrieve it first.

In the meantime, the Allied command structure was setting new priorities, and
the men of the 416th would be slowly moving to their new base, which would be north
of Paris. By the middle of February 1945, the Laon-Athies aerodrome—Airbase A-69—
would hold the entire group. A-69 had been visited before by men of the 416th, when
flak damage had forced emergency landings there. They had also visited in early February when Command sent a group of officers and ground crews there for an advance
evaluation. The airbase had been extensively cratered by Allied forces when it was in
the Luftwaffe's hands, and then bombed by the Luftwaffe and the Wehrmacht during its
tenure as an American airfield. With such shelling, the advance party was not surprised
when they found only one runway out of three usable and five hangars damaged but
operable.

The advance group also came to understand why this piece of terrain had been
the starting point for so many invasions and wars. Any army with foot soldiers, cavalry or
wheeled machinery could move quickly over this treeless, glacial, prairie-like landscape.
Hitler had exploited it just as the Allies were doing now with their mechanized, highly
mobile military. The countryside reflected this exploitation, having become one big battlefield that had been ground under foot and wheel twenty-five years ago in World War I.
The terrain stretched for what seemed liked hundreds of miles; from the air the trenches
from that war were still visible. Now the country and countryside, having survived World
War I, had to endure the Wehrmacht blowing up everything coming into France, only to
be followed by the Allies—Montgomery in the north, Patton in the south and Bradley in
the middle—blowing up everything as they ran the Germans out of France.

The Air Corps couldn't escape its share of responsibility either. The signs of the
air war were everywhere—from dead animals in the fields to bomb craters and smashed
villages. Destroyed and abandoned equipment from both sides littered the countryside,
including crashed aircraft from every country flying missions into combat. The good
news was that there were still small areas of undefiled land with intact villages. These areas were sought out by the servicemen of all ranks. It was a welcome change of scenery,
and everyone jumped at the chance to get off base.

The 416th's new home was next to a small town located on a round knob of land
rising close to 350 feet out of a flat, fertile plain. Just four kilometers away from their
base, Laon was topped by an ancient cathedral with four spires surrounded by the businesses and houses on its slopes. The entire town sat on a hill shaped liked a tear drop
lying on its side that sloped from high to low into the flat plains surrounding Laon. It
all seemed oddly out of place, as if dropped there from above. The architecture of the
city indicated its extreme age, and you almost expected knights to come riding out
on horseback. "Either it was out of place or the bomb group is going to be," joked the
advance crew when it initially poked around the town, The town made for a great land-
mark when flying, which is probably why the airbase was built here before the war.

Laon

Laon, France, suffered during the war, as did many of the
French villages, towns and cities. Dropping bombs from ten
thousand to twenty-five thousand feet was as much an art as a
science.
Reproduced with permission of Wes Chitty

And so the 416th began the process of moving to a new home again. Between February 1st and 14th, the 416th moved in waves from Melun. As with any relocation, it was organized chaos. Some hangars became mess halls, while another became a training and photographic building. As at Melun, any structure of any value was taken first by those at the top. What was left went to those sequentially down the chain of command. Rank had its privileges. By the time the move was completed, everyone knew his place.

Since the move was undertaken in waves, the 416th was still able to complete missions. So, during early February, many men reached their magic sixty-five, while many others experienced their first and, in some cases, final mission. Lieutenants Jack Smith, Ralph Conte, and Bill Tripp would see that magic number hit their flight records. Captain Dick Wheeler, who also reached sixty-five missions, would be transferred to group operations.

Surviving 65

Judging from the smile, this was the sixty-fifth and final
mission for Lieutenant Jack Smith of the 669th Squadron
Personal collection

During this time, the 416th was making deep incursions into German territory, but also suffering losses. A sortie to Euskirchen took the lives of Sergeant R. DeStafano and two other crewmen—Lieutenant C. H. Stead and his gunner Sergeant C. E. Transhina—of the 669th squadron while they flew in support of the Canadian and British ground forces. Over the Mechornish repair depot, bombardier-navigator Lieutenant L.A. Eckard sacrificed his life. On February 16th the Unna ordnance depot, well protected by flak guns, would exact the life of a young lieutenant, W.D. Wilson, who was on his eighth mission. His gunner Sergeant E.F. Berks would survive to be returned to duty.

The losses piled up. On the afternoon of February 21st the group flew on the Lage bridge. Some moderate success was achieved, but Lieutenant R.J. Johnson would lose an engine to flak. On return to the base he attempted to land, but on final he turned the plane into the dead engine, contrary to the single-engine flying rules for the Invader. After losing lift, he stalled the Invader in the turn. In a no-lift, wing-down configuration the Invader began its slide to the earth, crashing into the bivouac area of the 670th squadron and killing Lieutenant John Cook and injuring Lieutenants V.S. Merritt and S. Shelly. The men aboard—Lieutenant Johnson and gunner Sergeant H.E. Brandt—suffered fractures of various bones, but survived.

Crash Landing

The crash landing at the end of mission #209, February 1945.
Returning to base on one engine, Lieutenant R.K. Johnson of
the 669th crashed into the bivouac area of the 670th squadron.
Reproduced with Permission of Ralph Conte and Wayne
Downing

The very next day brought bombing and strafing runs that demonstrated the destructive firepower of the heavily armed Invaders. After destroying a rail bridge in formation, the strafing teams of two broke off to begin their hunt. They began looking for targets of opportunity and finding them, destroying one tank train, four motor transports, a rail station, five barges, wagons and oil tanks—all in a good day's work. They denied the enemy the use of weapons of war manufactured by the labor of their countrymen and of slaves from the concentration camps.

As 1945 developed, the focus of the war was changing in many venues, from military to political, which would have far-reaching consequences that were unforeseen at this time. It was clear that the Allies would win the war in Europe, and now the world powers were already considering who would govern and shape postwar Europe. On February 4th, the Yalta Conference began, with one Allied leader, Roosevelt, suffering congestive heart failure and supporting another, Churchill, who was totally dependent on the aggressive use of the former's power. As Stalin brokered for more land during the Yalta meeting, it became increasingly clear that an "Iron Curtain" would—as Churchill prophesied—fall on Europe. Like the western Allies, the Soviet Union was already positioning itself for the postwar era. Among other concessions at Yalta, Stalin negotiated hard for the transfer of Poland to his country. The spread of communism in the wake of the war, however, was not a foregone conclusion. Stalin kept to one aspect of his Yalta agreement, by suspending support for the Communist guerrilla forces in Greece. There, disguised British military power helped bring the end of the civil war, and forced the capitulation of Communist forces, but the conflict would last until 1949.

While political realities were reshaping policy, changes in the war were reshaping military tactics. As Germany was surrounded, continued interdiction missions by all branches of the air corps began to blur into generalized destruction of towns and communities. The American Eighth Air Force would find itself following in the shadow of British Bomber Command, destroying cities, as opposed to "military targets of strategic value." For example, on February 2, one thousand B-17s bombed Berlin, killing an estimated twenty-five thousand civilians. February would also bring the fire-bombing of Dresden, which took the lives of ten of thousands of civilians. Incendiary bombings on the city by British Bomber Command on the evening of the 13th were followed by the Eighth Air Force the following morning and afternoon. They destroyed some sixteen hundred acres of the city and created a firestorm that would rival the coming napalming of Tokyo. Dresden was bombed at the request of Soviets operating in the area, who implied the city was a legitimate military target. By the end of the war eight missions were flown over Dresden, which received comparatively little tonnage of bombs and effort but suffered massive destruction. The destruction of civilians would continue on February 23rd, with the bombing of the city of Pforzheim by the RAF. Some twenty thousand citizens perished.

With orders to bomb Germany, the 416th and every other Allied air group was in the business of destroying the enemy. The enemy was now Germany and Germans, in a change of tack that amounted to total war. Life itself had become the enemy. Indeed, total war had become the synthesis of eugenic principles. In their drive to stop the country's ability to wage war, the Allies destroyed anything, including the enemy's civilian populace, both in Germany and Japan. In fact, as conflict in Germany was clearly winding to its inevitable conclusion, preparations were being made for the destruction of Tokyo with conventional weapons, which would bring tremendous loss of life. Complete destruction and capitulation of the enemy had become the absolute goal of the Allies.

While the Allies rained eugenic hatred from above, the Germans enforced it on the ground. Recognizing that the end was close, the SS began to accelerate its killing. As January closed out, SS guards at the Königsberg concentration camp marched seven thousand prisoners to their deaths. Many guards aided the annihilation at the end of the march, when the four thousand survivors were shot.[262, 263, 264, 265, 266]

---

262   Attack Bombers We Need You: A History of the 416th Bomb Group; Ralph Conte; Copyright 2001; Chapter 12

263   Chronology of Jewish Persecution: 1945; http://www.jewishvirtuallibrary.org

264   Timeline of Pacific War; http://www.historyplace.com

265   The Bombing of Dresden; http://airforcehistory.hq.af.mil

266   1945: Information from Answers.com; http://www.answers.com/topic/1945

February's losses were felt among the 416th, but energetic new faces were rotating in as the old guard moved out, as they reached the required mission number, as they became POWs or as they were found by death. Those who had survived were ready to go home or at least change their mission, all except Lieutenant Wayne Downing, who was well into his second rotation of sixty-five missions. But most of the old guard felt their fatigue. War carried with it the weariness that fell only to the warriors. Somehow, day after day the majority of men would continue their charge into the teeth of death, isolating their fear from the reality of their mortal lives. Something greater than their own sense of self-preservation overcame their fear and allowed them the ability to crawl into their aluminum flying machines to face an enemy with the same fears.

By denying the possibility of their own death, these men could enter into battle watching other men die; they were sad to see their comrades passing but uncontrollably glad it wasn't them. Eons of evolutionary pressures had given humans the ability to overcome fear through a series of integrated neuronal rationales that function only for the preservation of one's self. Those hidden parts of the mind—one couldn't feel them working or know of their existence, but all the same they were doing their job of protecting the mortal body while hiding and suppressing the pain and visions of the world of aerial combat and death. Some men's minds couldn't suppress the realities of their existence, which pulled them over the threshold into combat or flak fatigue, making them useless as airmen and men. Some men consumed the drug of availability to help them deal with the internal conflicts, consuming in large quantities their monthly ration of alcohol as well as others' rations. Other men would never show any signs of problems until they were asked to reunite with their families, communities, and churches again. Their hidden pain would always separate them from others. The causalities of this war would continue. These losses and their effects would endure for some time, well into the peace.

❧

"Who ya writin', Roland?" Bill asked as walked into the tent after mess.

"Just a letter home," Roland said.

"Not a bad idea. I haven't written one in a while myself." Bill said, pondering when he might take care of it. "Some of the guys are getting up a baseball game, thought I might join 'em. You wanna play?"

"Maybe, after I finish this." Roland collected his pen and paper and sat down at the little table under the light.

"See you there, and don't forget your glove." He went toward the door. "Oh, if you see Carl, tell him to get his butt over there. We'll need him. Darn gunners kick the stuffing out of us every time."

Roland chuckled and agreed, "Roger that."

Bill walked out.

No longer thinking about the ball game, Roland looked at the blank paper on the table in front of him. It seemed so long ago that he came over here. He wasn't so sure any more about his decision to leave the shipping industry to fly around in planes. In shipping at least you could jump in the water if things went bad. Up there, you had to jump from ten thousand feet and hope your chute opened while praying the Krauts didn't kill you on the way down. Roland took up the pen.

March 1945
Northern France

Dearest folks,

Hello everybody and how are you all feeling these fine days? Everything over here is just as fine as could be expected under the circumstances, but I'm still just as anxious as ever to return, and when eighteen more missions are finished I'll be raring to go. Yep, they are beginning to pile up behind me. It's like looking at a long hill which is right in your path to an object you want to reach. From the bottom of the wrong side it looks like an insurmountable obstacle but when you get the biggest half over, it seems to have been not half as bad as it appeared to be.

A couple of days ago I received the box of fudge and it arrived in wonderful condition. Needless to say it didn't last long with the hungry bunch of wolves here; but I can tell you that we all enjoyed it very much and that it was very much appreciated.

I'm having a little trouble with my left eye these days, but it is nothing serious. The flight surgeon says it is only a low-grade infection. Up until recently I've been able to keep it from being known by the big shots, but during a recent mission the darn thing clouded up and leading a flight of men throughout the flak positions of Germany without all your faculties is not fair to them. So I was grounded for a day or two till it cleared up.

Next month I expect to be sent to England for a week or ten days on what is called flak-leave. It is just a short leave to take a little of the tension out of fliers which they all acquire after a number of missions. This combat fatigue, as the tension is called, is said to cut down a man's ability by 50%.

How are all the children and do you still hear from Marge regularly? I get a letter darn near every day from her and I think I'm safe in saying that over 90% of all my mail comes from her. Yes, folks, I am sure and I think you agree with me, Marguerite and I are meant to be together and upon my return we will be married. The divorce should be final by then. She has really worked wonders with me, after everything including the army failed, and I don't think I am bragging when I say that you can feel as proud of me as you'd like to; and I'll not let you down. Please even though you are busy, and I realize you are, try and write her once in awhile. Look, folks, it must be hard for her knowing that I am married, even though in the middle of the divorce, and yet she is still waiting for me, and writing me every day. But every bit of knowledge she gets which will prove to her that I am being true to her and really love her will help a lot, I know. So please write her and tell her that you are sure I really love her, and it is the truth. Please write her soon and incidentally I could use a letter, and also photos.

Well, folks, my eyes are troubling me quite a bit so I'll close.

With my
Love & respect, Brother

P.S.

It may be a little early but—start planning for the party in late July or early August, and be prepared for one guest. (That's right!)

B.

P.P.S. Take care of yourselves & the children. The days of the tin solders are over, Dad.

Roland's thoughts were interrupted when Carl and Earl noisily entered the tent joking about something.

"Hey, Roland…hey, Enman," said Carl and Earl sequentially.

"Hey, guys," Roland replied, while licking the envelope and then sealing it closed by pressing it between his fingers and the table top. "Carl, the guys were hoping you'd come play ball with them today. Bill already headed over, and it sounds like they want you pretty bad."

"Sounds good." Grabbing his glove, Carl moved toward the door.

"What about you, Earl?"

"No, I'm gunna write Helen a letter."

"What about your girl back in Torquay, you still writing her?"

"Yeah…but not as much."

Getting up from his seat, Roland walked to the door after grabbing his glove. "Well, I'll see you later."

"Yeah, see you later, Roland."

Some of the 669ᵗʰ's Finest

Lieutenant Bill Tripp, (fourth from left), Lieutenant Earl
Hayter (sixth from left), Lieutenant Leo Poundstone (second
from right), and Jimmy Farley (far right) pose beside an A-26
Invader of the 416ᵗʰ / 669ᵗʰ squadron (2A) Note the heavy
flight boots used for warmth in the unheated planes.
Reproduced with permission of Earl Hayter

Changes accelerated around the globe as killing became the way. Manila fell to
General Douglas MacArthur, with a hundred thousand civilian casualties—a number
exceeded only by the losses in Berlin and Stalingrad. Six days later, Tokyo was peppered
with napalm incendiary bombs from three hundred B-29 Flying Fortresses, creating firestorms that destroyed 16 square miles of the city at temperatures approaching eighteen
hundred degrees. Civilian causalities approached one hundred thousand. Japan's cities
would burn one after the other as mid-altitude missions below the newly discovered jet-
stream proved to be the forte of the B-29. After a bloody battle, the Americans took the
Pacific island of Iwo Jima, a strategic location for fighter escorts to be stationed. Iwo Jima
would not only provide for fighter escorts over Japan, but it would also become a safe
haven for damaged B-29s to land.

All across the world, death's scythe was falling from the sky, hurtling from artillery, rifling from barrels of guns or swinging indiscriminately in hand-to-hand combat.
This level of carnage was about to be surpassed, as the ability to bring death in one massive explosion was about to become a reality for the United States. Nazi Germany was
still in the quest to produce the atomic bomb, as they detonated the first in a series of

attempts at a nuclear weapon on March 3rd at the Ohrdruf military testing grounds. The race was on, with the Americans clearly in the lead by having produced more fissionable material than the Nazis. America's weapon would work when tested. But Germany had the ideal means to produce more fissionable material, with its gaseous nuclear centrifuges, which were developed by Dr. Erich Bagge in 1944. However, the Nazis were unable to produce enough material to make a workable bomb. This centrifuge would later become the world's model for producing nuclear-grade material, with countries around the world using it to make the bomb.

The pressure to end the war was weighing heavy on all armies on both sides of the globe. Pressures were also being exerted to hide the extent of the eugenic death machine.[267, 268] The 416th would feel these pressures too. March brought missions flown with GEE-equipped B-26 Marauders to bomb when cloudy, or the men would bomb by sight when clear. Radar technology allowed the group to fly a record number of missions, and thereby drop a record tonnage of bombs in March. Missions over ordnance depots, transport depots, and marshaling yards continued, as the Allied armies on the ground below advanced eastward for the Rhine. March 7th brought the first push across the Rhine, at Remagen.

⟩W⟨

As the air war in March of 1945 progressed for the 416th, several men completed their commitments. Bombardier-navigator Lieutenant Bob Basnett of the 671st Squadron would hit his magic number on March 5th after bombing the Bingen marshaling yard, along the Rhine. He would be joined by Lieutenant Charles Mish on the 13th. Both men were happy they could see this day come. Roland Enman was closing in on the magic sixty-five. He was leading boxes and flights over German cities now. Others who had done their duty had received orders that they were to be rotated back to the states.

Sipping black coffee, Jack opened his orders from Wing. He found himself assigned to a recruiting-bond tour. He'd be flying a B-25 around the states for a while. "Ralph, what they gunna have you doing?"

Ralph discovered that he'd be delivering documents between headquarters units and such. Meanwhile, Bill Tripp found out that he'd be ferrying aircraft. All three were happy to be doing something different.

Roland looked up from the mess table: "You lucky stiffs."

No one commented. They sipped their coffee.

After breaking up, the group headed to the tents. No one was much in the mood for the trip into Laon. March was still a little chilly at this latitude, so it was too cold to walk or bike. A warm fire and stiff drink sounded better.

---

267   How Close Was Hitler to the A-Bomb?; Klaus Wiegrefe; Der Spiegel 11/2005-March 14, 2005; http://www.spiegel.de/international/spiegel/.html

268   1945: Information from Answers.com; http://www.answers.com/topic/1945

Leaving the final tent, the adjutant was ready to head back to the Operations building, get a cup of coffee, and begin his other preflight duties. Roland watched as the adjutant exited his tent, and then he grudgingly threw back the covers and rolled out. He stretched widely, with a big yawn, to wake up. He turned to the stove to wash his face. "Heck fire!" They had forgotten to put the wash basin on the stove last night. Roland braced and then dipped his hands into the water to wash his face. He placed the bowl on the stove. He knew the guys would appreciate the warm water when they rolled out of the sack. Looking around the room at his snoring buddies, Roland realized that he, Earl and Carl were the only ones still on flight status in the tent. Some new faces would be here soon to replace his buddies. He left the tent for the early briefing, knowing he would see Carl and Earl at the main briefing later this morning.

Roland's mission that day was without incident. He released his payload over the Dillerburg-Neiderscheld marshaling yard just as the Pathfinder B-26 leading the group dropped its salvo on the GEE reading. The bombs fell through the cloud cover onto their target. The trip home was uneventful, as the A-26s landed in the order they had taken off.

In March, missions were flown every day, and so the days passed quickly. Enman quickly found himself flying with Earl and Carl again, on the town of Pirmasens. Although not far from the base or deep inside Germany, the town was the next target of American ground forces, and they wanted any Wehrmacht resistance there destroyed. At the briefing Roland, Brownie, Kerns, Earl and Carl were surprised to find that the Ninth Bomber Command had assigned eleven bomb groups to the target. They all were soon to learn that overwhelming force was to become standard operating procedure, since fewer and fewer targets were available and the battlefield shrank. The good thing about it, from the airmen's point of view, was that when that many aircraft hit a target there was very little of it left. Pirmasens was to be no exception, as hundred of thousands of pounds of bombs rained down on the small southwest German town. Civilians died by the thousands as the town exploded around them. For the 416th and all the other groups that flew on Pirmasens that day, it was a milk run—no losses, no flak damage and no fighters.[269]

Rolling to a stop at his hardstand after the mission to Pirmasens, Earl secured his aircraft and then looked for the debriefing truck that would run him up to Operations. Patting *Classy Lassy Helen* on the nose, he thanked her once again for bringing him home safely. Seeing the truck, he walked out on the taxiway and jumped in. He extended his hand over the back and helped his gunner over the tailgate.

"Roland, good mission," said Earl to Enman, who was already in the truck.

The truck jerked to a fast start.

"We hit those guys pretty good."

"How's the eye?" Earl asked.

---

269   Milk run – American slang for an easy bomb mission with little or no chance for people being killed or encountering resistance

"No sweat, Doc says it will be fine. Need to stand down for a couple days, but will be back on flying status the 18th."

"Me too. This damned ringing in my ears is driving me crazy."

Approaching the next Invader, the truck slowed. Brownie and Kerns clambered over the tailgate and into the truck. Both were talking about the burning town they had just helped destroy. The Allies had quickly occupied the town, and then moved on to other objectives.

Two days passed quickly; the group visited the cities of Alten Kirchen and Bad Homburg. Neither mission went well. Then came March 18th—and the attack on Worms.

Chapter Seventeen

Worms, the Taker of Souls

*Undertake this journey eagerly for the remission of your
sins, and be assured of the reward of imperishable glory
in the Kingdom of Heaven.*

– *Pope Urban, 1095*

The morning of the 18th seemed like any other, but the flight crews had no idea this was the start of five days of intense missions designed to open the way for the Third Army, which was primed to cross the Rhine and push deeper into Germany.

At mess that morning the conversations were light, with no mention made of the morning mission briefing they had just completed. Breakfast went fast. Few ate their eggs, but the SPAM was tolerable today, so the men pushed it down. Coffee was consumed in large quantities; everyone was looking for their edge to be sharpened as they prepared to do battle. Almost in unison the squadrons would finish their meal and then start moving in their well-conditioned manner to the trucks that would take them to the briefing hut and the full briefing. Conversation wasn't necessary in the early-morning darkness; the glowing embers from the nervous pulls on cigarettes showed what was on the airmen's minds. The men moved slowly toward the trucks.

"Good morning, gentlemen," said the Operations officer. "As you all know, the early bird gets the Worms." There were a few subdued obligatory chuckles from the now-anxious officers. Most everyone's focus was on the ingress and egress routes pinned to the map. One colored yarn was pinned to the map going one direction until it stopped at the target, Worms, Germany. The color changed for the return route home. From start to finish, the yarn zigged and zagged its way across eastern France and western Germany. Pins dotted the important waypoints, where the group would change direction. Plans A and B and the coordination of routes with the other bomb groups' arrival times were reviewed.

The men of the 416th began to realize the complexity of today's mission was really becoming the routine, with so many groups scheduled over the target on very tight intervals. One mistake could put your group in the middle of a bomb drop.

The bomb-run from the IP quickly drew everyone's attention.

"Maps today are first G.S.G.S. 4414, sheet 6316, with 1:12,500 Rhine River, Mainz to Mannheim, sheet number 13 and the town plan of Worms am Rhein." After giving everyone time to locate the proper maps, the Operations officer moved to his next well-rehearsed comments. The navigators wrote down the coordinates for each turn in Plan "A"—base to P-8340, followed by L-5860, then L-8554, then L-9433, to the IP M-2018 to TGT (target). They filled in the new headings and times off each turn to the next waypoint. After they computed the bomb-run from the IP, they all cursed silently. Each pilot and navigator reviewed the Plan A logistics as they were being discussed by the Operations officer.

PLAN A VISUAL

3.   A. 97TH COMBAT WING:
                (1) (A) M-448160
                (B) G-543189
                (2) (A) ONE GROUP MAX. EFFORT.
                (B) 2 GROUPS MAX. EFFORT.
(4)   (A) BASE TO P-8340 TO L-5860 TO L-8554 TO
                L-9433 TO M-2018 TO TGT.
                B)   BASE TO 8587 TO F-6801 TO F-9220 TO G-1819
                TO G-3013 TO TGT.
(5)   (A) TGT. LEFT RETRACE LOSE 1000 FT.
          (B) TGT. LEFT TO G-1819 1ST GROUP LOSE 1000 FT.
                2ND GROUP CLIMBS 1000 FT.
(6)   (A) 12,500 FT.
          (B) 1ST. GROUP 12,000 FT. 2ND GROUP 10000 FT.
(9)   (A) GSGS 4414 SHEET 6313 REF: COVER RD/JNS IN
                AREA 44851533, 45901530, 45751475,
                44801400, ALSO SEE GH5545
          (B) ILLUS: 5 (A) 46A/2 REF: IST GROUP COVER
                M/Y FROM 048045 TO 064056, 2ND GROUP COVER
                M/Y FROM 039045 TO 048048 ALSO SEE US31/
                4362 NO. 1081-84 TTF ILLUS. US7GR/ 3270 NO.
                3196-97
(10)   (A) 18 X 150 GP FUSED 1/10 X 1/40
          (B) 1ST GROUP 6 X 500 GP. FUSED 1/10 X 1/100
                2ND GROUP 4 X 1000 GP FUSED 1/10 X 1/100
(12)   (A) AND (B) DESIRED INTERVAL 50 FT.
(13)   (A) TOT: ZERO PLUS 15
          (B) TOT: 1ST GROUP ZERO PLUS 15 2ND GROUP ZERO
                PLUS 45

"Hey, Cornell, that's gotta be a mistake on the run. Whattaya think?"

"I damn sure hope so, Roland," Cornell whispered back.

"Listen up, fellas," said the Operations officer. The mumbling and grumbling died away as everyone refocused. "As usual, the bomb line is the Rhine River. Worms sits on both sides of the river, so be careful. The marshaling yard is on the west bank and the communications center is just to the south of it." He tapped the map with his three-foot wooden pointer. "Now, those Third Army guys have been moving forward damned fast these days, so listen for any change in the bomb line before takeoff." The Third Army sat several miles from Worms on the west bank of the Rhine.

He tapped the map again. "You will cross it here. No bombs dropped before that line. Everyone got that?" He knew he had made his point—he got no responses from the tight, focused, cigarette-wielding faces staring back. He turned, and signaled to the briefing officer to proceed.

Before beginning, the assistant Operations officer acknowledged his superior: "Thank you, sir." He cleared his throat. "G-2 has determined that flak will be light to moderate over the target zone. There should be sporadic 88s and 105s mixed with some 150-mm cannons, along with the usual small-caliber anti-aircraft fire from the 20- and 37-mm guns on the way in and out. We suspect they may put a few 109s up your way, but fighter escorts from the Ninth, Twelfth, Nineteenth, and Twenty-Ninth TAC will meet up with you here."

The pilots and navigators wrote down the coordinates, and calculated the flight times.

"They should keep the bandits off you. Sounds like a milk run, gentlemen. Times and routes are outlined. Sir." The assistant turned to his superior.

"Thank you, Lieutenant." The commander resumed the body of the briefing. "It's critical that everyone stay on course and on time. This is a big one today, gentlemen. It is a combined attack with B-26s from the 98th and 99th combat wings. Looks like it will be the 387th, 394th, 397th, 391st, and the 334th Bomb Groups. The 416th will have the only A-26s on the mission, so let's do it right. There will be six waves, with each group attacking at fifteen- to thirty-minute intervals. Each group will bomb with at least one Pathfinder from the First Pathfinders Squadron out of Perrone, A-72. Navigators, keep them on schedule and follow the Pathfinders. We will be bombing off OBOE-equipped Marauders. If you can't bomb visual, that's Plan B, which is as follows."

PLAN B OBOE

3.   A. 97TH COMBAT WING:
                (1) (A) M-448160
                (B) G-543189
                (2) (A) 1 GROUP 33 A/C PLUS 1 PFF A/C
                (B) 2 GROUPS 30 A/C PLUS 2 PFF A/C EACH
                (4) (A) BASE TO P3640 TO L-5971 TO M-1367 TO TGT.
                (B) BASE TO P6567 TO F-6801 TO F-9831 TO TGT.
                (5) (A) TGT TURN RIGHT TO M-2015 TO L-9433 TO L- 8554
                        TO L-5860 TO BASE: LOSE 1000 FT.
                (B) TGT TURN RIGHT TO F-9220 TO F-6501 TO BASE. LOSE
                        1000 FT.
                (6) (A) 13,000 FT.
                (B) BOTH GROUPS FIRST BOX 13,000 FT. 2ND BOX 12,500 FT.

(9) (A) GSGS 4414 SHEET 6314 REF: 45091462
(B) FIRST GROUP ILLUS: 5 (A) 46/2 COVER M/Y
FROM 064056 TO 048045 SECOND GROUP COVER
M/Y FROM 048045 TO 039048
(10) (A) 150 GP FUSED 1/10 X 1/40
(B) FIRST GROUP 500 GP FUSED 1/10 X 1/100
2ND GROUP 1000 GP FUSED 1/10 X 1/100
(12) (A) AND (B) DESIRED INTERVAL: 50 FT.
(13) (A) ZERO PLUS 15 MIN.
(B) FIRST GROUP ZERO PLUS 15 MIN SECOND GROUP ZERO
PLUS 45 MIN.

"The B-26s will rendezvous with you at the RP. Don't go without them. This is where you will rendezvous with your fighter cover too. After you link up with them, turn onto the first leg of the mission on this heading."

A junior Operations officer entered the room, walking quickly to the front of the seated aircrews. He saluted and then handed the senior Operations officer a teletype.

Stopping his briefing, the officer read. "Thanks, Lieutenant. Dismissed."

Directing his attention back to the briefing, the officer continued, "Each group will be flying with three Window aircraft from their own group. One last thing, gentlemen, this just came in from Wing: Plan B is in effect. Use Plan A only if visual bombing is capable. Plans C and D are canceled. Repeat, Plan B in effect, and use Plan A only if visual on target. C and D are canceled. Recognition code words for the day are one, Bestman – Blizzard – Quickstart; two, Pallmall – Sleepy – Sleepy; and three, Ripsaw – Sweepstake – Sweepstake."

The Window mission and the three crew assignments were reviewed, showing their position relative to the group's route on ingress and egress. Lieutenant Harry Popeney let out a groan when he heard his name called for the Window mission. Turning to his crew, he said, "Well, guys, I guess we're the targets today." His crew and the other two crews assigned to Window shook their heads in a slow, affirmative fashion, pulling harder now on their Chesterfields and Luckies.

⊶∿⊷

This already had been and was continuing to be a busy day for the USAAF all around the world. Sunday, March 18, 1945, had seen the Fourteenth Air Force in the China theater send six B-24 Liberators to sink a freighter in the South China Sea. Two P-51 Lightnings over northern French Indochina had strafed trucks, troops and horse-carts. The Tenth Air Force in the India-Burma area put twelve P-47 Thunderbolts up, flying support for Chinese ground troops. Eight P-47s dropped napalm northeast of Mogok, Burma, in support of British troops, while eleven B-25 Mitchell bombers accompanied by twenty fighter-bombers attacked troop concentrations and supplies behind the enemy lines there. In the same area sixteen P-38 Lightnings swept a road south of the bomb line. Later that day the Eleventh Air Force out of Alaska would fly a weather sortie.

The war in the Pacific was busy. Exactly 290 B-29 Super Fortresses from the Twentieth Air Force, XXI Bomber Command, firebombed the Japanese city of Nagoya, destroying the Nagoya arsenal, Aichi engine plant, and freight yards. The Mitsubishi plant escaped major damage, but three square miles of Nagoya were incinerated. This mission was flown in conjunction with fourteen B-24 Liberators from the Seventh Air Force out of Guam; the Liberators bombed Susaki Airfield on Chichi Jima Island. Sixteen Seventh Air Force Fighter Command P-51 Mustangs dive-bombed radar and radio installations on Chichi Island, and also claimed some hits on enemy barges. That evening five B-24s attacked Susaki again. Earlier that day the 392nd Bombardment Squadron (Heavy) of the Thirtieth Bombardment Group (Heavy) moved from Saipan Island, in the Marianas, to Hawaii.

The Far East and Southwest Pacific air forces sent B-24s, A-20s and fighters to support ground forces in the Batangas Province of the Philippines. B-24s also bombed Bacolod, Sepinggang and Jesselton airfields on Borneo, Cebu Island, Taiwan, respectively, and the emergency airfield at Koshun. P-61 Black Widows from the 419th Fighter Squadron, XIII Fighter Command, stationed in Puerto Princesa were sent to operate their night missions out of Zamboanga, Philippines.

Despite all the missions flown in Asia and the Pacific, the men flying in the European Theater of Operations were not to be outdone that day. P-38s from the Fifteenth Air Force attacked the Varazdin, Yugoslavia, railroad bridge. This attack was followed by multiple strafing missions against airfields and communication centers in Yugoslavia, Austria, and Hungary. Bad weather limited many operations in the region. The Twelfth Air Force in Italy attacked the Po Valley river bridges with A-20s and A-26s. Meanwhile, B-25s bombed railroad bridges and fighter-bombers flew ground-support missions and attacked communications centers. Fourteen locomotives were destroyed that day at the Novara, Italy, marshaling yards.

That morning the Eighth Air Force was flying two major strategic missions, which helped crowd the skies over Germany. Mission number 894 for the Eighth Air Force saw 1,329 heavy bombers accompanied by 733 fighter escorts bomb rail stations and tank factories in Berlin. These missions were made with both visual bomb-runs and with H2X radar-guided releases. The bomber group was met by a vigorous, concentrated attack of Luftwaffe Me-262 jet fighters as well as piston-driven fighters.

The three Berlin targets took their share of men and material. First, over the Schlesischer rail station and the two secondary targets, Zehdnuk and Vechta, five B-17 Flying Fortresses were lost, eight were damaged beyond repair and 268 received significant battle damage. The sortie took one crewman's life, while eighteen were wounded and forty-nine were listed as missing in action. The P-51 Mustang escorts lost two aircraft. The Eighth Air Force and their escorts claimed a total of ten enemy aircraft destroyed.

The second sortie consisted of 530 B-17s escorted by 219 P-51s, and flew on the Nord Rail Station. The attack resulted in seven B-17s being shot down, six damaged beyond repair, and 319 receiving battle damage. More importantly, one airman was killed, twelve were wounded in action, and seventy-nine were listed as missing in action. Two P-51s were lost. The Allies claimed eight enemy aircraft downed.

The third sortie, to the industrial areas of Tegel and Henningsdorf tank factories, involved 347 B-24 Liberators escorted by 254 P-51 Mustang fighter-bombers. One B-24 was lost, one damaged beyond repair, and 127 received severe battle damage. The mortal loss was one, one was wounded and eleven were missing in action. Two P-51s were lost, while three enemy aircraft were destroyed.

That day featured still other missions in Europe, including two B-17s flying scouting missions, twenty-seven P-51s flying scouting missions, and five F-5s escorted by one P-51 on photo-recon missions over Germany. Mission number 895 for the Mighty Eighth that day was a leaflet mission over the Netherlands and Germany at night. The mission was without loss.

Tactical flight operations were carried out as well. The First Tactical Air Force (Provisional) moved the 415th Night Fighter Squadron, Sixty-Fourth Fighter Wing, flying Beaufighters, to St. Dizier, France, from Ochey.

The Ninth Air Force participated in the day's attacks, by putting up over 660 A-20 Havocs, A-26 Invaders and B-26 Marauders over Germany. They hit the marshaling yards at Wetzlar, Worms, Kreuztal, and Bad Durkheim as well as a communications center at Bad Durkheim and Worms. Four different town areas were targeted, with the aim of hampering enemy movement and communications. These assaults were accompanied by fighters who escorted the bombers, attacked assigned targets, flew patrols, and armed reconnaissance. They also cooperated with the US III Corps at Remagen as the XII Corps began an assault on the Mainz-Worms sector of the Rhine River. The Ninth Air Force also assisted the XX Corps as it moved rapidly eastward through the Sankt Wendel area toward Kaiserslautern. HQ Seventieth Fighter Wing moved from Verviers, Belgium, to Brühl, Germany.[270]

In all, Sunday, March 18, 1945, was a busy day of combined air operations that required tremendous logistical coordination and timing among the men and women of the United States Army Air Corps. Operations like this had been coordinated every day from well before the start of the war, throughout the war, and well after its end. The United States Navy and Marine Corps conducted their own air operations, as did Bomber Command with the Royal Air Force. Adding up the combined operations of every Allied and Axis air operations on any given day made the skies around the globe a very crowded and deadly place. The only operation that would approach such logistical coordination before the onset of the Korean War was the Berlin airlift—a massive demonstration of the power of air control, but thankfully a peaceful humanitarian demonstration.

⚜

---

270   USAAF Chronology; http://paul.rutgers.edu/~mcgrew/wwii/usaf/html/mar.45.html

"It is critical that you hit the IP on time, since there will be a fifteen-minute interval between each group's TOT (time over target). We've been assigned to follow the 387th to hit the Worms' communication center here." Tapping the map with his pointer as cigarette tips glowed brighter, the Operations officer punctuated the groans escaping from the airmen, when they heard that they were second in the order. No one wanted to be second or last over the target.

"Calm down," said the officer and regained order. "The good news is there shouldn't be much flak on this one. Keep on your toes, anyway. Use your evasive maneuvers to avoid the flak bursts, till you hit the IP. Window should draw most of the Kraut fire, keeping those darned 88s busy.

"Turn right at the IP onto the run in flights of six. Bombardiers, here is your aiming point. Pilots, intervalometers are on zero. Bombardiers, we want you to put all the ordnance on this aiming point, with everyone dropping in flights of six. Keep tight intervals. Now…the communications center is here," he said, tapping a photo that showed the target. "Here's your aiming point and target. You will be dropping a mixture of 150-pound GP, 500-pound HE and 1,000-pound HE. Check your aircraft when you get there to calculate your takeoff and emergency speeds."

He paused.

"Remember, the 387th will be fifteen minutes ahead of you, so bombardiers notice the landmarks around the aiming point and target in case the MPI is covered with smoke. Watch out for their aircraft and stragglers. We don't want any midair collisions." The officer looked around the room at the somber faces to make his point. "Pilots in A-Box, once the bombardiers give you the all-clear, turn left and drop a thousand feet. Then retrace out at 12,500, got it?"

He looked around.

"B-Box, turn left and gain a thousand feet while turning to G-1819 and retrace at twelve thousand feet. Get out of the target area fast. Remember, the other four groups are coming over right behind you to hit the marshaling yard. That's it for Plan A—any questions?"

Pausing to look around before starting into Plan B, the Operations officer gave the crewmen time to digest the data.

"OK, if the weather is lousy, then everyone will drop off the OBOE-guided Pathfinders. The way points to target are as follows—base to P-3640 to L-5971 to M-1367 to target. Drop on the Pathfinders in box formation." He waited. The navigators and pilots were plotting and timing it on their maps.

"Weather says it's going to be cloudy, so you'll probably be dropping off the Pathfinders' mark. The Krauts jammed us pretty well last time, but the Brits think they can force-transmit through any jamming this time to get a good signal for a drop. Besides, they have a few tricks the Krauts don't know about yet. Pilots and bombardiers, remember if you can bomb visual with the Nordens, do it. Gentlemen, this is going to be a long bomb-run because of all the other groups hitting the site. Wing doesn't want you hitting the MPI together. The run is down this valley at 13,000 for A-Box and 12,500 for B-Box. Form up tight and put the eggs on the target; the ground forces coming in behind this mission are counting on you to make it hard for the Krauts to stop 'em."

He caught his breath.

"Again, the flak concentrations, based on the F-5's recon photos from the Thirty-Third flown four days ago, show the majority of the AA are protecting the marshaling yard in the northeast here. One more time, our target along with the 387th's thirty-eight Marauders is the communication center here." He pointed to the photo that showed the collection of buildings where Wing believed the command structure was located. They believed it was coordinating what was left of the Wehrmacht in the Worms area of operations.

"The 387th will hit the drop zone at 1000 hours on this heading and will be followed by you on the same heading at 1015 hours. There's no reason to bring any bombs back with you, since we have all we need. So let's give it to the Krauts. Remember, if all else fails, go for a visual with the Norden bombsight. The aiming point is here," said the officer as he tapped the recon photo of the target again.

"Study it and look for these landmarks as you fly in on the bomb-run if you have visual on the target. Your navigation maps have your coordinates with flight times. Your box assignments will be posted as usual in the pilots briefing. Any questions?"

The major turned the briefing over to Weather and G-2, who gave a quick update. The briefing broke up, and most men first went for the latrines; twelve thousand feet was a terrible place to be in need of an outhouse.

Now, nineteen-year-old gunner Sergeant Jack Sittarich had just finished pulling all the safety pins out of the bombs in the bomb bay, and was settling back into his gunner's periscope station. Reaching up, he activated his throat interphone microphone and called, "Lieutenant Kenny, all the safety pins are out and the bombs are secure."

"Roger that, sergeant, closing bomb bay doors now." Kenny listened to the hydraulics groan as they pulled against the cold, tight hinges and pulleys of the doors. He looked at his instrument panel until he saw the green light come on.

As Kenny closed the doors, Sittarich completed his final preflight priority, which was not on the Army Air Forces checklist. On finishing the Lord's Prayer, Sittarich began the Apostles' Creed: "I believe in the Holy Spirit, the holy Catholic Church…and life everlasting…Amen."

"Amen," said a voice behind him. Kenny had listened to his affirmation.

Both men were ready for battle.

After an uneventful taxi, Kenny and Sittarich had come off the runway behind Lieutenant Cornell. Kenny immediately began his turn to join up with A-1 flight, and took the number-six slot.

The next Invader coming through the overcast on schedule was Lieutenant Cornell, who would start the number-two flight, in slot A-2-1. The Invader continued its one-minute trip out and then turned to orbit back for the next plane to fill the number-two slot.

Lieutenant Wes Chitty and Staff Sergeant Raccio slid into the run-up spot at the head of the runway. Wes put his hand on his right coat pocket feeling for his pipes. He counted four, plus the one he was smoking. "Yeah, got 'em all." Wes took a deep draw from his pipe as he advanced the throttles and held the brakes. Feeling the plane wanting to go, he released the brakes. Like all the ones before, the Invader leapt forward and started its roll to the sky. Wes climbed out and slid into the A-2-2 slot ten seconds later. He was followed by Invaders that filled out the flight.

Carl Weinert should have been in this flight, at A-2-2, but during his taxi he had come across a piece of ground equipment that had been left in the way, forcing him to turn the Invader hard right and apply a right brake and then reverse the maneuver to get around the misplaced equipment. When he turned back to the left, the right wheel rolled off the edge of the tarmac. Once it was onto the soft French soil, the wheel immediately sank to the rim's edge, stopping the plane in its tracks. The right wing jolted to a stop, causing the plane to list to the right. Carl throttled back and applied brakes equally.

Beginning to worry, Carl thought that he must have forgotten something. This shouldn't have happened. Reviewing the taxi and takeoff procedure in his mind as well as covering his personal preflight ritual, he considered what could have gone wrong. He had done his traditional takeoff ritual in the cockpit, putting three pieces of gum in his mouth before takeoff. He had also been introduced to another preflight ritual. After having given ground crewman the thumbs-up to show he was ready to taxi, he had been waved off from taxiing by his new crew chief. Climbing up on the plane, the crew chief had opened Carl's cockpit hatch and patted him on the head three times. The ground crewman had leaned over and said, "I've never lost a plane when I've done this before." Carl would have felt better if he had said that he'd never lost a pilot. Saluting the ground crewmen who were lined up saluting him, Carl had begun his taxi.

Now, Carl called the tower to inform them of his predicament, asking for a tow. All available ground crews were alerted and arrived at the floundering Invader for the hard work of getting its wheel freed from the hole it had made. Some thirty thousand pounds of plane could make a surprising dent in soft earth. Carl wanted to get back onto the taxiway too, first of all, so it wouldn't look bad on his record, but more importantly he wanted this mission to count. He would have only thirty-two more after this one. Carl was a capable pilot, but he had lost the boundaries of the taxiway. He realized again that this wasn't training.

Reida Rae idled to a stop, as Lieutenant Jack Buskirk was forced to wait in the taxi formation until the Invaders ahead of him could navigate past the obstruction.

"What's going on, Lieutenant?" heard Buskirk over his interphone. It was Buskirk's gunner Herman Fessler.

"Don't know. Something happened to a plane in the taxi order."

"Hope they get it cleared up fast. Operations hates it when we get off schedule," said Lieutenant Bob Hanna to Buskirk.

"I know, I know," Buskirk replied as he craned his neck out the window to see what the problem was.

The ground crew had a tractor out now trying to pull the Invader free. The tractor pulled while Carl revved the engine. Finally lurching forward, the big plane rolled up onto the taxiway. The success brought a back-slapping cheer from the ground crew which had been working hard in a dangerous environment to get it free.

Carl quickly pulled back on the throttles, realizing he was free to keep the plane under control as he looked to the ground crew chief again to see if he could go to the head of the runway. This delay, though, had cost Carl his customary number-two slot, which Lieutenant Wes Chitty and Staff Sergeant Raccio now held.

Moving onto the runway, Carl saw Father Penticoff blessing the planes and crews as they went by. Not being one to pass up what he was beginning to realize was a series of preflight rituals that had to be followed, he happily accepted the blessing and then roared off down the runway. Carl easily completed his takeoff roll, and transitioned into flight. He cleaned up his flight surfaces, enjoying the feel of this big bird as it ascended into the sky. Carl was the second to last to join his flight, in the A-2-5 slot. He felt a little out of position, but adapted quickly as the flight turned to the staging point after the number-six slot was filled.

The next flight leader, Major M.W. Campbell, completed his climb, and contacted Cornell. Campbell watched as A-2 headed off for the group staging area, while the rest of his flight joined up. Ross was happy to fill out his flight and headed to the group's staging zone.

At the staging zone, Captain Evans flying box lead in A-1-1 slot watched as the three B-26 Marauders moved out in front of his box. Once it was in position, he followed as the Marauder turned onto the first leg of the mission. The group followed in tight precision. Scanning the horizon, Evans noted that so far things were as advertised. Cloud cover was preventing visual bombing.

Getting his new heading from his navigator, Evans eased the combined fighter and bomber groups onto the new heading toward the bomb line and German airspace. They knew every mile of ingress would be heavily defended and contested. No one talked except when the pilot would check with his gunner to make sure he didn't see any fighters or flak. All the pilots were busy synchronizing their engines and adjusting the fuel flow and air mixtures to maximize their engine's performance on the steady climb up to twelve thousand feet. The pilots and gunners watched each other so as to avoid a midair collision. The pilots worked hard to hold a tight formation, which was designed for protection from enemy fighters, but also for mutual comfort and a good bomb pattern. Concentrating on keeping the flight in formation was therapy as well, helping the men to avoid thinking about that imaginary line shown only on maps but clearly demarcated in the hearts of Deutschland's *hausfrauen*,[271] *Volkssturm*,[272] Wehrmacht, and the unforgiving SS, who were all determined to destroy anyone who crossed it.

It was then that radio silence was broken by the voice of "Axis Sally." The propagandist said, "This is Berlin calling. Hello, boys of the 416th. We are sorry to see that you are still fighting for those British and their Bolshevik-loving leader, Churchill. You know they do not like you, yet you persist in fighting for them while your wives and girlfriends play behind your backs at home. You know I love America, but I don't know why you

271   German – housewives
272   German – German people's attack force, generally older men and young children

fight for that Jewish-loving Roosevelt. They send you here to die, while they grow fat back home. Don't you know the Luftwaffe and Wehrmacht are waiting for you at your target? Yes, we know all about your mission to Worms today. We received the same tele-type briefing as the group from the tapped telephone lines, and we have been listening to your so-called chatter all morning—"

"To all air crews, to all air crews," interjected Evans. "Bestman, blizzard, quick-start. Repeat, bestman, blizzard, quickstart," said Evans to all aircraft. "All crews switch to alternate channel one on my mark three, two, one—mark." He switched his channel selection switch. Axis Sally left the headsets of the flight crews.

⌇⌇

The SS, with the help of the Luftwaffe, had taken notice of the US Army Air Corps' exploitation of the light attack bombers' ability to devastate high-value targets such as marshaling yards, bridges, and in particular communication centers. Because of this ability, the SS had intensified all air defenses around these type of targets. With most of the heavy military production safely underground and hidden from the heavy bombers, the SS could focus on protecting the smaller, more-valuable targets. This change in tactics had started the night of the last daylight American photo-recon flight over Worms. That evening, under orders from the SS, the Luftwaffe had begun moving large numbers of AA units into Worms' air defense corridor. They had also brought up well-trained, radar-directed SS anti-aircraft units. In addition, they had increased the number of veteran gunners and *hauptwachtmeister* to man the cannons. The SS had re-quested the newer "Heinrich" advanced GEE-jamming units in hopes of misdirecting or separating the enemy planes. This intensification of radar defenses was to provide the SS with its greatest success in the defense of the installations today.

Following the success of the Normandy invasion, the SS knew that every battle would be harder to win, but they also knew that they were not without some tricks left to make their adversary pay. The *Dolchstosslegende*[273] was alive and well in the SS. The weath-er was on their side today too. It had forced the Americans to break radio silence, which had given the radio direction-finders time to identify their location and ultimately their direction of flight. Those two things coupled with knowledge of the type of aircraft, range and origin gave the Germans a reasonable estimate of the general vicinity of the target. Once the heading was confirmed they would be more accurate. The shortwave radar systems would provide advanced targeting information to the gunners. The weak-ness of the system now lay with the lack of qualified radar technicians that were manned by foreigners, teenage boys, and young women (*Flakhelfer* and *Flakhelferinnen*). The ra-dar systems were manned by some experienced operators too, but the system had its

---

273   German – The German military theory that the defeatist attitude of the civilian popula-tion had caused the military to lose WWI, even though the German army was never defeated on the battlefield. It was used as a political tactic by Hitler to win votes.

weaknesses. There were constant repair problems, but the Luftwaffe adapted and kept the system operating by moving repair technicians from site to site.[274, 275]

The Germans lay in wait smelling their prey approaching. Their trap was about to be sprung. The Luftwaffe had calculated the most logical bomb-runs and had deduced the Allied IP on the nose. They had plotted the exact bomb route the group was going to have to take, and lined that flight corridor with 20-mm, 37-mm, and 88-mm cannons. The SS had taken advantage of the mountains, by positioning quad 20s and track-mounted 37-mm guns on the mountaintops along the approaches. The guns would be more effective if the aircraft were concentrated in a narrow area. The SS was ready to deploy carpets of exploding steel and the cold hands of *Tod* around the necks of the Americans.

Using their short-wavelength radar, the German radar technicians noted the large formation of planes approaching from the southwest at twelve thousand feet and fourteen thousand feet. They had learned to ignore the decoy signals that came in at various altitudes with shifting directions, recognizing them for the Window decoys. The Würzlaus radar's Doppler effect aided the radar operators in identifying their intended targets. They wanted the real thing today and were determined to get it. Targeting information was passed from the gun-laying radar system to the slaved 88-mm artillery pieces. Zeroing in their 88s, the *kanoniers* cut the fuses on the shells, using the radar-guidance information to set altitude, azimuth and direction coordinates.

Surveying the sky for the scattered clouds Weather had promised, Evans didn't see any scattering—all he could see *was* clouds. This didn't help the crews if they were heading into mountainous terrain.

"Captain, we're approaching our next turn just south of Bingen," said McCartney over the intercom.

"Roger that, navigator. Watch out for those bandits, and call out any flak, since we're in Germany now," called Evans to his gunner. He looked for his fighter escort, and felt reassured when they were at their proper altitude and location above the bomber group. Evans was as worried about bandits and flak now that he was about to make the last turn to reach the IP. Each flight would have to settle into an approach flying straight and level along the bomb-run until the target crossed below the crosshairs of the OBOE or the Norden bombsight. Either way, the bombardier had a dangerous and thankless job ahead.

274   *The Invention That Changed the World*, Robert Buderi; Touchstone Books, Simon and Schuster, copyright 1996
275   *A Radar History of World War II*, Technical and Military Imperatives, Louis Brown; Institute of Physics Publishing, copyright 1999

The location of Worms in the Rhine River valley, nestled against the edges of a mountainous area, made it the Luftwaffe's friend. Unfortunately, the mountains were to become the pilots' and crews' worst nightmare. Worms had been the target of many Allied air missions throughout the war, and the Luftwaffe had learned how to protect it on the bombing approaches. Worms had also been the site of many changes over the last two thousand years.

Before the 416th's mission to Worms and well before the rise of fascism, Worms had been the source of many religious, economic, and social transitions as well as many anti-Semitic clashes. Its history was rooted in the commerce of the Rhine River and as a location on the frontiers of the Roman Empire that allowed escape from prying eyes. Recorded as one of the first Jewish communities to be established in the Germanic regions in the fourth century, Worms became a thriving center for early Judaism. The Jewish communities prospered and helped form the local governments. Jews held office and supported the local economies. Many members of Germanic tribes converted to Judaism at this time. In spite of later Germanic nationalization, Charlemagne's unification of Europe in the eighth century, and the destructive feudal wars that followed his death, the Jewish communities continued to succeed. Christianity and Judaism prospered side by side, even with the Church's attitude that Jews were a rejected people.

It was at the turn of the first millennium that the cities of Worms and Mainz were home to Germany's yeshivas. These yeshivas developed into premier centers for Jewish study of the Talmud. Aided by the efforts and intellect of Rabbeinu Gershom ben Judah, these cities became the center of Jewish thought, even surpassing the traditional Persian centers of study. This recognition resulted in the immigration of many students, resulting in the growth of the Jewish community there.

This peaceful coexistence with the Catholic community was not to last, though. In the 11th century, the age of Christian holy pilgrimage had arrived, and Jews were mistakenly associated with Persian territories. As the Turkish Muslims swept across Asia Minor and occupied Jerusalem in 1070, Pope Urban II felt threatened from abroad, while close to home the centers of Jewish study grew in Germany and France. These fears were fed by the religious tolerance that occurred in Jerusalem once the Turks ran the supportive Fatimids. These developments conflicted with Pope Urban's desire for a papal dynasty stretching over the vast Euro-Mediterranean-Persian world with Rome as the fountainhead.

Knowing that such ambition would require great numbers of unquestioning followers, the French pope began his own personal crusade. With the help of delegates sent to the Council of Piacenza by Byzantine Emperor Alexius I, the perceived defender of the gates of Constantinople, Urban began sounding the horn of battle. Playing on the desire of many to expand commercial trade, preserve religious pilgrimage and tolerance, and guard the gates of Christendom, Urban began his whistle-stop tour during 1095. In November, in the town of Clermont, France, Urban's efforts culminated in the following speech: "O race of Franks! Race beloved and chosen by God!….A grievous report has gone forth that an accursed race, wholly alienated by God. On whom, then, rests the labor of avenging these wrongs, and of recovering this territory….Undertake this journey eagerly for the remission of your sins, and be assured of the reward of imperishable glory in the Kingdom of Heaven." That day was born the battle cry of the Crusades—*Dieu li volt* (God wills it).

Recruitment to the cause grew, as did the bloodlust fervor, as Germans, Rhine-landers, and others joined the fold. Soon a poorly led group of German and Rhineland recruits was slaughtering thousands of Jews in Worms, Mainz, and Cologne as a warm-up to the coming Middle East crusade. While time faded the memories of the horrors and truths of two hundred years of Crusades, the propensity for wholesale persecution of a displaced people for unfounded reasons did not.

Worms played a still greater role in anti-Semitism during the medieval period. As the ability to print and spread the written word grew, the ability of words to incense grew still larger. In the early sixteenth century, after surviving the inquisitional Diet of Worms, Martin Luther used the new ability to print as a vehicle to distribute anti-Semitic pamphlets after he failed to convert the German Jews to Protestantism. His intolerant and inappropriate condemnation of them resulted in violent assaults on the German Jews for centuries. All the reason that the Enlightenment and the Reformation brought did little to abate the Jewish suffering and persecution. The groundwork had been laid for continuing anti-Semitism. Despite a brief period of political revival in the mid-1800s, Jews never enjoyed complete equality with the average German. This historical disparity helped the resurrection of the same unsupportable, quasi-religious bigotries in the twentieth century, which allowed the growth of the unscientific eugenic ratio-nales that were to haunt Jews, gypsies, homosexuals, the genetically unfit, and political non-conformists. This time, however, the "fervor" was prosecuted with meticulous ruth-lessness.

Armed now with the pontifications of the eugenicists, another unifier of hate preached to the masses. From his alliance with and adulteration of the church, Hitler threatened the Jewish community of Worms, even using the pulpits of Martin Luther. After the Nazis gained power by taking the Chancellery in 1933 and enacting the 1935 Nuremberg Laws, they orchestrated *Kristallnacht* (Crystal Night). This pogrom against the Jews was promulgated by using the assassination of Ernst Vom Rath, Third Secretary of the German Embassy in Paris, by a German Jew, Herschel Gryneszpan, as an excuse. Centuries of anti-Semitism of fluctuating intensity was now coupled with the rise of eu-genics; Hitler ordered the Final Solution in 1941, which resulted in the virtual elimina-tion of the eleven hundred Jewish inhabitants of Worms by 1945.

Their eradication from Worms did not occur before the Allied air forces had flown their missions over the city. R.A.F. Bomber Command had flown a night mission on the 21st and 22nd of February, a month before the Ninth Air Force's 416th Bomb Group flew its mission. The RAF mission consisted of 288 Halifax bombers, 36 Lancast-er bombers and 25 Mosquito bombers. Exactly 10 Halifax and one Lancaster were lost. The mission was an area saturation bombing with 1,116 tons of bombs dropped, result-ing in 39 percent of Worms' developed area being destroyed. The mission laid waste to 64 percent of the town's structures, including cathedrals, museums, and most of the churches in the historic district—all of questionable military priority. In addition, most of Worms' industry was destroyed, including a factory that made sprocket wheels for

Panzers and the Cornelius Heyl A.G. and Heylesche Lederwerke GmbH facilities, which were both part of the designated military leatherworks industrial complex of Worms. The fires in these complexes raged for days. The net effect was the displacement of 35,000 people and the deaths of 239.

Eugenics teachings and philosophy had hit their high-water mark, as civilians on both sides of the issue were dying like in no war ever before. Both sides targeted civilians, in an attempt to deny the opposing military the population base needed to continue the war. War itself had become the ultimate mechanism of genetic cleansing. The Luftwaffe wasn't happy about the military loss at Worms, nor was the German High Command. But the British had paid a high price for their mission, as would anyone else who dared to target the city. The 416th was about to find this out.[276, 277, 278, 279, 280]

⚜

The cloud cover cleared some fifty miles out as the aerial armada began their turn south at Bingen, Germany. The clearing of the clouds gave the bombardiers a visual bomb-run with their Norden sights. The B-26s were just as happy, since the Oboe signal was distorted in spite of the Brits' claim that they could burn their signal through any jamming put up by "Jerry." The Brits were confident that there would be little jamming in the Worms' area since the March 2nd destruction of the Taunus Mountain jamming site.

Captain Evans' bombardier, Lieutenant McCartney, saw the cloud cover disappear, and started recalculating his position the old-fashioned way. McCartney said, "Captain, we're fiver minutes out from the IP, repeat, fiver minutes out from IP."

"Roger that, McCartney, fiver minutes to IP. You can have her then."

The *Luftschutzwarndienst* sounded the air-raid alarm at 1000 hours calling the central command area and bringing the city to life. The German civil-defense machine went to work as the *Reichsluftschutzbund* wardens began moving the citizenry into their assigned bomb shelters. Roof spotters began calling in the location, altitude and direction of the approaching bombers, which had become visible when the clouds cleared. Aware of the intended target now, the Luftwaffe alerted the *Sicherheits und Hilfdienst* mobile units for this sector. The German machinery was in motion now, as the *Amerikanische*

276   Jewish Virtual Library: Germany and The Crusader Period (1095–1291) http://www.jewishvirtuallibrary.org/jsource/vjw/germany.html

277   Wikipedia: Kristallnacht; http://en.wikipedia.org/wiki/Kristallnacht

278   Wikipedia: Worms: Judaism in Germany; http://en.wikipedia.org/wiki/Worms %2C_Germany

279   The Story of Civilization IV: The Age of Faith: A History of Medieval Civilization From Constantine to Dante-A.D. 325–1300; Will Durant; pp 585-613; Simon and Schuster; Copyright 1950

280   The Story of Civilization VI: The Reformation: A History of European Civilization From Wycliffe to Calvin 1300–1564; Will Durant; pp 337–379, 720–747; Simon and Schuster; Copyright 1950

bombenleger[281] approached their target. Worms prepared for its fate as the American air crews between eleven thousand and thirteen thousand feet fortified their resolve.

Up to this point the Luftwaffe's *Flugabwehrkanonen*[282] under SS command had been silent. The SS knew where the bombers were and more importantly where they were going to be in just a few minutes. The radar operators manning the Würzburg gun-laying radar had been tracking the bomber group, continually updating the altitude and position of the bombers to the *kanoniers*. The *kanoniers* were ready for the order to open fire when it came. They knew their rounds would find their targets, even though they could only barely see the planes through the haze.

Roland and the other navigators had given up on the Oboe system, and decided to follow orders to bomb visually, if possible. They were following McCartney's lead, with a visual run-up to the target from the IP. They were also calculating their positions in case Evans' ship was hit and went down.

Roland was worried about being in the lead. Even though he had led many times, his left eye was still infected. It kept him from tracking the flak bursts consistently at altitude, and for some reason the eye would haze over so he couldn't see as well. Navigators really needed depth perception when identifying and maneuvering the flight through a barrage of flak. Right now it didn't matter, though, as he leaned over the eyepiece of his Norden preparing to uncage his gyros. Roland was happy to stay behind the lead flight, and waited for Evans to make his turn from the IP onto the bomb-run.

Approaching the IP, Evans noted a gradual clearing of the skies. It was hazy at first, and the bombardiers could barely see down to the ground through it. As Evans made his final run up to the IP, he and McCartney were relieved to see the skies clear. The bomb-run opened up below McCartney just like the recon photos and film had shown. Roland planned his turn at the IP, and fell in behind Evans. The A-3 flight was making its starboard turn right behind him.

The other trailing flights saw the first flight turn onto the bomb-run, and prepared to execute their own turn soon. They watched as the bomb bay doors opened on all the first flight's planes after hitting the IP.

The Luftwaffe knew what the turn meant as well, and waited until the second flight completed its turn onto the bomb-run. It was better than they had hoped for: clear skies, radar guidance for half the AA *kanoniers*, and targeting information from the radar technicians for the other *kanoniers*.

The group settled into its assigned altitudes while slowing to 260 miles per hour. The slower speed made the 20- and 37-mm AA *kanoniers* positioned around the city on either side of the bomb-run very happy. They were going to make the experience painful.

Roland advised Cornell of the turn at the IP, and then leaned over the Norden bombsight as Cornell applied right rudder with some right aileron. As he did so, he

---

281   German – American bombers
282   German – Anti-aircraft cannon, 88 mm

pulled back slightly on the yoke to keep the nose up, thereby turning the speedy Invader and the rest of his flight into a ten-degree bank, as if they were a flock of geese moving onto the bomb-run. He leveled out and looked down the run, watching the other flight that was only ten seconds ahead of them. Cornell dropped the group to assigned altitude while slowing to 260 mph. Roland opened the bomb bay doors, and unpinned his gyros. The rest of the pilots in Roland's flight flipped their door switches to open.

Completing the turn onto the bomb-run, Cornell called Roland, "She's all yours."

"Roger, I've got her. Keep that PDI centered."

Roland and McCartney almost couldn't believe their eyes when they saw the number of flashes from the ground through their bombsights. "Here it comes!" they both yelled almost simultaneously to their flights.

"This is going to be heavy," Roland followed.

Nothing to do now except hold course and sweat it out.

Jack Sittarich saw the bursts of German resistance as the flak peppered another plane.

Lieutenant James Kenny and Sittarich had just completed their turn with the first flight at the IP and were heading down the bomb-run.

"My god, Creeden took a hit," Sittarich said to his pilot, just seconds before he and Lieutenant Kenny felt the starboard wing of their aircraft rise violently into the air. The blast and shockwave of the direct hit on their right engine disoriented the two men. Slamming against the fuselage of his gunner's compartment, Sittarich was dazed.

The blast had nearly severed the right wing off their plane, but had separated part of the engine and most of its nacelle instead. The fire had begun immediately. The heat was so intense that it was melting what little aluminum superstructure was keeping the plane's wing on. The steel had instantly brought Kenny's life to a quick but violent end. His body sat strapped into the pilot's seat. His hands still grasped the yoke.

Sittarich struggled to reorient himself. Out of the hatch at the right wing he could see the damage. He called for Kenny on the interphone, but heard nothing. Jack could see the plane was falling out of formation to the right. The wing wouldn't last much longer. He had to get out.

Crawling into the bomb bay that was crowded with bombs, Jack looked for the switch that would open the bomb bay doors. The flames began to lap their way into the bomb compartment. Finally he found it and flipped it. Nothing happened.

"Holy cow!" He looked again and found a switch behind the one he had just thrown. After flipping that switch, he waited to hear the hydraulics, but no such luck. Jack was not aware that his pilot had failed to flip the bomb bay door switch back to the neutral position, which would have allowed him to open the doors from inside the bay.

He crawled back to his compartment and grabbed his chute. He snapped it on to his harness, but then looked at it closely. "Oh, heck!" It was reversed; the D-ring was on the left instead of the right. He popped it off, spun it around, and then snapped it back into place. Sitting at his periscope, he resolved not to die here. "Dang it, I'm going."

He grabbed the emergency handle to open the hatch on the top of the fuselage over the gunners compartment that was used for escape. Jack watched as the hatch was ripped open by the 220-mph slipstream. Feeling the plane roll more to the right, he knew he had to hurry. If the plane started to spin before he got out, there wouldn't be any getting out. He could see the flames coming from the right engine and wing as he slid out the hatch and fell off the left side of the plane, hoping to avoid the tail structures when he fell. But he had held on to the plane just long enough that the fire had reached over the wing and burned the left side of his face.

As he fell, he thought how he had never actually jumped from a plane before, thinking and then hollering, "Helluva way to learn!" The wind hit him hard, and he tumbled head over heels through the air. He sailed away from the side of the plane, paralleling it momentarily until his airspeed fell. Catching a glimpse of the falling plane as he spun, Sittarich could see that the fire was doing its duty. In spite of all the other engine noise from the amassed planes and the flak bursts, Sittarich heard the few remaining aluminum support struts and bulkheads begin to give way on the right wing. Some seconds after he cleared the tail structures, the right wing ripped away from the fuselage, forcing the dying Invader into a spin. Sittarich's hand firmly clasped the D-ring as he completed his count to ten. He pulled the rip cord, and the chute popped open, sending its contents streaming out above him. His head snapped back, and his body stopped its tumbling. He was afraid to look up, fearing that he would see his chute on fire. That's when he realized how close to the ground he had already fallen.

The plane had been falling from the sky as soon as it was hit by the burst. By the time Sittarich had correctly snapped his chute on, opened the escape hatch and fell away from the plane, it had fallen to slightly more than two thousand feet. If he had waited any longer, he couldn't have jumped. The good thing was that he had started counting as he crawled out of the hatch, before he actually left the plane. Three or so counts were gone by the time he actually began his fall, so he ended up pulling the cord at a little more than twelve hundred feet. This actually turned out to be a blessing. So intent on shooting the planes out of the sky, the 20- and 37-mm AA *kanoniers* hadn't seen Sittarich's small body plummeting.

Jack was happy for his escape. A pilot buddy of his, Lieutenant Harry Hewes of the 669th, had been shot up pretty bad over Amiens, France, as he floated down. Word was that he had nearly had his legs shot off by the 20-mm. He had been repatriated after Paris was liberated, where he had been found in a hospital recovering.

Jack watched as the tracers flew past him, but not at him. Fortunately for Jack, by the time the gunners saw the chute, it was too difficult to redirect their fire at him. Besides, they wanted more aircraft to fall out of the sky today.

Spiraling down, the burning Invader plowed inverted nose first into the ground, as the impact detonated the bombs. With tremendous brutality the bombs destroyed what was left of the aircraft and Kenny's body. The fuel created a tremendous fireball, matched only by an equally large shockwave that shattered windows in the town that was under the bomb-run. What happened to his body didn't matter; Kenny's essence had been granted the opportunity to sit at the right side of Captain Battersby and Private Coleman in that heavenly pew.

Before hitting the ground Sittarich felt the concussion from the plane's explosion. "Dear God, where's Kenny?"

He had no more time to worry about Kenny, though, as the ground was only a second or so away. Hitting the ground rolling as he'd been taught, Jack felt the concussion of large-caliber guns firing. He looked up to see the flames and smoke from a battery of 88s in a ravine not fifty yards in front of him. They were the very guns that had killed Kenny and put him here. After getting control of the chute, Jack sat up and began to release himself from the harness. While struggling with the harness, he suddenly found himself staring at two soldiers with obvious intentions of securing him as a prisoner.

"*Stehen Sie auf, Amerikaner! Für dich ist der Krieg vorbei.*"[283]

Sittarich had no idea what they were saying, but it didn't matter. The rifles and the looks on their faces were enough to make him raise his arms in the air and hope that they didn't kill him. The soldiers roughed him up while looking for weapons, and Jack began to worry about his safety. He briefly thought about his sidearm, but realized all he had in his pockets were the arming pins and flags of the bombs. He had left his gun in the tent, thinking he would never need it. He was glad he didn't have it with him now.

The soldiers made Jack get out of the parachute harness, and then stripped him of his flight boots, flight pants and gloves—leaving him with his GI issue shoes, pants, shirt and heavy flight jacket. He knew about the Geneva Convention stuff, but who would know or care about what was happening out here?

Looking for his .45-caliber sidearm and his survival pack, the soldiers turned to Jack and made gestures of a gun with their hands. Jack finally convinced them that he didn't have a gun. All the while, the 88s in the ravine were firing. The soldiers started him on his long march to multiple prison camps, but first to a château just over the hill from the batteries. He spent the first night in a small hut with a window, and slept on the ground.

Completing the IP turn on Evans' left wing in the A-1-3 slot, Lieutenant W.B. Jokinen had been watching the lead so he could drop his bombs. He hadn't noticed the ground flashes, but did catch a glimpse of some flashes out of the corner of his right eye that seemed to come from the mountaintops. Then he felt the plane violently jump fifty feet. Regaining his composure after the blast, he looked at the instrument panel. All the instruments were giving crazy readings. The hydraulic pressure was dropping. The manifold pressure was declining, and the precious engine rpms were plummeting. "Creeden, you OK? You there?"

"Yessir, I seem to be in one piece. You OK?" asked his gunner.

---

283   German – Get up, American! For you the war is over.

"I'm fine, but this plane isn't. We're losing altitude and the engines are barely holding their own. What do you see from up there?"

"It looks pretty bad. No fire, but both engines are smoking. We have fuel and hydraulic fluid draining from both wings." Creeden looked around at both engines and realized neither was running properly. The smoke poured out. The wings were badly shredded, and holes pocked the flight surfaces. That wasn't the worst of it, though. Fuel mixed with the red hydraulic oil was pouring from what seemed like every hole in the wings and running off the trailing edge of the wings. "Looks bad. What do you think?"

Jokinen didn't need to think too hard. The fuel gauges were dropping, and the precious hydraulic pressure was falling just as fast. There was very little manifold pressure, and they were dropping altitude. He knew it was only a matter of time, and they didn't have much of it. The plane fell in an easterly direction, while he tried to turn west. He was heading away from the bomb line, and deeper into the German countryside.

"Boat deck lead, boat deck lead, this is two…three…seven…D…dog, dropping out of formation. I'm making a run for the bomb line, over and out," Jokinen radioed. But he never made the near-180-degree turn to head west. He struggled to keep the mass of the Invader in the air.

Still flying east and deeper into Germany, Jokinen's Invader kept losing altitude faster than he could cover countryside below them. Jokinen knew they weren't going to make it to Allied territory at this rate of descent. "Creeden, I think you should jump before we run out of altitude. I can't keep her in the air much longer!"

"What are you going to do?"

He thought before answering, "I'm dumping the bomb load now. I'm going to stay with it!"

"Then I'm with you!"

There was a brief silence from the other end of the intercom. "Hold on, then, I can't promise anything." The voice was sober and focused.

The odds were against a successful landing in the mountains under the best of conditions, but with no flaps, hydraulics, and no engines there weren't any odds. Jokinen doubted his decision—not for his own life, but for Creeden's, for whom he was flying more than ever before. Looking for someplace to crash-land or just crash, Jokinen kept hoping he could make it over the Rhine to American-held territory. He threw the switch to open the bay doors, and salvoed the bombs. Feeling the bombs rippling out of the bay, Jokinen didn't care where they fell. They exploded on the outskirts of Lohr am Main, destroying three homes and killing five townspeople, two of whom were children. Another child was orphaned. For the casualties, their prayers for protection were answered on their arrival into the loving hands of God on the other side.

The plane responded briefly to the lightened load, but Jokinen knew it was not for long. It was becoming more like a flying death trap every second.

"Oh, damn it! Did you see that! Jokinen and Creeden bought the farm! They blew up!" hollered Earl Hayter as he refocused his attention on the flak field in front of him.

"Damn right, I did! Poor bastards!" said Ralph Hoffman, Earl's gunner.

Others in the formation shook their heads in guilty pity, feeling sorry for those guys but still glad it hadn't been them.

The blast was actually the detonation of the jettisoned bombs dropping from such a low altitude and exploding only seconds behind Jokinen's plane, making it appear as if they had augered in.

Jokinen had lost a lot of altitude flying the severely damaged A-26 through the mountainous valleys on a due-east course. It was getting harder and harder to keep the wounded bird in the air. Looking at his instrument panel with every gauge reading zero or damn near it, he realized there were only a couple of options. "Creeden."

"Yeah, Lieutenant."

"I can't keep this thing in the air much longer. We either need to jump, or I can try to land this thing. We need to do one or the other quick, cause we're gunna crash."

"Hell, I can see the birds in the trees from here, how we gunna jump?"

"That settles it then. Hold on. I'll try to find us a spot to set her down!" Wrestling the plane over the next ridge top—and not twenty feet over the trees—he spotted a clearing on the downhill slope. Pulling back on the throttles while raising the nose of the plane, he bled off energy so that the plane slowed down. This maneuver allowed Jokinen time to quickly estimate his approach. Then he threw the flaps lever to full, but no flaps came down, as he expected. With a belly landing, he didn't want the wheels down. Trees flashed past below them. He was on the meadow clearing in an instant. At this point, he cut and feathered his engines while pulling back on the yoke to flare the nose, which created drag to help slow the approach. He didn't want the plane to stall, but to fly into the ground instead, letting the tail contact the ground first. "Say your prayers, Creeden, here we go!"

"Put her down!"

The Invader's tail struck the ground and acted as a plow, opening up the soft soil of the German homeland. Even though this was rapidly reducing the plane's speed, it was also destroying the pilot's ability to control the plane's attitude. Jokinen held the yoke back, trying to keep the nose up to allow the plane to settle onto the ground. He cut the fuel flow and the magnetos. The plane began falling forward, and the propellers cut into the ground, causing the plane to slow rapidly and jerking the fuselage down. When Jokinen felt the props hit, he knew his role in this controlled crash was over. "Dear God, hold on, Creeden."

Creeden said his blessing out loud so Jokinen could hear: "Our Father who art..."

The props were digging their trenches as the rear of the engine nacelles impacted. The speed degraded quickly as the ground absorbed the energy of the moving body. With the wings still level the nose fell straight down, striking the ground and causing the bomb bay doors to crush inward. Jokinen and Creeden foolishly tried to resist the tremendous shock of the impact and were jolted. Skidding forward toward the opposite tree line of the clearing, Jokinen sat watching the tree trunks grow larger and larger, and realized that he was heading straight toward one of the sturdy, pilot-killing trunks.

Wrapped in his flak jacket, Creeden grimaced and wedged himself tighter inside the gun turret. He hadn't seen the wall of ancient trees.

The trees became huge, and Jokinen threw his arms up in front of his face and ducked to the right, waiting for the impact that he imagined would kill him. He prayed: "…for thine is the kingdom, and the power, and the glory, forever. Amen." He ended at the exact moment the plane stopped. Restrained by his seat harness, he was spared injury. Out the cockpit window he saw the three-foot-diameter tree trunk just several feet in front of the nose of the plane. "Thank you, God. Now let's go. Get the hell out of here, Creeden!"

"I'm right behind you, let's get," Creeden replied, starting to his escape hatch, only to find it wedged closed. The airframe had bucketed so badly that the only exit was through the cockpit. He crawled through the bomb bay and followed Jokinen out.

Running to the edge of the woods, they took cover behind a large tree and waited for the inevitable concussion of the plane exploding. After several minutes things seemed OK. Carefully they stuck their heads around either side of the tree to confirm it.

The plane had stopped short of the tree because of a ridge running along the downhill side of the meadow. Jokinen looked at the plane and then along the crash line. "Damn, would you look at that." He realized he'd made a near-perfect downhill belly landing. He stood up and walked toward the plane, and then fell back down on the small ridge that had saved his life. Putting down is exactly what Jokinen had done—sixty miles due east of Worms, unfortunately well inside German territory.

"Good job, damn good job. I'll fly with you any time, sir. Hell of a landing, but whatta we do now?"

Jokinen gathered his senses and realized they were far from being out of trouble. "Well, let's salvage what we can and then destroy the ship with our grenade. The front lines should be," looking around briefly to get his bearings, "thatta way." He turned and then pointed west.

Stripping off their flak jackets, they went to work. Jokinen pulled the pin from their only grenade and tossed it into the cockpit. They dove for cover and waited for the explosion. After several seconds nothing had happened.

"Oh, hell, can it get any worse? The darned grenade was a dud. What a screwed-up day," Jokinen lamented.

Indeed, it could get worse and did. Germen patrols who had also witnessed the crash landing were hurrying to the site. With the two crewmen working around the plane, they had been able to sneak up unnoticed on their soon-to-be prisoners. They surrounded both men and started the process of making Jokinen and Creeden prisoners of war.

"Achtung! Nicht bewegen. Hände hoch! Ihr seid jetzt Gefangene vom Dritten Reich und der Wehrmacht. Nicht bewegen!"[284] shouted the *unterfeldwebel*. Both Jokinen and Creeden were hit in the back of the head with the butts of German field rifles, and fell to the ground.

"Bergen diese Maschinengewehre und alle Munitionen!"[285] barked the *unterfeldwebel* to the *obergefreiter*,[286] who promptly turned to his *soldaten* and passed the order downhill.

The crews in the A-2 flight were watching as the first salvo of German anti-aircraft fire had decimated the first flight. Witnessing the systematic destruction of the first flight was bad enough, but knowing they were going to have to fly into it was unnerving even to the most seasoned of the pilots and crews. Cornell continued his flight forward unwaveringly, and the crews braced for the worst. Cornell could see the fires burning and smoke billowing from the target area inside Worms. It looked like the boys from the 387th had done OK. Now it was their turn.

Everyone had watched, except Roland, who was hunched over the Norden bombsight and concentrating on the target-approach landmarks. Roland was struggling to just stay on the Norden's eyesight as the Invader was knocked around the sky by the repeated bursts of flak.

"Damnit, Cornell, can't you watch out for that flak? Tell those sons of bitches down there to stop shooting at us," said Roland in anger to Cornell.

"I'll get Hitler on the radio right now for you."

"Well, get on with it then," Roland retorted almost seriously.

Having unpinned the gyros from the Norden, Roland became more angry when another flak burst knocked them out of synch, forcing him to repin them. As the flak bursts continued to rock the ship, Roland reoriented himself and then unpinned the gyros, beginning the process of killing the rate again.

Sitting in the gunner's compartment, Ashton Carter had listened to the officers' banter, but did not respond. He tightened his flak jacket and scanned the sky around him through his periscope, noting the intense and accurate flak around them. His thoughts drifted to his time with the Ninetieth Bomb Squadron in the Pacific war, before they had transferred him back to the states to be an instructor in Lincoln, Nebraska. Pulling away from the periscope's oculars, Carter glanced over to the photo of his wife and his new baby, Cheryl, whom he had never touched and only seen in photos. He remembered the evening in February when Cheryl's life was conceived, his reassignment to the 416th Bomb Group's 669th Squadron in August '44, and her October delivery. He was ready for this mission and tour to end. He had resolved to not do a third tour. It was time for others to take the fight to the enemy.

---

284   German – Attention! Do not move. Hands up! You are now prisoners of the Third Reich and the German army. Do not move!

285   German – Salvage those machine guns and all the ammunition !

286   German – corporal

Cornell saw, felt, and heard the flak exploding around his plane; the continuous ping of metal on metal constantly reminded him of the intensity of this barrage. The smell of the powder was now filling the air inside the aircraft, mixing with the ever-present odor of sweat, oil, aviation fuel, and fear. He never remembered anything quite like it. The Germans were very angry, he could tell, and they were sending their anger via 88s. This was one hell of a milk run.

The 20-mm rounds would pass with great thuds through the thin skin of the airplanes but unless they hit something vital the plane could absorb the punishment. For those planes that made it back, the ground crew would be impressed by the amount of punishment these new Invaders could absorb.

"Flak burst nine o'clock," Raccio announced over the intercom.

Lieutenant Wes Chitty and Staff Sergeant. Raccio knew it was a bad hit, as the plane, reacting violently, began to fall out of formation. They both felt the plane shudder in midair and then settle back down.

Chitty had no time to answer; his left engine was out of commission, and he instinctively increased the manifold pressure in the good engine while feathering the left. After regaining control, Wes pulled the Invader back up into formation; the right engine was able to keep the airspeed at 260 miles per hour.

Trying to complete the feathering procedures, Wes looked up only to see a blinding orange and black flak burst shower the front of his aircraft with shrapnel. The nose guns and magazines of *For Pete's Sake* absorbed the brunt of the metallic assault, but several large pieces of shrapnel had impacted the windshield and canopy. The metal had powdered the glass of the windshield, spraying Chitty. He had instinctively ducked when the shell exploded, preventing any facial injury. The cold air rushed into the already-cold cockpit through three gaping holes in the windshield.

The bad news kept coming, as the left engine wouldn't feather, causing the propeller to windmill on the engine. This not only slowed the plane, but risked a fire, or the engine seizing, or the propeller burning up the bearings and breaking off from the crankshaft. The propeller could go anywhere after that. Pressing on down the final minutes of the run, Chitty wrestled to keep the plane under control as he set the left prop control at full decease rpm to cut down drag and hoped to slow the windmilling prop.

Turning onto the run, Lieutenant Carl Weinert witnessed Chitty and Raccio take the two flak bursts. For the first time, he began to understand the true meaning of "sweating bullets." He was glad, because, for whatever twist of fate, he was in the A-2-5 slot instead of his usual slot, where Chitty was flying.

The *Flugabwehrkanone* were unrelenting as the A-Box continued on its run. Lieutenant McCartney in A-1-1 was glued to the bombsight as he traced the target path below, and matched it up with the briefing landmarks. As the ground in his sight slid by, he started seeing the fires and smoke from the first hits dropped by the Marauders. He was close now, but he still had no idea how few planes were left in his flight to bomb the target.

As they flew down the run, McCartney kept wiping sweat from his face, while the flak kept pouring up at them. Evans made no evasive maneuvers, flying only straight and level into the blackening cauldron of death. The clock was ticking, just not fast enough for anyone.

Seeing the drop sight come into view and then slide under the center of his sight's crosshairs, McCartney sounded off, "Bombs away!" He then counted the green lights as the eggs fell from the nest. When the last set of lights went green, he hollered to Evans, "Let's get the hell out of here!"

But another 88 exploded nearby, jarring the Invader and knocking McCartney against the glass nose of the bombardier's compartment. Another salvo of 88s detonated around the remains of the formation.

The rest of the flight needed no encouragement to pickle off their eggs, waiting for the all-clear to close the bomb bay doors, and then they followed Evans into a steep left-hand dive. Evans was high-tailing it for the cloud cover, pushing up the throttles even more than usual. The others were happy to follow, finally diving into some cloud cover. They knew it was only a temporary respite from their adversary.

The A-2 flight was next. Cornell waited as the black, menacing flak continued to bounce them around the sky. Enman was watching the bomb-run passing below his sight's crosshairs. The release point came into his field of view, and he started his countdown. "Three, two, one...bombs away," was heard throughout the interphone.

Bombs were unshackled in all of that flight's Invaders. All the planes shuddered slightly as the thousand-pounders slipped one after another out of their racks. Cornell almost couldn't wait for the bombs to finish falling from the plane.

"All clear," said his gunner.

"Roger, making the turn—"

Cornell was cut off by a direct hit from an 88 that had exploded inside the open bomb bay. The detonation pulverized the vital organs of the Invader; every vital piece of equipment took a hit. Both engines began failing, as aviation fuel, oil, and hydraulic fluid flowed from every opening. Any chance for communication between the crewmen and other planes was lost; the hungry steel had ripped through the radio and communication system. Cornell's left leg felt the barrage, and his blood immediately started running on to the floor of the cockpit after a piece of shrapnel passed through it. Cornell pushed through his pain. Struggling to make sense of his readings on the instrument panel, he soon realized there was no sense to be made.

Roland made his way into the cockpit, "Cornell, you OK?"

"Heck yeah, but I've taken a hit in my left leg. It doesn't look too bad."

"Can you fly?"

"I think so. Give me a heading."

Roland backed his way into the navigator's position in the nose and looked at the chart and compass. They were heading at forty degrees, almost due east into Germany. Roland tried the intercom again, and then made his way back to the cockpit.

Cornell heard the left engine over-revving. The prop governor had gone out, and the oil pressure was dropping to zero in that engine. He quickly feathered the engine, fighting all the time to keep the plane in the air as they dropped farther out of formation.

Roland returned and informed Cornell of the heading. "We have to turn to a heading of 2-7-0 degrees to get out of here!"

Cornell checked his magnetic compass to confirm Roland's readings. It showed a heading of 250 as he continued his turn to 270 degrees due west.

Roland looked at it and agreed. "Let's stay on that heading. My equipment is shot up pretty bad down there." Roland returned to his glassed-nosed haven, and waited for something good to happen.

Cornell had not heard from his gunner, Carter, and tried several times to raise him on the intercom. He finally realized that it must be out.

With all the damage, the A-26 had fallen into dangerous airspace.

The smaller-caliber AA gunners were zeroing in on this lone bomber limping along at five thousand feet and still falling fast. The first round of 37-mm fire to reach the ship ripped through the starboard wing and engine. As it passed through the wing, it severed the primary fuel line to the engine and then destroyed several cylinders on the outboard side of the Pratt and Whitney radial. The burning phosphorous from the tracer immediately ignited the high-octane fuel pouring from the open fuel line. The *kanoniers* continued to hammer away at the lone plane, wanting the kill.

The plane started to nose over—the beginning of its death spiral to the ground. Cornell saw the left engine feathered and smoking. Glancing to the right, he was shocked to see the starboard engine burning. Smoke was filling the cockpit. He tried all the control surfaces, anything to get control of the plane. The airspeed bled off, and he knew what was to follow. The plane continued falling, and he realized then and there that there was no recovery from this disaster. The fire was worsening in the starboard engine nacelle. Without a fire-extinguishing system, there was no controlling the fiery death raging inside the nacelle. He knew it was time to go. How could he tell the crew?

"Bail out, repeat, bail out, abandon ship!" He repeated it three times into the intercom with no response. He reached to the emergency panel and flipped on the alarm, when he heard Roland's escape hatch open. *Thank God, someone heard it,* he thought.

But only two people heard it; the alarm was unnecessary for Carter. The blast of the 88 had sent a massive fusillade into his compartment, mercifully and instantaneously releasing his essence onto a different flight path with a decidedly different destination.

Cornell reached up and pushed the emergency escape hatch. The airstream ripped it away and it sailed past the gunner's turret and bounced off the rudder. Red lights came on in the nose and gunner compartments indicating the escape hatch had been opened. With great pain in his left leg, Cornell dragged himself out of his seat to the hatch. Pushing and pulling up out of the cockpit, he fell out over the right wing, and safely cleared the tail structures. As he pulled the rip cord and saw the chute open, Cornell thanked his God and stared in amazement. Just as he fell free of the fuselage, the wing tore off. The fire had finally melted the starboard wing supports. The plane continued its plummet and passed through three thousand feet.

Having released his escape hatch, Roland shed his flak jacket and secured his chute. As he tried to crawl out of the burning Invader, he uncontrollably thought of Marguerite and his family, and wondered how it had come to this. This wasn't supposed to happen to him; he was going home to a party to see his family again. Among these thoughts were prayers to his Savior. He reached the edge of the open hatch and hesitated as he considered how to fall through so as not to become a victim of the propellers. But this hesitation was a hesitation too long.

While Roland calculated his escape, a barrage of 20- and 37-mm shells in unison hit the nose and fuselage of the plane. They ripped the thin aluminum shell to pieces. The 37-mm rounds pulverized the glass and shell of the bombardier compartment. Roland's body suffered the same fate, and his spirit joined his crewmate on their journey over, no longer having to worry about the propellers, his family, or Marguerite. The plane increased its rate of spin as it fell into the pulling arms of mother earth.

The jerk of the parachute when it had opened had given Cornell an overwhelming sense of security and thankfulness. "Oh, God, thank you," he declared, while watching his plane spiral down. He hollered and prayed for the other guys to jump. "Bail out….Jump….Dear God, jump!" He was quickly brought back to his own reality as tracers zipped past him.

"You damn Krauts," he screamed. He reached for his sidearm as if he were going to shoot at them. Looking down, he could make out the *kanoniers* who were shooting at him. His prayers changed—he asked to fall faster amid requests for the *kanoniers* to miss. They did miss, but when he hit the ground, pain shot through his body; he did still have a leg wound. He couldn't run, which really didn't matter. By the time he got out of the parachute harness, he was surrounded by soldiers who took him prisoner. They actually rescued him from a mob of angry civilians, who had arrived just before the five soldiers.

Everyone in A-2 flight witnessed Cornell's plane take the hit and drop like a stone from formation. They all also realized they wanted out of here. Lieutenant Earl Hayter flying A-2-4 called the flight on the radio and informed them he was moving up to the lead and for everyone to follow. Kicking up the throttles, Earl eased back on the yoke, pulling the Invader's nose up, so he could move up into the lead spot. As Earl was moving up, a well-fused salvo of 88 fire was just reaching their altitude. The air erupted with black, orange-centered bursts all around the flight.

Now in the lead slot, Earl wasted no more time, and banked hard to port and then dove out of the killing space called the bomb-run. He was happy to be turning off the run and gaining speed in the dive. At three hundred miles per hour, he leveled off at eight thousand feet and headed for the cover of the clouds. He hadn't had time to look around to see if the flak had done its duty, and he wouldn't until he found some safer airspace. The remaining pilots in the flight followed Earl's lead, except Lieutenant Chitty.

Earl called the flight for a heading to the RP, and received a heading from every remaining pilot and navigator in the flight almost immediately. "OK, I got it," he responded. Turning onto that heading, he pulled the nose up and climbed to the assigned altitude, while he looked for flares from the lead ships to zero in on.

Meanwhile, Chitty had made a hard banking right-hand turn once he had dropped his bombs. He powered up the one engine and then pulled back hard to the left or right, evading the menacing tracers laced with death. He knew with one engine he would not be able to maneuver with the rest of the squadron. Turning off target with the nose down to gain speed, Chitty headed back toward the Rhine River bomb line on his own. He was holding his pipe tightly between his teeth and making promises he would keep if the good Lord got him out of here alive. He dove through the merciless anti-aircraft fire and listened as rounds intermittently penetrated the wing or fuselage.

He and his gunner were deliriously happy when they hit some cloud cover to hide in. They stayed in it as long as they could. Turning for the rendezvous point while still in the protective covering of the clouds, Chitty hoped to find some friends there before the fighters or the flak found him. Struggling to keep the A-26 heading toward the RP, Chitty noted that his fuel flow was down in the left engine. Taking a chance, he switched the full booster on to the fuel pump that supplied the intake manifold. The engine sputtered and then fired off with about ten pounds of precious manifold pressure.

At least the damned prop is spinning, giving us some extra speed and lift, Chitty thought. Any performance from that engine was better than nothing. The German border was his next goal now.

Taking a Pounding

Worms, Germany, March 18, 1945
Railyard and surrounding community taking hits from 416th
and combined units from the Ninth Air Force. The Germans
got their licks in also, as this was a costly mission for the 416th.
Reproduced with permission of Heinz Leiwig

The Aftermath

Bomb damage photos of Worms, Germany, marshaling yard
after March 18, 1945, mission.
The aerial bombardment was very successful, and was followed
three days later, on March 21, 1945, with Patton's Third Army
crossing over the Rhine River at Worms. Patton's Third Army
quickly pressed the attack on into Germany.
Reproduced with permission of Heinz Leiwig

The B-1 flight had entered the bomb-run as the first flight in A-Box was turning off target, and were now coming up on the drop zone. They had seen 18 planes go in ahead of them, and only fourteen come out. Fear was battling resolve in the hearts of every crew member in every ship. An all-consuming fear was kept at bay with the painful reality of their losses on this mission and the desire to avenge them.

The Wehrmacht's day wasn't free of casualties either. The people of Worms suffered painful losses as well. The A-Box bombs had not fallen on Worms without accomplishing a good part of their mission, and even accomplished a little more. The first salvo had fallen on the area of the map referred to as the communications center, which was one of the primary targets. Between the 387th's hits and now the 416th's, the target was nearly destroyed, leaving it useless for the rest of the war.

The bombs continued to fall from the other flights in A-Box as well. High explosives landed on a railyard that had been heavily defended by 88s. The *kanoniers* and *soldaten* were cut down in the prime of their earthly experience. They were scattered about like tin soldiers, being ripped apart just as easily by the blasts. Two 88 batteries were shattered into unusable piles of metal and their *kanoniers* suffered the same fate. The flying steel from the blasts showered more deadly shrapnel for the killing fields all around. The secondary detonations of the 88s' ammunition helped destroy the target to a lesser degree. The remainder of the mindless projectiles landed beyond the railyard, destroying a road junction the Wehrmacht was using to keep the artillery crews supplied with ammo. The loss of the junction meant ammunition had to be rerouted, with a considerable loss of time. This interruption of ammo and the loss of several guns did not stop the continued darkening of the sky with *Deutscher Pulver und Stahl*[287] from the *Flugabwehrkanonen*.

Captain Anderson leading B-Box waited for his bombardier, Lieutenant Babbage, to complete his obligation to the crew, the flight and the group. Anderson had seen the green light on his panel come on when the doors had opened. All he could do from then on was keep the PDI needle in the middle and wait for Babbage's words to bomb, which the whole flight was waiting to hear. Four minutes were stretching into an hour, as German death was exploding all around them, delivered via high-velocity flak shells.

"Bombs away," came in over his headset. He felt the bombs ripple out through his controls, and was pretty sure he counted them all clear.

"All gone, sir, good drop," filled Anderson's headset.

The planes were still bouncing as the flak exploded around them. The clouds were no protection from the radar-directed 88s.

In only a few minutes B-Box was forming up with the lead box. Approaching from behind and below, the B-Box crews could see that A-Box had faired as poorly as they had. Everyone in B-Box was counting the planes missing from the formation.

---

287   German – German powder and steel

"Hell of a mission. What was so important back there it was worth all this?"

The SS, Wehrmacht and Luftwaffe knew why it was important. It was the defense of their *geliebtes Deutschland*, which every day became harder and harder to accomplish.[288] They knew the relentless and deadly assaults form the air and ground on their Wehrmacht, Luftwaffe, and infrastructure were a long, slow death march of attrition upon their war machine. *Lebensraum* had failed.[289] Even with *Lebensborn*,[290] which was designed for the *Eindeutschung*[291] of the occupied territories, the country could not continue these losses. Hitler had staked a lot on the success of such plans as *Lebensborn*.

The *Lebensborn* Project relied heavily on the strength of the eugenics movement from the 1920s. The project was operated by a division of the SS designed by Heinrich Himmler himself—the *Rasse und Siedlungshauptamt*.[292] The program had sought out children and people of reproductive age from Germany and its occupied territories whose physical traits conformed to the ideal Aryan appearance—blond hair and blue eyes. The women who met the selection criteria were impregnated by the ideal Aryan male; the newborn was taken from her at birth. The abducted children and newborns were placed in *Lebensborn Zentrums* and raised and educated in the Aryan way, even if this required physical abuse to the children by the SS overseers to succeed. This nightmarish project had started back in 1935, and was thought to have contributed to other atrocities. Supposedly, in 1942 a special SS unit killed every male in the Czech village of Lidice in reprisal for the successful assassination of SS Governor Heydrich in Prague by the Czech underground. From the same town the unit allegedly abducted ninety-one children who met the ideal Aryan genetics. The rest of the children were sent to *Ausrotten Zentrums*.[293]

Continuing on their evasive flight back to base, Captain Evans saw multiple P-38 and P-47 fighters appearing around them twenty miles out from the RP. Taking a deep breath, he made a headcount of who was left, and faced the fact that it had been a costly day.

Earl looked around and saw that Carl's plane was not in the flight any more. He just shook his head and said, "It's always the new guys buying the farm."

The airwaves were silent, since no one had cared to tune in the Armed Services Radio on this trip back. Contemplating their situation instead, everyone was grateful to be still among the living. Friends mourned the loss of friends, giving short blessings on

---

288   German – beloved Germany
289   German – Literally, living space. The word signified Hitler's plan to expand Germany's borders into the Rhineland, Sudetenland, Ukraine, and the Caucasus in order to feed and grow the ever-enlarging Germanic population and war machine.
290   The German SS's program to breed and raise children in the Aryan way. The Lebensborn were the first generation of the population that was to cleanse the European continent of "lesser races."
291   German – Germanization
292   German – Race and Settlement Head Office
293   German – extermination centers

their behalf. Occasionally the pilots would check on their gunner, but on the whole it was a somber flight home.

Flying into the changing weather patterns of partially clearing sky, the crews could feel the intensity of the mission lifting from them for every mile farther away from Worms they flew. When the crews finally came up on the RP, they could see the fighter escort form up about two thousand feet above. Somehow the crews couldn't get as excited about seeing their little friends circling up above. Then they heard in their headsets over the combat frequency, "Bandit, nine o'clock low, coming out of the clouds." That quickly changed their appreciation for the fighters.

Snapping his head left and looking down through scattered clouds below his wing, Earl spied a twin-engine aircraft approaching with a very familiar shape. Relieved it wasn't an enemy fighter, he radioed, "Hold on, it looks like one of ours."

Indeed, it was. Lieutenant Chitty spoke up. "Boat deck...pallmall...sleepy... sleepy....Repeat, pallmall...sleepy...sleepy. Don't shoot, it's me."

"Roger, join up in the low box, over," ordered Evans happily. "Good to see ya again."

"Oh, not nearly as good as seeing you guys, over and out," Chitty echoed.

Climbing on one and a half engines to the group's altitude, Chitty slid into position beside Lieutenant Sorrels at the end of the second box. He felt an odd sense of relief in being back with his buddies, which conflicted with his anxiety over the thought of future missions needed to hit the golden number sixty-five.

The west side of the imaginary line that separated France and Germany gave relative safety and was a welcome navigational sight. As they crossed that imaginary bomb line while they went west out of the teeth of the Wehrmacht and Luftwaffe war machine, the pilots, navigators and gunners all began to feel the perspiration that had soaked their clothes in spite of the cold. On one side they could bomb at will and take flak until they ceased to exist; on the other they were unlikely to encounter any resistance. The skies opened ahead of them, helping a little more pressure slip away from their bodies. Those with stable, flyable aircraft felt the best. Those pilots and crews still flying in damaged aircraft were not as confident of their "happy landing" yet. The wounded waited. They would land first.

"Boat deck control, boat deck control, this is boat deck one, do you read, over?" Evans broadcasted out into the static-filled air on the prearranged channel. Amid the same static a voice came back, "Roger, boat deck one, this is boat deck control, over."

"Boat deck one on return route with three damaged ships and wounded, over."

"Roger, will have fire and rescue crews available. Land all injured personnel first, over."

Having heard the responses, Wes Chitty settled in for the final miles home to Laon, only to be startled back to apprehension by his gunner's call, "Lieutenant, we got smoke coming in back here!"

"See if you can find it and put it out!"

"Yessir!" Raccio learned that the smoke was coming from the burning bomb bay fuel tank. The gas was burning through the holes that had been punched in it by the flak and ignited by the flak as well.

Chitty's theory had proven true. He had always saved his bomb bay auxiliary tank until last, fearing that if he drained it near empty early in the mission and left only fumes, it could explode if it were hit by a hot round or tracer. So many of his fellow pilots would burn the auxiliary dry first, leaving a vapor-filled bomb in the plane. Today, Wes's choice had been the right one. The fuel had ignited but not exploded, and was just burning off as it came out of the full tank.

"Can you put it out?" Chitty relayed.

"I'm damn sure gunna try!"

"The last thing we need is a fire! Get up here and get this extinguisher!"

Raccio made his way to the cockpit as Chitty relayed his problem to Evans.

"You follow Downing in," said Evans, "and get out of that that plane quick when you stop. Bail out if you have to. Do you copy?"

"Roger, boat deck one, I'll follow second, over and out."

Pulling in behind Downing as he turned on final, Chitty watched his approach speeds and kept his landing distance from Downing.

Meanwhile, Raccio was fighting the fire back into the bomb bay with the hand-held fire extinguisher. He was unable to quench it, even after emptying the contents onto the burning tank.

"I can't get it out!"

"How are the straps holding?"

"They're burning but look OK."

"Get up here, we're going in anyway!"

Raccio made his way to the cockpit, as he sent a little prayer upward.

Wes found himself promising God so many things if He would just get him through this mission. He thought about all the other times he'd said this same prayer with all the same promises. Wes pulled deeply on the last pipe he had for the mission, hoping it wouldn't be his last time.

Turning on final, Chitty set his glide path and touched down. Taxiing off the runway and onto the grass as soon as he was slow enough, he hit the brakes, cut the engine's fuel and magnetos, and instinctively pulled the emergency brake. The fire crews were racing up as Chitty flipped the switch to open the bomb bay doors, allowing access to the burning tank. "Get the hell out of here, Raccio!"

Raccio popped the escape and crawled out followed by Chitty. They had wasted no time getting themselves out. They had no interest in sitting in a burning plane any longer than they had to.

Smoke and steam billowed out as the crews hosed down the tank.

The group began its final approach to their home called Laon. Evans started his traditional and well-disciplined pattern around the base to allow the planes to peel off one by one and land. Evans touched down with no problems. The other planes followed.

Wes watched the returning Invaders land, with three at a time on the runway—one pulling off at the end, one in the middle and one landing. It was a beautiful sight.

Later, as Chitty and Raccio were leaving the debriefing hut, they saw the flight surgeon. They gratefully accepted his offer. Drinking down the Methuselah, they hoped they got half a chance to live as long as the liquor's namesake. Thanking the surgeon, Chitty walked toward the resting spot of *For Pete's Sake*, and watched the fire crews wrap up their duties. The fire was out.

Walking up to the plane, Wes looked into the bomb bay, where the fire from the fuel had burned off three of the four asbestos straps holding the tank in place. Shaking his head back and forth in disbelief, he comprehended just how lucky he and Raccio had been today. He reached for a pipe in his chest pocket, but found the pipe empty. He slid it between his teeth anyway.

A ground crewman said, "This one's done, Lieutenant. Airframe is shot up too bad and the fire burned up most of the bomb bay circuitry. She's headin' to the boneyard."

Wes shook his head and thought about how many missions *For Pete's Sake* had brought him home from. He wondered what or who would go next.

The airfield and hardstands seemed unusually empty as the ground crews set to work repairing every ship. Not one had come home without some damage.

"So many losses in one day," said Roland Dullnig in his thick Texas drawl. He was walking down the line supervising his crew's activities. Not one aircraft didn't need repairing. The aluminum-sheet-metal crews were going to be exceptionally busy today and tonight. The boneyard was going to get fat after this one.

The mission debriefing wasn't quick for any of the air crews, since Operations wanted all the details about the mission from takeoff to landing. Lots of questions went back and forth over the same details until all the crews had provided G-2 and Operations with a clear and detailed picture of the entire mission. It was one for the books, and one that no one wanted to repeat ever again.

It was then that the men around the base heard the sound of a twin-engine plane approaching. There was no flare, so the base personnel watched the approach and waited for the air-raid siren that never came. Instead, the tower crew fired a green flare, which put the base at ease. Everyone watched as the now recognizable Invader turned in on approach, and followed it up with a nice three-point touchdown. Taxiing to a hardstand, the pilot followed the traditional shutdown protocol. The hatch popped open. Carl Weinert's head came through slowly, while his ground crew ran up. The same ground crewman who had patted him on the head three times hollered, "See, sir, it works every time." Helping him out, they found him soaking in sweat. He climbed down the ladder quickly and was picked up by the debriefing crew.

Seeing Earl and Hoffman walking out after their debriefing, Carl jumped out of the debriefing truck and trotted over to them. "What a mission, huh?"

"What happened to you?" asked Earl.

Carl looked for a place to start. It was all so real and intense that he wasn't sure what was important and what wasn't. "Well, we had just dropped on the target and I followed Earl's lead after…after…I saw Roland's plane take a hit…and go down. We all dove off the target and I put the nose down hard to really get some speed. Earl led us into some cloud cover. I got separated from the group somehow. I was afraid I was going to collide with someone so I put the nose down a little more and turned out of formation. It gets a little hazy from here. I was flying instruments, and the artificial horizon started to tumble or somethin'. I think the airspeed was frozen. I could tell I was in a hard dive and losin' altitude fast. I remember pulling back on the stick real hard. I put my feet on the instrument panel and wrapped my arms around the wheel, and pulled and pushed as hard as I could to get out of that dive. I remember some green grass and I blacked out…"

He paused to catch his breath.

"Things kinda started coming back to me when I woke up—back in those damn clouds of all places. I called for my gunner who said I'd pulled out so hard I ripped the bomb bay doors open and he had lost his flak helmet when it flew out the bay. I flipped the switch to close 'em, and told him to come up to the cockpit with me. I remember getting a heading somehow and turned on to it and flew for a while. I was pretty much with it by then. I popped out of some cloud cover and headed west around five thousand. I thought I was past the bomb line by then, but that's when all hell broke loose! There were tracers everywhere. Heck, I thought I was in friendly territory by then. I slid open my window, and shot the day's colors out with my flare pistol. Golly, that was a hell of mistake. That damned triple-A fire doubled up on me. I pushed up the manifold pressure and got the hell out of there. I actually put the nose down for speed, and then I climbed up out of that valley. After I rolled over the valley edge, the shooting stopped. That's when I got back on my heading. I flew for a while and finally picked up a friendly. It was a P-38 with a shot-up port engine. He flew with me a while, and then took off for his own base, I guess. I headed on to base and here I am."

"Damn, you're one lucky stiff," said Earl with a chuckle, as Hoffman shook his head and smiled in agreement.

After Carl finished his debriefing, he walked back to his plane to talk with his crew chief. He found Dullnig and Bailey underneath his plane looking at the superstructure inside the bomb bay.

"Everything OK, Sergeant?"

"Hell, no, sir! Everything ain't OK! What the hell did you do up there today? I don't think this one will ever fly again. Do you know how many of my planes we lost today, sir?"

Carl had just relived the battle with G-2. He still wasn't sure what the true account was. All he remembered was the little piece of the fight he was in.

Looking up under the plane with Dullnig and Bailey, Carl could see what Dullnig was talking about. Apparently, when he had pulled up out of the dive, the plane's airframe buckled, causing the skin to wrinkle just aft of the bomb bay. When he saw the wrinkles, he realized why he couldn't keep the plane in trim and had been constantly struggling to go in a straight line on the way back.

"Another one for that damned boneyard," mumbled Dullnig walking away.

Carl felt a little guilt, but quickly overcame it. They could always build another plane. He was happy to be alive.

A few men walked over to the flight surgeon, who then emptied his last bottle. *Hell of a day,* he thought. *The boys really needed it today.* He couldn't remember ever pouring so much whiskey before. He wondered, as he did after every mission, how the hell we got to this point in time on this earth that we had to do this to each other. He was a lettered man who still wondered whether humans were innately good or evil, and why we suffered a wanton need for power and an inability to control it. He sometimes didn't hold out much hope. Not seeing anyone to offer the last shot of whiskey to, he took the liberty, swigging it down and feeling the burn of being alive.

Earl and Carl turned in their parachutes and sidearms, and collected their personal effects from the sergeant behind the table. Putting their wallets in their back pockets, they headed out toward the Red Cross tent and exchanged conversation, mostly about Carl's experience.

Earl poured himself a cup of coffee and grabbed a donut from the tray. He wasn't on the afternoon mission, so he didn't rush. He enjoyed the coffee, the donuts, and the conversation with the Red Cross ladies, who had been assigned to their group since Wethersfield. The faces had changed, but it was always a pleasure to escape from the war for a few minutes.

"How'd it go today?" Jack asked as he and Bill walked up to join Earl and Carl.

"Not good. Roland bought the farm along with Cornell and Carter."

This quickly quieted Bill Tripp and Jack Smith, who had just poured a cup of coffee.

Earl continued, "It was pretty bad up there today. Sittarich went down with Kenny. Jokinen and Creeden got it too." Earl took a long, slow slurp of his coffee. The others did the same and said nothing.

Earl thought about the few remaining missions he had left. He was a little jealous of Bill and Jack, who had already hit the magic number.

Finally Carl broke the silence. "Those dang Kraut gunners shot us up pretty good today. I sure ain't in no hurry to go back over there any time soon."

By the end of their brief conversation, the four men found themselves nearly alone in the Red Cross tent. Men flying the afternoon mission had already gone to the mess hall. Others had just gone back to their tents. The four sat finishing their coffee, and then went to their separate destinations.

Walking back to the tent, Jack was in no mood for much of anything. He nursed his sore left elbow and wondered if he should drop by to see Old Saw Bones. He decided against it while working his arm back and forth. If anything, the doc might ground him, not that it really mattered now. *What next,* Jack wondered. He ran into Earl, who was coming back from Operations.

"No news," he said to Jack without looking.

"Don't matter, what can we do anyway?"

"Nothing. Just hoping the Red Cross finds him in one of their POW camps."

"Hope so. A lot of guys saw it though. Only one chute. Might have been Roland." Jack ended the conversation as they entered their significantly less-crowded home.

Bill walked to Roland's cot and started separating his personals out. He separated the stack of letters into a pile that would go home.

Earl looked at the empty cot and walked over to help out. He put Roland's clothes into the B-4. Some candy, a liquor ration, a deck of cards, and a half pack of Chesterfields were put on the table. The rest was put into the B-4 and set beside the door on his footlocker. The cot was folded up and laid next to Roland's personal things. In just a few minutes the process was done. They all knew the quartermaster would come by to pick up the stuff.

Bill looked at the stuff. "This is all they have to show for their sacrifice? Damn, what a waste, Earl!"

Saying nothing, Earl fell back on his cot.

Jack was trying to sleep, but it wouldn't come.

Walking back to the tent, Carl kept recounting the day's mission and always came back to his luck. He was fortunate to be alive. "Hell," he thought, "how many more to sixty-five?"

When he walked into his tent, Carl noticed Roland's cot was gone. No one even looked up. Carl lowered his eyes, and a cold shiver ran down his spine. One hour ago he had never felt more alive; now he never wanted that feeling again. Carl threw his heavy flight jacket onto his cot and laid down to stare at the canvas ceiling.

The process of notifying the Enman family had already begun. Within three weeks the telegram had been delivered. ·

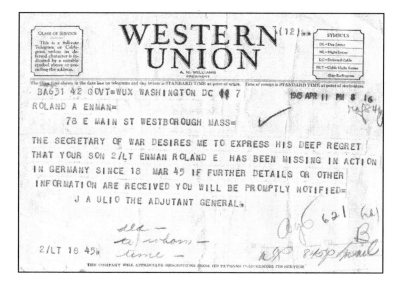

A Sad Day and Telegram for the Enmans

Western Union telegram delivered to Roland Enman's family
almost one month after his death in the skies over Worms.
Reproduced with permission of Doug and Jane Enman

Chapter Eighteen

If the international financial Jewry within and outside Europe should succeed once more in dragging the nations into a war, the result will be, not the Bolshevization of the world and thereby the victory of Jewry, but the annihilation of the Jewish race in Europe.

– Hitler, 1939

Mourning for the Worms' mission losses was over quickly, as it had been for any other mission's losses over the last year, and the A-26s roared down the runway at ten-second intervals to start the afternoon mission to the Kreutztal marshaling yard. This was followed by three more missions over the next two days—all rail-line interdiction missions. March 21st brought an incendiary raid on the town of Coesfield, Germany, which contained a Wehrmacht command center. Coesfield suffered near-complete destruction, as thirty-seven heavily bombed Invaders dropped their incendiaries on target, facing little flak. The afternoon mission on the 21st to the Vreden communication center in Germany would not be as painless.

Captain Robert Rooney jokingly showed off his new captain's bars to his ground crew after jumping from the jeep.

"Congrats, sir," said several men.

He saluted back to each sergeant. Turning to Captain Chester C. Slaughter, Rooney instructed him on how to climb the ladder and where to sit.

"I'll join you up there in a minute," said Rooney as he started his walk-around.

Climbing up the ladder after finishing his duties, Rooney ran down his preflight checklist. Then he energized the starter and cranked off the starboard then port radials. He gladly waited his turn in the taxi order. With the new rank came the responsibility of leading the B-Box.

"You guys ready?"

Getting two quick affirmatives back over his headset, Rooney saluted the ground crew and pushed his cylinder head pressures up to eight pounds of mercury, which started the Invader rolling forward. The smell of high-octane exhaust mixed with oil and hydraulic fluid covered the flight line and drifted over the base, adding to the sense that a mission was starting. Turning out onto the runway, Rooney pushed the throttles forward, accelerating his Invader with its crew toward their fate. He guided his Invader out, with 17 other A-26s lining up behind him.

Once in the air, Captain Rooney's attention turned to Captain Chester C. Slaughter, who had asked a question. Slaughter sat in the jump seat beside Rooney. He was an infantry officer from the Twenty-Ninth Infantry Division who was flying with the group today. Also in Rooney's plane were navigator Lieutenant Robert L. Kirk and gunner Sergeant Robert J. Kamischke.

Operations had decided some time ago that officer exchanges between the air corps and infantry would be helpful in improving communication for close-in air strikes. There were regular exchanges now. Captain Slaughter was the observer today. On an earlier exchange mission, Lieutenant Don Sorrels of the 416th had visited the Thirty-Fifth Infantry Division of Patton's Third Army near the front. He was billeted in a pillbox with a company of soldiers who were not all so happy with the accuracy of the 416th's bombing. They accused the group of having bombed their infantry division. In the good tradition of his group, Don denied the charges and emphasized that the 416th had never bombed US soldiers. As it turned out, Don had a lot of history to learn that day. The infantry troops were happy to bring him up to speed.

Just three months earlier, on December 23rd, the Battle of the Bulge was grinding on. Aircraft from the 416th had just lifted off and were heading to bomb the Waxweiler marshaling yard. It was an afternoon mission led by Captain Morton, with Lieutenant "Punchy" Moore as BN. Captain Hulse and BN Lieutenant Conte were flying deputy in the second box, and would take over if Lieutenant "Punchy" Moore got in trouble. Punchy was being moved up to flight lead BN for the first time. The group had made all the rendezvous and approach routes as planned, but at the IP there was a change.

In the flight with Punchy, Lieutenant Claude Brown called to his BN Lieutenant Jim Kerns, "They called the IP."

"I'm sorry, Brownie. I don't see a damn thing I recognize!"

Brown continued on the run behind Moore. It seemed odd that there was no flak coming up to greet them. "They opened their bomb bay doors."

"Brownie, I'm sorry, just don't see anything I recognize."

"Bombs away," came in from Lieutenant Moore's plane.

Lieutenant Brown responded, "They dropped their bombs."

Kerns closed his bomb bay doors without dropping his eggs, and the flight turned off the run and headed for home. Brownie cussed Jim all the way home, sure that they were going to have their butts chewed out by Command after they landed.

Back at base everyone learned Moore had dropped on a marshaling yard already in Allied hands. Brown apologized to Kerns. As it turned out, Moore had flown toward the wrong city and marshaling yard off the IP. In spite of Conte's efforts to raise him on the radio and stop him, Moore dropped on the wrong marshaling yard. Conte had then taken control and led the rest of the flight and group to the correct target, where they scored multiple direct hits. What made the mistake worse was that the unintended target was being used as a staging area for Patton's Third Army. Patton lost the majority of his gasoline reserves and supplies, not to mention American soldiers' lives.

On touchdown Hulse and Conte were ordered before General Backus to explain the situation. Moore was demoted, but the rest of the squadron was commended for recognizing the error and not dropping on the wrong target. This certainly wasn't the first, nor the last, episode of "friendly fire" committed by the Army Air Corps in the ETO.

Don remembered the incident. He didn't win his argument, but eventually he did win the infantry soldiers' confidence by sharing his month's ration of gin with them. This little act of charity went a long way to calming the situation. For Don and his crew, this newfound camaraderie would come in handy a few days later, when they were being escorted toward the frontlines through a German minefield. An infantry tech sergeant, with whom the airmen had shared the pillbox and gin, was leading the patrol.

"Walk in the footprints of the man in front of you," stressed the tech sergeant over and over again all along the march. The seriousness of this advice was brought home to the airmen when a loud explosion was heard from near the front of the line of men. As the group of men advanced forward, Sorrell and his gunners saw firsthand the grisly effects of a land mine. It made them appreciate their air role more than ever before, and they developed a greater understanding of the foot soldier's day-to-day existence, which was punctuated by his constant fight for survival with every step.

❧

Rooney responded to Slaughter's question. "Yes, it's usually just like this on take-off. We generally have smooth takeoffs with the same routine, so we know where everybody is. From here we'll orbit the base in a predetermined pattern picking up each plane that comes up, until we have six planes in our flight and then three flights in the box. It shouldn't take long now."

Lieutenant Robert Bower took Rooney's left wing. Lieutenant Downing filled in B-1-4 behind him. Rooney's right wingman had already settled in, and two more A-26s rose into the afternoon light and joined in at the five and six slots.

Captain Anderson, the flight lead in B-2, saluted Father Penticoff—Anderson's ritual as he started his roll down the runway. Climbing his Invader to altitude without any problems, Anderson circled toward base after sixty seconds while watching Rooney lead his flight toward the group staging area. As he turned back to the base, he saw one A-26 after another rise to assume their flight positions. Anderson slid his flight in behind and slightly below Captain Rooney's flight, and was soon followed by the B-3 flight. Anderson informed Rooney of the status of his flight and Rooney acknowledged. Eighteen planes had formed up in just less than five minutes. Anderson was worried about this afternoon's mission because each flight in the second box was attacking a different target. There were three different targets with three different runs.

Rooney's B-Box progressed toward the bomb-run after hitting its IPs. Light flak greeted them as the three flights diverged toward their separate targets. Rooney led his flight down the bomb-run, noting that the flak was intensifying. Each Invader began to take substantial structural damage, but none of the planes dropped out of formation. Rooney was hoping his luck would hold for a few more turns of the prop, as detonations from another salvo of *Deutscher Tod* reached them.[294]

Slaughter wasn't so sure about being an aerial target up here in this cockpit with Rooney. He was a veteran of many artillery attacks during the advance across

---

294   German – German death

France, but felt like a sitting duck. He nervously asked, "How much longer are we going to be in this artillery fire?"

The Invader felt the concussion of another explosion, followed almost instantaneously by metal-on-metal impacts.

"Hard to say. If we kill the rate and drop our eggs soon, then we'll turn off target and maneuver for some safer airspace. We'll pick up some fighters around the RP when we come out of the flak. Maybe ten to twenty minutes or so at the most," answered Rooney.

Slaughter had been through his share of artillery barrages, but this was the worst he had ever experienced. Here he was eleven thousand feet in the air with cold hands, fingers, and feet, and pieces of steel coming through the airplane everywhere and no place to hide. "Heck, they aren't even trying to dodge the explosions any more," he thought. "At least when I was on the ground I could crawl under a log or rock or even into a hole." He realized he missed the comforting feel and smell of mother earth and wanted no more of this flyboy stuff. He yelled out, "Let's get this over with, you guys can have it. I'll never talk bad about you guys again!"

Having opened the bay doors at the IP, Lieutenant Kirk was ready to release the payload. Watching all the artillery flash through his bombsight made him plenty nervous, but he held the course. He watched for the right landmarks to slip into view through his Norden, so he could finish killing the rate. He waited anxiously; he didn't want to come back here.

Unfortunately, the Luftwaffe was having some success with their *Flugabwehrkanone;* shrapnel was ripping through the control surfaces and wings of the Invaders in Anderson's flight. Thirty seconds into the bomb-run an 88 round exploded behind and above Anderson's right wing. He and his gunner instinctively flinched. Hot steel peppered Anderson's ship. A large piece slammed into the upper edge of Anderson's rear armor plate, and fragmented when it hit the top of the armored bulkhead plate that formed the back wall of the cockpit. The plate was designed to protect the pilot from bullets and shrapnel attacking at lesser angles of attack than the one it had just encountered. It had stopped several potentially lethal rounds. However, a small sliver of steel had still entered the cockpit. Undeterred by the Anderson's flak jacket and thin clothing, the tiny piece entered into Anderson's back slightly above his right shoulder blade, ripping through muscle and then tearing between the second and third ribs. Glancing off the third rib, it changed direction and passed through the apex of the right lung. It tore through the anterior pleural lining and passed between the third and fourth ribs, tearing the intercostal artery and vein as it exited the chest cavity. It came to rest in the pectoralis major muscle. The event happened so fast that Anderson didn't notice anything except a sharp burning sensation in his right arm and chest. Then he felt increasing pain and muscle cramping. The pain became so intense that it doubled him over on his right side, and he groaned, "Oh, God." His face grimaced in contorted pain.

"You OK, Captain?" called his gunner over the interphone.

With sharp grunting short breaths Anderson replied, "Yeah...yeah, I'm OK.... But I think I've taken a hit. God, does it hurt." In spite of his pain, Anderson found he could maintain control of his plane and hold his position in formation. Slowly he began to collect his senses. Aside from the pain, he felt OK. He figured he had been hit, but was surprised at how little blood there was. "Maybe just a flesh wound," he prayed, echoing the prayers of his crew. He proceeded and maintained radio discipline as the muscle spasms in his back and chest slowly relaxed.

Unaware of the true nature of the injury, Anderson pressed on with the mission. The size and severity of the wound was really quite deceptive. With every breath he took, the torn alveoli and bronchioles of the lung slowly and steadily leaked air into Anderson's right pleural cavity. The leak had its allies too, in the slow and steady flow of blood from all the torn arteries and veins along the course of the wound.

Flak exploded all around them and jarred Kirk with each blast. The target zone finally passed under the bombsight. He recognized the drop point as it crossed the Norden's crosshairs. Steadying his hand, he flipped the cover on the arming switch and swung it to arm. Seeing the green light, Kirk started his countdown via radio. "Three... two...one...bombs away."

Rooney waited for the all-clear from his gunner, who was watching the death-filled projectiles slide out of the racks. "All clear, Captain," Rooney heard.

"Roger."

Rooney banked left and pushed the nose down to get some airspeed. The rest of the flight gladly followed, having dropped their payload when Rooney did.

Seconds after Rooney's bombs began their fall, Anderson's flight released its payloads over their target. Struggling to get a good breath, Anderson hesitated to begin evasive maneuvers after the bomb drop by only a second or two. He found it harder to catch his breath. Then Anderson noticed his heart was beating faster than usual, and the pain in his chest was just as bad. He executed the diving escape maneuver, let the Invader speed up to 320 mph, and pulled back the yoke to bring the A-26s in his flight out of the dive.

As Anderson pulled the Invader's nose out of the bottom of the dive, he felt strange. The plane was creating negative G force. Gravity did not want to give up its grip, pulling the plane, its occupants and Anderson's blood corpuscles back toward the earth. Anderson's depleted blood volume, his heart's compromised pumping capacity, and gravity starved his brain of blood. He felt himself slipping away; his vision was becoming darker and darker until he passed out.

With Anderson unconscious in the pilot seat, the Invader climbed upward as it had been set in motion to do. Five other ships followed in tight formation. Eventually Anderson slowly woke up. He was stunted by a pounding headache and a shortness of breath. He had no idea how long he had been out. He scanned his instrument panel and saw that the plane's attitude was still good. The plane was well-trimmed and climbing, and he led his flight on. Still very lightheaded, he didn't have time to think about his spell, since the flak was following them.

Anderson turned his flight toward Rooney's, noting that he found it harder to focus now. His breathing was becoming more difficult, and while laboring for each breath he could feel his body changing and his mental awareness altering. As he brought his flight in under Rooney's flight, Anderson focused on Rooney's lead plane and slid in from below and behind. Anderson's vision blurred at first, and then worsened as he saw two of Rooney's Invaders flying above him. His diplopia was suddenly followed by darkness as the blood flow to his brain dropped, and he quickly lost consciousness.

Finally, all the blood and air that had escaped from his lung into his right chest cavity had compressed his right lung and heart, inhibiting its ability to pump what little he had left in his vessels. Due to his high heart rate and blood flow from the adrenaline-pumping mission, his body was unable to clot the blood. The adrenaline had been able to make the muscles in his arteries squeeze tightly enough to keep his blood pressure up long enough to get him through the mission, but only to this point and no further. Eventually his blood volume dropped so low that even a young man's heart and blood vessels couldn't constrict enough or his heart beat fast enough to supply blood to the brain. The brain then did what it will always do when it doesn't have blood and is starved for oxygen and glucose, it stopped working. Anderson's body convulsed in the pilot's seat as he slowly passed into the world of those granted peaceful eternity. The German steel that had penetrated his right chest had completed its mission.

As his soul was slipping away silently, the well-trimmed and climbing Invader hadn't noticed his passing. It kept to its assigned duty of climbing toward Rooney's formation.

Wayne Downing, flying the number-four slot behind Rooney, recognized that something was wrong. He radioed to Lieutenant Robert Bower on Rooney's left wing. "Bower, move out!"

Bower heard the strong command, but didn't recognize the voice. It didn't matter; he understood the order instantly and jammed hard right rudder with strong left aileron, to slide out of formation. As he did, he was dumbfounded to see the nose of an A-26 slipping up through the spot he was just in. Bower bled off energy and airspeed so the interloper would pass by.

Rooney, flying straight and level, was a sitting duck.

Downing throttled back and eased backward, slightly out of formation. He called to alert Rooney, who couldn't see any of this, to break right.

Anderson's ship merged quickly into the flight, and pushed into Rooney's airspace. His right wing clipped the left wing of Rooney's plane. Rooney looked to his left in time to see the climbing nose of the Invader turning in toward him. Glancing up at Bower' ship, Rooney smiled a smile of excruciating comprehension. Bower could see in the smile and eyes that Rooney knew things were out of his control now, even as Rooney tried to slip under the life-threatening intruder.

The wing-tip collision stalled the right wing of Anderson's ship, but the plane continued its upward angle of attack, only now turning into Rooney's ship. The nose slid over Rooney's cockpit. Anderson's navigator was staring in sickening disbelief, as his and Rooney's eyes locked on each other—not ten feet apart. Rooney's port propeller cut into the aluminum shell of the assaulting A-26's aft bomb bay, starting the final death dance of this midair collision. The pieces of shredded aluminum were slung out in every direction, as more and more of the shiny Invader was consumed by the impartial propeller, which acted like a pair of high-speed scissors cutting paper.

"Dear God!" said Downing, staring in disbelief. He immediately cut power again and jerked the nose up so as to drop back, but not out, of formation. Aluminum was already raining down on his plane, as the death dance ahead continued.

"What the hell," called Sgroi over the intercom, as he bashed around inside the gunner's compartment. He had injured his right thigh because of Downing's rapid maneuvering.

"Hold on, buddy, this is gonna be a close one!"

Wayne maneuvered his Invader out of the path of the falling aluminum and the two inseparable aircraft. Reaching up, Wayne laid his hand on his front pocket, which held the four-leaf clover that he had had since the start of the war. Downing said a short prayer for the fellows in the two ships.

The two planes continued to fall faster out of formation, as Anderson's craft rolled over even more onto Rooney's plane. The move locked Anderson's cockpit and nose just in front of Rooney's right wing against the fuselage. Both planes were entangled now in a slowly accelerating death spiral. The Invaders resembled a pair of eagles fighting for a fish as they swirled through the air and fell. The two planes gnawed at each other. The propellers spit out aluminum as fast as they could, leaving a trail of metal reflecting in the sunlight as it fell.

"Bail out, guys, get out!" radioed every pilot to Rooney and Anderson.

After they had fallen through six thousand feet of sky, Lieutenant Kirk called Rooney, "I'm getting out. What about you?"

"Go ahead" came the reply, the last words Kirk would ever hear from Rooney. Kirk rolled out the escape hatch and fell away from the spiraling death dance, praying he didn't become a meal for the hungry propellers or get knocked unconscious by the spinning fuselages. Realizing he had escaped from the hands of death, he pulled the rip cord on his chute. His fall seemed to come to a momentary stop, and he watched the two planes spiraling faster and faster on their descent. No other chutes had opened.

Kamischke—still able to talk with Rooney——asked him what to do.

"Bail out, Kamischke! Get out of here!"

Kamischke pulled his headphones out of the turret jack, grabbed his chute and headed for the bomb bay. He threw the switch to open the doors, but nothing happened. The pistons that open the door groaned and then stopped completely. The twisting of the airframe had locked the bomb bays, just as it had to the escape hatches. After crawling down into the bomb bay, Kamischke jumped on the doors hoping to help the pistons push them open. After a few moments of futility, he plugged his headset into the bomb bay jack and called Rooney, "No good. The doors are frozen closed and the other plane's propeller has cut off my other route. Any suggestion?"

"We have the same problem here. Do the best you can!"

"Roger!"

Rooney wanted desperately to bail out, but the force of the collision and the twisted airframe had sealed the cockpit escape hatch. No matter how hard he tried, he couldn't open the hatch. Even if he could, he realized there was no getting out without being hit or killed by these two falling hunks of metal or the whirling propeller right outside the hatch.

Slaughter was working to open the hatch and wanted out with all the human desire he could muster, but this was not his or Rooney's fortune today.

"Try to get to the navigator's escape hatch, Slaughter!"

"Where the hell is it?"

"Down through that opening…there, on the right!"

"Hell, I'm on it!"

Rooney unstrapped himself from his pilot's seat and watched as Slaughter tried to overcome the increasing centrifugal force caused by the spinning of the two Invaders. Rooney knew it was becoming useless to try, since he could barely pull himself from his seat. Struggling to lift his arms and legs that seemed to weigh tons now, he realized that both of them were trapped inside the cockpit. They tried desperately to drag themselves through the small opening into the navigator's compartment, but to no avail. The laws of spinning bodies were starting to work against them now.

The sad truth was that, even if Rooney had been able to get the hatch open, there was no way out for any of them. It would be impossible to survive the fall between the two tightly married aircraft. Man-eating propellers, bone-crushing fuselages and back-breaking tail structures were all falling in unison and waiting for their prey to exit the plane. The cockpits and fuselages had now become their sarcophagus.

The crew inside Anderson's ship was trapped as well. Rooney's propeller had not only sealed the escape route of Anderson's gunners, it had chewed him up as it had the plane. He was spared the agony of the spiraling death fall to terra firma. His mortal remains, bloodied by the propeller, lay motionless and did not resist the increasing centrifugal force.

Anderson's crew had been trying to reach the pilot since seconds before the wings had collided. After the collision, the bombardier and gunner had been talking with each other and then realized they had waited too long to jump. The gunner witnessed the propeller chewing its way through the fuselage of his plane. Babbage continued to call for Anderson, hoping to get orders to bail out. He hadn't seen any of the bail-out failsafes go off, and assumed that Anderson was still alive. Continuing to call, Babbage ultimately waited too long before deciding to jump on his own. The plane was upside down now and rested on the back of Rooney's plane. It was spinning so fast that the centrifugal force pinned him in the nose compartment. He prayed for salvation, struggling with all his might to escape his coming fate. The rules of physics and of centrifugal force glued him to the outside wall of the now-spinning tomb.

Kamischke was crawling back to his turret and tried to think of a way out. As he crawled, he slowly realized that more of his energy was just being used to overcome the spin of the ship.

Realizing they were trapped, the content of their prayers changed as they saw the ground approaching at an ever-accelerating rate. God, heaven, hell, family, and death all crossed their minds and lips at one time or another before the two planes slammed with tremendous violence into the German landscape and exploded in an inferno of aviation fuel. Babbage had resolved himself to God's plan, and joined Battersby and Coleman's heavenly pew, which was now filled with so many fellow souls. That afternoon six more men ended their war and their search for peace, having found both. The passing over of all the men's souls was quick and painless, and therefore welcomed by all of them.

B-Box had witnessed a painful and dumbfounding loss that left the lead flight scattered across the sky. Lieutenant Downing in B-1-4 had held his relative position, for fear of flying into the five or six planes if he had moved either way. From his position Downing had been forced to witness the whole fatal ballet of the midair collision. After it became obvious that there was no recovery for either plane, he had radioed for the guys to jump. Seeing no one escape, he had then endured the painful vision of the two entangled earth-bound aluminum coffins as they ended their final landing on earth. Downing appreciated that by staying in formation he had saved both his life and the life of his gunner, Sergeant Sgroi. Sgroi, however, was not without injury, as some of the falling aluminum from Anderson's ship had shattered the top turret's glass and showered Sgroi with fragments of glass and aluminum. He had suffered lacerations to the face, arms and hands, as well as his leg. Looking at all the blood, he thought, "Hell of a way to earn a Purple Heart."

On the way back to base, the lead bomber group's gunners saw the B-Box moving in from below and behind, and advised their pilots. The lead bomber's group held course and speed. The group was waiting to rendezvous with the fighters for the flight back.

Downing turned on final to the base, and slid his left window open in order to fire a red flare out. The appropriate ground rescue crews started their vehicles rolling for the final taxi position for planes with injured crewmen. It wasn't going to work out for Wayne and Sgroi so easily though. About 250 yards out, the tower radioed, "This is the tower to the plane on approach, over."

"Roger tower, this is fiver-six-one G golf"

"Fiver-six-one, you have a problem. Your left tire is flat."

"Shit, not now," said Downing. He was now less than fifty yards out from touchdown. "Roger that, tower. Will try to crab her in. This is fiver-six-one, over and out." He immediately hit a little left rudder with some reverse aileron pressure in order to raise the left wing. Wayne was keeping the flat left tire off the ground for as long as possible. It was made harder because he still needed to keep the plane flying straight. This was going to be tough. Wayne bumped up the manifold pressure in the left engine, knowing that he was going to have to cut power soon.

He crossed the start of the runway and then touched down in a near-perfect two-pointer. All the while Wayne struggled to keep the left wheel off the ground. The last thing he wanted was a ground loop. He cut power while pulling the yoke back gently and to the right, with continued left rudder. Wayne hoped he could keep the wheel up long enough to slow down. Watching the airspeed decrease, he felt the nose start to settle and the left wing begin to fall. Any second now the wheel was going to hit.

"Whump!"

The flat hit the tarmac and refused to roll. Wayne knew better than to hit the brakes now. It had bitten into the runway, causing the left wing and wheel to act as if the brake was on full. The right wing immediately swung around, as the left wing slowed faster than the right. The big Invader started spinning in circles, right wing around the left, as it looped and skidded off the runway to the left.

"Holy shit!" yelled Sgroi.

"Hold on!"

Spinning out of control, the plane moved farther from the runway, digging circular trenches in the ground as it went. The left wheel's undercarriage buckled under the stress, which caused the left wing to slump and the propellers and wing to dig trenches. Dirt and smoke flew. With the left wing partially buried in the ground, the Invader shuddered to a stop, angled downward to the left. Oily smoke burned off the port-engine exhaust manifolds. Oil had exploded out through the engine casing when the propeller hit the ground. Fortunately for Downing and Sgroi, no fuel lines had been ruptured, only oil had escaped. Downing had cut the fuel pumps the second he cut the throttles.

With the plane now facing 180 degrees from its landing approach, Downing hollered to his gunner, "Let's get the hell out of here!" Then he realized that Sgroi might not be able to escape. Downing called back again as he hurriedly unbuckled his restraint straps, which were now his enemy holding him inside this potential death trap. "Can you get out, Sgroi?"

"I'm damn sure tryin', sir!"

He released his straps, then shut off all the fuel pumps and electrical power to help prevent or worsen a fire. Downing was halfway out the escape hatch when he saw the rescue and fire teams arriving.

Once there, the rescue team began attacking the plane before the oil fire had been extinguished by the fire crews. They removed Sgroi and attended to him quickly. It was a mission they had dealt with too many times this morning.

Downing sat on the ground a hundred yards from his *Pink Lady*. His head sat in his hands, and he was thankful that everything was OK. Lifting his head, he watched as Sgroi was loaded into the ambulance. *Another Purple Heart,* he thought as the ambulance roared off.

Chitty, Raccio, and Downing were taken to the debriefing and forced to relive the past several hours. Downing went first, recounting as best he could the details up until Anderson and Rooney's midair collision. He stopped for a while to light a Chesterfield, taking a deep draw before going into the details. After he finished his account, Downing was dismissed from the debriefing. Standing up and walking out into the evening sun, he saw the flight surgeon sitting in his jeep just outside of Intel's hut.

"Downing!"

Wayne looked the flight surgeon in the eyes.

"Tough one today?"

Wayne hesitated as he looked on. "Yeah."

"Come here." The surgeon poured a shot of Old Methuselah and then offered it to Downing.

Without hesitation Downing accepted the drink, something he rarely did after missions. The shot glass was empty in one quick, hot swallow, and he held it out for a refill.

Looking Downing in the eyes, the surgeon filled the glass to the rim a second time. It disappeared as quickly as the first, and Downing handed the glass back.

"Thanks, Doc." Downing felt the heavy burn in his esophagus and stomach while waiting patiently for the whiskey to enter his brain. Then he walked to the Red Cross tent for some coffee and conversation.

Turning to the medic sitting in the jeep, the flight surgeon said, "Here are the keys to the medicine closet. Bring me that case of whiskey; we're going to need it today."

Wayne sat with Bower in the Red Cross tent and quietly sipped his coffee. He wished it was another shot from the doc. He couldn't bring himself to take a doughnut. The thought of food wasn't appealing right now. Bower hadn't said anything since sitting down several minutes ago. Wayne wasn't pressuring him to speak anyway.

Ralph Conte walked in to talk with his two pilot friends. "Did you two hear about Anderson and Rooney?"

"About Roland, Sittarich, Jokinen, and all the others too," Downing replied, saving Bower the need.

"I hope you fellas don't have to do that one again."

Looking Downing in the eyes, Ralph asked, "Wayne, how long you going to keep doing this?"

"Hell…I guess till they don't need me…or this thing ends."

"Or you buy the farm," Ralph added.

"I guess that too."

"Heck, guys, what went so bad to start all this anyway?" Bower asked rhetorically, causing everyone to shake their heads in a silent, unknowing reply.

Wayne and the fellas knew people had been dying for years before America's official entry into this global struggle. Unknown to them and most Americans, the United States had already been engaged in combat long before the official entry date.

❧

Every war has its historical revisionists—some right, some wrong. This war was no different. Clearly the foundations and responsibility for this war lay in the hands of the many masons of international diplomacy and treaty-writing that preceded it. Some say this war was destined after the treaties ending WWI gave Adolf Hitler the framework for gaining power. Others feel that the war was destined after the 1935 Nuremberg Laws in Germany created the laws of "eugenic fascism." The laws allowed Hitler to pass the

Reichsburgergesetz,[295] which deprived Jews of their German citizenship, and the *Gesetz zum Schutze des Deutschen Blutes und der Deutschen Ehre.*[296] Both laws prevented Jews from owning real property and having civil rights and also prevented marriages and sexual relations between Jews and "Aryans." Hitler's National Socialism was built on and around the framework of his eugenic cleansing. For him, all the social, economic, anti-German injustices were clearly the result of and going to be solved by the correction of this racial imbalance. Hitler was able to bring this single unifying issue to the suffering German citizenry, thereby mobilizing it by directing the simplest of all emotions—hate. The "lunatic" was now breaking out of his asylum and had found "That Someone to Blame" for the German citizens to vilify. His eugenic-driven[297] godless architecture, supported by many outside of Germany, now had the victims to purge. Misguided organizations of hate pushed for legislative change (not just in Germany) as genetic-ethnic anti-immigration laws were being passed all around the world. Governments and private-sector organizations became unquestionably aligned with the belief that "the unfit" hurt society. The circle of genetic fascism had just about been closed.

With the gradual acceptance of birth control linking itself to the eugenicists' push for immigration control, isolation of the "unfit and criminal types" and sterilization, the birth control movement would soon embrace abortion as the next step. The value of life had been established by the commodity market of eugenics, with life itself being devalued to the point that the final extension of the eugenicists' beliefs were brought to the establishment of the legislatively imposed Final Solution. Mass genetic, ethnic, behaviorally justified murder became the solution, since even the embryo was a meaningless collection of defective genes. The circle was closed. Capitalizing on this increasing global perception, Hitler began the campaign to protect Germany from eugenic decay, and combined it with the people's desire to regain self-respect, to recover their "lost lands," and to rescue their genetically isolated brethren.

None of these pseudo-justifications seems like reason enough to go to war, unless these reasons can be linked to the concept of economic self-sufficiency, or becoming an autarkic state. As Stephen Roberts argues in *The House That Hitler Built,* Germany suffered a severe paucity of natural resources. He writes, "Germany is worse off than any other great State in so far as these the thirty four vital materials a nation must have… Germany has only two in ample quantities—potash and coal." Similarly, as an island nation, Japan was no better off. So in order to become independent nations, they both needed to control the oil, iron, silver, gold, copper, and every other necessity a modern nation must have to be among the world's "First Rate Nations."

Germany relied on its scientists to develop the resources that the country did not contain. Roberts discusses Germany's reliance on its chemists to transform the nation's industries into self-sufficiency. For example, Germany developed synthetic rubber, produced oil from coal, and burned a mixture of benzol, alcohol, and gasoline in their

---

295   German – Law of the Reich Citizen
296   German – Law for the Protection of German Blood and German Honor
297   *From Darwin to Hitler: Evolutionary Ethics, Eugenics and Racism in Germany;* Richard Weikart; page 15; Palgrave Macmillan; copyright 2004

cars. To facilitate this process, the Nazis purged the nation's key independent research institution, the Kaiser Wilhelm Institute, of nonparty members, and mobilized it for the investigation and production of substitute natural resources to replace those not in the nation's geography and geology. Success in the production of synthetic substitutes for materials such as leather, rubber, mineral oil, fertilizer, and explosives had already been achieved. The party now wanted to expand on this success by designing and producing experimental weapons. This included the development of sarin nerve gas, jet aircraft, remote-control bombs, rockets, nuclear fission, and the atom bomb, though, fortunately, they had little sustained interest in the latter two.[298]

While Germany was busy arming itself on xenophobic grounds, America too had become a nation that was far from open-minded about outsiders. FDR was wrestling with the isolationist policies of a Congress and a citizenry that were not fully informed about the rising darkness of war. Roosevelt had to navigate the political waters of these isolationists' policies while still trying to aid America's allies, who, by 1939, were becoming victims of the Nazi and Japanese war machines. By the end of September 1939, Poland had fallen, and America's Congress would pass a neutrality law on top of the isolationist laws of 1935.

America and Americans continued to profess neutrality and practice isolationism while good people, innocent children, women, and men were dying or being sacrificed in the name of eugenic fascism. After Poland fell, France was soon conquered, in early 1940, leaving Britain to fight for its life on the beaches of Dunkirk between May and June of that year. Britain fought the Luftwaffe to a standstill, while the German air force rained death down on its cities. People were being forced into slave labor camps, and the systematic killing of races of people was starting in Germany. Victory in Europe and over Japan couldn't have come quickly enough, but how could it occur with an isolationist America?

While trying to navigate the difficult waters of what was correct for the world and still maintain power at home, Roosevelt had become trapped in his own rhetoric as well as his promise that he would not send Americans to fight. Yet, Roosevelt wrangled some aid for Europe and other Allies, through the Lend-Lease Act. The Lend-Lease Act required votes from both sides of the aisle and both houses of Congress to pass, in spite of the neutrality and isolationist policies that were in existence. It was a perfect example of FDR's wrestling from the Congress and the American people the materials for war so desperately needed by the Europeans, Chinese, and, soon, Russians. Speaking at the White House Correspondents' Association Dinner on March 15, 1941, FDR stated, "Nazi forces are not seeking mere modifications in colonial maps...They openly seek the destruction of all elective systems...The aid-to-democracies bill was passed by... Congress...I signed it one half hour later. And so our country is going to be...the arsenal

---

298   Laying the Foundation for Wartime Research: A Comparative Overview of Science Mobilization in National Socialist Germany, Japan, and the Soviet Union; Walter E. Grunden, Yutaka Kawamura, etal; Politics and Science in Wartime: Comparative International Perspectives on the Kaiser Wilhelm Institute; Editors, Carola Sachse and Mark Walker; OSIRIS, Second Series, Vol. 20; 2005

of democracy." Roosevelt also defended his assistance to future allies in economic terms: "The British people…need ships. From America, they will get ships. They need planes. From America they will get planes. From America they need food…they will get food. They need tanks…they will get tanks and guns and ammunition and supplies of all kinds…China likewise." America was producing things that those nations needed, and FDR didn't have to defend the mechanism by which they were produced. It was a near-perfectly balanced global "Keynesian aggregate." By the end of the war America had produced:

Warplanes…	296,429
Tanks…	102,351
Artillery pieces…	372,431
Trucks…	2,455,964
Warships…	87,620
Cargo ships…	5425
Aircraft bombs (tons)…	5,822,000
Small arms…	20,086,061
Small-arms ammunition (rounds)…	44,000,000,000 [299]

All this war material was produced by employees of the companies not engaged in war, unlike the Japanese and soon the Germans who were forced to press the peoples of occupied countries into slave labor to just maintain their armies in the field. The Americans could produce with enthusiastic workers the instruments of war for the wanton consumers. The inefficient war production of the Axis countries prevented them from growing their economies.[300]

America's involvement in the war increased as 1941 sped along. In August, President Roosevelt met with Prime Minister Churchill in a small bay along the coast of Newfoundland. The two laid out a framework for their two nations in the postwar era, even though the United States had not even entered the war, except indirectly through Lend-Lease.[301] In the so-called Atlantic Charter, Britain and the United States promised to not seek new territories after the war and reaffirmed their belief that all people had a right to self-determination, among other agreements. It was clear that Roosevelt was angling to get America involved in the war. Indeed, later Churchill remarked of the "astonishing depth of Roosevelt's intense desire for war," and cabled his cabinet that "[FDR] obviously was very determined that they [the United States] should come in." Why would Churchill want anything less than America's involvement? He was trying to survive a grueling air war at home and a growing ground war against two of the world's most powerful nations.

299   *The Glory and The Dream: A Narrative History of America- 1932–1972*, William Manchester, Chapter 10, pp 296
300   On Lend-Lease (March 15, 1941), Miller Center of Public Affairs, Scripps Library and Multimedia Archive; http://millercenter.virginia.edu/scripps/diglibrary/prezspeeches/roosevelt/fdr_1941_0315.html
301   Atlantic Charter, The Avalon Project at Yale Law school; http://www.yale.edu/lawweb/avalon/wwii/atlantic.htm

The early months of this European contest were when America's involvement in the war became critical. FDR was faced with the potential loss of many constructive democracies in Europe. What was the right thing to do? How should the president, who has knowledge of the plans and objectives of the enemies of humankind, get America to engage two powerful enemies with governments that are conducting atrocities of unspeakable deprivation while conquering the lands of valued and trusted democracies? These problems abroad were troubling enough, but America still faced the Depression, which was far from over.

In such a situation, what allows the right response from the public to occur? The same way it has for all wars, with a seminal inflammatory event. Maybe it was the shot heard 'round the world that heralded America's Revolutionary War. Or a border dispute over land—either a "Remember the Alamo" or "Remember the Maine" battle cry or perhaps a rallying cry for the *Lusitania.* For World War II it was the Japanese attack on Pearl Harbor on December 7, 1941, that galvanized the public to enter the war.

Because Roosevelt was already inclined to involve the United States in the conflict, some have questioned whether he or the military knew beforehand of the attack on the Hawaiian military base. The US military should have been well aware of the possibility of attack. The military had conducted extensive exercises over Pearl Harbor in 1932 and 1938, and had demonstrated the vulnerability of a fleet inside the harbor. The vulnerability of fleets in the harbor should have been well known also from the 1940 Royal Navy assault on the Italian Navy at Taranto. The British destroyed the Italian navy with shallow-water torpedoes dropped from old torpedo biplanes.

In fact, the surprise attack at Pearl Harbor was not such a surprise at all. Well before December 7 the War Department or our allies were supposedly decoding nearly every encrypted message intercepted from Japanese radio traffic. These intercepted and decoded messages built a dynamic picture of the coming storm. In May 1940, FDR correctly stated, "The Atlantic and Pacific oceans were reasonably adequate defensive barriers when fleets sailed under sail...But the new element—air navigation—steps up the speed of possible attack to...three hundred miles per hour...So-called impregnable fortifications no longer exist."[302] FDR had been warned of the possibility of attack by Churchill himself, yet the event still occurred. Records indicate that even the Soviets' top spy, Richard Sorge, alerted the Kremlin in October 1941 of an attack, and they supposedly stated they would alert Washington. The enemies and other allies were aware of the vulnerability of fleets in harbor, and the United States certainly should have been as well.

But, still, how would FDR justify going to war in Europe if Japan attacked the United States on the other side of the world? Now, it's well known that Hitler had assured Japan that if America declared war on Japan, he would declare war on America. Indeed, it seems that the Japanese had already decided in 1940 to engage America at Pearl Harbor. But the Americans, British, and Dutch were aware of the potential

---

302   *Pearl Harbor: Mother of all Conspiracies*, Mark Emerson Willey, Chapter one, page 14; 2000

Japanese threat, having imposed an oil embargo in July 1941, which had prevented the Japanese from invading Russia.

Also, America had been providing some, but not all, of the materials for Japan's war in the Far East. Roosevelt had slowly started curtailing America's support for the Japanese after seeing Germany's aggression succeed and Japan's enlarging sphere of control. So, well before 1941 America had begun to control the exportation of goods to Japan that were considered of strategic military value. The controlled exports were far more than oil. Between July 1940 and July 1941, Roosevelt signed proclamations based on the definition of military material dated May 1, 1937, that limited or curtailed the export of the following items: aluminum, antimony, asbestos, chromium, cotton linters, flax, graphite, animal hides, industrial diamonds, manganese, magnesium, manila fiber, mercury, mica, molybdenum, optical glass, platinum-group metals, quartz crystals, quinine, rubber, silk, tin, toluol, tungsten, vanadium, and wool. Roosevelt also limited chemicals, manufactured goods, and machinery. The chemicals included ammonia and ammonium compounds, chlorine, dimethylaniline, diphenylamine, nitric acid, nitrates, nitrocellulose with a nitrogen content of less than 12 percent, soda lime, sodium acetate anhydrous, strontium chemicals, and sulfuric acid fuming. The manufactured goods included aircraft parts (equipment and accessories other than those listed in the 1937 proclamation), armor plate, glass (nonshatterable or bullet-proof), plastics (optically clear), and optical elements for fire-control instruments (aircraft instruments, etc.). The machinery included metal-working machinery for melting or casting, pressing into forms, power-driven cutting or grinding, and welding.

These proclamations were based on the action taken by Congress on July 2, 1940, titled "An Act to Expedite the Strengthening of the National Defense." All these military material embargos were further subdivided, which gives an even-broader picture of the extent of the materials being withheld from Japan, and ultimately the American people. On July 26, 1940, President Roosevelt signed proclamation No. 2417, which allowed for the controlled export of petroleum products, tetraethyl lead, iron and scrap steel. These proclamations were accordingly noted by Japan in its communication to the Department of State on August 3, 1940. Japan responded,

> As a country whose import of American aviation gasoline is of immense volume, Japan would bear the brunt of the virtual embargo. The resultant impression would be that Japan had been singled out for and subjected to discriminatory treatment. While reserving all rights of further action, the Government of Japan wishes to protest against the policy of the Government of the United States set forth in the announcement under review.

So, in slowing or eliminating the flow of vital supplies to Japan, Roosevelt had skillfully navigated the frontiers of war.

In a radio address to the nation on July 25, 1941, FDR explained why America was suffering gasoline shortages and how he was trying to slow the spread of war. Note the diction that suggests the relative isolation of Americans. Roosevelt stated,

> Now the answer is a very simple one. There is a world war going on, and has been for some time…nearly two years. One of our efforts, from the very beginning, was to prevent the spread of that war in certain areas where it hadn't started. One of those areas is a place called the Pacific Ocean…one of the largest areas of the earth. There happened to be a place in the South Pacific where we had to get a lot of things… rubber… tin…and so forth and so on…down in the Dutch Indies, the Straits Settlements, and Indochina. And we had to help get the Australian surplus of meat and wheat, and corn, for England…It was very essential from our own point of view of defense to prevent a war from starting in the South Pacific. So our foreign policy was…trying to stop a war from breaking out down there…We wanted to keep that line of supplies from Australia and New Zealand going to the near east…[because] all their [Britain's] troops, all their supplies they have maintained in Syria, North Africa and Palestine. So it was essential for Great Britain that we try to keep the peace down there in the South Pacific…All right. And now here is a nation called Japan. Whether they had at that time aggressive purposes to enlarge their empire southward, they didn't have any oil of their own up in the north. Now, if we cut the oil off, they probably would have gone down to the Dutch East Indies a year ago, and you would have had war…Therefore, there was…you might call…a method in letting this oil go to Japan, with the hope…and it has worked for two years…of keeping war out of the South Pacific for our own good, for the good of the defense of Great Britain, and the freedom of the seas.

Roosevelt clearly explained the balancing act that was going on in the Pacific to maintain the British defenses in Europe, Africa, and the Mideast. It wasn't long, however, before Americans were doing their bit. By the start of the war, rationing of most things had begun in America, with distribution to the populace based on the product's availability and the allotment allowed by their ration stamps.

These presidential statements were not made, of course, without some insight into the current global situation. On July 24, 1941, around 5 p.m., slightly less than five months before the Japanese attack on Pearl Harbor and one month after Hitler's invasion of Russia, President Roosevelt received the Japanese ambassador in the Oval Office. During this audience, the president tried specifically to reason with the ambassador. In a memo from Secretary of State Cordell Hull outlining the substance of the meeting, Roosevelt noted,

The Ambassador undoubtedly knew that there was a very considerable shortage in the oil supply in the eastern part of the United States...when Japan during these past two years had given every indication of pursuing a policy of force and conquest in conjunction with the policy of world domination which Hitler was carrying on...If Japan attempted to seize oil supplies by force in the Netherlands East Indies, the Dutch...would resist, [and] the British would immediately come to their assistance...In view of our policy of assisting Great Britain, an exceedingly serious situation would immediately result.

He went on:

This new move by Japan in Indochina created an exceedingly serious problem for the United States...The cost of any military occupation is tremendous and the occupation itself is not conducive to the production by civilians in occupied countries of food supplies and raw materials of the character required by Japan [exactly one of Japan's major economic burdens at his time]...This Government, consequently, could only assume that the occupation of Indochina was being undertaken by Japan for the purpose of further offense and this created a situation which...must give the United States the most serious disquiet.

The president did offer to supply Japan, through treaty, all the food, materials, oil, and sovereign security it needed, if the nation would suspend its aggressive activity.

In the meeting FDR also mentioned that the United States was of the belief that "such policies as those Japan was now pursuing were due to German pressure upon Japan." The Japanese ambassador reacted by saying, "Japan was, of course, an independent country and that while such pressure might be exercised, decisions on the policy she was pursuing were solely her own and no one else had any responsibility for them." The president then tried to impress upon the Japanese ambassador the truth of the situation:

One thing the Japanese Government did not understand as clearly as this Government was the fact that Hitler was bent upon world domination and not merely the domination of Europe or of Africa...If Germany succeeded in defeating Russia and dominating Europe and then dominating Africa, there wasn't the slightest question in his mind that Germany thereafter would turn her attention to the Far East...The navies of Japan and of the United States would be cooperating together against Hitler as the common enemy.

By way of reply the ambassador quoted a Chinese proverb: "He who continuously brandishes the sword eventually kills himself." It was a profoundly prophetic observation, and quite possibly Japan should have heeded his words.[303]

---

303   Papers Relating to the Foreign Relations of the United States: Japan: 1931-1941; Vol. II; pp 208-265

The war might have gone much differently, if not for the embargo of oil. By the start of August 1941, with the embargo basically complete, the Japanese were forced into the Pacific. This was sooner than the nation expected, and the Dutch colonies, under duress, would provide the needed oil to continue the war. The Japanese had been prepared to invade eastern Russia, but with the embargo they were forced to cancel this operation. Therefore, Russia was able to transfer numerous divisions from the east to the west, to fight the Germans. If Russia had been assailed on two fronts, the outcome of the war could have been drastically changed. With a successful invasion of southwestern Russia, Hitler's Wehrmacht could arguably have been able to capture the Russian oil reserves, since it would not have had to face the numerous divisions transferred from the east. Then, if Russia were defeated, clearly, it would not have been difficult for the Japanese to take the Pacific islands later.

Roosevelt was well aware of what action the Japanese might take in response to the embargo. He had stipulated in the Atlantic Charter that an invasion of the Dutch colonies would be an act of war against the United States. But the Japanese wanted oil, and they weren't going to wait on America to turn off the spigot before conquering lands that would provide it. On the other side of the diplomatic coin, Japan could have taken the total embargo as a way to conclude a peace. Describing the embargo in "The Grand Alliance," Churchill stated: "It was evident that this was a stranglehold, and that the choice before them was either for Japan to reach an agreement with the United States or go to war." Japan's peace settlement would have entailed the withdrawal from China and all conquered lands. The choice of war or peace was for Japanese leaders to make. Japan had ignored all the progressive sanctions placed on it, starting with the League of Nation's demands in the early thirties. As military theorist Carl von Clausewitz argued in the nineteenth century, "War is politics continued by different means." In a different form or in reality "diplomacy is war in a different form." Japan chose war.

On December 4, 1941, the Japanese army violated the ADB (American-Dutch-British) agreement from the Atlantic Charter, by crossing the 100° east and 10° north line, thereby invoking the treaty's recourse. But Roosevelt wisely did not "bite," because it would mean nothing to America and Americans. Three days later settled the issue. Pearl Harbor was attacked, and the extent of Japanese's need for oil revealed. The preemptive strike attempted to prevent America from curtailing Japan's seizure of oil in southeast Asia, by eliminating the US naval capabilities in the Pacific. While they did significantly disable ships, obliterate planes, and kill or wound over three thousand, the Japanese aircraft did not destroy the military oil reserves on the island, the loss of which might have been more detrimental to American power in the Pacific.

Some argue that the attack on Pearl Harbor was known to the administration. Such a wholesale conspiracy would require a massive and well-designed coverup, to the depths of the Executive branch, State Department, and War Department. Yet, American military strategy was based on information derived from decoded enemy strategies, while keeping Japan and Germany in the dark about America's knowledge of their codes and plans. If the administration did know, and reacted to its knowledge of the possible strike, Japan would have recognized it before the attack. Japanese radio codes and tactics would surely have changed, and quite possibly a totally different outcome to the Pacific war may have occurred, and possibly greater loss of life. Intelligence implies deception, deception of the enemy and possibly your allies. Sun Tzu's spies were at work.

If foreknowledge of the attack were there at the highest levels, it was used to minimize the disaster. Informed military men were aware of the price to be paid. However, the important thing to remember is that the sailors and soldiers were already at war. They were at war from the day they joined the military. Even though the American military was not in a clearly defined shooting war until after December 7, 1941, worldwide tensions had been mounting since the thirties. The Japanese sinking of the *USS Panay* in China in 1937 is testament to those tensions. Before that, the war consisted of intelligence-counterintelligence, failing diplomacy and protection of America's global interests and safety. As Admiral Stark wrote to Admiral Hart a month before Pearl Harbor, "The Navy is already in the war of the Atlantic, but the country doesn't seem to realize it…Whether the country knows it or not, we are at war." Pearl Harbor was just the first calculated battle of a long war. Regardless of the motives, this seminal event occurred.

However, by no means does that lessen the value of the soldiers' and sailors' lives. The human losses were great at Pearl Harbor, when judged by the number of irreplaceable lives taken from us. Yet, their sacrifices ensured the ultimate victory. Because of this painful shocking event, Americans' consciousness awoke to the reality of the world that was closing in around them. Without the attack on Pearl Harbor, the liberation of the world from the most heinous destroyers of humanity known to date quite possibly might not have occurred at the price of "just" fifty-eight million lives. It would have cost many more, but that Roosevelt and the Allies played Sun Tzu's game well. They could have reacted to every intercepted message, and tipped their hand to the enemy that they were reading the Japanese codes. Japan would have changed them, leaving the Allies in the dark. As it was, America decoded later messages from the unsuspecting Japanese about attacks on a target code-named "AF," which was actually Midway Island. Access to the code helped the United States gain a decisive victory there. Otherwise, the likely outcome was for America to have lost its aircraft carriers there instead of Japan losing its carriers. So, the sacrifices of those at Pearl Harbor were vital to the effort. From the first day of their tenure the soldiers and sailors were in harm's way, and every person in the service is a diplomatic or military tool. As the old saying goes, "When you're in the military, your butt belongs to Uncle Sam." With the attack, the American people's consciousness awoke to the reality of the world that was closing in around them.

In the end, FDR and the military men had made good but difficult decisions in an atmosphere of informed leadership, and had understood the consequences of those decisions. The material losses for the navy during Pearl Harbor were, according to many, acceptable losses. World War I vintage battle wagons and cruisers were lost, but conveniently (or by design) many ships and the newer vital carriers with all their escorts were out at sea. A well-planned military tactic? Well, many planes were lost too, because they had all been placed on the airfield to be protected against sabotage. A similar loss was endured nine hours after Pearl Harbor, when Japanese planes destroyed General Douglas MacArthur's air force on the ground. MacArthur, then commander in the Philippines, was accused of ignoring radar reports of approaching Japanese planes.

Roosevelt's destiny was war, but war on our terms and with our goals. America entered the war with the express desire to prevent Germany and Japan from conquering Russia and then closing in and hoarding resources under their tyrannical rule. Otherwise, the Axis powers would have controlled the resources that America and what remained of the free world would need just for their economic survival.

If America had reacted to the intelligence and not entered the war, it would have given the Axis powers the opportunity to consolidate their territories in Europe, North Africa, Persia, and quite possibly all the way to India. Imagine the magnitude of the effort it would have taken to dislodge them. Their control of the world's oil reserves and being in a position to delegate their terms are much scarier thoughts than the United States waiting to enter the fray. Imagine the genocide that would have been perpetrated all around the world if the United States had not entered. If foreknowledge of the coming Pearl Harbor attack existed, as several congressional and military commissions investigating the tragedy near the end and after the war suggested, [304] (and as many high-ranking military leaders and statesmen obviously already knew), then is it not up to the judgment of the Almighty to rule on guilt or innocence of the conspirators? Good men and women had allowed a war to start so it could be, as Churchill said, "the beginning of the end."[305]

After the attacks, the floodgates on the war let loose. December 7 brought declarations of war against America and Great Britain by Japan, while the Dutch East Indies and Canada declared war against Japan. December 8 offered more of the same—Britain, the United States, Nicaragua, Honduras, Guatemala, Haiti, the Dominican Republic, the Netherlands, the Free French, and Panama took up arms against Japan. The next day offered still more, with declarations of war against Japan by Costa Rica, Australia, South Africa, and New Zealand. Also, China declared itself against Germany, Italy, and Japan. Over the next week the nations of the globe declared their allegiances. Diplomacy in the guise of war sprouted its colors all around the world as the global cataclysm began in earnest.[306]

As it had before the war started, extensive planning was undertaken before the war ended. Well before the conflict was won, the Allies had been planning the shape of the globe after the war was over. During difficult and complex discussions at various summits, Allied statesmen had created broad outlines of a democratized world that would be enacted as soon as the war could be terminated. The first of such summits was the Atlantic Conference in August 1941, during which Roosevelt and Churchill

---

304   Pearl Harbor, Mother of All Conspiracies, Mark Emerson Willey; http://www.geocities.com/Pentagon/6315/pearl.html
305   *Pearl Harbor: Mother of all Conspiracies*, Mark Emerson Willey, Xlibris Corporation; 2000
306   Chronology of International Events: March 1938 to December 18th 1941; Department of State, Bulletin, December 27, 1941, p. 590; http://www.ibiblio.org/pha/events/events.html

outlined the grand design for the democratization of the postwar world. The fruit of the conference was called the Atlantic Charter, which specified the goals of the western powers for the war. The document discussed the mechanisms of America's entry into the war, and guaranteed mutual assurances of security, since the intelligence that was flowing into the security offices all around the world mandated joint security. The charter also served as the foundation for the follow-on organization to the League of Nations—the United Nations. At subsequent meetings among Allied Western powers, the principles of the charter were adopted unanimously. The Atlantic Charter was particularly significant for laying out the Allied vision, since it was referenced frequently in all future documents produced by the Big Three—the United States, Great Britain, and the Soviet Union.

Another significant summit was the Casablanca Conference held in Morocco in January 1943. During the eleven days of the conference, Churchill, Roosevelt, and de Gaulle—but not Stalin—plotted the European strategy. The Casablanca Declaration detailed the results of the conference. It called for unconditional surrender from the Axis powers, reiterating previous declarations. It also promised Allied aid to the Soviets and outlined the invasion of Sicily and Italy. The document further noted that the "authority of government" came from the people only, and referenced the Atlantic Charter again, by arguing that "the conquered populations of today be again the masters of their destiny." Also of note, the Casablanca document refers to the propagandists of the Axis powers who had predicted that "a cat-and-dog fight" would erupt among Russia, China, Britain, and the United States if the Allies won the war.

Throughout the war, the summits continued, and sketched in greater detail the Allied plans for the war and the postwar world. In August 1943 in Quebec, Canada, Roosevelt and Churchill outlined broader plans for China, Japan, and France during and after the war. October 1943 brought the Moscow Conference among the United States, Great Britain, the Soviet Union, and China. From this conference, the Moscow Declaration expressed, among other things, the desire for the formation of the United Nations. The document also stated that postwar Italy and Austria would be democratic and free of fascism in all its forms. Also significant, the statement noted the atrocities of Hitler's forces, and made it clear that the Allies would enforce justice against the perpetrators when the war was over.

The Moscow Conference was soon followed by the Cairo and Tehran meetings in November 1943. The Cairo summit, with Roosevelt, Churchill, and Chiang Kaishek of China, outlined the return of territories conquered by Japan to their rightful countries. Moreover, it stated that Korea was to become "free and independent." This last clause set up the field for the Korean War, in the early fifties. Just on the Cairo meeting's heels, the Tehran Conference planned how the war against Germany would be wrapped up, including the broad outlines for the American and British invasions of Europe. The conference was the first that Stalin attended, and spoke of the inevitable destruction of the enemies of the Allies. It also outlined the Big Three's commitment to Iran, and referenced the Atlantic Charter. The conference also expressed the desire for Turkey to enter the war, and guaranteed mutual security for the nation.

The final summit before the end of the conflict in Europe was the Crimea Conference held in Yalta in February 1945. Attended by Churchill, Stalin, and an ailing Roosevelt, the conference established the further outline for the United Nations, the democratic processes in postwar western Europe, the division of Germany, and the estimated cost of Germany's reparations—upward of twenty-two billion dollars. In addition, the conference discussed other matters, such as the conclusion of the war in the Pacific and how eastern Europe would be reorganized. Each leader had come with his own agenda: Roosevelt wanted Soviet help against Japan, while Churchill wanted free and democratic governments in eastern Europe. Stalin insisted on a sphere of influence in eastern Europe as critical to the Soviet Union's security. Throughout the documents from the Yalta conference, references are made to the ideals of the Atlantic Charter, which of course Stalin had not been party to.

While the United States and Britain would have liked to negotiate from a position of strength at Yalta, in truth they were in no position to demand anything from the Soviet Union at this time. The weakness of their position is outlined in the transcript of Operation Unthinkable, Churchill's survey of what it would have taken to defeat the Soviet Union after the war was over. At the time of the conference the nuclear bomb had not been tested yet. So the situation required "mutual dependency." Roosevelt was left to deal with the reality that the Soviet Union had three hundred divisions, representing some twelve million soldiers. The Soviet force was estimated to be some three times larger than what General Eisenhower commanded, and Japan had yet to be defeated. The reality was that the Soviet Union was unbeatable at that moment, and as Roosevelt described his actions, "It was a compromise."[307,308]

Well aware of his position, Stalin was able to drive a hard bargain. As one of his concessions, the Soviet leader was allowed to annex territory from eastern Poland. Moreover, the outline for Poland's postwar democracy were laid, with the administration of such changes under the control of the Soviet Union. (After the war, the Soviets would essentially force Poland toward communism.) In exchange for opening a second front against Japan, the Soviet Union would receive territories currently occupied by Japan. Some dispute whether such concessions were necessary.

The final conference held among the Big Three took place in Potsdam, Germany, during July and August 1945. Germany had been defeated, and now Japan remained. Stalin again was in a position of power. Roosevelt had passed on, leaving the relative newcomer Harry Truman to deal with the wily Soviet leader. Churchill was in a poor position as well, facing political defeat in the polls back home. Later in the proceedings, Churchill was replaced by Clement Atlee. The summit produced the Potsdam Agreement, which included agreements on how to organize and administer Germany and establish order in the postwar world.

307   Cold War Transcripts, National Archives Learning Curve/ Cold War; http://www.learningcurve.gov.uk/coldwar/g2/cs3/s4_t.htm

308   Cold War Transcripts: Operation Unthinkable, Report By The Joint Planning Staff; National Archives Learning Curve/ Cold War; http://www.learningcurve.gov.uk?coldwar/g2cs3/S6_t.htm

Also of note, at Potsdam Truman mentioned the existence of the nuclear bomb, and is supposed to have made the decision to use it here. A few days later, on August 6, the United States dropped the first atomic bomb, on Hiroshima. Three days later, Nagasaki was bombed, and Japan finally surrendered. The world had moved into the nuclear age.

By the end of the war, the 416th had flown over two hundred missions, and dropped over 100,000 tons of bombs. The group had flown missions from England—bombing No-ball sites, air bases, railroad yards, communication centers, and participated in D day. The airmen had successfully destroyed the Oissel Bridge over the Seine River, trapping the retreating German army in the Falaise Gap, leading to one of the greatest routs in military history. They had flown 2,554 sorties during the Battle of the Bulge. After the last mission, the total cost in lives for the 416th stood at 115 killed or missing in action. At war's end, forty-two men who had been listed as POWs were repatriated from the stalag-luft camps.

The time and contribution of the men of the 416th to the war effort, like that of so many other men, is now lucky to be a footnote in the history books.

Chapter Nineteen

Counting the Cost

I suppose if I had lost the war, I would have been tried as
a war criminal.

– *Gen. Curtis Lemay*

Upon entering their canvas home, Captain Rooney's tentmates were saddened even more by the sight of the makeshift decorations and the small cake they had managed to have baked by a local Frenchwoman. It was almost incomprehensible that Rooney, who had just been promoted to captain, was flying his "lucky" sixty-fifth. How was it that it was his time? Heck, he had made it to sixty-five. *What are our odds then*, everyone thought. He was going to be moved up the chain, even get some time back home after today. The guys had planned a big surprise party, which now had become a wake. The senior man in the tent walked over to Rooney's cot and gathered his personal effects, and threw out anything that might be remotely embarrassing to the family.

After Worms, personal effects were being collected all around the base and then turned over to the squadron adjutant. Crews were being listed MIA or KIA, if known. POWs would be listed once the Red Cross got access to the names, and any mistake in MIA or KIA status would then be corrected. Letters to the mothers and fathers had to be written. No one wanted that responsibility, but it was assigned and completed.

March missions continued on at a record pace, as communication centers, factory areas, gun positions, railroad bridges, oil storage areas, marshaling yards, and ordnance depots fell under the Norden crosshairs of the 416th. March also brought the group's first use of napalm, which was dropped over the Dinslaken factory area. At the same time, Patton's Third Army began pushing across the Rhine. By month's end, three more men from the 416th were to go missing in action, and Patton's soldiers had pushed past the Rhine.

The planes from the afternoon mission began arriving back at base. They had targeted the Marienburg storage area this afternoon using GEE-equipped Pathfinders with good results. Fortunately there were no red flares as the planes began their approaches. The ground crew was happy about that. They were still trying to get a grip on the repairs from all the damage on the morning mission. The debriefing was quick and painless, and everyone learned that the group had set some new record in March. Some officer was coming to the base to give them a commendation tonight.

The days were getting longer and warmer now. Everyone made plans to listen to Joe Bananas and his group tonight down on the flight line by the photo hangar. The men were looking forward to the fun.

Earl and Bill were walking back to the tent when they ran into Carl.

"How was it up there today?" Bill asked in the routine way.

"No sweat."

Earl looked at Carl's somber face, which now showed the realities of this war. "How many under your belt?"

"Not enough. Still on the back side of thirty-two."

"They'll go by quick enough. Besides, this war can't last forever."

"Thanks."

Entering the tent, the guys were greeted by Jack, who was stretched out on his cot listening to Lord Haw-Haw on the radio. Distemper had somehow made the trip from Melun, and was sleeping beside him on the floor. Jack was rubbing the dog's head.

Lord Haw-Haw was trying to convince the Americans of the senselessness of their efforts. He ranted, "It is a lost cause for you to continue this futile war, fighting and dying for your leaders who don't care about you. Fighting to help those Russians, the Bolshies who laugh at you every day behind your back. The German Army has captured Moscow, yet you Americans still resist us. When will you learn?"

"When's this crazy Kraut going to wake up and smell the roses? Adolf and company are finished. No one believes this Lord Haw-Haw crap anymore," Bill said.

Not that they ever did believe anything he said. Mostly the guys listened to it for the laughs. It had gotten to the point that they just wanted the music. Nearly everyone at the base believed now that the war was going to wind down sooner than later.

The propaganda came to an end when Haw-Haw said, "This is Germany signing off, station Bremen and station DBX signing off the thirty-one meter band. Our regular program in Gallic will follow."

"Listen, Bill, this guy is just doing his job," said Jack agreeably. "They know we were over the Rhine at Ludendorff in February. Heck, since that Worms' mission, has anybody heard about their 109s coming up at our guys?"

The reference to Worms had more meaning than Jack or the others knew. When Patton's Third Army had pushed over the Rhine in the region of Worms seven days earlier, they had attacked and captured a town named Gemunden, which was to provide the squadron with some good news.

Earl could feel it too. "Just the other day our guys pushed across at Wesel. Golly, I read in the *Stars and Stripes* that Patton went over with the Third Army some days before that at...Nier-stein...or something like that."

Bill interjected in an obviously happy, revengeful tone, "Heck, I've heard the Russians are almost in Berlin, not fightin' in Stalingrad anymore, that's for dang sure. The *Stars and Stripes* is already starting to write about Europe after the war. We're pushing those Krauts off the map."

"Yeah, I've heard that too." Carl got caught up in the enthusiasm of the conversation and chimed in. "Hope Patton beats them to Berlin."

Jack and Bill were already on easy street. They were done with their sixty-five, and both held orders to rotate back to the states. They were ready too. Things seemed very different to all of them now. Even with Carl's presence, the tent was empty without Roland and Hiram. They all five had fought from England, flew together on D day, and fought across France. Now it seemed incomplete, an empty victory. Bill, particularly, hadn't been the same.

"Any you guys going to hear Joe play tonight?" Carl asked.

"I don't know, probably," Bill replied. "You going?"

"I'm thinking about it. It will be my first time. Are they any good?"

Ralph Conte knocked on the frame of the tent's door and walked in. "You guys going?"

"Carl, ask Ralph about them," Bill said.

"Are Joe Bananas and his Boys any good?"

"Oh yeah, they play it all. Good swing sounds. They got a good brass group, but the piano is a little out of tune. What can you expect, though? It's survived a lot here." Ralph sat on the cot next to Jack and rubbed Distemper's head. "Funny, he doesn't shake when he sleeps."

Earl chuckled. "Yeah, I noticed that too. What do you think happened to him?"

"Doc thinks he's got something like that shakin' disease people get. What's that called?"

"I think it's...like Parkin's sickness...some-thun...Some-thun like that," Bill said.

"Yeah, that's it, Parkinson," Ralph confirmed. "Damn shame, he's a good dog." Ralph stroked the sleeping dog's back. "Hey, if we're going to get a good seat we need to get."

"Let's get," said Jack, rolling out of his bunk. Distemper immediately opened his eyes, rose up on his hind legs while bowing his back and stretching out his front legs. He whined a big yawn and then struggled up on all fours, shaking and wobbling as he moved toward the door. All the guys took what little remained of their month's liquor ration from their B-4s and poured a short one.

"Here's to the end of this war, going home, and our fallen friends," said Bill, pursing his lips in a defiant toast. Everyone else responded, "Here, here." The tin cups were raised to everyone's lips, and the whiskey went down.

One by one the men walked out of the tent, while lighting up a few Luckies. They started the walk toward the flight line where Joe and the Boys were to perform. Distemper wobbled out of the tent, in a walk of sorts alongside the guys. After a short distance he ambled over to the side of a tent and smelled it. Not recognizing the odor, he balanced on three shaky legs and raised the other to mark the tent.

"Crazy dog. Even with the shakes, dogs will be dogs," Earl joked. Everyone laughed.

The walk to the flight line was pleasant, as they all finished their smokes and tossed the butts into the proper sand-filled buckets. Walking out on the flight line, the group began to break up, as they each saw someone they wanted to say hello or good-bye to. Distemper made his own rounds, picking up strokes of affection as he wobbled through the growing crowd. Occasionally he got lucky, and was rewarded with a snack.

"Hey, Cooke, how was the trip today?" Jack asked as he walked up and extended his hand. Lieutenant Cooke accepted it with a firm grip.

"It was OK, but you won't believe what we found. Earl, Bill, Ralph, you need to hear this too," Cooke hollered.

The three officers walked over, followed by Don Sorrels and Ralph Conte. All five congregated around Cooke. Carl, having overheard the invitation, walked toward the group.

Cooke began his story. As kismet, luck, or divine intervention would have it, Cooke and his gunner Sergeant Russell Redding had been putting in some jeep time today around the town of Gemunden, Germany. "So let me tell you what Redding and I found today. You won't believe it. We were driving around with some of Patton's Third Army guys. Redding spotted an Invader that had crash-landed in a clearing off the road about three hundred yards uphill from us. Whose squadron do you think it was from?"

"How the heck would we know that?" Bill answered with a serious inflection of interest.

"I guess you're right. Anyway we pulled off the road and drove uphill straight to it. Hell, when we got there, we found out it was one of the ships Redding and I had flown. It had our group's black rudder markings and our ship's number, 237-D. The Army guys didn't believe us until we showed them Redding's jacket number that matched the number on the ship."

"Well, you weren't flying it, so who went down in her?" Earl asked.

"I found out today, when we got back. After checking the loading lists at Operations, I discovered it was Jokinen and Creeden in her. Heck, I think they're probably still alive. My guess is POWs. Anyway, Redding looked inside while I looked around outside. He didn't find any blood or bodies. The plane was shot up really bad, not to mention the landing, which tore it up pretty bad too. Both engines were full of holes, I don't know how he flew her that far. One thing's for damn sure—he set her down perfectly in that little clearing. All the bombs had been salvoed. Krauts had stripped all the 50s out of her, and took some of the flight maps too. We found the escape hatches popped open, and their flak jackets were in the woods out in front of the plane."

"Has Command heard from the Red Cross about their status or anything?" Ralph asked.

"Not that I know of, but I passed it up the chain, so at least they would know they probably aren't dead."

"Sounds good, let's hope they're OK," Jack optimistically interjected.

Officers with crews from all around the base began to show up, filling up the flight line. Bomber groups mixed with a number of different fighter and recon groups. Joe Bananas and the Boys had become a welcome relief to the daily routine as well as being local celebrities among the different groups and squadrons.

"Hey, Conte, I thought you were on the way home."

Ralph turned to see Captain Dick Wheeler walking his way. "Well, I don't leave until tomorrow, but I know you were gone. What brings you down here from Operations?"

"Came to hear Joe and the Boys and catch up with you guys."

"What's new?"

"Well, I finally found out what happened to Meagher."

"Oh, yeah, what?" Ralph was interested.

"He's in a hospital in Paris, been there since he went down. Just about lost his foot, I hear."

"At least he's still alive," Ralph said, happy to hear the news. "I'll need to tell the guys."

"OK, Ralph, good seeing you. I'll catch up with you in a bit," Dick said, as they shook hands.

The band settled in to their seats making the usual tuning sounds that bands make as they get ready. Joe walked up onto the bandstand, talked to a few of the guys, and then checked the microphone. The crowd started moving to their seats.

As Dick shuffled over to his spot, he recognized a fighter-group insignia on a pilot's jacket. He walked over and introduced himself. "I want to thank you guys for all the cover you provide for us. I owe you a big one. Back in December I was on a mission…" Dick related the story of how some Lightnings had come out of nowhere to save him and some of his flight. He also told how the last P-38 had been hit by flak, and then having flipped over, disappeared down into the clouds. "I feel really bad for that guy who saved our asses, then bought the farm."

The smiling young fighter officer looked Dick straight in the eyes and said, "Hey, it's OK, that's our job. Besides that guy's OK. It was me flying that 38. It scared the shit out of me too! When I took that hit, my plane rolled over before I could correct for the loss of lift. I pulled some G's while putting her into a steep dive to get away from the Krauts, then pulled her up on one engine. I powered the engine up, getting back to land her over at the 410th's field. Damned lucky really, but thanks for the worrying though."

"You betcha, and thanks," said Dick, and then saw Sorrels. "Hey, Don." He waved him over as he vigorously shook the 38 pilot's hand. "Don, this is that 38 pilot who saved our butts on that mission in December!"

He shook the pilot's hand too. "Thank you, it's good to see you made it. That was a tough one, a real tough one." Don thought of his good friend Svenson, who was lost about that time along with all the others.

"Yeah, I heard."

The band settled down as Joe approached the microphone.

"Gentlemen, if I can have your attention, please. We have an old friend here to address us today. He has a few words to share with us all tonight." Joe turned to the guest and directed him to the microphone. "Sir, it's all yours."

"Thank you, Joe. Hi, boys." The familiar phrase rolled from the group's old CO, Brigadier General Harold L. Mace, who was now the Ninety-Eighth Combat Wing commander. "You guys have been busy since I left."

A gentle understated laugh came from the crowd; followed by applause that drowned out any conversation. Dick, Don, and their new fighter buddy waved goodbye and headed off to find their fiends who were already enjoying the general's comments.

"Lieutenant General Omar Bradley sends his commendation for all the outstanding work the Ninth Bomb Group has done this record month. He thanks you for the fifteen thousand sorties and twenty-four thousand tons of munitions you've dropped on the enemy. The division was operational more than twenty-eight days this month, with one unbroken period of nineteen days. Two-thirds of your air offensive was directed at communications centers, marshaling yards, and bridges. These successful operations prevented the movement of the enemy troops into positions to resist our ground assaults. Your group is credited with destroying nine major railroad bridges, multiple marshaling yards, and countless rail lines and rail facilities. A four-day assault against gun positions in the northern area of the Ruhr freed the Twenty-First Army Group to expand its Rhine River bridgehead."

Mace paused and looked out over the crowd of young faces. Some smiled and others stared back with a look hardened by many combat sorties.

"As you all know, these successes do not come without a price…a price that you are all aware of…a price that commands us to stop…to remember our fallen brothers in arms…men who have gone to the peaceful skies beyond. We honor them by praying for a rapid end to this war, so that no more need leave this earthly existence before their time. As you know, this has been a costly month. Twenty-three bombers were lost to flak and enemy fighters, but we got our licks in too, destroying nine of their fighters and accomplishing all we had set out to do. General Bradley and I want to tell you how proud we are of this division. The country sends its great thanks. God bless America." With that, the general looked out over the crowd. Cheers and applause rose from the large crowd. Distemper howled his approval too, bringing laughter from small groups close by him. Waving a high hand toward the crowd, the general turned away from the microphone.

Walking to the microphone, Joe looked at the band. "Alright, boys, a one, a two, a three, and a four." The band hit its first note right on time, and belted out Dorsey's "Birmingham Bounce." The crowd cheered and applauded louder as the band played on. Missing hardly a beat, Joe and the boys rolled right into Dorsey's "Beale Street Blues," as the crowd began to settle down.

Unwilling to miss out on this event, Distemper made his way through the crowd shaking and wobbling his way up to the front. After sitting down just in front of the bandstand, he looked up at the band. Joe and the Boys finished "Beale Street Blues" and jumped right into Benny Goodman's "One O'clock Jump," bringing a cheer from the crowd. About halfway through the song, the crowd and then the band noticed that Distemper's head was bobbing or shaking, or whatever move his head made, in perfect time with the song. Everyone—including the band—was laughing so hard that the music stopped until the band members could get their composure back.

It was a day of good news and good humor. It had been worse before. It would be again in the future.

Chapter Twenty

Coming Home

*The death of one man is a tragedy. The death of
millions is a statistic.*

– *Joseph Stalin*

Well into 1945, the remaining strands of the Nazi attack on humanity were quickly unraveling. The infamous Auschwitz death camp was liberated by the advancing Russians around 3 p.m. on January 27, 1945. This stopped Dr. Josef Mengele's eugenic-inspired studies on twins, which involved all manner of barbarity and cruelty on his subjects. Notoriously known as the "Angel of Death," Mengele escaped ahead of the Russian assault. In April, the Buchenwald camp was also liberated by the Russians. With the capture of the camp, the American-inspired eugenicist Dr. Katzen-Ellenbogen was prevented from further barbarity on the inmates.[309] On April 30, Hitler committed suicide in Berlin, as the Allies rapidly approached from every side. Admiral Karl Dönitz took over the presidency for the remainder of the Third Reich's days. May 5 saw the liberation of the Mauthausen concentration camp, followed two days later with the unconditional surrender of the Nazi government. Poles, Jews, gypsies, homosexuals, and the mentally defective, as well as religious and political undesirables were freed from the camps that epitomized the successful institution of the world's eugenic movement through governmental policy. But the war claimed other lives as well, with more civilians than combatants dying in this eugenic struggle.

Atrocities were not, however, an exclusive practice of the Third Reich.[310] At the end of the war, Japan was the only country to have used chemical and biological weapons. The Japanese deployed such weapons at a variety of sites in China. These sites include the documented 1939 biological experiments in Harbin that left ten thousand dead, the 1940 bombing of Quzhou with bubonic plague and the bombing of Yunnan with cholera and anthrax, which attacks took two hundred thousand lives combined. Over the course of the war, POW deaths in Japanese prison camps approached 31 percent, compared to 1 percent for German camps. The Japanese were stopped in August 1945, just three months after the Germans surrendered.

The victory was one that President Franklin D. Roosevelt was unable to witness. He passed on before seeing the completion of the great efforts he had presided over during the last four years. He had been a heavy smoker and was plagued by hypertension in the later years of his life. On April 12, 1945, the president was having his portrait

---

309 *War Against the Weak: Eugenics and America's Campaign to Create a Master Race*, pp 320, 375; Edwin Black; Copyright 2003; Publisher, Four Walls Eight Windows
310 A Timeline of World War II, Deaths in World War II, http://www.scaruffi.com/ politics/wwii.html

painted in Warm Springs, Georgia. He was absorbed in his reading and had not been able to hold the pose, telling the artist Madame Shoumatoff, "We've got just fifteen minutes more." He lit a cigarette, then pressed his temple with his left hand. The hand fell and twitched.

Seeing the movement of his fingers, his confidante Miss Suckley asked, "Did you drop something?"

Placing his left hand on the back of his neck, he whispered softly, "I have a terrific headache." At 1:15 p.m. his arm fell and his head drooped to the left. He slumped in the chair. That morning his blood pressure had been 180 over 110 to 120, and had risen to over 300 systolic near the end.[311] The president passed, his spirit moving on to greet the many who in the last four or more years had gone on before him. He greeted many young men and women as well as the vast sea of children and innocents who had been killed in a war where more civilians had died than combatants. The goal had been noble and the cost painfully worth it. Those greeting him knew that then and now.

America was shocked along with the whole world, as Winston Churchill broke down during a speech describing to the House of Commons the loss of Roosevelt. Nearly sixteen years of domestic and world leadership had come to an end, the only leadership some young Americans had ever known. Roosevelt had helped rid the world of his evil counterpart's intent to change the world's values. It was a war that, regardless of the higher virtues it advanced, was won with the blood of good men and women.

⚜

At long last the war had come to an end, and for each man of the 416th it had ended differently. Some were returning home more or less whole, others were still recuperating well after the conflict was over, and many didn't return home at all. Those who made it out alive were anxious to get back to their lives.

Joe Meagher was recovering slowly from his ankle injury. He was still in a cast, and there was talk of surgery. The pain was finally almost gone, and bothered him mainly when he tried to walk or move around. He still couldn't put any weight on the leg, because the ankle was so severely shattered. He'd been told by the sawbones not to put weight on it anyway. Besides, it hurt too badly when he did, so the pain reminded him not to walk on it.

Joe enjoyed the attention of the nurses in the Paris military hospital, but all the while still wanted to get home. He had been told the war was over for him in more ways than one. He had completed his sixty-five, which was enough, but with the ankle injury he had been told it was unlikely he'd be able to stay in the military. Joe adapted to this new reality as he had adapted to all the situations this war had pushed on him and his fellow soldiers. The ankle injury ultimately kept him in the hospital for many months after the war was over. Joe did get home to start his new life.

311   The Glory and The Dream: A Narrative History of America- 1932–1972, William Manchester, Chapter 11, pp 349–354.

⚜

Jack Sittarich had listened to the sounds of battle off in the distance for some time as he stood in the compound of his stalag luft. It was near the end of April, and in spite of the sounds of battle, he was sad to learn of President Roosevelt's passing from a guard. Still, he was happy that it was spring. The stories he had heard about the winters were very scary, and he knew his blanket tent that he shared with two others would not hold up through a real winter. He prayed every day that the war would end soon, since he didn't like the idea of frostbite or being cold all winter.

Jack was annoyed about being confined, but surprised that his captors seemed to be treating them all pretty well. All in all, they had been a decent group of captors, and had shared tobacco and occasionally food. God knows, he was tired of sauerkraut and black bread. He was also surprised by how badly they spoke of Hitler. He had grown to know a few of the guards, all of whom were forty years old or better, and with families. "Have these guys always treated you this well?" he asked one of the senior camp members.

"No, it started getting better here a few months ago. Red Cross packages started coming through regular. Heck fire, we even got extra blankets. The food ain't much better, but at least it's regular now. We thought sumthun was up, some kinda inspection or sumthun. What's been going on with the war, we still winning?"

Jack didn't hesitate, "Oh, yeah! We've kicked their asses back inside Germany. Our group has been bombing in Germany for some months now. That's where I got shot down, over Worms."

"Maybe that explains all the old men and kids guarding us now," said the veteran prisoner as he looked around at all the goon towers and gate guards.

Not knowing any different type of prison, Jack couldn't relate to the changes the gaunt young sergeant was referring to. Jack was just happy it wasn't any worse.

All the senior prisoners were delighted with the news about the war that came in with every batch of new prisoners brought to the stalag luft. New prisoners kept the camp rumor mill going, especially about when their liberation would come. The veteran prisoners were delighted to know that the Allied armies were in Germany and driving toward Berlin. Talk began again among themselves of being home by summer, but never around the goons. Jack had been taught that the goons would even hide under the prison barracks at times, to try to overhear plans for an escape or any meaningful conversation.

In spite of all the difficulties here, the reality was that their freedom was drawing closer. The thought of it brought a guarded smile and a bouncier step into the prisoners' lives. They even held their shoulders straighter now. The guards noticed the change as well, and a few enterprising guards actually discussed helping some prisoners escape in exchange for surrendering themselves to the Americans. No German soldier or officer wanted to be taken by the Russians.

Recently he had noticed too that some of the guards had disappeared as the sounds of war drew closer. He wasn't sure if it was the Americans, British or Russians making all the noise off in the distance, but he hoped they were heading his way. Jack was concerned that things would get bad if the guards resisted the approaching Allies.

One day around noon the cannon fire and explosions ended. Jack hoped the right side had won. Later that day Jack heard the rumble of engines approaching. He waited to see if they were American tanks or German Panzers. He was relieved when a large Sherman tank rolled into the area outside the compound, and stopped at the gate just as the barrel of the turret poked through the wire. Jubilation filled the camp as the few remaining German guards laid down their guns and helmets, and walked down the road out of camp. Jack smiled as the US Army soldiers opened the gate.

Jack went to the gate to greet the tank sergeant, "Golly, are we happy to see you guys!" He shook the young sergeant's hand.

"Good to see you guys too. We woulda gotten here a little sooner 'cepten some of them SS Krauts put up a little fight back down at the bridge. Wouldn't surrender, won't be worrin' 'bout them no more."

"Heck fire, we're just happy you made it," Jack smiled, as he finally let the tanker's hand go.

Jack and his fellow POWs spent the next week in the camp as the repatriation process began. They were happy the ordeal was over. He and some of his fellow patriots were flown to La Havre, France, and then trucked to the harbor to be shipped home to New York. After a train ride to Minneapolis and a week in Fort Snelling, he was discharged from Uncle Sam's service and sent home.

❦

Lieutenants R.A. Wipperman and W.H. Palin finished the duration of the war in their stalag luft. They were treated well, but as in most camps, food was never in good supply. Both officers lost weight, but were confident that they would be free soon, along with all the other prisoners being held by the Wehrmacht and the Luftwaffe.

❦

Lieutenant Ross Cornell spent time at dulag luft, near Frankfurt, as all the aircrews did. His stay was prolonged there due to his injury, but after recovery he was shipped to a couple of stalag lufts. First, he spent time at Stalag Luft 3 and then his final destination 7A, near Moosburg, Germany, before his liberation on April 29th. His leg wound healed, but he lost twenty pounds over that short period of time. After his transition back to the states and a visit to his family, Ross contacted Roland Enman's parents and Marguerite in response to a letter that she had sent to Ross's folks.

Childers, Texas
May 18th, 1945

Dear Mr. Connell,

Lt. Roland Enman's father, who lives in Mass., sent me your address.

Roland and Ross were together and always in my letters from Roland he mentioned your son's name.

Sunday I went to see Lt. Jack Smith who has recently returned from combat duty and knew both our loved ones very well; however, Smith completed 65 missions and returned to the states after they went missing in March. Of course, he could give me no information but he does feel sure he can write a friend who is still there and perhaps find more definite information.

Mother and I talked to Lt. Smith for about three hours and I can assure you it was very nice to talk to someone who has recently been with Roland & Ross. Smith said Worms, Germany, is mountainous country and doubted they could make a crash landing. If they bailed out, the Germans would have continued shooting 'til the fellows got down. Certainly doesn't sound good.

Each day I continue looking for a letter. If you learn any news won't you please let me know? I will appreciate it so very much and I will do the same.

Sincerely,

Marguerite

Ross found himself in the difficult position of writing a painful but necessary letter to inform the families and loved ones of the bravery their son had exhibited and the event causing his loss.

Portland, Oregon

August 5, 1945

Dear Mr. & Mrs. Enman,

It isn't easy for me to write this letter to you, but I'm sure that you deserve to know the details of March 18th. A few days ago a letter came from Marguerite in which she mentioned that she had received no news of Roland. I am writing a letter to you, Marguerite, and the Carters explaining as best I am able what happened. I'm sorry that I can't say definitively what happened to Roland or Carter.

On March 18th we took off in our A-26 light bomber to attack a target at Worms, Germany. The mission had been planned to be a P.F.F. mission. That is, the bombs were to be dropped on the target though a cloud layer by means of a special target-locating device. About 50 miles from the target, however, the weather cleared and we could see our target clearly and, of course, the flak gunners could see us as well. We were in the second "flight" of ships. Over the target we received "moderate accurate" flak and two ships were seen to explode to bits from direct hits. Our lead bombardier finally found the target and we dropped our bombs O.K. As we turned off the target, we had a shell burst very close to the cockpit, sending shell fragments through the ship. I was momentarily dazed by the shock. Roland evacuated back to the cockpit and asked me if I was hurt. I felt my stinging left leg and found it bloody but still in working order, so I told him that I thought we could make it. Just then the left engine oil pressure dropped to zero and the prop governor failed. I stopped the engine. By this time we had fallen out of formation and were losing altitude. Several instruments, including the airspeed indicator, were shot out. Roland again came back to call my attention to our *course of 40*, which would take us on into Germany. I checked this against my magnetic compass which read 270* and we decided that his compass was out. Roland again went back to the nose.*

It was then that the right engine caught afire from a severed gas line. With the engine on fire and smoke coming into the cockpit, I ordered the crew to "abandon ship." Called this three times but received no answer from Roland or Sgt. Carter. Also turned on the emergency alarm bell. It was then I realized that Carter hadn't said a thing since being hit. It is my opinion that he was knocked out or killed by shell fragments. I heard Roland salvo his emergency escape door and assumed that he had jumped. By this time we were down to about 3,500 ft. and the fire was eating the wing away. I jumped out and opened my chute. I was in the air about 45 seconds and in that time I saw the ship crash and burn, but did not see other chutes. Roland could have jumped enough ahead of me that I couldn't see him or possibly his chute failed to open properly. Another possibility is that he got tangled up in the escape hatch and didn't clear the ship. If he did bail out O.K. and was captured as was I, he could have been killed by the German civilians. I can tell you that it is only by the mercy of God that they didn't kill me. The civilians were very hostile. Fortunately, though, five German soldiers also were with the civilians that captured me and they prevented violence and took me to prison. I looked for Roland in prison camps but never found a trace of him.

Had Roland been captured and taken to prison, surely you would have heard from him or the government by now. Between this and the other possibilities, Roland's return looks hopeless to me. I know this is hard for you, and you can be sure it is also hard for me. From talks with my wife and parents I know what you are going through.

Roland and I went to Paris and other places together and I found him to be an outstanding officer. He put everything into his work of being a good bombardier and his record proved it.

I will be glad to hear from you again in regard to any news from Roland or in regard to additional details about March 18th.

Sincerely your friend,
Ross

Painful acceptance was not reserved just for Roland's family. America was dealing with the loss of loved ones everywhere. Letters like this were exchanged daily.

Roland Enman

Left: the newly commissioned officer in the Merchant
Marines stands on deck of the *SS Uruguay*; Right: a fresh
second lieutenant in the US Army Air Corps.
Reproduced with permission of Doug and Jane Enman

Lieutenant Roland Enman and Staff Sergeant Ashton Carter never came home. Like so many American boys, their bodies were recovered after the war. Their resting spot as well as the Invader's was found five kilometers west of Birkenfeld and fifty-five kilometers west of Worms by the Dutch group of Bomber Command. During excavation of the site, the mortal remains of the two were exhumed and repatriated. Roland's and Ashton's families received the news that their children had been buried in St. Avold, France, in January 1947. The "tin soldier" was home. Roland's father always remembered and regretted the comparison he had made. He was equally unhappy with the US military for returning Roland's violated uniforms, which had been stripped of their insignias.

Staff Sergeant Carter's family experienced similar grief, but every family's experience was something uniquely their own. As with so many families of the time, Carter's entire family had been committed to the war effort. His two brothers were in the fight, as were his two sisters. Warrant Officer Wright V.B. Carter had been stationed in New Guinea. His other brother, Corporal Arthur N. Carter, was at home on leave the day the Air Corps notified the family of Ashton's MIA status. His two sisters—Sergeant Ruth Wright stationed in Great Falls, Montana, and Private Addie Sinclair stationed in Washington—learned of the news later. Families all across America accepted the reality of their painful losses.

⚜

When the war ended, Al Damico had been home for some time. After his or-
deals, he was very happy to be with his family. He married, raised a fine family, and
enjoyed the rich gravy of life, including becoming a valued member of the future 416th
reunion group.

⚜

Sergeant Lee yelled out to his gunners: "Hey, guys, only one more. I'm heading out today and I'm not in any hurry to have a hangover." They were celebrating his
orders to go home. He was to report to Scotland, and then ship out to New York. He
was scheduled to attend Officer's Candidate School (OCS) at Perrin Field in Sherman,
Texas. It was a major training center for the Army Air Corps and a historic base, first
established after December 7, 1941.

After some R&R in Miami with his wife, Lee attended OCS, intending to become
a gunnery officer and instructor there. However, when he reported, he was advised by
the adjutant at the base that he had 137 points, well above the required minimum number for discharge. He was given a choice—be promoted to captain or be mustered out.
Lee chose the latter and went home to Pulaski, Tennessee. After some time back home,
he moved with his wife to Knoxville, Tennessee, to attend law school at the University of
Tennessee. His life then took him back to Pulaski, where he moved from law to a construction business, and on to an elected judgeship. Most importantly, he and his wife
raised three children.

⚜

After they had landed in England, Ralph Conte said good-bye to Jack and Bill.
Shaking hands with no fanfare, they all three headed off in different directions to their
new assignments, since the war was still going on. Ralph had been assigned to the Adjutant's Office as a courier. Bill was scheduled to ferry aircraft in the Air Transport Command. Jack was looking at flying some recruitment tours in B-25s. How they got home
wasn't important; just getting there was.

Ralph reported to his new assignment as a courier. He did a lot of flying in
his new assignment, and eventually was scheduled on a flight to New York that came
with some R&R. Ralph could hardly wait. He watched out the window of the C-47 as
it banked in on final to land at Mitchell Field, Long Island. Ralph was delighted to be
home. After he delivered his messages, he immediately went about completing the tasks
he had set for himself. *First things first,* Ralph thought. Heading for the nearest soda
fountain, he sat down at the counter and ordered an ice-cream float. The taste of the
ice cream mixed with soda was heavenly, a taste he hadn't experienced for many years
and never took for granted again. Draining the last drop of melted ice cream from the
glass, Ralph wiped his mouth and looked around the shop for a pay phone. Spying one

near the back of the store, he slid off the stool and reached into his pocket for a dime. He dropped the dime in and dialed.

A voice answered, "Aircraft Engineering, can I help you?"

"May I speak with Norma, please?"

"May I tell her who is calling?"

"Lieutenant Ralph Conte."

"One moment please, Lieutenant Conte." Norma's secretary put Ralph on hold, and then rang Norma's phone.

"Put him right through!" said Norma.

Norma snapped up the phone, not even letting it finish the first ring. With unreserved excitement she talked with her lifelong love, and immediately made arrangements for them to meet that evening. After finishing the long-awaited call, she turned to her typewriter and drafted a letter of resignation, which she submitted that day. Leaving the office, she never looked back.

After the call, Ralph caught a taxi to his home in Paterson, New Jersey. Arriving at his father's corner butcher shop, he was greeted by his mother, "Raffie, si arrivato!"[312] Ralph battled with the taxi driver to finally accept the fare, then turned to greet his mother and father. His mother gave him a hug and kiss, while his father stood in the shop window with tears. His father was crying because several of the neighborhood boys had been killed and many more were still at war. After a loving homecoming, Ralph journeyed that evening to Norma's hometown, which was just down the road. There he learned of the wedding plans. He and Norma were married three weeks later in Clifton, New Jersey, in Norma's hometown Catholic church. Their honeymoon was a whirlwind to New York City and then a transfer to Atlantic City and then to Texas for instructor training.

In August the Manhattan Project proved to be the deciding factor for the end of the Pacific war, and gave Ralph the opportunity to reflect on his goals. Ralph mustered out in November '45. He had more than enough points now, and wanted to attend Rutgers University. After graduating from Rutgers, Ralph continued to lead by being elected to community government. He and Norma raised a family and participated in the 416th reunion organization.

⚜

Bill Tripp finally made it home in May '45. He met his love Joanne first thing. They had been together since high school, and wanted no more than to spend the rest of their lives together. He and Joanne were married May 13, 1945, in their hometown of Dedham, Massachusetts, at the Allen Congregational Church. Their honeymoon was a week in Savannah, Georgia, followed by a week at the Ritz Carlton in Atlantic City, courtesy of the Army Air Corps leave. An outstanding time it was too!

When the honeymoon was over, Bill was assigned to his duty station at Romulus Field Air Transport Command in Michigan. From there he ferried aircraft to the East Coast. On the return trip to Romulus, he could generally make time to get to LaGuardia

312   Italian – Ralph, you came home.

Field. Meanwhile, Joanne would leave her job at R.H. Macy & Co. and meet Bill at a park bench close by the field. They would spend precious moments there together until he had to leave again.

After ferrying aircraft from Romulus to various locations on the east coast, Bill received orders reassigning him to a post in Europe. His new orders were to fly war-weary B-24 Liberators home to the states for their new roles. In due course, most of the Liberators—as well as Havocs, Invaders, and every other make of plane—ended their distinguished careers in the salvage yard or on the target range.

Bill and Joanne

Lieutenant William Tripp and new bride Joanne on May 13, 1945. Many returning soldiers and airmen took the leap after returning stateside.
Reproduced with permission of Joanne Tripp

When Bill discussed the new assignment with Joanne, she reminded him of an opportunity he had with American Airlines. As Bill contemplated the future with his new wife, the two of them decided he had pushed his luck long enough in the military. As it did for many returning veterans, the new points system gave them a way to resign their commissions. Bill had accumulated plenty of points to submit his resignation, so he did. All at once, Bill was a civilian again, after five tough years of service to his government and the good people of this nation. Bill began what was to become a thirty-year career with American Airlines management. Joanne and his family were always at his side.

Jack Smith finally made it home. His first mission was to visit with the family. The second order of business was to see his girl, Rosalie. Jack drove his Studebaker down the winding dirt roads toward the old home place. The same roads he and his brothers had walked to town and back on many times before the war. Pulling into the old home place Jack pulled on the brake and turned off the ignition. Sitting in the car he took a deep draw on his Lucky and looked into the graveyard thirty yards from where he sat listening to the birds and noting a gentle breeze rustling the leaves. Getting out of the car Jack dropped the butt and crushed it under his right shoe then walked toward the Winton chapel graveyard. He walked to the two freshly covered graves and read the two headstones, one engraved with his father's name the other with his older brother's name. He missed them both. It saddened him to know that his brother's body was really somewhere in the deep blue Pacific Ocean "on eternal patrol" with so many other good men. It brought the most painful price of war home to Jack. Standing over the graves, Jack began to realize the type of world he had been living in for so many years, a world of death and unrelenting destruction. The Godly lessons and concepts about the realities and penalties of killing had been repressed these many years. It made Jack see another cost of war to its participants. He thought of his two other brothers. Bill was flying Superfortresses over China, and Pat was still serving in the Navy. Bill was being forced to kill civilians in Burma who sneaked into their bombers at night to steal things. If they were caught, they killed you or had to be killed while trying to escape. War degraded us all.

Jack turned from the headstones and looked toward the one-room Methodist chapel. He turned toward the old home place and began a prayer for the safe return of his brothers. He didn't want his family to end up like the Sullivan family from the early days of the Pacific war. Jack hoped the statistics were in his family's favor. In the end, the family was blessed, and that prayer answered. His brothers returned home safely, although not without some hidden wounds.

Leaving the graveyard, he headed back to town to talk with Rosalie and his family about many things and about staying in the military. Sitting at the kitchen table, they all talked for a while and drank coffee and smoked. After having covered all the news about the family and the local townspeople, finally the conversation rolled around to his plans for the future. His current orders included flying goodwill tours around the states to boost recruitment. He was looking forward to it, since there was nothing he enjoyed more than flying. He seemed to enjoy it more when people weren't trying to kill him. Jack helped everyone understand how much he enjoyed the Air Corps, particularly the flying. He felt he had found a home with them. With the war winding down, he thought a career in the service would be good for him and that he could serve his country in a meaningful way.

His leave came to an end, and Jack reported for duty. His recruitment tour was brief, but then he began a long career of transfers in and out of Greenland,

Newfoundland, and the states, while racking up tens of thousands of hours flying all types of aircraft from the Air Force inventory.

All this time Jack continued to court Rosalie. In 1950, Jack realized he wanted her and a family, and proposed. They both knew it was time to start a family, since their love for each other had survived the test of time, distance, and war. She accepted. They were married in Panama City, Florida, in a small military wedding. Over the next thirteen years, during what seemed to be as many transfers, Rosalie gave birth to five children in four pregnancies. Between all the moves, Jack and Rosalie worked hard and yet still somehow raised their five children. Jack continued his flying while rising through the ranks in the USAF, ultimately being assigned to Kelly Air Force Base, near San Antonio, in the early sixties. There an untimely heart attack prematurely grounded him in 1961. It ended a career in the Air Force that had lasted through two hot wars and the first fifteen years of the cold one. He and Rosalie then made their final transfer, back home to Tennessee.

❦

Dean Vafiadis rotated out of the group, and was sent home to a happy family and an equally happy future. After arriving stateside, he did what so many other veterans did, and mustered out of the service, because the points system allowed them that choice. Dean had had an interest in motorcycles before the conflict, and now decided to build on that by opening a motorcycle shop in his hometown. Over the years he sold many types of motorcycles. Every Sunday you could see him riding through town on the way to church dressed in a white tuxedo with a bow tie and his wife on the back. It was the signature mark of his business. Dean had a good life and raised a fine family with his wife.

❦

"Thy will be done," Earl said with more sincerity and intensity than ever before, as he rolled the Invader to the takeoff line, He was on his last mission, and he had no reason to alter his ritual now. The throttles were advanced and the bird responded, starting down the runway. Earl unfailingly continued the tradition that had safely brought him this far, singing,

> It is not mine to question the judgment of my Lord,
> It is but mine to follow the leadings of His Word;
> But if to go or stay, or whether here or there,
> I'll be, with my Savior, content anywhere!

Earl rotated the Invader into its takeoff climb, and turned his attention to cleaning up the airframe. Gear up at fifty feet and flaps up at 140 mph, as he climbed to altitude, and instinctively found his slot in formation. He wasn't excited about this flight leader he was assigned to fly with today, some new academy grad learning the ropes at his expense. He tried flying all over the place to avoid the flak, making it hard to keep the planes in formation. It also burned a lot of fuel. Fuel that Earl knew was critical, having experienced being without it one time. He thought back to that eventful day in February '45.

"You ready to go back there, over? Earl radioed to Frank Basford, his gunner on this Window mission.

"Roger, got all the aluminum strips ready to go. Seems kind of funny dropping strips of aluminum instead of bombs, don't it, sir?"

"Yeah, you just wait. Once those Germans start targeting us instead of the group, you'll wish we had some bombs to drop."

"You've done this before?"

"No, but I've heard enough to know we're gunna be flying all over Germany trying to keep our butts alive."

"Holy shit, Lieutenant, I would have flown with someone else if I knew that."

"It's too late now, Basford. Get ready to push some of that stuff out. Opening bomb bay doors now." Earl reached for the lever.

The doors swung open into the slipstream, and the wind immediately whistled around Basford. Freezing February air was made colder by the twelve thousand feet altitude.

"Doors open and ready to go."

"Roger, give 'em a load now," Earl ordered.

"Bombs away," Basford joked, as he let the first load of aluminum strips fall.

The chaff tumbled out of the plane and spread across the sky like a flock of aluminum birds reflecting the sunlight. It began its slow, fluttering descent to the ground, all the while reflecting not just the sunlight but also the radar waves back to the German oscilloscopes.

In seconds, exploding shells changed the sky from a blue tranquil world to a deadly smoke- and metal-filled maelstrom. Each explosion caused the Invader to shudder in fear. Earl knew that was the signal to get the hell out of here. "Hold on, Frank."

Earl nosed down and rolled right. While powering up the manifold pressure, he descended and turned to a new heading and altitude to avoid the deadly accurate flak.

"Give then some more…now, Frank," Earl ordered, as they turned out fifteen hundred feet lower and headed ninety degrees off their original course.

"Out the door, sir." Frank watched the shiny strips spread over the sky below and behind the Invader.

Seeing the new location of the "planes," the Germans redirected their *flugabwehrkanonen* to that altitude and heading. The detonation of perfectly fused and well-aimed 88s was again the clue for Earl to move, which he did by giving up altitude or climbing back up as he headed away from the target area, pulling the 88s along with him. He just prayed they wouldn't encounter any bandits.

After several close calls, Earl finally checked his watch and noted that the mission should be over if the group had hit the IP on time. Earl scanned his instrument panel; everything looked good until he saw his fuel gauges. "Holy cow! Boat deck one, this is Window, over."

"Roger, this is boat deck one."

"I'm low on fuel, and request alternate landing sight. Don't think I can make it to base, over."

Boat deck one gave Earl a heading to a closer airbase in Belgium and the radio settings to reach it, if needed.

Turning onto the heading, Earl looked down and saw nothing but cloud cover below them. Checking the fuel gauges, Earl knew he had no other choice. He eased back on the throttles, and began his slow descent toward the Belgian base. "Frank, we're just about out of fuel. If we start to have problems, you should bail out. Do you understand?"

"I get it. Let me know how it goes."

The Invader entered the cloud cover; Earl watched the fuel gauges drop. If he had to bail, he knew how he was going to get out, and hoped Frank was ready too. Earl had no idea when he would break out of this cloud cover, and hoped he didn't fly right into the ground as he finished the third verse of his favorite hymn. At fifteen hundred feet the cloud base formed, and the Invader popped out. Earl and Frank both breathed a sigh of relief, and Earl radioed the base for landing instructions.

"Roger that, Window, you're cleared on runway 2-1 right, over."

"Roger, 2-1 right, on final now," said Earl, as he lowered the gear and then the flaps. As he reduced airspeed, he watched the needles bounce off the stop peg of his fuel gauges. He saw the start of the runway now, and prayed that he would just get over the end of it before he ran out of fuel. He could feel the sweat on his forehead as he reached up to wipe some out of his right eye.

"How we doing?" It was Frank checking in.

"OK, so far. Nothing we can do now at this altitude anyway 'cept pray."

"I'm doing plenty of that for both of us."

"Me too," Earl replied, as the Invader slid over the start of the runway. He pulled back on the throttles, and touched down. He cut the throttles and idled the engines, and the Invader settled down on all three landing gear. Both men counted their blessings, and Earl called the tower, "Tower, this is Window, need taxi instructions, over."

"Roger, taxi to hardstand in northeast, turn to zero-three-six, over."

As Earl was turning off the runway onto his ground heading, the engines quit. Not with a sputter, they just quit. All the tanks were bone-dry now. The propellers spun down to a stop. Earl tried to crank the port engine several times, and then realized he needed to get a tow. Both men now saw how blessed they were. Two or three minutes earlier and they could have been dead. As the Invader rolled to a stop, Earl called the tower to report the situation.

Next day, on returning to base, Earl found out this mission had turned into a snafu. The plan had been to bomb the Kemper Command Headquarters. Somehow, most of the flights had gotten separated, which was made worse because the PFFs that were carrying the GEE equipment got jammed over the primary target. What was left of the group tried to drop visually. The lead in A-Box made a second run, but there was a foul-up in the release mechanism in the bomb bay, so none of the planes dropped. The B-Box went to the secondary target, Lingen, and had a successful GEE drop with the Pathfinders. But half the group going out that day had ended up bombing Scherfede. Earl wondered why he had risked his and his gunner's life for this.

Earl followed the group lead all over the sky on his sixty-fifth, as they headed toward the target. Würzburg was well-protected with flak, so it was going to be hairy once they got to the IP. The group had been assigned to destroy some warehouses, for whatever reason, and that's what they were going to do. Earl was up for it, though. He wanted to end this sixty-fifth and final mission at the base, safely on the ground and nowhere else. Earl found himself sweating more than he had in a long time. His prayers were coming a little more frequently on this mission too. He knew why though. The orders back at the base for his reassignment were tucked into his B-4.

At the IP the group began its starboard turns onto the bomb-run. Carl was in the flight behind Earl's and watching as Earl's flight turned in and leveled out at twelve thousand feet for the two-minute run in. The flak was pretty heavy, but by now Carl categorized it as moderate, compared to what he'd lived through in the past. Worms never was far from his mind or any of the others' now.

While watching Earl make his turn onto the bomb-run, Carl thought how he was going to be the last man in the tent after today's mission. He found himself hoping Earl might get assigned to some base duty for a while. He didn't really know any of the new guys, and even though he had been here only a short time, he felt closer to Earl than anybody. Carl eased on the right rudder with a little right aileron, and followed Earl's lead onto the run. He threw the bomb bay lever. His ship was buffeted and shaken more, as the ever-increasing flak sent out shockwaves.

"Doors open," his gunner called back.

"Roger."

Carl looked ahead at Earl as an 88 exploded in front of Earl.

Earl felt his ship hesitate in midair as the shockwave hit the nose. The control surfaces shook through his yoke as the shockwave passed over. The Invader stormed into the cloud of black smoke and German steel right in front of him. Hot steel pinged off or penetrated the nose.

"Thy will be done," said Earl pushing on. He sang,

It may be I must carry the blessed Word of life
Across the burning deserts to those in sinful strife;
And though it be my lot to bear my colors there,
If Jesus goes with me, I'll go anywhere!

As Earl sang, he noticed over the intercom that his gunner was singing with him. He was happy for the extra, uplifting voice.

Earl saw the lead pickle off the first salvo, and instinctively with perfect timing he pushed his release button. "Bombs away!" Feeling the bombs ripple out, he waited.

"All clear."

"Roger." Seeing the green lights, Earl reached for the last time to close the much-lighter Invader's bomb bay. Then he kicked hard left rudder while pushing down on the elevators and applying left aileron. The Invader turned down into the evasive maneuver and pushed the manifold pressure up. Earl was ready to get the hell off this bomb-run when an 88 round detonated under his right wing, throwing the Invader upward onto its side. Earl and his gunner heard the hot breath of death penetrating the left wing and fuselage. Earl quickly and efficiently scanned the instrument panel—everything was green. *Two more hours,* Earl thought, as he pulled the Invader out of its dive at nine thousand feet and leveled out at 300 mph. He stayed on his lead's course, and turned his weapon toward the bomb line and RP for the final time.

The flight back to base was uneventful. Earl knew the skies had been swept clear of any enemy aircraft. P-38s, P-47s, P-51s and the Brits' Spitfires owned the sky now, that was one bit of comfort, along with the radio broadcast he had tuned into. As he listened to Duke Ellington's "Mood Indigo," he thought that the war couldn't go on much longer.

Before touching down, he had one more thing to do. Watching the plane land ahead of him, Earl banked in behind him and put the Invader into a shallow dive and then leveled off one hundred feet over the field. He was performing the traditional base-buzzing that every pilot did at the end of his sixty-fifth mission. Everyone from the Red Cross to the base commander watched as the Invader zipped across the field. Then Earl pulled the plane into a steep climb, rolled to the right, and leveled out to begin his approach. After touching down perfectly, Earl taxied to his revetment.

After methodically going through his shut-down routine, he unstrapped himself and popped the hatch. Earl crawled out of the cockpit, happy to be back safe and sound. He turned to look at his plane and placed his hand against the fuselage of the nose below the words *Classy Lassy Helen* and closed his eyes whispering, "Thy will be done." The debriefing truck pulled up. Turning away, Earl walked over to it and never looked back.

Stepping out of the debriefing, Earl was ready for a cup of joe. As he walked to the Red Cross tent, he was greeted by the smiling, familiar faces of the ladies who had been here so many times after the good and bad missions. He smiled too as they brought a tray with doughnuts spelling out "sixty-five", and a cup of hot coffee. Earl began to realize that it was over now, and felt the reality set in as the pressure slipped away. Smiling broadly while receiving congratulations and handshakes from his comrades and the Red Cross ladies, Earl took his cup of coffee.

The Best Doughnut Ever

A happy Lieutenant Earl Hayter holds his 65th mission
doughnut, which the Red Cross ladies at Laon, France, had
made for him. Earl was one of the last of the tentmates to
rotate out.
Reproduced with permission of Earl Hayter

Earl's remaining time on the base was spent casually, and Carl was glad for it. The last week of April brought Earl's orders home. On V- E Day he was in England boarding the Liberty ship *USS General Brooks*. While reading the *London Daily Mirror*, Earl watched England vanish over the horizon as the troop ship steamed west.

Mirror of the Times

Lieutenant Earl Hayter's reading material as he left England
on his troop ship home to New York.
Reproduced with permission of Earl Hayter

In the press

Newspaper articles about the German surrender
and the Goebbels' family suicide
Reproduced with permission of Earl Hayter

When he arrived in New York, he was greeted with celebrations from a boat in the harbor that had a band playing "One Meatball" by Hy Zaret and Lou Singer. Earl smiled as he listened.

A little man walked up and down,
He found an eating place in town,
He read the menu through and through,
To see what fifteen cents could do.
One meatball, one meatball,
He could afford but one meatball.

Earl's reception in the harbor was never forgotten, nor was the song.

After he stepped ashore, Earl filled his time visiting with family, and then was sent to Santa Ana, California, for therapy for ringing in the ears. The problem wasn't surprising given that when he did his duty for nearly four years, two 2,000-hp engines were located within arm's length and were running full-bore.

Victory over Japan ended Earl's relationship with the military. His relationship with Helen had ended before that. Uncle Sam was equally as cold in its separation, giving Earl a discharge and a ticket home. He spent one year at the University of Washington, hoping to fly for the Forest Service if he achieved a degree in forestry. But, he found out that the Forest Service outsourced those jobs, so he moved back home to help his family reunite and move off the stump ranch.

After returning home, Earl became a flight instructor, and then worked for the Boeing Aircraft Company. An opportunity to own and operate his own flying company came along, and before he knew it, he owned a couple airplanes with a fellow flyer. The company was dismantled, however, after an unfortunate crash killed his friend and a terrible winter destroyed his planes.

It wasn't long before Earl met Juanita Stanaway, who became his wife of thirty-eight years and the mother of their two girls. But Earl still missed flying, so he joined the Air Reserve, and after twenty years retired from it. He also worked for Puget Sound and Light, from which he retired in 1982. All along the way he used the skills he was taught in the CCC.

Since then, Earl's time has been filled with family, the loss of his first wife and his marriage one year later to another good woman named LaVerne, who had lost her husband ten days before Earl lost Juanita. They travel, dance, and enjoy life together. He makes it a point to attend the 416th reunions, and continues his tradition of singing "If Jesus Goes With Me" and quoting the Lord's Prayer whenever they fly.

⚜

Carl Weinert wasn't happy to see Earl ship out. Earl was the last of his original tentmates. He didn't look forward to making new friends, realizing now how his old tent mates must have felt about him when he arrived. Carl was to be rewarded soon by the armistice. By then he had flown forty-three missions and was happy to spend his time after the armistice around Paris, until he was ordered to fly to northern France to have Tokyo fuel tanks installed into the bomb bay, to lengthen the plane's range for the flight home.

The flight home was a long one. First, he flew south to Marseilles for refueling, where Carl learned the Japanese had surrendered. Then, he and his crew moved on, past the Rock of Gibraltar and on to Marrakech, Morocco for rest and fuel. The next leg took him to Dakar, Senegal, for fuel, so they could complete the flight over to Fortaleza, Brazil. It was on the flight north to Hunter Field in Savannah, Georgia, that Carl and his crew discovered singing radio commercials, which they found very entertaining.

Neither the Armed Forces radio nor the German radio stations played commercials throughout the war.

Carl mustered out of the Air Corps, and focused his life on his wife Mickie and raising a family. He pursued his education and then worked many years as an engineer at Boeing Aircraft. Retirement did not slow him and his wife down. They have spent their golden years enjoying life, the 416th reunions, and their children and grandchildren.

∾❦∾

Wayne Downing was reunited with his wife and Army nurse, Norma, after the war. Just as his commitment to the cause had carried him on eighty-six missions during the war, so would his commitment to his country carry him to protect our freedoms in a long career in the USAF. He and his wife raised a family and supported America throughout the Cold War. In the early 1950s, he participated in Operation Tumbler-Snapper, which investigated and tested atomic bombs in Nevada. Later, he flew B-47s with the Forty-Third Bomb Group from Davis Monthan AFB, and then transitioned into B-52s with the 4038th Strategic Wing at Dow AFB. Wayne protected our country like so many others, during one of the most difficult times in the world's history. It was a time when humankind's ability to destroy all of humanity almost outweighed its ability to control the forces and pressures constantly pushing toward using the bomb.

∾❦∾

At the end of the war, Wes Chitty went home to start his life anew. Family, friends and happiness filled that time, as it did for so many of the others who came home from the conflict.

∾❦∾

Richard V. Wheeler, a West Point graduate, went on to a distinguished career in the USAF, including setting a record for a high-altitude parachute jump.

∾❦∾

Amidst America's rapid postwar demobilization, the 416th went into the history books. After the war the airmen flew their planes to Camp Miles Standish, Massachusetts, where the group was disbanded on October 24, 1945. Many of the Invaders went on to see combat in Korea and Vietnam with new pilots and new missions. The longevity of the A-26 airframe as a good weapons platform was due to its ability to loiter over targets and its high speed. But piston-driven aircraft were losing the edge to faster jet-powered fighters and fighter-bombers. The traditions of the 416th were honored in the fifties, as a wing of B-52s were named after the 416th and in the sixties served over the skies of Vietnam.

It is impossible to thank the multitudes of men who sacrificed their precious lives unselfishly in the skies, on the beaches or in the countryside of Axis-held territory to crush the vile belief of eugenics.

∝W∾

The Third Reich's organized propaganda machine had attacked the belief systems in one country that had freed so many in America less than a hundred years before. This misguided hate-filled machine had adulterated humankind's personal responsibility to itself and ultimately its God. The successful destruction of these beliefs in Germany allowed the formation and operation of the death camps, because the public turned an approving yet fearful eye. The Holocaust succeeded, because through science the lunatic Hitler found the "people" to blame. Eugenics had found its perfect model, and it was called the Holocaust.

Besides the vast number of men and women that it affected, the war, of course, had many other far-reaching consequences, especially on the eugenics movement and international politics. One would like to say the study of eugenics and the racism it inspired ended with the war. However, even though the study of eugenics on a broad scale had started declining before the war, it never completely disappeared. The ultimate death-filled expression of eugenics was ended with the defeat of its Nazi practitioners but sadly, elements of the ideology live on today.

Even before the war, in the late thirties, American private funding of the eugenic organizations was coming to an end, as the financiers began to realize the racism that the organizations were actually producing and supporting. The public organizations, from Congress on down, were slower but supported the private sector's efforts to escape the grips of "negative eugenics" and the fearmongering associated with it. By 1938 the Carnegie Institute had had enough of the pseudoscience of eugenics. It withdrew its support of the publication *Eugenical News*. In 1939 Vannevar Bush, then president of the Carnegie Institute, told Harry Laughlin of the Eugenics Record Office not to expect funding from them that year. In spite of slackening support for the ideology, Laughlin testified before Congress in 1939 in favor of restrictive immigration legislation for Jews and other peoples entering America from oppressive nations. After speaking, Laughlin received a reprimand of sorts from an informed American citizen, who castigated him for citing and supporting the material published in *Mein Kampf* to Congress.[313]

In the face of a hostile environment, other eugenics efforts transformed themselves. From the early forties on, Charles Davenport struggled to receive funding for his eugenic practices. His influence waned but did not vanish, since the foundations of the modern study of genetics had been established. Similarly, the American Eugenics Society (AES) transformed into a "more respectable" organization. The AES was founded by Madison Grant and his fellow eugenicists Harry Laughlin, Harry Crampton, and Henry Osborn in 1926. By 1930 it reached a small membership of 1,250. The organization

313   War Against the Weak: Eugenics and America's Campaign to Create a Master Race; Edwin Black; Copyright 2003; Publisher, Four Walls Eight Windows, pp 393–396

eventually transitioned into the The Society for the Study of Social Biology, with an academic following and membership. Similarly, the Eugenics Records Office and its goals metamorphosed into The Pioneer Fund. Openly acknowledging its links to the eugenic past, The Pioneer Fund advertises its study of behavioral genetics, intelligence, social demography, and group differences that include sex, social class and race.[314] Its rhetoric has earned the group a spot in the Southern Poverty Law Center's list of active United States hate groups, along with over a hundred more such organizations.[315] The Pioneer Fund has funded many race differences studies over the last fifty years and appears ready to fund more.[316]

The real face of the racist pseudo-intellectual egocentric eugenicists of today is best revealed in a statement made by Nicholas Agar in the defense of eugenics in his book *Liberal Eugenics*. He states, "The embryo does not yet have a life plan…Those of average intelligence can enjoy uncomplicated pleasures denied to some with superior intelligence. They can develop parts of their characters that highly intelligent people tend to leave relatively undeveloped."[317] It becomes obvious that eugenic racism is alive and well and needs to be kept in check.

A positive consequence of the war was a growing, powerful, and worldwide Zionist movement, that advocated the creation of a Jewish state, a home where Jews could live without fear of persecution. War's end brought the Jewish mass migration to Palestine, further destabilizing long-standing Middle Eastern instability. Territorial, religious and familial rivalries escalated into wars fueled by outside world powers for their own agenda. Having escaped the Holocaust, the Zionists found themselves in a near constant state of war that they fight to this day.

Other after-effects of the war on international politics were also profound. Charles de Gaulle's France surrendered more civil independence to the Communist Party, as financial institutions, transportation companies, and labor were nationalized. At the same time France tried to re-establish its imperial desires in Vietnam, Algeria, and other pre-war possessions. France's efforts to reclaim the resources of these countries fell victim to independence movements in each country. Both Vietnam and Algeria were violent conflicts. As the French succumbed not only to the Communists in their own country, the Vietminh[318] destroyed their last foothold in Vietnam at Dien Bien Phu. Vietnam's division into north and south led to continued civil strife between the Communist north and democratic south. The North's leader, Ho Chi Minh, eventually drew

---

314   Pioneer Fund; http://www.pioneerfund.org
315   Southern Poverty Law Center; Active US hate Groups in 2005; http://www.splcenter.org/intel/map/hate.jsp
316   The Nazi Connection: Eugenics, American Racism and German National Socialism; Stefan Kühl; Oxford University Press; copyright 1994; chapter 1; pp 5–11
317   Liberal Eugenics: In Defense of Human Enhancement; Nicholas Agar; Blackwell Publishing; Copyright 2004; Chapter 5; pp 108–109
318   Vietminh – The name given to the Vietnam resistance fighters who defeated the French. Later, it would be renamed "Vietcong," after the Americans entered the Vietnam conflict.

the United States into a protracted "police action" that ultimately brought civil unrest in America.

Surprisingly, the postwar Communist conflicts in Greece, Sicily, Korea, and Vietnam, aided by independence conflicts in Israel and Algeria, built the framework for guerrilla and terror warfare that haunt the Western powers to this day.

Afterword

In World War II, many fine men and women gave up the remaining years of their earthly existence in a worldwide campaign to free people enslaved by eugenic ideologies while fighting to fulfill the broad democratic goals of the Atlantic Charter. The ideals of democratic self-determination in the charter have been carried out as much as possible in the once Nazi-occupied countries that fell under Allied control after the war. They are all practicing some interpretation of democracy today. Even many of those countries that were once under the direct influence of the Soviet Union are now participating in some form of democracy. With these new democratic freedoms has come the right for individuals to pursue their beliefs in a higher purpose and power unfettered by the blind grasp of science or the controlling state.

Yet, the push for the scientific-based society is still with us. Instead of opening their minds to all the possibilities that science affords us, scientists and other proponents of the eugenic legacy have closed their minds, while ridiculing the very people who have respected their freedom to express themselves in a scientific manner. Because Americans fought and died for these freedoms during World War II, these freedoms need to be respected and protected for believers of whatever faith is closest to them, be it science, God, or even both. "Science for society's sake" is a deadly combination that the world fought to end in the 1940's, but its legacy hasn't escaped us, as evidenced in the ongoing study of eugenics and a scientifically justified culture of death that pervades America and much of the world. Allowing science to control political thought is as dangerous as allowing Thomas Jefferson's priest-craft or the Nazi Blood and Soil religion to control all political thought.

The eugenics agenda is alive and well in America; numerous popular magazines show its infiltration. For example, Madison Grant's old stomping grounds, the American Museum of Natural History, in its November 2005 magazine spends more time debasing religion than promoting its religiously unfettered, scientific findings. Indeed, the magazine's mission seems to be more one of promoting the organization's agenda than its findings. Evolutionary biologist Dr. Richard Dawkins, an Oxford University professor, discusses science as a religion in his article in *The Humanist* of January/February 1997. His impassioned "faith" is also outlined in a debate with geneticist Dr. Francis Collins, M.D., Ph.D., in the November 13, 2006, *Time* magazine. Collins (a believer and committed scientist) was also featured in a February 2007 *National Geographic* interview. One could see past the article's façade to its real intent—to push the boundaries of science against the religious beliefs of others in spite of Collin's best efforts. Might these arguments be examples of Sir Francis Galton revisited? Let us hope not. With hate organizations like the New Black Panthers, the KKK, skinheads, and other supremacist organizations still producing literature that is infiltrating the minds of the young, it is not a stretch to see such groups combining their beliefs with science into a religious dogma of racist and religious hate. Could this be the Nazis revisited?

Science as the new belief is still heavily proselytized, not only by Richard Dawkins but also by respected and "non-controversial" popular magazines such as *Scientific American*. In a December 2006 article called "Bowling for God" that sounds alarmingly similar to the debates of the 1920's, author Michael Shermer separates society into the secular "enlightened" left and the religious "uninformed" right. Then he goes on to explain how "the religious" on average support the poor through charity, support non-religious organizations and provide a framework for community interaction, as opposed to the secularist positions. Interestingly, he implies through his analysis that religious democracies tend to score higher on the scale for homicide, sexually transmitted diseases, teen pregnancy, and abortion.[319] He fails, though, to disclose whether it is the secular left or the religious right who are the offenders. However, the results are more likely a reflection of the freedoms that democracies offer. Shermer also fails to compare these numbers to societies that violently punish these behaviors. Eerily, this debate is not new, but now the religious right has lost ground to the discourse of science, which had such fatal consequences in the early and mid-20th century.

Such issues of genetics are also opening a Pandora's box of civil rights concerns. In the same December 2006 issue of *Scientific American,* author Sally Lehrman, in the article "Partial to Crime," discusses linking a known criminal's DNA to family members as a way to alert police agencies to the possibility of someone's criminal potential or culpability in a crime. The legacy of eugenics is upon us, as one family member's behavior genetically links and damns the other family members to his or her destiny.[320] Is this new application of science going to lead to more judges like Oliver Wendell Holmes who wish to save us from "generations of imbeciles"? Isn't this the logical progression of a scientifically classed society? The authority of our civil rights stops when someone else decides they are better positioned to judge the value to society of others. As humankind has seen in the past that it is the start of the devaluing of human life.

Americans fought to free the imprisoned and genetically devalued from the Nazi concentration and death camps, only to find themselves today destroying the very future of their society at will using the same logic as the Nazis. The legacy of eugenics lives on as we see Margaret Sanger's control of the "unfit" through birth control programs growing into the Planned Parenthood organizations of today. Knowledge of and utilization of birth control certainly provides for planned parenting, but abortion has become birth control too. Unfortunately, today's cultural genocide through abortion is the civil standard that many organizations use on their banners for individual civil rights and birth control. We justify the wholesale abortion of fetuses, by rationalizing that their DNA is less important than our own. Abortion, the last vestage of the holocaust is alive and well within many societies around the world today. The pluri-potential cells of the fetus now form the instruments of our future immortality. Stem cells, which hold the

---

319   Scientific American; Bowling for God: Skeptic; Michael Shermer; p-44; December 2006
320   Scientific American; Partial to Crime: Families Become Suspects as Rules on DNA Matches Relax; Sally Lehrman; p-28; December 2006

life force of a human being, have become just another scientific tool to the (I daresay) non-believing. Have we justified the destruction of a human population before they are even born? Are our own "needs" being used to justify the sacrifice of the unborn, or is it that the "unfit attitude" has become the "unwanted attitude"? The eventual devaluation of human life to nothing more than an unwanted gene pool is the legacy of the world's and the Nazi's eugenic programs. We as a society can't seem to escape the reality of our ongoing legacy of World War II, and have established a culture of death.

In the process, science has shown us at least one powerful thing. By saying long enough and loud enough that single cell or complex multi-cellular collections of DNA are nothing more than instruments of evolution, science has allowed humankind to justify the killing of humans at any level of development. The eugenic culture's focus on birth control coupled with Sanger's goals of peri-natal intervention—all for race improvement—have left us with a confused populace. But improved living standards, quality public-health programs, public education, and social hygiene have all lead to a healthier society too. They would have succeeded without eugenics.

Science—in the study of the human genome—has allowed parents to predict the sex and the likelihood of a genetic condition in their child. But it has also put on them a new burden—to choose whether to abort the unborn. Parents can test for the genetic health of their child through paternal and maternal genotyping, maternal blood testing, chorionic villus sampling, amniocentesis, or even ultrasound. By knowing the genetic condition, the family then has to decide the fate of their child. Even with these results, not all genetic aberrations could or should warrant the killing of the child. Imagine if physicist Dr. Steven Hawking, who suffers from Amyotrophic Lateral Sclerosis, had been terminated because of the results of peri-natal genetic testing. Wouldn't humankind have suffered from the loss? Moreover, advances in fetal surgery now allow for the repair of many structural abnormalities that, before, would have handicapped children. Although not 100 percent successful, fetal surgery affords the child and the family a better opportunity for a productive life.

However, all this is not to say that there are not arguments and indications for genetic studies with the selective termination of nonviable life. Pregnancies as a result of rape and incest certainly would warrant the opportunity for termination, but require proof and represent only 1 percent of such terminations. But, herein lies the heart of the problem. Even with the best of intentions, our cultural acceptance of killing has expanded at the expense of the silent unborn. All these issues now infiltrate our political lexicon and dialogue.

Other types of killing also benefited from the spoils of World War II. The war's military legacy—like its eugenic legacy—has infiltrated our way of thinking. America and its allies now have the capability to target a building, a bridge, a tank, or an individual with just one bomb. This highly selective power has thankfully lessened the likelihood that soldiers today will have to live with the memory of the accidental death of uncounted orphans. But, even with this selective power there still exists side by side the ability to destroy an entire city with just one bomb, instead of using thousands. The lethality of weapons today has guaranteed that the United States and its allies are unlikely to lose any head-to-head conflict with any other belligerent military or nation in the world. It provides a tremendous advantage from the point of view of negotiations. But it also puts the militarily developed nations into the position of being the world's police force. One would think this power would and should be used benevolently, but when coupled with the legacy of the World War II, such power puts us at risk for losing our compassionate realism if the scientific infuses itself too deeply into the equation.

America and the developed world are not the only ones suffering from the results of the war. Its legacy is still practiced in the recent conflicts of Bosnia, Darfur, and the Middle East. The scientific and eugenic legacy has led to governments such as Iran's—which is on the verge of harnessing the atom as a weapon—to hold a conference whose intent is to deny the Holocaust, while justifying Iran's religiously based anti-Semitic agenda. The conference was attended by the former grand wizard of the Ku Klux Klan, David Duke, and leaders of organizations around the world, including Jewish clerics.

Despite the persistence of the eugenic legacy, the world still owes so much to all those men and women from every walk of life, nationality, and religious belief who destroyed the seething monsters of National Socialism and Japanese Imperialism. A great debt is owed to the Italian-American, Jewish-American, Irish-American, Latino-American, African-American, Polish-American, the supposedly genetically inferior Appalachian-American, and every other warrior from around the world, regardless of their "race," who served or sacrificed to bring an end to the racist regimes of the Axis powers. Let us all hope we as a society are using their sacrifices to prevent history from repeating itself.

Perhaps the intent and spirit of the Atlantic Charter were carried on after the war through the Berlin airlift, the Korean War, the Vietnam War, and into the height of the Cold War. For sure, the 416th Strategic Bomb Wing carried the 416th standard and the flag of freedom in Vietnam and throughout the Cold War. Let us hope we are experiencing the continuation of the spirit of the 416th in Afghanistan, Iraq, and across the Middle East. There are changes coming and the 416th is there again to see that they succeed. Stationed at Karshi-Khanabad Airfield, Uzbekistan, the 416th Air Expeditionary Group is supporting Operation Enduring Freedom in Afghanistan while providing humanitarian relief to schools and orphanages in Uzbekistan. Let us hope the changes occur as peacefully as possible, because the spirit of a eugenic-free democracy is strengthened by those who have given their lives to ensure and defend it. It has become obvious that within the worlds of science, politics, warfare, and faith there is always going to be the need for sacrifice.

Glossary

Abteilung – (German) – Labor Service Unit (equivalent to Army Battalion)

Abteilungsführer – (German) – Labor Service Unit leader

Achtung! Nicht bewegen. Hände hoch, ihr seid jetzt Gefangene von dem Dritten Reich und der Wehrmacht. Nicht bewegen – (German) – Attention do not move, arms up, you are now prisoners of the Third Reich and the German Army. Do not move.

Américain, ne se déplace pas. Nous sommes ici pour vous aider. Faites comme nous disons – (French) – American, don't move. We are here to help you. Do as we say.

Arbeit – (German) – Job, work

Artillerie – (German) – Artillery

Ausrotten Zentrum – (German) – SS extermination centers for the non-Aryan peoples

Befehl – (German) – order or command

Befehlen – (German) – To command

Bergen diese Maschinengewehre und alle Munitionen – (German) – Salvage those machine guns and all the ammunition

Beordern – German – to order with authority

Bewegung! Er ist unser Gefangener – (German) – Move back. He is our prisoner.

Bodenpersonal – (German) – The ground crew

Chesterfield – American cigarette brand popular with the troops in WWII

Deutsch – (German) – German

Deutsche-Armee-Dolchstosslegende – (German) – The German military theory that the defeatist and social-democratic attitude of the civilian population had caused the military to lose WWI, even though the German Army was never defeated on the battlefield. Used as a political tactic by Hitler to win votes.

Deutschland – (German) – Germany or German homeland

Deutsche Landschaft – (German) – German landscape

Deutsche Pulver und Stahl – (German) – German powder and steel

Durchgangslager der Luftwaffe – (German) – German transit camp of the Luftwaffe for captured American and Allied Air Force crews

Eindeutschung – (German) – The idea of Germanization, or the idea to make all things Germanic that were under German control

Englisch – (German) – English

Eroberung – (German) – Capture, conquest

Escape and Evasion (EET) – Every air crew was given training in how to evade the enemy and escape techniques to avoid capture. It was a requirement of every captured soldier to try to escape. Soldiers were also taught how to contact the Free French Underground if shot down over France.

Exekutionskommando – (German) – German firing squad

Fallschirm – (German) – Parachute

Feuerbefehl – (German) – Order to open fire

Feldwebel – (German) – Senior Sergeant Infantry

Flugabwehrkanonen – (German) – 88 mm Anti-aircraft Canon

Flugzeug – (German) – A plane or aircraft

GEE – Radio-frequency guidance system designed by the British to allow for more accurate bomb drops.

Gefangen halten – (German) – To keep imprisoned

Gefangen nehmen – (German) – To arrest, capture, catch, take prisoner

Geliebtes Deutschland – (German) – Beloved Germany

Genauigkeit – (German) – Accuracy

Generaloberst Stab Offiziers – (German) – General Staff officers

Gruppenführer – (German) – Labor service group leader

Hauptwachtmeister – (German) – Battery Sergeant Major, Artillery

Hausfrau – (German) – Housewife

Im Radio übertragen – (German) – To broadcast by radio

Infrastruktur – (German) – infrastructure

Jagdflugzeug – (German) – Fighter plane

Jawohl – (German) – Yes, sir or yes, indeed

Jawohl, Herr Unterfeldwebel – (German) – Yes, sir, Sergeant (Infantry)

Jerry – British slang name for Germans, thought to be a common German name

Kanone – (German) – Artillery piece, either anti-aircraft or assault cannon

Kanonier – (German) – Gunner in artillery unit; artillery private

Kismet – fate

Kommunications-Zentrum – (German) – German communication center

Krauts – American slang for German soldiers

Kriegsgefangener – (German) – Prisoner of war

Ladungen – (German) – Rounds or artillery rounds, bullets

Lebensborn – (German) – The Third Reich and Himmler's SS program to breed "Aryan" men with Aryan women, then to raise their children in the Aryan way. The objective was to allow for the cleansing of the European continent of "lesser non-Aryan races."

Lebensraum – (German) – Literally, Living space. Hitler's plan to expand Germany's borders into the Rhineland, Sudetenland, Ukraine, and the Caucasus in order to feed and grow the ever-enlarging Germanic population and war machine.

Luckies – American cigarette brand popular during the war

Luft – (German) – air

Luftwaffe – (German) – German Air Force

Luftwaffefluchtkommandeur – (German) – German Air Force flight commander

Marsch, Amerikaner! Der Krieg ist für dich vorbei. – (German) – Get going, American! The war is over for you.

Maschinengewehr – (German) – Machine gun

Mausergewehr – (German) – German 8 mm German rifle

Milk Run – American slang for an easy mission to fly and complete

Munitionen – (German) – Ammunition or bullets

Nehmen die drei am links, Gruppe zwei. Gruppe eins, kommen mit mir und greifen die zwei am rechts an. Gute Jagd – (German) – Take the three on the left, group two. Group one, come with me and attack the two on the right. Good hunting!

Nicht mehr sprechen, ihr drei – (German) – No more talking, you three

No-Ball – (German) – Code name for a German V-1 rocket launch site, a common target early in war for the 416th

Nun, aufstehen. Wieder in die Aufstellung. Schnell, schnell. Marschen. – (German) –Alright, everyone up. Back into formation now. Hurry, hurry, start walking now.

Obergefreiter – (German) – Corporal

Oberkanonier – (German) – Private First Class Artillery

Oberleutnant – (German) – First Lieutenant

Obersoldat – (German) – Private First Class Infantry

Oberstleutnant – (German) – Lieutenant Colonel

Oberstleutnant führend die Verteidigung Worms – (German) – Lieutenant Colonel in command of Worms's defense

Östliche Front – (German) – Germany's Eastern front with Russia

Oui – (French) – Yes

Panzer – (German) – Tank

Porcelaine – (French) – China plates or dinner ware

Raffie, Si arrivato – (Italian) – Ralph, you came home

Rasse und Siedlungschauptamt – (German) – Race and Settlement Head Office

Russin – (German) – Russian woman

Schutzstaffel or Schwarzhemden – (German) – Literally, Blackshirts (Schwarzhemden), but better known as the "SS." Originally an elite group of Hitler's bodyguards, they became Himmler's private army. Later divided into the Allgemeine SS (black uniforms) and the Waffen SS (gray uniforms). The Waffen SS fought as combat soldiers alongside regular Army units, but they remained part of the SS under Himmler. The Allgemeine SS supplied concentration-camp guards rather than combat soldiers.

Schwarzbrot – (German) – Black bread

Soldat – (German) – Soldier

Stalag – (German) – German POW camp or prison

Stalag Luft – (German) – German POW camp for Allied aircrews

Steh doch auf, Amerikaner – (German) – Get up now, American

Technikers – (German) – Operators or technicians

Tod – (German) – Death

Töten – (German) – To kill

Unterfeldwebel – (German) – German Sergeant Infantry

Unteroffizier – (German) – German Lance Sergeant

Unterwachtmeister – (German) – German Sergeant Artillery

Venez avec nous. Nous nous cacherons dans la forêt pendant le jour et voyagerons seulement pendant la nuit. Vous comprenez? – (French) – Come with us. We will hide in the forest during the day and travel only at night. Do you understand?

Venez ici maintenant – (French) – Come here now.

Viel Glück – (German) – Good luck

Vier – (German) – Four

Volkssturm – (German) – "People's Attack Force," composed of overage men and used principally for defense.

Von grösster Wichtigkeit – (German) – Of vital importance

Vom Kommunikations-Zentrum, Eisenbahnen, Bereitstellungsaum, Flugabwehrkanonen, und noch wichtiger die Leben und Seelen von Deutschlands junge wollende Männer und Frauen – (German) – from communication centers, rail lines, marshaling yards, anti-aircraft cannons, and more importantly the lives and souls of Germany's young, willing men and women.

Wachtmeister – (German) – Senior Sergeant Artillery

Wehrmacht – (German) – Germany's armed forces

Wehrmacht Generaloberst Stab – (German) – German Army General Staff

(Er) würde nicht aufgeben – (German) – (He) would not give up

Wehrmacht-Verpflichtung perfekt – (German) – Obligation to the German army perfectly completed

Wir werden die Amerikaner niederschlagen – (German) – We will teach those Americans.

Ziel – (German) – Target

Bibliography and Footnotes

1. OD, Officer of the Day
2. R&R, Rest and Relaxation, military slang for time off
3. It was a standing order for the ground crews to salute as the planes began their taxi.
4. *The Wall Street Waltz, 90 Visual Perspectives*, By Kenneth L. Fisher, Chapter 29, A Clear Warning, Pgs. 70-71; 1987
5. American President, President Herbert Hoover; http://www.americanpresident. org/history/herberthoover/biography/printable.html
6. Fair Labor Standards Act of 1938: Maximum Struggle for a Minimum wage; Jonathan Grossman; US Department of Labor; http://www.dol.gov/oasam/programs/ history/flsa1938.htm#content
7. *The Wall Street Waltz, 90 Visual Perspectives;* Kenneth L. Fisher, Chapter 74, In the Know, Or Heavily Snowed?; pages 168-169; 1987
8. Readers Companion to American History, New Deal, Houghton Mifflin; http:// college.hmco.com/history/readerscomp/rcah/html/ah_064200_newdeal.htm
9. The Dust Bowl, http://www.usd.edu/anth/epa/dust.html
10. An Open Letter to President Roosevelt, John Maynard Keynes; http://newdeal.feri. org/misc/keynes2.htm
11. Secret City History: A World War II Secret City; http://smithdray.angletowns.net/ or/sch.htm
12. Secret City History: A World War II Secret City; http://smithdray.angletowns.net/ or/sch.htm
13. TVA: Electricity for All, The Origins of the Tennessee Valley Authority, Opposition to TVA, The Dams and Their Builders, Agriculture and Conservation, The Displaced Peoples of Norris Basin; http://newdeal.feri.org/tva/tva01.htm
14. A Short History of TVA: From the New Deal to a New Century; http://www.tva .gov/abouttva/history.htm
15. The Boulder Canyon Project, Hoover Dam; William J. Simonds, http://www. nevada-history.org/boulder-project-by-simonds.html
16. History link Essay: Grand Coulee Dam- a Snapshot History; File # 7264 http://www .historylink.org/essays/output.cfm?file-id=7264
17. Woody Guthrie Biography; http://www.woodyguhtrie.org/biography.htm
18. Woody Guthrie; http://en.wikipedia.org/wiki/Woody-Guthrie
19. Daily Worker; http://en.wikipedia.org/wiki/Daily_Worker
20. Japan; Contributor: Gary D. Allison, Ph.D., Ellen Bayard Weedon Prof. of East Asian Studies, Univ. of Virginia; www.pushsd.k12.ca.us/chana/staffpages/Mr._Eichman/ worldhistory/wwii/japan

21. *Soldiers of the Sun: The Rise and Fall of the Imperial Japanese Army*; Meirion and Susie Harries; Random House; copyright 1991; Part 3; chapter 13; page 139

22. *The Last Lion, Winston Spencer Churchill, Alone 1932-1940*; William Manchester, pages 1 to 350

23. *The Wall Street Waltz, 90 Visual Perspectives*, Kenneth L. Fisher, Chapter 22, The Silent Crash No One Noticed, pages 57-58; 1987

24. History of the Civilian Conservation Corps, www.cccalumni.org/history1.html

25. *The Glory and the Dream, A Narrative History of America-1932-1972*; William Manchester pages 1 to 93

26. James F. Justin, Civilian Conservation Corps museum, An online Museum of Histories, Items, Stories, links and Photographs regarding the CCC's. ; pages 1-8

27. Japanese Economic History 1930's; www.emayzine.com

28. Commander Submarine Force, US Pacific Fleet; USS Corvina; http://www.csp.navy .mil/ww2boats/corvina.htm

29. Luckies and Chesterfield – Two very desirable brands of American cigarettes popular among the aircrews at the time. Phillip Morris was also a popular brand.

30. No-ball missions were to German V-1 Rocket (buzz bomb) launch sites. The 416th was effective at destroying these sites but the Germans were equally effective at rebuilding them.

31. Vergeltungswaffe – German meaning "vengeance weapon." They were nicknamed "buzz bombs" or "doodlebugs" by the Londoners.

32. *Peenemunde:* 1943: Weapons of Mass Destruction; Global Security; http://www .globalsecurity.org/wmd/ops/peenemunde.htm

33. Initiation Point – IP, navigational point where the bomb-run to target begins

34. United States Army Air Force Chronology: Tuesday, April 11, 1944; http://paul. rutgers.edu/~mcgrew/wwii/usaf/html/Apr.44.html

35. Kill the Rate – Term used to describe the rate of closure and alignment as the Norden bombsight's crosshairs moved toward the target; one crosshair moved toward the other fixed crosshair. The phrase "rate of closure" signifies the aircraft's rate of closure towards the target's Maximum Point of Impact (MPI). When both crosshairs crossed on the MPI of the target, the bombs dropped automatically.

36. The 416th would make two more trips to Bonnieres and one to Beauvoir and would give up five lives and two POWs. The photo of Jedinak's plane afire amid ships displayed at the USAF Museum was shot on this mission.

37. *Kanonier*, Gunner in artillery unit; artillery private

38. *Oberkanonier*, artillery private first class

39. *Unterwachtmeister* – artillery sergeant

40. *Hauptwachtmeister* – artillery battery sergeant major

41. *Oberleutnant* – infantry first lieutenant

42. *Unteroffizier* – infantry lance sergeant

43. *Soldat* – infantry private

44. German 88mm anti-aircraft artillery battery

45. *Papaver somniferum* – the poppy flower.

46. *The Pharmacological Basis of Therapeutics*, Ch. 22, Opioid Analgesics and Antagonists, pp 494 to 501; Alfred Goodman Gilman, M.D., Ph.D., Louis S. Goodman, M.A., M.D., D.Sc.(Hon.), Alfred Gilman, Ph.D., D.Sc.(Hon), et-al; Sixth edition.

47. *War Against the Weak: Eugenics and America's Campaign to Create a Master Race*; Edwin Black; Copyright 2003; Publisher, Four Walls Eight Windows

48. *From Darwin to Hitler: Evolutionary Ethics, Eugenics, and Racism*; Richard Weikart; Copyright 2004; Publisher, Palgrave Macmillan

49. *A Life of Sir Francis Galton: From African Exploration to the Birth of Eugenics*; Nicholas Wright Gillham; Copyright 2001; Publisher, Oxford University Press, Inc.

50. *Struggle for National Survival: Eugenics in Sino-Japanese Contexts, 1896-1945*; Yuehtsen Juliette Chung; Copyright 2002; Publisher, Routledge

51. British National Archives; Correspondence between EES and MRC 1925 to 1932; Ref: FO 1/1734 268033

52. Statement by the British National Committee for Human Heredity; British National Archives; Ref; FO 1/1733 268033

53. National Socialist Workers Party of Germany

54. *The Last Lion, Winston Spencer Churchill, Alone 1932-1940*; William Manchester, page 112

55. Goddard History, Robert H. Goddard: American Rocket Pioneer, http://www.gsfc.nasa.gov/gsfc/welcome/history/history.htm

56. Robert H. Goddard, father of modern rocketry, by Paul Jarvey; http://www.eworester.com/extra/goddard/

57. *Eugenics and Other Evils: An Argument Against the Scientifically Organized Society*; G. K. Chesterton; Copyright 2000; Editor, Michael W. Perry

58. *A Life of Sir Francis Galton: From African Exploration to the Birth of Eugenics*; Nicholas Wright Gillham; Oxford University Press; copyright 2001

59. *Preaching Eugenics: Religious Leaders and the American eugenics Movement*; Christine Rosen; Oxford University Press; copyright 2004

60. Germany: Zone Handbook No. V: Rhine-Ruhr; Part 1: People and Administration; January 1944; Imperial War Museum, London, England

61. Events preceding World War II in Europe; www.WorldHistory.com

62. Causes of World War II; www.WorldHistory.com

63. Chronology of World War II, 1918 to 1939, Copyright © 1998-2004 Ken Polsson, pages 1 to 23; www.islandnet.com

64. Commanding heights: The German Hyperinflation, 1923, By George J. W. Goodman, Copyright © 1981; www.pbs.org/wgbh

65. World War II Commemoration, Colonel Vincent J. Esposito, US Army; Head, Dept. of Military Art, United States Military Academy; www.grolier.com/wwii/wwii

66. John Maynard Keynes, His radical idea that government should spend money they don't have may have saved capitalism, By Robert B. Reich; http://www.time.com/time/time100/scientist/profile/keyens.html

67. *The House that Hitler Built*, By Stephen H. Roberts, chapters; 3, 4, 8; Harper, 1938; reprint by Gordon Press, 1975

68. *Eugenics and Other Evils: An Argument Against the Scientifically Organized Society*; G. K. Chesterton; Copyright 2000; Editor, Michael W. Perry ; pp151-152; (Social Hygiene, Vol. 6)

69. Darwin & Evolution: Good Breeding: Darwin Doubted His Own Family's Fitness; James Moore; *Natural History* pp 45-46; November, 2005

70. *War Against the Weak: Eugenics and America's Campaign to Create a Master Race*; Edwin Black; Copyright 2003; Publisher, Four Walls Eight Windows

71. Eugenics: America's Darkest Days, Sterilization; http://iml.jou.ufl.edu/projects/ Spring02/Holland/Sterlization.htm

72. Eugenics: A Faultline in History: Eugenics in America: Public Policy: Sterilization; Buck v. Bell Supreme Court case of 1927; http://129.41.238.103/eugenics/ content/section_03/sterilization.htm

73. Racial Science in Social Context, John R. Baker on Eugenics, Race, and the Public Role of the Scientist by Michael G. Kenny; Isis, Vol. 95, number 3, Sept 2004, pp 394-419.

74. *The Unfit: A History of a Bad Idea*; Elof Axel Carlson; copyright 2001; Cold Spring Harbor Laboratory Press, Cold Spring Harbor, New York

75. Casti Connubii, section 68

76. *War Against the Weak: Eugenics and America's Campaign to Create a Master Race*; Edwin Black; Copyright 2003; Publisher, Four Walls Eight Windows

77. *The Unfit: A History of a Bad Idea*; Elof Axel Carlson; copyright 2001; Cold Spring Harbor Laboratory Press, Cold Spring Harbor, New York

78. *The Works of Thomas Robert Malthus; Vol. I*; Copyright 1798; The Pickering Masters; William Pickering; copyright 1986

79. *The Auto Biography of Margaret Sanger*; Margaret Sanger; Dover Publications; copyright 1938; pp 375-377

80. *War Against the Weak: Eugenics and America's Campaign to Create a Master Race*; Edwin Black; Copyright 2003; Publisher, Four Walls Eight Windows

81. *The Nazi Connection: Eugenics, American Racism and German National Socialism*; Stefan Kühl; Oxford University Press; Copyright 1994; Chapter 8; page 85

82. *The Passing of the Great Race or The Racial Basis of European History*; Madison Grant; Copyright 1916; Charles Scribner's & Sons; Fourth revised edition, page 211–215, 222

83. *Mein Kampf*; Adolf Hitler; copyright 1925, Houghton Mifflin Company; chapter XI, Vol. I

84. *War Against the Weak: Eugenics and America's Campaign to Create a Master Race*; Edwin Black; Copyright 2003; Publisher, Four Walls Eight Windows

85. Germany: Zone Handbook No. V: Rhine-Ruhr; Part 1: People and Administration: The Health Castes; January 1944; Secret 1943; Imperial War Museum, London, England

86. MSN Encarta Premium-Multimedia-Summer Olympics Medal Standings, Berlin, 1936;   http://encarta.msn.com/media_701701849/Summer_Olympics-Medal_ Standings.html

87. *War Against the Weak: Eugenics and America's Campaign to Create a Master Race;* Edwin Black; Copyright 2003; Publisher, Four Walls Eight Windows

88. *From Darwin to Hitler: Evolutionary Ethics, Eugenics, and Racism;* Richard Weikart; Copyright 2004; Publisher, Palgrave Macmillan

89. *Struggle for National Survival: Eugenics in Sino-Japanese Contexts, 1896-1945;* Yuehtsen Juliette Chung; Copyright 2002; Publisher, Routledge

90. *The Unfit: A History of a Bad Idea;* Elof Axel Carlson; copyright 2001; Cold Spring Harbor Laboratory Press, Cold Spring Harbor, New York

91. *Preaching Eugenics: Religious Leaders and the American Eugenics Movement;* Christine Rosen; Oxford University Press; copyright 2004

92. *The Glory and the Dream: A Narrative History of America, 1932-1972,* William Manchester pp 57-58, pp 107-111. 1973

93. American Bund: The Failure of American Nazism: The German-American Bund's Attempt to Create an American Fifth Column; Jim Bredemus; http://www.traces.org/americanbund.html

94. Hooded Progressivism: The Secret Reformist History of the Ku Klux Klan; Jesse Walker; http://www.reason.com/links/links120205.shtml

95. *Voyage of the Beagle;* Charles Darwin; Henry Colburn Publisher; 1839

96. *On the Origin of Species;* Charles Darwin; J. Murray: publisher; London; 1859

97. Has Mendel's Work Been Rediscovered?, R.A. Fisher, MA., SC.D., F.R.S., (1890-1962), Galton Professor of Eugenics, University of Eugenics, University College, London, From Annals of Science,1, 1936, http://www.men.org/c/irapilgrim/men01.html

98. Gregory Mendel; Wikipedia, The Free Encyclopedia; http://en.wikipedia.org/wiki/Gregor; Experiments in Plant Hybridization (1865), Gregor Mendel; English translation, http://www.mendelweb.org/Mendel.html

99. An American Military History, Army Historical Series, Office of the Chief of Military History, United States Army, The War of 1812; Chapter 6; http://www.army.mil/cmh-pg/books/amh/amh-06.htm

100. War of 1812, The History Channel; http://www.historychannel.com/perl/print_book.pl?ID=225473

101. The History Guy: The Mexican-American War; http://www.historyguy.com/mexican-american_war.html

102. An American Military History, Army Historical Series, Office of the Chief of Military History, United States Army, The Mexican War and After; Chapter 8; http://www.army.mil/cmh-pg/books/amh/AMH-08.htm

103. *Voyage of the Beagle;* Charles Darwin; Published by Henry Colburn 1939; Penguin Books 1989

104. *Japanese Militarism: Past and Present;* Dr. Harold Hakwon Sunoo; Nelson-Hall, Inc.; copyright 1975; Chapters 1–5

105. *Negotiating with Imperialism: Unequal Treaties and the Culture of Japanese Diplomacy;* Michael R. Austin; Harvard University Press; Copyright 2004

106. Mathew Perry & The Opening of Japan 1848-1860; http://www.navyandmarine .org/ondeck/1800perryjapan.htm

107. *A Social Basis for Prewar Japanese Militarism: The Army and the Rural Community*; Richard J. Smethurst; University of California Press; copyright 1974

108. *Japanese Militarism: Past and Present*; Dr. Harold Hakwon Sunoo; Nelson-Hall, Inc.; copyright 1975; Chapters 1-5

109. *The Rising Sun: The Decline and Fall of the Japanese Empire: 1936-1945*; John Toland; Modern Library Publishing; copyright 1970, 1998 and 2003; Part 1; chapter 1; page 5

110. *Japanese Militarism: Past and Present*; Dr. Harold Hakwon Sunoo; Nelson-Hall, Inc.; copyright 1975; Chapters 1-3

111. *The Black Stork: Eugenics and The Death of "Defective" Babies in American Medicine and Motion Pictures Since 1915*; Martin S. Pernick; copyright 1996; Oxford University Press

112. *War Against the Weak: Eugenics and America's Campaign to Create a Master Race*; Edwin Black; Copyright 2003; Publisher, Four Walls Eight Windows

113. *The Unfit: A History of a Bad Idea*; Elof Axel Carlson; copyright 2001; Cold Spring Harbor Laboratory Press, Cold Spring Harbor, New York

114. *War Against the Weak: Eugenics and America's Campaign to Create a Master Race*; Edwin Black; Copyright 2003; Publisher, Four Walls Eight Windows

115. *The Nazi Connection: Eugenics, American Racism and German National Socialism*; Stefan Kühl; Oxford University Press; copyright 1994; Chapter 4; pp 48-50

116. Clash of Cultures in the 1910s and 1920s, *The Ku Klux Klan*; Immigration Restriction & The Ku Klux Klan; http://history.osu.edu/projects/clash/imm_KKK/ KKK%20pages/KKK-page1.htm

117. Between the Wars: The Klan Rides Again; http://chnm.gmu.edu/courses/ hist409/klan.html

118. *Dixiecrats Triumphant*, The secret history of Woodrow Wilson, By Charles Paul Freund, senior editor, Reason on Line; http://www.reason.com/0303/co.cf. dixiecrats.shtml

119. *Ku Klux Klan*, Wikipedia, the free encyclopedia; http://en.wikipedia.org/wiki/ Ku_Klux_Klan

120. *The Auto Biography of Margaret Sanger*; Margaret Sanger; Dover Publications; copyright 1938; pp 317- 326

121. *War Against the Weak: Eugenics and America's Campaign to Create a Master Race*; Edwin Black; Copyright 2003; Publisher, Four Walls Eight Windows

122. *Struggle for National Survival: Eugenics in Sino-Japanese Contexts, 1896-1945*; Yuehtsen Juliette Chung; Copyright 2002; Publisher, Routledge

123. *Eugenics and Other Evils: An Argument Against the Scientifically Organized State*; G.K. Chesterton; Edited by Michael W. Perry; copyright 2000

124. *Architects of the Culture of Death*; Donald De Marco and Benjamin D. Wiker; Ignatius Press; copyright 2004

125. *Killer Angel: A Short Biography of Planned Parenthood's Founder, Margaret Sanger*; George Grant; Cumberland House Publishing, Inc.; Copyright 1995, 2001

126. *Struggle for National Survival: Eugenics in Sino-Japanese Contexts, 1896-1945*; Yuehtsen Juliette Chung; Copyright 2002; Publisher, Routledge

127. *A Social Basis for Prewar Japanese Militarism: The Army and the Rural Community*; Richard J. Smethurst; University of California Press; copyright 1974; Ch II, pp 22–23

128. Louisiana Purchase, www.gatewayno.com/history/LaPurchase.html

129. The Louisiana Purchase, http://lsm.crt.state.la.us/cabildo/cab4.htm

130. The Avalon Project at Yale Law School; Thomas Jefferson- Message to the Senate of January 11, 1803 Regarding Louisiana; www.yale.edu/lawweb/avalon/presiden/messages/tj003.htm

131. Manifest Destiny: An Introduction; www.pbs.org/kera/usmexicanwar/dialogues/prelude/manifest/d2aeng.html

132. John L. O'Sullivan on "Manifest Destiny", 1839, Excerpted from "The Great Nation of Futurity," The United States Democratic Review, Vol. 6, Issue 23, pp. 426–430. www.mtholyoke.edu/acad/intrel/osulliva.htm

133. Manifest Destiny and Expansion in the Americas, http://humwww.ucsc.edu/gruesz/manifest.htm

134. Japan's March Toward Militarism, Bill Gordon; March 2000: http://wgordon.web.wesleyan.edu/papers/jhist2.htm

135. Japan's Economic Expansion into Manchuria and China in World War Two (part one and two), James Graham, May 2004; http://www.historyorb.com/asia/japan_economic_expansion.shtml

136. Armed Conflict Events Data, First Italo-Abyssinian War 1895-1896, http://www.onmar.com/aced/data/india/italyethiopia1895.htm

137. Mussolini Justifies War Against Ethiopia, Benito Mussolini, Scritti e Discorsi di Benito Mussolini, vol. IX (Milano, 1935), pp218-220; http://www.dickinson.edu/~rhyne/232/EthiopiaSpeech.html

138. Events preceding World War II in Europe; www.WorldHistory.com

139. Causes of World War II; www.WorldHistory.com

140. Chronology of World War II, 1918 to 1939, Copyright © 1998-2004 Ken Polsson, pages 1 to 23; www.islandnet.com

141. Commanding heights: The German Hyperinflation, 1923, By George J. W. Goodman, Copyright © 1981; www.pbs.org/wgbh

142. World War II Commemoration, Colonel Vincent J. Esposito, US Army; Head, Dept. of Military Art, United States Military Academy; www.grolier.com/wwii/wwii,

143. *The Last Lion, Winston Spencer Churchill, Alone 1932-1940*; William Manchester, page 1 to 350

144. Spive – name of British black-market person who could supply most anything someone wanted.

145. *Radartechniker*, German: radar technician

146. *Flugabwehrkanonen*, German anti-aircraft canons, generally 88 or 105 mm canons

147. The History Place: World War Two in Europe Timeline; http://www.historyplace .com/worldwar2/timeline/ww2time.htm

148. The History Place: Holocaust Timeline; http://www.historyplace.com/ worldwar2/holocaust/timeline.html

149. The History Place: July 31, 1941: Heydrich ordered to prepare for Final Solution; http://www.historyplace.com/worldwar2/timeline/ww2time/order1.htm

150. Wannsee Protocol; The Jewish Virtual Library; http://www.jewishvirtullibrary .org/jsource/Holocaust/Wannsee_Protocol.html

151. World War II in the Pacific: Japanese Unit 731: Biologic Warfare Unit; http:// www.ww2pacific.com/unit731.html

152. *Jug* – Cylinder head in which the piston resides. It provides a chamber for fuel and air to enter and exhaust to be pushed out of.

153. *Tod* – (German) – death

154. *Fallschirm* – (German) – parachute

155. *Gefangen nehmen* – (German) – to take prisoners

156. *Generaloberst Stab Offiziers* – (German) – General Staff Officers

157. *Attack Bombers We Need You!: A History of the 416th Bomb Group*; Ralph Conte; copyright 2001, pp 48-49

158. *Oslo Report* – The validity of the report was questioned for some time but eventually was verified and the information put to use

159. *The Grand Alliance, The Second World War,* Winston S. Churchill, pages 45-46;

160. *The Invention That Changed the World,* Robert Buderi; Touchstone Books, Simon and Schuster, copyright 1996

161. *A Radar History of World War II, Technical and Military Imperatives,* Louis Brown; Institute of Physics Publishing, copyright 1999

162. *Feuersturm* – (German) – firestorm

163. *The Invention That Changed the World,* Robert Buderi; Touchstone Books, Simon and Schuster, copyright 1996

164. *A Radar History of World War II, Technical and Military Imperatives,* Louis Brown; Institute of Physics Publishing, copyright 1999

165. *The Invention That Changed the World,* Robert Buderi; Touchstone Books, Simon and Schuster, copyright 1996

166. *A Radar History of World War II, Technical and Military Imperatives,* Louis Brown; Institute of Physics Publishing, copyright 1999

167. *Rickenbacker,* Edward V. Rickenbacker; New York; Fawcett Crest; Copyright 1967

168. My tribute to Tom Ferebee, bombardier on the *Enola Gay,* http://home.att.net/ ~sallyann4/ton-ferebee.html

169. Soviet Aims in Korea and the Origins of the Korean War: 1945-1950 New Evidence from Russian Archives; Woodrow Wilson International Center for Scholars; http://www.wilsoncenter.org/topics/pubs/ACFB76.pdf

170. The Atomic Century, The 1940's, http://www.dpi.anl.gov/dpi2/timelines/1940s. htm

171. *The Glory and the Dream, A Narrative History of America 1932-1972*, William Manchester, Chapter 11 pp 308-311, Chapter 12 pp 371-388.

172. *Attack Bombers We Need You: A History of the 416ᵗʰ Bomb Group*; Ralph Conte, copyright 2001

173. The History Place: World War Two in Europe Timeline; http://www.historyplace .com/wordwar2/timeline/ww2time.htm

174. The History Place: Timeline of Pacific War; http://www.historyplace.com/ unitedstates/pacificwar/timeline.htm

175. The History Place: Holocaust Timeline; http://www.historyplace.com/ worldwar2/holocaust/timeline.html

176. *The Art of War; Sun-tzu*; Translation by Ralph D. Sawyer; copyright 1994, pp 163–229

177. *The Wall Street Waltz: 90 Visual Perspectives: Illustrated Lessons From Financial Cycles and Trends*; Kenneth L. Fisher; copyright 1987; pp 168 & 186

178. *Great Battles of World War II*; John MacDonald; copyright 1986; pp 132–143

179. Army Air Forces in World War II: Combat Chronology of the US Army Air Forces: June 1944; http://www.usaaf.net/chron/44/jun44.htm

180. D-Day 1944: Air Power Over the Normandy Beaches and Beyond: The US Army Air Forces in World War II; Richard P. Hallion, Air Force Historian; http://www .ibiblio.org/hyperwar/AAF/AAF-H-DDay/

181. Frequently Asked Questions for D-Day and the Battle of Normandy: http://www .ddaymuseum.co.uk/faq.htm

182. Eighth Air Force Historical Society: Timeline; http://www.8thafhs.org/ combat1944a.htm

183. Analysing and Forecasting the Weather of Early June 1944; ECMWF; http://www .ecmwf.int/research/era/dday

184. *Great Battles of World War II*; John MacDonald; copyright 1986; pp 132-143

185. Doctor on D-Day; Claude Matuchansky; *Annals of Internal Medicine*; 2001;134: 1075–1076

186. *Maschinengewehr* – (German) – Machine gun

187. *Noch mehr Munitionen* – (German) – More ammunition…more ammunition

188. Franz Gockel was taken prisoner on Omaha Beach and later wrote a book about his experience, *The Gate to Hell*

189. The World at War: Operation Overlord; Richard Doody; http://worldatwar.net/ article/overlord/

190. *Great Battles of World War II*; John MacDonald; copyright 1986; pp 132-143

191. Second World War History: D-Day: The Normandy Invasion (June 6- 25, 1944); http://www.secomdworldwarhistory.com/battle_of_normandy.asp

192. Kriegsgefangene – (German) – prisoner of war

193. *Runde* –(German).– rounds or artillery shell

194. *Wehrmacht verpflichtung* – (German) – German army obligation

195. Gefangen halten –(German) – Take them prisoner

196. Jawohl, Herr Unterfeldwebel – (German) – Yes, sir, sergeant (infantry)

197. Ground loop—when a plane spins in circles on the ground without flipping over

198. British nickname for V-1's or buzzbombs

199. United States Air Force Museum-WW-II Combat Europe-V-1 Buzz Bomb; http://www.wpafb.af.mil/museum/history/wwii/ce28.htm

200. Fighter Factory: Aviation Institute of Maintenance: German V-1 Buzz Bomb; http://www.fighterfactory.net/airworthy-aircraft/buzzbomb-v1.php

201. V-1 Flying Bombs; http://spartacus.schoolnet.co.uk/2WWv1.htm

202. Antwerp X: The AAA War Against the Buzz Bombs: Skylighters, The Web Site of the 225th AAA Searchlight Battalion; http://www.skylighters.org/buzzbombs/index2.html

203. *A Radar History World War II: Technology and Military Imperatives*; Louis Brown; Institute of Physics publishing; pp 395-396 copyright 1999

204. *Américain ne vous déplacez pas. Nous sommes ici pour vous aider. Faites comme nous disons* – (French) – American don't move we are here to help you, do as we say.

205. *Venez ici maintenant* – (French) – Come over here now

206. Venez avec nous. Nous nous cacherons dans la forêt pendant le jour et voyagerons-seullement la nuit. Vous comprenez – (French) – Come with us. We will hide in the forest during the day and travel only at night. Do you understand?

207. *Great Battles of World War II*; John MacDonald; copyright 1986; pp 120-131

208. The History Place: World War Two in Europe: Timeline; http://www.historyplace.com/worldwar2/timeline/ww2time.htm

209. *Conseil National de la Résistance* (CNR); http://www.spartacus.schoolnet.co.uk/FRenr.htm

210. The History Place: Holocaust Timeline; http://www.historyplace.com/worldwar2/holocaust/timeline.html

211. The Jewish Virtual Library; http://www.jewishvirtuallibrary.org/jsource/holo.html

212. *Majdanek*; The Jewish Virtual Library; http://jewishvirtuallibrary.org/jsource/Holocaust/maidanek.html

213. The History Place: Holocaust Timeline; http://historyplace.com/worldwar2/holocaust/timeline.html

214. The History Place: World War Two in Europe: Timeline; http://www.historyplace.com/worldwar2/timeline/ww2time.htm

215. The US Army Air Forces in World War II: D-Day 1944: Air Power Over the Normandy Beaches and Beyond; Richard Hallion; Air Force historian; http://www.ibiblio.org/hyperwar/AAF/AAF-H-DDay/

216. World War II Timeline 1939-1945: Western Europe 1944; http://www.worldwar-2.net/timelines/war-in-europe/western-europe/western-europe-inde

217. Personal Historical Record of Oissel Rail Bridge; Fabrice Dhollande

218. PDI – Pilot Directional Indicator, which was used to control left and right drift of the plane on the bomb-run. Drift was relayed to the pilot's instrument panel's PDI by the Norden bombsight.

219. MPI – Main Point of Impact on the target for the salvoed bombs

220. *Das Korridor des Todes* – (German) – The Corridor of Death

221. *Great Battles of World War II*; John Mac Donald, pp 140–143; Macmillan Publishing Company, 1986

222. *Attack Bombers We Need You: A History of the 416ᵗʰ Bomb Group*; Ralph Conte; copyright 2001; chapter 7

223. Western Europe; World War 2 Timelines 1939-1945; http://www.worldwar-2.net/timelines/war-in-europe/western-europe/western-europe-inde

224. History of the Oissel Rail Bridge and Battle for Rouen, France; Fabrice Dhollande; Personal Records and Historical Research

225. The Normandy Campaign: June-August 1944: Great Battles of World War II; John MacDonald; copyright 1986; pp 132–144

226. Anne Frank 1929-1945; Jewish Virtual Library; http://www.jewishvirtuallibrary.org/jsource/biography/frank.html

227. World War II Timelines:1939-1945: Western Europe 1944; http://www.worldwar-2.net/timelines/war-in-europe/western-europe

228. The History Place: World War Two in Europe Timeline; http://www.historyplace.com/worldwar2/timeline/ww2time.htm

229. Pratt and Whitney R-2800 Double Wasp- USA; http://www.aviation-history.com/engines/pr-2800.htm

230. The History Place: World War Two in Europe Timeline; http://www.historyplace.com/worldwar2/timeline/ww2/ww2time.htm

231. The History Place: Timeline of Pacific War; http://www.historyplace.com/unitedstates/pacificwar/timeline.htm

232. The History Place: Holocaust Timeline; http://www.historyplace.com/worldwar2/holocaust/timeline.html

233. Sonderkommando; The Jewish Virtual Library; http://www.jewishvirtuallibrary.org

234. Statistics on American Jews in World War II; http://www.jewishvirtuallibrary.org

235. Statistics on American Jews in World War II; http://www.jewishvirtuallibrary.org

236. The History Place: Holocaust Timeline; http://www.historyplace.com/worldwar2/holocaust/timeline.html

237. *The Ardennes: Battle of the Bulge: The European Theater of Operations*: United States Army in World War II; Hugh M. Cole; Chapters 1; http://www.army.mil/cmh-pg/books/wwii/7-8/7-8_Cont.htm

238. Germany Zone Handbook No. V: Rhine-Ruhr: Part I: People and Administration: January 1944: Secret 1943: Chapter III

239. RAF History: Bomber Command: Campaign Diary, December 1944; http://www.raf.mod.uk/bombercommand/dec44.html

240. Tidal Wave, The August 1943 Raid on Ploesti; Air Force Historical Studies Office; http://www.airforcehistory.hq.af.mil/popTopics/ploesti.htm

241. Ploesti Oil Raid Operation Tidal Wave; http://www.ww2guide.com/oil.shtml

242. *The Ardennes: Battle of the Bulge: United States Army in World War Two: The European Theater of Operations*; Hugh M. Cole; Office of the Chief of Military History, Department of the Army; 1965; http://www.army.mil/cmh-pg/books/wwii/7-8/7-8_2.htm;

243. *The Ardennes: Battle of the Bulge: United States Army in World War II: The European Theater of Operations*; Hugh M. Cole; http://www.army.mil/cmh-pg/books/wwii/7-8/7-8_2.htm ; Chapters 2 & 25

244. The History Place: Holocaust Timeline: Nazi Euthanasia; http://www.historyplace.com/worldwar2/holocaust/h-eitanasia.htm

245. The History Place: World War Two in Europe Timeline; http://www.historyplace.com/worldwar2/timeline/ww2/ww2time.htm

246. *The Ardennes: Battle of the Bulge: The European Theater of Operations*: United States Army in World War II; Hugh M. Cole; Chapters 22-24; http://www.army.mil/cmh-pg/books/wwii/7-8/7-8_22.htm

247. The History Place: Holocaust Timeline: Nazi Euthanasia; http://www.historyplace.com/worldwar2/holocaust/h-eitanasia.htm

248. The History Place: World War Two in Europe Timeline; http://www.historyplace.com/worldwar2/timeline/ww2/ww2time.htm

249. The Ardennes: Battle of the Bulge: The European Theater of Operations: United States Army in World War II; Hugh M. Cole; Chapters 22-24; http://www.army.mil/cmh-pg/books/wwii/7-8/7-8_22.htm

250. *Nehmen die drei an das links, gruppe zwei. Gruppe ein, kommen mit mir und angreifen die zwei an das rechte. Gut jagen, Gr.,* Take the three on the left, group two. Group one, come with me and attack the two on the right. Good hunting!

251. *Luftwaffe fluchtkommandeur* – (German) – air force flight commander

252. The Ardennes, Battle of the Bulge; http://www.army.mil/cmh; Ch 25

253. *Attack Bombers We Need You, A History of the 416th Bomb Group*; Ralph Conte; Ch 11; Copyright 2001

254. A Matter of Some Urgency, Lois Eveland memoirs of Col. Ivan Wayne Eveland, Retired officer, 2002

255. "If Jesus Goes With Me"; Gospel song written by C. Austin Miles, 1908; http://www.cyberhymnal.org/htm/i/f/ifjesusg.htm

256. Chronology of Jewish Persecution, 1945; http://www.jewishvirtuallibrary.org

257. Army Air Forces in World War II; http://www.usaaf.net/chron/45/jan45.htm

258. Timeline of Pacific War; http://historyplace.com/unitedstates/pacificwar/timeline.htm

259. Federal Bureau of Investigation; FBI History; http://www.2.fbi.gov/libref/historic/history/historicdates.htm

260. White House Statement on the Sentence of Nazi Saboteurs; August 8, 1942; http://www.jewishvirtuallibrary.org

261. Rhineland; http://www.army.mil/cmh-pg/brochures/rhineland/rhineland.htm

262. *Attack Bombers We Need You: A History of the 416th Bomb Group*; Ralph Conte; Copyright 2001; Chapter 12

263. Chronology of Jewish Persecution: 1945; http://www.jewishvirtuallibrary.org
264. Timeline of Pacific War; http://www.historyplace.com
265. The Bombing of Dresden; http://airforcehistory.hq.af.mil
266. 1945: Information from Answers.com; http://www.answers.com/topic/1945
267. How Close Was Hitler to the A-Bomb?; Klaus Wiegrefe; Der Spiegel 11/2005-March 14, 2005; http://www.spiegel.de/international/spiegel/.html
268. 1945: Information from Answers.com; http://www.answers.com/topic/1945
269. Milk run – American slang for an easy bomb mission with little or no chance for people being killed or encountering resistance
270. USAAF Chronology; http://paul.rutgers.edu/~mcgrew/wwii/usaf/html/mar.45.html
271. German – housewives
272. German – German people's attack force, generally older men and young children
273. German – The German military theory that the defeatist attitude of the civilian population had caused the military to lose WWI, even though the German army was never defeated on the battlefield. It was used as a political tactic by Hitler to win votes.
274. *The Invention That Changed the World*, Robert Buderi; Touchstone Books, Simon and Schuster, copyright 1996
275. *A Radar History of World War II, Technical and Military Imperatives*, Louis Brown; Institute of Physics Publishing, copyright 1999
276. Jewish Virtual Library: Germany and The Crusader Period (1095–1291) http://www.jewishvirtuallibrary.org/jsource/vjw/germany.html
277. Wikipedia: Kristallnacht; http://en.wikipedia.org/wiki/Kristallnacht
278. Wikipedia: Worms: Judaism in Germany; http://en.wikipedia.org/wiki/Worms%2C_Germany
279. *The Story of Civilization IV: The Age of Faith: A History of Medieval Civilization From Constantine to Dante-A.D. 325-1300*; Will Durant; pp 585–613; Simon and Schuster; Copyright 1950
280. *The Story of Civilization VI: The Reformation: A History of European Civilization From Wycliffe to Calvin 1300-1564*; Will Durant; pp 337–379, 720–747; Simon and Schuster; Copyright 1950
281. German – American bombers
282. German – Anti-aircraft cannon, 88 mm
283. German – Get up, American! For you the war is over.
284. German – Attention! Do not move. Hands up! You are now prisoners of the Third Reich and the German army. Do not move!
285. German – Salvage those machine guns and all the ammunition !
286. German – corporal
287. German – German powder and steel
288. German – beloved Germany

289. German – Literally, living space. The word signified Hitler's plan to expand Germany's borders into the Rhineland, Sudetenland, Ukraine, and the Caucasus in order to feed and grow the ever-enlarging Germanic population and war machine.

290. The German SS's program to breed and raise children in the Aryan way. The Lebensborn were the first generation of the population that was to cleanse the European continent of "lesser races."

291. German – Germanisation

292. German – Race and Settlement Head Office

293. German – extermination centers

294. German – German death

295. German – Law of the Reich Citizen

296. German – Law for the Protection of German Blood and German Honor

297. *From Darwin to Hitler: Evolutionary Ethics, Eugenics and Racism in Germany*; Richard Weikart; page 15; Palgrave Macmillan; copyright 2004

298. Laying the Foundation for Wartime Research: A Comparative Overview of Science Mobilization in National Socialist Germany, Japan, and the Soviet Union; Walter E. Grunden, Yutaka Kawamura, etal; Politics and Science in Wartime: Comparative International Perspectives on the Kaiser Wilhelm Institute; Editors, Carola Sachse and Mark Walker; OSIRIS, Second Series, Vol. 20; 2005

299. *The Glory and The Dream: A Narrative History of America- 1932–1972*, William Manchester, Chapter 10, pp 296

300. On Lend-Lease (March 15, 1941), Miller Center of Public Affairs, Scripps Library and Multimedia Archive; http://millercenter.virginia.edu/scripps/diglibrary/prezspeeches/roosevelt/fdr_1941_0315.html

301. Atlantic Charter, The Avalon Project at Yale Law school; http://www.yale.edu/lawweb/avalon/wwii/atlantic.htm

302. *Pearl Harbor: Mother of all Conspiracies*, Mark Emerson Willey, Chapter one, page 14; 2000

303. Papers Relating to the Foreign Relations of the United States: Japan: 1931–1941; Vol. II; pp 208-265

304. Pearl Harbor, Mother of All Conspiracies, Mark Emerson Willey; http://www.geocities.com/Pentagon/6315/pearl.html

305. *Pearl Harbor: Mother of all Conspiracies*, Mark Emerson Willey, Xlibris Corporation; 2000

306. Chronology of International Events: March 1938 to December 18th 1941; Department of State, Bulletin, December 27, 1941, p. 590; http://www.ibiblio.org/pha/events/events.html

307. Cold War Transcripts, National Archives Learning Curve/ Cold War; http://www.learningcurve.gov.uk/coldwar/g2/cs3/s4_t.htm

308. Cold War Transcripts: Operation Unthinkable, Report By The Joint Planning Staff; National Archives Learning Curve/ Cold War; http://www.learningcurve.gov.uk?coldwar/g2cs3/S6_t.htm

309. *War Against the Weak: Eugenics and America's Campaign to Create a Master Race*, pp 320, 375; Edwin Black; Copyright 2003; Publisher, Four Walls Eight Windows

310. A Timeline of World War II, Deaths in World War II, http://www.scaruffi.com/politics/wwii.html

311. *The Glory and The Dream: A Narrative History of America- 1932-1972*, William Manchester, Chapter 11, pp 349-354.

312. Italian – Ralph, you came home.

313. *War Against the Weak: Eugenics and America's Campaign to Create a Master Race*, Edwin Black; Copyright 2003; Publisher, Four Walls Eight Windows, pp 393-396

314. Pioneer Fund; http://www.pioneerfund.org

315. Southern Poverty Law Center; Active US hate Groups in 2005; http://www.splcenter.org/intel/map/hate.jsp

316. *The Nazi Connection: Eugenics, American Racism and German National Socialism*, Stefan Kühl; Oxford University Press; copyright 1994; chapter 1; pp 5–11

317. *Liberal Eugenics: In Defense of Human Enhancement*, Nicholas Agar; Blackwell Publishing; Copyright 2004; Chapter 5; pp 108–109

318. Vietminh – The name given to the Vietnam resistance fighters who defeated the French. Later, it would be renamed "Vietcong," after the Americans entered the Vietnam conflict.

319. Bowling for God: Skeptic; Michael Shermer; *Scientific American* p-44; December 2006

320. Partial to Crime: Families Become Suspects as Rules on DNA Matches Relax; Sally Lehrman; Scientific American; p-28; December 2006.

A

C

I

259, 261, 267, 274, 276, 277, 278, 279,
280, 282, 283, 286, 291, 292, 293, 296,
299, 301, 302, 304, 309, 310, 311, 312,
315, 317, 318, 320, 321, 324, 326, 327,
328, 330, 332, 333, 334, 351, 352, 360,
366, 370, 371, 376, 377, 378, 379, 382,
383, 384, 385, 391, 406, 407, 411, 412,
413, 414, 417, 421, 422, 425, 426, 427,
431, 432, 437, 438, 448, 449, 450, 451,
452, 453, 455, 473, 490, 495
Pilot direction indicator (PDI)   13, 61,
134, 245, 248, 250, 251, 320, 425, 518
Pirmasens   402
Plankton   303, 319
Planned Parenthood   101, 500
Plexiglass   14, 74, 113, 116, 131, 134,
197, 204, 223, 225, 245
Ploesti, Romania   304
Plutonium   47, 161, 162
Pointe du Hoc   190
Poisonous gas   119
Poland   79, 118, 228, 265, 303, 395,
457, 467
Policy of Fulfillment   80
Polish   75, 87, 175, 215, 300, 309, 502
Poontang   166, 350
Pope Pius XI   86, 89
Pope Pius XII   86
Pope Urban II   417
Port Arthur   97
Portsmouth, England   153
Potbellied Stove   34, 42, 50, 111, 163,
165, 270
Potsdam Agreement   467
Potsdam Conference   467, 468
Powdered eggs   53, 111, 270, 295
Prayer   50, 64, 67, 116, 121, 127, 141,
177, 190, 191, 201, 204, 210, 215, 216,
221, 224, 245, 250, 253, 255, 260, 262,
277, 296, 308, 309, 311, 318, 319, 327,
328, 337, 338, 351, 374, 383, 385, 389,
412, 424, 425, 431, 438, 449, 451, 452,
485, 489. 494

President
  Hindenburg   82
Priestcraft   86
Prisoner of War (POW)   199, 504, 517
Private policy   1, 117
Proclamation No. 460, 696, 697
Propaganda   80, 84, 91, 92, 93, 99, 100,
158, 164, 164, 271, 273, 286, 470, 496
Protestants   84, 85, 86
Proximity fuse   152, 214, 215
Public policy   1, 87, 88, 117, 301, 512
Public Work Commission   46
Puerto Rico   42
Pulaski, Tennessee   224, 225, 482
Purple Heart   33, 50, 71, 116, 205,
453, 454

Q

Quebec, Canada   466
Quincy, Massachusetts   37
Quonset hut   13, 26, 31, 33, 34, 157,
178, 270, 274

R

R. DeStafano   394
R.A. Wipperman   203, 204, 205, 478
R.B. Prentise   261
R.C. Morehouse   275
R.J. Johnson   394
R.J. Lackner   381
R.J. Troyer   275
R.P. Chustz   195
R.V. Jones   146
R.W. York   274
Rabbeinu Gershom
  ben Judah   417
Racial Purity   81, 82, 88, 90, 91, 99, 101,
118, 456, 512
Racism   2, 80, 87, 88, 90, 92, 93, 99,
100, 456, 496, 497, 511, 512, 513, 514,
522, 523

X

Y

Z